THE RESURRECTION OF HOMER IN IMPERIAL GREEK EPIC

This book offers a radically new reading of Quintus' *Posthomerica*, the first account to combine a literary and cultural-historical understanding of what is the most important Greek epic written at the height of the Roman Empire. In Emma Greensmith's ground-breaking analysis, Quintus emerges as a key poet in the history of epic and of Homeric reception. Writing as if he is Homer himself, and occupying the space between the *Iliad* and the *Odyssey*, Quintus constructs a new 'poetics of the interval'. At all levels, from its philology to its plotting, the *Posthomerica* manipulates the language of affiliation, succession and repetition not just to articulate its own position within the inherited epic tradition but also to contribute to the literary and identity politics of imperial society. This book changes how we understand the role of epic and Homer in Greco-Roman culture – and completely re-evaluates Quintus' status as a poet.

EMMA GREENSMITH is Associate Professor of Classical Languages and Literature at St John's College, Oxford. She specialises in imperial Greek literature. She previously held a Research Fellowship at Jesus College, Cambridge, and a Visiting Assistant Professorship at Colgate University, New York. She was a member of the collaborative project 'Imperial Greek Epic: A Cultural History', funded by the Arts and Humanities Research Council.

GREEK CULTURE IN THE ROMAN WORLD

Series Editors: Jaś Elsner, University of Oxford
Simon Goldhill, University of Cambridge
Constanze Güthenke, University of Oxford
Michael Squire, King's College London

Founding Editors: Susan E. Alcock, Jaś Elsner, Simon Goldhill

The Greek culture of the Roman Empire offers a rich field of study. Extraordinary insights can be gained into processes of multicultural contact and exchange, political and ideological conflict, and the creativity of a changing, polyglot empire. During this period, many fundamental elements of Western society were being set in place: from the rise of Christianity, to an influential system of education, to long-lived artistic canons. This series is the first to focus on the response of Greek culture to its Roman imperial setting as a significant phenomenon in its own right. To this end, it will publish original and innovative research in the art, archaeology, epigraphy, history, philosophy, religion, and literature of the empire, with an emphasis on Greek material.

Recent titles in the series:

The Resurrection of Homer in Imperial Greek Epic: Quintus Smyrnaeus' Posthomerica *and the Poetics of Impersonation*
EMMA GREENSMITH

Oppian's Halieutica*: Charting a Didactic Epic*
EMILY KNEEBONE

Preposterous Poetics: The Politics and Aesthetics of Form in Late Antiquity
SIMON GOLDHILL

Greek Epigram and Byzantine Culture: Gender, Desire, and Denial in the Age of Justinian
STEVEN D. SMITH

Painting, Ethics, and Aesthetics in Rome
NATHANIEL B. JONES

Dionysius of Halicarnassus and Augustan Rome: Rhetoric, Criticism and Historiography
Edited by RICHARD HUNTER and CASPER C. DE JONGE

Author and Audience in Vitruvius' De Architectura
MARDEN FITZPATRICK NICHOLS

Visual Style and Constructing Identity in the Hellenistic World: Nemrud Dağ and Commagene under Antiochos I
MIGUEL JOHN VERSLUYS

THE RESURRECTION OF HOMER IN IMPERIAL GREEK EPIC

Quintus Smyrnaeus' Posthomerica *and the Poetics of Impersonation*

EMMA GREENSMITH

University of Oxford

CAMBRIDGE
UNIVERSITY PRESS

University Printing House, Cambridge CB2 8BS, United Kingdom

One Liberty Plaza, 20th Floor, New York, NY 10006, USA

477 Williamstown Road, Port Melbourne, VIC 3207, Australia

314–321, 3rd Floor, Plot 3, Splendor Forum, Jasola District Centre, New Delhi – 110025, India

79 Anson Road, #06–04/06, Singapore 079906

Cambridge University Press is part of the University of Cambridge.

It furthers the University's mission by disseminating knowledge in the pursuit of education, learning, and research at the highest international levels of excellence.

www.cambridge.org
Information on this title: www.cambridge.org/9781108830331
DOI: 10.1017/9781108907200

© Emma Greensmith 2020

This publication is in copyright. Subject to statutory exception and to the provisions of relevant collective licensing agreements, no reproduction of any part may take place without the written permission of Cambridge University Press.

First published 2020

A catalogue record for this publication is available from the British Library.

Library of Congress Cataloging-in-Publication Data
NAMES: Greensmith, Emma, author.
TITLE: The resurrection of Homer in imperial Greek epic : Quintus Smyrnaeus' Posthomerica and the poetics of impersonation / Emma Greensmith, University of Oxford.
DESCRIPTION: Cambridge ; New York : Cambridge University Press, 2020. | Series: Greek culture in the Roman world | Based on the author's dissertation (doctoral)–University of Cambridge, 2017. | Includes bibliographical references and index.
IDENTIFIERS: LCCN 2020014745 (print) | LCCN 2020014746 (ebook) | ISBN 9781108830331 (hardback) | ISBN 9781108820653 (paperback) | ISBN 9781108907200 (epub)
SUBJECTS: LCSH: Quintus, Smyrnaeus, active 4th century. Posthomerica. | Homer–Appreciation–Rome.
CLASSIFICATION: LCC PA4407.Q6 G744 2020 (print) | LCC PA4407.Q6 (ebook) | DDC 883/.01–dc23
LC record available at https://lccn.loc.gov/2020014745
LC ebook record available at https://lccn.loc.gov/2020014746

ISBN 978-1-108-83033-1 Hardback

Cambridge University Press has no responsibility for the persistence or accuracy of URLs for external or third-party internet websites referred to in this publication and does not guarantee that any content on such websites is, or will remain, accurate or appropriate.

To Anthony

Contents

List of Figures	*page*	viii
Acknowledgements		ix
Editions, Translations and Abbreviations		xi

1	Beginning Again (Introduction): The Poetics of Impersonation	1

PART I QUINTUS AS HOMER: ILLUSION AND IMITATION		47
2	Enlarging the Space: Imperial Doubleness, Fixity, Expansion	49
3	Writing Homer: Language, Composition and Style	93

PART II QUINTUS AS QUINTUS: ANTAGONISM AND ASSIMILATION		155
4	When Homer Quotes Callimachus: The Proem (not) in the Middle	157
5	Selective Memory and Iliadic Revision	189
6	Prodigal Poetics: Filiation and Succession	226
7	Temporality and the Homeric Not Yet	280

Bibliography		345
Index Locorum		374
Subject Index		381

vii

Figures

1 Papyrus fragment depicting a figure in armour, probably representing a *homeristes* with accompanying verse text, second century CE. *POxy.* XLII 3001, 'Homeric Verses' ed. P. Parsons. Reproduced with the permission of the Egypt Exploration Society. *page* 74

Acknowledgements

This book began life as a PhD thesis, written as part of the Imperial Greek Epic project at the University of Cambridge. I am indebted to the Arts and Humanities Research Council (AHRC) for funding the project, to Peterhouse for providing a supportive graduate (and undergraduate!) home and to the team of researchers who brought later Greek epic to life. Pavlos Avlamis, Emily Kneebone, Laura Miguélez-Cavero and Leyla Ozbek offered insights, intellectual encouragement and copious amounts of fun along the way. I can think of no better environment in which to have begun this research.

To Tim Whitmarsh, the project's Principal Investigator and my doctoral supervisor, I owe more thanks than any acknowledgement could express. He has been unfailingly generous with his time and enthusiasm, his instincts about my research are always uncannily right and he has become in all respects an inspirational mentor and, I hope, a lifelong friend.

Richard Hunter and Thomas Schmitz, the examiners of the thesis, provided numerous helpful suggestions on points large and small. I thank them for a stimulating and (actually) hugely enjoyable *viva*, which I shall always remember fondly.

Since then, the book and I have travelled to a number of classics departments, near and far: Colgate University in New York, Jesus College, Cambridge, and finally St John's College, Oxford, which I now proudly call my academic home. I am immensely grateful to my colleagues and friends at all three places – especially to Robert Garland, Talitha Kearey, Franco Basso, Rosanna Omitiwoju and, now at Oxford, Georgy Kantor, the late, inimitable Donald Russell, Constanze Güthenke and 'the team' (Karolina, Pan, Pippa and Dan) – for their intellectual community and great friendship. It is often said that academia can be an isolating place. I have never found that to be true.

x   *Acknowledgements*

I have benefited from the input of all those who have read chapters and listened to papers during the course of the book's preparation. Michael Sharp, Michael Squire and Jás Elsner provided fantastic editorial advice and fresh ideas, as did the manuscript's two external readers. Thanks also to Mary Morton for her meticulous copyediting. For their attention to, (re) readings of and comments on the project at so many stages, two people deserve particular thanks. Calum Maciver – whose book on the *Posthomerica* was the first thing I ever read on Quintus – has been an invaluable interlocutor from my PhD days to the present. It is a privilege to share ideas about Quintan poetics with him. Simon Goldhill, whose infectious enthusiasm for imperial Greek epic first burst into our 2014 reading group on Nonnus, has since become a cherished friend and intellectual ally, and his razor-sharp comments on the book's macro- and micro- ideas have enriched the finished version tremendously.

I am so lucky to know Daisy Dixon and Hannah Woods (my best friends): they share in the *mēnis*, and, in the true spirit of *nostos*, always make me feel that I am home.

My final and deepest thanks go to my family, and above all to Anthony, for everything.

Editions, Translations and Abbreviations

The text of Quintus is that of Vian; of the *Iliad* and *Odyssey* that of Murray; of Callimachus' *Aetia* that of Harder. Editions of other ancient works are indicated in the footnotes beneath the relevant text. Translations of Quintus are adapted from Hopkinson, of Homer from Murray and Dimcock. All other translations are my own unless indicated. Other editions are indicated in the footnotes beneath the relevant text. Ancient authors and works are abbreviated after those listed in the *Oxford Classical Dictionary* (4th edition).

CHAPTER I

Beginning Again (Introduction)
The Poetics of Impersonation

1.1 Prologue: Still Homer?

At an unknown place and time in the imperial Greek third century,[1] an epic picks up from the last line of the *Iliad*. This poem, known to posterity as the *Posthomerica* and whose author goes only by 'Quintus of Smyrna',[2] begins without a proem, Muse invocation or stated subject, but with a temporal conjunction – a 'when' – which implies not so much a start but a continuation:

> Εὖθ' ὑπὸ Πηλείωνι δάμη θεοείκελος Ἕκτωρ
> καὶ ἑ πυρῆ κατέδαψε καὶ ὀστέα γαῖα κεκεύθει,
> δὴ τότε Τρῶες ἔμιμνον ἀνὰ Πριάμοιο πόληα
> δειδιότες μένος ἠΰ θρασύφρονος Αἰακίδαο·
> ἠΰτ' ἐνὶ ξυλόχοισι βόες βλοσυροῖο λέοντος   (5)
> ἐλθέμεν οὐκ ἐθέλουσιν ἐναντίαι, ἀλλὰ φέβονται
> ἰληδὸν πτώσσουσαι ἀνὰ ῥωπήια πυκνά·
> ὣς οἱ ἀνὰ πτολίεθρον ὑπέτρεσαν ὄβριμον ἄνδρα
> μνησάμενοι προτέρων, ὁπόσων ἀπὸ θυμὸν ἴαψεν
> θύων Ἰδαίοιο περὶ προχοῇσι Σκαμάνδρου,   (10)
> ἠδ' <ὁπ>όσους φεύγοντας ὑπὸ μέγα τεῖχος ὄλεσσεν,
> Ἕκτορά θ' ὡς ἐδάμασσε καὶ ἀμφείρυσσε πόληι,
> ἄλλους θ' ὡς ἐδάϊξε δι' ἀκαμάτοιο θαλάσσης
> ὁππότε δὴ τὰ πρῶτα φέρε Τρώεσσιν ὄλεθρον.
> τῶν οἵ γε μνησθέντες ἀνὰ πτολίεθρον ἔμιμνον.   (15)
> ἀμφὶ δ' ἄρα σφίσι πένθος ἀνιηρὸν πεπότητο
> ὡς ἤδη στονόεντι καταιθομένης πυρὶ Τροίης.
>
> Q.S.1.1–17

When godlike Hector had been vanquished by the son of Peleus and the pyre had consumed him and the earth had covered his bones, the Trojan forces stayed

---

[1] On this dating and its controversies, see 1.7.
[2] On the names, both much later, non-biographical conjectures, see Baumbach and Bär (2007): 1–2 for an overview. Further discussion below.

2   Beginning Again (Introduction): The Poetics of Impersonation

inside the city of Priam terrified of the noble might of bold-hearted Achilles, grandson of Aeacus. Like cows which, unwilling to face a grim lion among the thickets, flee pell-mell and cower in the dense undergrowth: just so, inside their city, they shrank from the mighty warrior, remembering the many lives he had already cut short in his rampage around the streams of Scamander whose source is Mount Ida, the many men he had slaughtered as they fled under the great wall, his killing Hector and his dragging him round the city, and all the others he had slain in his passage through the restless sea when first he came bringing death to the Trojans. Such were the memories that kept them inside the city; and bitter grief fluttered all around them, as if Troy were already being burned with grievous fire.

This non-beginning contains an intense and carefully constructed nexus of allusions to Homer's first poem, signalling its status as a direct link – an 'Anschluss' – to the *Iliad*.[3] The first line specifically reminds us of the first *and* last lines of the *Iliad*. Πηλείωνι evokes the patronymic naming of Achilles in line 1 of the *Iliad*, and the verb δάμη, 'tamed', echoes the final adjective of Book 24, ἱπποδάμοιο '(Hector) tamer of horses'. The first adjective applied to Achilles in the *Iliad*, δῖος, is also perhaps cued and glossed by the adjective θεοείκελος, 'god-like'. In Homeric exegesis from the Alexandrian era onwards, the sense of δῖος as an epithet was much debated (does it mean 'god-like', 'noble' or 'descended from Zeus'?), whereas θεοείκελος means, definitively, 'godlike': Quintus' choice could be answering this Homeric question.

The narrative then continues (18–19), 'And then from the streams of the broad-flowing Thermodon came [ἦλθε] Penthesileia. . .'. This verse takes its cue from the alternative ending of the *Iliad* included in some manuscripts; where instead of the usual last word, ἱπποδάμοιο, one finds ἦλθε δ' Ἀμάζων, 'There came an Amazon'. The plot here slips into the first line of the *Aethiopis*, and the next phase of the saga.[4] This sequence thus takes place within the space opened by these two readings. Hector's death (line 1) is separated from the arrival of the Amazon (line 18) by an expansion that covers in a nutshell the whole narrative from Achilles' arrival in the war to the fall of Troy, which is imagined as 'already' (ἤδη) burning: the flashback to the Iliadic past is joined with a prolepsis to the cyclic future, which every reader of this poem will already know.

---

[3] This is by now the well-established interpretation of the epic and its opening, stretching as far back as Köchly (1850). Discussion of these and other allusions in Keydell (1963) (especially at 1273), Schenk (1997) (who uses 'Anschluss'), Kakridis (1962), Bär (2007), Maciver (2012b): 29–33 and now Goldhill (2020): ch. 3.

[4] Further treatment of Quintus' relationship to the Epic Cycle in 1.10. All of my comments in Chapter 1 are designed to foreground and anticipate later, sustained analysis.

Prologue: Still Homer?

This is therefore an opening which simultaneously claims to be 'still the *Iliad*' and also a highly self-conscious reading of the *Iliad*, which revels in its own oblique relationship to the Homeric critical tradition. Just as the frightened Trojans recall the earlier heroes (μνησάμενοι προτέρων, 9) so this passage is forged from poetic memory. Here is an epic beginning without the expected invocation of the Muses, but which repeats the verb associated with the mother of the Muses, and thus with 'the memorializing function of epic'.[5]

However, these echoes do not, *qua* the usual logic of referentiality, urge the reader just to look back to the mythological and literary past. Instead, at the correlative δὴ τότε (3), the opening shifts across the sequence of tenses, and moves the *Iliad*'s narrative situation back closer to the present. With ἔμιμνον in line 3, the aorist gives way to the imperfect, and the verb's meaning mirrors its move to the past continuous: an indication of the poem's position, in which the characters 'remain' in the *Iliad*. With the participle δειδιότες (4) the aorist is further overturned, and the past completed now becomes perfect. The Trojans were scared and are scared: their fear is triggered by an event in the past, but one which has a consequential state in the present.

The description then yields to a simile (Q.S.1.5–7), the first instance of the feature of which this poem will go on to make such frequent use. But why start with *this* simile? Why put it precisely here? There is a heavy denseness to these lines, not only in the image (the huddling and the thickets), but also in its construction: the subject (βόες) is conjoined with the aggressor (βλοσυροῖο λέοντος, 5); the verbs run together, a mass of *etas* and *thetas* (ἐλθέμεν οὐκ ἐθέλουσιν ἐναντίαι, 6); the bushy thickets shrink into themselves (πτώσσουσαι ἀνὰ ῥωπήια πυκνά, 7) . . . everything is squashed. This emphasis on proximity, set at odds with the desire to 'go out' or stand opposed (ἐναντίαι), could offer an opening indication of the poem's whole relationship to the Iliadic narrative: they will not be set apart, but joined together closely. When the aorist is reasserted (ὑπέτρεσαν, 8) its sense of a past completed has thus been destabilised by the multitextured presentism of the intervening lines. This antagonism between past and still-present also operates in the linguistics of memory: the aorist μνησάμενοι (9) again yields to the perfect μνησθέντες (15). This is a literary recapitulation framed as a memory – but an act of remembering which, the repeated ἔμιμνον stresses, is itself set to 'remain'.

---

[5] Goldhill (2020).

4   Beginning Again (Introduction): The Poetics of Impersonation

The epic thus begins by raising as a *question* the possibility of its status as 'still Iliadic': it thematises as well as narrativises the 'seamless' progression from Homer's first poem to this familiar and yet eerily new here and now. Its story then proceeds to tell in fourteen books the events of the Trojan War which took place between the *Iliad* and *Odyssey*, and ends with a proleptic gloss to the start of the *Odyssey*'s narrative – the first lines after the proem:

> ...οἱ δ᾽ ἐνὶ νηυσὶν
> Ἀργεῖοι πλώεσκον, ὅσους διὰ χεῖμα κέδασσεν·
> ἄλλη δ᾽ ἄλλος ἵκανεν, ὅπη θεὸς ἦγεν ἕκαστον,
> ὅσσοι ὑπὲρ πόντοιο λυγρὰς ὑπάλυξαν ἀέλλας.
>
> Q.S.14.665–8

Meanwhile those Argives still aboard ship sailed on, scattered by the storm; and they arrived in different places, where a god guided each one, as many as had survived the voyage through that disastrous storm.

> ἔνθ᾽ ἄλλοι μὲν πάντες, ὅσοι φύγον αἰπὺν ὄλεθρον,
> οἴκοι ἔσαν, πόλεμόν τε πεφευγότες ἠδὲ θάλασσαν·
>
> Od. 1.11–12

Now all the rest, as many as had escaped sheer destruction, were at home, safe from both war and sea.

The 'safe' returns of the *Odyssey*'s own opening recapitulation are closely predicated and anticipated in these closing scenes: the *ad hoc* 'arrival' on random shores (ἄλλη δ᾽ ἄλλος ἵκανεν) is the first, necessary stage of the real Odyssean homecomings (οἴκοι ἔσαν); and the indeterminate group contained in the Homeric ὅσοι φύγον (the generalised many to contrast particularly with the singular, particular 'man' [τὸν δ᾽ οἶον νόστου κεχρημένον, *Od.* 1.13]) is echoed and enabled by Quintus' ὅσσοι ... ὑπάλυξαν – the escape the destruction of the stormy sea allows the safe and dry presentism of those lucky ones who have reached the start of the *Odyssey*.

The so-called *Posthomerica* thus proclaims in fact a profoundly *inter*-Homeric position: not just a piece of the cyclic saga, a 'slice of Homer's banquet',[6] but a carefully construed narrative location, it seems, precisely in between the *Iliad* and *Odyssey*. Quintus occupies the complex, tense Homeric middle. And the Homeric relationship does not end there. Not only is language throughout thoroughly indebted to Homer, but the narrative also features in enormous numbers many defining Homeric

---

[6] Cf. Athenaeus' oft-quoted 'quotation' of Aeschylus (*Sophists at Dinner* 8, 347e).

Prologue: Still Homer?

features – particularly similes, *gnomai* and ekphrasis – including, most starkly, a certain shield of Achilles, which appears 'again' in Book 5 of this poem. Stressed as being the same shield (the same object) as appeared in the *Iliad*,[7] this unique piece of Homeric description is narrated here once more in its full ekphrastic glory, but with different, 'later' aspects of its cosmological story emphasised; imagined as elements which were always already there:[8]

> ἄλλα δὲ μυρία κεῖτο κατ' ἀσπίδα τεχνήεντως
> χερσὶν ὑπ' ἀθανάτης πυκινόφρονος Ἡφαίστοιο·

Countless other scenes had been skilfully wrought on the shield by the hands of the ingenious god Hephaestus.

Q.S.5.97–8

Then, most drastically of all, the poet uses his singular moment of self-description to represent himself *as* Homer: a programmatic self-identification that occurs in a strikingly late proem in Book 12:

> τούς μοι νῦν καθ' ἕκαστον ἀνειρομένῳ σάφα Μοῦσαι
> ἔσπεθ', ὅσοι κατέβησαν ἔσω πολυχανδέος ἵππου·
> ὑμεῖς γὰρ πᾶσάν μοι ἐνὶ φρεσὶ θήκατ' ἀοιδήν,
> πρίν γε μοι <ἔτ'> ἀμφὶ παρειὰ κατασκίδνασθαι ἴουλον,
> Σμύρνης ἐν δαπέδοισι περικλυτὰ μῆλα νέμοντι. . .

Q.S.12.306–10

Muses, I ask you to tell me precisely, one by one, the names of all who went inside the capacious horse. For you were the ones who filled my mind with all song even before down was spread across my cheeks, when I was tending my renowned sheep in the land of Smyrna. . .

In what would be the mid-point of a Homeric epic, before he embarks upon his own catalogue of heroes, Quintus claims most directly to be Homer; *not* by saying 'I am Homer', but instead by preserving Homer's

---

[7] See Maciver (2012b): 40: 'The shield, more than any other part of the *Posthomerica*, represents the poem's intertextual dialogue with the Homeric poems. . . since the shield of Achilles in Q.S.5 is the same shield as that given to Achilles in *Iliad* 19 and made by Hephaestus in *Iliad* 18' (although of course, as he clarifies with notable directness [n. 9]: 'strictly speaking, of course, the shield of Achilles does not ever exist.'). Thus the actuality which we are talking about here exists on the level of fictional physicality, in the realm of illusion.

[8] On the conceit here, see the excellent discussion of Maciver (2012b): 47: 'the expression ἄλλα δὲ μυρία implies that there are an inexhaustible number of scenes on the shield of Achilles, and that neither the Iliadic nor post-Homeric narrator described all [of them], but rather only decided to describe some of them, according to their own interpretations of the world of the shield'. Also now Maciver (2018): 79.

6   Beginning Again (Introduction): The Poetics of Impersonation

renowned anonymity, and evoking Smyrna, one of his most famous birthplaces in the biographical tradition. However, alongside this Homeric proclamation, this proem also includes some strong allusions to later Greek poets; most outstandingly in line 310, which near-on quotes the *Somnium* of the *Aetia*, where Callimachus re-presents Hesiod's meeting with the Muses (ποιμένι μῆλα νέμοντι παρ' ἴχνιον ὀξέος ἵππου/'Ησιόδῳ Μουσέων ἑσμὸς ὅτ' ἠντίασεν [...], *Aet.* fr.2.1–2).

This dynamic merging of Homeric mimesis and Homeric biography, making 'Homer' quote Hesiod and Callimachus, epitomises the dramatic form of identity poetics on display. As is traceable first and foremost through these central pivots – the opening sequence, the closing verses, the 'still Homeric shield', and the delayed proem – this epic voice is characterised by a fundamentally paradoxical stance towards its primary and overwhelming model. In a move that renders it unique among surviving imperial Greek epic, its relationship to Homeric epic is one of impersonation, not just imitation. And yet at every stage of this impersonation, the reader encounters obstacles which disavow these authoritative authorial claims: philological quirks, contemporary references and later literary allusions; all loitering just beneath the Homeric surface, constructed so as to almost – but never quite – escape detection.

The reason for starting with these essential passages (each of which will return as a central focus point in the chapters to come) stems from the questions about the aesthetics and politics of Homeric reworking that they so powerfully raise. That Quintus is 'Homerising' is commonly accepted by any scholar who has looked at or worked on this text. But what is far less understood is what this Homerising means: for the poet, for his reader and for the imperial culture in which he was composing. It is not possible to appreciate any of the recent re-evaluations of Quintus unless the intensity of his relationship to Homer is more deeply interrogated.

This book therefore puts forward a new way of understanding this remarkable epic, its poetics, agenda and literary identity. It is my central contention that Quintus' response to Homer represents a new formative poetics. To be characterised neither by 'second sophistic' epigonality, nor by Hellenistic allusiveness, nor silver Latin belatedness, the *Posthomerica* involves inserting oneself *within* fixed, pre-existing literary boundaries, occupying the space in between antiquity's oldest pillars, Homer's two canonical poems. This type of response should be conceptualised instead, I suggest, as a **poetics of the interval**: a mode of continuation which does not start from where the old poet left off, but intervenes non-linearly, engaging with Homeric epic as a text internally and inherently incomplete, canonically bounded and finished, but conceptually a living work to be expanded and re-embodied.

I turn first to constructing and analysing, through a number of different vectors, this interval poetics of the *Posthomerica*, and aim to trace the *consequences* (literary and cultural) of this strong, sustained and self-conscious interstitial Homeric position.[9] This programmatic middleness, the drive to find a space within what is already there, to revivify Homer and re-animate the past, emerges as an intense form of meditation on a specific strand of cultural politics in the third century, involved in the shaping of Greek erudite identity in the East. To access these consequences, however, also requires a departure from the critical discourse in which the poem, and imperial Greek epic more broadly, is currently situated. By making this departure, my second major intention is to demonstrate how Quintus' poetics could be pivotal for rethinking prevailing scholarly conceptions of this era of epic, suggesting what it meant to resurrect the Homeric idiolect in the later Roman Empire.

1.2   Opposition in Imitation

'One useful approach to great "imitative" texts is to see them as re-readings of the works imitated.'

– Martindale, *Redeeming the Text*, 35

'Roman literary-historical self-fashioning operated through a revision of previous Hellenising revolutions, a revision which can simultaneously be an appropriation and a denial ... these poets carved out cultural space for themselves by consigning their predecessors to the dustbin.'

– Hinds, *Allusion and Intertext*, 10

'The poet is always challenged to be supreme in the supreme genre ... the ever-present desire and its attendant anxiety.'

– Hardie, *The Epic Successors of Virgil*, 119

---

[9] A note on terminology is required at this early stage: throughout this book, I shall use both the notions of the 'interval' and the 'interstitial' to define Quintus' Homeric self-positioning, in full awareness that the terms are not synonymous, but rather offer a mutually fruitful double act for discussing the types of 'middleness' at play. The brevity usually associated with an 'interstice', for instance, will capture the ways in which Quintus works to reduce the space (narrative and chronological) between Homer's two epics, and between Homeric time and imperial time. And the perceived inter-ludic nature of the 'interval' (*qua*, for instance, toilet breaks in a modern theatre performance) will work to show how the *Posthomerica* ironically anticipates derogatory assessments of its poetic quality in relation to Homer – simply a text to 'pass through', to fill in the gaps in the cyclic story between Homer's masterpieces – and turns the idea of liminality and transition into an active, culturally relevant, temporal statement.

8   Beginning Again (Introduction): The Poetics of Impersonation

'Opposition in imitation' or 'contrast imitation' has long been considered an important type of literary response in antiquity, becoming increasingly self-conscious with the Alexandrian poets. Thus, to take an initial but paradigmatic case, the now seminal work on Apollonius and the Hellenistic poetic tradition has revealed quite definitively how this literary era's 'self-conscious textuality' unleashes a dynamic tension with its Homeric epic model: thus Apollonius' poem 'proves to be a meditation upon the problems of "epic" ... within the parameters bequeathed by Homer.'[10] In a ground-breaking series launched at the end of the twentieth century, the authors of *Roman Literature and its Contexts* sought to demonstrate how this Alexandrian adversarial style of imitation was specifically harnessed by Augustan and post-Augustan Latin literature.[11] Focusing on theories of hermeneutics, supplementarity, reader reception, historical contingency and the Anxiety of Influence, the project presented the principles of a creative emulation to characterise the poets of the Latin tradition, and used it to cast new insights on both the emulating poets and their original models.

Charles Martindale borrows from Harold Bloom and Derridean deconstructionism to sketch his particular way of conceptualising the interpretative process; namely that 'any interpretation, unless it is mere tautology, must be a re-stating, and thus *different* from whatever is interpreted.'[12] The notion of supplementarity, that 'a signifier is so charged with an excess of energy that it generates further fictions, which serve to answer unanswered questions, fill "gaps", explain perceived contradictions, provide sequels and allow for appropriations in view of new circumstances'[13] helps to account for the process of continued interpretative revision that Martindale reads as acutely present in the Latin tradition and its inheritors: the constant striving for, but refusal of, textual closure.

---

[10] Hunter (1993): 36. To Hunter's tide-turning analysis of Apollonius can now be added a mammoth number of studies and readings in this (still on-going) 'golden age' of Alexandrian criticism in the classics. See the bibliography compiled by Cuypers for an overview of the volume of work done on these poets up to July 2012: sites.google.com/site/hellenisticbibliography/empire (date last accessed 13.04.20).

[11] The whole series spans 1993–2016. My interest is principally in the first and second wave of publications, from 1993–8, which are the most influential and are also considered the most 'radical.' The following discussion does not aim to suggest that this group are the only voices in this discussion, nor the most important: see also for instance the invaluable contributions of Henderson (1987), Barchiesi (1986), Feeney (e.g. 1991) and Bartsch (1994) – each of whom will also appear as interlocutors in the chapters to come. My reason for focusing on this series here is due to the specific and often specifically stated impact that it has had on imperial Greek epic studies (see discussion and examples in 1.3).

[12] Martindale (1993): 37.   [13] Ibid.

Opposition in Imitation

Stephen Hinds applies many of these tenets to his now (in)famous study of allusion in Roman poets.[14] Following Conte's conception of allusion as an analogical figure,[15] Hinds characterises the patterns of reference in Ovid, Statius and Lucan as 'tendentious re-readings' of their literary models, expressed through a range of 'tropes', which he defines as figural symbols (words, images, characters) used to characterise authorial engagement. From Ennius onwards, and no doubt before, Roman writers create old poets in order to proclaim their newness, and thus concepts such as 'new', 'old', 'secondary' or even 'decline' are not just modern labels, but inherent to these writers' literary self-conceptions.

The work of Philip Hardie has anchored this model most firmly to the epic tradition. In his incisive readings of post-Augustan Latin epic, Hardie shows how the successors of Vergil 'at once respectful and rebellious, constructed a space for themselves through a creative imitation that exploited the energies and tensions called up but not finally expended or resolved in the *Aeneid*'.[16] Theories of supplementarity and Oedipal struggles also loom large for Hardie, but he goes one step further by demonstrating the epic genre's innate hospitality to these processes. Epic, by its very nature, must be rivalrous, because of the fundamental ambition of its undertaking: attempting to compose within the most foundational of literary genres, this is a power game played for the highest of stakes.[17]

As Hardie's study also shows, the process of contrast imitation has strong political potential. As writers responding to the problems and contradictions of the principate, poets such as Ovid, Lucan, Statius and Silius Italicus reveal 'anxiety' about imperial as much as poetic succession: their re-readings of the *Aeneid* bring to the fore its questions about the viability of a lasting age of peace, the relationship between power and the sacred, and the chaos caused when an empire turns in on itself. This political dimension has been explored most capaciously by David Quint in *Epic and Empire*.[18] In his account of how the epics of the western tradition responded to the two different narrative modes offered by the *Iliad* and *Odyssey*, Quint centralises and politicises the idea of 'continuity', and the creativity triggered by the desire for its avoidance. Thus Lucan, in his

---

[14] Cf. Hinds (1998): 47–51.   [15] Conte (1986): 23–4; 52–69. Hinds (1998): 120–1.
[16] Hardie (1993): xii.
[17] Ibid: 118–19. Cf. Steiner (1989): 13: the successor poet is always 'answerable to the original' because it 'puts at eminent risk the stature, the fortunes of his own work'.
[18] Quint (1993).

10   Beginning Again (Introduction): The Poetics of Impersonation

anti-Vergilian, anti-imperial epic, mounts a critique on 'the conservative tendency of the epic genre to perpetuate, through imitation, its own formal structures of narrative and diction, its motifs and commonplaces of plot: the same story told over and over'.[19]

This framework has had a momentous impact on readings of ancient epic: the critical rewards which are now associated with contrast imitation are rich and abundant. This form of intertextuality, once pitched as revolutionary by its champions, has now become deeply entrenched in the industry of classical scholarship; a means of recuperating a poem's quality by a demonstration of how it imaginatively re-works the language of its predecessors – the same story told over and over. It has provided a particularly positive stimulus for studies in silver Latin,[20] doing much to increase interest in these once neglected works by revealing their complex literary-political textures. Since the turn of the century, however, it has found a further epic test site, to which I now turn.

1.3   Silver Latin, Imperial Greek?

A surge in interest in the Greek literature of the Roman Empire has seen scholars gradually direct attention towards the epic composed during this period. Between the second and sixth centuries CE more Greek hexameter verse was composed (and survives) than during any other comparable era of antiquity. Whilst statistics alone, admittedly, can mean little in litera-ture, what this density begins to suggest is that epic remained, as it was for Greeks throughout antiquity, the most prestigious literary form, the apex of the hierarchy of genres. The Homeric epics themselves stood at the centre of imperial Greek culture: the avatar of *paideia*, Homer was studied at every stage of the education system.[21] Despite these facts, epic – and poetry in general – was for a long time almost entirely neglected by scholarship on this period in comparison to prose: only thirty-five years ago did Habicht feel confident to declare that in imperial Greece, 'poetry

---

[19] Quint (1993): 8 using Greene (1963). Quint's is of course far from the only – or the overbearing – version of Lucan as politics. Henderson's account of Lucan's 'Word at War' (1987) remains indispensable and unsettling. For Masters (1992) Lucan's obsessive poetics comes to embody, rather than merely describe, the political discord of civil war.

[20] I use this term here as I shall throughout this book, in a non-pejorative sense as a shorthand for the post-Augustan poets of the first two centuries CE.

[21] We return centrally to the topic of Homer and imperial education in Chapter 2.

was dead'.[22] The situation is now very different. The importance and impact of the work of Francis Vian on two imperial poets, Quintus and Nonnus, remain difficult to overstate. His editions of Nonnus' *Diony-siaca*[23] and Quintus' *Posthomerica*[24] gave rise to a number of further studies,[25] and greatly facilitated detailed research on these two epics. Ewen Bowie's series of articles[26] offered the first serious attempt at a broader account of imperial Greek verse, bolstered by a conference on this poetry in 2007 which resulted in the aptly titled volume *Signs of Life?*.[27] The imperial Greek Epic project at Cambridge (2014–17) has further raised the profile of this material, through the compilation of a complete database of the poetry,[28] the first comprehensive set of translations[29] and a public-facing website.[30] Verse is thus increasingly being recognised as a living medium of expression in imperial Greek culture; and epic in particular is emerging as a powerful vehicle through which traditional language and themes were renegotiated.[31]

If the lamentation of scholarly neglect has thus become a genuinely outdated trope for imperial Greek epic, then I have resurrected it here because it is worth considering not just why this material was understudied for so long,[32] but what the study of it now has uncovered: what ideas have emerged which make it matter so much. On the one hand, the themes of imperial hexameter were no less varied than that composed in any other

---

[22] Habicht (1985). Bowie (1989b): 198 also cites *The Short History of Greek Literature* ('only two names deserve mention – Quintus and Nonnus'), and *The Cambridge History of Classical Literature*, which stops in the middle of the third century and has only two pages on imperial Greek poetry.

[23] 1976–2006, nineteen volumes.

[24] 1963–9, three volumes: the first edition based on a complete collation of all relevant manuscripts. See Baumbach and Bär (2007): 18–19 for further discussion. I return to Vian's editorial work centrally in Chapter 3.

[25] Further references given below in this section and *passim*. For a detailed overview of recent scholarship on the *Dionysiaca*, see the introduction by Accorinti in the recent *Brill's Companion to Nonnus of Panopolis*: 2016: 1–7. Vian himself published two monographs on the *Posthomerica* (1959); and, together with Battegay, a Greek-French *Lexique de Quintus de Smyrne* (1984).

[26] Bowie (1989a), (1989b), (1990).   [27] Hunter and Carvounis (2008).

[28] Which has collated c. 1000 poems, fragments and references in the literary, papyrological and epigraphic records.

[29] Forthcoming by the University of California Press.

[30] www.imperialepeios.wordpress.com/ (date last accessed 18.4.20).

[31] See the 'imperial Greek poets' section of Cuypers' bibliography for an overview for an indication of the work done to date on these authors up to 2012: sites.google.com/site/hellenisticbibliography/empire (date last accessed 18.4.20). As is the case with the Hellenistic poets, to this list can now be added a number of important works, which, rather than listing superfluously in a footnote, I shall cite and engage as they become relevant in the chapters to come.

[32] This question has been amply addressed and variously answered. For a deft summary of how so, see particularly Hunter and Carvounis (2008): 1–2.

12   Beginning Again (Introduction): The Poetics of Impersonation

period.[33] We have examples of works on material as diverse as imperial lion hunts,[34] hymnic prayers[35] and world history – Dionysius of Alexandria's *Periegesis* describes the globe in 1187 hexameters. Didactic themes were also common – manuals on hunting, fishing[36] and medicine –[37] which Bowie suggests constituted the most dominant type of poetry at least in the Antonine age.[38]

However, within this diversity we may detect a particular thematic penchant: the explicit engagement with Homer and the return to the narrative world of Troy. 'Engagement with Homer' is, of course, a notion which could be applied to almost any ancient Greek poem; and Trojan mythology was also likely to have been a popular theme at all times in antiquity,[39] including in the lost Hellenistic epics against which Callimachus allegedly railed.[40] But the *combination* of these features – the extremely close recapitulation of Homeric language and forms, and the direct return to his mythological subject-matter –[41] does seem to unite a number of texts from the imperial Greek period specifically. There is something dramatic and direct in the Trojan texture of these epics which is worthy of further attention.

The *Posthomerica*, if dated to the third century (a hypothesis to which we shall soon return) represents the earliest surviving example of this imperial penchant. Its highly Homeric lexicon and narrative straddling of Homer's poems represents a stark illustration of this type of epic production. It must also be comprehended within the larger matrix of mythological epics from the era, which take on similar cyclical themes and use Homerising language, but mobilise these elements to achieve their own effects and agenda. I shall here outline a few of the most important and contrastive examples, which will provide crucial interlocutors in the analysis to come.

About a century after the *Posthomerica*,[42] Triphiodorus penned a hexameter poem also richly steeped in Homeric language which narrates the sack of Troy. Unlike Quintus' elliptical fourteen books, this poem tells its

---

[33] For this brief survey I draw from Bowie (1989a), (1989b) and (1990) and the Cambridge database, which has uncovered material to add to this picture.

[34] Pancrates wrote a hexameter poem on the lion hunt of Hadrian and Antinous.

[35] Macellus of Side wrote hexameters encouraging Roman women to offer cult to Regilla's statue and praying to Athena and the Nemesis of Rhamnous to punish anyone who encroaches on Herodes' estate.

[36] Most extensively the works of the Oppians.

[37] Marcellus of Side wrote a 42-book *Iatrika*, of which 101 lines survive; and Heraclitus (see Bowie (1990): 69) was dubbed the 'Homer of medical poetry.'

[38] Bowie (1990).   [39] Cf. e.g. Miguélez Cavero (2013): 5.

[40] For the relevance of Callimachus' accusations to imperial Greek poetry, see Chapter 4.

[41] On the place of the Epic Cycle poems in this model, see 1.10.

[42] On the direction of influence between Triphiodorus and Quintus, see discussion below.

Silver Latin, Imperial Greek? 13

tale in just under 700 lines. In fewer verses than most single books of Homer, this story is over and done with. It provides a characteristic example of what in modern literary criticism is known as epyllion: a little epic.[43] 'Little epic' is in one sense an ironic oxymoron – epic by nature is anything but diminutive – and since there is no Aristotelian or other ancient version of this typology, scholars remain divided as to whether or not it should be usefully considered a type of epic at all.[44] And yet the sorts of play with size encapsulated in the epyllion of course have a long history in ancient written and visual representation. From the 'potted stories' of the songs of Demodocus[45] and, in the Latin tradition, Catullus 64, to the compressive dynamics of the epigram, to the games with medium, narrative and scale set forth by Callicrates and Myrmecides – said to have inscribed either Homer's whole epic, or a single couplet, on a 'sesame seed' –[46] and on the Iliac Tablets (of which we shall hear more soon), the underlying conceit of the epyllion, of 'rescaling epic', must take its place among this long line of forerunners and interlocutors.[47] Triphiodorus' text seems distinctly to address just such issues of genre and form: to draw attention to its own 'oxymoronic' status as a miniature epic. This knowingness is at its clearest in the proem (1–5), which immediately turns the process of compression into a question of speed.[48] Treating the sack of Troy as a tired, completed story, Triphiodorus resolves to accelerate through his version of the tale: the justification for re-telling is found in the rejection of the indulgence of delay.

Another epyllion, Colluthus' account of the rape – or abduction, or seduction –[49] of Helen (c. sixth century CE), returns to the start and cause of the entire Trojan War. Unfolding in miniature the origins of the most canonical conflict of all, Colluthus repeatedly foregrounds concepts of primordiality and inception, asking from the outset: ὠγυγίη δὲ τίς ἔπλετο νείκεος ἀρχή; (10). But the poem also makes clear that this beginning belongs to the past. As Eris the goddess of Strife hurls her golden apples to

---

[43] On this poetic type in antiquity, see Baumbach and Bär (2012) and Fernandelli (2012).

[44] If one consults, for instance, the recent *Brill's Companion to Greek and Latin Epyllion* (Baumbach and Bär (2012)) there will be found some excellent readings of individual poems, but little to no sense of the self-identity to which these poems do or do not make claim.

[45] See Hunter's contribution to Baumbach and Bär (2012).

[46] Respectively Plut. *Mor.* (*Comm. not.*) 1083d–e and Aelian *VH* 1.17.

[47] See particularly Squire (2011): ch. 1, from where 'rescaling' (p. 2) is taken.

[48] I defer detailed discussion of this proem to the chapters to come, which tackle directly its issues of acceleration and form: see particularly Chapter 4 and Chapter 7.

[49] On the definition(s) of *harpage* in this context, see discussion in Morales (2016): 61 with further references.

14   Beginning Again (Introduction): The Poetics of Impersonation

disrupt the wedding of Peleus, there begins a series of events which from the point of view of the reader has long since 'already' occurred:

ἤδη δ᾽ Ἑσπερίδων χρυσέων ἐμνήσατο μήλων·
ἔνθεν Ἔρις, πολέμοιο προάγγελον ἔρνος ἑλοῦσα
μῆλον, ἀριζήλων ἐφράσσατο δήνεα μόχθων.
Abduction of Helen 59–61

And already now she recalled her golden apples of the Hesperides. Then Strife took the fruit, the harbinger of war, the apple, and devised the plans for conspicuous woes.

Nonnus' sprawling *Dionysiaca* (fifth century CE) concerns not the pointedly small but the gargantuanly big. This compendious poem, the longest surviving work from late antiquity, and one of the most influential,[50] narrates – to summarise absurdly – the birth of Dionysus, his love affairs, travels and battles (most notably the Indian campaign) and final apotheosis into Olympus. The centrality of Homer to this poem is overwhelmingly apparent. Its forty-eight books deliberately match the *Iliad* and *Odyssey* combined, and its poetics, as we shall discuss, obsessively thematises rebellion, filiation and (dis)continuity in relation to Homer, appropriating and transforming Homeric style, scenes and skin[51] for a new polymorphic agenda. The narrative chronology of the *Dionysiaca* also positions itself in the mythological era before the Trojan War. This timing itself opens up an intense space for Homeric foreshadowing and retrospective echoing; as Nonnus constantly exploits his simultaneous position as pre- and post-Homeric.

In addition to these major later testimonies, references to non-surviving texts also reveal that the production of mythological epic was continuous in the centuries preceding the *Posthomerica*. Triphiodorus' other works, according to the *Suda*, included a lipogrammatic *Odyssey* and *Paraphrase of Homer's Similes*. In the second century, Areios composed a cento on Memnon using Homeric phrases, signed by 'the Homeric poet from the Museum'.[52] And the poets of Laranda, the Homerically named Nestor and his son Pisander (both third century CE) both wrote large-scale mythological works. The former produced a lipogrammatic *Iliad*: a bold and novel move to create a 'new' *Iliad* missing successive letters in successive books,

---

[50] On the influence of Nonnus and particularly the so-called Nonnian School in the fifth century, see Accorinti (2016) and Tissoni (2016), which represent two of the most recent treatments.
[51] Nonnus in his preface asks the Mimallons to leave the rancid seal-skins to Homer for Menelaus (*Dion.* 1.34–8).
[52] See Bowie (1990): 65.

Silver Latin, Imperial Greek? 15

which won him great fame across the empire.[53] The latter in turn offered up the largest poem of antiquity, the *Heroic Marriages of the Gods*, sixty books in length. By the time the *Posthomerica* was composed, we may thus rightly speak of a distinctive trend of Homeric-imitative, mythological epic.

Another related strand of the late antique epic tradition must also be comprehended in light of this 'trend': a continuation of it, but also an alternative interpretation of its ambitions. Cento poetry has attracted copious attention in recent scholarship on later Greek and Latin poetics.[54] Defined most straightforwardly as a patchwork poem composed from hemistichs or whole lines of pre-existing poetry, typically Vergil and Homer, the cento has been recognised as a distinctive imperial literary phenomenon,[55] which strikes at the heart of some of the particular concerns surrounding tradition and creativity in the (particularly post-Christian) phases of the Roman Empire. As Elsner well puts it, like the use of *spolia* in monuments of material culture, the cento takes fragments from earlier canonical poetry to create new poems which operate on a double level: they are both poems in their own right and 'an audacious intertextual commentary' from the past (the corpus of Homer or Vergil) on the present (e.g. Ausonius' *cento nuptalis* about intercourse in the marital bed, or the Empress Eudocia's tales about her Christian life, and Genesis and the New Testament): 'the ways that centos valorize a lost and unattainable or palpably passing classicism ... helps us understand the larger question of the transformation of the classical tradition within late antique culture'.[56]

Such penchants make clear that within and throughout the rapidly changing conditions of the Greek world under Roman rule, the distant mythology of Troy and the ancient idolect of its 'original' storyteller Homer was not redundant or arcane. On the contrary, it appears to have acquired a new – or renewed – relevance and authority, articulated most

---

[53] See the excellent discussion by Ma (2007). Triphiodorus' later decision to produce a lipogrammatic *Odyssey* has rightly been considered to be directly influenced by Nestor's groundbreaking creation: Triphiodorus wanted a slice of this action, and of the resultant high praise.

[54] I shall not here attempt to recapitulate the full bibliography on the cento as a poetic technique and the individual works within it. Particularly important publications include Usher (1998), Sandes (2011), Hinds (2014) Pelttari (2014): especially ch. 3, and the various chapters in Elsner and Hernández Lobato (2017). An excellent new contribution on Eudocia is forthcoming by Sowers (2020).

[55] While some centos date to the late classical period, most were written during the imperial era, and come from across the empire: Gaul, Italy, North Africa, Constantinople and Palestine have claim to at least one cento poet.

[56] Elsner (2017), quotations at 178.

16   Beginning Again (Introduction): The Poetics of Impersonation

vociferously by the epic poets, who chose to return directly to the Homeric world and or use the language of its original song. This 'return to Troy' will be central to my reading of Quintus. I shall use the *Posthomerica* to interrogate its heightened relevance and suggest reasons for the particular authority that it held: a parallel or rival to alternative forms of literary-cultural hegemony being displayed and contested.

1.4   Homeric Poetics at the Dawn of Christianity

Nonnus' story, and that of many of the centos, add a further crucial dimension to imperial Greek epic's relationship to Homer and to Trojan time. Nonnus was also the author of a twenty-one-book verse paraphrase of John's gospel,[57] and the *Dionysiaca* guides a suspiciously but never quite overtly Christian Dionysus through his ante-Homeric adventures. The issue of Christianity is thus brought to the fore for the *Dionysiaca* in a way much more direct than for the other imperial mythological poets discussed here. And amidst the boom in critical interest in the poet in the past two decades, scholars remain divided about why Nonnus would write this 'pagan' epic at all. The traditional recourse to a conversion explanation – that Nonnus embraced Christianity after finishing the *Dionysiaca*, and then wrote the *Paraphrase*, or recanted it after the *Paraphrase* and then wrote the *Dionysiaca* –[58] is increasingly dismissed as circular and facile, and replaced with more holistic interpretations and possibilities. How far, for instance, can we read coded references to Christianity in the *Dionysiaca*, with the Dionysiac symbols of the vine, virgin births and resurrection offering ripe material for typological, syncretic reworking?[59] The (anti)-Christian position of Nonnus is thus far more than a biographical question: it makes the poet critical for considering the potential *religious* dimensions of a return to distant mytho-poetics – the extent to which the recourse to a Trojan Homeric world should be read as a reactionary

---

[57]   Editions have been produced of, thus far, eight books of the Paraphrase (the most recent in Spanoudakis 2014b (ed.)). Shorrock's seminal work on the *Paraphrase* and the *Dionysiaca* (2011) was joined in 2016 by another monograph dedicated to the Christian poem (Doroszewski 2016). See also Part III of Accorinti (ed.) (2016).

[58]   On this traditional narrative, and its dependencies on the relative dating of the *Dionysiaca* and the *Paraphrase* (itself a matter of contention), see the cogent summary of the state of play in Accorinti (2016): 37–46.

[59]   See particularly the influential work of Shorrock (2011) on this topic. For a negative view of the 'Christianity' of the *Dionysiaca*, see Vian (1994) and Deckers (1986). Accorinti's discussion ((2016): 37–46) also provides a full synthesis of the range of scholarly positions on this debate.

Homeric Poetics at the Dawn of Christianity　　　17

(re)turn at a time when sacro-intellectual authority was contemporarily being renegotiated.

These questions, posed so explicitly for Nonnus, must also be applied to Quintus. Amidst the vast output produced on the *Posthomerica* in recent years, scholars have (almost without exception) found no traces of Christian themes or engagement. Aside from the biographical possibility that Quintus' son was a Christian – a certain Dorotheus, to whose poem on the Vision of God we shall shortly return – his epic seems, from all internal evidence, to be either pre- or conspicuously non-Christian. And yet the story perhaps does not end there. We have already seen in Chapter 1.1 how Quintus establishes a careful policy of Homerising self-occlusion, deliberately and pointedly immersing himself in the world of Homeric stylistics and Trojan narrative, and deeply embedding any contemporary gestures. If this is the case for literary allusivity and Roman-political issues, why should religious discourse be any different? In terms of religiosity, too, we should be primed in this text for significant silences and more covert or conceptual nodes of interaction.

What is more, if we continue to pursue the connotations of Quintus' likely dating to the third century, then there is much *external* evidence which supports taking seriously the possibility that his text is formed and informed by a nascently Christianising world. The total number of Christians in the third century is a topic of much debate: in the Severan period, for example, estimates range from less than 250 literate Christians in Tertullian's Carthage,[60] to about a tenth of the overall population.[61] Yet whatever the demographical truth in terms of statistics (and this is not an issue that I shall debate further here), it is undeniable that the period gave rise to a number of instrumental Christian Greek and Latin authors – Clement, Origen, Hippolytus and Tertullian himself – whose output attests to a significant and varied conversation surrounding Christian identity, textuality and authority in this transitional, pre-institutional phase.[62]

A number of these issues are of intense relevance to Quintus' project – and vice versa. As has been (predictably) far better explored for the prose authors of this period than for the poets, both Christian and non-Christian writers were engaged in the shared endeavour of demonstrating a 'vicarious

---

[60] Dunn (2004)　　[61] Edwards (2007).

[62] What follows is not intended to be a comprehensive account of the vast and contentious topic of Early Christianity in the Graeco-Roman Empire. Rather, it traces some particular strands of development which are fruitful for consideration against Quintus' project.

18   Beginning Again (Introduction): The Poetics of Impersonation

antiquity' as a form of cultural superiority and hegemony. Thus the genealogical claims of Diogenes Laertius, for instance, (who insists that wisdom and the human race itself originated with the Greeks) and the 'polemically Hellenocentric'[63] works of Philostratus (who explores in the *Vita Apollonii* the complex Greek claims to antiquity and universalism; and in the *Heroicus* the precarious projections of Greek heritage and tradition) can be read in competitive concert with the similar moves undertaken by Hippolytus and Julius Africanus, who were simultaneously developing sophisticated chronologies to drive Christianity's foundational origins home.[64]

A number of these Early Christian texts and artworks also attest to a concentrated renegotiation of mythic models – a 'reprogramming of the familiar' for new religious adepts.[65] Thus for example, as Zahra Newby has recently shown, the trend in the third-century sculptural sphere to focus on key figures, often relegating or ignoring the wider myth, encouraged Christian artists to make their own use of pagan iconography (such as the use of Endymion to represent the favoured story of Jonah) without doing away with it completely.[66] The Sermons of Origen have been read as revealing a similar confidence in adapting Graeco-Roman literary forms as vehicles for present ideological and moral exhortations.[67]

And perhaps most pertinently, third-century Christian evidence also bears witness to a strong concern with the complex relationship between literary status and textual unity in the formation of scripture. It was not long before the turn of the third century that the idea of a canonical 'new testament' had emerged into being – a fixed, 'inelastic canon of four gospels', 'the received designation of a body of writing from the apostolic age which had already been used as touchstones in great questions', and 'a recognition of widespread unanimity of what constituted sacred texts.'[68] And yet this consensus and 'inelasticity' did not preclude, and in fact

---

[63] Phrase from Whitmarsh (2007) and Swain (2007): 2.

[64] For these and the subsequent examples I am particularly indebted to the collected essays in Swain, Harrison and Elsner (2007), which make the convincing case for the emergence of Christianity 'on its own terms' in the Severan period, and its conceptual engagement with the writings of many of the second sophistic authors and other imperial Greek and Latin thinkers.

[65] Swain (2007): 14.   [66] Newby (2007).

[67] See, for instance, Finn (2007) on the sermons on the Book of Joshua, productively read in this light.

[68] Respectively, Edwards (2007): 411 and Swain (2007): 19. Edwards (2007) (with further bibliography for and against this position) makes the convincing case that there appears in fact to have been more unanimity in this epoch than in the fourth century, before the clear bifurcation between 'heretics' and 'orthodoxy' enshrined by Nicaea in 325.

Homeric Poetics at the Dawn of Christianity

encouraged and facilitated, processes of mediation, temporary expansion[69] and above all experimental amalgamation of the scriptural texts: zooming in and widening out from a shared conception of what constituted the fixed Christian canon.

A remarkable text from the late second century best exemplifies this practice.[70] The so-called *Diatessaron* of Tatian (c. 160–75 CE) sought to combine the texts of the four canonical gospels into a new, single, running work.[71] The resultant composition, which was probably originally composed in Syriac and survives in a Greek fragment of only a few verses,[72] not only speaks to the desire in some Early Christian quarters to create, from the four gospels, 'one continuous whole' but also occupies a tellingly liminal position between a number of different textual spheres: 'canonical' or 'apocryphal'; Gospel 'supplement' or 'substitute'; subordinate to and dependent on the texts which it joins together, and/or invested with an independent authority on its own.[73] The recognisable content of the fourfold gospel was conjoined in this work, but also transformed, existing in a radically altered context, and the product of the 'bridging' agenda of an apologist and (supposed) heretic.

The huge potential relevance of these themes to the *Posthomerica*, though never before actively considered, is clear even from our initial foray into the epic's poetic motivations. The resolutely past-facing surface temporality of the poem (it is hard to imagine a work with a greater interest in 'vicarious antiquity' that one which purports to be by Homer) and its intensive 'reprogramming' of Trojan myth reveal this to be a work deeply invested in the same sorts of concerns as Philostratus *and* his Early Christian counterparts. But above all, Quintus' programmatic agenda of joining the Homeric epics together brings the *Posthomerica* and the

---

[69] To take just one example from this period, Origen includes in his gospel canon the second-century *Shepherd of Hermas*, but states his awareness that many others do not (*De principiis* 4.2.4.).

[70] The *Diatessaron*, if dated correctly, is from a time when texts were more actively vying for position as authoritative scripture (before being rejected by ecclesiastical authorities), but which still has great resonance with the situation closer to Quintus' era of composition, probably less than a century later.

[71] See, from a large bibliography, Peterson (1994), Joosten (2001 and 2017), Schmid (2013) Crawford (2015) and (2016).

[72] For the Dura Parchment, see Kraeling (1935) who published the fragment 24 with extensive discussion; also Plooij (1934–5), Burkitt (1935), Parker et al. (1999), Crawford (2016).

[73] See for instance the interesting suggestions in Watson (2013) on the 'genre' of the *Diatessaron*: it lurks between gospel 'harmony' (a subordinate, comprehensive supplement which sees how the texts can best be co-ordinated) and a gospel itself (which can be selective in its use of sources, and can add new material, or present old material with a new slant).

20 Beginning Again (Introduction): The Poetics of Impersonation

Diatessaron into a productive conceptual conversation.[74] Creating one unified Homeric epic (a Homeric 'trilogy' of the *Iliad*, the *Posthomerica* and the *Odyssey*), a text which is both inescapably 'Homer' and also evasively independent, and which claims an authority *through* a cohesive attachment to its source, Quintus' poetics of the interval discloses a programme of *Homeric* liminality, akin to Tatian's earlier textual position within and between the Christian scriptures.

Pursuing this 'analogy' with Early Christian textuality will thus emerge as another major strand of this book. Without making the claim that Quintus is covertly Christian *or* anti- Christian, I want to suggest instead that his interstitial position has a *religious* cultural dimension too. The *Posthomerica*'s mode of Homeric engagement makes the epic a crucial testimony for charting the early, accumulating and *shared* development of textual practices and 'canonical' ideas in this transitional period, before the total shift in cultural values brought about by Christianity, but whilst this shift was gradually emerging and extending its influence across Greek literature and its composers. Quintus' epic deserves a voice in these conversations, just as the role of the *Dionysiaca* is being increasingly recognised in the different religious discourse of the fifth century; and by setting out this context at such a pointedly early stage of this introduction, I intend for it to serve as an important part of my roadmap, which will closely condition the analyses to come.

1.5 Silver Latin $\neq$ Imperial Greek?

First, however, we must now return to the connection with which we began: between contrast imitation and critical redemption. From such an overview it is not difficult to comprehend how all the imperial 'Trojan epics' have become the great new beneficiaries of this style of reading. Due to their direct appropriation of a canonical source and claims to innovation in the face of such dependence, the self-conscious allusivity of Alexandrian poetics and the belatedness associated with silver Latin have become the two main paradigms used for redeeming these texts. Rob Shorrock's study of the *Dionysiaca* shows how closely analogies have been drawn.[75] In his account of 'the poet of Dionysus', Shorrock draws explicitly on 'recent

---

[74] I am not claiming any direct engagement with or even, necessarily, knowledge of Tatian by Quintus (for my stance on the intertextual rabbit holes surrounding the *Posthomerica*, see 1.10). It is rather their connectivity in stance, textual practice and literary co-ordination that makes these works from two different traditions worth thinking through together.

[75] Shorrock (2001).

Silver Latin ≠ Imperial Greek? 21

work on Latin epic poetry which has done much to focus attention on the figure of the epic poet'; and decries the fact that 'this approach has [yet] been little explored with regard to the Greek poets of the later Roman empire'.[76]

The *Posthomerica* – which, alongside the *Dionysiaca*, has so far received the most attention in the scholarly turn towards this poetry –[77] has itself gained much critical traction from being placed in this framework. Methodological statements from the two most influential recent studies of the poem will serve as examples. In the first monograph in English on Quintus since the turn of the twentieth century, Calum Maciver aims to defend the poet against his traditional detractors[78] by stressing the *Posthomerica*'s Alexandrian qualities, demonstrating how 'Quintus imitates, manipulates, comments on, differs from, and revises Homer'; an appropriation which, 'in Hardie's terms', is also a rejection.[79] The 2007 volume edited by Manuel Baumbach and Silvio Bär, *Quintus Smyrnaeus: Transforming Homer in Second Sophistic Epic* (a title which itself implies the Bloomian misreading process), is also underpinned by this reckoning. Most explicitly, Thomas Schmitz argues that Quintus' use of anachrony draws attention to his belatedness in the epic tradition; the *Posthomerica* becomes 'a text that reflects upon the poetical situation of a literary latecomer who has to navigate through the masses of prior treatment of his subject matter'.[80] Under the care of this interpretative treatment, the *Posthomerica* is emerging as the example *par excellence* of the antagonistic, creative capabilities of imperial Greek epic, helping to usher in these texts from the canonical wilderness which they once inhabited.

There are, however, problems with this critical cross-application. There is first an issue of heterogeneity. As Hunter and Carvounis rightly stress,[81] whereas Vergil's silver successors all composed within a few generations of one another and of Vergil himself, producing epics of comparable size and style, the timespan between the earliest and latest texts which we call

---

[76] Shorrock (2001): ch. 3, quotations at 113.

[77] For a summary of scholarship, see Baumbach and Bär (2007): 15–26.

[78] Detractors such as Lloyd-Jones whose famous condemnation – that Quintus has served up 'an anaemic pastiche of Homer, utterly devoid of life' ((1969): 101) – has become emblematic. I return briefly to this tradition of scholarship in relation to the poem's style in Chapter 3. However, in general, I shall emphatically not follow the now-conventional model of first narrating and then refuting the negative twentieth-century reception of the poem; hence my decision to relegate this Lloyd Jones-ism to a footnote. The quotation has served as the rallying cry and opening epitaph for many recent works on the poem (e.g. Maciver (2012b): 7 and 25; Baumbach and Bär (2007): 23–5; Boyten (2010): 8) and has enjoyed its time in the spotlight for long enough.

[79] Maciver (2012b): 9.   [80] Schmitz (2007b): 65–85, quotation at 67.

[81] Hunter and Carvounis (2008): 2–3.

22   Beginning Again (Introduction): The Poetics of Impersonation

'imperial Greek epic' is more than 400 years, and they encompass, as we have seen, a number of styles and forms: from the epyllion to the longest surviving epic. There is then the related question of context. Whilst the epics analysed by Hardie and Quint are tied to specific and often directly articulated ideological backgrounds,[82] the chronological diversity and contextual uncertainties surrounding many imperial Greek poems make it harder to capture their 'political dimensions' in anything like the same way. Thirdly, the contrast imitation rubric does not alone promote sufficient reflection on the centrality of Trojan mythology as subject matter for these works, nor the directness with which they reach for a model far more ineffably distant than was Vergil for his early imperial inheritors. In order to account for this focus, and explain the intensity of the Homeric imitation, this poetry must be approached on its own terms.

My reading will focus attention on these problems, and suggest that the *Posthomerica* offers a uniquely important vehicle to redress them. Quintus' new poetics does *not* fit the paradigm of Alexandrian-derived contrast imitation and rejects the belated self-labelling of silver Latin. The poet reveals himself to be highly alert to the techniques and 'tropes'[83] associated with these traditions. But he employs them deviantly, to affirm rather than reject continuity with his Homeric source. This affirmation is a crucial component of the poetics of the interval and also suggests the relevance of such a position to works beyond the *Posthomerica*. Quintus' distinctive response to Homer, in other words, can and must in turn be contemplated against the other 'Trojan epics' – 'pagan' *and* 'Christian' – from the imperial period, which chronologically follow Quintus and diversely interact with his endeavour. In the course of this analysis, I shall therefore ultimately reconsider the place of the *Posthomerica* within the development of imperial Greek epic, addressing the extent to which the poem can cast insights into the 'collective' identity of this era of hexameter verse: whether, despite its heightened heterogeneity and colourful disparities, this may rightly be considered a 'corpus' of poetry, with a distinct – and dynamic – literary agenda.

Before turning to the context of this poem of the interval more directly, let us first examine its features in greater detail.

---

[82] Cf. e.g. Quint (1993): 8: 'Vergil's epic is tied to a specific national history, to the idea of world domination, to a monarchical system, even to a particular dynasty.'

[83] I use 'tropes' here in Hinds' sense of the word – 'figural symbols (words, images, characters) used to metaphorize authorial engagement –' as defined in 1.2. For the ways in which I depart from Hinds' allusive methodology, see 1.8 and Chapter 4.

1.6 (Non) Parallels: Poetic Impersonation

I began this book by claiming that Quintus displays a 'unique', 'distinctive' and 'formative' approach to Homer through his impersonatory stance. And yet his assertion to be 'still Homer' may in fact at first seem far from exceptional, and thus needs to be comprehended within the long tradition of ancient pseudepigraphic and apocryphal writing. As Irene Peirano has demonstrated, such a tradition encompasses a vast continuum of literary existentialism: 'from forgeries, to playful hoaxes, to anonymous misattributed writings, to derivative works that become attributed to the author whose style they sought to recreate'.[84] However whilst such a continuum is frequently dissected into neat sub-categories and internal genres (Peirano herself proceeds to focus on a specific group of Roman pseudepigraphia, largely concerning the *Appendix Vergiliana*, which make active claim to 'fake' authorship),[85] in the case of Homer and his poetry the situation is uniquely diffuse and difficult. As Barbara Graziosi has shown, until and after the Homeric corpus was reduced to a duo in the fifth century, a number of works were attributed to the famous poet: the Epic Cycle, the Homeric Hymns, the *Margites* and even the parodic *Batrachomyomachia* were all at one stage deemed to be the product of Homer.[86] These texts, however, make no discrete claims to Homeric identity *of their own*.[87] Unlike the 'faux-Vergilian' exempla,[88] the explicit identification as Homer

---

[84] Peirano (2012): 3. For an earlier and more comprehensive study of these types of pseudepigraphia in the Graeco-Roman world, see Speyer (1971).

[85] See also and conversely Paratore (1976) who coins the subcategory 'pseudofakes' ('pseudo-falsi') as a means for considering texts that become attached to a famous name during the course of transmission, but do not show the demonstrable intention of being passed off as thus.

[86] Graziosi (2002).

[87] The *Hymn to Apollo* may be argued to prove an exception: 'whenever anyone on earth, a stranger who has seen and suffered much, comes here and asks of you: "Whom do you think, girls, is the sweetest singer that comes here, and in whom do you most delight?" Then answer, each and all, with one voice: "He is a blind man, and dwells in rocky Chios: his lays are evermore supreme".' (165–70). This refrain does not, however, imply an identification with Homer, but rather a desire to be considered as '*a*' Homer: the singer is cementing his claims to superlative greatness by evoking the generalised prestige of the blind bard.

[88] Indeed, the extent to which one can question Peirano's identification of her chosen texts as 'fakes' under her own rigid criteria (cf. e.g. the pertinent challenges raised by Kayachev (2013) over whether either the *Ciris* or *Catalepton* 9 really does pretend to be Vergil) demonstrates the caveats in applying a tight typology to texts with such slippery and unstable identity politics. The most instructive approach, as Kayachev also suggests, is not to ask 'what unites this "genre" of inauthentic texts?' but rather to ask of each member of this 'group' 'what kind of texts is this?' That is precisely the question that I hope to pose here.

24   Beginning Again (Introduction): The Poetics of Impersonation

is a phase of their reception history, a reading imposed upon them,[89] and in many cases their original anonymity is highly unlikely.[90]

The same notion applies, albeit differently, to the *Anacreontea*, commonly hailed as Greek impersonation poetry *par excellence*. In her analysis of these lyric pretenders, Patricia Rosenmeyer argues that we find in them a *modus scribendi* quite alien to the ancient literary norm of antagonism, as multiple authors submerge their personalities in a selective vision of Anacreon, whose persona, attitudes and verse they openly imitate. Through this 'unique' aesthetic, which centres on an eschewal of independence, embrace of conformity and absorption into the Anacreontic voice, the new poet aims at something 'more valuable than the individual, namely tradition', to achieve 'a timeless and universal literary status'.[91]

However, whilst relentlessly anonymous, the *Anacreontea* in fact resist the move of appropriating Anacreon's own identity. What was originally the first poem in the collection – moved to the twenty-third position by West to suggest a more genuine affinity with the real Anacreon –[92] contains instead a strong statement of independence: it describes a dream where Eros led Anacreon by the hand. In this dream – a well-known symbol of literary handover, from one poet to another – Anacreon is conceived as a separate figure, the product of the current singer's imagination, and not an extension of him.

What distinguishes the *Posthomerica* from all of these literary imposters is thus the explicit contradiction of its claims. If the *Anacreontea* are entirely subordinating in their aesthetic but make no assertions to be Anacreon, then the reverse is true for our epic. For as we have seen in the discussion in 1.1, Quintus *does* lay claim to Homeric identity, but he does not subordinate his sense of difference completely. The poem is centred on an unapologetic doubleness: a stark juxtaposition of traits.

1.7   Homer and the Performance of the Past

We have seen how scholars of silver Latin epic have linked its adversarial response to the cultural and political concerns which drove the projects.

---

[89] Ps. Herodotus (*Vit. Hom.* 24), Statius (*Silv.* 1. *Praef.*) and Martial (*Ep.* 14.183.1) all take the *Batrachomyomachia* as a work of Homer; though in the two Latin examples, we may rightly suspect that tongues are firmly in cheeks. Ps. Plutarch (*Vit. Hom.* 1.5) cites, but refutes, the attribution.

[90] This is particularly true for the Epic Cycle poems: see Davies (1989); West (2013); Fantuzzi and Tsagalis (2015). As Peirano (2012): 71 discusses, later poets, particularly in the Roman tradition, often engaged with the cyclic poems in a manner which betrays their perception of them as ancient and yet un-Homeric, and of a secondary status in the canon. On Quintus and the Cycle, see 1.10.

[91] Rosenmeyer (1992): 69.   [92] West (1993).

Homer and the Performance of the Past

To attempt a better understanding of this paradoxical stance of the *Post-homerica*, we must similarly now turn more directly to the question of the environment which might have informed it. Our preliminary discussions of Quintus' place in the imperial Greek poetic world, and particularly his potential relationship with Early Christianity, have worked upon the premise of a third-century dating. Let us now consider this premise in more detail, so that this position, and this relationship, can be more thoroughly interrogated.

This is, of course, not an easy task. If the contextual opacity of many surviving imperial Greek epics precludes the easy assertion of direct political readings, then for the *Posthomerica*, this problem is particularly acute. The question of Quintus' date and biography is the subject of much detailed and, at times, tenuous scholarship, and remains unresolved.[93] Despite its otherwise confident tone, much of the recent critical output on the poem therefore remains tentative regarding its cultural positioning. Baumbach and Bär's volume, for instance, poses the question of whether Quintus could have been a member of the second sophistic 'phenomenon', a declaimer and *pepaideumenos* who also turned his attention to composing epic poetry.[94] However, they concede pre-emptively that 'the observations made are not clear enough to prove (this) link'.[95] Maciver strongly contests such a second sophistic context for the poem, but is hesitant to supply an alternative. He instead roots his conclusions in the terms of reader reception: 'my Quintus is only a reading'.[96]

It is, however, possible to ascertain some broad dating parameters for the poem. I have so far acknowledged these parameters, but since they will be critical starting points for my argument, they now require some detailed exposition. Ideas about the timing of the *Posthomerica* have swung from the sixth century BCE, to the Hellenistic era, to the late fifth century CE.[97] The current *communis opinio* dates it indeed to the third century. This conclusion is based on a number of premises, ranging on a spectrum from firmness to flimsiness. Oppian's *Halieutica* – which, thanks to its dedication to the emperor Marcus Aurelius and his son Commodus can be dated with some precision to 176–180 CE – offers an uncontentious *terminus post quem*. Scholars have identified at least three allusions in the

---

[93] Evidence, viewpoints and conjectures are summarised in Baumbach and Bär (2007): 1–8.
[94] I return to this hypothesis centrally in Chapter 2.   [95] Baumbach and Bär (2007): 15.
[96] Maciver (2012b): 12.
[97] See summary in Gärtner (2005): 23–6. Brief discussion in Maciver (2012b): 3. I have no new evidence *per se* to offer on these existing points; but rather will use and augment them to inform my own reading.

26   Beginning Again (Introduction): The Poetics of Impersonation

Posthomerica to the *Halieutica*, where Quintus mobilises quite directly Oppianic technical-nautical language and imagery of fishing to infuse his similes.[98] As a *terminus ante quem*, some slightly shakier boundaries can be suggested. Nonnus' awareness of and engagement with the *Posthomerica* has long been accepted,[99] which must place Quintus' poem before the fifth century CE.[100] The possibility of zooming in further within this 300-year range comes from the suggestion, made with increasing conviction, that Triphiodorus is indebted to Quintus (as opposed to the other way around).[101] Since a papyrus fragment (*POxy.* 2946) now enables us to date Triphiodorus' epyllion to no later than the end of the third century,[102] we can tentatively seal off the composition of the *Posthomerica* as having occurred before then.

Two passages from the poem itself further affirm a Roman imperial dating: a simile (Q.S.6.532–6) detailing the use of wild beasts for public executions in an amphitheatre; and a prophecy made by Calchas foretelling Aeneas' role as the founder of Rome – or at least, a city with universal rule (Q.S.13.366–41).[103] Such 'contemporary' allusions, of course, are shadowy, so as to maintain the Homeric veneer of the poetics at large. Quintus' Roman *praenomen*[104] is shadier still: it is found no earlier than in a Homeric scholion on *Iliad* 22.220 (which refers to 'Quintus the poet')[105] with a number of references in Eustathius and Tzetzes in the twelfth century.[106] The manuscripts of the poem which use the name come from

---

[98] Q.S.7.569–75 (~*Halieutica* 4.640–6); 9.172–7 (~*Halieutica* 3.567–75); 11.62–5 (~*Halieutica* 4.637–9). See Vian (1954): 50–1; James and Lee (2000): 6; Kneebone (2007): 285–305 and Maciver (2012b): 3 n. 10. I return to this connection, and suggest further passages of a potential Oppianic inheritance, in Chapter 7.

[99] Restated in Baumbach and Bär (2007): 2.

[100] On Nonnus' own dating, see Vian (1976): LX–XVIII who narrows down the dating of the *Dionysiaca* to 450–70 CE, a position which is still generally accepted.

[101] The direction of influence between the two poets has long been contested: see the summary of debates in Miguélez Cavero (2013): 4–6. On the currently prevailing view of Quintus as the anterior poet, see chiefly Gerlaud (1982): 8, *pace* e.g. Gärtner (2005): 25.

[102] Published by Rea (1972). See discussion and further bibliography in Dubielzig (1996): 9–10 and Miguélez Cavero (2013): 4–6.

[103] I discuss this passage in detail in Chapter 7.

[104] It was not of course uncommon for Greek citizens in the Roman Empire to be known by a Latin first name.

[105] *Schol. Gen. Il.* 2.119, dated to the twelfth or thirteenth century: 'You must know, then, that Achilles finishes him [= Thersites] off, as Quintus the poet reports in his *Posthomerica.*'

[106] Eustathius: introduction to *Iliad*, A468 (136.4), B814 (352.2), θ501 (1608.1), λ546 (1698.48), λ592 (1702.11). Tzetzes: *Post.* 10, 13, 282, 522, 584, 587; Prooem in Iliadem 482; schol. ad. Lycophron, Alex. 61, 1048; Exeg. in Iliadem p. 772.20 (Bachmann (1835)); Chiliad. 2.489f.; schol. to Tzetzes, *Post.* 282. See James and Lee (2000): 3–4 and Boyten (2010): 10.

Homer and the Performance of the Past

no earlier than the beginning of the sixteenth century.[107] As a biographical marker the name 'Quintus' thus remains annoyingly anonymous: possibly anachronistic, and certainly inconclusive.[108]

A further and final consideration is a papyrus from the fourth/fifth century CE, discovered in 1984. Written on this papyrus are 384 hexameters, in a hybrid of *koine* and Homeric Greek, which tell the first-person story of the vision of Dorotheus, a gate-keeper in God's palace. The potential relevance of this text for our epic derives from the two instances at the end where the author mentions a poet called Quintus: ὁ Κυντιάδης Δωρόθεος (line 300), and, in a subscription, τέλος τῆς ὁράσεως/Δωροθέου Κυίντου ποιητοῦ.

'Dorotheus' thus seems to identify himself as, firstly, the son of Kuintos[109] and secondly as either 'Dorotheus the son of Quintus the poet' or, less probably, 'Dorotheus Quintus the poet'.[110] Based on this *sphragis*, many recent scholars have happily concluded that 'in the absence of any rival candidates and of any historical difficulty', the Quintus to whom Dorotheus refers is the poet of the *Posthomerica*; and 400 CE has therefore been used as another *terminus ante quem* for the 'paternal' poem.[111] Whilst some of the counter-arguments to this theory are equally baffling (Vian has suggested that the severe 'linguistic deficiencies' of the *Vision* make it unlikely that its author was someone sufficiently versed in Quintus' poetry: but why a son should be literarily or proficiently close to his father remains unclear)[112] this scepticism in general is sensible. That Quintus Smyrnaeus is the only surviving imperial Greek poet to bear this name is not satisfactory grounds to draw a filial-biographical link with Dorotheus' text. The *Vision* does provide a productive cross-comparison for the *Posthomerica*, as another, later, Homerically derived hexameter work, and it suggests how Quintan poetics could indeed be put to work in a now overtly Christian context; however, I see neither the basis nor the need to connect the texts in ways more tenuous than these.

---

[107] Further details and exact references in Vian (1963): vii–viii.

[108] On the second part of the poet's name – Smyrnaeus – with its obvious Homeric connotations and strong poetological implications, see full discussion in Chapter 4.

[109] A common enough alternative for Kuintos: see also Maciver (2012b): 4.

[110] The genitives could of course work both ways; although given the self-identification in the first of these passages, taking the latter genitive as paternal-possessive rather than appositive is the more persuasive reading. For alternative views on this colophon, including on how the ambiguity *could* be removed by the restoration of the definite article between 'Quintus' and 'poet', see the brief but helpful comments of James (2006).

[111] See e.g. James and Lee (2000): 8, from whom I draw the quotation.

[112] Vian (1985): 48, with further discussion in Baumbach and Bär (2007): 6 n. 28 and Maciver (2012b): 5.

28   Beginning Again (Introduction): The Poetics of Impersonation

From the evidence summarised and evaluated here,[113] there are thus threads of evidence – not definitive in isolation, but in aggregate sufficiently suggestive – that enable us to date the *Posthomerica* between 200 and 300 CE. I have traced the strongest of these threads not just to re-establish or reiterate this chronological framework, but so that I may now proceed to interrogate the poem further within it. For this timespan does in fact provide some pieces of information about our mysterious poet. Firstly, he was a literate Greek speaker alive during the third century. Secondly, he was – we can assert to within a small degree of doubt – a Roman citizen.[114] And thirdly, he was a well-educated member of society, highly familiar with the staple classroom exercises of rhetorical training, with an intimate knowledge of Homer. This story, admittedly, does not make for the densest *Vita Poetae*. It does, however, provide the impetus to attempt to think less 'anonymously' about the *Posthomerica* and to approach the question of its context in terms less restrictive than those posed by current scholarship. Seizing this impetus, my account will take seriously the possibility of reading the *Posthomerica* within a specific intellectual environment and cultural background; and by so doing, it will reinforce the validity and the value of conceiving of the epic as a product of this particular time.

If we are prepared to adopt this bolder approach, we may now turn to two areas of imperial Greek culture, active in the first two centuries CE and continually but differently pressing in the third, which have recently received vast scholarly attention, and seem particularly relevant to Quintus' endeavour. The first is the centrality and authority of Homer. Throughout antiquity the influence of Homer upon Greek literature and culture was so tremendous that scholars have eschewed any large-scale attempt to chart his ancient reception.[115] However, the particularly special position which Homer occupied in the Roman Empire has been well demonstrated. Kindstrand examines the Homeric self-positioning of Dio, Aristides and Maximus of Tyre.[116] Kim considers the attitudes towards the poet in revisionist prose works.[117] Buffière treats his use in mainly the allegorical tradition.[118] Lamberton traces a more specific form of this

---

[113] For further considerations of less weight, which nevertheless steer towards a similar dating conclusion, see Baumbach and Bär (2007): 3–8.

[114] The Constitutio Antoniniana, issued in 212 CE, predates Quintus' poem according to most estimations.

[115] Cf. Kim (2010): 4–5.   [116] Kindstrand (1973).   [117] Kim (2010).

[118] Buffière (1956). See also Hillgruber (1994 and 1999) for enlightening comments on this allegorical penchant in the period.

Homer and the Performance of the Past

allegorical bent, telling the remarkable story of how Neoplatonist philosophers came to view Homer as a sage 'theologian', and used such allegorising forms of exegesis to reconcile the parts of his poetry most discordant with their Platonic worldviews and to plough the epics for what they deemed the most fundamental forms of truth.[119]

In the realm of visual representation, both the figure of Homer and his prodigious poems continued to occupy a central and increasingly complex place in the artistic mindset of the empire.[120] Thus, to introduce two examples which will be of particular and continued relevance, the Pompeian mosaics and mural cycles of the *Iliad* and *Odyssey*, most elaborately at the Casa di Octavius Quartio (Pompeii II 2.2), reveal an interest in displaying, re-ordering and dissecting the narrative scenes of Homer's monumental work: bringing its grandeur into the domestic dining room.[121] And the Iliac Tablets – twenty-two Greek-cum-Roman miniature marble reliefs from the early imperial period signed by a certain 'Theodorus', which depict panoramic vistas from Homeric and cyclic epic – give a different sense of how Homer's all-encompassing grandeur could be provocatively combined with those previously mentioned issues of form, compression and scale.[122] This whistle-stop tour of some (though certainly not all) of the major imperial testimonies seeks to emphasise for now some simple but fundamental points: the broad and irreducible significance of Homer in this era; from the Greek perspective, his importance for the assertion of Hellenic 'affiliation' under Rome – however slippery that term may be; and from all directions, the sheer variety of responses on offer: a full spectrum ranging from sacralising to satirising.

---

[119] Lamberton (1986).

[120] The Archilaos relief dated to the Hellenistic period and discussed in the light of Homeric 'vision and revision' by Zeitlin (2001) provides an earlier example of many of the same penchants of Homeric reception: a figure of awe, fleshed out, personified (and accompanied by personifications) and deified; of textual and material literary status; of intense contestation and competition (poetic contests and geographical ones). Homer's perennial importance, present in all phases of ancient Greek culture, is concretised and concentrated on this sculpture – given a visual and visceral edge. Beyond her excellent discussion of this piece, Zeitlin (2001) also remains the key (anglophone) analysis of Homer's broad place in imperial viewing culture (textual and, to a lesser extent, material).

[121] On the house generally, see *Pompeii, Pitture e Mosaici*, vol. III: 42–108. The original key publications on the house and its decoration are Aurigemma (1953), with useful discussion in Brilliant (1984): 60–1, Clarke (1991): 201–7 and Squire (2011): 145–7. For an excellent discussion of the epic 'vision' that the friezes convey, see now Lorenz (2013). For other Pompeian Homeric friezes, see Stefanou (2006).

[122] These tablets are now familiar to the modern classicist through, from a now ever-expanding field, the influential treatments of Squire (2011) and Petrain (2014). I shall return to them from a different perspective below.

30 Beginning Again (Introduction): The Poetics of Impersonation

That the *Posthomerica* is saturated in the Homeric style clearly reflects this imperial obsession with the figure of Homer; and also offers an extreme response to it. There was clearly appetite for the type of hyper-Homeric poetry which so many imperial Greek epicists composed; and for the well-trained and ambitious writer, penning an epic which goes so far as to join itself to the seams of Homer's works provides a significant opportunity – to give a learned readership some *more* Homer to play with.[123]

The second related sphere is what may be called the 'performance of the past.' A number of studies have revealed the emphasis placed on role-playing and play-acting in second sophistic declamations: the re-enactment of scenes from history and the close 'immediate' representation of figures from the mythological and historical past.[124] The school exercises of the *progymnasmata* also involved creative tasks centred on this kind of representation: in *prosopopeia* or *ethopoeia* the student had to construct a speech in the words of a character in a certain situation, such as Ajax losing the arms contest, or Niobe after the loss of her children; and in *eidolopoeia*, a subset of this exercise, the aim was a dramatic personification of an abstract notion or a character who was absent, far away or dead – a 'verbal necromancy'[125] of classical themes or celebrated figures. Nor was role-playing restricted to rhetorical spaces. The Atticising tendencies of the prose works of this era demonstrate what Anderson calls a 'communing with the classics' – a textual mimesis of canonical texts.[126] Surviving works also bear witness to 'close encounters'[127] with resurrected figures from the past. Homer or Socrates were available to be consulted in speeches; famous figures would appear in dreams and even in the less fleeting, waking world via epiphany.

In the material sphere too, the 'artistic'[128] representations of Homer which I introduced above display their own versions of these performative penchants: a vivacious and complex Homeric mimesis which both encompasses and extends beyond the textual. Thus the Iliac Tablets, as Squire has convincingly demonstrated, are concerned not only with miniaturising Homeric epic, but also with programmatically combining the verbal and the visual methods of conveying it, as the text inscriptions and figurative

---

[123] Cf. Tomasso (2010).
[124] See Anderson (1993); Zeitlin (2001); Schmitz (1997) and (1999): 71–92; Connolly (2001a): 339–72; Konstan and Säid (2006).
[125] Zeitlin (2001): 208 n. 26 and Anderson (1993): 138–9.   [126] Anderson (1993): ch. 3.
[127] A term used productively in Late Antique contexts by Lane Fox (1986).
[128] I use 'artistic' here, imperfectly, to draw a distinction between the tactile and material objects discussed here and the book-based or literary productions in the previous paragraph.

Homer and the Performance of the Past   31

reliefs work together to command their viewer to partake in the game of Homeric reconstruction, 'flirting self-referentially with grand dialectics of . . . the original and the copy'.[129] For a term which encompasses all of these forms we might consider '**re-animation**': a desire to resuscitate into the present figures and words from bygone temporal spheres.[130]

More significant still is how this output reflects critically on the very possibility of its endeavour. In Schmitz's radical formulation of declamatory mimesis, for example, the personality of the sophist completely disappears behind the figure he is embodying, in an articulation of the crushing weight of the past felt by elite performers in second-century Greek cities.[131] Webb augments this model by borrowing from the vocabulary of acting – in which an actor is 'not and not not' the character s/he is playing –[132] to suggest that in these speeches imitation intersects with a consciousness of difference: 'on the one hand, the audience were Athenians listening to Demosthenes or Pericles. On the other hand, they were the audience of the contemporary sophist judging that sophist's skill, comparing him to others they had heard, or heard of, comparing his technique to a notional ideal or ideals.'[133] Connolly considers instead the internal conflicts in Greek imperial educational writings which bespeak a 'profound ambivalence' about the classicising tendencies of *paideia*. Putting democratic Athenian texts to work inculcating an imperial elite *habitus*, she argues, could only happen through a process of selection, revision and censorship. If classical texts were thus divorced from their original context and subject to strict ideological controls, then recapturing the past was not always what it seemed.[134] Likewise the Iliadic representations on the Pompeian walls and the miniature tablets compel their viewer to undertake a similar critical re-evaluation of their emulative manoeuvres. The scenes from the Homeric texts are defiantly recombined, expanded and recontextualised: merged with wider material from the Trojan cycle, turned upside and down and inside out (the tablets' structuring, for example, of the vistas of the *Iliad* around scenes from the

---

[129] Squire (2011), quotation at 19. See also Squire (2014) for the tablets as a springboard for thinking through the relationship between art and rhetoric in this period, of obvious and continued relevance for my analysis of the *Posthomerica*'s complex relationship to the imperial rhetorical sphere.

[130] Further discussion of this term in relation to the book's title in 1.8.   [131] Schmitz (1999): 78.

[132] Webb (2006) from Schechner (1985). It is also a near-direct quotation of Dicaeopolis in Aristophanes' *Acharnians* (440–1). I return to these formulations centrally in the next chapter.

[133] Webb (2006): 39.   [134] Connolly (2001a).

32 Beginning Again (Introduction): The Poetics of Impersonation

Ilioupersis,[135] or in the Casa di Octavius, setting the Iliadic frieze directly below the one depicting the labours of Heracles – placing 'Heracles on top of Troy'[136]) and set in a complex and at times contradictory relationship with their Homeric textual antecedents.[137] As Squire puts it, 'these self-referential objects contest a system of representation even as they perform and enact it'[138] – a constantly shifting interpretative game which is more than just funny.

All eras, of course, may claim to take an interest in the 'past'; and agents throughout history have been involved in the performance of complex identities: one may be tempted sharply to question the exceptionalism of these traits to the early imperial period alone.[139] However, not all epochs are equally given to this *type* of reflexive relationship with their history. Different conditions elicit different styles of self-representation, and it has been argued that moments of crisis in particular evoke a tendency to imitate one's forebears so directly and discursively. We therefore need only consider the nature of those opening centuries CE to see the significance of the mobilisation of antiquarianism in Greek culture at this particular time. After the *Pax Romana*, the Greek east was involved in just such a crisis – of cultural as well as political identity.[140] As a result, this was an age intensely self-conscious about its relation to 'the before', which manifested itself in both a reverence for antique models and also (simultaneously) new constructions: ethnic identities, educational and religious institutions, and political interactions with, even among, the Romans.[141] Konstan and Säid summarise these effects: 'continuities were perceived and invented, differences were grafted onto the past to create new figures, in the way that grids on two superimposed transparencies produce elaborate and unexpected moiré patterns'.[142]

This narrative of 'Greece under Rome' is, to be sure, a highly familiar one. Horace knew it and captured it succinctly in his famous dictum: *Graecia capta ferum uictorem cepit et artes/intulit agresti Latio.*

---

[135] As is the case on the Capitoline Tablet (which I shall return to later) and in tablets 2NY, 3C, 6B and 9D. On these issues of order and arrangement in the tablets (particularly the Capitoline), see Squire (2014).

[136] The title of Lorenz (2013).

[137] I defer further specific examples to the analyses in the chapters to come, where these tablets will often recur as important interlocutors.

[138] Squire (2011): 19.

[139] See, for instance, the critique of precisely such exceptionalism by Dench in the recently published *Oxford Handbook to the Second Sophistic* (2017): 99–114.

[140] This crisis has been well delineated by a number of studies: particularly, for our purposes, Alcock (1993) and (1997); Hekster (2008); Ando (2012).

[141] Konstan and Säid (2006): ix–xii.   [142] Ibid: x.

(Epist. 2.1.156). It has also formed the basis of a number of modern scholarly accounts of the relationship between Greece and Rome under the empire; accounts often centred specifically around the 'second sophistic',[143] where, so the story goes, erudite Greeks used the historical prowess of their literary heritage to provide a 'peaceful', bookish resistance to the more tangible loss of hegemony experienced under Roman rule.[144] However, this is a story which has been told predominantly in prose. That is, the evidence-base most consistently tapped consists of the prose declamations and witty treatises of writers such as Lucian, Philostratus and Dio Chrysostom, whose penchant for the Attic dialect, use of classical allusions and imitation of figures from the historical or mythological past are hailed as the tools by which a space for the authority of Greek culture was reclaimed and contested. Despite the surging interest in imperial Greek poetry, verse – and epic most strikingly – has not yet been fully amalgamated into this picture.[145] Given the continued dominance of epic in imperial education and culture, and the backwards-facing temporality displayed in many of the surviving hexameter works, this taciturnity is particularly resounding. The role of epic poetry in articulating imperial Greek self-positioning, and its connection to this culture's intensely reflexive relationship with the past, remains significantly under-interrogated.

By reading the *Posthomerica* in light of these conditions, I shall aim to begin this interrogation. Considering more fully Quintus' voice in the

---

[143] The usefulness of the term 'second sophistic' as a descriptor for a specifically demarcated period (conventionally c. 60–230 CE, see e.g. Swain (1996): 1–6) now has a long recent history of debate: see particularly Whitmarsh (2013) and Richter and Johnson (2017). It is not my intention to enter fully into such reflection. I shall use the term in what follows with the inverted commas always tacitly understood, in the acknowledgement that what is at stake is inevitably a more complex web of artistic production and socio-political events than a watertight literary period, and that the phrase 'second sophistic' more generally must designate 'an era centred on the second century with defining characteristics that go well beyond Greek sophists or even Greek literature'. (Richter and Johnson (2017): 4).

[144] In addition to the works cited in the discussion above, other prominent tellers of this story include Whitmarsh (2001), with/versus (2013); Bowersock (1990); Schmitz (1999); and the collected papers in Goldhill (ed.) (2001).

[145] There has, certainly, been interest in the practice of individual poets along these lines, particularly in some of the aforementioned major studies of Quintus (e.g. Baumbach and Bär (2007), which instigated the 'second sophistic' reading of the poem) and Nonnus (Shorrock 2001 and 2011; Spanoudakis (2014 b)). Particular mention should be made of Shorrock (2011), as discussed in the notes to 1.4, which attempts to read Nonnus as a mediator between the Graeco-Roman tradition and Christianity, and of Alan Cameron (2016) who considers various aspects of poetic and philosophical culture in the fourth to sixth centuries CE; though the latter scholar is chiefly concerned, in his own words, 'less with poetry and philosophy than with poets and philosophers' (xi). In general, however, the larger questions have not yet been consistently posed.

34 Beginning Again (Introduction): The Poetics of Impersonation

imperial Greek discourse on the past, we shall see, not only adds an important poetic dimension to current scholarly treatments based around an interpretation of 'crisis and response'; it also *challenges* the basis of these interpretations. Quintus' integrative, collaborative approach to the (Homeric) past suggests how the re-animating techniques of the imperial Greek third century can bespeak something other, or something more, than repression, bitterness or resistance. The connection between 'performance' and poetics in the epic will therefore be explored at a deeper level than it has been by scholars so far; through its engagement with the various forms of mimesis on display in areas including *but not limited to* second sophistic declamation: the politically inflected re-animation at large in the Greek third century.[146]

1.8   (Post) Latourian Quintus

There is, however, a counter-argument to this model. In the 'doubleness' which I have here outlined, the reader cannot truly accept both parts. As Hinds puts it, 'a case can be made that full dialogue is always an unattainable ideal – that it is *impossible*. A privileging of one text/side/interpretation over another is *required* by the minimal linearity of response necessary to define reading as reading.'[147] In other words, because, as Maciver states, 'the reader *knows* that the *Posthomerica* is not the *Iliad*, and its poet is not Homer, but a much later writer of a different cultural and literary background'[148] then whatever claims it makes to Homeric affiliation are ultimately irrelevant to our real experience of the text. Therefore, in expounding this interval poetics, I shall in the end be led to the same conclusions of contrast-imitation as Martindale, or Hinds, or Maciver – that the *Posthomerica* tacitly reveals its newness and presents a self-differentiated 'reading' of Homer. I shall have merely arrived there by a different route; or worse, by different metaphors.

There are, however, grounds to challenge the idea that such a 'full dialogue' is impossible. The attempt to formulate a break with the past is characteristic of much postmodern thought on temporality.[149] Such

---

[146] Chapter 2 is devoted to this argument. This broader approach will also attempt to address the potential problems arising from reading the *Posthomerica* as inherently connected both to the particular identity conflicts of the third century *and* the penchants of the second sophistic, which is usually associated tightly with the two centuries before this time.

[147] Hinds (1998): 102.   [148] Maciver (2012b): 33, my italics.

[149] Cf. e.g. Jameson (1991): 1: postmodern theories that emerged at the end of the twentieth century are 'marked by an inverted millenarianism in which premonitions of the future, catastrophic or redemptive, have been replaced by senses of the end of this or that'.

(Post) Latourian Quintus

theories have in turn triggered responses which seek instead of a rupture with the past entrenched lines of continuity. Bruno Latour's *We Have Never Been Modern* offers a drastic example of this counter-position. Latour argues that we are not moving into a radically new age, because *the very notion that time passes* is a deluded construct of modern thought. Anthropology reminds us that the passage of time can be interpreted in several ways – as a cycle or a decadence, as a fall or as instability, as a return or a continuous presence – in a way that is incomprehensible to the moderns, for whom 'time's forward arrow is unambiguous'.[150]

There is a typically Latourian irony that this theory is based precisely on drawing a contrast between 'modern' and 'premodern' ways of conceptualising time. This contrast is no doubt a peculiar vision of history; and ideas about the succession of distinct eras are readily found in ancient literature. Hesiod's *Works and Days* takes as its *raison d'être* the exposition of the difference between ages.[151] When Latour writes that 'the moderns have a peculiar propensity for understanding that time passes abolishing the past behind it; they take themselves for Attila, in whose footsteps no grass grows back'[152] he may as well be quoting the famous line from Vergil's *Georgics*: 'time flies, never to be recovered' (3.284). And his notion of the 'false' dichotomy of moving forwards versus going back is exactly what is interrogated in Vergil's Fourth Eclogue, which heralds the return of the Golden Age under Augustus – a newness achieved by repetition – but also makes clear that this return is to be past-effacing, as is visualised in the opening poem of the collection by the farmers who are forced to pack up and leave their fields behind.

What this critique of Latour's critique serves to emphasise is the simple but crucial point, that 'ancient literature' can offer profound deliberations on the forward arrow of time. If we return to the re-animating culture of imperial Greece, we may see how the output from this period conducts such deliberations particularly intensely: confronting the conflict at the heart of this not-so-modern concept of temporality:

> One can go forward, but then one must break with the past; one can choose to go backward, but then one has to break with the modernising avant-gardes.[153]

If the *Posthomerica* can be read as a product of this culture, then the simultaneous presence of Homeric and later elements in the poem

---

[150] Latour (1993): 69.
[151] Compare e.g. Vernant (1980): ch. 8 who argues that Hesiod has a circular view of time.
[152] Latour (1993): 68.   [153] Ibid: 68–9.

36   Beginning Again (Introduction): The Poetics of Impersonation

represents Quintus' own meditation on that past-present divide; a divide whose limits must lie at the core of his poetics of the interval. The paradoxical doubleness of the text suggests that this poet too sought a way to integrate his work into the traditional past without sacrificing his contemporaneity; and rather than using one to cancel out the other, he aims at a positive co-operation between the Homeric 'then' and his own *hic et nunc*. The title of this book, *The Resurrection of Homer*, expresses the profound results of this enterprise. In an era *just* before the term 'resurrection' had an indelibly Christian overtone, Quintus embarks upon a twofold temporal hermeneutics, a polemical simultaneity of the old and the new, which re-animates into and for the present a figure, a text and a form which (contrary to Habicht's grumbling) never really died.

In what remains of this 'beginning' chapter, I shall now delineate my strategy of reading: its structure, scope and critical methodology. These final opening remarks will also serve to make clear in what ways this interpretation will depart from the *methods* of recent treatments of the poem, as well as their conclusions.

1.9   Structure, Scope and Sources

There are two strands to this book. Part I, *Quintus as Homer: Illusion and Imitation*, expands the notion of the interval established in this introduction: considering how such a position is constructed on a macro- and micro-scale. After a detailed study of what I term the 're-animating' culture of imperial Greece, I offer a detailed re-analysis of the compositional techniques of the text: how and why, this first section asks, does this poet 'write Homer'? Part II, *Quintus as Quintus: Antagonism and Assimilation*, considers four metapoetic[154] vehicles – the programmatics of the proem; the trope of memory; the metaphor of filiation and the narrative agent of time – which Quintus co-opts from a range of genres and texts to advance his incorporative style of poetics, turning the symbolic toolkit of poetic antagonism into a *new* Homeric mode.

Any such reading of the *Posthomerica* must address the contentious question of its sources. Identifying Quintus' literary models beyond Homer is, like his dating, another task which continues to provoke and frustrate scholars. It is not my intention to re-enter these old arguments either in full.[155] I shall instead adopt a broadly maximalist approach to

---

[154] On this term, see 1.10.
[155] For the fullest treatments of Quintan *Quellenforschung*, see Vian (1959) and the useful summary of the state of play in the introduction to Baumbach and Bär (2007).

Structure, Scope and Sources 37

Quintus' sources. I shall make the case for the epic's engagement with a wide range of literary interlocutors, particularly those which are openly antagonistic to Homeric epic, against whom Quintus launches his response. Interactions will be considered positively rather than rejected *a priori*. But I shall also posit instances where I believe a specific and direct connection is likely and has not before been suggested. I shall shortly address the intertextual implications of this approach.[156] It is first necessary to set out my position regarding the two most problematic areas of this literary background, which are also most relevant to my arguments: Quintus' familiarity with the Epic Cycle and his use of Latin material.

If Quintus positions his poem in the Homeric middle, an obvious question arises regarding his relationship to the Cyclic poems, another group of texts which may be considered as doing the same thing. The *Posthomerica* covers the same narrative ground as several of these lost epics;[157] and the *Aethiopis*, also begins straight after the end of the *Iliad*, and led to an alternative final line for the poem (ὣς οἵ γ' ἀμφίεπον τάφον Ἕκτορος· ἦλθε δ' Ἀμαζών,/Ἄρηος θυγάτηρ μεγαλήτορος ἀνδροφόνοιο, fr.1 W); an alternative which, as we have seen, Quintus mobilises pointedly in his own opening sequence. A persistent line of scholarly thought thus runs that Quintus chose to write a poem on this theme to replace the Epic Cycle; which, it is argued mainly on the basis of the *Posthomerica*'s numerous divergences from its stories, was by his time no longer extant.[158] My stance on the matter aligns with that of Maciver, who offers surely the most common-sense take on this rather illogical argumentation:

> Quintus, as a creative poet, need not follow the traditional version of events, just as Euripides felt that he could manipulate traditional myths for the purposes of his plays. A poet does not need an excuse to write a poem.[159]

Whereas for Maciver the availability of the Cycle is important for qualitative reasons – invalidating suggestions that the poem only

---

[156] See 1.8.

[157] The events of the *Aethiopis*, the *Little Iliad*, the *Ilioupersis* and part of the *Nostoi* all feature in Quintus' narrative.

[158] Gärtner (2005): 28 n. 10 lists the scholars for and against engagement with the Cycle. See also relevant discussion in Baumbach and Bär (2015).

[159] Maciver (2012b): 8–9. I also agree with Maciver that it is likely, on balance, that the Epic Cycle was in Quintus' time still 'around' at least in portions (ibid: 9) and, as Bär and Baumbach suggest (2007: 1 n. 2), should not necessarily be thought of as a unified text, but a collection which may have still existed in some regions. Where relevant my argument shall proceed on this basis.

38   Beginning Again (Introduction): The Poetics of Impersonation

survived through the Middle Ages as a guide to what happened after the *Iliad*[160] and affirming that it was appreciated for its literary merits too – what is crucial for me is that Quintus' manoeuvres of completing Homer's story reflect the poetological aims of the poem, not any 'supply and demand' replacement job.

The so-called Latin question, whether Quintus made creative use of Latin poetry, has even larger implications for my reading. As I define the poem's techniques against the methods of response mainly (but not exclusively) identified with Roman writers, the possibility of Quintus' direct engagement with these poets must be actively considered. The level of Latin knowledge among erudite imperial Greeks has been the subject of much recent scholarship.[161] It is an interesting – and frustrating – quirk of cultural history that despite evidence for widespread bilingualism[162] and the overwhelming influence of Greek literature on Latin works, it is difficult to make a watertight case for Greek poetry's sustained use of Latin models in this period. Difficulty arises not only from the obvious and perennial problems with searching for intertextual parallels between different languages,[163] but also, in the imperial literature more specifically, from the fact that in the Greek and Latin poems which cover the same themes, divergences seem to outweigh similarities. This situation has led many scholars to conclude that these Greek poets either did not know the Latin material at all, knew it insufficiently closely to make detailed use of it – a possibility 'corroborated' by the existence of a number of Greek translations of canonical Latin works from the third and fourth centuries –[164] and/or relied on now-lost Alexandrian material to construct their narratives: the durable adage of the 'lost Hellenistic source' still exerts a particularly strong hold in this field.

For the imperial Greek mythological epics, these Latin debates are especially frequent and strident. Given that Triphiodorus covers the same ground as the story told by Aeneas to Dido at the Carthaginian banquet, his epyllion is frequently compared with the narrative of *Aeneid* 2, especially the respective roles of Sinon, Laocoön and Cassandra as the horse

---

[160] *Pace* e.g. James (2007): 145 'It was probably the recent loss of [the Epic Cycle] poems that motivated Quintus' undertaking ... Certainly the fact that he successfully replaced them was the main reason for his work's survival.'

[161] Particularly instructive here are Fisher (1982) and Sánchez-Ostiz (2013).

[162] Recent engaging interventions in this vast topic include Adams (2003); Adams, Janse and Swain (2002); and Mullen and Elder (2019).

[163] We return to the difficulties of intertextuality in 1.10.

[164] See especially Fisher (1982), who shows that many of these are dated to the fourth century.

Structure, Scope and Sources

enters Troy.[165] In its kaleidoscopic style and erotic fixations, the *Dionysiaca* has triggered comparisons not only with Vergil but particularly with Ovid's *Metamorphoses*: scholars are increasingly considering how Ovid's drastically topsy-turvy epic could have offered a model of formalistic deviance, embedded storytelling and transitional mythmaking for Nonnus' ample innovations in hexameter verse.[166]

In the case of Quintus himself, as with Triphiodorus, the subject matter and characters in the *Posthomerica* make questions of Vergilian inheritance most prevalent. The traditional consensus regarding his direct use of the *Aeneid* – particularly for the account of the destruction of Troy – has been negative: in the nineteenth and twentieth centuries, Tychsen, Köchly and Heinze all argued against the likelihood of a Vergilian-infused *Posthomerica*.[167] That Quintus chose not to include many prominent features of Vergil's narrative is rejected as inconsistent with an author who, in line with the prevailing assessment of his Homeric imitation, would surely have copied 'anaemically' any models available to him.[168] Vian confirms this line;[169] although at least with the concession that 'on ne saurait affirmer que Quintus ignorait les Latins'.[170] Recent attempts have been made to revise this position.[171] The book-length study of Gärtner[172] and the detailed chapter by James[173] have re-analysed all of the relevant passages of the *Posthomerica* against their potential Vergilian counterparts, and reached the more generous conclusion (still stated, however, particularly by Gärtner, with perhaps excessive ambivalence) that Quintus could well have been working creatively – and *deviating* creatively – from the *Aeneid* as a source for the sack. Elsewhere in the poem, recourse to more minor

---

[165] Relevant parallels and divergences are set out in Miguélez Cavero (2013): 64–71.

[166] See Braune (1935) and Shorrock (2001): 110, with many more studies to come in Verhelst and Scheijnen (forthcoming). For a negative view, see Knox (1988) and Hopkinson (1994b): 3. Shorrock (2001): 110–11 and (2008): 105 is more ambivalent. Nonnus' engagement with the *Aeneid* has also been discussed: see e.g. Harries (1994), Duc (1990): 38–42, and Frangoulis (1999).

[167] (1807): LLXXVII; (1850): XXVI and (1915): 63–81 respectively.

[168] Of these scholars, Heinze argued most strongly for derivations from a lost Hellenistic epic to explain features common to the *Posthomerica* and the *Aeneid*'s accounts of the fall of Troy.

[169] Vian (1959): 17–109.

[170] Vian (1963): XXXIV. He concludes nonetheless, however, that 'même si par endroit ces lectures ont laissé des traces, la mise en oeuvre a été opérée avec des matériaux grecs et d'après la technique traditionelle de l'imitation'.

[171] Keydell, in a series of publications – (1931), (1954), (1961) and (1963) – offers an earlier positive reading of direct dependence of Quintus on Vergil. His arguments were strongly contested by Vian's analysis (1959).

[172] (2005).   [173] (2007).

40   Beginning Again (Introduction): The Poetics of Impersonation

scenes and imagery from Vergil's epic[174] also points strongly towards intimate knowledge and engagement.

Based on the existing evidence and the status of such debates, my overall position is as follows: the existence of Greek translations of Latin works does not by any satisfying logic preclude knowledge of the original versions (modern readers honed in Latin still enjoy English translations...); those recent suggestions about the connections between other imperial Greek epics – particularly Nonnus – and the works of Ovid and Vergil are increasingly convincing; and in the case of Quintus, his divergence from the *Aeneid* in certain key passages should be read, as is the case with the Cycle, as indicative of creative independence, not ignorance. Now that Quintus is more firmly recognised as, to reuse Maciver's catch-all phrase, a 'creative poet', many of the traditional arguments against Latin influence based on a low estimation of his abilities can be confidently disregarded. Since it is not the aim of this book (rather, it is the aim of this book not) to produce another defensive reading of a work whose value as a text 'worth reading' has now so often been demonstrated,[175] I shall proceed with regards to the 'Latin question' without further justification along these lines. My premise is that Quintus did in all probability know Latin literature; that there are a range of ways in which a Greek or Roman reader would perceive significance in the overlap or the *absence* of overlap when, for instance, Quintus and Vergil share a storyline; and that the *Posthomerica* also engages with themes recognisable from the broader Latin tradition (literary and also, as should already be clear from our discussion of the Pompeian houses, material) and reworks the tropes used by many individual works within it.

---

[174] Namely: the entry of Penthesilea into battle (Q.S.1.355–41) with the Vergilian description of Camilla (*Aen.* 11.648–55); the simile of boiling water at Q.S.5.379–85 for Ajax' madness via Allecto's intoxication of Turnus (*Aen.* 7.461–6); and the description of the Greeks' shield-formation (Q.S.11.356–407) *testudo* at *Aen.* 9.505–18. On these examples, in my opinion the strongest cases available, see respectively Gärtner (2005): 53–6; 96–100 (with James (2007): n. 29); and Keydell (1954) and James (2007): 151–2. On the possible connections between Quintus' Penthesilea and Camilla, see also the recent article by Fratantuono (2016), which posits a very direct engagement: 'Quintus manipulates and reverses the plot of Book 11 of Vergil's *Aeneid*, the account of the equestrian battle in which the Volscian Camilla plays the central role' (207). The *testudo* scene will be the most crucial for my argument: I return to it centrally in Chapter 7.

[175] Thus Maciver (2012b): 1 'My purpose in this book is to examine the *Posthomerica* as a *poem* worth reading and interpreting in its own right.' Of course, dismissive voices remain: see for example the introductions to Lelli (2013): xi–xiii and Gärtner (2005). However, since the counter-arguments against such negative views are both prevalent and, largely, successful, I seek not to assert once more *that* the post-Homeric poet is 'creative', but to define more fully *how* he is so.

1.10 Terms of Engagement: 'Intertextuality', 'Theory', 'Metapoetics'

I have referred and will continue to refer to this book as an 'argument' about the *Posthomerica* and its place within imperial Greek epic (I do not like the term 'study': it often has connotations which are too descriptive for the style of approach adopted here). This is an argument based, of course, on a *reading* of the text. 'Reading', however, is a fluid term and should be defined further.[176] My reading will be situated within both ancient reading considerations – the notion of Quintus as an educated reader from the imperial Greek third century, and the possibility of texts which he and his contemporary audience would have encountered – and modern theories and critical discourse. My notional 'reader' will therefore shift, in ways which are intentional and self-conscious, from the conceptual to the concrete, the hypothetical to the situated, with the aim of understanding the poem on the multiple sites in which it is, could be and must be read. There are more specifically three main strands to this reading – the intertextual, the theoretical and the programmatic – and I shall briefly treat each of these here.

As will already be clear from my discussion of the sources, this reading will actively posit connections between the *Posthomerica* and a wide range of Greek and Latin texts. That concept of 'connections', however, itself inevitably raises questions about intertextuality; and since this remains a loaded and contentious concept in literary criticism, there requires some initial comment on my position towards it. Since the term was first coined by Julia Kristeva,[177] 'intertextuality' has been the subject and method of a vast cascade of studies in classical scholarship; often used, as Pucci remarks, 'indiscriminately by students of allusion of every stripe and critical inclination'.[178] In spite – or perhaps because of – this ubiquity, there is no one fixed and universally accepted definition of the theory; and as Pucci's comment makes clear, its relationship to its evil twin of textual praxis, 'allusion', remains particularly fraught. This is not the place to rehearse such battles at great length. But most relevant to my purposes is the divide between 'allusion' as describing a tight verbal imitation by one author of another, associated (positively or negatively) with Alexandrian and Roman poetry and signalled in concrete and linguistic terms, versus 'intertext' as based predominantly on the interpretative capabilities of the

---

[176] As Maciver (2012b): 9 also pertinently notes.   [177] Kristeva (1969).   [178] Pucci (1998): 15.

42 Beginning Again (Introduction): The Poetics of Impersonation

reader – associated with the so-called death of the author,[179] a vision of the text as an inescapably multi-dimensional space, and the idea that meaning is released (only) at the point of reception.[180]

When accounting for the literary layers in the *Posthomerica*, the former, more rigid practice has traditionally prevailed. Attempts to identify the literature with which this elusive poem makes contact have led to the objectives of *Quellenforschung* taking on a leading role. The term 'intertextuality' – so central to the 'Roman Literature and its Context' series – was first applied extensively to the *Posthomerica* by Maciver. Based, as discussed, on a heavily outlined theory of 'historically informed reader reception', his book proceeds on the premise that 'a constructed Quintus alludes, and we read this activity and interpret it, according to our capacities of reading.'[181]

There is, of course, ample space for a 'middle ground' between these philologically concrete and reader-oriented modes of textual contact. And yet there is also a deep ideological investment in maintaining a division between them. Whilst most classicists are deeply aware of how flawed these existing taxonomies are, it remains the case that the vocabulary of intertext 'vs.' allusion conceals genuine differences in approach between continuity and change in ancient literature and its inbuilt reception of its inherited tradition. Such difficulties are particularly palpable in those highly influential intertextual studies of classical works that we have already discussed so much. Conte and Hinds quite clearly rebel against the tightly demarcated limits of 'allusion' in favour of more open-ended markers of textual interaction. And yet for all their Kristevan resonances, one may rightly question how far Conte's 'poetic memory' or Hinds' 'tendentious annotation' really roam from an expanded sense *of* allusion: both rubrics are subsequently employed by their coiners to posit a range of tight linguistic connections between one ancient author and another. Maciver too dedicates his opening pages to outlining how intertextual his Quintan study will be; and yet after this excursus, there is little that is Kristevean about his arguments, and plenty (convincingly) philological in the literary connections which he suggests.

This book is not a study of allusion or intertextuality. However, since it is an account of a poetics deeply rooted in literary engagement, it cannot

---

[179] Barthes (2001).

[180] Cf. e.g. Fowler (2000): 127: 'what counts as an intertext and what one does with it depends on the reader'. For influential proponents of this approach in the classical field, see also Martindale (1993); Hinds (1998); Conte (1986); Pucci (1998); Lyne (1994).

[181] Maciver (2012b): 13, with further description of his methodology at 9–13.

Terms of Engagement

deny the significance of working within these terms and their mutual controversies. As it seeks to read the *Posthomerica* not just in terms of Quintus' references to Homer but as a uniquely rich site for exploring the relationship between Quintus and Homer as whole textual systems, my approach may indeed be termed 'intertextual' in a more critically defined sense. That is, it will treat Quintus' 'references' to Homer as indicators of this ideological and aesthetic transposition of one set of signs onto another, a process which I believe is crucial to the overarching aim of reading the poem as both a text and a cultural artefact.[182] I have already stressed how historical lacunae have held back imperial Greek epic, and particularly Quintus' epic, too far for too long. If it is not only a critical truism but a fundamental truth that in the process of reading literature any historical alluding poet is a phantom figure, impossible to recover fully, then textually as well as contextually our reading of this 'alluding poet' can be far bolder.

The second strand of my reading moves from assessing Quintus' use of material from his own time to our own use of material more contemporary in nature to inform our assessment of him. As is clear from the discussion of intertextuality, the recourse to modern theoretical models developed in other disciplines for the analysis of ancient literature is now a standard prospect in much classical scholarship. The odious and paradoxical idea that it is radical or gimmicky for a classical philologist to 'do theory' is one that needs no further detraction here.[183] More deserving of comment are the *types* of theoretical model upon which this book will draw. In addition to interrogating the hermeneutic strategies favoured by recent scholars of Roman poetry – of obvious relevance to my arguments regarding Quintus vis-à-vis silver Latin studies – I shall also use tools drawn from further a-'field'.[184] Latour's critique on millennial-dystopian linear time has already been posited as a useful way to elucidate the particular temporal reflexivity on display in imperial Greek works. The social sciences will continue to inform my approach. In Chapter 6, to take a major example, I discuss the *Posthomerica*'s expansive vision of heroic succession and its rejection of a

---

[182] Cf. in this vein the pertinent argument of Hardie (2007) on the imperial cento as a 'healthy anecdote' to Bakhtinian and Kristevean ideas: for intertextual 'extremists' who (in his words) set readers and authors drifting in a 'sea of fragmentary citations and uncontrolled referential relationships', the cento does not work, because it is tightly controlled and very clear about its use of allusion from an authoritative authorial source.

[183] For the persistence of this idea in some quarters, see e.g. (discussion in) Schmitz (2007a) whose aim of providing a handbook for applying 'modern literary theories' to 'ancient texts' (to use his title's terms) arguably serves also to perpetuate the artificial divide between them.

[184] That is, less familiar to traditional classical studies.

44   Beginning Again (Introduction): The Poetics of Impersonation

one-man-centred model of epic narrative using discourses of relationality drawn from art criticism and 'posthuman' anthropology. These formulations are powerful ways of conceptualising multiplicity and deviation from a monocentric model of thought. By reading with them, I seek not to 'apply' the theories to this text, but to show how they capture something distinct and idiosyncratic in the techniques already present within its poetics, and simply provide the best language to articulate it.[185]

The third and final strand concerns more specifically a mode of reading. As is apparent from the outline of chapters, there is a programmatic tone to many of my arguments: my assessment of Quintus' literary agenda will, by the very nature of its questions, centre on the poetological, the epic voice and – dare I say it – the 'metapoetic'. 'Metapoetics' is not a popular term anymore. Matthew Leigh wryly dubs it 'the dreariest of contemporary approaches to ancient verse',[186] and Pramit Chaudhuri warns against its 'overfamiliarity' in modern readings of ancient poets, which 'works against the thrill of [their] gambit'.[187] However, as Leigh and Chaudhuri's own work well shows,[188] literary symbolism was a crucial means by which particularly post-Alexandrian writers conceptualised the paradigms of power under negotiation in their verse. Programmatics continued to dominate imperial Greek epic, in ways connected with but ultimately radically different from their imperial Latin equivalents. As my overview of these poets has suggested in preliminary form, writers such as Nonnus and Triphiodorus relentlessly centralise questions about the literary identity of their works, and reconfigure a number of symbols from their inherited tradition to visualise these concerns. Quintus, I shall argue, plays a pivotal role in this programmatic bent of imperial Greek epic. As my account of the proem – the locus for poetic reflexivity in the *Posthomerica* – will argue centrally, but as all of my readings will suggest, this is a text which revels in the programmatic and explores new routes for literary self-consciousness through Homeric imitation which are anything but dreary. The book will thus in one respect be unapologetically 'metapoetic',[189] in

---

[185] In the adoption of newer models than those to which classical studies is usually indebted, one must be alert to charges of extraneousness. This book uses the models it does in full awareness of such potential charges, and aims actively to combat them.

[186] Leigh (2006): 238.   [187] Chaudhuri (2014): 2.

[188] Classical scholars have their own anxieties of influence, of course, and one may detect a knowing irony in Leigh's protestations, prefacing as they do a piece which teases out some excellent programmatic connotations in Statius.

[189] However, as for 'intertextuality' and 'allusion', I shall not use the terms as a major piece of vocabulary in my analysis, so as to circumvent the continual debates over the words themselves, and focus instead on the effects of the reading strategies which they open up.

Terms of Engagement 45

that it will argue that these Trojan poets are reflexive *about being reflexive* and that a deep engagement with programmatic ideas is one of the features which can unite these seemingly disparate works.

I shall have succeeded in this approach if the (potential) reader of Quintus gets a sense of the breadth of literary-cultural references on display in this poem and emerges more attuned to the nature of its engagement with them: participatory rather than parroting, reactionary and even radical in its treatment of Homer and positioning of itself. In this way, the elusiveness of the *Posthomerica* does not fail to signify. Quintus' slippery identity, his refusal to be contained by one or other existing critical paradigm, his lingering status 'in the middle' *is* a way of understanding his poetics. Exceptions can destabilise the rule, and for the modern scholar of ancient epic, the *Posthomerica* should prompt some important self-reflections. Two decades on from its launch into mainstream classical criticism, the model of adversarial re-reading has indeed become the blueprint for studying creative imitation in epic. In a poem previously taken as a serene conformer to this model, Quintus' rejection of antagonism towards Homer, his (re)-embrace of continuity and culturally informed criticism of Homeric criticism contains a pertinent warning against its universal applicability; a timely reminder that there are other ways of dealing with poetic rivalry than the Oedipal.[190] In creating a picture of epic succession which repeats, to varying degrees and combinations, the same moves of competition and change, and in translating this theory, such a successful fit for silver Latin, directly onto imperial Greece, have we thus really struck interpretative gold, identifying a system of unifying characteristics which are 'always' 'ever present' for 'all'? Or are we in danger of subscribing to another breed of unambiguous thinking,[191] in our own anxiety to quench that ever-present desire for exegetical closure?

---

[190] As Hardie also concedes, (1993): 118. But cf. his final remarks (119) on the persistence, nonetheless, of the 'ever-present anxiety'.

[191] Cf. Latour (1993): 68.

PART I

Quintus as Homer: Illusion and Imitation

CHAPTER 2

Enlarging the Space
Imperial Doubleness, Fixity, Expansion

Chapter 1 described the need to rethink Quintus' literary position – to move away from the post-Homeric to the inter-Homeric. It outlined the framework for the cultural narrative which could be driving this shift: the imperial Greek interest, cemented but complicated in the third century, in creative re-animation – carving out new space within fixed boundaries of language, convention or tradition. We turn now to reconstructing that narrative; to exploring discrete spheres of imperial Greek culture which offer crucial new perspectives on the *Posthomerica*'s project.

There are three areas of this culture which together will form a central, but strikingly under-considered matrix for comprehending Quintus' epic: sophistic declamation; the creative exercises in the *progymnasmata*; and new imperial styles of Homeric performance. These modes combine ideas of mimesis with self-conscious adherence to their source texts: re-enacting their models, they expand from within clearly demarcated limits. They constitute major examples of and inspiration for what the *Posthomerica* attempts on the boldest of scales: a full-scale epic inserted within a Homeric frame.

In order to demonstrate the points of contact between these spheres and the *Posthomerica*, we must consider not – as per the conventional approach – speculative biographical possibilities (Was this poem performed? Does it show the influence of ethopoeiae? Is it the work of a sophist?) but instead turn to the text's own portrayal of Homeric song. The scenes of internal performances contain in miniature Quintus' approach to expanding Homeric epic. The poet displays in his songs within the song a version of the interstitial worldview in which the *Posthomerica* is claiming a part.

2.1 Being and Not Being

We have begun to consider the heightened interest in play-acting in the Greek culture of the early empire, and seen how concepts of 'doubleness'

50 Enlarging the Space: Imperial Doubleness, Fixity, Expansion

were crucial to such acts: being and not being the subject impersonated.[1] Let us now interrogate this concept more fully, and turn to its particular, peculiar manifestations in this period.

The very idea of doubleness conceals a web of complex and contradictory connotations. Its jagged relationship to other terms in the typology of duality helps to reveal its nuance. If 'doubling' denotes a process – the reduplicative transformation of one thing into another, the sliding and colliding of opposites – and if the 'doublet' defines a twin-*set*: the combination of two identical terms, the heroic formula of Homeric narrative or a line of verse occurring twice,[2] then 'doubleness' both draws upon and deviates from such formulations. Closer consideration of the most readily quoted examples of the concept illustrates the difference.[3] When Aristophanes' Dicaeopolis exclaims that 'today I must be a beggar; to be myself and yet not seem to be' (δεῖ γάρ με δόξαι πτωχὸν εἶναι τήμερον,/ εἶναι μὲν ὅσπερ εἰμί, φαίνεσθαι δὲ μή, *Ach.* 440–1), his words make clear the calculated, correlative nature of this 'change': the thrice repetition of the existential verb; the precarious reinforcement of ὅσπερ; the equal but opposite pulls of being and appearing, balanced in the μέν and the δέ all bespeak the shift, but not the loss, of the original self. Richard Schechner's (in)famous description of the conceit of acting, in which Olivier is both 'not Hamlet' and 'not not Hamlet' as he delivers his lines on stage relies on a similar possibility of movement forwards *and* back between two ontological states. This is not a one-way shift from actor to character, nor a straight, lateral transformation from impersonator to his object: doubleness is an inherently *liminal* position – an existence in the interval between the being and the not being.[4]

This position, so crucial to the actor-character dialectic, can recur in a number of different forms. Barstch's concept of 'doublespeak' sketches a framework for how this type of multiplicity can take hold in language

---

[1] Chapter 1.7.

[2] The term 'doublet' has been used in Homeric scholarship for many, often interrelated, types of repetition – from individual phrases and verses, to speeches, character types and extended sections of narrative. See Sammons (2017): ch. 3 with up-to-date bibliography. On doublets in later poetry denoting an intentionally occurring, non-formulaic, line repetition, see the clear discussion in Wills (1997).

[3] We return here to the examples sketched in preliminary form in Chapter 1. For the use of these examples in discussions of mimesis and performance, see Webb (2006) with further bibliography.

[4] Schechner himself corroborates such a conception when he describes the 'not not' process (and although he uses the word 'process', he admits that neither side is lost in the transformation) as 'transitional', and taking place 'in a liminal time/space and in the subjunctive mood.' (1985): 111–12.

Being and Not Being   51

itself.[5] The second paradigm to explain the demise of sincerity during the first centuries of the Roman Empire (the first being theatricality, which for Bartsch delineates the performativity of an audience: the need for the subjects of the emperor, and even at times the emperor himself, to act out a script in their dealings with each other), 'doublespeak' unveils the ways in which the very act of writing adjusted and responded to the lack of freedom felt under imperial rule. A method of determining textual meaning by hunting for hidden criticisms of a regime, 'doublespeak' makes clear the potential for linguistic invention offered by the notion of 'being both'; as an author can occupy two seemingly irreconcilable positions, and embody in a single text the safety of praise and the empowerment of blame. Such formulations help to reveal above all the two-fold temporality which lies at the heart of what doubleness can do. Occurring in ways both diachronic and synchronic, simultaneous and successive, its two parts are joined in constant antagonism, entwined like μέν and δέ.

This slippery concept has a long history in ancient modes of performance and praxes of imitation – complex manifestations which stretch well beyond these initial paradigms *par excellence*. It lies at the core of Plato's complex, multiform definitions of mimesis:[6] in the dangerous act of impersonation of *Republic* 3; the illusionistic copy-making from *Republic* 10; and the fraudulent mimicry of the sorcerer sophist (*Soph.* 235a), the falseness of representation, the genuine but ambiguous gap between imitated character and imitating artist are notions which connect all three taxonomies[7] – notions which can elsewhere be exploited to expose their profound psychological connotations. For example, in the memorable story of how Leontius desires to look at a pile of corpses, and at the same time feels disgust and turns his eyes away (ἅμα μὲν ἰδεῖν ἐπιθυμοῖ, ἅμα δὲ

---

[5] Bartsch (1994). I am taking her term 'doublespeak' as an alternative means of conceptualising the key characteristics of doubleness. Further general discussions on subtle criticism in Ahl (1984a) and (1984b); Dominik (1994): ch. 4. For more sceptical approaches, see Johnson (1987) and Vout (2007): ch. 3. We return to this notion in 2.3.

[6] The discussions to follow will often take 'performance' and 'mimesis' as a double act, in that I focus on how they work together within the larger terminological cluster of ancient concepts impersonation (cf. the much-dissected chains of near-synonyms such as *mimema* [imitation], *eikon* [image], *homoioma* [likeness]). For these purposes, 'mimesis' will be defined primarily as 'imitation', with the acknowledgement that such a definition does not cover all possible aspects of what mimesis – as a process or an outcome – does. Further helpful discussion along these terminological lines in Sörbom (1966); Belfiore (1984); Porter (2010); and Pappas (2017) with further bibliography.

[7] By emphasising this link, I am consciously bypassing the contentious issues surrounding the other points of convergence and divergence in Platonic definitions. Bibliography on this topic is voluminous. See especially the clear summary of the proposals in Naddaff (2002), and more extensively, Belfiore (1984); Halliwell (1988); Nehamas (1982); Lear (2011).

52   Enlarging the Space: Imperial Doubleness, Fixity, Expansion

αὖ δυσχεραίνοι) but is eventually overcome by his urge to watch (*Resp.* 4.439e–441b)[8], Leontius' double position (he is not and not not an indulger of the spectacle) represents a yearning, an urge to break free from one or other state – watching and not watching; compulsion and reason or shame – achieved precisely and paradoxically by occupying them *both*.

Such notions remain just as central to modern terminology. In his attempt to provide a general definition of 'performance', Richard Bauman describes it precisely as a 'consciousness of doubleness', in which 'the actual execution of an action is placed in mental comparison with a potential, an ideal, or a remembered original model of that action'.[9] In this formulation once again we find the pliancy of temporality (the future implied by a 'potential'; the past to be recovered by remembering an original) and the significance of desire – here, the striving for an 'ideal' – which encapsulate the practice at large. Nowhere perhaps is such a definition more powerfully reflected than in classical Athenian theatrics. A domain acutely aware of the borderline between being the self and the clouding or submerging of oneself into a separate performed identity, Athenian drama actively thematises the motivations and mechanisms behind such acts. The *Bacchae* has long been recognised as the *locus dramaticus* for ideas of the double: 'playing the other',[10] 'seeing double'[11] and being double are all integral to the experience of the play's victims (and) audience: an experience which collapses into 'an irresolvable interplay of sameness and difference.'[12] This interplay is also explored differently in a number of paradigmatic examples from comedy and 'tragicomedy'; as, Dicaeopolis is joined by a host of other 'dramatists' such as Aristophanes' Agathon[13] and Euripides' Helen all of whom take on various metatheatrical roles in their plays, stage-crafting their parts with extreme explicitness and hyperbole so that the audience is made, as Lada-Richards puts it, to 'reflect self-consciously upon the twofold way in which the

---

[8] Quotation at *Resp.* 4.439e. The anecdote is explicitly introduced to illustrate the conflict between parts of the soul, and to identify a third part, here called *to thumoeides* (*Resp.* 441a). On the episode, see particularly Liebert (2013) and von Reden and Goldhill (1999). The latter piece convincingly relates the story to Socrates' own vocabulary of conflict between honour and control and, most relevantly for our purposes, the agonistic tension between 'the performance of the Socratic dialogue [and] the paradigm of performance' (260).

[9] s.v. 'performance' in Barnouw (ed.) (1989).   [10] Zeitlin (1985).

[11] Segal (1982) is essential reading: on the two sets of Maenads, two versions of Dionysus; or the double vision of Pentheus, who sees outside the palace two suns, two cities. Further discussion and analysis in Goldhill (1988): 141–2.

[12] Goldhill (1988): 153.

[13] The meta-theatrical player *par excellence*, who explains how he, as a tragic poet, constructs stage characters, all the while being a character himself in a play (*Thesm.* 146–72).

Being and Not Being

elements of "actor" and of "character" can co-exist in a performer's stage presence'.[14]

This brief tracing of doubleness from the Platonic dialogue to the Athenian stage begins to cement its cross-generic ramifications: the duality inherent in ancient acting could readily acquire a symbolic authority to be drawn upon in other intellectual spheres. In the *Helios* volume on 'unmasked performance'[15] Stehle argues that doubleness also has a special valence for performers *in propria persona* and their spectators, because 'on the one hand, since the performer acts as himself or herself, such "unmasked" performances are public performances of identity, (but) on the other hand, the identity projected is an "ideal" or "potential" one ... constructed, rather than natural'.[16] The impulses central to doubleness – multiple temporality; the desire for escapism; a fluid position in between two states or beings – thus offer distinct opportunities to those engaged in these *particular* mimetic fields.

Apprehending these facets of doubleness is a crucial first step to grasping its specific and spectacular impact on our period under question. For whilst the concept finds expression across such a vast range of ancient spaces, it appears to have acquired an especial relevance in the performative output of imperial Greece. This sharpened attention can be observed through three avenues. First, the period saw the development of new genres focused directly on such conceits. Mime and pantomime, the new and highly popular entertainment forms which emerged during the Hellenistic and Roman periods, derived their power from their unnerving mimetic manipulations, as actors simultaneously appeared as characters in a role and performers displaying their virtuoso technique – a paradox which lay at the heart of the anxiety that they produced.[17] Libanius for instance is obsessed by how dancers' individual bodies can act as an index of a successive series of characters (διὰ δὲ Ἡφαίστου τὴν Ἀθηνᾶν, διὰ δὲ Ἄρεος Ἥφαιστον, διὰ δὲ Γανυμήδους Δία, διὰ δὲ Ἀχιλλέως Πάριν. *On Behalf of Dancers* 113). And in Lucian's famous account of a disastrous performance of the story of Ajax, the actor's madness spills out into reality as he attacks the audience, a *faux pas* described explicitly as mimesis gone

---

[14] Lada-Richards (2002): 396.

[15] In *Helios* 28 Stehle (2001): 3 defines 'unmasked performance' as 'more or less formal performances conducted by performers who are not disguised or standing in for fictional figures' – although acknowledges that such a categorisation is 'slippery'.

[16] Stehle (2001): 4.

[17] On this point, see the extended discussion by Webb (2008), who analyses the polemics on mime and pantomime which fill the ancient source material on the subject.

54   Enlarging the Space: Imperial Doubleness, Fixity, Expansion

too far (ἐκ τῆς ἄγαν μιμήσεως, *On Dance* 83–4). The combination of these two vignettes makes clear the fluid temporal possibilities of the double technique: the shifts which captivate Libanius occur with mesmerising diachrony – one character is embodied 'through' (διά) another – whereas for Lucian it is the refusal to stop being *simultaneous*, after the appropriate dramatic moment has passed, that causes such dismay.

Secondly, many imperial performances – 'unmasked' sophistic speakers declaiming *in propria persona*, to use Stehle's terms – also, as we have discussed, infused their routines with the imitation of figures from the distant past – mythical figures in the rhetorical exercises; Demosthenes or Solon in the speeches of the declaimers; Homeric heroes in 'close encounters'[18] – in a particularly intense and particularly bold form of performative fantasy. This fantasy also finds full embodiment in the rhetorical schools and training, which, as we shall see, provide a central locus for the collusion between the performance of impersonation and the assertion of contemporary knowledge and skill.

Thirdly, the era is marked by an increased slippage between literary texts and theatrical performance. Bartsch's twin paradigms of doubleness point to a conceptual version of this slippage for the early empire in Rome, as a text's duality of meaning manifests the same concerns and insecurities as the theatricality of spoken communication. We may perceive even more concrete examples of such a symbiosis in the imperial Greek scene. Poems were recited at agonistic contests which became increasingly institutionalised under the empire,[19] and many new works were specifically composed for performance at such events.[20] Traditional epic poetry was put to use at various theatrical occasions: either as background songs for pantomime displays or in the rhapsodic shows which continued well into the third century CE.[21] Poetry was also read out at community reader gatherings: both private, in a house, or public, in a library or auditorium, such as those recently excavated in Kom el-Dikka in Alexandria.[22] School exercises, particularly at the level of the *progymnasmata*, involved the composition of prose texts or epic hexameters and the performance of them to a classroom audience. And in shows of sophistic oratory, declaimers – for all their pretences of spontaneity – would frequently incorporate into their speeches quotations or paraphrases of classical texts and even original

[18] Cf. Lane Fox (1986).
[19] Further discussion and examples in 2.5. On these contests generally, see Spawforth (1989); Roueché (1993); Gangloff (2010); Remijsen (2015).
[20] Cf. especially González (2013).   [21] Collins (2004); González (2013); see 2.4.
[22] See overview in Cavallo (2007).

Being and Not Being 55

verses.[23] The conventional Aristotelian divide between the narrative and dramatic modes is thus increasingly fractured and frayed by such activities, as the bookishness of erudite literary culture made space for the mimetic possibilities most familiar to the world of performance.

How then do we account for this heightened interest in 'being both'? We have seen how performances of impersonation can take on new meaning in the context of political hegemonies: how in the dynamic and fluctuating relationship between Greek identity and Roman rule, such acts were profoundly influenced by the vital and authoritative role that literature and history played in defining the elite sense of self-worth and social position. Such mimetic enactments could thus become sites for more general questions about the validity and authority of ancient tradition in imperial culture. What is at stake in a movement backwards? What is the place of the past in the culture of the present? What role, if any, should the distant past and the mythological age play in the definition of 'Greekness'? One of the central reasons that such efforts intensified in this period is thus precisely because they provide possibilities for raising these broader issues. If doubleness afforded throughout its long history the escapism of alternating time, the enactment of an ideal and the performance of liminality, if the duality of being and not being made possible Leontius' hidden desire to outrun the confines of 'control', or the Bacchic release from secure Athenian masculinity, then such acts of impersonation in this setting offer an intense expression of the specific forms of desire, transition and restraint produced by the multiple options for and perspectives on Greek self-positioning 'under' Rome. Doubleness became a way of testing the limits of the imperial Greek obsession with the past.

Quintus' own Homeric enactment – his interstitial status as 'Homer and not Homer' – must be re-interrogated in light of these conditions. Three case studies of imperial Greek impersonation will form a setting for this re-interrogation: declamation; the *progymnasmata*; and Homeric performance on stage and page. Chronologically, these works span the first three centuries CE. They all provide examples of the imperial move towards enacting the past: they reflect, and help to construct, the deep entrenchment between literature and spectacle in the period. However what marks them as a coherent group within this larger field[24] is their distinctive combination of two interests: self-conscious doubleness and a

---

[23] On sophists and poetry Bowie (1989a) remains seminal.
[24] Mime, pantomime and other forms of theatrical and literary mimesis will thus remain in the background in the subsequent sections of this chapter, but will cease to be the main focus.

56   Enlarging the Space: Imperial Doubleness, Fixity, Expansion

strong *textual* focus. That is, all three of these areas continue the heightened trend of being and not being one's mimetic subject. But crucially, this double-being intersects with a close adherence to the source material being impersonated; an expression of the boundaries created by this adherence; and a delight in displaying creative effects within the constrictions imposed by their models.

Such an approach, of course, should by no means be limited to this group of works. Compositions that elaborate their sources via dependent, not independent, reworking find precedent at least as far back as Homeric epic itself – the scholia describe the *Odyssey* as addressing the missing pieces of the *Iliad* –[25] and continue through a range of genres throughout the rhetorical, educational and high poetic traditions.[26] As Peirano puts it, such techniques reveal across a diverse literary field 'a shared interest in treating [canonical] authors and texts as stretchable containers, potentially capable of expanding to accommodate the responses and points of view of their readers'.[27] The practice of 'opposition in imitation', she adds, whereby a poet alludes to a predecessor's version whilst simultaneously correcting their account, 'has much in common with this reading strategy'.[28]

These Quintan case studies will thus take their place within this long and strong continuum of 'creative supplementation',[29] and reveal its particular manifestations in the imperial Greek cultural space; but they will also – and crucially – redefine the terms of this process for the output of this time. Rather than displaying a combative drive analogous to poetic contrast imitation, these works combine mimesis and expansion in such a way that cohesion, not correction, becomes the prevailing force. Through their distinct exploitation of the literary opportunities of doubleness, the forms display their own narrative of the interval; which must radically inform our approach to Quintus' new poetics.

2.2   Declamation: What Demosthenes Would Have Said

The Greek sophists of the imperial period were 'walking exemplars of elite Greek culture',[30] whose epideictic displays were central to their cultural capital. The very persona of a sophist conveys their central preoccupation with ideas of doubleness. To take a perplexing and pertinent example, the

---

[25] Σ E. ad. Od. 3.248; Σ. MV Od. 24.1.   [26] Examples and references in 2.3.
[27] Peirano (2012): 24.   [28] Ibid: 21.   [29] A term which Peirano favours ((2012): 12).
[30] Connolly (2001b): 76.

Declamation: What Demosthenes Would Have Said

flamboyant Favorinus of Arles is said to have described his life in terms of three paradoxes: he was a native of Gaul who spoke Greek; a eunuch who was accused of adultery; and a citizen who quarrelled with an emperor and yet lived to tell the tale (Γαλάτης ὢν ἑλληνίζειν, εὐνοῦχος ὢν μοιχείας κρίνεσθαι, βασιλεῖ διαφέρεσθαι καὶ ζῆν, Philostratus, *V S* 489). This embodied sequence of opposites draws together a number of the diverse facets of the double position that we have seen thus far: linguistic, gendered and political in theme; simultaneous (Gaul-being and Greek-speaking, an apposition strengthened by the syntax – the nominative participle ὤν can carry both a descriptive and concessive force) and successive (first quarrelling and then surviving – the only one of the paradoxes linked with a καί) in temporal range.[31] By their strident commitment to *enacting* Greek erudition, sophists are destined to occupy that liminal 'not not' space of being: they demonstrate the full extent of Stehle's notion of the 'constructed' persona of the performer unmasked.

This sense of duality central to the sophists' self-fashioning is also widely displayed in their speeches. As has been much discussed in recent scholarship, sophistic oratory achieved its power by employing a particular sense of cultural conservation. Not only do the declamations (particularly the *suasoriae*, advanced rhetorical exercises in deliberative oratory)[32] arise from a centuries-old pedagogical tradition, but they are also bound by strict rules of linguistics and subject matter: a fidelity to classical theme, historical scenario and the Attic dialect.[33] Within this ring-fenced repertoire, the sophist would showcase his skills of elaboration through methods such as rephrasing, prosification of verse material and, most distinctively, the insertion of ethopoetic sections: block speeches which gave advice in the voice and persona of a fictional character, or, more commonly, a figure from the mythological or historical past.

This process was marked above all by an intense self-consciousness about its own imaginative pretence. Just as the *Bacchae* offers an exemplum of the thematisation of theatrical performance, so too does declamation pursue its own model of intra-generic reflexivity. Isocrates provides a

---

[31] On the fascinating identity of Favorinus, see particularly Gleason (1995), Beall (2001) and, on the quarrel with Hadrian, Swain (1989).

[32] The second type of declamation, the *controversiae*, which involved fictional legal cases aimed at training the speaker in forensic oratory, also provides ample, if different, opportunities for doubleness and engagement with canonical texts.

[33] On this aspect of second sophistic declamation, see especially Anderson (1993): chs. 2–5; Whitmarsh (2005); Enos (2008): 164–200; Connolly (2001b); Schmidt and Fleury (2011); Eshleman (2012): ch. 4.

58   Enlarging the Space: Imperial Doubleness, Fixity, Expansion

provocative early precedent. In his mammoth *Panathenaicus,* a piece written for the Panathenea festival of 342 BCE, he ends by disclosing how as he was revising what we have just read, he showed his draft to some of his pupils, and goes on to narrate vividly the sequence of events that then took place: their general praise of the speech, one boy's piercing criticism and his subsequent revision of it, which was finally performed aloud and interpreted by the same student-cum-critic.[34] This story brings into sharp relief Isocrates' concept of 'rhetoric in action':[35] dramatising the value of educative oratory, the process of training students is itself turned into a performative act of self-display.[36] Such a meta-rhetorical bent became a defining feature the imperial Greek practice of the trade.

Philostratus provides numerous significant examples. Many of his sophists are recorded as admiring and actively imitating the oratory of Demosthenes – of constructing a 'Demosthenic quality' (τὸ Δημοσθενικόν) of thought.[37] His praise of Lollianus of Ephesus includes a speech which carefully rephrases Demosthenes' *Against Leptines* 30:[38]

> κέκλεισται τὸ στόμα τοῦ Πόντου νόμῳ καὶ τὰς Ἀθηναίων τροφὰς ὀλίγαι κωλύουσι συλλαβαί, καὶ ταὐτὸν δύναται Λύσανδρος ναυμαχῶν καὶ Λεπτίνης νομομαχῶν· Philostr. *V S* 527

> The mouth of the Pontus has been locked up by a law, and a few syllables keep back the food supply of Athens; so that Lysander fighting with his ships and Leptines fighting with his law have the same power.

Philostratus' Lollianus preserves key details from the original oration: both the overall theme of the problematic law, and finer details such as the use of τοῦ Πόντου in the genitive (as per *Lept.* 20.30–1: ἐκ τοῦ Πόντου σῖτος

---

[34] The pupil in question apparently read the speech thus to show that Isocrates had in fact concealed a hidden meaning therein which only the truly sophisticated reader would pick up: covert praise for Sparta. On this and many other aspects of the speech, see Goldhill (2002a): 76–7 and, more extensively, von Reden and Goldhill (1999) with further bibliography.

[35] Goldhill (2002b): 77.

[36] *V S* 527. At the end of the speech (Isocrates 5. 271–3) Isocrates makes this point explicit: he explains that this speech has been written for those who believe that orations which are *didaskalos kai tekhnikos* (composed for educational and exemplary purposes) have greater weight than epideictic or forensic oratory.

[37] Philostratus uses the phrase specifically to describe Polemo (*V S* 542). Whitmarsh (2005) discusses briefly but pertinently the particular appeal of Demosthenes to Polemo and other sophists.

[38] Whilst the following discussion relies on Philostratus' depiction of such techniques – admittedly stylised, fictitious and the product of a reporter with his own intellectual and cultural agenda – this should not disqualify his account from shedding light on the dynamics of imperial Greek culture. On the credibility of Philostratus' depictions of the sophists, see particularly Swain (1991) and Eshleman (2012): 135–9, and brief but pertinent comments in Connolly (2001b): 89–90.

Declamation: What Demosthenes Would Have Said 59

εἰσπλέων ἐστίν). The speech, in this sense, is 'still Demosthenes'. Having established this frame, the sophist then expands: adding metaphors (the mouth of the Pontus locked up), metonymy (the συλλαβαί of the law) and poetic compound doublets (ναυμαχῶν καὶ Λεπτίνης νομομαχῶν). Lollianus also enlarges his source material via a deft shift in time: his version imagines that the law of Leptines was now in force, and the evils predicted by Demosthenes had actually come about. Mobilising the temporal flexibility afforded by his double position – as Athenian orator and contemporary sophist – his speech becomes both an impersonation of Demosthenes and a continuation of him.

Philostratus similarly recalls how Polemo gave voice to Xenophon's imagined plea to be executed alongside Socrates (*V S* 542). Revealingly, he cites this theme in order to combat the sophist's critics, who claim that he was unable to sustain ἐσχηματισμέναι ὑποθέσεις.[39] The ability to speak ἐσχηματισμένως (a term difficult to translate; but inherently containing connotations of the artificial, the disingenuous, speech marked by the possession of *form*),[40] a crucial skill in rhetoric, forms part of a long-standing tradition of thought and practice. The bT-scholia on *Iliad* 9.17, for example, argue that Agamemnon's speech before the assembly advising that the army retreat, which triggers resistance from Diomedes, is in fact a second 'test', because 'he puts up with Diomedes' rebuke when he did not put up with the speech of Achilles'. In Book 1, Agamemnon is known to have spoken without the σχῆμα of concealment, whereas his silent reaction here to Diomedes is taken for tacit acquiescence with his position, thereby showing that Diomedes' reaction was secretly just what the king wanted. Agamemnon's speech was therefore a λόγος ἐσχηματισμένος: a 'figured speech'.[41] The λόγος ἐσχηματισμένος is thus a particular form of 'doublespeak'[42] which exploits in a number of forms the craft and

---

[39] *V S* 542: τὴν αὐτὴν ὁρῶ διαμαρτίαν καὶ περὶ τοὺς ἡγουμένους αὐτὸν ἐκφέρεσθαι τῶν ἐσχηματισμένων ὑποθέσεων εἰργόμενον τοῦ δρόμου, καθάπερ ἐν δυσχωρίᾳ ἵππον. Polemo is then accused by his critics, according to Philostratus, of deprecating these themes by quoting Achilles' famous rebuke of Odysseus in the Iliadic embassy (ἐχθρὸς γάρ μοι κεῖνος ὁμῶς Ἀΐδαο πύλῃσιν, ὅς χ' ἕτερον μὲν κεύθῃ ἐνὶ/φρεσίν, ἄλλο δὲ εἴπῃ, *Il.* 9.312) which aligns this attack-and-defence with the scholiastic musings on Homer discussed here.

[40] Cf. LSJ s.v. ἐσχηματισμένως.

[41] Eustathius offers further indication of this conception in his comments at *Il.* 732.68–733.2, where he draws a contrast between speaking ἐσχηματισμένως and speaking ἀληθῶς. This ancient interpretation of the passage is convincingly set out by Hunter (2015): 700–2.

[42] For Bartsch's own discussion of such related 'schema', which can also denote both a reading and writing strategy of searching for hidden meanings and criticisms, see ch. 3 especially 67–71.

60   Enlarging the Space: Imperial Doubleness, Fixity, Expansion

elusiveness of language in the interests of both tact and safety;[43] enabling the speaker-author confidently to say one thing and think another (in fact, Zoilus, the fourth-century critic of Homer, describes the figure by mobilising precisely this famous insult of Odysseus by Achilles – σχῆμά ἐστιν ἕτερον μὲν προσποιεῖσθαι ἕτερον δὲ λέγειν).[44] By defending Polemo in these terms, Philostratus thus shows firstly how concealing, multivalent language was and remained a central desideratum for the sophist's reputation and success. But most importantly, the choice of this particular speech as an exemplum for his ability suggests how ethopoetics, the art of declaiming *in character*, could well encapsulate the skills and protective opportunities that figured speech entailed.

This figured speech of Polemo's would have pursued a similar pattern to Lollianius' enactment of Demosthenes: the close appropriation of a pre-existing speech – but also, here, a well-known historical story (the trial of Socrates) – and the creation of new material set within this narrative range. The same technique is central to Dio Chrysostom's ethopoetic orations (*Or.* 2, 3, 4). These, respectively, conjoin the structure of a Platonic dialogue with a conversation between the young Alexander and his father (2); mimic the Xenophontic Socrates' speech on the happy man (3) and re-enact an imagined exchange between Alexander and the Cynic Diogenes (4). But Dio's examples also directly display the reflexive bent behind this rhetorical act, as he frequently emphasises the conceit behind the impersonations. In introducing the Socratic speech, he remarks that 'in discussing this subject I shall endeavour to set forth the view of Socrates' (3.29): a sign-posted announcement of doubleness. In *Or.* 4, he also displays in a more extended manner the manipulations of time found in Philostratus. The meeting between Alexander and Diogenes is described as a widely reported event, with a place in collective memory (Φασί ποτε, . . . ταῦτα δὲ λέγουσι καὶ γράφουσι πολλοί, 4.1). Diogenes then meets his interlocutor 'with an abundance of time on his hands' (οὐ πάνυ τι σχολάζοντα πολλὴν ἄγοντι σχολήν, 4.1); and before they begin their discussion, there was a pause (ὀλίγον ἐπισχών, 4.16). Within the frame of this well-known event, space for imaginative supplementation is produced by the drawing-out of time itself: a means of stretching a narrative which becomes a significant characteristic of Quintus' epic.

---

[43] The figure is frequently linked directly to dealing with sensitive subjects: Demetrius, for instance, suggests its use in dealing with tyrants (*De elocutione* 287–95). Ahl (1984a) centralises the notion of safety in his extensive account of figured speech.

[44] Phoeb. de Fig. 1 (Walz (1832)); cf. Quint. *Inst.* 9.1.14.

2.3 The *Progymnasmata*: Practising Expansion

Ethopoeia is therefore a technique whose success insists on the insertion of new material within the lines of what pre-exists – imagining, and then actually creating, what an ancestral or mythological figure *would have said*. Nowhere is this process more discernible than in the *progymnasmata* exercises which comprised the final phase of imperial education and provided transferable techniques and material for declamatory performance.[45] The ethopoetics of the classroom, however, offer more than the backstory to sophistic orations. They provide in their own right significant and at times sophisticated examples of the enlarging of conventional models as undertaken at this earlier level of literary society: a level through which Quintus himself would undoubtedly have passed.

Classical themes provide the raw material for composition across the *progymnasmata*. As Webb puts it, 'mythological stories from the classical canon are elements of a common cultural property, to be exploited as a demonstration of the art of argumentation. Their utility for this purpose lies precisely in the fact that they are well known.'[46] The exercises were based on extremely close reading of these source texts, ploughed for the minutest signs which could be used as ammunition for or against a point of view. The paired exercises of encomium and invective, for example, frequently take Homeric characters as their subjects. In Libanius' substantial list of topics, alongside such concepts as 'righteousness' and 'anger', occupations such as farming and items such as 'the date palm and the apple tree' are found the Homeric heroes Diomedes, Odysseus and Thersites (for praise) and Hector (for polemic), with Achilles as the only character to feature in both categories.[47] Tellingly, both the encomium *and* invective speeches for Achilles are closely based on his behaviour, descriptions and characterisation in the *Iliad*. Thus to take just two illustrative examples, Achilles' sense of social responsibility and public service is substantiated by his decision to call an assembly in *Iliad* 1: 'when the plague struck and the ranks were being emptied, the man who saw fit to rule...did not seek a way to set them right, nor did the most clever Odysseus or the most wise Nestor experience any grief, but instead they stood idly by as they watched the army being destroyed. Achilles alone convened an assembly,

---

[45] See particularly Morgan (1998); Cribiore (2001); Amato and Schamp (2005); Webb (2001) and (2006).

[46] Webb (2001): 302.

[47] See Gibson (2008): 195–320, from whom I take the translations of Libanius.

62   Enlarging the Space: Imperial Doubleness, Fixity, Expansion

summoned the prophet, promised to help him, encouraged him to be confident and did not stop until he had found a cure for the evils.' (Lib. *Prog. Enc.* 3. 12). Synthesising and summarising this Homeric sequence of events (*Il.* 1.9–91), Libanius also draws upon the language of the Iliadic account: the report that Achilles παρεκάλει πρὸς τὸ θαρρεῖν converts into indirect discourse the strong imperative of Achilles' original speech to Calchas ('θαρσήσας μάλα εἰπὲ θεοπρόπιον ὅ τι οἶσθα', *Il.* 1.85), which itself is echoed by the Homeric narrator's description of his response (καὶ τότε δὴ θάρσησε καὶ ηὔδα μάντις ἀμύμων, *Il.* 1.92).

On the other hand, in the Achilles invective, the same Homeric behaviour, episodes and language are deployed to show instead that the hero had 'rushed into wickedness' (Lib. *Prog. Psog.* 1.2). Thus his summoning of an assembly becomes an act of headstrong insubordination, and, linguistically, his paradigmatic incipit wrath is converted into a durational verbal action (ἀθάνατα ἐμήνιεν, Lib. *Prog. Psog.* 1.11).[48] Laying bare the perceived duality, the 'doubleness', of the Homeric Achilles – his ability to occupy both sides of the praise-blame dichotomy *at the same time* (and in the same handbook) – Libanius shows how through such set pieces of rhetorical imagination, the opposing, contradictory elements of this character could be juxtaposed, accommodated and expanded.

On the other end of the spectrum, the famous encomium of Thersites in Libanius' repertoire, an instance of adoxography (the praise of things which are bad or ugly),[49] also directly establishes itself as working from inside Homer's account: 'begging Homer's pardon', it will 'attempt to praise this man of whom the poet wished to speak badly...offering Homer himself as witness to certain points' (Lib. *Prog. Enc.* 4.1).[50] These points include the broad components of the Iliadic episode – the fact that Thersites was not expelled from the assembly is redeployed as evidence that the Greeks agreed with him – and also its very words. The encomium keeps the Homeric *hapax* φολκός (*Il.* 2.216) used to describe Thersites' bandy legs; and when arguing that Thersites found fault with Odysseus and Achilles due to their shirking of military service, not through envy of their speaking skills, for in that case he would surely vie with Nestor, it takes up the well-known phrase from *Iliad* 1 to describe Nestor's words as 'sweeter than honey' (μέλιτος γλυκίων ῥέεν αὐδή, *Il.* 1.249).

---

[48] The verb in the imperfect occurs only seven times in Homer, and of the (six) Iliadic occurrences, five are referring to Achilles' anger and one (*Il.* 1.247) to Agamemnon's continued rage against him.
[49] On this sub-genre, see Billerbeck and Zuber (2000).
[50] Foerster (1963). See also Gibson (2008).

The Progymnasmata: Practising Expansion

It is, again, from within this frame that Libanius moves out, incorporating details drawn from external mythological accounts. Thus both the encomium and invective to Achilles begin not with the calling of the assembly, but with stories about his education by the centaur Chiron; teasingly aligned with a reminder of his 'real', and really Homeric, parentage ('This centaur gave instruction to all heroes,[51] but with the son of Peleus and Thetis he was more ambitious', Lib. *Prog. Enc.* 1.2; and 'Let no one suppose that I will contend that Aeacus was not good or Peleus not prudent... but under his guardian Chiron his food was the marrow of lions rather than milk', Lib. *Prog. Psog.* 1.3). Likewise, to prove Thersites' noble parentage, he cites his kinship with Diomedes, as is attested in the Iliadic scholia and in Apollodorus (*Bibl.* 1.8.6, 1.7.10), and which also finds a place in Quintus' continuation of Thersites' story (Q.S.1.716–824). The encomium moulds these extra-Homeric details back into Iliadic genealogy – Argius is named as Diomedes' paternal grandfather, a link which comes from *Il.* 14.118 – and even Iliadic quotation: in imagining that Thersites might have proclaimed how 'to Portheus were born three glorious sons' (τρεῖς παῖδες ἀμύμονες ἐξεγένοντο) the writer turns the *Iliad*'s description of Diomedes' family tree (*Il.* 14.115) into a line available to his cousin – what Thersites *could* have said. The composition thus 'corrects' Homer's account of his villain, not by writing over him, but by reconfiguring the narrative and linguistic points already on his textual map.

The exercise of ethopoeia, the later and more complex task in the *progymnasmata*, provides the most crucial paradigm for this type of reconfiguration, as the impersonating drives revealed in the declaimers' block speeches-in-persona are given extensive and central attention in this task. The subjects of Libanius' ethopoeiae include tragic themes, such as Ajax or Medea, which weave quotations from the source text into a new speech, and feature variations of mythological subjects – such as the words of Chiron on hearing that Achilles was hidden among girls on Skyros. The process of composing an ethopoeia, as we have seen, involved a combination of listening to models (drawn from classical literature or written by the teacher), reading out loud, and active imitation: students had to think themselves into their mythological role and situation. This is thus the educational task most directly centred on ideas of 'doubling' and performance, and also with the closest affinity to literature: the compositions indicate neatly the impact of dramatic doubleness on the budding writerly

---

[51] This particular extra-Homeric detail is from Xenophon (*Cyn.* 1.2)

64   Enlarging the Space: Imperial Doubleness, Fixity, Expansion

culture of this time. As has been widely explored by scholars,[52] this two-way flow of influence revealed in ethopoeia between rhetorical display and literary text suggests how, in both modes, source literature could be seen as a repository of themes that existed in order to be reworked:[53] it displays the impulse to respond in new ways to scenarios and motifs in such literature perceived as *already* – on some level – to be there. The student composing such texts thus participates in 'a literary continuum'[54] with their classical models, moving alongside, rather than against, the words of the sources.

This connection between tradition and exploitation perceptible across all levels of the *progymnasmata* and acutely evident in ethopoeia is central to the impersonatory power that these compositions could achieve. It is precisely because the source material texts are so established, recognisable and fixed in collective literary memory, that such a continuum becomes possible. Brimming with identifiable reference points to which students can anchor their creative ideas, the traditionality of these works enables the dual conceit of 'still being' them and extending beyond them to take form. Only through the objectification of this body of literature can it become re-embodied and changed from within.

A particularly instructive snapshot of this connection is found among the collection of verse ethopoeiae from Roman Egypt. Written in Home-rising hexameter, they are of especial relevance to our building consider-ations for Quintus' project.[55] Many of these pieces start from Homeric scenes. Others, like the Thersites encomium, treat a situation with which Homer deals at length.[56] One example establishes an even closer link with the Homeric original:

> εἰ μὲν [ἐ]πὶ Τρώεσσι κορύσσεο χε[ῖρ]ας, Ἀχιλλεῦ,
> καὶ ξίφ[ο]ς, ἀστυφέλικτον ἐρυσσ[ά]μενος κοτέεσκες,
> προφρονέως κεν ἔγωγε συνείρυ[σ]α φασγανον αὐτή·
> εἰ δὲ τεοῖς Δαναοῖς θωρήσσεα[ι, ο]ὐκέτ' Ἀθήνη
> πείθεται οὐδ' "Ηρη βασιλήιος · ἴσχεο θᾶσσον,   (5)
> ἴσχεο καὶ μῆνιν πολυπήμον[α π]αῦσον, Ἀχιλλεῦ·
> μηκέτι δ' ἀργυρέης ἐπιμάσσεο χ[είρ]εσι κώπης,
> μιμνέτω ἐν κολεῶι σέο φάσγαν[ον]· οὐκ ἐπ' Ἀχαιοῖς

---

[52] Such explorations have focused predominately on the Roman literary tradition. The example *par excellence* is Ovid's *Heroides*, once treated as actually being, and still often discussed as analogous with, versified scholastic exercises: see Knox (1995): 15–16; Jacobson (1974): 322–38; Webb (2001): 306 and Peirano (2012): 14 and 19. On the Greek side, the work of Webb (particularly (2001) and (2006)) is formative. See also the collected papers in Too (2001).

[53] Tarrant (1989): 159, with discussion in Peirano (2012): 14.   [54] Webb (2001): 306.

[55] On these texts, see particularly Fournet (1992).

[56] See the examples collected in Parsons (ed.) (1974): 12f.

The Progymnasmata: *Practising Expansion*   65

ἀνδροφόνον σε πατὴρ μενεδή[ιος] ἔτρ[[ε]]αφε Πηλεύς,
οὔ σε Θέτις προέηκε θεὰ βασιλῆι [φ]ονῆα·   (10)
μᾶλλον δυσμενέεσσι κορύσσε[ο], μὴ Δαναο[ῖ]σι[ν]
σοῖς ἑτάροις Πριάμῳ δὲ καὶ υἱάσ[ι] πέμψον. . [.] . . ην·
μήνιδος ἀργαλέης πλῆσον μένος, εὖτε νοήσῃς
Ἕκτορα καὶ Τρώων κρατερὸν στρατόν· οὐκ ἐπ᾽ Ἀχαιοὺς
φάσγανον ἐν κλισίηισιν ἐθήξαο· θυμὸν ἀχεύεις   (15)
σοῖς ἑτάροις; ἐπέεσσι κορύσσεο · ἀντὶ δ᾽ἀκωκῆς
κ]αὶ ξιφέων μύθοισιν ἐριδμαίνουσιν ἑταῖροι,
δ]υσμενέας κτείνουσιν ὀρινομένους περὶ χαλκῶι·
φ]είδεό μοι Βασιλῆος, ἵνα Τροίην ἀλαπάξηι
σὺν σοὶ μαρνάμενος καὶ ὑποδρήσσων σεθεν ἀλκῆι·   (20)
μῆνιν ἀποσκέδασον πολυπήμ[ο]να, μή σέ τις ἀνηρ
Αἰα]κίδην βαρύμηνιν ἐν ὀψιγό[νοις]ιν ἀείσηι·
οὐ]χ ἑτάροις κρατερόν σ[ε] γέρων [ἐδιδά]ξατο Χείρων,
ἀ]λκήεντα δ᾽ ἔτευξεν .[.].αντ.[. . . .].λεμι. . . []
ἠ]θείηισι θεῆις ἐπιπείθεο· σοὶ δ[έ κεν α]ὐτὸς   (25)
λισσόμενος καὶ δῶρα πόροι βα[σιλεὺς] Ἀγαμέμνων.
        (*POxy.* 3002 Parsons (ed.) (1974))[57]

If it had been the Trojans against whom you were arming your hands, Achilles, and raging with your invincible sword drawn, I myself would willingly have drawn sword along with you. But if it is against your own people, the Greeks, that you arm yourself, Athena no longer agrees, nor does queenly Hera. Restrain yourself quickly, restrain yourself and put an end to the wrath which brings so many sorrows, Achilles. No longer clutch the silver hilt with your hands; let your sword remain in its scabbard. It was not against the Greeks that your father, valiant Peleus, brought you up a slayer of men; it was not as killer of the king that the goddess Thetis bore you. Arm against the enemy instead, not against your comrades the Greeks; send a (threat?) to Priam and his sons; fill your spirit with painful wrath, when you see Hector and the strong army of the Trojans. It was not against the Greeks that you sharpened your sword in your tent. Do you feel bitterness in spirit against your comrades? Arm yourself with words: comrades strive with words, instead of sharp edge and swords; their enemies they kill in rout with bronze weapons. You should spare the king, so that he may sack Troy, fighting alongside you and assisting your valour. Dispel the wrath which brings so many sorrows, lest some man in later generations sing of you as Aeacides heavy in wrath. It was not to be forceful against your comrades that aged Chion taught you; he made you valiant. . . Obey the goddesses your friends; and king Agamemnon himself would beseech you and give you gifts.[58]

---

[57] In this and subsequent papyri examples, I am following the reconstruction of Parsons. I have omitted subscript markers from my transcription.
[58] Translation adapted from Parsons (1974).

66   Enlarging the Space: Imperial Doubleness, Fixity, Expansion

In the *Iliad*, Athena restrains Achilles against Agamemnon in a speech of eight lines (*Il.* 1.207–14). This text takes that moment and elongates it into a twenty-six-verse intervention. It first fixes itself to its Iliadic source: lines 1–24 treat the first six lines of Athena's Homeric speech, and her parting two verses in Homer are rendered by 25–6. Then around this base it forms an elastic, forcefully repetitive new version. For Parsons, however, the resultant text 'makes no substantive additions' to the *Iliad* scene, and thus 'comes close to the alternative exercise of the paraphrase'; although, he concedes, all examples of that classroom exercise are in prose.[59] In fact, we may discern three striking modes of addition in this composition – wholly substantive – which render its techniques much more constructive.[60]

The writer laces, but does not saturate, Athena's words with extra-Homeric vocabulary.[61] ἀστυφέλικτος is found first in poetry in Callimachus, where it describes, contrastingly, at one time a god (*Del.* 26) and at another time the underworld (*Epigr.* 540.3). Here, describing the sword, it is redeployed for a far more tangible object: but one which, in Achilles' hands, will take on its own hubristically destructive capabilities.[62] By adopting a word whose earlier history had existed only in prose and redeploying it in Homeric poetry, this writer combines linguistic innovation with a recalibration of form: its post-Hellenistic newness is also signalled by its very appearance in verse, and yet it also becomes retroactively ancient by its insertion into this original Iliadic scene. The composition thus achieves its own topsy-turvy moves through time by playing with the doubleness of a singular piece of language. In a similar fashion, the compound βαρύμηνις, originally found in Aeschylus to describe the exceeding wrath of the δαίμων (*Ag.* 1482), is another Alexandrian favourite, becoming increasingly popular in imperial poetry and favoured particularly by Nonnus, who expands and diversifies its uses across his furious Dionysiac

---

[59] Parsons (1974) (*POxy.* vol. XLII): 13.

[60] It is also bizarrely reductive to suggest that the paraphrase – both as an elementary exercise in the school curriculum (centred on the recasting of poetic texts into prose) and as a full literary 'genre' – makes no substantive additions to a source text. Quintilian in fact explicitly praises the exercise as providing ample scope for not only *aemulatio*, but also *improvement of* the model (*Inst.* 10.5.5). Establishing the typologies of these different forms of creative expansion remains an ongoing and difficult task (see also discussion on the cento below). My continual aim here is to delineate what my chosen texts do in complex relation to such other modes.

[61] On this idea of moderation in linguistic innovation in the *Posthomerica*, see Chapter 3.

[62] The adjective appears once pre-Callimachus: in Xenophon, to describe the king's firm resolve (*Lac.* 15.7). It occurs in the Anthology to describe the joy of sleep (ὕπνου χάριν *AP.* 9.764) and in the Orphic fragments to describe the body (fr.168.22). Only here is it found to describe such a concrete, practical item.

tale.[63] By choosing it here, our author thus updates and, literally, deepens the Iliadic μῆνις, which he elsewhere echoes twice (v. 6 and 21), with an expanded form of the concept drawn from a later literary time.

The piece also amends genuine Homeric terms. κρατερός (a loaded term for Achilles, of course, in its alternative form καρτερός, in the famous contrast drawn by Nestor between him and Agamemnon [*Il.* 1.280–1]) is never used for the army in Homer; συνείρυσα, active here, for Homer is always in the middle voice; and ἀχεύεις is formed as a main verb, when Homer only uses the participle.[64] And whilst carefully stretching out his language in this way, the work also reconfigures Homer's narrative time. 'Later' in Homeric epic, Athena in the *Odyssey* advises Telemachus to be brave (ἄλκιμος ἔσσε) so that he will be praised by many men who are yet to be born: ἵνα τίς σε καὶ ὀψιγόνων ἐὺ εἴπῃ *Od.* 1.302. In line 22 of our text, this statement is adapted forwards so that it refers *to* Homer himself; who becomes the later man who will sing of Achilles and his μῆνις.

This piece of imperial schoolwork, far from being 'a piece of threadbare sub-Homer',[65] strikingly demonstrates the specific methods of manipulation afforded by the ethopoetic mode: simultaneously remaining inside a Homeric scene and using this familiar fabric boldly to gesture outside. It provides an intricate example of this process in *poetic* form: verse which self-consciously attaches itself to its model to become inter-Homeric, not sub.

2.4 Homeric Performance: Scripts and Spoofs

As the papyrus shows, many of these examples of expansion focus their energies intensely on Homer: using his language, speaking on behalf or in the persona of his characters. We have discussed the special, all-encompassing and super-lative position of Homer in the education and culture of imperial Greece: through such a position, he represents objectified tradition *par excellence*. The apex of Hellenic 'common cultural property', the *Iliad* and *Odyssey* offer a set of communal markers which can be variously reached for, activated and re-enacted by those who choose creatively to engage with the poems; expansions were carried out, in other words, based on a shared and activated understand-ing of what was and was not Homer. The third and final set of works to be considered reveal this practice of Homeric expansion in its most insistent form.

---

[63] The term occurs fifteen times in the *Dionysiaca* to describe subjects as wide ranging as Pentheus (*Dion.* 44.94), the gods (Nonnus is particularly attached to the term for Hera, who is called βαρύμηνις on five occasions [*Dion.* 6.171; 6.202; 9.38; 8.109; and 9.69] and again as a 'wrath heavy stepmother' at *Dion.* 30.200) and even Eros (47.415).
[64] Cf. e.g. *Il.* 5.869.   [65] Parsons (1974) (*POxy.* vol. XLII): 13.

68   Enlarging the Space: Imperial Doubleness, Fixity, Expansion

Performances or compositions which deal with Homer specifically and exclusively, and delivered in the poet's own voice, they comprise perhaps the most important set of interlocutors for Quintus' endeavour.

The communal traditionality of Homer as figure and concept in the imperial Greek world[66] finds an analogue in the status of the Homeric text, which by the imperial period was largely fixed and 'fenced'.[67] Whilst the detailed permutations of this textual history have preoccupied and divided generations of scholarship, an overall narrative can be maintained with some confidence: that with the completion of Aristarchus' editorial work in c. 150 BCE and the disappearance of fluid, orally derived alternatives, the Homeric epics had reached a more rigid and stabilised state: they had even 'evolved', in Nagy's continually contestable terms, from 'song' to 'script' to 'scripture'.[68] The most crucial part of this story for our purposes, however, is that in this post-fixation period, the poems continued to be performed and recited. Thus whilst in the earlier stages of Homeric transmission, performance marks a space where fluidity and variations continued to occur even as the epics were moving towards the status of a written text,[69] by the era in question the situation is very different, even reversed: in this time of high collusion between drama and literature, these were not performances turned into a text, but a text turned (back) into performances.[70] Yet these imperial enactors of Homer found remarkable new ways to achieve expansion, now within the confines of a text otherwise immovable and predetermined.

Rhapsodic shows themselves, after all, offer from their earliest stages another intense example of 'doubleness.' Analyses of rhapsodes throughout their long history have first stressed the strong mimetic connection that they claimed to the 'original' Homeric bard or bards. In Pindar's *Nemean* 2, the *locus classicus* for the mechanisms of rhapsodic performance, the name *Homeridai* applies to a lineage of rhapsodes in Chios who traced

---

[66] On the broader notion of Homer as a concept, Porter (2002) offers a significant and lucid account.

[67] Terminology favoured by Allen (1924) e.g. 281–2; and adopted and adapted by Nagy (1996): e.g. 155–6.

[68] See the self-summary at Nagy (1996): 110. This is not the place to debate the merits and shortcomings of Nagy's system of textual fixation (its criticisms are well documented; as succinctly summarised and further evinced by Powell (1997)). I use it rather to point to one way of conceptualising the general stages of movement towards a fixed text.

[69] Cf. Nagy (1996): 155 on the Athenian stage of transmission (sixth–fourth centuries BCE): 'we can in principle accept Allen's notion of an *unfenced* text [in this period] – provided we restrict the description "unfenced" to Homeric *Koine* texts as *transcripts* of performances'.

[70] That is to say, in the argument that follows I am not positing any imperial version of the 'Ptolemaic papyri' argument (cf. e.g. Collins (2004): ch. 20) – that there was any long-term textual variation or destabilisation caused by their amendments and additions. I suggest instead the *conceptual* enlargement to which their additions bear witness.

Homeric Performance: Scripts and Spoofs 69

themselves back to an ancestor called *Homeros*. In Pindar's poem, it is these *Homeridai* who first perform the songs of Homer, and yet they are not Homer himself. Instead, they represent a continuum of descendants who keep on restarting his song: a continuum of which Pindar himself is now part, as the first word of the ode, ὅθεν, reveals.[71] Plato's *Ion* adds a further nuance to this relationship by accounting for the role of the audience, and the rhapsode's keen self-reflexivity as a performer to a crowd. On the one hand, Ion is fully possessed by the 'divine power' of the Muses (θεία δὲ δύναμις, *Ion* 533 D); but on the other, he possesses sufficient self-control to keep an eye on his spectators, scrupulously observing their reactions. Alongside this mimetic connectivity, modern studies have emphasised the aspects of skilled improvisation in rhapsodic displays. Building on Nagy's challenge of the 'reduplicative' rhapsode model,[72] Collins has argued convincingly for the creative elements inherent to the art. Rhapsodes, he shows, could competitively recite memorised verses, spontaneously improvise verses anew for elaboration or embellishment, and take up and leave off from the narrative of Homer wherever they saw fit.[73]

In the imperial era, however, it is traditionally considered that these creative elements withered and died. According to the conventional line of scholarly thought, the skilled, improvising rhapsodes dwindled in significance and were replaced by the raucous *homeristai*: costumed, histrionic enactors of Homeric battle scenes, for whom we have some limited inscriptional evidence,[74] but who survive most famously in Petronius' *Cena Trimalchionis* (*Sat.* 59.2–7) where they entertain the party with a performance from the *Iliad* which is ham-fistedly misinterpreted by the host. These performers have been understood either as actors who followed a select Homeric sequence,[75] or else a type of mime artist specialising in Homeric material:[76] silent or slavish reciters of a tight Homeric script.

---

[71] On this aspect of the ode, see Nagy (1996): 62.
[72] Nagy (1990): 42 and (1996): 113. Cf. also Pavese (1998).   [73] Collins (2001) and (2004).
[74] See: Robert (1936); Husson (1993), with catalogue; Nagy (1996): 157f; Hillgruber (2000); Starr (1987); González (2013): 447–78.
[75] Cf. Nagy 1996: 170: the *homeristai* fit into his schema of textual fixation by confirming that 'what was already "scripture" for Aristarchus may have continued to be a "script" for the later Homeric performer'. They treat Homer as an obviously excerpted 'script' which was memorised in advance to be performed in a stylised mimetic format, and thus represent 'the final, terminal stage in the history of Homeric performance'. This stance is followed by Parsons (2012): 23 ('these performers have learned their lines by heart, from a written text more or less marked up for comprehension'), and González (2013): 415: 'the average *homeristes* [uses] slavish memorisation and reproduction – and hence strict adherence to a performance script'.
[76] This is the view of Husson (1993) and Hillgruber (2000). The assumption, however, that a similarity to mimes would justify considering the *homeristai* silent and lacking in verbal creativity is equally

70   Enlarging the Space: Imperial Doubleness, Fixity, Expansion

There are grounds to question this story. What the *homeristai* in fact reveal is another, extreme method of creativity in mimetic performance. On the one hand, they continue the rhapsodic tradition of imitating facets of the Homeric bard's identity: the very verb connected to their name, ὁμηρίζω, which the *Suda* defines as 'to act Homer or use Homeric verses', contains just such connotations of pretence and otherness.[77] But they also, in the vein of the imperial declaimers and classroom composers, focus their impersonation on the text of the Homeric source: this too was both a textual *and* a dramatic doubleness. The 'script' used by the *homeristai*, the Greek verses which they recited in their shows, was drawn from the post-Aristarchan, standardised Homeric text, from which they would select excerpts, memorise them in advance and act them out in stylised format.[78] However the result was *not* simple recitation – the Homeric script followed word for word without variation. Closer analysis suggests that the *homeristai* recombined and elaborated this textual base, creating 'more Homer' through their own supplementations inserted within the canonical script. They thus offer a remarkable, proactive example of the imperial process of expansion from within: performing the Homeric interval.

Let us briefly consider the examples even within the limited surviving evidence which can highlight these creative techniques. The enduring image of the *homeristai* as a band of boisterous mime actors can first be challenged by at least two (and possibly three) of the papyrological sources, which record the presence of a single *homeristes*. One, from the second century CE, describes expenditure for a theatrical performance (*POxy.* III 519). Here a *homeristes* is named as a paid entertainer alongside, but emphatically separate from, a mime. The same may be true of a further festival inscription (*POxy.* VII 1050, third century CE) which also lists a *homeristes* as an independent

---

discordant with correct understanding of what the mime performance art entailed. Webb (2008): chs. 5 and 6 rightly stresses the importance of the mimes' verbal dexterity alongside the slapstick and the crude stereotypes. She also, following Wiemken (1972), points to the evidence for the combination of written scripts and improvisation in mime shows, arguing that within a limited number of basic plot types and characters, these performers too elaborated them as they went along.

[77] As is the case for βαρβαρίζω, and Ἑλληνίζω (cf. LSJ s.v. Ἑλληνίζω, II): in the latter case we may consider again Philostratus' description of Favorinus: he may *speak* Greek but he is not Greek himself. In Achilles Tatius 8.9.2–3 ὁμηρίζων is explicitly linked to duplicity: playing Homer becomes a metonym for *faux paideia*.

[78] A process well-demonstrated by Nagy (1996) and González (2013): chs 11 and 12.

Homeric Performance: Scripts and Spoofs

performer.[79] A fragmentary calendar (*POsl.* III. 189) offers further confirmation of this singularity, as it lists two individual Homeric performers (first a *homeristes* and then an *allos homeristes* three lines later).[80] Now, this evidence for solo-performance must affect our conceptions of what the *homeristes* did on stage: whilst individual artists, of course, could feasibly enact single-handedly scenes which would ordinarily involve multiple actors or participants (lovemaking, for instance, was a popular topic for mime shows), the named presence of this entertainer as having a role in festivals in his own right – a role defined in a prosopography as *distinct* from a mime – suggests that his 'Homeric-ness' could have as much to do with declaiming Homer's poetry as acting it out: one can certainly declaim alone. A passing remark in Achilles Tatius' *Leucippe and Clitophon* affirms the link between solo-performance and textual recitation in this profession. When Satyrus tells the story of a ship attacked by pirates, he lists one of its passengers as 'one of those who performs orally Homer's poetry in the theatres' (τις ἐν αὐτοῖς ἦν τῶν τὰ Ὁμήρου τῷ στόματι δεικνύντων ἐν τοῖς θεάτροις, 3.20). In the very phraseology of the anecdote, the 'showing', 'displaying' and 'explaining' of poetry (with the choice of the verb δείκνυμι neatly capturing all three of these senses) and the serene juxtaposition of Homeric material (τὰ Ὁμήρου) and the theatrical space, we can perceive the sharp relevance of the *homeristai* to the performative textual culture of their time.

The performance at Petronius' dinner party itself, usually cited as the ultimate testimony for the conventional picture of the *homeristes*[81] as an unsophisticated battle mime, provides some of the strongest indications of their techniques of Homeric textual expansion, if read another way. The scene is characteristically opaque and disorientating – difficult to interpret on many levels. And yet the description of the start of the show is revealing:

> *Ipse Trimalchio in puluino consedit, et cum Homeristae Graecis uersibus colloquerentur, ut insolenter solent, ille canora uoce Latine legebat librum.*
> Sat. 59.3

---

[79] If, as González (2013): 459 argues, the identity in the relative order between the *homeristes* and the mime can be extended to the number of artists involved in the show.

[80] Husson (1993) pairs the two together to argue for a troupe performance, but this interpretation ignores the structure of the list, which clearly maintains the separateness of their appearances, with two other items intervening between them.

[81] For the purpose of consistency, I continue to use the Greek term for the performers, despite the Roman context.

72   Enlarging the Space: Imperial Doubleness, Fixity, Expansion

> Trimalchio sat up on his cushion, and when the reciters talked to each other in Greek verse, as their conceited way is, he intoned Latin from a book.[82]

The statement makes clear first that declamation remains a component of the *homeristai's* set, corroborating the inscriptional suggestions that this is no silent mime act. The note that they performed 'in Greek verses' is a striking detail: the actors are not only speaking, but speaking Homeric Greek. Trimalchio's *liber* also implies some adherence to a written text: this could be a Latin transcription of Homer from which he can, with irreverent incompetence, attempt to follow along.[83] Trimalchio's own description of the show is then suggestive of the textual manoeuvres which took place:

> *Diomedes et Ganymedes duo fratres fuerunt. Horum soror erat Helena. Agamemnon illam rapuit et Dianae ceruam subiecit. Ita nunc Homeros dicit, quemadmodum inter se pugnent Troiani et Parentini. Vicit scilicet et Iphigeniam, filiam suam, Achilli dedit uxorem. Ob eam rem Aiax insanit et statim argumentum explicabit.* Sat. 59.4–5

> Diomede and Ganymede were two brothers. Helen was their sister. Agamemnon carried her off and took in Diana by sacrificing a deer to her instead. So Homer is now telling the tale of the war between Troy and Parentium. Of course, he won and married his daughter Iphigenia to Achilles. That drove Ajax mad, and he will show you the story in a minute.

The hapless host is, of course, wrong in his conflated interpretation: his blatant misallocation of mythological roles is the anti-paideutic joke at which everyone can keep on smirking. And yet as a spectator of *this* type of Homeric performance, he may be accidentally right about one thing: that the contents of the *homeristai* show encompasses more than the 'proper' Iliadic plot. For in this final line of his wayward speech, Trimalchio describes the madness of Ajax, which *statim explicabit*. And once the show is over, a slave brings in a boiled calf for the feast, and 'Ajax', still in character, attacks the meal with his sword:

> *Secutus est Aiax strictoque gladio, tanquam insaniret, concidit, ac modo uersa modo supina gesticulatus mucrone frusta collegit mirantibusque uitulum partitus est.* Sat. 59.7

---

[82] Translations adapted from Heseltine (1975).
[83] For the possible contents of this book, see Hillgruber (2000): 64.5 and González (2013): 453. Whether or not this book closely followed the Greek spoken by *homeristai*, what is important here is that Trimalchio attributes the words to Homer, and must have expected his guests to *consider* them as a Latin equivalent.

> Ajax followed and attacked it with his sword drawn as if he were mad; and
> after making passes with the edge and the flat he collected slices on the
> point, and divided the calf among the astonished company.

The spilling over of mimesis beyond the realm of performance is akin to Lucian's account of the pantomime gone awry. Such a spillage suggests that we are indeed to imagine the madness of Ajax as a component of the *homeristai*'s routine: the joke only works if we maintain the connection between the madness 'on stage' and what unfolds beyond it, as Ajax' frenzied slaughter of the sheep acquires an extra layer of insanity, since now he strikes cattle which are already dead. If we accept that Ajax' downfall was indeed a part of the show, we have an instance where this type of performer, whose very existence is based on an exclusive commitment to the *Iliad* and *Odyssey*,[84] includes an episode that is emphatically extra-Homeric.[85] If Lollianus' extension of Demosthenes' law and the ethopoeia's embellishment of Athena grafted extra lines onto pre-existing textual moments, then we have here an example of an entire scene inserted into the Homeric middle, construed so as to form an extended part of what *Homeros dicit*. Just as the Homeric depictions on the walls of the Casa di Octavius Quarto – that other, real life dinner-party setting – combined in one vista a clearly Iliadic and clearly *non* Iliadic frieze (of Heracles' labours), a visual arrangement whose aim, as it has been well argued, was neither to prioritise *nor* erase associations with the Homeric text, but rather to play with narrative direction in all sorts of innovative ways,[86] so too does the performance at this *Cena* require of its participants (internal and external) an engagement with culturally relevant ideas about Homeric narrative expansion. The exercise for the *homeristai*'s viewers is (as Squire puts it of the Casa) 'to pull apart the stories and then put them back together anew during the course of the dinner'.[87]

A little-known papyrus fragment offers further justification for viewing *homeristai* performers as inter-Homeric expanders:

---

[84] See Husson (1993) and González (2013): 449, with references at n. 57.

[85] Hillgruber (2000): 65 notes this expansion, and suggests that Petronius' account must therefore imply that the *homeristai* of later times adopted a broader repertoire than the *Iliad* and the *Odyssey*. This would, however, contradict all other evidence (including that dated later than the *Satyricon*) which strongly suggests that part of what defined the *homeristai* was their sole focus on the Homeric oeuvre.

[86] See Squire (2011): 145f with further citations and bibliography.   [87] Ibid: 147.

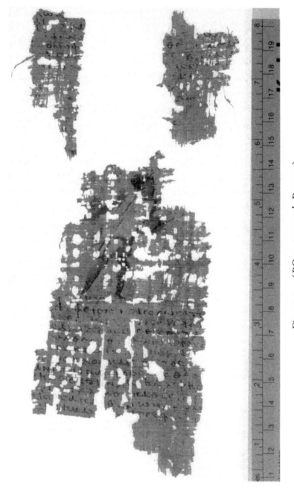

Figure 1 (*POxy.* 3001 ed. Parsons)

Homeric Performance: Scripts and Spoofs

..] ιδευλ . [] .. [.] . η. .. ε. . ροκ[
ψυ]χὴ ἐφε{ι}στήκει γοόωσά τε [μυρομένη τε

Il. 23.106

(5)   Πηλεΐδην ... ουσα κατατ[
ὁσ]σάκι δ᾽ ὁρμήσειε πυλάω[ν

Il. 22.194

..]σελεθειν θυ[ρ]έων μ αρου . [
τοσσάκι μιν προπάροιθ[εν ἀποστρεψασκε παραφθὰς

Il. 22.197

Πάτροκλος και . [.] ... ρος ... [
(10)   ᾽μνῆσαι πατρὸς σε[ῖ]ο, θεοῖ[ς ἐπείκελ᾽ Ἀχιλλεῦ

Il. 24.486

μηδὲ Θέτιν χή[ρ]ην λ<ε>ίψῃς [
πρίν τι κακὸν παθέειν· ῥε[χθὲν δέ τε νήπιος ἔγνω

Il. 17.32, 20.198

μή τις ἀπ᾽ἀθαν<άτ>ων .ριαμ[
ἐμβήῃ· μάλ[α] τ[ού]ς γε φιλεῖ [ἑκάεργος Ἀπόλλων

Il. 16.94[88]

The papyrus, dated to the second century[89] shows a figure in armour, perhaps Achilles, above hexameter verses. West first suggested a connection with the *homeristai*,[90] but the document has not found its way into any of the recent surveys of the profession.[91] And yet there is much to support such an identification. The costume, the arms (stage props?) and the staging of a specific Homeric scene all accord with what we can reconstruct from other sources about the craft.[92] If the figure is indeed a *homeristes*, then the text beneath him can correlate to what he would have performed.[93] The scene takes off from *Iliad* 23.65, where the ghost of Patroclus appears to Achilles, discussing his funeral and prophesying his death. Here Achilles tries

---

[88] Transcription by Parsons (1974) (*POxy.* vol. XLII).

[89] Parsons (1974) (*POxy.* vol. XLII): 8 thus assigns it, based on the hand.

[90] As discussed by Parsons (1974) (*POxy.* vol. XLII): 9.

[91] González (2013) does not include this papyrus in his prosopography.

[92] Compare for instance the inscription from Aphrodisias (see Roucaé 1993: 18) which was found on a doorway leading into room 6 behind the stage front of the theatre, which identifies the performer who occupied the room as a *homeristes*; refers to the equipment that he uses (διασκεύη); and describes how he Ἐγενήσθη Ἀλέξανδρος – 'became' Alexander (Paris). This suggests an image of a costumed, Homeric character equipped with stage props, which could closely correspond with the scene depicted here. I return to this inscription in Chapter 6.

[93] That the scene depicted here is not a battle episode could thus be a further suggestion that the *homeristai*'s oeuvre was not limited to Iliadic battle scenes.

76   Enlarging the Space: Imperial Doubleness, Fixity, Expansion

to set out, and each time the ghost turns him back and gives a speech of warning. This sequence thus provides a further example of the techniques adopted in the Athena ethopoeia, as new lines and narrative developments are fused directly onto a famous Iliadic exchange. The process also works on the level of language: as indicated on the transcription, half the lines are taken verbatim from different contexts of *Iliad* 16–24, reconstructed into a new amalgamation, fused with new Homerising material.

Parsons is baffled once again, by what he calls this time an 'odd confection', and explains it as a 'half-cento'.[94] Half-cento, however, is oxymoronic, or at least imprecise. Just as his likening of the Athena ethopoeia to a paraphrase failed to account for the specific techniques of that text, so too does a quasi-cento label insufficiently capture the effects on display here. Verses 6–8 best illustrate the difference. This section begins with *Iliad* 22.194 and ends with 22.197; but between these points the writer replaces Homer's two intervening lines with a single new verse of his own creation. He thus compresses the original interval between the Homeric statements and chooses alternative vocabulary which seems provocatively to reject the lexica of the original Iliadic scene: Homer's well-built towers (ἀντίον ἀΐξασθαι ἐϋδμήτους ὑπὸ πύργους, *Il.* 22.195) are now displaced for more down-to-earth, undecorative stone (]σελεθειν θυ[ρ] ἐων). Centos, as we have seen, recombine the lines of their sources to serve entirely different thematic aims: they tell, for instance, stories from the Bible using lines of Homer.[95] This text pushes and pulls the lines of its source, and creates more Homer whilst remaining thematically within his remit.[96] If we accept West's *homeristes* hypothesis, then this papyrus provides further evidence of what is implied in the festival inscriptions and Petronius' slippery fiction: that these Homeric actors align with the approach to the epic palpable in other outputs of this era – a form of textual experimentation set within the drive for doubleness and the reflexive impersonation of tradition.

Such experimentation is also on display in the more 'literary' Homeric compositions from the period: texts composed primarily to be read, not performed, but which still, like Bartch's Roman exempla and the conflicted dialogues of Plato, make provocative use of the techniques of doubleness recognisable from the dramatic spheres. In the *True Histories*,

---

[94] Parsons (1974) (*POxy.* vol. XLII): 8–9.   [95] See discussion in Chapter 1.3.

[96] Parsons (1974) (*POxy.* vol. XLII: 11) implicitly acknowledges this difference. In his rejection of εἰ]σεθ in line 6, he remarks that it 'hardly suits the context'. He is correct, but this comment confirms that an Iliadic context is there to be maintained.

Homeric Performance: Scripts and Spoofs

during Lucian's meeting with Homer on the Island of Dreams, the bard twice composes new material. Lucian first teases us with the premise of another book of Homer, which never made it back to the real world:

> συλλαβόντες οὖν τοὺς νενικημένους καὶ δήσαντες ἀπέπεμψαν ἔτι μᾶλλον κολασθησομένους. ἔγραψεν δὲ καὶ ταύτην τὴν μάχην Ὅμηρος καὶ ἀπιόντι μοι ἔδωκεν τὰ βιβλία κομίζειν τοῖς παρ' ἡμῖν ἀνθρώποις· ἀλλ' ὕστερον καὶ ταῦτα μετὰ τῶν ἄλλων ἀπωλέσαμεν. ἦν δὲ ἡ ἀρχὴ τοῦ ποιήματος αὕτη, νῦν δέ μοι ἔννεπε, Μοῦσα, μάχην νεκύων ἡρώων. *Ver. Hist.* 2.24

> Arresting the losers and putting them in irons, they sent them off to be punished still more severely than before. An account of this battle was written by Homer, and as I was leaving he gave me the book to take to the people at home, but later I lost it along with everything else. The poem began:
> This time tell me, O Muse, of the shades of the heroes in battle![97]

With ἔγραψεν, Homer becomes a writer, who composes τὰ βιβλία: a nod to the fixed, bookish, nature of Homeric verse as it was received thanks to the work of Aristarchus and company: the 'pedants' whom Homer corrects earlier in the interview with his visitor (*Ver. Hist.* 2.20). The ἀρχή of this new tome starts by recycling the opening of the *Odyssey*; but its first words replace the metonymic ἄνδρα with νῦν δε: this would have been an epic which started with a temporal conjunction, the same signal of continuation as we find in the *Posthomerica*. And 'now', we are told, it is the battle of dead heroes that is being sung – with the shades like those at the *end* of the *Odyssey*, and a new noun in the feminine accusative (from Iliadic μῆνιν to post-Odyssean μάχην) taking up the narrative mantle.

In a brilliantly cynical comment on the literary tradition, Lucian's Homer here acknowledges the deep antiquity, the inescapable oldness, both of all traditional epic – its heroic subjects themselves are now corpses, long, long dead – and of the writers who composed it. The setting of this encounter is a veritable dead poets' society, filled with shadowy, ethereal heroes and celebrities plucked from the classical canon; who never grow old, but wander 'like shadows...upright and dark' (*Ver. Hist.* 2.2). This static existence of the island's inhabitants, caught in a strange middle state between life and death, can reflect, as Kim has argued, their situation in canonised texts 'who remain the same every time the text is read, never aging, never developing'.[98] And yet it is also in this very setting that *new* poetry is composed, that the Homeric canon *is* developing, by the original

---

[97] Translation from Harmon (1913).   [98] Kim (2010): 161.

78   Enlarging the Space: Imperial Doubleness, Fixity, Expansion

bard himself. The canon is thus ever old but not getting any older; a new book complete but not 'transmitted' to the land of the living; and the dead corpses become the subject of the epic tradition revivified. In her recent account of Lucian's fictive techniques, Karen ní Mheallaigh has highlighted his obsession with what Umberto Eco calls 'hyperreality': an erasure of the lines between authorial origin and contemporary copy 'to give torsi, fragments, relics and all that seems to count in constituting cultural tradition, a new, splendent and overwhelmingly "real" allure'.[99] Through this remarkable play of paradoxes, Lucian displays here Homer's own 'hyperrealistic' potential. Harnessing the recurring power of doubleness to thematise liminality – here, powerfully and sinisterly, between life and death – and to occupy two conflicting temporal modes, he can simultaneously re-animate Homer into the present and issue a powerful reminder of his perennial association with the past.

As Lucian prepares to leave, he begs Homer to compose once more:

> Τότε μὲν οὖν τὰ περὶ τὸν πλοῦν παρεσκευασάμην, καὶ ἐπεὶ καιρὸς ἦν, συνειστιώμην αὐτοῖς. τῇ δὲ ἐπιούσῃ ἐλθὼν πρὸς Ὅμηρον τὸν ποιητὴν ἐδεήθην αὐτοῦ ποιῆσαί μοι δίστιχον ἐπίγραμμα· καὶ ἐπειδὴ ἐποίησεν, στήλην βηρύλλου λίθου ἀναστήσας ἐπέγραψα πρὸς τῷ λιμένι. τὸ δὲ ἐπίγραμμα ἦν τοιόνδε·
> Λουκιανὸς τάδε πάντα φίλος μακάρεσσι θεοῖσιν
> εἶδέ τε καὶ πάλιν ἦλθε φίλην ἐς πατρίδα γαῖαν. *Ver. Hist.* 2.28

> Well, I made preparations for the voyage, and when the time came, joined them at the feast. On the next day I went to the poet Homer and begged him to compose me a couplet to carve up, and when he had done so, I set up a slab of beryl near the harbour and had the couplet carved on it. It was:
> One Lucian, whom the blessed gods loved, beheld what's here, and home again did go.

Here it is Lucian who fixes this new Homeric poem into writing (ἐπέγραψα turns now into the first person). And once again, the composed piece sticks closely to Homer's originals: in its metre – from ἐπίγραμμα we might expect elegiacs, but instead we get hexameters – and in its language: μακάρεσσι θεοῖσιν is a frequent Homeric formulae,[100] and the phrase φίλην ἐς πατρίδα γαῖαν occurs twenty-nine times across the *Iliad* and *Odyssey*.[101] Within these parameters the new composition

---

[99] ní Mheallaigh (2014). Quotation from review by von Möllendorff (2016).

[100] *Il.* 1.599, 5.340, 14.72, 15.38; *Od.* 1.82, 5.186, 8.326. Cf. also its occurrence in Q.S.14.186, as I discuss in Chapter 6.

[101] *Il.* 2.140, 2.158, 2.174, 2.454, 4.180, 5.687, 7.460, 9.27, 9.47, 9.414, 11.14, 15.499, 16.832, 18.101, 23.145 23.150; *Od.* 1.290, 2.221, 5.37, 5.204, 10.562, 11.455, 14.333, 15.65, 18.148, 19.258, 19.290, 19.298, 23.340.

Homeric Performance: Scripts and Spoofs

displays its humorous creativity: with linguistic re-orientations – the verse, for instance, only uses the aorist, which just may be a nod towards the completed nature of Homer, who is now posthumously composing again –[102] and the glaring neologism of Λουκιανός, our new heroic subject. In another intensely ironic gesture, the author whose own signature appears a mere six times in a corpus of over eighty works[103] chooses (and uses) the famously anonymous Homer to engage in a rare act of self-naming; and the prose writer who relentlessly circumscribes verse in his treatises and who never publishes poems himself[104] here momentarily becomes a poet: the composer, scribe and subject of Homeric verse.[105]

Homer versifies again in a group of epigrams from the same generation as the *True Histories*, inscribed on a pair of herms of Homer and Menander found in Rome outside the *Porta Trigemina*. Of the three Homeric poems, the first and third address Homer.[106] The second speaks in his voice:

> Οὐκ ἔθος ἐστὶν ἐμοὶ φράζειν γένος οὐδ' ὄνομ'αὐτό,
> νῦν δ'ἔνεχ' Αἰλιανου πάντα σοφῶς ἐρέω·
> πατρίς μοι χθὼν πᾶσα, τὸ δ'οὔνομά φασιν Ὅμηρον,
> ἐστι δὲ Μουσάων, οὐκ ἐμὸν οὐδὲν ἔπος.

The epigrammist evokes a typical Homeric scene – question-and-answer sessions about name and lineage – and engages an Iliadic topos: the notion of poetry belonging to the Muses, not the poet, echoes Homer's deferral in *Il.* 2.484–93. He then expands on this invocational material using ideas drawn from Homer's later biography and elaborates the Iliadic Muse call to have the poet, finally, self-naming. Like Lucian's (un)Homeric moment of nomenclature, this poem delights in toying with the famous and feted notion of Homer's silence about himself in ways which, we shall subsequently see, come strongly to the fore in Quintus' own delayed invocation. In this careful blend of impersonation and extension, the present epigram creates, as Bowie puts it 'just the sort of verse one might expect a declaimer

---

[102] Lucian's Homer here also resolutely uses the augment: a pointed deviation, perhaps, from the 'real' (or, better, 'older') Homeric practice?

[103] On the significance of this reticence, see Goldhill (2002b): ch. 2 esp. 61–7.

[104] On the extent and manner of Lucian's quotation of and allusion to poetry, see Householder (1941) (who in table 41 lists all the references in order of frequency), and, on his attitude to poetry more conceptually, Bowie (1989a): esp. 210–11 and Anderson (1978).

[105] Here, in a similar way to the use of ἀστυφέλικτος in the Athena ethopoeia, we see how an imperial author uses the retroactive re-engagement of Homer to make a comment on form: poetry versus prose. We return to this issue fully in Chapter 5.

[106] The first is an adaptation of a poem known from the Anthology originally by Antipater of Sidon; the third discusses the view that Homer is divine. Further discussion of this pair in Bowie (1989a): 244–5.

80   Enlarging the Space: Imperial Doubleness, Fixity, Expansion

to produce'.[107] He is right of course, but the connection goes much further.[108] Although these verses, like Lucian's, could be dismissed as little more than potted Homeric spoofs, such snippets – the epic that could have been; the valedictory sphragis; what Homer would have said if asked about his lineage – bear witness to the same games with Homeric temporality and language as found in sophistic and educational texts. Taken together, these works help to define the distinctive tone of the imperial Greek participation in the practice of doubleness and expanding from within: a participation based on a shared and objectified tradition, common techniques and, crucially, a specific cultural drive. It is therefore on this basis, and according to this drive, that we must now consider Quintus' Homeric project.

As we turn now to address directly Quintus' participation in these practices, we can see how the terms of the question must be fundamentally reframed. Whilst the question of how 'second sophistic' Quintus is has continued to divide scholars, the precise nature of this relationship has been consistently underexplored. It is not (and cannot be) a question of whether the poet of the *Posthomerica* 'was' a sophist, or whether the poem was performed in any located contemporary setting. It is rather the *conceptual* links – in persona, technique and effects – that place Quintus in conversation with these spheres. The *Posthomerica* too insists on carving the closest relationship to its source text and works to expand it into a new composition which speaks in the resurrected poet's voice. If 'second sophistic epic' is a contradictory term,[109] then it is because of this combination of interests that Quintus can be aligned with the declaimers, rhetorical training and wider spheres of Homeric performance. He is a member of *this* 'group.'

The following chapters of this book, insofar as they aim to reveal Quintus' own methods of expanding Homer from within, will make frequent recourse to this group. The ways in which our epic reformulates Homeric language, literary tropes and notions of temporality will suggest the significant contribution that it makes to this imperial discourse of doubleness, and how Quintus' liminal poetics constitutes a significant response to the cultural and political conditions which lie behind it. In the final section of this chapter, however, we must first consider some internal evidence for such a connection.

---

[107] Bowie (1989a): 245.

[108] For Bowie, the point is primarily that sophists were interested in composing poetry.

[109] Since we have no concrete surviving examples of full-scale poems composed by sophists. See chiefly Bowie (1989a) on this point, in contrast of course to the title of Baumbach and Bär (2007).

2.5 Quintus' Homeric Performance: Songs within the Song

The interface between imperial Greek epic and the performative culture of the Roman Empire has been increasingly probed in recent scholarship.[110] Links have been suggested between the shows depicted in many of the poems and the contemporary poetic contests at large in the imperial period, although conclusions regarding actual performative contexts for the texts remain limited. In Quintus' case, Baumbach and Bär consider the possibility that the *Posthomerica* could have been performed 'by a sophist on stage in the third century', reading its scenes of *agōn* as reflective of such declamatory shows.[111] Carvounis has suggested a connection between the poem's internal songs and imperial poetic competitions,[112] and has also read Quintus' presentation of character speech as directly defined by the rhetorical tradition.[113] Stimulating as such suggestions may be, the inevitably tentative nature of their conclusions ultimately affirms that, given the many contextual lacunae surrounding the epic, straight-up biographically based readings are unlikely to get us far.

There is, however, a different route through. We have seen how both Athenian drama and imperial declamation make great use of generic reflexivity – the play within the play; declaiming about declamation – to embed in the very act of performance a deliberative commentary on the impersonating manoeuvres on display. The *Posthomerica* offers its own version of this mimetic self-reflection; moments where the text metaphorises its own undertaking of impersonating Homer. On three occasions, Quintus describes a performance in which Homeric scenes and material are turned into spectacle or song. Now, the device of the performed song within epic is a well-known moment where poetics are often programmatically on display: internal singers can function as emblems for the activities of the composing poet.[114] Without demanding a direct biographical reading, Quintus capitalises on this collusive potential to present the *type* of poet that he aims to be.

---

[110] Agosti (2006); König (2005); Miguélez Cavero (2008).

[111] Baumbach and Bär (2007): 13. See also Appel (1994a): 9–13.

[112] Carvounis pursues this connection centrally in a forthcoming chapter entitled 'Poetry, Performance and Quintus' *Posthomerica*', which collates much of the material evidence for agonistic contexts for imperial Greek poetry and reads such evidence alongside the literary features of Nestor's song in the *Posthomerica*. The piece will undoubtedly aid contextual hypotheses of its kind. My analysis here aims to consider the poetic ramifications of such a position, beyond such specific contextual 'what ifs'.

[113] Carvounis (2019).

[114] They can also represent for ancient epic a classic example of the *mise en abyme* in the vein of Dällenbach (1989). See e.g. Segal (1994) – 'the *Odyssey* loves to talk about poetry' (126); Redfield (1973): 173, Thalmann (1984) esp. 158f; Goldhill (1991): 66 and Mackie (1997).

82   Enlarging the Space: Imperial Doubleness, Fixity, Expansion

Read in this way, the poem's performance scenes can display not a mirror-image of its setting, but an analogue for comprehending its techniques of doubleness: of embodying and enlarging the Homeric text.

The first internal performance takes place at the funeral games of Achilles, which begin with a verbal rather than physical display of prowess.[115] Nestor, who cannot compete in strength but excels in verbosity, sings an extended song in honour of Thetis (Q.S.4.128–80). This song, reported in indirect speech, clearly evokes the tradition of the Homeric *aoidos*, and the performances of Phemius and Demodocus in the *Odyssey*. Such an echo immediately flags the reflexive potential of this scene. The bardic songs in the *Odyssey* have long been understood as moments of concentrated Homeric self-awareness, as the rhapsode reflects consciously and competitively on the mechanisms of his own craft.[116] Quintus' use of the model is thus significant in more ways than one: not only does he choose to reach for an 'obvious' Homeric framework for a performed song in epic as the basis for his scene, but by the same choice he also mobilises the instance where Homer himself comes closest to the 'generic' consciousness favoured by later dramatists and declaimers – a 'meta-meta poetic' gesture.

This immediate comparison with the Homeric singers, however, also creates an interpretative opportunity when any differences exist.[117] The most fundamental of these differences is the identity and position of the singer. Nestor is *not* a bard, and never was in Homer. Instead, he has from the *Iliad*'s early reception onwards been associated with the reflexes and results of *rhetorical* performance: the scholion on *Il.* 3.212–6, for instance, suggests that the three styles of oratory have their representatives in Nestor, Odysseus and Menelaus (AbT 3.212–6), and Quintilian uses Nestor as the Homeric model for the 'middle style' of Hesiod.[118] Thus in his very choice of mouthpiece, Quintus not only employs but reformulates the metapoetic inheritance of the epic song.[119] Nestor will go on to prove himself to be a very different type of performer from those in Homer, both in terms of what he sings and how he sings it. In line with his rhetorical 'background', his piece will be showy, self-conscious and deeply invested in displaying its own knowing artificiality.

---

[115] This oral opening contest, of course, immediately sets these games apart from their obvious Homeric counterpart – the games for Patroclus in *Iliad* 23.

[116] To take just one recent return to this extremely well-trodden point, see e.g. Hunter (2012a), on what he neatly terms 'agonistic performance and cultural metapoetics', interestingly read in the context of the epyllion, and with further bibliography.

[117] See recently Maciver (2018): esp. 79.   [118] Further discussion of this style in Chapter 4.

[119] Nestor can exert a further different type of 'metapoetic' energy through his very status as an old man: cf. Dällenbach (1989): 52 on the status of old people as 'organs of truth' and therefore embodiments of the poet, discussed also in Maciver (2017): 271 n. 54.

Quintus' Homeric Performance: Songs within the Song   83

Immediately striking is the increased emphasis on spectacle itself, and the multiple processes involved in creating it. The event is introduced in a mixture of the language of vision, participation and competition:

καὶ τότ' ἄρ' ἐκ πόντοιο κίεν Πηλῆος ἄκοιτις
αὔρῃ ὑπηῴη ἐναλίγκιος· αἶψα δ' ἵκανεν
Ἀργείων ἐς ὅμιλον, ὅπῃ μεμαῶτες ἔμιμνον,
οἳ μὲν ἀεθλεύσοντες ἀπειρεσίῳ ἐν ἀγῶνι,
οἳ δὲ φρένας καὶ θυμὸν ἀεθλητῆρσιν ἰῆναι.
Q.S. 4.110–14

Then out from the sea arrived the wife of Peleus, like a morning breeze. She quickly came to the assembly of waiting Argives, some keen to compete in that immense event, others to take pleasure in watching the competitors.

Nestor's primary involvement is likewise construed as a competitive practice: οὐδέ τις ἄλλος ἐριδμαίνεσκεν Ἀχαιῶν/κείνῳ, ὅτ' εἰν ἀγορῇ ἐπέων πέρι δῆρις ἐτέχθη – none of the Achaeans could compete with him in oratory when an argument arose in public (123–4). The Iliadic assertion of Nestor's superlative speaking abilities (directly appropriated, as we have seen, by the Thersites encomium) is here given an explicitly agonistic edge.[120] And whereas the Odyssean bards attempt to gain control of their narratives so that the external audience can forget that theirs is not the voice of the primary narrator, but must ultimately endure Homer's carefully timed punctures of their song with reminders of their external status,[121] Nestor's account is much more densely crammed with assertions of its secondary, performative mode: verbal cues (ἔνισπε, 131; μέλπε μέσῳ ἐν ἀγῶνι, 147; καὶ τὰ μὲν Ἀργείοισιν ... μέλπε, 161–2) and audience reactions (ἡ δ' ἀΐουσα τέρπεθ', 130; πολὺς δ' ἀμφίαχε λαός/ἀσπασίως, 147–8).

The direct integration of traditional epic funeral games with competitions of dramatic or melic skill drawn from the entertainment world of late antiquity is often hailed as a palpable feature of Nonnus' *Dionysiaca*; where, most strikingly, the funeral of Staphylus includes contests in singing and pantomime (*Dion.* 19.59–348).[122] These reflective, competitive and performative nodes in the *Posthomerica* suggest that whilst – characteristically – less

---

[120] In the original *Iliad* scene, by contrast, such competitiveness is only explicitly present in Nestor's own speech (*Il.* 1.254–84) where it is based on his supremacy in age and longevity of experience, not rhetoric.

[121] Such reminders include the song introduction and conclusion formulae (e.g. *Od.* 1.325; 8.521), strategically placed third person verbs (ἤειδεν δ' ὡς ... *Od.* 8.514) and descriptions of the instructions given to compel these bards to sing (8.43–5 and 8.485–11).

[122] On the background to the presence of these features in Nonnus, particularly the *Paneia* games in Panopolis, see Miguélez Cavero (2008): 258–60; Remijsen (2015): 115; Van Minnen (2016): 59–60.

84   Enlarging the Space: Imperial Doubleness, Fixity, Expansion

explicitly 'contemporary',[123] Quintus' games can also be read in this light, as an updating of the Homeric games with signs of the imperial penchant for dramatic spectacle and agonistic song.[124] Having established this different context for this show and its central performer, Quintus moves to exploit the poetic opportunities afforded by such a shift. His imperial Nestor sings ἔνθεν ἑλών … ἀρηραμένοις ἐπέεσσι (148–9). This performance style appears again to be in keeping with the practice of the Homeric *aoidos*, and the wording precisely echoes the phrase used to describe Demodocus' technique (ἔνθεν ἑλών, *Od.* 8.500).[125] However, what follows undermines this purely 'archaic' framing:

> καὶ τὰ μὲν Ἀργείοισιν ἐπισταμένοισι καὶ αὐτοῖς
> μέλπε…
>
> Q.S.4.162–3
>
> Thus he sang to the Argives songs that they already knew.

Here most clearly of all, Nestor is not performing *qua* Homeric *aoidos*, who provokes joy, sorrow or *thauma* by giving new information to his hearers.[126] He is instead, like the sophist in his ethopoetic declamations, reciting well-known and much-loved stories, instantly recognisable to the audience gathered to hear them. The choice of the verb μέλπε, adds to this impression. The word firstly has strong associations with lyric: Nestor is aligned with the poetic performers most renowned for their self-conscious techniques and reflexive appropriation of traditional song. And yet there is also an already-Homeric edge to this appropriation. The verb's related noun, μολπή, is used in the shield of Achilles to describe the famous Linus song; the earliest reference to the song in Greek poetry:

> τοῖσιν δ᾽ ἐν μέσσοισι πάϊς φόρμιγγι λιγείῃ
> ἱμερόεν κιθάριζε, λίνον δ᾽ ὑπὸ καλὸν ἄειδε

---

[123] Subtly in keeping, of course, with the Homerising scheme of the poem.

[124] Thus König (2005): 237: 'Quintus modernises the Homeric games by presenting many more events than we find in *Iliad* 23 … as if to bring his games in line with contemporary agonistic programmes, in a way which contributes to the impression that his poem has taken us into a new world which the heavy sense of closure within the final books of the *Iliad* can only hint at.' I would suggest, however, that the relationship between the 'modernised' Quintan world and the Iliadic-Homeric one is less linear than this reading implies.

[125] Collins (2004): 167–75 reads this technique as an embedded reflection of the strategies of the archaic rhapsode.

[126] See the interesting take of González (2013): 365–6 on this aspect of the Homeric singer's craft, which is particularly true for Phemius' song (the subsequent search for news is motivation for Telemachus' journey, first to Nestor and then to Menelaus) but arguably more problematic for Demodocus.

Quintus' Homeric Performance: Songs within the Song

λεπταλέῃ φωνῇ· τοὶ δὲ ῥήσσοντες ἁμαρτῇ
μολπῇ τ' ἰυγμῷ τε ποσὶ σκαίροντες ἕποντο.

Il. 18.569–72

And in their midst a boy made pleasant music with a clear-toned lyre, and thereto sang sweetly the Linos-song with his delicate voice; and his fellows beating the earth in unison therewith followed on with bounding feet mid-dance and shoutings.

This passage of the Homeric ekphrasis, which 'presents more than one context for poetry in a double gesture . . . enclosing non-epic forms like the fair Linus song within the larger framework of the *Iliad*'[127] has great relevance to Nestor's performance here. In the book immediately before Quintus' own re-enactment of the cosmic-poetic shield, Nestor's subtle allusion to this moment showcases his ironic awareness of his own status as a re-crafter of traditional epic song. ἔνθεν ἑλών thus takes on a whole new meaning once refracted through this statement. Rather than the spontaneous (re)composition of a Homeric singer, Nestor selects ('takes up', 'seizes')[128] excerpts from a pre-conceived oeuvre of mythical material to fashion a song sufficiently well-known to his audience so that they can easily follow along.

In terms of content, the middle of the song (154–60) is Homeric: Nestor recounts Achilles' killing of Polydorus and Asteropaius, his *aristeia* at the Xanthus and the slaughter of Lykaon, and finally the death of Hector. Also included in these lines is the death of Troilus, not narrated in the *Iliad's* primary narrative but mentioned by Priam at *Il.* 24.257: another instance of Homeric and para-Homeric blending. Framing this section are excerpts of mythology which lie outside Homer's tale: the wedding of Thetis (130–45), a story, which, from the point of view of the listeners, is in the distant 'plupast';[129] the cities sacked by Achilles before his arrival at Troy, much more recent 'history' (161–2); and the hero's killing of Penthesilea and Memnon, events experienced first-hand by the show's audience, and the poem's readers – the content of the first two books of the *Posthomerica*. The song thus combines an Iliadic core

---

[127] Stephens (2002): 13.

[128] Cf. e.g. Murray (1919 ad loc.) who renders the phrase 'taking up the tale'. Neither Way's translation of the term in the *Posthomerica*, 'from that beginning with aptly chosen words' (1913 ad loc.), nor Hopkinson's, 'in apt words' (2018 ad. loc) sufficiently capture the force of the phrase.

[129] On this term in ancient historiography, see Grethlein and Kreb (2012), with further discussion in relation to imperial Greek epic in Chapter 7 of this book.

86 Enlarging the Space: Imperial Doubleness, Fixity, Expansion

with earlier and later mythological stories to create a potted epic cycle; and these different layers of material are not separated into discrete sections, but merged seamlessly so that the Homeric and the post-Homeric even share a line:

> Ἕκτορά θ᾽ ὡς ἐδάμασσε, καὶ ὡς ἕλε Πενθεσίλειαν,
> ἠδὲ καὶ υἱ<έ>α δῖον ἐϋθρόνου Ἠριγενείης.
>
> Q.S.4.160–1

How he slew Hector, Penthesileia and the divine son of fair-throned Erigeneia.

We have seen how the Iliac Tablets provide a visual-verbal emblem of the techniques of enlarging Homeric narrative into a wider cyclic frame. Thus, for example, the Capitoline Tablet (1A) combines a number of scenes drawn from across the *Iliad* (such as Zeus' supplication by Thetis and Priam's interview with Achilles) with a central panel depicting the Sack of Troy – material obviously external to Homer's primary narrative and accompanied by text inscriptions from a variety of poetic sources: the *Iliad* is joined by quotations from the *Aethiopis* and Lesches of Pyrrha's *Little Iliad*. Through such amalgamations, the tablet 'encapsulates not just the whole *Iliad* – from *alpha* to *omega* – but an epic cycle that stretches beyond that single poem'.[130] Here Quintus provides his own (re)-textualised visualisation of this conceit: the Homeric and cyclic *alpha* to (not quite) *omega*, 'shrunk' into a clearly Homeric-emulative microcosm (the internal song), miniature in form.

Likewise in its language, the song contains a mixture of Homeric phrases and new linguistic combinations in a Homerising style. Quintus 'reports' Nestor's use of distinctive terms from the Homeric corpus: ἐνὶ χρυσέοισι κυπέλλοις (139) occurs only in the ninth book of the *Iliad* (*Il.* 9.670); and ποταμοῖο ῥέεθρα (156, describing the Xanthus) is used only once in the *Iliad* (*Il.* 14.433) and once in the *Odyssey* (*Od.* 6.317). Ἕκτορά θ᾽ ὡς ἐδάμασσε (160) is another type of 'quotation' – a variation on the opening line of this current poem (Q.S.1.1: Εὖθ᾽ ὑπὸ Πηλείωνι δάμη θεοείκελος Ἕκτωρ): Nestor quotes from the start of 'the *Iliad* part two'.

Homer's *Odyssey* provides, of course, the paradigmatic 'original' model for incorporating wider cyclic events into the frame of a single poem.

---

[130] Squire (2011): 171. Squire also makes the convincing case that the missing section of this frieze on the left side is likely to have contained, like tablet 3C, a scene which prefigured the start of the *Iliad* (possibly something from the *Cypria*) which would add to its parallelism with Nestor's song here.

Quintus' Homeric Performance: Songs within the Song   87

Demodocus' song and, more elaborately, Menelaus' tale (*Od.* 4.332–592) bring episodes from the sack of Troy and the *nostoi* into contact with the narrative present. Quintus' Nestor does not only mimic this process; he adds a further dimension to it. Now Homeric epic itself becomes part of the 'cycle' to be incorporated – the *Iliad* takes its place within the storytelling tradition to be told and retold in song. When the verse ethopoeia from Egypt turned Homer himself into the fulfiller of Athena's prediction to Telemachus, and when Lucian composed 'new' Homeric poetry on an island filled with ghosts and the literary long-dead, we saw how such manoeuvres brought to the fore the double status of Homer as an always-old original and an up-to-date new-model, able to be resurrected and continued. In the same way Nestor's song marks its paradoxical self-identity in relation to its source: by acknowledging the canonical status of Homer as part of an 'already known' tradition, the composition conveys *through* this tradition its embedded alterations. The contemporary flavour of the funeral games, with their echoes of festivals familiar from Quintus' own era, cements this 'imperial' reading. The internal bard expands Homeric narrative in the same way as Quintus himself inserts the death and funeral of Achilles into his Iliadic continuation.

After the sack of Troy, a band of Greek bards performs another epic song:

τοῖς δέ τις ἐν μέσσοισιν ἐπιστάμενος . . . .
. . . . .οὐ γὰρ ἔτ' αὐτοῖς
δεῖμα πέλεν πολέμοιο δυσηχέος, ἀλλ' ἐπὶ ἔργα
εὐνομίης ἐτρέποντο καὶ εὐφροσύνης ἐρατεινῆς.
ὃς δ' ἤτοι πρῶτον μὲν ἐελδομένοισιν ἄειδε,   (125)
λαοὶ ὅπως συνάγερθεν ἐς Αὐλίδος ἱερὸν οὖδας,
ἠδ' ὡς Πηλείδαο μέγα σθένος ἀκαμάτοιο
δώδεκα μὲν κατὰ πόντον ἰὼν διέπερσε πόληας,
ἔνδεκα δ' αὖ κατὰ γαῖαν ἀπείριτον, ὅσσα τ' ἔρεξε
Τήλεφον ἀμφὶς ἄνακτα καὶ ὄβριμον Ἠετίωνα,   (130)
ὡς <τε> Κύκνον κατέπεφνεν ὑπέρβιον, ἠδ' ὅσ' Ἀχαιοὶ
μαρνάμενοι μετὰ μῆνιν Ἀχιλλέος ἔργα κάμοντο,
Ἕκτορα δ' ὡς εἴρυσσεν ἑῆς περὶ τείχεα πάτρης,
ὡς θ' ἕλε Πενθεσίλειαν ἀνὰ μόθον, ὡς τ' ἐδάμασσεν
υἱέα Τιθωνοῖο, καὶ ὡς κτάνε καρτερὸς Αἴας   (135)
Γλαῦκον ἐυμμελίην, ἠδ' ὡς ἐρικυδέα φῶτα
Εὐρύπυλον κατέπεφνε θοοῦ πάις Αἰακίδαο,
ὡς δὲ Πάριν δαμάσαντο Φιλοκτήταο βέλεμνα,
ἠδ' ὁπόσοι δολόεντος ἐσήλυθον ἔνδοθεν ἵππου
ἀνέρες, ὥς τε πόληα θεηγενέος Πριάμοιο   (140)

88   Enlarging the Space: Imperial Doubleness, Fixity, Expansion

πέρσαντες δαίνυντο κακῶν ἀπὸ νόσφι κυδοιμῶν.
ἄλλη δ' ἄλλος ἄειδεν, ὅ τι φρεσὶν ᾗσι μενοίνα.

Q.S.14.121–42[131]

And in their midst a skilled <singer stood up to perform> now that the troops no longer had reason to fear the clamour of war and could turn to peaceful activities, enjoyment and good cheer. First of all he performed for his eager audience an account of the army's mustering on the sacred ground of Aulis; then he told how that great and mighty man, the tireless son of Peleus, sacked twelve cities during his voyage across the sea and eleven more once he reached the boundless mainland; also his exploits against King Telephus and the mighty Eëtion and his slaying of the arrogant Cycnus; how the Achaeans had struggled in the fighting after Achilles became angry; how he had dragged Hector round the walls of his city, slain Penthesileia in battle, and vanquished the son of Tithonus; how mighty Ajax had slain Glaucus of the fine ash-wood spear, the son of swift Aeacides had slain the renowned warrior Eurypylus, and Philoctetes' arrows had vanquished Paris; and he named all those who had taken part in the ambush by going inside the horse, and told how they sacked the city of Priam, descendant of the gods, and were now dining far from cruel conflict. And throughout the army men sang about whatever they liked.

As in Nestor's song, this miniaturised account of the events at Troy combines pre-Iliadic, Iliadic and post-Iliadic material into one composition. The post-Iliadic portion (134–41) contains even more material from the *Posthomerica* itself: the killings of Glaucus by Ajax, and Eurypylus by Neoptolemus; the death of Paris and the sack of the city; and the current celebrations which followed. In line with its later chronological position in the poem, the song's mythological range encroaches even further on the internal audience's present-tense. This section also contains quotations and paraphrases from earlier in *this* epic. ὁπόσοι δολόεντος ἐσήλυθον ἔνδοθεν ἵππου (139) echoes Quintus' request to the Muses (ἔσπεθ', ὅσοι κατέβησαν ἄσω πολυχανδέος ἵππου, 12.307) and the bards' reported words borrow concepts and even an entire phrase (ἕλε Πενθεσίλειαν) from Nestor's earlier song.[132] The poet who is 'still Homer' merges self-quotation with Homeric imitation.

Preceding this post-Homeric excursus is another central Homeric section (131–3). The bard's reported language here lifts creatively from its Iliadic antecedents. When describing how Achilles dragged Hector's body (Ἕκτορα δ' ὡς εἴρυσσεν ἑῆς περὶ τείχεα πάτρης, 133) the song both

---

[131] I have quoted this song in full because of its more compressed length in comparison to Nestor's, and also because of the textual difficulties which it contains: the poem here features a considerable lacuna, on which see Vian (1969): 181.
[132] Q.S.4.160.

Quintus' Homeric Performance: Songs within the Song 89

provides an alternative focus for Hector's demise to that given in Nestor's song – forfeiting an explicit description or even a verb for the killing itself, taking it as the well-established precondition for this part of the story – and follows Quintus' own practice at the start of the *Posthomerica* in altering a locational detail from *Iliad*, where Hector is dragged not around the city walls, but behind Achilles' chariot and around Patroclus' tomb.[133] He also sings, remarkably, of μῆνιν Ἀχιλλέος (132). Mobilising the incipit title of the *Iliad*, this phrase gives it a morphological twist (Ἀχιλλέος for Ἀχιλῆος) to fit the metrical requirements of the new line and a thematic suppression – as the wrath is speedily elided into new scenes and events. Like the writer of the ethopoeia on Athena, this composer uses μῆνιν and its immediate Iliadic triggers to locate his shift in Homeric temporality: as Achilles' anger becomes not *the* subject of the song, but one small part of its extension.

Our final performative episode concerns not a song but a show. After the funeral games for Achilles, Odysseus and Ajax embark upon a lengthy verbal contest for his arms (Q.S.5.180–316). Quintus' version of this famous scene accentuates many features of an *agōn*: the two contenders compete in front of an audience (175–9) and spar off one another by performing set 'chunks' of speech in turn. This performance is one of Baumbach and Bär's major examples of how the poem reflects imperial declamation: 'like two sophists competing on stage with μελέται about the same topic, the two heroes use their rhetorical skill in order to persuade the audience of their claims'.[134] Their reading has been strongly resisted by Maciver, who stresses instead the scene's continuity with Iliadic flyting contests.[135] The episode has thus become the crux of the *Posthomerica*'s 'second sophistic' debate.

Perhaps, however, the division between 'Homeric' and 'post-Homeric' has been drawn too bluntly. The Odyssean structure of Nestor's song was mobilised to align it with the generic self-consciousness of later dramatic and rhetorical forms. Quintus puts the same idea to work in this scene. We have seen how sophistic ethopoetic declamations were themselves obsessed with forging links with ancient textual models and that their innovations occur within this particular form of conservatism. Odysseus and Ajax here compete using highly Homeric techniques and formulations, and this fact in itself can align them with more contemporary modes of performance: *through* its commitment to Homer, the show becomes 'imperial'.

---

[133] Q.S.1.12. Cf. *Il.* 22.395–404; 463–5; 24.14–21. I return to this altered detail in Chapter 5.
[134] Baumbach and Bär (2007): 13.   [135] Maciver (2012c).

90 Enlarging the Space: Imperial Doubleness, Fixity, Expansion

These rhetorically Homeric, Homerically rhetorical heroes recount their achievements in a tone infused with poetic touches like similes and epithets.[136] They also offer a neat example of how Quintus himself plays with the opportunities and the criticisms of figured speech.[137] When Ajax here rebukes Odysseus for his hypocrisy he, like Zolius, mobilises the Homeric Achilles' famous notion of saying one thing and thinking another, now given an added sting in this reflexive, rhetorical context:

> …νῦν δ' ἄρα μύθων
> ἰδρείῃ πίσυνος μεγάλων ἐπιμαίεαι ἔργων·
>
> Q.S.5. 222–3

But as it is, you are relying on your way with words to lay claim to great deeds.

Like Nestor and the bards, in the examples which they employ, the two heroes intertwine details from Homeric epic with new additional material:

> …ἐπεί νύ σε γείνατο μήτηρ
> δείλαιον καὶ ἄναλκιν, ἀφαυρότερόν περ ἐμεῖο,
> ὅσσον τίς τε κύων μεγαλοβρύχοιο λέοντος·
> οὐ γάρ τοι στέρνοισι πέλει μενεδήιον ἦτορ,
>
> Q.S.5. 186–8

The truth is, your mother bore you feeble and cowardly, weaker than me just as some dog is weaker than a loud-roaring lion. It's no brave heart that you have in your breast.

> …ὅς σ' ἐνὶ χάρμῃ
> ἐξεσάωσα πάροιθεν ὑποτρομέοντα κυδοιμὸν
> δυσμενέων, ὅτε σ' ἄλλοι ἀνὰ μόθον οἰωθέντα
> κάλλιπον ἐν δηίων ὁμάδῳ φεύγοντα καὶ αὐτόν.
>
> Q.S.5. 202–5

I rescued you in the mêlée when you were trembling with fear at the enemy's clamor, when everyone else was fleeing the din of the foe just like you, and you were all alone in the fighting.

> ἀλκῆς γὰρ τόδ' ἄεθλον ἀρήιον οὐκ ἀλεγεινῶν
> θῆκεν ἐνὶ μέσσοισ ἐπέων Θέτις ἀργυρόπεζα.
>
> Q.S.5. 232–3

[136] It may be added that if this debate does reflect a sophistic performance, it is one conducted in verse…

[137] The narrative of the *Posthomerica* also contains some fine examples of λόγος ἐσχηματισμένος in action: for example, in Helen and the Trojan women's public lamentation over Paris (Q.S.10.389–410), which is explicitly contrasted to their true inner feelings. Helen speaks falsely of her grief for own safety, and thus strategically, self-protectively, says one thing and thinks another.

Conclusions

It is a dispute over warlike strength, not of wounding words, that Thetis of the silver feet has set up here.

> ἀμφὶ παλαισμοσύνῃ πολυτειρέι πολλὰ μογήσας,
> ὁππότε δὴ περὶ σῆμα δαϊκταμένου Πατρόκλοιο
> Πηλείδης ἐρίθυμος ἀγακλυτὰ θῆκεν ἄεθλα.
>
> Q.S.5. 314–6

I gave you a hard time in the wrestling when the glorious Pelides held those memorable games at the tomb of the slain Patroclus.

Recognisably Homeric themes, moments (the funeral games of Patroclus, Odysseus' precarious moment in battle [*Il.* 11.411–88]) and language (the retention of Thetis' famous epithet ἀργυρόπεζα) are interspersed with extra-Homeric moments – some of a particularly explicit kind:

> οὐκ οἴῳ δ᾽ ἄρα τῷ γε λυγρὴν ἐπεμήσαο λώβην,
> ἀλλὰ καὶ ἀντιθέῳ Παλαμήδεϊ θῆκας ὄλεθρον,
> ὅς σέο φέρτερος ἔσκε βίῃ καὶ ἐύφρονι βουλῇ.
>
> Q.S.5.197–9

And he (Philoctetes) is not the only one you have injured with your tricks: you also managed to get godlike Palamedes killed, a man superior to you in both strength and wise counsel.

In mentioning Palamedes, Ajax insults Odysseus by evoking the hero whom the Homeric poet forgot.[138] Like Trimalchio's *homeristai*, who include in their performance, fittingly enough, this very *krisis* story, the contenders in this *apodeixis* expand their Iliadic excerpts with stories known unequivocally to lie outside of the bounds of their source text: splitting open the Homeric and inserting the paradigmatically non-Homeric within.

2.6 Conclusions

These internal shows embody in summary form the Homerising tendencies of the *Posthomerica*, by demonstrating above all its integrative relationship to its primary source. The analogies in technique between Quintus' composers and the imperial declaimers, classroom ethopoeiasts and Homeric enactors confirm his poem's status as a product of a deeply reflexive performative culture – a culture in which the notion of 'still being' a figure from the past was not just a game or parody, but a genuine

---

[138] I defer detailed discussion of this Palamedes reference, and its importance to Quintus' strategy, to Chapter 5, where this practice of Iliadic alteration will become my central concern.

92   Enlarging the Space: Imperial Doubleness, Fixity, Expansion

and complexly articulated mode of actualisation. The *Posthomerica* does not merely reflect this preoccupation, but literalises it into a momentous new form: composing not just a speech, excerpt or δίστιχον ἐπίγραμμα, but a full epic of the interval, which expands not only between Homer's lines but between his whole poems.

The much-cited conception of Quintus as 'still Homer' achieves deeper significance when comprehended through this context. Perceived as part of the discourse of doubleness, the poetics of the interval starts to disclose its full and expanded connotations: the *Posthomerica* exploits the 'in between' of not only the *Iliad* and the *Odyssey*, but also between the origin and the contemporary, the fixed and the fluid, the Homeric poet and the poetic self. In the chapters to follow, these multiple positions will increasingly reveal themselves to be deeply intertwined with contemporary concerns over liminality: the duplicitous relationships between past and present and the political opportunities afforded by being one thing and appearing another which were under particular pressure and negotiation in the Greek third century. The poem in the middle offers its readers a paradigm for experiencing this dynamic multiplicity of identities; the critical re-embodiment of the deep past, with the seams still defiantly on show.

How Quintus creates this paradigm – his methods of enlarging the middle space, beyond the prototypes in the emblematic songs – is the question to which we must now turn. To locate these methods, we must ask: what is Quintus' inter-Homeric text?

CHAPTER 3

Writing Homer
Language, Composition and Style

3.1 Introduction: Omerico Ma (Non) Troppo?

To ask, as we did in the previous chapters, what an imperial epic is, inevitably requires us to investigate what 'form' this epic will take: to define the aesthetic, stylistic attributes which mark and drive the texts from this period. This formal aspect of imperial Greek hexameter poetry is, certainly, an area to which scholars are increasingly devoting attention. The last two decades have given rise to a cascade of studies focused on the compositional features of individual works.[1] In the desire to characterise these epics as a 'corpus' a spectrum of stylistics has gradually begun to emerge, which places on one end the tradition of imperial Homeric-imitative epics – exemplified above all by the large-scale works of Nestor and his son Pisander from Laranda: heroic, mythological and hyper-Homerising –[2] and on the other the bold stylistic and metrical innovations of Nonnus and his successors.[3] As transitional points on this spectrum, the surviving works from the third century have been analysed for the ways in which they bridge this aesthetic gap: between the conservative, 'Homeric' style epics and the self-proclaimed originality which marks the *Dionysiaca* as so new.

Triphiodorus has particularly benefited from such treatment. Recent analyses of *The Sack of Troy* have shown how the text is both a continuation of the imperial trend of traditional epic composition and a diversion from that trend. Miguélez Cavero's commentary, for instance, focuses on how Triphiodorus 'preferred a Homer with fewer repetitions than the

---

[1] References ad loc. in this chapter. 'Compositional' will here be defined as lexematic, morphological, dialectical, formulaic, metrical and stylistic features.

[2] See overview and discussion of these works in Chapter 1.3. Nestor's lipogrammatic poem was of course innovative in its own sense, but also inextricably Homeric, in that it was *the same poem*, done differently, again.

[3] On Nonnus' stylistic reforms, see particularly Hopkinson (1994a); Whitby (1994), who suggests at 118–19 this idea of a spectrum; Miguélez Cavero (2008).

94   Writing Homer: Language, Composition and Style

vulgate text, and shunned any element that had been overused by Homer: his Homer was a master craftsman of the language, whose use of literary σχήματα was worth studying and imitating'.[4] Within a predominantly Homeric lexical range (Gerlaud calculated that about 80 per cent of his words are Homeric)[5] Triphiodorus displays his innovation through creative use of Homeric vocabulary, by using non-Homeric words and by introducing his own neologisms into the mix.[6]

This type of practice has, unsurprisingly, been tightly linked to Alexandrian aesthetics; Triphiodorus' style has become quickly aligned with the *imitatio cum variatione* and *Selbstvariation* so prevalent in the philological games of Hellenistic poets.[7] Maciver has recently run with this connection. In his extensive account of Triphiodorean poetics, he argues that it is through the use of Alexandrian techniques that the poet states his claim for independence: 'Triphiodorus carefully entwines within his overwhelmingly Homeric fabric an aesthetic which proclaims its poetics of difference.'[8] The epyllion is read as updating its Homeric tenor with the sorts of differentiating moves later undertaken on a vast scale by Nonnus, thus representing a pivotal point in the development of Greek epic in the imperial period.

As the Homerising epic *par excellence*, the *Posthomerica* may seem another highly suitable candidate for this line of reading. Its chronological proximity to Triphiodorus – both works were written after the Laranda epics but before Nonnus' –[9] similarly Homeric vocabulary (79 per cent of Quintus' words are Homeric)[10] and traditional Trojan theme all suggest that it too could be tested for points of innovation which push against a dominant Homeric style. Current work on the poem has begun to construct just such a critical narrative. As has been increasingly recognised, the tradition of considering Quintus as lacking in poetic innovation is a distinct product of the twentieth century.[11] It was at that time when

---

[4] Miguélez Cavero (2013): 48. Hence her assessment that he can be governed by the motto 'omerico, ma non troppo'.

[5] Gerlaud (1982): 51–2 = 1061 out of 1556 words.

[6] For examples and analysis, see Miguélez Cavero (2013): 42–6.

[7] Compare Rengakos (1993)/(1994) on the use of glosses by the Hellenistic poets.

[8] Maciver (2020).

[9] As per the dating and direction of influence between the poets set out in Chapter 1.3.

[10] Paschal (1904). He also argues that 'many of the remaining [words] are compounds formed on Homeric analogy' (22), which would make the total even higher.

[11] See particularly Baumbach and Bär (2007): 21–5, who rightly note that 'in former times' (and particularly during the Renaissance) 'the *Posthomerica* was much more admired', and even as recently as the nineteenth century 'as a rule, the poem was either ignored' or, when it was read, actually rather 'appreciated' (24).

Introduction: Omerico Ma (Non) Troppo? 95

Quintus' style came to be viewed as 'monotonous' and (this even from Vian) defined by a 'frostiness' and lack of 'personality':[12] Posthomeric stylistics thus became associated with a flattened Homeric *koine*, lacking in the monumentality and directness of its mighty primary model. In response to such disparagement, newer readings have predictably stressed how the *Posthomerica* shows its innovation by means of significant stylistic deviations. These deviations for Quintus have been traced through two main strands. Firstly, in a manner similar to Triphiodorus, studies have emphasised his 'intense' reconfiguration of Homeric language: specifically, the tendency to vary Homeric formulae, using Homeric elements but rarely repeating them exactly, and avoiding common Homeric adjectives in favour of rare ones.[13] Secondly, other scholars have stressed his amplified use of poetic devices, particularly ekphrasis, similes and *gnomai*, which appear in far greater number in the *Posthomerica* than in either of the Homeric texts. In this respect, the epic has been read as 'a poem of extremes',[14] displaying an aesthetic of excess which aligns it with Late Antique literary fashion,[15] refracted through Alexandrian philological practices.

The contradictions in these readings, however, should immediately give pause. It appears that on the one hand Quintus is being read as a bedfellow of Triphiodorus, another innovative precursor of Nonnus. And yet on the other, he is considered 'too Homeric', saturating his poem with rare words and devices poached from his literary hero. He is somehow both *omerico, ma non troppo* and *omerico troppo*, depending on the features upon which one chooses to focus. These paradoxes make clear the problems with trying to fit the *Posthomerica* in to a linear, developmental epic chronology: conservative in some respects and 'radical' in others. In order to assess the real position of our poem in the landscape of imperial Greek epic, its idiosyncrasies need to be directly confronted and comprehended.

This chapter represents such a confrontation. It is my contention that the *Posthomerica* does not fit the picture of stylistic contrastive imitation in the same way as Triphiodorus; that the case for linguistic innovation in the poem has been greatly overstated; and that its refusal to fit this mould is

---

[12] Vian (1959): 250.   [13] Examples and analysis in 3.2.
[14] Phrase from Maciver (2012b): 13. For such a viewpoint on the *Posthomerica*, Mehler (1961): 38 is illustrative: Quintus' 'lack of self-control' with regard to similes and other such features leads to 'exaggeration and pompousness'.
[15] For the (problematic) idea of a Late Antique aesthetic, see Roberts (1989); Cameron (2004); Elsner (2004).

96 Writing Homer: Language, Composition and Style

meaningful, and vital for assessing the real aesthetic agenda of the work.[16] I shall therefore be returning afresh to the two main areas of Quintus' Homeric deviation usually cited by scholars; firstly, his 'innovative' language and formulae, and then his 'excessive', similes and *gnomai*.[17] If the contradictions presented by such elements are acknowledged, interpreted rather than ignored, they begin to reveal a coherent stylistic strategy. In his use of Homeric language and formulae, Quintus avoids filling his poem with linguistic novelties and adapted versions of Homeric terms: he pursues in fact a programme of *moderation* in change, actively resisting the discourse of excess with which his poem has now become associated. This restraint gives heightened significance to any change that does occur, and invites reflection upon the way in which words and formulae have come to acquire new meaning within Homeric epic itself.

In the case of similes and *gnomai*, which in terms of their numbers do represent a case for poetic saturation, Quintus favours these features not to create a sense of hyperbole, but because of their highlighted interpretative function in imperial Greek literary and pedagogical thinking. Quintus capitalises upon the reflexive potential of these devices, well-expounded in other imperial genres, to express his agenda of literary conservatism: his examples become a means of communicating ideas of likeness, markers of his assimilation into Homer. Taken together, these features construct the textuality of Quintus' epic of the interval: a stylistic expression of the Homeric middle way.

3.2 Language and Formulae

Language

Quintus' close replication of Homeric language is one of the most well-known features of his epic. 'No other poem on a comparable scale reproduces the language of its models as closely as does the *Posthomerica*

---

[16] In this respect, my position is to *return* to the pre-twentieth-century judgements of the *Posthomerica*, particularly e.g. that of Köchly (1850), but to suggest new and *positive* significations for Quintus 'non-innovative' style.

[17] I have chosen to focus on these devices rather than ekphrasis for two main reasons. Firstly, their sheer number makes for a more expansive analysis addressing the question of a poetics of excess. Secondly, the issues raised by the use of ekphrasis in the *Posthomerica* – of visuality, personification, representation – whilst connected to the topic of this chapter and indeed to this book's interest in Quintus' connections to the world of material culture, really do require full study in their own right, which I have undertaken elsewhere (Greensmith forthcoming a), as has, from a different perspective, Maciver (2012b): ch. 2.

Language and Formulae

that of the Homeric epics.'[18] It is this claustrophobic closeness of imitation that drove the now traditional conception of the Quintan lexicon as a flattened Homeric *koine*;[19] and it is from the desire to resurrect the text from such pejorative dismissals that those more recent readings have emerged, which emphasise instead the elements of adaptation and innovation in Quintus' lexical choices.

Before assessing this re-assessment in depth, we must first consider the data which has driven it. The most exhaustive presentation of Quintan language is provided by the lexicon of Vian and Battegay, and, most significantly, the analyses of Vian in his *Recherches*.[20] In the latter work, Vian painstakingly uncovered a number of features of change in Quintus' text from its Homeric antecedents, many of which had been previously suppressed by the over-correction of manuscript editors based on recourse to Homeric precedents.[21] These changes are concentrated in three distinctive forms: Homeric rarities and particularly *hapax legomena*, 150 of which are found in the poem;[22] Homeric variants (usually grouped in certain books, the only more systematically occurring example being θέλω for the Homeric ἐθέλω); and neologisms.

Vian's findings have proven hugely influential on current thinking about the linguistic style of the poem, promptly triggering the identification of further patterns and penchants. In the case of *hapaxes*, Appel demonstrated how they most often take the form of 'unexceptional' compounds, with 'glosses' far less frequent –[23] there is, for instance, only one gloss in the whole of Book 5, ἠϊόεν (5.299), where Quintus, using it for a plain (πεδίον), makes a clear choice between disputed Homeric meanings –[24] and they are almost always used in different syntactical

---

[18] James and Lee (2000): 21. Although the lexica of Triphiodorus is marginally even more Homeric (cf. the statistics in Tomasso (2012): 290) it is scale that renders Quintus' lexical imitation so distinctive.

[19] Köchly (1850) with discussion in Vian (1959): 145–6.

[20] Vian (1959): chs. 5–6. Vian builds upon the standard and (still) only systematic treatment of the language of the *Posthomerica*, that of Köchly in the *prolegomena* of his edition ((1850): xliv–xciii).

[21] For a full survey, see Vian (1959): ch. 5. The recent commentary of Ferreccio (2014), drawing on the work of Bär (2009), offers pertinent discussion of Quintus' 'Lieblingswörter' (see esp. xxxii–xxxiii).

[22] Vian (1963): xli, following Paschal (1904). Appel (1993)/(1994a) calculated that roughly one in ten Quintan words is a Homeric *hapax*.

[23] Appel (1993) and (1994a). This distinction is intended to mark the difference between the sorts of 'standard' Homeric compounds, but which count as *hapaxes* because they are used only once, and the more striking singularly occurring words on which the Hellenistic scholars focused their critical attention. Cf. also Köchly (1850): xlix; Campbell (1981): Index a 1 (iii) a.

[24] The word is alternatively associated with rivers, assuming a derivation from ἠϊών, describing their high or alternating banks. Cf. LSJ and Autenrieth (1995) s.v. ἠϊόεις.

98   Writing Homer: Language, Composition and Style

and grammatical contexts from those in Homer.[25] Many of the Homeric variants have been associated with the *variae lectiones* of Aristarchus and in one case Zenodotus: for example Quintus' use of the verb ἔκθορον to convey the rampant charge of the horses during the race at the funeral games (Q.S.4.522) reflects Zenodotus' suggestion for the verb in *Il.* 23.759; a line which describes the foot race at the Iliadic version of these contests. By employing a variant, Quintus – so the current interpretative story goes – marks his learned and 'later' appropriation of the original Homeric scene. And the neologisms have been read as displaying predominantly the influence of tragedy and Hellenistic literature on the poem, since Quintus seems to borrow the majority of his 'new', non-Homeric word choices from these genres.[26]

As such interpretations make clear, these linguistic deviations, which 'in a more or less conscious way have slipped their way into the Homeric frame',[27] have been associated above all with an Alexandrian style of poetics: Quintus is deemed to show his critical dexterity and self-differentiation by means of clever philological twists and 'corrections' derived from the tradition of Homeric scholarship.[28] Such innovations certainly stand in contrast to the poem's metrical system, which is conservative and largely avoids irregularities: Quintus is not among the later epic poets who significantly show the influence of Callimachus' metrical reforms.[29]

However, in constructing this narrative of linguistic change, scholars have now tended to go much too far. Although Vian and his successors are undoubtedly correct in their identification of *some* rarities, variations and neologisms in the epic, the total amount of such material is actually, unavoidably, comparatively low. Deviations are far less prevalent, for instance, than in the multifarious, compound-heavy vocabulary of Nonnus, or the lexical adaptations of Triphiodorus. For example, Triphiodorus uses proportionally far more *hapax legomena* in his tiny poem, 115 for Quintus' 150, and Nonnus saturates the *Dionysiaca* with glosses, using for example καλαῦροψ (*Il.* 23.845) – an esoteric term for an esoteric

---

[25] Appel (1994a).
[26] Vian (1959): 168. List of terms provided in Köchly (1850): xlix; Paschal (1904): 22–7. Further examples in Vian (1959): 168–74.
[27] Translation of Vian (1959): 268: 'd'une manière plus ou moins consciente se sont glissés dans la frame Homérique'.
[28] Appel (1994a) takes this view. See also Bär (2009): 62f; Maciver (2012b): 15; Ferreccio (2014).
[29] For the Quintan metre, see Köchly (1850); Vian (1959): 212–49; James and Lee (2000): 30–1. This chapter does not focus in detail on metrical matters, for the simple reason that it aims to analyse the features which seem to suggest the greatest deviation from Homeric practice.

Language and Formulae 99

shepherd's crook – no fewer than nineteen times throughout the epic, in a brazen proliferation of Homeric idiosyncrasy.[30]

When faced with this comparative paucity in Quintus, the terms of inquiry must shift. The obsessive focus on the features of change, the desire to answer, in line with the much-fêted, still-trending readings of Alexandrian poets, the question of 'why the innovation?' has occluded the messier but most pressing issue of hesitation and reticence: 'why not *more* of it?'. We have seen in the previous chapter how the *Posthomerica* displays a deep interest in the reflexive potential of language: how Quintus invests his internal singers with a carefully selected repertoire of words to indicate their interstitial relationship to the primary Homeric source. In the epic's wider lexical system, the same approach is palpable. Rather than applying sweeping labels to this system – 'Homeric *koine*' or 'Alexandrian *uariatio*' – it seems that the 'middle ground' that it represents should be read as pointed, considered and productive. That Quintus includes rarities and neologisms, but does not overwhelm his poem with them, suggests that there is a marked specificity to his individual choices: his adaptations are marked and exceptional, assuming a singular, isolated energy rather than working in aggregate to signify an agenda of innovation. Precisely because of their infrequent occurrence, the specific narrative *context* of Quintus' Homeric deviations gains greater significance than has yet been suggested.

To reveal this significance, however, requires a certain twist in strategy. The recent influx of work on Quintan language has harnessed the power of totals: statistics have been re-collated and refined, and conclusions based around overall numbers – general and thus, supposedly, all-encompassing. In the readings to follow, I shall not be replicating or replacing such a methodology.[31] Instead, I shall trace an alternative perspective by delving inside such vast statistical conglomerations to focus on case studies which are particularly suggestive of Quintus' agenda of moderation in change. Now, 'exemplarity' of this kind in any linguistic analysis may well raise calls for caution. When defining the formal characteristics of a composition at large, the individual paradigm can surely carry little conclusive weight: not all language will produce the same marked effects. And yet one of the most hallowed techniques for 'characterising' ancient poetry, as the Homeric scholia's famous catchphrase puts it, is to read a poet using his

---

[30] A full study of Homeric *hapaxes* in Nonnus remains to be undertaken. For a starting point, see Ojeda (2002); Spanoudakis (2014a): 5–6; Bannert and Kröll (2016): 485.

[31] My readings have undoubtedly benefited from and been made possible by this methodology and its recent practitioners.

100   Writing Homer: Language, Composition and Style

own internal cues: 'Homer from Homer'. Given the cues of our particular poet – his refusal to write a poem overwhelmed with features of change; his distinctive interest, as displayed in the internal songs, in the process of paradigmatic selectivity (ἔνθεν ἑλών ... ἀρηραμένοις ἐπέεσσι, 4.148–9; ἄλλα δ' ἄρ' ἄλλος ἄειδεν, ὅ τι φρεσὶν ᾗσι μενοίνα, 14.142); and his tantalising abnegation of an easily definable innovating mode – it seems that a self-conscious focus on examples can in fact represent a quintessentially Quintan method for analysing the Quintan style.[32]

Homeric Rarities

The Homeric *hapaxes* uncovered by Vian in the *Posthomerica* attracted so much attention not only because they provided more evidence of this word type in the poem (affirming that *hapaxes* are indeed a salient feature of the text) but also because, freed from the obscuring mist of over-emendation, they appeared to offer examples far more 'distinctive' than those previously identified: they either denote rare instances where Quintus opts for a Homeric 'gloss' rather than a conventional once-occurring compound; or else they are solo-occurring words in Homer which did not themselves receive much attention in Alexandrian criticism, but are given a distinctly increased weight in Quintus' poem. What remains virtually unconsidered however, is *where* these *hapaxes*-of-distinction tend to occur. In fact, two of the most striking cases are found in passages of pronounced prolepsis: moments which look forward either to the end of the poem, or to events which stretch beyond it.

During the battle with Eurypylus, the narrator remarks that Locrian Ajax did not meet his end because his day of doom was already fixed:

> Σὺν δέ οἱ ἦλθε Πάρις τε καὶ Αἰνείας ἐρίθυμος,
> ὅς ῥα θοῶς Αἴαντα βάλεν περιμήκεϊ πέτρῃ
> κὰκ κόρυθα κρατερήν· ὁ δ' ἄρ' ἐν κονίῃσι τανυσθεὶς
> ψυχὴν οὔ τι κάπυσσεν, ἐπεί νύ οἱ αἴσιμον ἦμαρ
> ἐν νόστῳ ἐτέτυκτο Καφηρίσιν ἀμφὶ πέτρῃσι·
>
> Q.S.6.520–4

---

[32] These examples will concentrate on rarities and neologisms. I have chosen not to focus extensively on Homeric variants for the primary reason that, in the vast majority of cases, correction back to the Homeric morphology is possible. This is particularly true for θέλω, the most prevalent 'variant' in the poem where, in virtually every instance, Quintus' use of the non-Homeric form is contestable, normally because the verb is preceded by the particle κε (cf. e.g. Q.S.10.263, 10.294, 11.140; and Vian (1959): 159–60.). I want therefore to focus on forms which are more firmly 'post-Homeric', and whose potential signification can therefore be interpreted with greater confidence.

Language and Formulae

He was joined by Paris and the spirited Aeneas, who quickly dealt Ajax a blow on his stout helmet with a huge rock. He was stretched out in the dust, but he did not quite expire, since he was destined to die on the Capherean Rocks on his homeward voyage.

This prediction is duly fulfilled at the end of the *Posthomerica*: at Q.S.14.558–89 Ajax is mangled by the storm and dashed upon the Capherean rocks. As he foreshadows that moment here, Quintus uses the *hapax* κάπυσσεν. In accordance with Appel's theory, the corresponding *hapax* in Homer is ἐκάπυσσε – a different morphological compound form (in the augmented aorist and in *tmesis*). But the timing of its Iliadic occurrence also suggests a deeper thematic relevance to Quintus' choice of it here:

> τὴν δὲ κατ' ὀφθαλμῶν ἐρεβεννὴ νὺξ ἐκάλυψεν,
> ἤριπε δ' ἐξοπίσω, ἀπὸ δὲ ψυχὴν ἐκάπυσσε.
>
> *Il.* 22.466–7

Then down over her eyes came the darkness of night, and enfolded her, and she fell backward and gasped forth her spirit.

As Andromache reacts to the death of Hector, (ἀπο) καπύω describes how she gasps out her ψυχή. The most logical subject for this phrase is Hector, who really has now 'breathed out his last';[33] but it denotes instead the visceral reaction of one who is still alive. The word in the Homeric passage thus offers a physiognomic hinge between the living and the dead, and strikes at the vicious intensity of a wife's grief, as she enacts the gaping expiration of her husband's more literal demise. Quintus capitalises upon this hinge, but transfers it to describe a death that has not happened *yet*. The term thus helps to emphasise the analeptic and proleptic forces at work in his statement, as the backwards-propelling movement of the Iliadic scene (the fall ἐξοπίσω, the compound in ἀπό) combines with the future-facing οὔ τι of the Quintan moment to encapsulate the liminal state of Ajax' own precarious ψυχή.

A second example makes even clearer this connection between *hapax* and narrative temporality. Still during Eurypylus' *aristeia*, the hero hurls a rock at the Achaeans, and the narrator describes the fear that took hold of them:

> σμερδαλέον δ' ἄρα πάντα περιπλατάγησε θέμεθλα
> ἕρκεος αἰπεινοῖο · δέος δ' ἕλε πάντας Ἀχαιούς,
> τείχεος ὡς ἤδη συνοχωκότος ἐν κονίῃσιν.
>
> Q.S.7.500–2

---

[33] As James (2004): 111 translates the phrase in Quintus.

102   Writing Homer: Language, Composition and Style

There was a terrific crash, and the towering structure was shaken to its very foundations, and the Achaeans suddenly became afraid that their wall had already collapsed in the dust.

Very few of the published English translations of the poem acknowledge the full force of ἤδη in these verses. Way ignores the word entirely,[34] and James construes the phrase 'they thought that the wall had completely collapsed in the dust'.[35] But ἤδη of course also means 'at this point', 'now', or 'already'.[36] ὡς has similarly pliant potential: construed with the implied verb of fearing, the phrase could mean that the Trojans were afraid 'as though the wall had collapsed' *or* 'that the wall had (actually) collapsed' – indicating, paradoxically, either a fact or a counterfactual. Such double meanings are particularly relevant given how closely these lines replay an earlier episode from the Iliadic *Teichomachy*, where Hector hurls a stone and succeeds in mounting the walls and shattering the Achaean gates (*Il.* 10.445–62). Quintus' Greeks thus think that their wall had been compromised, as indeed it once already had been. But as well as echoing that previous pressure-point in the war, ἤδη and ὡς can also serve to anticipate the other, *Trojan* walls which have not yet 'already' fallen, but are destined to crumble into the dust.[37] This is therefore another moment where analepsis and prolepsis collapse into one another. And once again it is in precisely this sort of moment that a Homeric *hapax* – συνοχωκότος – appears. Now, συνοχωκώς occurs in the *Iliad* in a particularly salient context to describe the appearance of Thersites: τὼ δέ οἱ ὤμω/κυρτὼ ἐπὶ στῆθος συνοχωκότε·...: 'his two shoulders were rounded, stooping together over his chest, *Il.* 2.217–8). The discussions in the scholia testify to the keen interest in ancient criticism in Homer's vocabulary choices for his most *hapax aeidomenon* of characters: the commentators pause over every term in his description and offer lengthy exegeses of what sort of physical shape ἐπὶ στῆθος συνοχωκότε should evoke.[38] We saw in the previous chapter through Libanius' encomium how distinctive words from

---

[34] Way (1913): 333: 'Terror gripped the Greeks, as though that wall had crumbled down in dust.'
[35] James (2004): 128.
[36] Vian's French translation is more accurate (1966): 125: 'comme si le mur avait déja croulé dans la poussière'; as is Gärtner's rendering into German (2005): 'als ob die Mauer schon zusammen gefallen *sei* um Staub' (my italics).
[37] Whilst ἤδη is, of course, a perfectly common word in ancient Greek, and may thus seem to have little place in a discussion of specifically Homeric lexemes, its loaded use here to denote ideas of specifically Homeric temporality justifies its inclusion.
[38] Σ *bT* ad loc.

Language and Formulae 103

this famous scene can be taken up by authors who wish to demonstrate their simultaneous adherence to and development of the Homeric model. Τείχεος … συνοχωκότος reveals Quintus' distinctive take on this practice. The lexical allusion to the stooping shoulders of a character, who voiced with such forcefulness the difficulties of the Greek campaign and caricatured the frustrating impotence of their inability to sack Troy, points in this new context both to the present-tense moment of Greek distress and to the real drooping wall of the losing side once the balance of the war has tilted.

The interpretative force of these two *hapaxes* recontextualised suggests how quantitative-based analyses can miss the crucially specific role of these words in action. The tabulated totals offered by Vian and Appel affirm the presence of *hapaxes* as 'a' component of the poem, but tell us little to nothing about why. In fact, their relative sparsity in the *Posthomerica* compared with other epics of its time suggests that for Quintus, the valence of the *hapax* is found not in its salient abnormality. The poet who is 'still Homer' does not seek to transform his model into a technicolour tapestry of his most unusual terms. Rather, the narrative positioning of two of the most critically significant examples reveals that their power for Quintus lies instead in their bendy conceptual potential. By definition both recognisably Homeric and distinctively different – non-'formulaic', sometimes obscure and bizarre – *hapaxes* present a key philological instance of Homeric doubleness.[39] Used in such passages which mark the precarious intersection of inevitability and anticipation, they help this poet to focalise the central tension of this poem, between looking back and recognising the Homeric, and glancing forwards to the disorientating, un-Homeric future which is destined to follow on.

Neologisms

If *hapaxes* can thus bespeak a complex poetic relationship to Homer by virtue of their dual status as both part of the original lexicon and marginal verbal 'outsiders', then neologisms present an even more capacious site for linguistic reflexivity of this kind. Occurring in a poem which professes to be 'still Homeric', they create bumps in the serene Iliadic continuation, by enacting, so it would seem, the real novelty of this poetic language through the widened vocabulary of its composer. However, once again, the placement of these bumps complicates such tidy conclusions. Vian's re-analysis

---

[39] On doubleness, see the extensive discussion in Chapter 2.

104   Writing Homer: Language, Composition and Style

of neologisms in the poem uncovered how they, like the variants, tend to be concentrated in certain books: all but two of his examples are found in Books 9–12 and almost half are in Book 14.[40] Vian himself is underwhelmed by such a pattern: the grouping of word types in particular areas of the text simply reveals what he deems 'un trait caractéristique' of the poet, whereby he uses and abuses a turn of phrase when it comes to mind, and then abandons it again.[41] And yet whilst such a conclusion may theoretically apply to the variants – that is, the use of a *particular* word form frequently in one section and then not in another – the concentration in the final books of a wide variety of neologisms, united only by the fact that they are non-Homeric, must signify more than clumsy compositional amnesia. In a poem which begins – purposefully and pointedly – with a connective of continuation, why wait to enact linguistic novelty until the very end? Read another way, this pattern of neologisms suggests that they are put to work by Quintus not to create a fissure between Homericness and newness, but rather to forge a connection between them. As we leave the story which continues the *Iliad*, an accumulation of 'new' terms helps to express the nature of this venture into Homeric unknowns. Linguistic gestures towards a later literary world are doubled back into the verbal texture of the poem which remains resolutely in the middle.

Let us consider an example of how this doubling-back takes place. In Book 12, Sinon responds to Odysseus' request for a volunteer in the Wooden Horse plan, and his commitment attracts the wonder of the other Greeks:

> καί τις ἔφη· Ὡς τῷδε θεὸς μέγα θάρσος ἔδωκε
> σήμερον· οὐ γὰρ πρόσθεν ἔην θρασύς· ἀλλά ἑ δαίμων
> ὀτρύνει πάντεσσι κακὸν Τρώεσσι γενέσθαι
> ἢ νῶϊν· νῦν γὰρ <καὶ> ὀίομαι ἐσσυμένως περ
> ἀργαλέου πολέμοιο τέκμωρ εὔδηλον ἔσεσθαι.
>
> Q.S.12.254–8

And some man said: 'What valour a god has given him today, though in the past he has not been valiant! Some divine power is prompting him to be a bane to all the Trojans – or to us; for no doubt there will soon be a clear conclusion to this cruel war.'

---

[40] Vian (1959): 168–74 gives a full list. The following analysis does not seek to suggest that *all* 'new words' in the *Posthomerica* are concentrated in the final books; merely that those uncovered by Vian (and which had previously been concealed by recourse to Homeric precedents) seem to be so and that neologisms in the later books of the poem provide a particularly interesting test case for proleptic connotations of this kind.
[41] Vian (1959): 149.

Language and Formulae

The adjective εὔδηλος ('quite clear, abundantly manifest'[42]) is un-Homeric, but is found frequently in tragedy,[43] and in Aristotelian and Platonic discourses.[44] Whilst many editors print ἀίδηλον,[45] εὔδηλον is contextually apt in this scenario, as it aims to express the Greeks' uncertainty now, against their hope for clarity in the future.[46] The term thus first provides a neat affirmation of Quintus' oft-cited penchant for borrowing his non-Homeric words from the tragic corpus. However, once again the pressing question becomes: why is it used here? Why now? Sinon's act of service is, from the viewpoint of his fellow Greeks, an unexpected and even shocking turn of events. Their speech then contains a further mix of precarious, unpredictable elements: the identity of the speaker (an anonymous τις); who is stirring; the conviction of the crowd's belief that the war will soon be over – as the assuredness of ἐσσυμένως περ is weakened by the prevarication in ὀίομαι. The mixing of familiar Homeric vocabulary with a 'new' word for clarity thus helps forcefully to underline this ironic juxtaposition of perspectives: between the internal expectations of the characters within the story, who remain suspended in this state of unknowing, and the external knowledge of the reader, for whom the *telos* of this story *is* already 'clear.' It is apposite in this light that the noun which the neologism describes, τέκμωρ, is 'particularly' Homeric – the spelling with *omega* occurs only in Homer's morphology –[47] furthering the vital mixture of familiarity and newness as the end of the war approaches.

This Sinon neologism is so suggestive because of the distinctly transitional nature of the moment which it is used to describe: the building of the horse, the gateway to the long-awaited 'end' of the lengthy Trojan War. The final book of the poem presents such transition in its most pressing form: the gateway from the Iliadic sequel to the *nostoi* and then to the *Odyssey*, it narrates the pivot between the triumphant Greek victory and the devastating later consequences of their success. With the intense concentration of neologisms in *this* book, Quintus does far more than simply display the 'influence of tragedy' on his work. During the sacrifice of Polyxena, Quintus describes Hecuba's lamentation of her family's fate (14.271–303). This scene of post-Iliadic aftermath had by Quintus' time acquired a long stage history: it is dramatised at length in Euripides'

---

[42] Cf. LSJ s.v. εὔδηλος.   [43] Cf. e.g. Aesch. *Pers.* 1009.
[44] Cf. e.g. Arist. [*Pr.*] 882b9; εὔδηλα γράμματα ('plainly legible'); Pl. *Plt.* 308d.: εὔδηλόν [ἐστιν] ὅτι...
[45] E.g. Köchly (1850) ad loc.; adopted by Way (1913): 504.   [46] Cf. Vian (1959): 170.
[47] It is unequivocally with *alpha* in later Greek.

106   Writing Homer: Language, Composition and Style

Troades, and Hecuba's specific reflections here also resemble those which she voices in *Hecuba* (154–61; 585). And yet in a passage imbued with such tragic inheritance, Quintus opts for a neologism – and, in that 'caractéristique' way which would cause Vian to roll his eyes, repeats it twice in quick succession–[48] but one *not* drawn from the tragic corpus:

> ὦ μοι ἐγώ, τί νυ πρῶτα, τί δ' ὕστατον ἀχνυμένη κῆρ
> κωκύσω πολέεσσι περιπλήθουσα κακοῖσιν,
> υἱέας ἢ πόσιν αἰνὰ καὶ οὐκ ἐπίολπα παθόντας,
> ἢ πόλιν ἠὲ θύγατρας ἀεικέας, ἢ ἐμὸν αὐτῆς
> ἦμαρ ἢ καὶ δούλιον; οὕνεκα Κῆρες
> σμερδαλέαι πολέεσσί μ' ἐνειλήσαντο κακοῖσι.
> τέκνον ἐμόν, σοὶ δ' αἰνὰ καὶ οὐκ ἐπίολπα καὶ αὐτῇ
> ἄλγε' ἐπεκλώσαντο...
>
> Q.S.14.289–96

Alas! What should I lament first and what last in my heart's grief, in my surfeit of trouble? My sons or my husband, who died dreadful and unforeseen deaths? My city, or my mistreated daughters, or my own fate, be it death or slavery? In how many troubles the grim spirits of doom have entangled me! And they have spun dreadful and unforeseen troubles for you, too, my child.

Ἐπίολπα is nowhere else attested in surviving literature. Many older editions of the *Posthomerica* thus correct it to the Homeric ἐπίελπτα.[49] However, the manuscripts unanimously give the former adjective,[50] and Vian has convincingly argued that this reading should be preserved. He connects the meaning of ἐπίολπα to the concept of ἐλπίς[51] and suggests that Quintus must have borrowed the word from lost authors. The most crucial point, therefore, is that Hecuba expresses the unanticipated traumas which her family have suffered using a word which morphologically distinguishes itself from normal Homeric *and* conventional tragic expressions of emotions of this kind.[52] Despite its elusive origins, the repeated term can thus work to create meaning in a passage such as this, which comes at the end of the epic, represents the final extended speech by

---

[48] This is, in other words, an unusual instance where Quintus repeats the *same* neologism in a passage (rather than concentrating the use of neologisms *per se* in particular areas), which Vian has noted as a driving trait for his use of Homeric variants. We shall treat Quintus' use of repetition in more detail later in this chapter.

[49] After Dausque (1614).   [50] Vian (1959): 171.   [51] Cf. *Theog.* 660 ἀνάελπτα παθόντες.

[52] It is possible, of course, that this lost back story to the word could include an occurrence in one or more non-surviving tragedies. However, the absence of the word in any surviving tragic texts suggests that it is not a common word in the genre and thus that Quintus is aiming at a different effect through his selection of it here.

Language and Formulae 107

a named human character,[53] and merges a range of events and actors. The Iliadic past (the suffering of Hecuba's sons), the Quintan present (the death of Priam) and the post-Homeric future (the Trojan women's bondage and new ἄλγεα) are here all combined and recalibrated. Invested with language which goes beyond her traditional repertoire, Hecuba can describe sufferings which are no longer confined to those that she voiced at the end of the *Iliad*.[54] But by using a non-Homeric *and* un-tragic term to emphasise this transition, our poet makes clear that this is not a linear replacement of the Hecuba of Homeric Troy with the Queen of the Tragic Stage: she is a composite hybrid whose language and position straddles both generic spaces, and also moves between them. Not a Hecuba after Homer; this is an aftermath enacted through the linguistics of continuation.

Quintus' approach to both *hapaxes* and neologisms is thus characterised above all by a tense mixture of concentration and restraint. The combination of these drives begins to account for the specific dynamics of interplay between language, narrative and poetics at work in the text. We saw in the previous chapter how sophistic declamations, educational exercises and Homeric performance scripts achieved their interstitial effects by including carefully chosen post-Homeric words and through topsy-turvy plays with Homer's narrative time. In his selective linguistic deviations, Quintus makes clear the nature of his participation in this practice: using subtle shifts of vocabulary to convey his distinctive double take on Homeric temporality.

Formulae and Epithets

If Quintus' divergences from Homeric language are remarkable chiefly for their paucity, a different mode of *imitatio* occurs in his use of the formulaic system. The *Posthomerica* employs noun and epithet formulae so extensively that, as Hoekstra noted in a passing remark which has been enthusiastically quoted by Quintan commentators ever since, it goes some way to disprove Milman Parry's conclusions about the essentially oral nature of the Homeric hexameter.[55] However, Quintus also extensively adapts this

---

[53] It is followed only by Neoptolemus and Nestor's very short speeches (Q.S.14.308–13; 14.339–45), and then Athena and Zeus' conversation (Q.S.14.427–48).

[54] Cf. *Il.* 24.747–59.

[55] Hoekstra (1965): 17: 'if the *Posthomerica* were the oldest surviving piece of poetry, the argument put forth [by Parry] would necessarily lead to the conclusion that this poem was an oral composition'. Discussion in James and Lee (2000): 24–7 and James (2004): xxiii–xxiv.

108   Writing Homer: Language, Composition and Style

system, varying the formulae of Homer in three main ways. Firstly, he does not consistently use exact Homeric formulae.[56] According to Vian's calculations, of 180 formulae involving adjectives in the *Posthomerica*, 76 are Homeric, and the noun-adjective combinations are almost always different from the Homeric examples.[57] Secondly, he rarely employs his own formulae in the Homeric fashion; that is, in exactly repeated phrases multiple times.[58] Thirdly, Quintus uses a far greater variety of epithets than Homer. Mansur's study of heroic epithets in the *Posthomerica* made the following three observations: the poem uses many more epithets per hero than his Homeric model; epithets which are commonly used for certain heroes in Homer are hardly ever applied to that person in Quintus; and very few epithets are applied by Homer and Quintus to the same characters.[59] To these conclusions James and Lee have added the suggestion that Quintus' epithets are like Homer's only in the respect that they are largely 'ornamental' and not invested with any contextual significance.[60]

Conceptualised in this way, Quintus' treatment of formulae has become one of the strongest indicators of his *imitatio cum uariatione*.[61] Such a verdict, however, leaves unresolved some fundamental questions about the interpretative effects of this variation, particularly, again, in a poem which claims to be a Homeric continuation. In other words, in contrast to his metrical conservatism and close adherence to Homeric lexica, why should Quintus choose formulae – a feature whose close imitation would most overtly affirm his work's ostensible claim to Homeric authorship – to showcase his difference? What is the impact of this break as an authorial methodology and what readerly reactions could it produce?

The key to answering these questions lies in the issue of 'ornamentality'. In their assertion that Quintan epithets are, 'like Homer's, predominantly ornamental', James and Lee under-emphasise the obvious but crucial fact that, for all the proto-Parryian claims that one can make about Quintus, as

---

[56] For the sake of consistency, I shall define 'formula' in the *Posthomerica* using the criteria proposed by James and Lee (2000): 25: 'any expression of two or more words used two or more times in the poem'. I shall also include noun and epithet combinations which appear only once in the *Posthomerica*, where these combinations include epithets which are frequently employed in the Homeric poems.'
[57] Vian (1959): ch. 6.
[58] There are only nine cases of a single line repeated once, one pair of lines repeated once (3.465–6 = 5.538–9, the longest verbatim repetition in Q.S.) and one line repeated four times (7.219 =7.700 = 8.146 = 12.66 = 13.237).
[59] Mansur (1940): tables 1–3.   [60] James and Lee (2000): 26–30.
[61] Vian (1959): ch. 6; Chrysafis (1985); James and Lee (2000): 25–30; Bär (2009); Ferreccio (2014): xxiv–xxvii.

Language and Formulae

a literate and literary poem his composition was not constrained by the same principles of formular economy in the same way.[62] On the contrary, when Quintus came to create his formulae, he inherited, of course, a deep and varied tradition of reading and manipulating Homeric epithets. Discussion surrounding πολύτροπον in the first verse of the *Odyssey* offers an extreme example of the debates, defence, categorisations and re-categorisations that could be put to Homeric adjectives in their context. The term provides a major hinge for Plato's complex excursus on Homeric characterisation, criticism and representation in the *Hippias Minor*, in a passage which has become, as Hunter recently lamented, 'stale with familiarity', but which is also, as the same reader recently proclaimed, revealing in its peculiarity:[63]

> φημὶ γὰρ Ὅμηρον πεποιηκέναι ἄριστον μὲν ἄνδρα Ἀχιλλέα τῶν εἰς Τροίαν ἀφικομένων, σοφώτατον δὲ Νέστορα, πολυτροπώτατον δὲ Ὀδυσσέα.
> *Hp. mi.* 364c4–7

> For I say that Homer made Achilles the bravest man of those who went to Troy, and Nestor the wisest, and Odysseus the most *polytropos*.

Hippias' answer to Socrates' conundrum – 'Which (of Achilles and Odysseus) do you say is better (ἀμείνων) and in what respect (κατὰ τί)?' (364b4–5) – both plays fast and loose with traditional Homeric character attributions (only Nestor, not Odysseus, is even contemplated here as qualifying for the adjective 'wise')[64] and also makes an emphatically *un*-traditional manoeuvre by calling Odysseus 'the *most polytropos*'. Turning this near-unique adjective (it occurs of course only twice in the Homeric corpus [*Od.* 1.1 and 10.330] on both occasions referring to Odysseus in the *Odyssey*) into a superlative, Plato creates a *hapax* from the Homeric almost-*hapax*, and thereby introduces the radical idea that it could potentially have a heroic antecedent other than the twisty ἀνήρ himself.[65]

---

[62] James and Lee's under-emphasis may be rhetorical, but it is nonetheless counter-productive. Visser (1987): 266–898 comes closest to appreciating this point, in a thesis which James and Lee dismiss (2000): 26.

[63] Hunter (2016) offers rich discussion of this passage and the wider impact of the strands of Homeric criticism traceable in the dialogue at large. Quotation here from 89.

[64] Contrast e.g. Eustathius' discussion of σοφία as a relevant term for Odysseus too: in the *Iliad* Odysseus was not yet 'wiser' (σοφώτερος) than Nestor, but his great wanderings after the war brought him huge ἐμπειρία, 'experience', which allowed him to surpass even Nestor (*Hom.* 1381.61–1382.2).

[65] Thus Hunter (2016): 90: 'The question "Which of the heroes was most *polytropos*?" would, on the face of it, be to anyone but the Platonic Socrates a nonquestion.' Socrates' subsequent claim that he has no idea whom Hippias meant by the 'most *polytropos*' thus presumably echoes the readers' own

110 Writing Homer: Language, Composition and Style

This discussion of the epithet had a strong influence on the rich tradition of later Homeric criticism,[66] not least through its complex relationship to the equally discombobulating remarks of Antisthenes, who worries that the term could be taken as an insult (οὐκ ἐπαινεῖν ... Ὅμηρον τὸν Ὀδυσσέα μᾶλλον ἢ ψέγειν, λέγοντα αὐτὸν πολύτροπον) and attempts to solve the difficulty by clinging to a very specific interpretation:

> λύων οὖν ὁ Ἀντισθένης φησί· τί οὖν; ἄρα γε πονηρὸς ὁ Ὀδυσσεύς ὅτι πολύτροπος ἐρρέθη; καὶ μήν, διότι σοφός, οὕτως αὐτὸν προσείρηκεν μήποτε οὖν τρόπος τὸ μέν τι σημαίνει τὸ ἦθος, τὸ δέ τι σημαίνει τὴν τοῦ λόγου χρῆσιν· *Schol. Hom. Od.* 1 l Pontani (2007) = Antisthenes fr.51 Caizzi (1966)

> Antisthenes' solution was as follows. What then? Was Odysseus a bad man because he was called *polytropos*? Rather, he called him this because he was wise. Is it not the case that *tropos* may signify 'character', but it also signifies 'the use of words'?

Lexicographical works such as the Homeric dictionary of Apollonius the Sophist, which themselves also exercised great influence on imperial reading patterns of Homer,[67] also pause and prevaricate on many Homeric epithets, discussing ambiguities of meaning, contradictory passages and polysemantic interpretations. For Quintus and his imperial readership, therefore, it cannot be emphasised enough that some Homeric epithets were always already contextually significant. In his persistent adaptation of formulae, Quintus mobilises this significance, not to tear up or rewrite the system, but to launch a critically informed discussion of what epithets 'mean' in Homeric epic. His formulaic system thus offers a key indication of his reception of the Homeric text as fixed and final and yet open for constant reinterpretation: a reaction to and embodiment of the culture of expansion-from-within at large in imperial Greece.

---

bafflement. For more on this aspect of the dialogue, see ibid. 91ff and Blondell (2002). See discussion below for responses in other and earlier genres, particularly through the role of Hermes in the Homeric Hymn, to the idea of an extra-Odyssean application for the epithet.

[66] We shall return to this discussion in more detail at the end of this chapter. See Giuliano (1995) and Hunter (2016) with further references.

[67] See especially Haslam (1994).

Language and Formulae 111

Variety of Epithets

To reveal this formulaic significance, a major case study presents itself in the epithets applied to one Homeric/Quintan hero. Achilles receives the largest number of epithets in both Quintus and Homer,[68] and in the *Posthomerica* his epithets conform to the pattern noted by Mansur for all major characters: Quintus uses a proportionally greater variety of terms than Homer does (32 compared with 36 in Homer);[69] he does not have a 'favourite' epithet for him; and he avoids using Homer's own favourites. Achilles is also one of the Homeric characters with the largest and most diverse literary receptions. Whilst the deep and murky waters of this reception cannot be dealt with at any length here,[70] let it suffice to recall that this is a figure who, by the time of Quintus' writing, had raged and reconciled with enemies, fallen in love, died at the hands of a man or a god, argued in the underworld or ascended to the Isle of the Blessed, been heroised and vilified, ridiculed and satirised, and whose words and character were studied fervently by scholar and student alike.[71] We have also seen in the previous chapter how Achilles' diversity of character within the *Iliad* itself – and the diversity of responses to it – could be pithily mobilised in declamatory exercises: the subject of both apologetic and polemic, Achilles became emblematic for the multiple, contradictory manoeuvres which rhetoric could apply to mythological foci. It has become by now a familiar move in Quintan scholarship to look at Achilles' 'characterisation' in the *Posthomerica* in light of this varied tradition.[72] But a more intricate and unanswered question is how Quintus uses formulae to inscribe his relationship with this tradition *as a tradition* and to demonstrate its impact on his poetic process. To describe Achilles with a formula is to tap a wealth of received and debated ideas. In his variation of epithets, Quintus showcases his awareness of this weight of literary inheritance and makes clear his methods of responding to it.

Let us begin by considering the rare occasions where Quintus does apply Homer's 'favourite' epithets for Achilles to his own version of the character: Mansur's assertion that this hardly ever happens obscures some

---

[68] Achilles is mentioned 196 times with an epithet in Homer (the only higher number is for the obviously exceptional case of Odysseus in the *Odyssey*) and 183 times without. In Quintus, he gets an epithet 66 times and does not 105 times. Cf. Mansur (1940): tables 1–3.

[69] Given the relative sizes of their poems and the number of references to Achilles.

[70] For a lively recent account, see particularly Fantuzzi (2012).

[71] Achilles was likewise a favourite for the character exercises undertaken by school pupils discussed in detail in the previous chapter. See e.g. Cribiore (2001): 223; Webb (2001): 301.

[72] See e.g. Boyten (2010); Scheijnen (2018).

112   Writing Homer: Language, Composition and Style

potentially important exceptions. Three common Achillean epithets from Homer are used by Quintus for Achilles, each only once: ποδαρκής, πελώριος and ποδώκης. The first occurs during Penthesilea's dream as she prepares to enter battle:

> ...Μόλε δ' αἰθέρος ἐξ ὑπάτοιο
> Παλλάδος ἐννεσίῃσι μένος δολόεντος Ὀνείρου, (125)
> ὅππως μιν λεύσσουσα κακὸν Τρώεσσι γένηται
> οἵ τ' αὐτῇ, μεμαυῖα ποτὶ πτολέμοιο φάλαγγας.
> καὶ τὰ μὲν ὣς ὥρμαινε δαΐφρων Τριτογένεια·
> τῇ δ' ἄρα λυγρὸς Ὄνειρος ἐφίστατο πατρὶ ἐοικώς,
> καί μιν ἐποτρύνεσκε ποδάρκεος ἄντ' Ἀχιλῆος (130)
> θαρσαλέως μάρνασθαι ἐναντίον. ἡ δ' ἀΐουσα
> γήθεεν ἐν φρεσὶ πάμπαν· ὀΐσατο γὰρ μέγα ἔργον
> ἐκτελέειν αὐτῆμαρ ἀνὰ μόθον ὀκρυόεντα,
> νηπίη, ἥ ῥ' ἐπίθησεν ὀιζυρῷ περ Ὀνείρῳ
> ἑσπερίῳ, ὃς φῦλα πολυτλήτων ἀνθρώπων (135)
> θέλγει ἐνὶ λεχέεσσιν ἄδην ἐπικέρτομα βάζων,
> ὅς μιν ἄρ' ἐξαπάφησεν ἐποτρύνων πονέεσθαι.
>
> Q.S.1.124–37

But Pallas ordered a dream of deceitful power to come down from high heaven; and her seeing it would result in misfortune for both the Trojans and herself by making her eager for the lines of battle. Such was the plan of warlike Tritogeneia. The baneful dream stood over Penthesileia in the guise of her father and urged her to go boldly into battle against Achilles. When she heard this, her heart was filled with joy at the thought of performing such a feat that very day in the fearsome fray. Poor fool, to trust that dream, malign though it was, coming at dusk! It beguiles the race of wretched mortals in their beds with words that mock all too well; and it deceived her then, when it urged her to take up the work of war.

The falseness of the vision – modelled on Agamemnon's οὖλος ὄνειρος in the second book of the *Iliad* – is prioritised and emphasised in this description. Agamemnon's dream was οὖλος (*Il.* 2.6), so here it is δολόεντος and λυγρός; this one is sent by Athena as Agamemnon's was by Zeus; and Penthesilea's dream is disguised in the likeness of her father, as in the *Iliad* it was Νηληΐῳ υἷι ἐοικώς (*Il.* 2.20). And as with Agamemnon, Penthesilea's belief in the message makes her a fool (νηπίη), and leads to a false optimism about her future (cf. *Il.* 2.48). It is within this context that we find Achilles described with a characteristic Homeric epithet, its only occurrence in the poem. Penthesilea is thus made to dream of Achilles in all of his terrifying, *Iliadic* horror. But this horror – though soon to be proven real enough for Penthesilea – is from the reader's perspective

Language and Formulae

refracted and set at a distance, confined to the realms of hallucination and filtered through layers of emphatic non-reality.[73]

πελώριος occurs later in the epic to describe the Trojan reaction to Neoptolemus as he arrives on the battlefield:

> Οἳ δ᾽ ἄρ᾽ ἀμηχανίῃ βεβολημένοι ἔνδοθεν ἦτορ
> Τρῶες ἔφαντ᾽ Ἀχιλῆα πελώριον εἰσοράασθαι
> αὐτὸν ὁμῶς τεύχεσσι·...
>
> Q.S.7.537–9

Shocked and helpless in their hearts, the Trojans thought it was mighty Achilles the man, armour and all, that they could see.

The description of Achilles with one of his common Iliadic epithets is again in the context of a fictional sighting: the Trojans only think that they see Ἀχιλῆα πελώριον before them, and the following line dismantles this false attribution. Achilles, the reader knows, is no longer living and the real αὐτός here is his son, dressed in the arms of his father.[74]

ποδώκης then occurs immediately after this battle scene, as Phoenix reacts to seeing Neoptolemus before him:

> ... τῷ δ᾽ αἶψα γέρων σχεδὸν ἤλυθε Φοῖνιξ,
> καί μιν ἰδὼν θάμβησεν ἐοικότα Πηλείωνι·
> ἀμφὶ δέ οἱ μέγα χάρμα καὶ ἄσπετον ἄλγος ἵκανεν,
> ἄλγος μὲν μνησθέντι ποδώκεος ἀμφ᾽ Ἀχιλῆος,
> χάρμα δ᾽ ἄρ᾽, οὕνεκά οἱ κρατερὸν παῖδ᾽ εἰσενόησε.
>
> Q.S.7.630–4

Old Phoenix soon came up to him and was astonished to see how like the son of Peleus he was; he felt great joy and unspeakable sadness – sadness from his remembrance of swift-footed Achilles, and joy at the sight of his son's prowess.

Once more, the Homeric epithet for Achilles forms part of the language of likeness: ἐοικότα suggests the strong similarity between father and son, but also stresses the fact that this is a comparison of two independent entities – to be alike is not to be the same.[75]

---

[73] Whilst in his decisive victory and brutal slaughter of Pentheseila (Q.S.1.538–653), Achilles proves himself just as belligerent and savage as in his most rage-filled Iliadic moments (and for further on such savagery, see Boyten (2010): 115–26 and Scheijnen (2018): 97–110), in his subsequent divinely inspired desire for her, his remorse for his actions and his wish to have 'married her' instead (Q.S.654–74), we see a very different form of the *mēnis/philotes* divide in his character. I have discussed this episode in depth and from a different perspective in Greensmith (forthcoming c).

[74] For this scene analysed in terms of Late Antique discourses of succession, see Chapter 6.

[75] See 3.3 of this chapter, on similes.

114 Writing Homer: Language, Composition and Style

On all three occasions, then, Homeric terms for Achilles are used in fantasy visions of the past: the sighting of something that is not there, or no longer there. Through the presence of these original epithets, the reader can recognise on a linguistic level the 'real' Iliadic Achilles and perceive his ongoing presence in this epic – as its inheritance, its ghost and its unavoidable memory. But this recognition is only a fleeting glimpse, re-focalised and set at a distance. The terms thus establish Homer's Achilles as something which can be momentarily captured, but never regained in its entirety.

To replace these Homeric epithets, now consigned to the sphere of the remembered past, the *Posthomerica* employs a wide range of adjectives. Achilles is described four times as ἀμείλικτος (Q.S.2.25; 8.335; 9.247; 14.268), the only individual human character in the poem to receive the term.[76] Homer uses this adjective in the singular only twice, in the formula ἀμείλικτον δ᾽ ὄπ᾽ ἄκουσεν, which is cited in Apollonius the Sophist's entry for the word (ἀμείλικτον πικρὰν καὶ οὐ προσηνῆ· ἀμείλικτον δ᾽ ὄπ᾽ ἄκουσεν).[77] The two passages in question both concern heroes' harsh responses to beseeching opponents: Agamemnon to the sons of Antimachus (*Il.* 11.137) and Achilles to the entreaties of Lykaon:

> ὣς ἄρα μιν Πριάμοιο προσηύδα φαίδιμος υἱός
> λισσόμενος ἐπέεσσιν, ἀμείλικτον δ᾽ ὄπ᾽ ἄκουσε·
> νήπιε μή μοι ἄποινα πιφαύσκεο μηδ᾽ ἀγόρευε·
> πρὶν μὲν γὰρ Πάτροκλον ἐπισπεῖν αἴσιμον ἦμαρ
> τόφρά τί μοι πεφιδέσθαι ἐνὶ φρεσὶ φίλτερον ἦεν
> Τρώων, καὶ πολλοὺς ζωοὺς ἕλον ἠδὲ πέρασσα.
>
> *Il.* 21.97–102

So the glorious son of Priam spoke to him with words of entreaty, but all ungentle was the voice he heard: 'Fool, do not try to ransom or address me. Until Patroclus met his day of fate it more pleasing to me to spare the Trojans, and full many I took alive and sold.'

The Lykaon episode has an important energy in the *Posthomerica*. It is mentioned on three separate occasions,[78] including in Nestor's song, which, as we have seen in the previous chapter, selectively recapitulates Achilles' feats from the war (Q.S.4.158). Quintus here transfers an epithet

---

[76] The other uses are for the Κῆρες (8.139); χέρες (3.83); ὀιστόι (6.290); the Argives (14.514); and twice πότμος (10.229 and 14.521). Quintus uses the (related but not fully synonymous) ἀμείλιχος (cf. LSJ s.v. ἀμείλιχος) much more frequently in his poem (thirty-nine times), but I am focusing on the former adjective due to its specific relationship to these Iliadic usages.

[77] Ap. Soph. *Lexicon Homericum.* s.v. ἀμείλικτος (Bekker 1833 p. 25.10).

[78] The other two: Q.S.4.384 and 4.393.

Language and Formulae

used in this Iliadic scene onto a description of Achilles himself. By so doing, he can demonstrate the effects of such famous moments in the *Iliad* on subsequent conceptions of the hero: Achilles now embodies the results of his behaviour towards Lykaon in his own heroic personality, as it is described by later singers of tales.

This sort of commentary on Achilles is suggested most provocatively in Quintus' use of 'divine' epithets for him. Recent scholarship has shown an interest in Achilles' 'non-Homeric' afterlife in the *Posthomerica*: his apotheosis, home on the Elysian Plains and ghostly final appearance.[79] What is more important for our purposes, however, and has not yet received comment, is how Quintus constructs this aspect of Achilles in his formulaic descriptions. δῖος Ἀχιλλεύς is one of Homer's favourite noun-epithet pairings: it is the first nominative epithet for the hero in the *Iliad* (*Il.* 1.7)[80] and goes on to occur thirty-six times in various metrical formulations. By Quintus' era, as I have discussed in Chapter 1.1, the meaning of the Homeric δῖος had been the subject of much debate.[81] Apollonius defines it as referring either to divine descent or to quality of character (δῖος (>) ἀπὸ Διὸς τὸ γένος ἔχων, ἢ ἀγαθός, ἢ γενναῖος, ἀπὸ τῆς τοῦ Διὸς ὑπεροχῆς).[82] The scholia gloss it as ὁ ἔνδοξος ἀπὸ τῆς Διὸς ὑπεροχῆς[83] and then list the many ways in which one could qualify for the term: Odysseus for wisdom; Paris and Clytemnestra for beauty; Eumaeus for goodwill (εὐνοία); and Achilles πάντων χάριν.[84]

Quintus does not use δῖος Ἀχιλλεύς at all. He employs δῖος for other heroes,[85] and in the (Homeric) formula δῖος ἀνήρ,[86] but never in direct pairing with Achilles' name or patronymic. He does, however, use far more epithets for Achilles which have divine connotations – more than are used for him in Homer or for any other character in the *Posthomerica*. Quintus' Achilles is θεοειδής (7.686; 11.234), ἰσόθεος (14.180), ζάθεος (14.304)[87]

---

[79] See especially Carvounis (2019); Maciver (2017).

[80] And the first hero's epithet full stop, if one discounts the genitive patronymic in the first line of the poem.

[81] On these discussions, see e.g. Vivante (1982) on epithets in context and Nagy (1997) on the scholia.

[82] Ap. Soph. *Lexicon Homericum*. s.v. δῖος (Bekker (1833) 59.8).

[83] Cf. also the comment after the descriptions of qualities: τὸν δὲ Ἀχιλλέα καὶ διογενῆ δίχα τοῦ κυρίου·' Φ 17). These opinions are often reflected in Apollonius' definitions.

[84] Σ. bT *Il.*1.7b. 2.

[85] Epeius (4.329; 12.151 and 12.329); Agenor (6.624); Odysseus (7.182); Neoptolemus (7.484); and Aegeus (13.510).

[86] 2.404 (re. Memnon), 10.236 (re. Philoctetes) and once (3.162) about Achilles himself, alluding to the original Homeric epithet combination, but still not using it directly with Achilles' name.

[87] An adjective which Quintus otherwise uses only for localities favoured by the gods, adhering to Homeric usage.

116 Writing Homer: Language, Composition and Style

and ἀντίθεος.[88] Now, it may be tempting to read this multiplicity as a reflection of these ancient critical debates about epithets such as δῖος: the Achilles of Quintus' epic is now 'godlike' in a greater range of ways, reflecting the many reasons (πάντων χάριν) for which he is deemed to be δῖος in Homer. Again, however, rather than simply 'reflecting' this tradition of exegesis, Quintus' formulae now work to *incorporate* such readings into the Achilles of his continuation poem. These epithets play out for the reader, attuned to such semantic slipperiness, the contradictions of Achilles' post-Homeric status in a still-Homeric world, where he is compelled to embody a series of complex double forms: illustrious and/or godlike; an actual god; or even an anti-god.

ἀντίθεος provides the most telling example of such contradictions. In Homer, the epithet means 'equal to the gods' or 'godlike' and only in later Greek did it come to denote 'contrary to the gods'.[89] Homer never applies the term to Achilles, nor usually to women, with the exception of once for Penelope,[90] but he does use it for a range of other characters, including the suitors (e.g. *Od.* 14.18) and even Polyphemus (*Od.* 1.70). This list of subjects suggested to some commentators an ambivalence fundamental to the word's meaning:

ἀντίθεον. τὸν ἰσόθεον. ἐπὶ δὲ τοῦ Κύκλωπος τὸν ἐναντιούμενον τοῖς θεοῖς. – Ap. Soph. *Lexicon Homericum*[91]

Quintus, like Homer, uses ἀντίθεος for a variety of characters.[92] But he uses it far more frequently for women, and particularly for one woman: it is thrice an epithet for Helen, occurring almost every time she appears in the poem (Q.S.2.97; 6.152; 13.595).[93] And he does use it – multiple times – for Achilles (4.385; 5.305; 12.288; 14.276). *This* particular combination of subjects sharpens the term's pre-existing semantic ambivalences: firstly, we are compelled now to consider its applicability to Troy's famously problematic woman, the offspring of Zeus and the contestable cause of the suffering of the war; and then its relevance for Achilles, in a disparate set of contexts – sometimes when he is being praised by other characters (5.305, by Ajax; 12.288 by Nestor) and other times when he is the object of their loathing:

καὶ τότε λευγαλέοις ἐπὶ πένθεσι κύντερον ἄλγος
τλήμονος ἐς κραδίην Ἑκάβης πέσεν· ἐν δέ οἱ ἦτορ

---

[88] See case study below for references.   [89] Cf. e.g. Ph. 1566; LSJ s.v. ἀντίθεος.   [90] *Od.* 11.117.
[91] Bekker 1833 33.15.   [92] Most commonly Memnon, Odysseus and Diomedes.
[93] Other female recipients of the epithet in Q.S are Kloinie (1.235) and Aithra (Q.S.13.503).

Language and Formulae

> μνήσατ' ὀιζυροῖο καὶ ἀλγινόεντος ὀνείρου,
> τόν ῥ' ἴδεν ὑπνώουσα παροιχομένη ἐνὶ νυκτί·
> ἦ γὰρ ὀίετο τύμβον ἔπ' ἀντιθέου Ἀχιλῆος
> ἑστάμεναι γοόωσα...
>
> Q.S.14.272–6

Then there fell upon the heart of poor Hecuba, on top of her bitter sorrows, a worse pain. There came back to her mind the unhappy and troubling dream which she had seen in her sleep the night before: she had stood lamenting at the tomb of godlike (?) Achilles.

If we take ἀντίθεος to mean 'godlike' in the Homeric sense, there is a serious disjuncture here. In the preceding narrative, Achilles has just been depicted as immortal as he appears in a vision to his son (Q.S.14.185–7 and 225–6): he is a god, not 'like' one.[94] The occurrence of the epithet so soon after this divinised appearance invites and then denies a comparison between the two descriptions: they do not add up. In this present passage, however, whilst spoken by the narrative voice, it is used in a scene focused on the vivid and emotional thoughts of Hecuba. If we take the epithet as a neat example of 'embedded focalisation', then we may detect instead a negative connotation: Achilles, now a god, is 'contrary to the gods' through the brutality of the action that he has just ordered, in the perception of those who suffer as a result of it. On this reading, Quintus not only acknowledges the duplicity of the word – meaning both like a god and/ or opposite to god, as later authors used it, and as Apollonius read it for the Homeric Cyclops – he also uses this double meaning to augment our perception of Achilles' divine status. He becomes one of the gods in the narrative, but in the lived experience of its characters, he is still (just) like the gods, or even acting against them. Through the doubleness of ἀντίθεος, the praise and blame dialectic that Achilles straddled in Libanius' manuals is brought to life in a new narrative situation: its consequences laid bear in his re-animated presence in this poem.

It thus appears that whilst Mansur's conclusion that Quintus had no 'favourite' epithets might hold up statistically, it is far less accurate as an assessment of the individual signification of the terms which the poem employs. The multiple epithets which Quintus gives to Achilles are often finely attuned to their previous Homeric connotations and alert to their subsequent tensions of meaning. They thus offer the reader a focal point

---

[94] A disparity which we are perhaps further encouraged to notice by the use of ἰσόθεος immediately before Achilles' deified speech (δὴ τότ' Ἀχιλλῆος κρατερὸν κῆρ ἰσοθέοιο... Q.S.14.180).

118   Writing Homer: Language, Composition and Style

though which to understand the changes that they are witnessing in this 'still Homeric' epic. An expanded catalogue of epithets becomes a method of communicating what it means to revivify Homer as a process of composition, as Quintus lays bare the responsibilities and repercussions of his task: of 'formulating' these Homeric characters in light of the varied and conflicting strands of their reception.

'Generic' Epithets

In this light, we may briefly consider whether a similar interpretative function is possible for the converse feature of the *Posthomerica*'s formulaic system: the high proportion of 'generic epithets', when a single adjective is applied to a number of different nouns with, apparently, no contextual significance. Given that so many Homeric epithets were invested with significance due to later philological and exegetical excursus, Quintus' broad application of a given term may also mark his participation in this reading process, inviting retrospective re-evaluation of some 'original' Homeric pairings. This may certainly be the case when Quintus, in a Homeric continuation, redeploys 'generically' an epithet which in Homer had – or came to have – very precise connotations.

To test the limits of this possibility, let us return to the adjective which in Homer is famously particularised, but for Quintus would, under the current terminology, qualify for the label 'generic'. As we have seen, πολύτροπος became one of the most loaded descriptive markers for Odysseus in ancient Homeric reception. Antisthenes felt obliged to defend the hero against its potentially distasteful implications, and Plato both affirms its intrinsic connection to Odysseus – whilst Achilles is truthful and simple (ἀληθής τε καὶ ἁπλοῦς), Odysseus is 'polytropic and lying' (πολύτροπός τε καὶ ψευδής, *Hp. mi.* 365b)[95] – and, through Hippias' baffling superlative, provocatively opens it up to a wider pool of assignees. Parry himself cited it as the first example of a 'particularised epithet', in that 'Homer's audience realised straightaway that the poet had special reasons for putting it into his song'.[96] But this almost unique tag can also be connected to the broader scheme of epithets relating to Odysseus'

---

[95] See Strauss Clay (1983): 29; Maronitis (1973): 81–5.
[96] A. Parry (1971): 154. Cf. derisively (?) Jones (1985): 178 'Poor old πολύτροπός suffers ... being invested with a glamorous significance quite out of keeping with its retiring nature. If we do not know exactly what a word means, that is no reason to infer that the Greeks found it loaded with subtle import.' Plato and Porphyry, it seems, would disagree.

mental versatility: πολύμητις, πολύφρων, πολυμήχανος and πολυκερδής.[97] These epithets in the *Odyssey* – all of which under James and Lee's definition would come under the heading 'generic', in that they are applied to more than one character – are inextricably linked to Odysseus: connected to the Greek term *mētis*, they drive at a central component of his ethos, which he shares in complex ways with the other characters who receive the terms.[98] The very concept of *mētis* suggests a web of conflicting ambiguities. As Detienne and Vernant put it, 'depending on the context, [*mētis*] can arouse contrary reactions. At times, one will consider it to be the result of deception in which the rules of the game have not been respected. In other occasions, it will excite all the greater admiration.'[99] It is thus paradigmatic and powerful that one of the earliest re-appropriations of *polytropos* in *poetry* gives the epithet to Hermes (twice, to equal Homer's number of uses for Odysseus: εἰπὲ πολύτροπε Μαιάδος υἱέ ...; καὶ τότ' ἐγείνατο παῖδα πολύτροπον, αἱμυλομήτην...– *Hom. Hymn Herm.* 4.13; 439) – capturing linguistically the conceptual link between the itinerant, trickster divinity and his shifty human 'equivalent'.

Such considerations make this epithet group particularly productive for Quintus. Tracing the instances in the *Posthomerica* of *poly-* compounds related to mental dexterity will firstly enable us to see how unhelpful labels such as 'ornamental' and 'generic' are for wide-ranging epithets in this poem. Secondly, it will allow us to consider how Quintus engages 'proleptically' with the particular themes of the *Odyssey*: the epic which, under the conceit of the poetics of the interval, 'Homer' has not yet composed. The epithets thus constitute a systematic example of language being used to move forward and back across Homeric time.

The *Posthomerica* features a large number of *poly-* compounds. The vast majority of these are connected to suffering and endurance: πολύστονος,[100] πολύκλαυτος,[101] πολύκμητος[102] and πολύτλητος[103] are most frequent. Compounds related to the mind are comparatively rarer, used proportionally far less than in either Homeric poem and compared with other imperial Greek epics: Nonnus, to take a dramatic example, sprinkles

---

[97] See Stanford (1950) and Strauss Clay (1983): 31 on grouping these epithets together.
[98] Especially Athena, Hephaestus and Hermes. See Strauss Clay (1983): 32; Rüter (1969).
[99] Detienne and Vernant (1974): 19.
[100] Q.S.1.300, 1.689, 2.361, 2.608, 5.535, 5.582, 6.412, 7.32, 7.82, 7.385, 11.272, 14.644.
[101] Q.S.1.806, 3.380, 6.263, 10.141, 11.315.
[102] Q.S.3.203, 5.649, 7.20, 7.424, 8.397, 9.173, 9,476, 11.310.
[103] Q.S.1.135, 1.182, 2.341, 5.45, 5.361, 8.411, 10.369, 11.25, 13.319, 13.477, 13.544, 14.557.

120   Writing Homer: Language, Composition and Style

his works with πολύτροπος – using it twenty-one times in the *Dionysiaca* (including to describe the programmatically slippery Proteus, *Dion.*1.14)[104] and a further seven times in the *Paraphrase.*[105]

Quintus, by contrast, uses *poly-* epithets to describe mental characteristics only four times.[106] On each occasion, however, these 'generic' terms[107] are specifically applied and loaded with substance. The first is voiced by Thersites during his rebuke to Achilles for desiring Penthesilea:

> καί τοι ἐνὶ φρεσὶ σῇσι γυναιμανὲς ἦτορ ἔχοντι
> μέμβλεται ὡς ἀλόχοιο πολύφρονος ἥν τ᾽ ἐπὶ ἕδνοις
> κουριδίην μνήστευσας ἐελδόμενος γαμέεσθαι.
>
> Q.S.1.726–8

The heart within you lusts so madly for women that you care for her as you would have for a prudent wife whom you aimed to marry lawfully with wedding gifts.

Thersites' reproach clearly replays his outburst during the Iliadic assembly – an incident to which Achilles makes explicit reference in his response (Q.S.1.757–65). But his use of πολύφρων – the only recorded instance of the epithet for a wife –[108] points towards another Homeric exchange, between Odysseus and Agamemnon in the underworld (*Od.* 11.404–53), where the topic is instead the wisdom and trustworthiness of women. In the Odyssean scene, a related epithet to πολύφρων is used about Penelope: περίφρων Πηνελόπεια (*Od.* 11.446). On the one hand, this wisdom is there presented positively, set in contrast to the evil cunning of Κλυταιμνήστρη δολόμητις (*Od.* 11.444–6).[109] But on the other, this compliment is qualified when Agamemnon asserts the contriving potential of *all* women (ὡς οὐκ αἰνότερον καὶ κύντερον ἄλλο γυναικός,/ἥ τις δὴ τοιαῦτα μετὰ φρεσὶν ἔργα βάληται, *Od.* 11.427–8), and warns Odysseus always to be on his guard (442–3).

Not one word of Thersites' speech echoes this exchange directly. περίφρων is, of course, a highly common Odyssean word,[110] and it may well be wondered how loudly we can really hear it echoed in Quintus' form. And yet we have seen how an expanded view of allusion is necessary for assessing the particular poetics of this epic: how, in constructing the ways

---

[104] Other occurrences: 1.366, 2.208, 5.527, 12.66, 19.219, 25.563, 27.72, 28.7, 28.304, 30.111, 30.299, 31.211, 37.186, 37.451, 39.46, 41.317, 41.388, 42.208, 43.247, 43.408.
[105] 3.12, 4.219, 9.82, 10.54, 12.149, 20.137, 16.35.
[106] Quintus does employ other adjectives without the *poly-* prefix to denote mental dexterity. I am however focusing on this group due to its particular connections with the *Odyssey* and its ancient scholarly reception.
[107] In that they are not distinctively applied to one hero.   [108] Cf. LSJ s.v. πολύφρων.
[109] As she is called at *Od.* 11.422.   [110] It occurs fifty-five times in total.

Language and Formulae 121

in which Quintus 're-routes' Homer's ideological and aesthetic signs, the reader must be open to encountering a variety of ways of configuring and articulating referentiality.[111] And we have also seen in the programmatic songs how the poet favours small tweaks in morphology (μῆνιν Ἀχιλλέος, 14.132) to signal his dual position within and outside the 'closed' Homeric canon. This switched compound provides a limit case for this type of reading. Under such conditions, the use of a wisdom-based compound with the suffix φρων, in such a distinctly female context, can cue the reader to this Odyssean debate. Taken as such a cue, Thersites' new insult becomes a reading of just how undesirable the Homeric 'wise woman' always was. Activating the Penelopean περίφρων, and the negative connotations of this sort of term, Quintus makes this comment a proleptic rehearsal of the 'later' warnings in the *Odyssey*, as the notion of female prudence becomes a sneering insult, refracted through the cunning Clytemnestra, *and* the prudent Penelope, *and* all women capable of such unruly thinking.

Through the focalised speech of Thersites, Penthesilea ultimately becomes a perverse proto-Penelope: perfectly suited to her (would-be) husband Achilles – their symmetrical names, both meaning 'grief for the people', suggest a deep-rooted *homophrosune* – but, via the embedded connections to Agamemnon's advice, inherently dangerous and never to be trusted. We thus perceive through this epithet another example of Quintan morphology combining the effects of retrospection and foreshadowing, as the seemingly antithetical characters of the Amazon Queen and the Odyssean Wife, far removed from one another on the Homeric timeline, are brought into a provocative diptych.

πολύμητις is also used just once in the *Posthomerica*, for Athena during the Wooden Horse ruse:

> Ὣς φάτο· τοῦ δ' ἐσάκουσε θεὰ πολύμητις Ἀθήνη,
> καί ῥά οἱ ἔργον ἔτευξεν ἐπιχθονίοισιν ἀγητὸν
> πᾶσιν ὅσοι μιν ἴδοντο καὶ οἳ μετόπισθε πύθοντο.
> Q.S.12.154–6

Thus he spoke; and Athena, the goddess of many counsels, heard him and made his work an object of wonder to all mortal men – those who saw it now and those who heard of it in later times.

Book 12 is the point where the notion of μῆτις takes on a pivotal role in the plot. Calchas' prophecy announces the need for δόλος καὶ μῆτις

---

[111] See Chapter 1.10.

122   Writing Homer: Language, Composition and Style

(12.20) and Odysseus' plan directly answers that call. The description of Athena here, and only here, using πολύμητις works as a fitting parallel to the shifting themes of the poem, highlighting the movement from military might to craft and deceit. However, the one-off nature of this epithet must affect how we interpret such a shift. (πολύ)μητις does not, like πολύτρο-πος for Nonnus, become a recurring term in the rest of Quintus' poem. Its singularity suggests a theme acknowledged but not obsessively pursued. Read as a marker of an Odyssean poetics of craftiness, the specific use of πολύμητις reveals Quintus' awareness of the epithet's potential to signify this poetics, and to denote a particular type of epic; but its exceptionality shows his reluctance to pursue this poetics to excess. As this Iliadic sequel moves closer to the *Odyssey*, this discourse of μῆτις winds its way into the poem's story, but its terms are emphatically not fully absorbed.[112]

What, then, of the ultimate *poly*-compound, πολύτροπος itself? The term appears three times in total in the *Posthomerica*– a mere increase of one from Homer's restrained usage – in a tightly controlled range of scenes. It is as though Quintus, like Nonnus, takes up Hippias' suggestion that one can legitimately ask 'who really *is polytropos*?'; but unlike Nonnus – who answers, with characteristic irreverence: '(almost) anyone!' – he responds with deep, and deeply Homeric, reservations. It is applied first in the context of Odysseus, not however directly to his name or patronymic, but rather to describe the contents of his mind:

> ὣς φάτο· τὸν δ' ἀλεγεινὰ παραβλήδην ἐνένιπεν
> υἱὸς Λαέρταο πολύτροπα μήδεα νωμῶν·
> Q.S.5.237–8

Thus he spoke; and the son of Laertes, using all of his versatile wiles, replied with wounding words in answer.

During the *hoplon krisis*, Odysseus' mental dexterity is one of the central points of contestation: it is ridiculed by Ajax as useless compared with the more tangible achievements on the battlefield, while Odysseus defends it as an essential counterpart to physical action. It is thus fitting that Quintus uses a term whose mental-physical connotations were so fiercely contested to apply here unequivocally to Odysseus' mental and *rhetorical* wiles: he is, as per the defensive interpretation of Antisthenes, performing as the man of many '*tropes*' in this sophistic contest of words. Employed in this way,

---

[112] The speech of Neoptolemus arguing against the use of this stratagem (Q.S.12.67–72), and his eventual capitulation (Q.S.12.93–103) is another way in which we can observe this idea: this is a poetics which is *persuaded into* accepting the need for *dolos*.

Language and Formulae 123

the term thus marks its participation in a debate on two different levels: firstly, on the level of interpretation, it takes a side in the exegetic disputes over the meaning of the word – clearly defining it as referring to mental rather than physical journeys; and secondly, on the level of narrative, it reflects and enacts the quarrel over thought-versus-action being staged in the contest for Achilles' arms.

The word then appears twice again, both times in Book 12. Despite his central role as architect of the horse trick, Odysseus does not receive the epithet in these scenes. Instead, it is given to Sinon, to describe the Trojans' split reaction after his deceitful speech:

> Ὣς φάτο κερδοσύνῃσι καὶ οὐ κάμεν ἄλγεσι θυμόν·
> ἀνδρὸς γὰρ κρατεροῖο κακὴν ὑποτλῆναι ἀνάγκην.
> Τῷ δ' οἳ μὲν πεπίθοντο κατὰ στρατόν, οἳ δ' ἄρ' ἔφαντο
> ἔμμεναι ἠπεροπῆα πολύτροπον, οἷς ἄρα βουλὴ
> ἥνδανε Λαοκόωντος. . .
>
> Q.S.12.387–91

Such was his cunning speech, and the agony did not wear down his spirit. For a strong man is able to withstand evils that cannot be avoided. Some in the army were persuaded, but others said that he was a wily deceiver, those who trusted Laocoön's opinion.

The connections between Sinon and Odysseus were frequently emphasised by poets interested in re-telling Troy's downfall. Vergil makes clear their shared skills in loquacity (*Aen.* 2.57–144); and Triphiodorus stresses their matching deceptiveness in an ostensibly similar manner to Quintus – giving Sinon two Odyssean epithets, ἀπατήλιος (Triph. 220) and πολυμήχανος (Triph. 291). Triphiodorus does not, however, use *this* epithet – so singularly connected to Odysseus – and nor does he do so in a poem which purports to precede the opening verse of the *Odyssey*. Quintus first intensifies the Odyssean quality of Sinon. The noun which this signature epithet governs, ἠπεροπεύς – a cheat or deceiver – is another key marker of Odysseus' *polymetis* skill in speech. It is used in the *Odyssey* by Alcinous (*Od.* 11.364), its only occurrence in the poem. Whilst the king employs it as an antithetical comparison, to reassure and compliment his guest on his upright character ('Odysseus, in no way as we look on you do we deem this of you, that you are a cheat and a dissembler. . .'), it also serves to remind the audience of the many ways in which such an accusation may in fact be true – in the *Apologoi* which Odysseus is in the middle of narrating, so many victims of his wiles (the one-eyed cyclops, the sun god without his cattle, the abandoned magical lovers. . .) would

124   Writing Homer: Language, Composition and Style

undoubtedly deem him ἠπεροπεύς. The word thus cues a similar ambivalence of characterisation to the term *polytropos* itself. Having established this embedded link between Homer's Odysseus and his Sinon, Quintus then reverses its direction. In this narrative and this poetic context, the πολύτροπος ἠπεροπεύς becomes a playful *anticipation* of Odysseus' complicated descriptors: Sinon was the cheater-in-disguise who received these labels first.[113]

The final instance of πολύτροπος comes after the construction of the horse. The narrator declares that the gods were prevented from destroying the contraption, or from razing the city themselves, because their minds were turned to mutual conflict:

> καί ῥ' οἳ μὲν δολόεντα κοτεσσάμενοι μενέαινον
> ἵππον ἀμαλδῦναι σὺν νήεσιν, οἳ δ' ἐρατεινὴν
> Ἴλιον· Αἶσα δ' ἔρυκε πολύτροπος, ἐς δὲ κυδοιμὸν
> τρέψε νόον μακάρεσσιν. . . .
>
> Q.S.12.169–72

One side, filled with anger, intended to burn down the horse together with the ships, and the other side had the same intention towards the lovely city of Troy. But Aisa of many turns checked them, and turned the mind of the blessed gods towards conflict.

Here 'Odysseus' particular epithet is applied neither to man nor god, but to Αἶσα.[114] The theological role of Fate in the *Posthomerica* has received much recent scholarly comment.[115] However, its unbreakable will can also function more poetically. A figure of restrictive narrative determinism, Fate enacts the predetermined imperatives of the cyclic plot.[116] At this point in the narrative, where the gods are prevented from taking an action whose completion would irrevocably change the course of the Trojan story, Αἶσα acts as just such a narratological border control, preventing the plot from derailing and allowing it to continue as it should. The horse cannot be destroyed, and the gods cannot sack Troy without it, because that is not how the story goes. Describing her as πολύτροπος thus opens up another, more profound, contradiction: this time between the iron grip of the fatalistic plot and the indeterminacy suggested by this twisty Homeric

---

[113] I am not counting Q.S.5.237 as an 'early' use of the epithet for Odysseus, because, as discussed above, there it is transferred from Odysseus onto his thoughts, set at a degree of separation from the hero and his name.

[114] Nonnus also uses the epithet (*Dion.* 41.317) to describe the threads woven by the *Moirai*, but only in Quintus is the adjective applied directly to the personified character of Fate herself.

[115] See especially Gärtner (2007) and (2014).

[116] We return to this concept centrally in Chapter 7.

Gnomai *and Similes* 125

word. The pairing helps to tease out the wider conflicts of this kind, on which the doubleness of the whole poem is based. The inter-Homeric story has to stay on its preordained course, so that we can get to the *Odyssey* and 'meet' the ἀνὴρ πολύτροπος himself. But it is also wandering and unpredictable in its details, derailing its own determinacy before arriving, finally and inevitably, at the final destination.

3.3 *Gnomai* and Similes

We now turn to the two literary devices which have most strongly contributed to the now-dominant interpretations in new readings of the poem: the picture of its non-Homeric 'poetics of excess'. That Quintus uses both similes and *gnomai* in staggeringly high numbers has caused the two features frequently to be grouped together in such discussions of the poem's style.[117] And yet the connections between the devices run far deeper than that.[118] Both *gnomai* and similes are firstly and fundamentally ways of describing the world. As we shall soon see in detail, they both depend on the notion of the *eikos*, a term which contains a complex cluster of meanings – what is reasonable, what occurs frequently or what *seems* true.[119] Hence the importance of both forms to rhetoric, where they are discussed as models for conceptualising persuasion and narrative – for getting the audience on side. For Aristotle, the *enthymeme*[120] represents the quintessential 'body of proof' precisely because it can win over an audience based on premises deduced from accepted public opinion,[121] and this notion of audience complicity – a mutual acknowledgement, a shared and constructed knowledge about how the world is – was central to what *gnomai* and similes could achieve. We have seen in the previous chapter

[117] See e.g. the introductory synthesis in James (2004): xxv–xxix and Hopkinson (2018): ix.
[118] To be clear, the purpose of these introductory remarks is to outline these lines of connection in the most general terms, before turning to the details – with definitions and examples – in the individual discussions below.
[119] See LSJ s.v. *eikos* which defines it as 'reasonable' or 'likely'. For Aristotle, it denotes 'what happens for the most part' (270, *Rh.* 1357 34); whilst in rhetorical contexts it can mean what appears to be true but may not be (cf. e.g. Pl. *Phdr.* 273 d 3–4). For the complicated relationship between *eikos* and other terms for verisimilitude – *pithanon*, and the Latin (not-quite) translations *veri simile* and *probabile*, see Wohl (2014) (esp. 1–14) with full bibliography. My reasons for focusing on *eikos* in this discussion are its origins in and intrinsic connections to rhetoric, which is crucial for my argument here.
[120] Of which, as we shall see, the *gnome* forms a part; and to which similes are conceptually related.
[121] This is particularly the case for the so-called third type of *enthymeme*: a syllogism with a missing premise that is supplied by the audience as an unstated assumption that would make sense of the argument. See Madden (1952); Weidemann (1989); and, on the third type specifically, Benoit (1982) and (1987) each with further bibliography.

126   Writing Homer: Language, Composition and Style

how Quintus harnesses not only the patterns and tropes of rhetoric but also its very impulses in order to enact his poetic agenda, as the reflexive conceit of doubleness persuades the 'audience' of the *Posthomerica* to embed themselves in the problematic reality of its re-animation of Homer. The role of similes and *gnomai* in constructing this reality – and testing the limits of our complicity in it – must therefore be considered as a crucial motivation for our poet's penchant for these forms.

There is, however, a second connection between these two features, of even greater import for the *Posthomerica*: they are both key methods of enlarging a textual space. In other words, similes and *gnomai* offer two ways of *not* progressing narrative but holding it in the stasis of description: through different methods, both devices demand the reader to stop and reflect, stretching out the gap between the progression of narrative events through suspension and delay, and at times grinding the action to a halt. These properties are paradigmatic for the poem of the in-between: taken up by Quintus, they can provide the raw material to construct his interstitial position.

These two shared qualities will thus provide a deeper explanation for the 'excessive' presence of *gnomai* and similes in our poem. Their role in engendering audience complicity in a given vision of the world and their ability to expand the inter-Homeric space render them vital to conveying the poetics as well as the aesthetics of the text; and it is for this reason that the inter-Homeric poet needs them so much.

Gnomai

The density of *gnomai* in the *Posthomerica* – 132 examples, compared with 154 in the *Iliad* –[122] is impossible to deny.[123] Of these *gnomai*, 33 are in the words of the primary narrator, compared with only 3 in the *Iliad*[124] and 2 in the *Odyssey*.[125] And whereas the narrator examples in Homer are

---

[122] Lardinois (1997): 215.

[123] I follow Maciver's total here for Quintus (in Maciver (2012b): 91) and Lardinois (1997): 215 for Homer (versus the smaller calculation by Ahrens (1937): 12–38, who counts only 81 gnomai in the *Iliad*). There are various disagreements and question marks over exactly what does and does not constitute 'a *gnome*' in both texts (should combinations of *gnomai* be counted together or separately? Is all enthememic material also gnomic material, and vice versa?). This is not the place to attempt to solve such debates, or overhaul the inevitably capacious terminology of wisdom sayings. For the sake of consistency, I shall retain Maciver and Lardinois' published figures and focus my discussion on how Quintus responds to the Homeric *concept* of gnomic material, rather than the difficulties of compartmentalising each and every example within the work.

[124] *Il.* 16.688–90, 20.265–6 and 21.264.   [125] *Od.* 5.79–80 and 16.161.

Gnomai *and Similes*

all concerned with the topic of man's inferiority to the gods, those in the *Posthomerica* cover a much greater range of themes: the gods, Fate, bravery and cowardice, social status, age, *kudos* through *ponos*.[126]

For Maciver, this abundance of *gnomai* represents '*the* aspect of the work that amounts to the greatest degree of modernisation of Homeric epic'.[127] His long analysis of the *Posthomerica*'s gnomic material, which remains the most substantial treatment of the topic to date, has provided a coherent outline of the role of *gnomai* in the *Posthomerica*, read through and against their Homeric function. Maciver stresses the importance of their context within the poem's narrative, and above all the ways in which Quintus 're-reads, changes and manipilates' the maxims from Homer to showcase the updated nature of his own 'wisdom'. Maciver roots this modernisation in the Stoic tenor of the sentiments.[128] Through them we gain insight, he argues, 'into the philosophical and ethical assumptions of the poet'.[129] This Stoicising, as we shall continue to see, is certainly a significant aspect of the what the poem 'does'. And yet an issue which remains strikingly unaddressed is the choice of the *gnome* as a poetic device – the vehicle employed so frequently to enact and communicate these 'assumptions'. It is not, in other words, just the Homeric content of the *gnomai* that Quintus appropriates and updates: in order to convey his new, inherited wisdom, he needs to 'modernise' their very *function* too.

We have noted the significance of the gnomic device to rhetorical discourse. It is defined variously in such arenas as a type of general statement: for Aristotle, it is close to a proverb or maxim, employed to prove something, and represents an important source for *enthymemes*, the *sine qua non* of the art of persuasion (*Rh.* 1394a22f). Quintilian prefers to consider it a *uox universalis* (Quint. *Inst.* 8.5.3) and points to Cicero to suggest that such sayings can have ornamental as well as authoritative function.[130] However *gnomai* also, of course, have a distinct *literary* presence. A feature of epic from its earliest (Homeric) origins, they function primarily as 'wisdom saying(s), mostly found in the climax of exhortatory speeches, spoken by those famous for wisdom or oratory, whose content is designed to add force to the main argument or add

---

[126] These categories are adapted from Maciver (2012b): 92 n.28.

[127] Maciver (2012b): 84–124. Quotation from James (2004): xxvii.

[128] Maciver (2012b): 87–124.   [129] Ibid: 93.

[130] See Morgan (2007): 84–121 and especially 84–90 on these sub–types of *gnomai*, and the different (and, as discussed above, often problematic) ancient and modern ways of categorising them.

128   Writing Homer: Language, Composition and Style

reason for action':[131] in line with the rhetorical assumptions, the *gnome* thus underlines epic's role in constructing a vision of the world. Because of these properties, a literary *gnome* has two types of application. On the one hand, it operates on a direct context-specific level: it functions within its textual setting and affects comprehension of that setting. On the other hand, it operates on the reader's perspectival level, its meaning interpreted through his or her literary-cultural background. It thus offers a fundamentally integrative mode of communication, which 'persuade(s) the reader to concretise the fictional world, to accept and engage with it as real.'[132]

In the imperial era, so obsessed, as we have seen, with the possibilities for symbiosis between different conceptual spaces, this double valence of *gnomai* caused them to acquire an even sharper cultural function. Gnomic material appeared in school texts at all levels – more educational papyri survive of this type than of any other type of exercise –[133] and *gnomai* provided the subject of numerous anthologies and became embedded in almost all kinds of literature.[134] This very range of uses suggests that the popularity of the device was also linked to its ability to be excerpted: these were parts of, for example, the Homeric poems which could be easily extracted, cut from their original scene, and collected and re-applied to suit any given new contexts. Given this potential, *gnomai* were also harnessed by imperial writers outside of the educational and anthological spheres as a means of communicating the different layers of meaning in their works. In her discussion of *gnomai* in the Greek novels, which also occur in saliently large numbers, Helen Morales has argued that far from merely showing off the author's rhetorical wares or personal philosophies, such material operates more profoundly by displaying the complex, often jagged relations between a story's different textual parts.[135] *Gnomai* in the novels thus act as intensely self-conscious moments, 'where the structure and texture of the texts are illuminated and the surface of the narrative is drawn attention to, defamiliarised'.[136] Such statements form part of the game of how the

---

[131] Maciver (2012b): 89. This section will accept, with qualifications, this 'working definition' of the epic *gnome*, in Homer and Quintus.

[132] Morales (2004): 108, discussing Jordanova (1989): 47. See also Lardinois (1997); Strenger (2004); Boeke (2007).

[133] Morgan (1998): ch. 4. She adds the caveat that an overwhelming quantity of school papyri containing gnomic sayings exists not necessarily because other themes were considered unimportant but because this kind of material was used particularly – if not exclusively – in primary education, a level at which school papyri can be identified comparatively certainly. See also Cribiore's review of Morgan's conclusions (1999).

[134] Homer and Menander were firm favourites as sources. See Morgan (1998): 120–51, (2007): 84ff.

[135] Morales (2000).   [136] Ibid: 70.

novel proceeds: *gnomai* in the mouth of sagacious or naïve characters can be proven false, knowingly undermined by the sequence of events unfolding in the plot, providing mischievous misdirection as much as assuring authorial guidance. Thus, to take just one playful example, Heliodorus' Cnemon both quotes and attacks the famous, unique Iliadic *gnome* on the topic of love (πάντων μὲν κόρος ἐστὶ καὶ ὕπνου καὶ φιλότητος *Il.* 13.636). Cnemon, acting as the novel's current internal narrator, as slippery and ostentatious as Odysseus in his attempts to manipulate a story to serve his own ends, uses this *gnome* to comment cynically on the subjects of his own 'novella': the story of Theagnes and Chariclea, he *thinks*, makes Homer wrong in the assumption that men can tire of love (*Aeth.* 4.4).[137] Through such techniques, the novels play with the basic strategy of audience complicity promoted by the rhetorical *gnome*: the universal applicability of the statement, its ability to 'persuade', is strained and tested as much as it is confirmed.

Quintus reveals himself to be deeply aware of these imperially inflected functions of the rhetorical (and) literary *gnome*: its doubleness both as universal and specific, its pliant and 'excerptable' nature, and above all its powerful potential to challenge the generalised reality it seems to promote. He, too, in ways just as sophisticated as the Greek novelists, his much-lauded contemporaries, takes up the device not just to indicate a philosophical programme but rather to mark and communicate a self-conscious compositional choice. However, what gives Quintus' gnomic reflexivity an extra edge, and distinguishes his practice from that of Achilles Tatius, Heliodorus and co., is that the text whose 'structure and texture is illuminated' is *Homer's* text, as it is re-embodied in this poem. Quintus thus uses *gnomai* in such large numbers because they can highlight his conception of Homeric epic itself, as something able to be reconfigured and recomposed through the creative mixture of its many different textual parts, to encourage *and* challenge the reader's complicity in the still-Homeric reality of the results.

An unusual but particularly revelatory example of this edginess occurs in a *gnome* spoken not by the omniscient narrator, but by a character with his own perspective and agenda. After the death of Penthesilea, Priam seeks to alleviate the Trojans' despair and rejects Thymoetes' suggestion (Q.S.2.10–25) that they should give up and flee:

---

[137] This same Homeric *gnome* is similarly provoked by Nonnus, who claims that Dionysus' unquenchable passion proves that 'the book of Homer lied' (*Dion.* 42.181).

130 Writing Homer: Language, Composition and Style

αὐτὰρ ὅ γ᾽ ἀσπασίως μοι ὑπέσχετο πάντα τελέσσαι
ἐλθὼν ἐς Τροίην· καί μιν σχεδὸν ἔλπομαι εἶναι.
Ἀλλ᾽ ἄγε τλῆτ᾽ ἔτι βαιόν, ἐπεὶ πολὺ λώϊόν ἐστι
θαρσαλέως ἀπολέσθαι ἀνὰ κλόνον ἠὲ φυγόντας
ζώειν ἀλλοδαποῖσι παρ᾽ ἀνδράσιν αἴσχε᾽ ἔχοντας.

Q.S.2.36–40[138]

But he undertook quite willingly to come to Troy and to fulfill all that I required.
And I expect that he is near. Endure, then, for a little while longer, since it is far
better to die bravely in battle than to live a shameful life among strangers.

On the one hand, Priam's *gnome*, the promotion of noble death over a
defeated life, is rooted in its immediate narrative context: it aims to add
force to his persuasion of the Trojans and is triggered by the hope/
expectation (ἔλπομαι) of Memnon's imminent arrival. However, the statement simultaneously reaches to other 'parts' of the reader's textual experience, by making connections of an intra- and inter-narrative kind. These
begin immediately after Priam's exhortation, as Polydamas' reply undermines the simple dichotomy that the statement sets forth:

Ἀλλ᾽ ἄγε μήτε πόληος ἑῆς ἀπὸ τῆλε φυγόντες
αἴσχεα πολλὰ φέρωμεν ἀνακλείῃ ὑπὸ λυγρῇ
ἀλλοδαπὴν περόωντες ἐπὶ χθόνα, μηδ᾽ ἐνὶ πάτρῃ
μίμνοντες κτεινώμεθ᾽ ὑπ᾽ Ἀργείων ὀρυμαγδοῦ·
ἀλλ᾽ ἤδη Δαναοῖσι, καὶ εἰ βραδύ, λώϊον εἴη
εἰσέτι κυδαλίμην Ἑλένην καὶ κτήματα κείνης,
ἠμὲν ὅσα Σπάρτηθεν ἀνήγαγεν ἠδὲ καὶ ἄλλα,
δισσάκι τόσσα φέροντας ὑπὲρ πόλιός τε καὶ αὐτῶν
ἐκδόμεν, ἕως οὐ κτῆσιν ἀνάρσια φῦλα δέδασται
ἡμετέρην, οὐδ᾽ ἄστυ κατήνυκε πῦρ ἀΐδηλον.

Q.S.2.49–58

But come, let us neither live a life of shame and foul dishonour fleeing in exile to
live in a foreign country, nor stay in our fatherland only to be killed in battle by
the Argives. It would be better, even at this late hour, to give renowned Helen
back to the Danaans, together with the property that she brought from Sparta,
and give compensation of double that amount on behalf of the city and ourselves,
before the swarms of the cruel enemy divide all our possessions between them and
our city is consumed in the destructive fire.

The presentation of a third, different, course of action by the seer who
alone sees both past and the future simultaneously (*Il.* 18.250) but whose

---

[138] This *gnome* is analysed under different terms by Maciver (2012b): 89–90, and thus provides a
useful starting point for my dialogue with his readings.

Gnomai *and Similes*

prudent advice Hector recklessly dismissed before his own death (*Il.* 18.284–314)[139] jarringly qualifies the universality of Priam's earlier utterance, in more ways than one. It firstly authoritatively acknowledges the alternatives that often remain un-vocalised in the face of this sort of generalising 'truth'. But, in the mouth of Polydamas, it also issues a powerful reminder that even such authority, the insights and foresights enshrined in the abilities of a seer, can *fail* to persuade, to predict or forestall the bendy turns of fate. The same qualification is later reinforced by the narrator himself. After the sack of Troy, the Trojan captives – those, that is, who did not perish, bravely or otherwise – are forced to depart to die indeed in foreign lands, and the description focuses on the humiliation that this situation brings:[140]

> . . . Ἕτερος δ' ἑτέρην γοόωσαν
> ἤγετο Τρωιάδων σφετέρας ἐπὶ νῆας ἀνάγκῃ
> αἳ δ' ἀδινὸν γοόωσαι ἀνίαχον ἄλλοθεν. . .
>
> Q.S.14.29–31

They each compelled a lamenting Trojan woman to go with them to their ships, and the women loudly lamented and cried out on every side.

Narrated in this way, the Trojan defeat glosses and actualises each part of Priam's nightmare antithesis in the *gnome* (the deaths, the exile, the disgrace), which came about despite or perhaps because of the Trojans' decision *not* in fact to flee. The reality of the sack and its aftermath can therefore prompt backwards reflection onto Priam's exhortation, laying bare just how empty and inconsequential it always was. Whilst cowardice itself is always – in Quintus as in Homer – pejorative in the epic worldview, the specific demand for courage from the post-Homeric Priam – who himself dies in Quintus' account without being θαρσαλέος or putting up any fight –[141] becomes a dark irony, a proleptic jibe at his naivety, which undermines rather than underpins his authority in the assembly, as his wisdom-saying turns out to be a prediction of defeat rather than a prescription for success. By playing with the parts of his own story and contradicting the sententiousness of his own character, Quintus thus begins to interrogate the very fabric of the gnomic device, holding up for questioning the advice that it contains and 'defamiliarising' even the most predictable parts and worldviews of this most predictable

---

[139] In this Iliadic passage it is Polydamas who advises retreat (after the death of Patroclus) – a scenario which Quintus' scene here ironically reverses.

[140] See also Hecuba's lament at 14.289–96, as discussed earlier in this chapter.

[141] Q.S.14.221–50.

132   Writing Homer: Language, Composition and Style

story. This process paves the way for an intertextual form of such contradiction, as the wisdom sayings of the *Iliad* and *Odyssey* – advice not just from an aging character but from a much more 'ancient' literary sage – are themselves subject to interrogation and, ultimately, re-integration.

It is in the poet's narrative voice that the interaction with Homeric truths becomes most insistent. That so many *gnomai* in the *Posthomerica* are spoken by the narrator signals an obvious didactic element: as Maciver remarks, 'the primary narrator points to his understanding of the way the world of the story works'.[142] However, Quintus also tests the breaking points of this didacticism: through the range of themes expressed within the narrator-*gnomai*, he signals that his poem contains, and merges, many different 'story worlds' – including the Homeric and the emphatically non-Homeric – and pushes to the limits his audience's belief in their seamless connectivity.

Towards the end of the first book of the poem, the Greeks allow the Trojans to bury Penthesilea and the other Amazons. Quintus gives the reason that Οὐ γὰρ ἐπὶ φθιμένοισι πέλει κότος, ἀλλ' ἐλεεινοὶ/δήιοι οὐκέτ' ἐόντες, ἐπὴν ἀπὸ θυμὸς ὄληται: no grudge is felt against the dead, but only pity; once they have breathed their last they are enemies no longer (Q.S.1.809–10). The *gnome* reflects a specific Homeric wisdom-saying: at *Il.* 7.409–10 Agamemnon allows the Trojans to bury their dead by expressing the same sentiment:

> οὐ γάρ τις φειδὼ νεκύων κατατεθνηώτων
> γίγνετ' ἐπεί κε θάνωσι πυρὸς μειλισσέμεν ὦκα.

For no man should grudge dead corpses, once they are dead, the speedy consolation of fire.

The fundamental scenario of burying a Trojan warrior killed by Achilles, however, may also conjure up the most famous Iliadic depiction of this sequence of events: the death and delayed burial of Hector, and the *lack* of pity shown by Achilles towards the dead there. Quintus moves to activate this association very specifically. The term κότος, not found in Agamemnon's statement, promotes a type of anger more inveterate than χόλος; an opposition which was frequently evoked in ancient discussions of Achilles' types of rage in the *Iliad*.[143] The verb ἐρύσασθαι (808) also echoes the

---

[142] Maciver (2012b): 93.
[143] Cf. Σ *Il.* 13.516–7: αἰεί καὶ ἐπὶ τοῦ ἐλαχίστου χρόνου τίθεται, ὡς "αἰεὶ δ' ἡνίοχον" (Ψ 502). κότος δὲ οὐκ ἐπὶ τοῦ ἀποκειμένου χόλου. *Il.* 1.81–3 cross-compares χόλος and κότος.

Gnomai *and Similes* 133

visceral aggression of Achilles towards Hector, as he dragged his body through the dust:

> ἀλλ' ὅ γ' ἐπεὶ ζεύξειεν ὑφ' ἅρμασιν ὠκέας ἵππους,
> Ἕκτορα δ' ἔλκεσθαι δησάσκετο δίφρου ὄπισθεν,
> τρὶς δ' ἐρύσας περὶ σῆμα Μενοιτιάδαο θανόντος.
> αὖτις ἐνὶ κλισίῃ παυέσκετο…
>
> <div align="right"><i>Il.</i> 24.14–17</div>

Then he would harness his swift horses to his chariot, and rope Hector's corpse to the rear, and when he had dragged him three times round the tomb of dead Patroclus, son of Menoetus, he would cease again in his hut.

Achilles' anger, the Quintan reader knows well, was not 'sated' by the end of the *Iliad*. After the scathing treatment of Lykaon, he performs the showpiece of his brutal treatment of the dead in this defilement of Hector; and even when ultimately showing pity to Priam, still he rises up in rage (*Il.* 24.559–71). And when he taunts Hector in the moments before his death, he does so by hijacking the communal language of funeral and burial, listing the usual rites and tropes in order violently to deny them:

> ὡς οὐκ ἔσθ' ὃς σῆς γε κύνας κεφαλῆς ἀπαλάλκοι,
> οὐδ' εἴ κεν δεκάκις τε καὶ εἰκοσινήριτ' ἄποινα
> στήσωσ' ἐνθάδ' ἄγοντες, ὑπόσχωνται δὲ καὶ ἄλλα,
> οὐδ' εἴ κέν σ' αὐτὸν χρυσῷ ἐρύσασθαι ἀνώγοι
> Δαρδανίδης Πρίαμος· οὐδ' ὡς σέ γε πότνια μήτηρ
> ἐνθεμένη λεχέεσσι γοήσεται ὃν τέκεν αὐτή,
> ἀλλὰ κύνες τε καὶ οἰωνοὶ κατὰ πάντα δάσονται.
>
> <div align="right"><i>Il.</i> 22.348–54</div>

No living man will keep the dogs from gnawing at your skull, not if men weighed out twenty, thirty times your worth in ransom, and promised even more, not though Dardanian Priam bid them give your weight in gold, not even then will your royal mother lay you on a bier to grieve for you, the son she bore, rather shall dogs, and carrion birds, devour you utterly.

Yet the *Iliad* ends, of course, with the fulfilment of exactly these moves: Hector's body is preserved, not mangled by dogs and, exactly as Achilles describes, it is ransomed, laid out and lamented. Achilles' wish for Hector's anti-funeral is thus emphatically disavowed: like Polydamas' positive wishes for Hector, so too does this threat about his corpse become part of the poem's knowing narrative of reversal, where predictions do not always come true. In this way, the Homeric universality of the plea for peace and the reciprocal respect for the dead is challenged by the echoes of these more belligerent moments from elsewhere in the epic. Quintus

134 Writing Homer: Language, Composition and Style

points to the *Iliad as* a collection of such contradictory moments and signals how, in creating his new narrative, the inter-Homeric poet must acknowledge that the parts do not always fit seamlessly together.

A similar contradiction occurs in a *gnome* spoken during Achilles' funeral games. After Epeius and Acamas clash in the boxing contest, their comrades tell them to lay aside their anger and make amends. As they do so, the narrator explains their compliance:

> ἀλλ' οἳ μὲν πεπίθοντο παραιφασίῃσιν ἑταίρων
> (ἀνδράσι γὰρ πινυτοῖσι πέλει νόος ἤπιος αἰεί)·
> Q.S.4.378–9

They obeyed their comrades' persuasive words (for men of sense are always good-natured).

This is the only *gnome* in the *Posthomerica* on the topic of gentleness: whilst it is marked as a generalising statement (with the explanatory γάρ and universalising αἰεί) it is also exceptional in its content. Gentleness is, however, expressed elsewhere in the narrative – most extensively during that ghostly advice of Achilles to his son Neoptolemus:[144]

> τῖε δ' ἀμύμονας ἄνδρας, ὅσοις νόος ἔμπεδός ἐστιν·
> ἐσθλῷ γὰρ φίλος ἐσθλὸς ἀνήρ, χαλεπῷ δ'ἀλεγεινός.
> ἢν δ' ἀγαθὰ φρονέῃς, ἀγαθῶν καὶ τεύξεαι ἔργων....
> ... νόος δέ τοι ἤπιος ἔστω
> ἔς τε φίλους ἑτάρους ἔς θ' υἱέας ἔς τε γυναῖκας.
> Q.S.14.192–4; 203–4

Treat with respect those who have a blameless character and good sense: good men incline to friendship with the good, wicked men with the bad. If your intentions are good, you will achieve good things... Be gentle toward your dear companions, your children and your wife.

The disjuncture between Achilles' advice to be gentle and his harsh conduct throughout the poem has often puzzled scholars.[145] Re-reading the passage through the *gnome* of the boxing match offers a route through such non-sequiturs. πινυτός (4.379) is the pivotal word for this reading.

---

[144] This speech is itself full of *gnomai*. Other occurrences of the theme of gentleness are found at: Q.S.3.424; 7.89–90; 9.522; 13.448–9.

[145] Cf. e.g. James (2004): 285 and 342; Carvounis (2019) and (2007). The Quintan passage is a certainly a provocative gloss on the famous scene during the embassy of *Iliad* 9, where Odysseus exhorts Achilles to show φιλοφροσύνη (9.256, a Homeric *hapax* not found extensively again in Greek literature until Plutarch): Quintus' Achilles breaks the term back up (φίλος ἐσθλός ... ἀγαθὸν φρονέῃς) and thus points to the original complexity of that compound term. I return to this scene in a different light in Chapter 7.

Gnomai *and Similes*   135

Meaning 'prudent' or 'discreet', the adjective is used far more frequently in Quintus than in Homer. In the Homeric poems, it usually describes Penelope in the *Odyssey*,[146] a specific, feminised use with which Quintus' ἀνδράσι immediately contrasts. There are only two occasions where the term is used for men in Homeric epic, both in distinctively *un*-gentle contexts.[147] In the first book of the *Odyssey*, Athena tells Telemachus that anyone who is πινυτός would be enraged upon seeing αἴσχεα like that of the suitors, with the fiery verb νεμεσσήσαιτο advocating an active, angry response (*Od.* 1.229). In Telemachus' visit to Sparta, he hears the adjective again, as Menelaus describes Nestor's sons as πινυτούς τε καὶ ἔγχεσιν εἶναι ἀρίστους (*Od.* 4.211), again pairing belligerence with wisdom.[148] Alternatively, during Agamemnon's advice in the Odyssean νέκυια we find the word in its 'conventional' Homeric sense (to describe Penelope); however, as we have seen, in the context of an exhortation *not* to be gentle at all:

> τῷ νῦν μή ποτε καὶ σὺ γυναικί περ ἤπιος εἶναι·
> ...ἀλλ' οὐ σοί γ', Ὀδυσεῦ, φόνος ἔσσεται ἔκ γε γυναικός·
> λίην γὰρ πινυτή τε καὶ εὖ φρεσὶ μήδεα οἶδε
> κούρη Ἰκαρίοιο, περίφρων Πηνελόπεια.
>
> *Od.* 11.441; 444–6

'So in your own case never be gentle even to your wife... However, Odysseus, death shall not come upon you from your wife, for very prudent and of an understanding heart is the daughter of Icarius, wise Penelope.'

In the combination of ἤπιος and πινυτός in the boxing *gnome*, Quintus evokes these hostile Homeric precedents. When set against them, his peaceful gnomic αἰεί becomes destabilised and insecure, as this universal decree for deference works simultaneously to remind us that Homeric epic, and Quintus' continuation of it, is also filled with 'wise' men who are anything but gentle.

A final case helps to illuminate what happens when a *gnome* includes not just mixed Homeric but also 'post-Homeric' sentiments, such as the philosophical tenets on which Maciver focuses. In Book 12, as the Trojans mutilate Sinon after his 'wonderous' act of enlistment, the narrator comments on his ability to endure under torture:

---

[146] *Od.* 11.445; 20.131; 21.103; 23.361.

[147] The possible exception of *Od.* 20.228, where Odysseus describes Eumaeus as ὅ τοι πινυτὴ φρένας ἵκει, uses the noun form of the term, with an accusative of respect, rather than an adjective.

[148] πινυτή in the *Iliad* gives a similar pairing, as Hector addresses Ajax as bestowed with μέγεθός τε βίην τε καὶ πινυτήν (*Il.* 7.289).

136 Writing Homer: Language, Composition and Style

Ὣς φάτο κερδοσύνῃσι καὶ οὐ κάμεν ἄλγεσι θυμόν·
ἀνδρὸς γὰρ κρατεροῖο κακὴν ὑποτλῆναι ἀνάγκην.

Q.S.12.387–8

Such was his cunning speech. The agony did not wear down his spirit: a strong man is able to withstand evils that cannot be avoided.

Maciver has naturally read this *gnome* as part of the poem's Stoic discourse, aligning it with the gnomic sayings of Nestor which promote similar ideas of acceptance in the face of suffering and the measured submission to one's Fate. So, for instance, just as Nestor does not grieve excessively upon the loss of a loved one (Q.S.7.44–55), so Sinon is able to withstand and withhold his emotion in the face of hardship. '[They] do not grieve because Stoic prudent men do not grieve. This sentiment echoes one of the basic tenets of Stoicism that the Stoic sage is able to withhold emotions, that he fulfils the ideal of *apatheia*.'[149] And yet this account underplays the plurality of this type of utterance in Quintus: its ability to inscribe multiple, often contradictory, layers of meaning, not just a single notional 'reality'.[150]

Another *Homeric* layer, which receives no explicit mention in Maciver's discussion, must be added to the texture of this passage. We have already seen how Quintus makes use of the long-standing connections between Sinon and Odysseus. In this *gnome* he activates the connection in a different way. Odysseus' association with Stoicism was a well-known strand of his reception in antiquity and became particularly pronounced in the imperial period, with authors such as Seneca, Epictetus, Musonius and Dio Chrysostom all transmitting a Stoic or Stoicising version of the hero.[151] As Montiglio argues, the popularity of a Stoic Odysseus at this particular time is unsurprising: some of his characteristic features, if properly reconfigured, were bound to appeal to a stoically minded 'subject' of Rome, and his endurance was particularly fitting to illustrate how to survive the blows of fortune – 'a universal condition', she acknowledges, 'but one that must have been poignantly felt under the sway of Roman rule'.[152] However, the relevance of the Stoic reading of Odysseus to the imperial psyche need not be limited to a narrow, negative conception of providing solace to Greece-the-oppressed. For through his dress-up games as the beggar, Odysseus can also encapsulate the Stoic exhortation to be like good actors: to interpret as well as we can the parts assigned to us by

---

[149] Maciver (2012b): 109. [150] Cf. Morales (2000): 70 on the idea of a notional 'reality'.
[151] See e.g. Buffière (1956): 316f. [152] Montiglio (2011): 66–94, quotation at 66.

Gnomai *and Similes*

fate, but never to forget that we are wearing masks and that each mask might be changed. Thus Montiglio, more cannily: 'Odysseus is and is not the character he plays: he is, as a committed performer of life's script; he is not, because his "moral purpose" extends beyond each role and protects him, so to speak, from them.'[153] It is precisely, then, Odysseus' 'doubleness', his ability simultaneously to embody multiple perspectives that makes him the perfect Stoic *avant la lettre* for the re-animating culture of this era.

Quintus mobilises just such an image of the imperial Stoic Odysseus to de- (or re-) familiarise his Sinon *gnome*, and by so doing brings the *Odyssey* into this 'later' philosophical statement. Immediately before the present scene, a mini-simile describes Sinon's endurance of blows:

> ...ἀμφὶ δὲ μύθοις
> μειλιχίοις εἴροντο πάρος, μετέπειτα δ' ὁμοκλῇ
> σμερδαλέῃ, καὶ πολλὰ δολόφρονα φῶτα δάιζον
> πολλὸν ἐπὶ χρόνον αἰέν. Ὃ δ' ἔμπεδον ἠύτε πέτρη
> μίμνεν ἀτειρέα γυῖ' ἐπιειμένος...
>
> Q.S.12.362–6

Gentle questioning gave way to violent threats, and they subjected the crafty hero to continual and prolonged torture; but he held firm like a rock, and his limbs continued tough.

The phrase ἠύτε πέτρη/ἔμπεδον occurs in only one other place in extant Greek literature: to describe Odysseus-the-beggar's tolerance of abuse by the suitor Antinous:

> ὣς ἄρ' ἔφη, καὶ θρῆνυν ἑλὼν βάλε δεξιὸν ὦμον,
> πρυμνότατον κατὰ νῶτον· ὁ δ' ἐστάθη ἠύτε πέτρη
> ἔμπεδον, οὐδ' ἄρα μιν σφῆλεν βέλος Ἀντινόοιο,
> ἀλλ' ἀκέων κίνησε κάρη, κακὰ βυσσοδομεύων.
>
> Od. 17.462–5

So saying, he seized the footstool and flung it, and struck Odysseus on the base of the right shoulder, where it joins the back. But he stood firm as a rock, nor did the missile of Antinous make him reel, but he shook his head in silence, pondering evil in the deep of his heart.

Quintus' echo of this scene firstly adds an almost comic note of deflation to Sinon's heavy endurance of gruesome mutilation: his withstanding of violent blows is described in the same way as Odysseus in rags coped with a footstool lobbed in the air. Secondly, it projects back into the Homeric

---

[153] Montiglio (2011): 74.

138   Writing Homer: Language, Composition and Style

original any straightforwardly Stoic reading of the *gnome*. By infusing this statement with an example of a Homeric character's ability to endure, and by merging the qualities of this pre-Odyssean character with Homer's 'later' hero (Sinon is Stoic, as well as polytropic, first),[154] Quintus insists on a stretched temporal setting, a diversity of models for this universal truth. If the post-Homeric Sinon is a Stoic, so too is the Homeric Odysseus, as the passage straddles the space between Homeric Troy and the imperial 'Stoa', and the wisdom of *apatheia* is refracted and re-blended with a different type of 'lesson' from Homer.[155]

Similes

We have so far been concerned with exploring the complexities of Quintus' stylistic 'likeness' to Homer. There is no more suitable place to end such a discussion than with the simile itself: the ultimate 'form' of comparison. The particular importance of the epic simile as a 'touchstone of poetic craft'[156] was vastly and varyingly acknowledged throughout antiquity. The ancient testimony preserved in Eustathius defines this importance in terms of the four main functions of the device: αὔξησις, to supply details and amplify the narrative; ἐνάργεια, to make things more vivid and 'actual'; σαφήνεια, to clarify; and ποικιλία, to vary the monotony or add variety.[157] Precisely because of their separation from the main narrative, similes are always self-conscious in their uniting properties. Like *gnomai*, they insist on the easiness of comparison of what things are like, only to play and subvert such assumptions with new meaning, constantly showing the seams in the links that they draw.[158] This self-consciousness has been detected particularly in the similes favoured by Alexandrian writers – both the scholars who dissected and analysed Homeric examples, and the poets who allusively manipulated them. Hunter, for instance, has shown how Apollonius gives his similes multiple overt correspondences

---

[154] Cf. Montiglio (2011): 74: 'The image of Odysseus the actor-of-life is grounded in his versatility and adaptability: the *polytropos* hero is best suited to interpret the *polyproswpia* of life as fortune or fate demands.'

[155] It is 'different' also in the sense that the original Odyssean passage is not a *gnome* but part of the main narrative.

[156] Hunter (2006): 83.

[157] Eustathius 176.20ff; 253.26ff; 1065.29ff van der Valk (1971). Translations from Snipes (1988): 208–9. See also Nünlist (2009a): 290–1.

[158] Cf. Maciver (2012b): 166: 'Simile, by its very nature, functions on a narratological plain that shows seams.' I agree with Maciver (2012b): 166f that, contrary to Lyne (1989): 68, the simile should be viewed as separate from the narrative.

Gnomai *and Similes* 139

with their subjects in a way that seems 'non-Homeric', and demonstrates how this tendency reflects the practices of the Homeric scholia, who were obsessed with finding narrative correspondences in the similes which they discuss.[159]

The most crucial aspect of the epic simile, however, recognised by both the theorists and practitioners alike, is its strong programmatic power. In manifestations as early as in the Homeric poems themselves, the simile demands to be read as symbolic 'for the cosmos of the whole poem, for it presents an icon of the relationship between human beings and the natural world, which in turn gives us an icon of the poem's relationship between order and disorder, chaos and harmony'.[160] Thus the first simile in Vergil's *Aeneid* (*ac ueluti magno in populo cum saepe coorta est/seditio...* 1.148–53), as has been often noted, reveals itself to be an emblem for regaining order after chaos, a theme set up to be continued throughout the rest of the poem. In its later guises, and particularly amidst the scholarly self-display of the Alexandrian poets-cum-critics, the programmatics of the simile acquired a specifically literary bent. Through its ability to convey a thematics of likeness, a coded form of analogy, the device was readily employed to inscribe a poet's own relationship to his craft and to those who practised it before him. So the scholia suggest that bees are chosen for the first extended simile of the *Iliad* (2.87–90) because there is an affinity between bees and poetry; and that first simile of the *Aeneid*, through its famous reversal of the second extended Iliadic comparison (2.144–9), also shows how Vergil uses the form to reflect both upon the relation between a simile and the narrative which surrounds it, and upon his own relation to Homer.[161] Likeness and difference within similes, therefore, become tools 'to focus issues of literary borrowing and imitation'.[162]

If these functions were long-enshrined in literary practice, similes came to occupy a particularly prominent position in the poetry composed during the imperial period. Oppian, for instance, crams his *Halieutica* with similes, with one occurring every 36.9 lines. The Oppianic similes also exhibit on an even larger scale the mannered parallelism between tenor and vehicle that has been centrally identified with Apollonius, often comparing highly similar items, such as blood described like mud which

---

[159] Hunter (1993): ch. 5; Fränkel (1997): 103. [160] Feeney (2014): 189.

[161] Many scholars have written finely on the first simile of the *Aeneid* as offering a complex programmatic statement about allusion, theme, plot and (poetic and political) power. See especially Pöschl (1970): 20–2; Perret (1977); and Harrison (1988) on the foregrounding of *pietas* and kingship; also Williams (1983): 70–1; Lyne (1989): 178; and Beck (2014).

[162] Hunter (2006): 85.

140   Writing Homer: Language, Composition and Style

looks like blood (5.727–8), or a turtle likened, via a radical leap of association, to a tortoise (5.403–9). Imperial Latin poetry shows a similar penchant: Claudian has 145 similes in his 8,468-line corpus, compared with 105 similes in the whole of the *Aeneid*.[163] Later Latin Christian poetics also found ways to exploit this programmatic correspondence game: to take one particularly bold example, *Prudentius' Peristephanon* 2 uses the simile as a bold *typological* device: amassing, like Oppian, a number of extremely close comparanda (all connected to the radiance of the vision of God), his similes jump around in time and order, so as to pointedly defy an earthly chronology:

> haec fante praefecto truces
> hinc inde tortores parant
> *nudare* amictu martyrem,
> uincire membra et tendere. (360)
> illi os decore splenduit
> fulgorque circumfusus est.
> talem reuertens legifer
> de monte uultum detulit,
> Iudaea quem plebs aureo (365)
> boue inquinata et decolor
> expauit et faciem retro
> detorsit inpatiens Dei.
> talemque et ille praetulit
> oris corusci gloriam (370)
> Stephanus per imbrem saxeum
> caelos apertos intuens.
> inluminatum hoc eminus
> recens piatis fratribus,
> baptisma quos nuper datum (375)
> Christi capaces fecerat;
>
> *Perist.* 2.357–76

While the prefect was thus speaking, the cruel tormentors all around were making ready to strip the martyr of his robe and bind his limbs and stretch them out. His face shone with beauty and glory was all around him. Such was the countenance that the bearer of the law brought down from the mountain on his return, and the Jewish people, having stained and tarnished themselves with thegolden ox, were greatly afraid of him and turned their face away because they could not bear the presence of God. Such again was the glory which Stephen presented shining on his face as amid the rain of stones he gazed at the open heavens. This was made

---

[163] Which at 9898 lines is longer than Claudian's entire corpus.

Gnomai *and Similes* 141

visible farther off to the breathren lately cleansed from sin, whom baptism given recently had made fit to receive Christ.[164]

Late Antique poetry was thus particularly alert to the functions and capabilities of the epic simile. Recurring in such high numbers, the comparisons in these texts work to push at the boundaries between what things are and what they resemble, constantly opening up and closing again the gap between signifier and signified. For Quintus, these ideas are overwhelmingly relevant. Once more, we can witness in the *Posthomerica* an 'early' instantiation of techniques which soon become so strongly but differently associated with Roman and Christian textual practices. As with *gnomai*, the high volume of similes is a demonstrable feature of the *Posthomerica*. With 226 long similes and 79 short, Quintus' text contains proportionally more similes than the *Iliad*,[165] and actually more long similes.[166] Book 1 contains the highest number (35 long and 5 short), and in general Quintus follows the *Iliad* by having similes huddled around battle narratives.[167] Their subject matter also generally aligns with the Homeric material: James estimates that only 10 per cent of the *Posthomerica*'s examples can be deemed 'thematically original'; these include topics such as the partial recovery from blindness (1.76–82); children frightened by thunder (7.530–2); the manufacture of charcoal (9.162–6) and movement of sows to different sties (14.33–6).[168] Quintus also has a tendency to conflate elements from two or more thematically related Homeric similes.[169] In terms of structure, he shows a fondness for 'clusters' – piling up multiple comparisons and including similes within similes –[170] and for parallelism, both between simile and narrative and between similes that occur successively.

---

[164] With thanks to Anke Walter for bringing this passage to my attention.

[165] Which itself has far more similes than the *Odyssey*. See the summary in James (2004): xxv.

[166] According to statistics from Lee (1964): 3–4 and Edwards (1991): 24, the *Iliad* has 197 long and 153 short similes. For the number and types of similes in Quintus, I am following the *communis opinio*, derived from culminating counts and studies. Way (1913): 627–8 provides an Appendix listing the similes in the *Posthomerica* organised by subject matter. Substantial studies on the topic offered by Vian (1954) and (2001). Maciver (2012b):127–8 adds to Way's (incomplete) lists. See also the most recent counts in Scheijnen (2018): 40–2.

[167] Cf. Moulton (1977): 50, and for the *Posthomerica* Maciver (2012b): 128.

[168] James (2004): xxvi.

[169] A process of variation similar to his merging of different nouns and epithets in his formulae, for which see 3.2.

[170] There are seven clusters of four similes (1.147ff; 1.516ff; 1.613ff; 3.170ff; 7.455ff; 7.530ff; 13.44ff); two of five similes (11.362ff; 14.33ff); six of six similes (1.37ff.; 3.353ff.; 5.364ff.; 8.28ff.; 8.167ff.; 8.36ff.); and one of eight similes (= 2.194ff.). For similes within similes, see below. Cf. also James (2004): xxvi.

142   Writing Homer: Language, Composition and Style

Quintan similes, given their intrinsically Homeric nature, always demand to be read against their Homeric templates: Quintus' use of similes in itself bespeaks his emulation of Homeric poetic practice. The literary programmatics of the post-Alexandrian simile is thus of supreme importance for the *Posthomerica*. In a text which so closely adheres to its Homeric source, similes offer the ideal medium to communicate the stylistic and conceptual dilemmas involved in this poet's task: visualising the ideas and implications of likeness. As Maciver puts it, 'the *Posthomerica*, through its extensive use of "Homeric" similes, behaves as a simile of Homer'.[171] This comment, however, is not only true in that, as Maciver would have it, 'it suggests that similes were a vital element in Homer to the constructor of the imitating text',[172] but also because Quintus uses this element as a symbol for expressing his entire relationship to the Homeric poetic space. If *gnomai*, through their claims to universality and excerptable status, demonstrate the poem's incorporation of competing literary-cultural parts, then through their programmatic function as devices of (dis)connectivity, similes help to communicate the nature of Quintus' Homeric verisimilitude: the techniques inherent to his space in between. They thus provide a crucial final example of how compositional features work to construct this *Homeric* 'typological' statement: removing the temporal distinctions between the Homeric world and the poet's own, and also drawing attention to these very distinctions, similes are crucial to driving the impersonation claims of this epic.

To explore this statement, let us take first the most 'extreme' set of similes: the largest cluster in the poem, used to describe the Greeks and Trojans entering the battlefield after the arrival of Memnon:

> ...μάλα δ' ὦκα πρὸ τείχεος ἐσσεύοντο
> κυανέοις νεφέεσσιν ἐοικότες, οἷα Κρονίων (195)
> χείματος ὀρνυμένοιο κατ' ἠέρα πουλὺν ἀγείρει.
> αἶψα δ' ἄρ' ἐπλήσθη πεδίον πᾶν· τοὶ δ' ἐκέχυντο
> ἀκρίσι πυροβόροισιν ἀλίγκιον, αἵ τε φέρονται.
> ὡς νέφος ἢ πολὺς ὄμβρος ὑπὲρ χθονὸς εὐρυπέδοιο
> ἄπληστοι μερόπεσσιν ἀεικέα λιμὸν ἄγουσαι·
> ὣς οἱ ἴσαν πολλοί τε καὶ ὄβριμοι, ἀμφὶ γαῖα (200)

---

[171] Maciver (2012b): 127. Maciver's lucid analysis of the poem's similes has, along with the narratological comments of Bär (2007): 97f, done much to dispel the negative judgements of Quintus' use of the device. However, as should now be clear from my approach to the poem's lexica, formulae and *gnomai*, my analysis here will seek to depart from the conclusions of these previous approaches, rather than merely to nuance their findings.

[172] Maciver (2012b): 127.

Gnomai *and Similes* 143

στείνετ' ἐσσυμένων, ὑπὸ δ' ἔγρετο ποσσὶ κονίη.
Ἀργεῖοι δ' ἀπάνευθεν ἐθάμβεον, εὖτ' ἐσίδοντο
ἐσσυμένους· εἶθαρ δὲ περὶ χροΐ χαλκὸν ἔσαντο
κάρτεϊ Πηλείδαο πεποιθότες· ὃς δ' ἐνὶ μέσσοις
ἦιε Τιτήνεσσι πολυσθενέεσσιν ἐοικώς, (205)
κυδιόων ἵπποισι καὶ ἅρμασι· τοῦ δ' ἄρα τεύχη
πάντῃ μαρμαίρεσκον ἀλίγκιον ἀστεροπῇσιν.
οἷος δ' ἐκ περάτων γαιηόχου Ὠκεανοῖο
ἔρχεται Ἥλιος φαεσίμβροτος οὐρανὸν εἴσω
παμφανόων, τραφερὴ δὲ γελᾷ περὶ γαῖα καὶ αἰθήρ· (210)
τοῖος ἐν Ἀργείοισι τότ' ἔσσυτο Πηλέος υἱός.
ὣς δὲ καὶ ἐν Τρώεσσιν ἀρήιος ἦιε Μέμνων
Ἄρεϊ μαιμώωντι πανείκελος, ἀμφὶ δὲ λαοὶ
προφρονέως ἐφέποντο παρεσσύμενοι βασιλῆι.
αἶψα δ' ἄρ' ἀμφοτέρων δολιχαὶ πονέοντο φάλαγγες (215)
Τρώων καὶ Δαναῶν, μετὰ δ' ἔπρεπον Αἰθιοπῆες·
σὺν δ' ἔπεσον καναχηδὸν ὁμῶς, ἅτε κύματα πόντου
πάντοθεν ἀγρομένων ἀνέμων ὑπὸ χείματος ὥρῃ·
ἀλλήλους δ' ἐδάιζον ἐυξέστῃς μελίῃσι
βάλλοντες, μετὰ δέ σφι γόος καναχή τε δεδήει· (220)
ὣς δ' ὅτ' ἐρίγδουποι ποταμοὶ μεγάλα στενάχωσιν
εἰς ἅλα χευόμενοι, ὅτε λαβρότατος πέλει ὄμβρος
ἐκ Διός, εὖτ' ἀλίαστον ἐπὶ νέφεα κτυπέωσι
θηγόμεν' ἀλλήλοισι, πυρὸς δ' ἐξέσσυτ' ἀυτμή·
ὣς τῶν μαρναμένων μέγ' ὑπαὶ ποσὶ γαῖα πελώρη (225)
ἔβραχε, θεσπεσίου δὲ δι' ἠέρος ἔσσυτ' ἀυτὴ
σμερδαλέη· δεινὸν γὰρ ἀύτεον ἀμφοτέρωθεν.
Ἔνθ' ἕλε Πηλείδης Θάλιον καὶ ἀμύμονα Μέντην
ἄμφω ἀριγνώτω. βάλε δ' ἄλλων πολλὰ κάρηνα.
εὖτ' αἰγὶς βερέθροισιν ὑποχθονίη ἐπορούσῃ (230)
λάβρος, ἄφαρ δέ τε πάντα κατὰ χθόη ἀμφιχέηται
ἐκ θεμέθλων· μάλα γὰρ ῥα περιτρομέει βαθὺ γαῖα·
ὣς οἵ γ' ἐν κονίῃσι κατήριπον ὠκέι πότμῳ
αἰχμῇ Πηλείωνος· ὁ γὰρ μέγα μαίνετο θυμῷ.

Q.S.2.193–234

They charged before the walls with great speed, like dark clouds which the son of
Cronus gathers in the heavy air as a storm is rising. Soon they filled the whole
plain as they swarmed onward like wheat-devouring locusts, which move insatia-
bly over the broad earth like a cloud or a torrent of rain, bringing horrid famine on
mortal men: so numerous and so powerful were they, and the earth was crowded
with men in motion raising the dust with their feet. From a distance the Argives
stood amazed to see them advancing. They at once donned their bronze armor,
putting their trust in the strength of Peleus' son, who went among them like the
mighty Titans. He exulted in his chariot and his steeds, and his armour flashed all

144 Writing Homer: Language, Composition and Style

around like lightning. Just as Helius, bringer of light to mortals, shines brightly in the heavens as he comes from the bounds of Ocean which surrounds the world, and the sky and the nourishing earth rejoice: just so the son of Peleus dashed among the Argives. Among the Trojans likewise moved the warrior Memnon just like a raging Ares; and his troops eagerly kept pace with their king as he led the charge. Soon the long lines of Trojans and Danaans alike were struggling, and the Ethiopians most notably of all. They fell all together upon their foes with a great clamour, like waves of the sea whipped up in the winter season by all the winds at once. Casting their polished spears, each side began slaughtering the other in a blaze of groans and clamor. Just as rivers in spate groan and roar as they pour down to the sea, when Zeus sends the heaviest rain among the rolling thunder of colliding clouds and fiery flashes of lightning: just so the broad earth resounded beneath the fighters' feet, and fearsome shouting sped up into the divine air, so dreadful was the clamour made on each side. Then Peleus' son slew Thalius and noble Mentes, both warriors of renown, together with many other victims: just as a violent subterranean wind strikes caves, and everything underground from its very foundations is at once reduced to rubble, and the earth quakes to its depths: just so quick death laid those victims low in the dust, killed by the spear of Peleus' son, so great was his anger.

A string of related similes creates a series of individual impressions, but when taken together, it also enlarges upon or varies (in the vein of the ποικιλία promoted by the rhetoricians) the overall picture to which the images contribute. In his analysis of a different cluster in the *Posthomerica* (Q.S.1.5–81) Maciver demonstrates the close connectivity between the different points of comparison and suggests that 'by a series of related similes (we don't get anything as measured or precise in Homer) the series also unifies the narrative on account of its tightly controlled thematic progression.'[173] The images in this accumulation also appear to be strongly internally motivated: gathering clouds prompt the image of a swarm of locusts, which itself prompts another image of an amassing cloud; Achilles' armour flashing like lightning produces ideas about the sun 'that lightens all the world from the furthest bounds of the Ocean', which relates the comparison of the sound of the armies colliding to the crash of waves of sea, triggering similarly watery ideas of rivers roaring; before we move to the man-made realms of knives and toppling buildings.

On closer inspection, however, the connections are more frayed and precarious than this initial movement suggests. The serene progression from one comparison to the next is first undermined by competing points of reference, creating a layered and overlapping effect. The Trojans

---

[173] Maciver (2012b): 139.

Gnomai *and Similes*

descend like a cloud *or* like a rainstorm (198); and miniature sub-comparisons are embedded into the fully elaborated similes (...τοῦ δ' ἄρα τεύχη/πάντη μαρμαίρεσκον ἀλίγκιον ἀστεροπῆσιν, 207–8). Quintus thus harnesses the use of alternatives in similes – a common method of elaboration –[174] to create a disorienting, not just reinforcing, effect. Some of the similes are also split between different characters, switching tenor as the perspective of the scene changes. For instance, after the series centred on Achilles, the object of comparison then becomes Memnon (211–2). Memnon, however, does not receive similes of his own. Instead with the parallel τοῖος Πηλέος υἱός. ὡς δὲ καί ... Μέμνων (211) he is made to share Achilles' imagery, as the same comparison serves heroes fighting on opposite sides of the war.

These techniques are, undoubtedly, not exceptional to the *Posthomerica* and much ink has been spilled on the artistry of simile groupings from the *Iliad* onwards.[175] What is distinctive, however, and most pertinent to the effects that Quintus is seeking to convey, is the contrast that emerges between the explicit 'closeness' of the similes – revealed in their structural density (occurring one after the other in close proximity) and straightforward thematic links – and the distance implied by the competing perspectives and differences in scale. The reader is thus simultaneously propelled forwards by the cluster's onward movement and pulled back by the momentary difficulty in ascertaining who or what is being compared to whom. Through such effects this hyper-cluster emphasises to the extreme (not, that is, to excess) the simile's function as a delayer of action and suspender of narrative: even when describing motion, as here, it makes things stand still. The sheer size of this simile segment, at such an early, fast-paced part of the story, forces such readerly stasis: we cannot, even if we wanted to, skim past it.[176]

In this way, the cluster simile and the simile-within-simile are forms which have a special power for the poetics of the interval: through their dizzying effects on narrative temporality (as images swirl but nothing moves), their aggressive multiplication, their constantly shifting points of comparison, they have an energy that extends beyond *enargia* – adding nodes of disorientation and doubt, not clarity. The ways in which these forms thus debase steady loci of comparison, and make it deliberately hard

---

[174] See e.g. the extensive discussion in Scott (2009), esp. 21–36 and 94–117.

[175] Cf. e.g. Moulton (1977): 27–33 and Edwards (1991): 31 and Scott (2009): 94–117 on the effects of cluster similes in the *Iliad*.

[176] We return to the temporal implications of these effects in Chapter 7.

146 Writing Homer: Language, Composition and Style

to pinpoint the exact likeness at play, operate on the same levels as the techniques of doubleness which characterise Quintus' mimetic effects: Quintus' position as 'still Homer', like the sophist who is not and not not Demosthenes. Imperial Greek doubleness too achieves its effects precisely by putting pressure on the mechanisms involved in 'being like'.

As an extended form of the extended simile – the archetypal epic device – this passage thus provides an embedded version of the generic self-referentiality that we witnessed, for instance, in the sophist's speeches and on the tragic stage. It becomes almost a simile of similes, a key for how to engage with the effects produced by the device in the rest of the poem. The tense, expanded space created by this sequence of comparisons offers a structural parallel for the contradictory forces underpinning the whole Quintan text, which from its outset is both intent on pressing forwards (ὡς ἤδη στονόεντι καταιθομένης πυρὶ Τροίης, Q.S.1.17) and obsessed with looking back to its complicated, shifting relationship with the Iliadic past (Εὖθ' ὑπὸ Πηλείωνι δάμη θεοείκελος Ἕκτωρ, Q.S.1.1).

Quintus also encourages a more reflexive reading of similes which overtly blend different Homeric models. The most frequent example of this kind is that of a rocky spring fed by melting snow, which occurs four times in the *Posthomerica*. It is first used to describe Briseis' mourning for Achilles:

> οὔ ποτε τέρσετο δάκρυ, κατείβετο δ' ἄχρις ἐπ' οὖδας
> ἐκ βλεφάρων, ὡς εἴ τε μέλαν κατὰ πίδακος ὕδωρ
> πετραίης, ἧς πουλὺς ὑπὲρ παγετός τε χιών τε
> ἐκκέχυται στυφελοῖο κατ' οὔδεος, ἀμφὶ δὲ πάχνη
> τήκεθ' ὁμῶς Εὔρῳ τε καὶ ἠελίοιο βολῇσι.
>
> Q.S.3.577–81

Her tears of sorrow never dried, but kept falling from her eyes to the ground like dark water from a spring among the rocks above which a mass of ice and snow lies on the hard ground until the frost is melted by the East Wind and the rays of the sun.

Then, Deidameia's sadness for her long-lost husband:

> εὗρον Δηιδάμειαν ἀκηχεμένην ἐνὶ θυμῷ
> τηκομένην θ', ὡς εἴ τε χιὼν κατατήκετ' ὄρεσφιν
> Εὔρου ὑπὸ λιγέος καὶ ἀτειρέος ἠελίοιο·
> ὡς ἥ γε φθινύθεσκε δεδουπότος ἀνδρὸς ἀγαυοῦ.
>
> Q.S.7.228–31

They came upon Deidameia grieving in her heart and pining away, just as snow melts away on the mountains under the unwearying sun and the east wind's shrill breeze: just so was she fading away now that her husband had fallen in battle.

Gnomai *and Similes*

Thirdly, Oinone's weeping for Paris:

> Οἵη δ᾽ ἐν ξυλόχοισι περιτρέφεται κρύσταλλος
> αἰπυτάτων ὀρέων, ἥ τ᾽ ἄγκεα πολλὰ παλύνει
> χευαμένη Ζεφύροιο καταιγίσιν, ἀμφὶ δὲ μακραὶ
> ἄκριες ὑδρηλῇσι κατειβόμεναι λιβάδεσσι
> δεύονθ᾽, ἥ δὲ νάπῃσιν ἀπειρεσίη περ ἐοῦσα
> πίδακος ἐσσυμένης κρυερὸν περιτήκεται ὕδωρ·
> ὡς ἥ γ᾽ ἀσχαλόωσα μέγα στυγερῇ ὑπ᾽ ἀνίῃ
> τήκετ᾽ ἀκηχεμένη πόσιος περὶ κουριδίοιο.
>
> Q.S.10.415–22

Just as in lofty mountain thickets there hardens into ice snow let fall by the squalls of Zephyrus and dusting the many hollows; and the tall peaks all around are wetted, pouring with watery streams; and the ice in the valleys, despite its great mass, melts into chilly water as a spring gushes upon it: just so she, in great distress and dreadful suffering, was melting away with grief for her wedded husband.

Lastly, and differently, during the blinding of Laocoön for the oozing discharge from his eyes:

> τοῦ δ᾽ ὀτὲ μὲν φαίνοντο μεμιγμένοι αἵματι πολλῷ
> ὀφθαλμοί, ὀτὲ δ᾽ αὖτε δυσαλθέα γλαυκιόωντες·
> πολλάκι δ᾽ ἔρρεον, οἷον ὅτε στυφελῆς ἀπὸ πέτρης
> εἴβεται ἐξ ὀρέων νιφετῷ πεπαλαγμένον ὕδωρ.
>
> Q.S.12.407–10

At times his eyes seemed much suffused with blood, and at others to be covered with an incurable glaucoma; and often they would run just as water mingled with frozen snow trickles down from some rough mountain crag.

The image in all four variations combines elements from three well-known Homeric similes.

> ἵστατο δάκρυ χέων ὥς τε κρήνη μελάνυδρος
> ἥ τε κατ᾽ αἰγίλιπος πέτρης δνοφερὸν χέει ὕδωρ·
> ὡς ὃ βαρὺ στενάχων ἔπε᾽ Ἀργείοισι μετηύδα·
>
> Il. 9.14–16

And (Agamemnon) stood up weeping even as a fountain of dark water that pours its dusky stream down over the face of a beetling cliff; even so with deep groaning he spoke amongst the Argives.

> Πάτροκλος δ᾽ Ἀχιλῆϊ παρίστατο ποιμένι λαῶν
> δάκρυα θερμὰ χέων ὥς τε κρήνη μελάνυδρος,
> ἥ τε κατ᾽ αἰγίλιπος πέτρης δνοφερὸν χέει ὕδωρ.
>
> Il. 16.2–4

148   Writing Homer: Language, Composition and Style

But Patroclus drew near to Achilles, shepherd of the host, shedding hot tears, just as a fountain of dark water that pours its dusky stream over the face of a sheer cliff.

> ὡς δὲ χιὼν κατατήκετ' ἐν ἀκροπόλοισιν ὄρεσσιν,
> ἥν τ' Εὖρος κατέτηξεν, ἐπὴν Ζέφυρος καταχεύῃ·
> τηκομένης δ' ἄρα τῆς ποταμοὶ πλήθουσι ῥέοντες·
> ὣς τῆς τήκετο καλὰ παρήϊα δάκρυ χεούσης,
> κλαιούσης ἑὸν ἄνδρα παρήμενον.

Od. 19.205–9

As the snow melts on the lofty mountains, the snow which the East Wind thaws when the West Wind has poured it down, and as it melts the streams of the rivers flow full: so Penelope's lovely cheeks melted as she wept and grieved for her husband who was sitting beside her.

Quintus' use of all three of these models has been duly noted.[177] But the way in which he blends them in his examples remains opaque. In the first three post-Homeric versions the correspondences between vehicle and tenor in each simile are strongly emphasised. In the Briseis example, the totality of her grief (οὔ ποτε τέρσετο) corresponds to the abundance of ice and snow (πουλὺς ... χιών) and the οὖδας of 577 is picked up by the same word in the simile (κατ' οὔδεος, 580). For Deidameia, the use of the same verb (τήκω) in the space of the single verse which joins narrative to simile (7.229) inscribes the close connection between the two contexts. Oinone's grief is described using a more 'systematic' description of melting ice. This elaboration must be related to the context of the particular lamentation – her harshness towards Paris, also lengthily depicted, which has now thawed far too late (Q.S.10.306–26).

However, in all three cases, this close correspondence on the level of narrative is disrupted on the level of intertext. The snow simile is unique in Homer's *Odyssey* and firmly connected to *its* particular tenor: Penelope weeping for the husband who sits beside her. Quintus acknowledges this context here, in these female versions of the simile: Briseis, Deidameia and Oinone are all women whose narratives are defined by the absence and presence of a man: through this simile they thus closely and obviously join ranks with Penelope as women who have lost their heroic 'partner'. However, the additional details of the icy river are drawn from an Iliadic simile which depicts, by contrast, *male* grief, triggered by the obstinate actions of Achilles. Quintus encourages a focus on this disparity in Homeric contexts through the wording of his amalgamations. In Briseis'

---

[177] See especially James (2004): 286.

Gnomai *and Similes*

lamentation, the word στυφελός (3.580), used here to describe the hard ground, can have two senses: either literal – hard, rough; or metaphorical – harsh, severe, cruel. The two meanings are shown in the different uses of the term across Homer's epic. Only found as a verb in Homer (στυφελίζω),[178] in the *Iliad* it invariably describes a physical strike;[179] but in the *Odyssey*, it always refers to the harsh treatment administered by the suitors to a ξεῖνος.[180] Employing this word of mixed Homeric meaning in a mixed Homeric simile, Quintus invites a reading of the term beyond its literal application and a reflection on what kind of hardness is really being evoked: the physical condition of the ground, and/or the emotional harshness of the Iliadic Achilles, as is continued in Quintus' version of the character.

Likewise, in the depiction of Deidameia's grief (7.229–31), the obvious Penelopean allusions (ἀνδρός in 231 provides a clear anchor to the Odyssean ἄνδρα)[181] are complicated by competing Homeric reference points. The overt similarities between Deidameia and Penelope underscore the contrasts in their real narrative situations: the Odyssean irony of Penelope mourning the husband who is sitting right beside her is replaced in Quintus by φθινύθεσκε δεδουπότος ἀνδρὸς ἀγαυοῦ (7.231). Achilles is dead and so, unlike Penelope, Deidameia will always, in the iterative, keep wasting away.

The Laocoön simile (Q.S.12.407–10), however, mixes its Homeric models to produce the opposite effect: not a sense of difference from Homer through superficial likeness, but likeness in the face of overwhelming difference.[182] Transforming material from two pathetic, emotional Homeric similes to describe the gory discharge of a disfigured socket is by any estimation a substantial reconfiguration of the source material. But Quintus also includes some surprising points of similarity to the original models. These all hinge on ἔρρεον (12.409). Here the verb describes the

---

[178] The adjectival form is found only from lyric and tragedy onwards.

[179] *Il.* 1.581 Hephaestus' warning to the Olympians lest Zeus strike them from their seats; 21.380 Hera's reprimand to Hephaestus that it is not right to strike a god; 7.261 and 12.405 Ajax striking in battle; 21.512 Hera to Zeus about Artemis' attack; 11.305 about the west wind striking a cloud of south wind.

[180] *Od.* 16.108; 18.416; 20.324; 20.318.

[181] Other similarities include the comparability of the contexts: a mother mourning the imminent loss of her son echoes that of Penelope in the early books of the *Odyssey* once she discovers that Telemachus has departed.

[182] This simile lacks the usual heavy correspondences between simile and narrative, which could perhaps further flag its 'dissimilar' nature to its Homeric points of reference.

150 Writing Homer: Language, Composition and Style

discharge seeping from Laocoön's eyes (hence the gruesome, in more ways than one, modern translations: James construes it 'from them came a frequent discharge'; for Way, 'with rheum they ran')[183] However, the antecedent of ἔρρεον found most frequently in poetry is not eyes but rivers[184] and is employed in precisely this way in the *Odyssey* 19 model: τηκομένης δ' ἄρα τῆς ποταμοὶ πλήθουσι ῥέοντες (*Od.* 19.207). In his retention of the term in this new simile, Quintus shows how, for all their horror and gore, Laocoön's running eyes – his weeping wounds – are still 'like' the snowy weeping of Penelope.

The Laocoön passage thus offers in reverse the interpretative process in the similes of weeping women. In the female versions of the comparison, the contexts in the *Posthomerica* are very similar to their Homeric models, but the language suggests a divergence, a shift of associations. In the blinding scene, the context is altogether different,[185] but the precision of the wording provides a connection to the Homeric source. Taken together, this group provides in miniature a version of the processes of Homeric similarity and difference operating within the *Posthomerica*, which remains entirely 'like' Homer, but also blends competing ideas from the Homeric texts and continues a Homeric essence using different formulaic combinations.

This same process occurs even when Quintus breaks from his usual practice and includes a simile not derived from Homeric material. The comparison in Book 7 has been considered the most original in the poem:

ὡς δ' ὅτε νηπίαχοι περὶ γούνασι πατρὸς ἑοῖο
πτώσσουσι<ν> βροντὴν μεγάλου Διὸς ἀμφὶ νέφεσσι
ῥηγνυμένην, ὅτε δεινὸν ἐπιστεναχίζεται ἀήρ·
ὡς ἄρα Τρώιοι υἷες ἐν ἀνδράσι Κητείοισιν
ἀμφὶ μέγαν βασιλῆα Νεοπτόλεμον φοβέοντο...

Q.S.7.530–4

Just as when young children cower round their father's knees when they hear great Zeus' thunder pealing from the clouds, and the sky rumbles frightfully: just so the sons of the Trojans took refuge from Neoptolemus' missiles among the Cetaeans around that great king.

This simile, describing the Trojans huddling round Eurypylus out of fear of Neoptolemus, has no obvious precedent, and is argued by James to be

---

[183] Vian (1969): 103 is characteristically subtler: 'souvent, ils se mettent à couler...'.
[184] Cf. LSJ s.v. ῥέω (1) (b) and (e).
[185] On this episode in the *Posthomerica* more broadly, and its possible relation to the Vergilian Latin tradition, see Bassett (1925).

Gnomai *and* Similes

Quintus' own invention.[186] And yet the very image of a child cowering near their father does in fact evoke a famous Iliadic scene – but one from the main narrative, not a simile: where the baby Astyanax cowers under his nurse, afraid of his father's gleaming helmet:

ὣς εἰπὼν οὗ παιδὸς ὀρέξατο φαίδιμος Ἕκτωρ·
ἂψ δ᾽ ὁ πάϊς πρὸς κόλπον ἐϋζώνοιο τιθήνης
ἐκλίνθη ἰάχων πατρὸς φίλου ὄψιν ἀτυχθείς
ταρβήσας χαλκόν τε ἰδὲ λόφον ἱππιοχαίτην,
δεινὸν ἀπ᾽ ἀκροτάτης κόρυθος νεύοντα νοήσας.
ἐκ δ᾽ ἐγέλασσε πατήρ τε φίλος καὶ πότνια μήτηρ·
αὐτίκ᾽ ἀπὸ κρατὸς κόρυθ᾽ εἵλετο φαίδιμος Ἕκτωρ,
καὶ τὴν μὲν κατέθηκεν ἐπὶ χθονὶ παμφανόωσαν·

Il. 6.466–73

So saying, glorious Hector stretched out his arms to his boy, but the child shrank back, crying, into the bosom of his fair-girdled nurse, afraid at the sight of his dear father, and seized with dread at the bronze and the crest of horse-hair, as he marked it waving dreadfully from the topmost helm. Aloud then his dear father and queenly mother laughed; and straightaway glorious Hector took the helm from his head and laid it all-gleaming upon the ground.

Quintus works hard to cue the readers to this very different Iliadic moment. His simile echoes Homer's accumulation of paternal and filial terms: πατρὸς ἑοῖο picks up the twice-repeated πατηρ φίλος in the Iliadic scene; the infantilising terms νηπίαχοι reflects the παῖς of *Il.* 6.466 and 467; and the φίλον υἱόν of *Il.*6.474 is captured in Quintus' reference to the Trojans as Τρώιοι υἷες when he resumes the main narrative (Q.S.7.533). The mention of Zeus, as the cause of the storm which triggers the children's fear, also nods to Hector's prayer immediately after the meeting: εἶπε δ᾽ ἐπευξάμενος Διί τ᾽ ἄλλοισίν τε θεοῖσι, ... *Il.* 6.475.

Now, the reunion of Hector and his family was renowned for its transferral of military imagery into a domestic setting. The scholia preserve a fragment which shows how Astydamas' lost tragedy *Hector* took full advantage of the double polemical/ pathetic potential of the scene, as Hector asks a servant to move his helmet completely out of sight, lest his son take fright – retroactively pre-empting the baby's response in the original Homeric encounter (σημειοῦνταί τινες τοῦτον διὰ τὸ τὸν τραγικὸν Ἀστυδάμαντα παράγειν τὸν Ἕκτορα λέγοντα †κοινήν μοι πρὸς

---

[186] James (2004): 310. If he is correct about the similarity here to three lines of a hexameter poem about an autumn day attributed to Pamprepius of Panopolis (fifth century CE) then the image may have had some literary influence.

152   Writing Homer: Language, Composition and Style

πόλεμον δὲ καὶ φοβηθῇ παῖς").[187] Likewise ἀτυχθείς (*Il.* 6.468) describes Astyanax's human fear in a term usually preserved in Homer for horses affrighted during combat, as the infant performs the battle sounds soon to be actualised on the fields of Troy. By evoking this scene, Quintus' simile flips around its pattern of transferal: bringing childlike imagery *into* the space of the battle, rather than using it to move outside of it.[188] He therefore highlights simultaneously the similarities *and* differences between Homeric similes and episodes as they recombine in his poem. We saw in our discussion of *hapaxes* how Quintus uses the specific qualities of that word type to express his methods of expanding the Homeric text. His treatment of similes provides a remarkable and extensive version of such self-expression: as an integral feature of Homeric poetry, and a key signifier of what epic 'is', the still-Homeric imperial poet returns to the feature time and again to signify what his epic is too.

3.4   Conclusions

Maciver's comment that the *Posthomerica* 'behaves like a simile of Homer' is thus true in more ways than he intended it. This chapter has focused on identifying features of Quintus' Homeric 'similarity': how the poet expresses what his text is like in relation to Homer. These aspects, usually cited as examples of un-Homeric contrast imitation, reveal how Quintus constructs his distinctive *Homeric* poetics: choices of language, use of formulae and favoured literary devices operate as indicators of the methods and intentions of the poetics of the interval.

I argued in the previous chapter that one of the driving components of this poetics is the multiplicity of perspectives and positions that it offers for imperial Greek self-expression 'under' Rome. Quintus' lexical system as I have read it constitutes a major example of such a position, engaging multiplicities of meaning, temporality, Homericity. It must therefore now be perceived as a crucial part of the *Posthomerica*'s cultural strategy; where old and new features are not pitted agonistically against one another, but folded back into an intricate system of meaning, mutually enforcing and invigorating. These formal aspects of the poem provide the essential

---

[187] Σ A. *Il.* 6.422a Ariston. = Astydamas fr.2, Snell and Kannicht (eds.) (1986) *TrGF* 1 (201–4). For detailed reconstruction and analysis of this play, see Liapis (2016).

[188] This transferral is similar to that discussed in the previous section regarding Quintus' use of καπύω.

Conclusions 153

grounding – literally, the textual basis – for its broader agenda of 'the middle', and a lens through which we can begin to comprehend its effects.

In characterising these effects, the most crucial conclusion for now is that, in the attempt to place the *Posthomerica* on a spectrum of imperial Greek stylistics, the poem has been identified with characteristics which it does not share. Quintus' means of updating Homer requires a different critical vocabulary than that used for the poets with whom he is too readily and closely aligned. The *Posthomerica* certainly does reveal, as per the now-traditional envoi in imperial epic scholarship, a deep and wide-ranging knowledge of Homeric language, and close familiarity with the props for its discussion.[189] However, he works this knowledge into his poem in a radically different way, harnessing the very function of verbal forms to convey the temporal ambiguity of his position: the duplicitous ambitions of his epic. So, emphatically *un*-like Nonnus, and even unlike Triphiodorus, Quintus uses stylistics not to correct or oppose his model, but to set forth a response more urgently assimilatory in tone, in which the prevailing concern becomes not how Homeric is the poet, but rather *how the poet is Homeric*.

---

[189] Cf. e.g. Miguélez Cavero (2013): 40 'Triphiodorus, like all the learned men of his age, knew his Homer extremely well, and like them, he also relied on certain props for a better understanding of the Homeric poems.' For the different types of *Homerica*, see ibid. n. 9 for full references.

PART II

Quintus as Quintus: Antagonism and Assimilation

CHAPTER 4

When Homer Quotes Callimachus
The Proem (not) in the Middle

The first part of this book has considered how Quintus' interstitial position is expressed in the compositional techniques of the text, and how this position intersects with a cultural environment of mimetic re-animation and performance. Through these aspects, we saw how the poem's relationship with Alexandrian aesthetics can be called into question: the now-familiar critical language of contrast imitation, *Selbstvariation* and linguistic innovation is proving increasingly incompatible with this epic system. The second part will now consider how this position is expressed in poetics: Quintus' engagement with the hyper-reflexivity which appears particularly pronounced in imperial Greek epics – making metapoetics a far from 'dreary' approach for re-analysing them.[1]

We have seen how recent work on Latin poetry has focused attention on the ways in which Roman writers adopt the self-conscious allusivity of the Alexandrians, and how these readings have now been transposed by critics onto the Greek epic of the empire. Therefore, in charting Quintan reflexivity – the ways in which our poet expresses through metaphor his ideas about allusion, identity and succession – we also return from another perspective to the question of his so-called Alexandrianism: this time, via his attitude to the programmatic techniques which have come to be strongly associated with those poets.

The *Posthomerica*, like all epics, has its own pronounced self-referential moments, in which it unveils its critical voice in a fully programmatic discourse. However, in these moments, Quintus does *not* just continue Alexandrian metaphorical techniques: he redrafts the markers of this shared tradition to serve his new integrative poetics, emphasising the Homeric origins of the programmatic mode. Here again is where Quintus

---

[1] Cf. Chapter 1.10, where I considered the revitalised programmatic energy on display in imperial Greek epic. This energy must prompt a revitalised, more reflective use of 'metapoetics' for reading them.

157

158 When Homer Quotes Callimachus: The Proem (not) in the Middle

stands out from other imperial epics: his specific self-placement in and against a poetic tradition shows a particular engagement with competing trajectories of 'modernist' Alexandrian techniques and a 'traditional' Homeric stance that offers a unique vision of how epic can be written, now.

To assess this redrafting, let us first turn to the most intensely programmatic section of the poem: the late proem in Book 12, where the poet's interaction with Alexandrian poetry is also most strikingly on display. The lines repay such close focus: as we must now expect from a poet so committed (on one level) to his Homeric disguise, who employs a mode of contemporary engagement and linguistic change so pointedly subtle and unobtrusive, Quintus' proclamation of his self-positioning is carefully veiled and thus requires careful disclosure.[2]

4.1 Introduction: Quintus' *Quale*

We have seen how through the unexpected absence of an invocation of the Muse(s) at the beginning of the poem, Quintus establishes his connection with the *Iliad*: dramatising the status of his narrative as a Homeric continuation. In Book 12, however, this continuity appears to be undermined. After his narrative of the construction of the Trojan horse, Quintus prepares to list the heroes who entered it before the sack of Troy. Before he begins, however, he breaks off to ask for help, precisely by invoking the Muses:

> τούς μοι νῦν καθ' ἕκαστον ἀνειρομένῳ σάφα Μοῦσαι
> ἔσπεθ', ὅσοι κατέβησαν ἔσω πολυχανδέος ἵππου·
> ὑμεῖς γὰρ πᾶσάν μοι ἐνὶ φρεσὶ θήκατ' ἀοιδήν,
> πρίν γε μοι <ἔτ'> ἀμφὶ παρειὰ κατασκίδνασθαι ἴουλον,
> Σμύρνης ἐν δαπέδοισι περικλυτὰ μῆλα νέμοντι
> τρὶς τόσον Ἑρμοῦ ἄπωθεν, ὅσον βοόωντος ἀκοῦσαι,
> Ἀρτέμιδος περὶ νηὸν Ἐλευθερίῳ ἐνὶ κήπῳ,
> οὔρεϊ οὔτε λίην χθαμαλῷ οὔθ' ὑψόθι πολλῷ.
>
> Q.S.12.306–13

---

[2] Many of these arguments first featured in Greensmith (2018). Since the publication of that article, my thoughts on the topic – as are now instantiated in this chapter – have developed in two main ways. Firstly, I suggest here some new evidence to support the deep and multiform Callimachean allusivity of these lines. Secondly and more broadly, I ended the article by suggesting that 'the proem functions as a map for the imitative strategies of the poem', and that. 'the next step will be now to use this map, and to apply its directions to the other elements of the *Posthomerica*' (Greensmith (2018): 274). By now reading the proem through and against *Posthomerica* as a whole, this book represents one way of rising to this challenge.

Introduction: Quintus' Quale 159

Muses, I ask you to tell me precisely, one by one, the names of all who went inside the cavernous horse. For you were the ones who filled my mind with all song even before down was spread across my cheeks, when I was tending my renowned sheep in the land of Smyrna, three times as far as the shouting distance from the Hermus, near Artemis' temple in the garden of Liberty, on a hill that is neither too high nor too low.

The programmatic significance of this invocation, recognised by all readers of the poem, is suggested by its position in the poem's architecture. Termed by Conte 'proems in the middle', such embedded invocations offer a specific declaration of poetics, dealing with the programmatic as opposed to the thematic, the *quale* instead of the *quid*.[3] Recent treatments of the passage have, consequently and inevitably, focused on this meta-poetic potential. Maciver and Bär, who have provided two of the most in-depth readings of the proem, have found its poetic declaration revealed in its intertextual patterning.[4] As well as echoing the Iliadic address before the catalogue of ships (*Il.* 2.484–92), Quintus' image of the inspired poet tending sheep recalls the invocation of Hesiod's *Theogony* (22–8). A further reference affects this relationship with the Homeric and Hesiodic proems: the allusion to the *Somnium* of the *Aetia*, where Callimachus re-presents Hesiod's meeting with the Muses:[5]

> ποιμένι μῆλα νέμοντι παρ' ἴχνιον ὀξέος ἵππου
> Ἡσιόδῳ Μουσέων ἑσμὸς ὅτ' ἠντίασεν (…)
>
> *Aet.* fr.2.1–2

When a swarm of Muses met the shepherd Hesiod who was tending his sheep by the footprint of the quick horse …

These three intertextual strands have been read as emblems of the main literary models of the *Posthomerica*. As is typical of imperial epic writers in Greek, Quintus does not name other poets,[6] but by alluding to the figures of Homer, Hesiod and Callimachus, he finds a coded way to chart his inheritance and thus constructs a tradition into which he places himself: as he is introducing a catalogue of heroes, he also catalogues his predecessors, those other writers of catalogues. The proem has thus emerged as a programmatic template for the allusive poetics of the poem; each reference

---

[3] Conte (1992): 147–59.
[4] Bär (2007); Maciver (2012a): 53–69 and (2012b): 33–8. See also Boyten (2010): 276–81.
[5] Cf. Vian (1969): 101; Campbell (1981): 100–5; Gärtner, (2005): 23; Bär (2007): 40–52.
[6] Quintus never names poets. Imperial Greek poets tend not to, unlike Late Antique Latin poets. See Maciver (2016): 529–48. Further discussion in Chapter 6.

160 When Homer Quotes Callimachus: The Proem (not) in the Middle

operates as part of a well-directed, emulative discourse on the nature and function of its imitation.

Such readings, however, focus on Quintus' integration of Alexandrian poetics into a predominantly Homeric-Hesiodic framework. The presence of Callimachus, it is argued, points to the Alexandrian influences (here Callimachean aesthetics)[7] in the poem, signalling the poet's aim to enrich his traditional epic by including Alexandrian intricacies among the generic Homeric elements.[8] For Maciver and Bär, Quintus comfortably acknowledges these 'newer' influences as part of his epic source and home.

This chapter will suggest that such readings ignore a far more complex and foundational paradox. For Quintus *both* claims a strong Homeric identity *and* engages with a later poetics that challenges that traditional stance. The proem at the interval of the Fall of Troy (after the horse, before the sack) is the most intense site for the expression of this fundamental doubleness and needs to be seen as a self-conscious commentary on this clashing use of models. By demonstrating the proem's more systematic engagement with Callimachus' programme, I shall suggest that Quintus co-opts symbolic imagery from the *Aetia* to make a highly *anti*-Callimachean statement about poetic assimilation and integration. For Quintus, Alexandrian techniques are deployed to defend a defiantly non-Alexandrian poem and Callimachean tropes are transformed into markers of the Homeric. Here the unique stance of Quintan epic is strenuously and proudly articulated.

4.2 Imperial Greek Epic and Callimachus: Locating the Slender Muse

After Callimachus, the traditional stance of a Homericising poet was certainly open to bitter and sarcastic criticism. The epigrammist Pollianus (first/second century CE) provides a scathing synthesis of the charges which could be levied against the imitation of traditional epic by imperial poets. Disparaging Homerising narrative epic as derivative and mundane, he enrols himself in the freer tradition of elegy and expresses his critique in distinctly Callimachean terms:

---

[7] For the use of Callimachus as a metonym for Alexandrian poetics, in this case in the *Posthomerica*, a method which I employ self-consciously and in full awareness of the issues at stake in such a move, see 4.2.

[8] For this view see Bär (2007): 47–51; Maciver (2012a): 64–8; Maciver (2012b): 33–8.

Imperial Greek Epic and Callimachus: the Slender Muse

Τοὺς κυκλίους τούτους, τοὺς αὐτὰρ ἔπειτα λεγοντας,
   μισῶ, λωποδύτας ἀλλοτρίων ἐπέων.
καὶ διὰ τοῦτ' ἐλέγοις προσέχω πλέον· οὐδὲν ἔχω γὰρ
   Παρθενίου κλέπτειν ἢ πάλι Καλλιμάχου.
θηρὶ μὲν οὐατόεντι γενοίμην, εἴ ποτε γράψω,
   εἴκελος, ἐκ ποταμῶν χλωρὰ χελιδόνια.
οἱ δ' οὕτως τὸν Ὅμηρον ἀναιδῶς λωποδυτοῦσιν,
   ὥστε γράφειν ἤδη μῆνιν ἄειδε, θεά.

Anth. Pal. 11.130

I hate these cyclic poets who say 'but nonetheless', plunderers of the verses of others, and so I pay more attention to elegies, for there is nothing I want to steal from Callimachus or Parthenius. Let me become like an 'eared beast' if ever I write 'from the rivers yellow king-cup'. But these epic poets plunder Homer so shamelessly that they already write 'Sing, O Goddess, the wrath.'[9]

Debates over how far the cherished modern generalisations about Callimachus' poetics stand up to scrutiny against real ancient conceptions of his work are deep-rooted and well-known. That is, can Callimachus' name really be taken as a metonym for the innovating intentions of Hellenistic poets? Does he really signal a radical break with the past and a shift away particularly from the large-scale, traditional conventions of Homeric epic? As Hunter, for example, rightly cautions, the poetry of Callimachus, his contemporaries and their successors, 'attempts recuperation [of archaic poetic forms] at least as much as it glories in difference'.[10] This fact, further complicated by our lack of much of the Greek poetry written between the high Hellenistic age and the Augustan era, means that it would be an overstretch – and perhaps even an anachronism – to assert without question that the subsequent poetic tradition (Greek and Roman) experienced Hellenistic poetry as drastically different from its archaic and classical forerunners.[11]

And yet Pollianus' poem also cautions against overstretching such cautions. His explicit attack on the repetition of Homeric structure,

---

[9] Translation adapted from Paton (1918).   [10] Hunter (2006): 4.

[11] Hunter (2006): 4–5: 'The idea that Alexander's death had wrought a profound change in poetry seems to be a later critical product than similar reflections in the history of rhetoric.' He pushes this point further in the Afterword (142–3), questioning how far Roman writers actually really experienced Hellenistic poets as *chronologically* different from their forebears either. See also the review of this argument by Clauss (2007). This is not the place to rehearse the wider tenets of such debates. On the importance to the Roman reception of Callimachus (on which Hunter's discussion is naturally focused) of the self-fashioning of the Roman 'neoterics', see Hinds (1998): 74–83, who offers a lucid synthesis and further bibliography. On the wider conception of the Alexandrian *avant garde*, see the survey in Fantuzzi and Hunter (2004): 462–7, again with further bibliography. On the Greek side more specifically, see discussion to follow.

162 When Homer Quotes Callimachus: The Proem (not) in the Middle

diction and form, and his explicit citation of Callimachus – both stylistically (in the choice of elegy) and personally, via the use of his name – as the antithesis to such a practice, provides a paradigm for reading Callimachean poetics as precisely signalling a radical break with the traditional epic past. Surviving evidence from the opening centuries CE suggests that, in the Greek tradition at least, Pollianus was swimming with the tide: Greek hexameter poets seem mainly to have followed, and fewer to have flouted, Callimachean precepts.[12] We have seen in the previous chapter how those who did take on Trojan themes and adopt the Homeric style often disassociated their works from notions of mindless plundering through lexical innovation. And it is being increasingly recognised that such poets actively associated these moves with Callimachus and his 'school' of new, small, scholarly-minded poetry. Gerlaud, for instance, reads Callimachus and especially the *Aetia* as an important model for Triphiodorus' *Sack of Troy*, expressed particularly in the poet's choice of epyllion and attendant short, compressed aesthetics.[13] Other scholars have highlighted the sustained presence of Callimachean phraseology in both Triphiodorus and Colluthus, suggesting an intertextual interest which both emphasises and extends beyond a poetics of brevity.[14] Just as the imperial Iliac Tablets 'visualize the thoroughly Hellenistic concern with *multum in parvo*' and embody 'the "contrast of extremes" that characterizes Callimachean *leptotes*',[15] so too does the imperial epyllion exploit the verbal and visual associations of Callimachus to articulate these authors' own concern with 'combining the big with the small, and the small with the big'.[16]

'Beyond such structural-lexical nods, imperial Greek poets further signal their self-conscious engagement with Callimachus through the use of the programmatic aspects of his *oeuvre*, particularly the symbolic imagery of the *Aetia*, and its central, but contentious, rejection of the long epics represented by 'one continuous song'.[17] Maciver's analysis of Triphiodorus discusses how he appropriates Callimachus in precisely this way: taking up the *Aetia*'s most programmatic passages to indicate that *The Sack of Troy* marks a shift from the epics which precede it, thus articulating his literary programme 'through the polemics and poetics' of Callimachean Alexandria.[18] To take just one illustrative instance,

---

[12] See Bowie (1990), especially 54–5 and 90.   [13] Gerlaud (1982).
[14] See de Stefani and Magnelli (2011): 553; Miguélez Cavero (2013): 62 on Triphiodorus; and Cadau (2015) on Colluthus. For a less convincing stance on Callimachus and Triphiodorus, see Tomasso (2012): 383–4, for whom '[Callimachus is relevant] only in terms of length'.
[15] Squire (2011): 23.   [16] Ibid.   [17] fr.1.3. Further sustained discussion in 4.3.
[18] Maciver (2020) as discussed in Chapter 3.

Imperial Greek Epic and Callimachus: the Slender Muse   163

beginning his poem with the word τέρμα – meaning both the 'end' and the turning post in a chariot race – Triphiodorus makes extensive use of the *Aetia*'s metaphor of chariot-as-poetry. The driving of the horse/poem – ἱππήλατον, line 2 – specifically recalls Callimachus' double use of the same verb:[19]

> πρὸς δέ σε] καὶ τόδ' ἄνωγα, τὰ μὴ πατέουσιν ἅμαξαι
> τὰ στείβειν, ἑτέρων ἴχνια μὴ καθ' ὁμά
> δίφρον ἐλ]ᾶν μηδ' οἶμον ἀνὰ πλατύν, ἀλλὰ κελεύθους
> ἀτρίπτο]υς, εἰ καὶ στειγοτέρην ἐλάσεις.
> *Aet.* 1 fr. 25–8

Besides, I also urge you to go where big wagons never go, to drive your chariot not in the same tracks as others and not along a wide road, but also untrodden paths, even if you will drive it along a more narrow one.

If Triphiodorus tracks in his miniature epic such footprints on Callimachus' pathways, then Nonnus stamps far more noisily across this terrain. The *Dionysiaca*, of course, exhibits anything but a poetics of brevity. However, Nonnus also draws deeply on ideas and images from Callimachus to set the tone of his paradoxical, polymorphic poetics.[20] Particularly striking in this respect is the figure of Typhon, who in the first two books attempts to overthrow world order by appropriating the thunderbolts of Zeus. Shorrock has read this assault as a metaphor for Nonnus' undertaking in his poem, and his challenge to the existing order of Homeric epic.[21] The thunderbolt is crucial to this image, as Nonnus taps the connection between thunder and epic poetry as it is formulated in Callimachus' famous dictum:

> μηδ' ἀπ' ἐμεῦ διφᾶτε μέγα ψοφέουσαν ἀοιδήν
> τίκτεσθαι· βροντᾶν οὐκ ἐμόν, ἀλλὰ Διός.
> *Aet.* 1 fr.19–20

Do not look for a loud sounding song to be born from me; Thundering is not my job but Zeus'.

The Dionysiac poet even literalises this connection – laying bare, in typical Nonnian fashion, the terms of his metaphorical language – when he compares the stolen weapons to musical instruments: πηκτίδα σὴν ἔχε

---

[19] This chariot imagery is traceable back to Pindar but given a specifically Callimachean flavour in Triphiodorus. I return more centrally to a discussion of Triphiodorus' programmatic imagery in Chapter 7.

[20] On such forceful paradoxes in Nonnus' self-conception, see generally Shorrock (2001); Lasek (2016); Acosta-Hughes (2016).

[21] Shorrock (2001): 121–5.

164 When Homer Quotes Callimachus: The Proem (not) in the Middle

μοῦνος, ἐπεὶ λάχεν ἄλλο Τυφωεύς/ὄργανον αὐτοβόητον Ὀλύμπιον. . .
Dion. 1.431–2.[22] Nonnus thunders out Callimachus in his 'self-shouted'
language.

As such examples make clear, despite all the unresolved debates surrounding Callimachus' ancient reception, and concerning the level of
'anti-epic' sentiment in the Aetia's own programme,[23] in terms of reception rather than conception, his stylistic proclamations could be activated
by later Greek composers as critiques of writing traditional epic poetry,
forming the implicit – and sometimes explicit – backdrop to charges of
bland imitation and their responses.

How, then, does Quintus engage with such a various engagement with
Callimachean principles? Compared with the fundamentally Alexandrian
epic of Apollonius, the epyllia's agenda of brevity, or Nonnus' multifarious
redrafting, the Posthomerica's compatibility with Callimachean aesthetics is
even more difficult to pin down.[24] At fourteen books, the poem could
certainly fall into the category of τὸ μέγα βιβλίον against which Callimachus railed. Its subject matter could also be described as 'cyclic' in,
potentially, the sense that incurred Callimachus' anger (ἐχθαίρω τὸ
ποίημα τὸ κυκλικόν).[25] Vian thus makes clear where he believes Quintus
lies in relation to Callimachus: in his reading, Quintus has no taste for the
learned poetics of the Callimachean school and his conception of epic is
exactly what Callimachus fought against.[26]

Recent work, however, has begun to question this conclusion. We have
seen how recent accounts, keen to rehabilitate Quintus into the canon of
admired authors, have connected the Posthomerica's philological techniques with the privileged practices of Alexandrian poets. Other scholars,
in the same spirit of reading, have drawn attention to further Alexandrian
aspects of the poem: references to Hellenistic authors, self-conscious

[22] Nonnus also makes use of the Callimachean imagery of the chariot: at Dion. 1.310–14 Typhon
becomes a novice driver trying to control a bit-shy horse.
[23] Among the strongest arguments against an anti-epic agenda remain those of Hutchinson (1988) and
Cameron (1995). Relevant discussion for the Posthomerica in Maciver (2012a): 67. The most relevant
points of contention in this 'anti-epic' question will be addressed in the discussion in 4.3.
[24] I am here adhering to Maciver's (2012a): 67–8 conception of Apollonius as 'typically Alexandrian'
from an imperial Greek poetic perspective, in this chronological sense at least.
[25] On the meaning of κυκλικόν in the epigram, see e.g. Hopkinson (1988): 86; Goldhill (1991):
223–34; and Cameron (1995): 387–402
[26] Vian (1969): xl: 'on a dit qu'il ne goûte pas la poésie savante et artiste de l'école callimachéene; sa
conception de l'épopée est celle-là même que combattait Callimaque'. Such a reading accepts
without any of the judicious demurrals which I have discussed above that the subsequent
Graeco-Roman tradition took these Callimachean terms as the same qualitative judgements on
poetic form as modern scholarship has done.

Imperial Greek Epic and Callimachus: the Slender Muse   165

techniques of allusion and learned intertextual intricacies.[27] Through the integration of such features, Quintus is once again aligned more closely with his imperial Greek siblings, this time on a poetic as well as philological level: putting forward his response to the charge of 'Homeric plundering', he augments his hyper-Homeric style and subject matter with elements aligned with the allusive techniques and slender Muse of Callimachus.

This line of reading, however, leaves unresolved one of the most fundamental aspects of the *Posthomerica*: its implicit claim to Homeric authorship and self-presentation as the middle part of Homer's epic canon. The previous chapters have stressed the importance and implications of this claim.[28] We return to now it from an intertextual perspective, since Quintus' self-depiction as 'still Homer' must also affect the tone in which we take his engagement with any later literature. If all intertextuality is paradoxical, in that an author signals the inclusion of a literary voice that is within and yet separate from their own, then in Quintus this paradox is all-engulfing and overwhelming.

The proem of Book 12 represents the most intense locus of this paradox. On the one hand, the passage contains a strong concentration of the 'Alexandrian' characteristics which have now come to be identified with the poem. Its very status as an embedded programmatic proem is a reflection of a mode of expression rooted in the influence of the Alexandrian poets.[29] Its literary nexus – referring to multiple sources, requiring a breadth of reading to unlock a culminating incorporation of texts – also suggests an Alexandrian-style intricacy of intertextual play.[30] And it contains the poem's most explicit 'quotation' of Callimachus, evoking a pre-existing intertextual relationship by alluding to a passage where Callimachus comments on his own place in the chain of literary reception. Yet this is also the moment where Quintus comes closest to making a direct claim to Homeric identity. The mention of Smyrna (310) has long been recognised as an allusion to one of Homer's most celebrated mythological birthplaces.[31] The surrounding details add intensity to this Homeric self-

---

[27] Vian himself, (1959): 101–10, suggests many Hellenistic models and sources for the poem. On the use of Apollonian material in Quintus, see Maciver (2012a), which focuses particularly on similes.

[28] See Chapter 1.3–6.

[29] Conte (1992):157: 'under the terms of the post-Alexandrian code of literary conduct, poets could no longer ignore their self-reflective consciousness'.

[30] So Maciver (2012b): 67–8.

[31] Cf. Pseudo-Herodotus *Vit. Hom.* 19–21; Pseudo-Plutarch *Vit. Hom.* 17–20; *A.P.* 9.672; 11.422; 16.295–8; 16.320. It was also an important culture centre in the second sophistic. Further discussion in Bär (2007): 52–5.

166 When Homer Quotes Callimachus: The Proem (not) in the Middle

indexing.[32] The Hermus (311) was a river closely associated in antiquity with Smyrna.[33] The reference to the Temple of Artemis (312) could also hint at the link between the goddess and Homer's birthplace on the river Meles, as is established in archaic poetry in the *Homeric Hymn to Artemis*:[34]

> Ἄρτεμιν ὕμνει, Μοῦσα, κασιγνήτην Ἑκάτοιο.
> παρθένον ἰοχέαιραν, ὁμότροφον Ἀπόλλωνος,
> ἥ θ᾽ ἵππους ἄρσασα βαθυσχοίνοιο Μέλητος
> ῥίμφα διὰ Σμύρνης...
>
> *Hom. Hymn.* 9.1–4

Sing, Muse, of Artemis, sister of the far-shooter, the virgin pourer of arrows, reared with Apollo, who after watering her horses at the reedy Meles drives her chariot all of gold swiftly through Smyrna...[35]

Now in one sense, such details may seem to *remove* any possibility of genuine Homeric authorship. The 'real' poet's voice of the *Iliad* and the *Odyssey* was of course frustratingly distant and famously anonymous – so the act of constructing his *Vita* was always already an act of reception. That is, it was precisely Homer's unknowability, what Jim Porter has deemed the sheer allure and *inaccessibility* of Homer, which gave rise to his mammoth and diverse ancient reception history, as readers, writers, scholars and cities would construct and contest this ever-imaginary identity.[36] However, as a result of this situation, the only way that Homer could be firmly 'known' was through his texts: he is formed in the fabric of his works, works which, by the imperial era, were increasingly 'fixed' and continuously engaged. Quintus, as we have seen in the last chapter, thoroughly immerses himself in this textual fabric of Homer. And so the biographical markers in *this* poem – a point to which we shall return in detail shortly – work differently. Taken up by Quintus, these details, as we have seen, both retain Homer's traditional 'anonymity' (what could be

---

[32] The fact that the epic 'I' remains cryptic and unnamed is in keeping with Homer's famous anonymity.

[33] Cf. *Il.* 20.392 and *Theog.* 343. For later references to the river in antique geographical writings, see Kaletsch (1998): 452–3.

[34] Scholars remain divided about the reasons for Quintus' choice of Artemis. For speculation about the temple's location, see Vian (1959): 131 and (1969): x. Bär (2007): 55–9 gives a metapoetic interpretation: that the goddess' occasional association with fertility enables Quintus to intimate that the Wooden Horse is the 'mother of evil', pregnant with soldiers. Artemis' early connection with Smyrna must surely also affect her function in this passage and has not been considered as the explanation for her presence; bar passing comment in Graziosi (2002): 77; noted by Boyten (2010): 280.

[35] Translation adapted from West (2003a).

[36] Porter (2002): esp. 58. The best account of Homer's ancient biographical tradition, its origins, development and cultural-political implications, remains Graziosi (2002).

One Continuous Song 167

more Homeric than *not* to say 'I am Homer?') and encourage, rather than undermine, a genuine affiliation with their canonical subject. This simultaneous Homeric ventriloquism and Callimachean allusion, therefore, crystallises for the reader the problems with placing the two influences side by side.[37] As Bär remarks, the pressing question becomes what it means for Quintus to revert to a model that is so critical of traditional epic poetry.[38]

Quintus uses his delayed proem to pose and answer this question. Towards the end of his epic (Book 12, the halfway of both Homeric poems, is *not* the mid-point of Quintus' tale), as the crisis of the fall of Troy approaches,[39] Quintus displays the conflicted place of his epic voice within the literary tradition – as a question. To appreciate the full depth of how this question is formed, and Quintus' self-solution is expressed, we need to read these lines in their full complexity. To begin with, it must be perceived that the interaction with Callimachus goes beyond the near-quotation of a *Somnium* line which critics have repeatedly recognised. Here we must return to the type of literary interplay coined by Hinds as 'tendentious annotation' and first interrogated in the introduction to this book. This process, by which poets forfeit direct citation of a source model in favour of more embedded ways of metaphorising their engagement,[40] is particularly relevant, and particularly *problematic*, for Quintus' proem. Like Triphiodorus and Nonnus, Quintus evokes a range of tropes from Callimachus' poetry, specifically those pertaining to his poetic programme. But rather than merely annotating his engagement, he hijacks and subverts this imagery so as to use it against its originating source. So, in another pointed contrast to Triphiodorus and to Nonnus, the metaphorical 'assault' in the *Posthomerica* is not on Homer via Callimachus, but on Callimachus, via the re-animated Homer. This technique – the most tendentious form of tendentious troping – enables this poet to define and defend his Homerising endeavour using, as he reads it, the tools of its most ardent detractor.

4.3   One Continuous Song

Let us look, then, in detail at how Quintus plays this double game with the authority of Callimachus.

---

[37] For an unpicking of this paradox, see 4.5.

[38] Bär (2007): 50: 'Zu fragen wäre hierbei, was es zu bedeuten hat, dass Quintus auf ein Vorbild rekurriert, welches der traditionellen epischen Dichtung derart kritisch gegenübersteht.'

[39] The issue of Quintus' ending and complex use of the Homeric 'mid-point' receives full treatment in Chapter 7.

[40] Hinds (1998): 3–16.

168 When Homer Quotes Callimachus: The Proem (not) in the Middle

Quintus begins his invocation by asking the Muses for clear and precise information about the identity of each hero and explains this request by asserting the Muses' status as the source of all of his song (12.306–8). The most salient phrase here in terms of allusion, and self-reflection upon allusion, is πᾶσαν ...ἀοιδήν. I have not translated this phrase yet here, because various and importantly conflicting interpretations have been offered. Its ambiguity centres on whether to render πᾶσαν as 'all' or 'the whole', and hence whether ἀοιδήν refers to the *Posthomerica* specifically or the act of poetic composition in general. Thus, James construes the line 'you were the ones who filled my mind with poetry', a general notion of inspiration;[41] whilst Maciver[42] and Hopkinson[43] translate the term as 'all my song', adding a personal pronoun where the Greek has none and making the inspiration more specific to the *Posthomerica* itself. However, when we recall that this passage has been read consistently as brimming with programmatic significance, it is surprising that critics have not considered how this very ambivalence could in itself provide a strong encouragement to interpretative reflection – that exploring the space in between (at least) two systems of meaning allows the reader to unlock a broader spectrum of symbolic associations.

One such association is with the idea of 'the whole song' – taking πᾶσαν as a totalising adjective describing the size, coherence and completeness of the present poem under composition. Vian's translation most closely reflects this meaning: 'est-ce vous qui avez mis en mon âme tout ce poème'.[44] This is a perfectly sensible rendering. Quintus uses the singular πᾶς to mean 'the whole' on ten other occasions in his poem, often when describing an area or space, such as the whole river bursting its banks, or the whole of Greece once covered by a flood.[45] Likewise, in all references to song in the poem's primary narrative, the verb or noun of singing relates to a specific 'composition' being performed: Nestor's song at the funeral of Achilles, the bards' tune after the sack of Troy and the Achaeans' victory ode as they return from razing the city.[46]

Taken in this sense, on the level of 'tendentious annotation' as I want to redefine it, Quintus' 'whole song' may trigger associations with the *Aetia*'s

---

[41] James (2004): 196. [42] Maciver (2012b): 34 [43] Hopkinson (2018): 601.
[44] Vian (1969): 100.
[45] Q.S.2.641, 3.602, 9.266, 11.125 (the whole ground or plain); 12.97 (the whole of Dardania); 12.181 (the whole of lofty Ida); 13.437 (the whole city); 14.406 (the whole Dardanian coast).
[46] Q.S.4.117–70; 14.121–42 and 14.85–93 respectively. A possible exception is the nightingale's song (Q.S.12.489–96), which could refer to the act of singing in general.

famous and frequently quoted[47] ἓν ἄεισμα διηνεκές (fr.1.3): that one continuous poem which Callimachus declined to write. If so, then the phrase sharpens the proem's crucial questions about poetic self-conception: in what sense is Quintus' epic 'whole' and how does such a claim of wholeness relate to Callimachus' dismissal of the one continuous song? However, before such questions are interrogated, it must first be established that these lines do, in fact, ask them. Given the centrality of the phrase to modern readings of Callimachus' poetics, it may at first seem unlikely that had Quintus really wanted to tap the significance of ἓν ἄεισμα διηνεκές here, he would 'refer' to it quite so obliquely. And yet in a passage which displays by its very existence (as a proem in the late-middle) its investment in the reflexive, the embedded and the covert, what better way to cement this agenda than through a liminal mode of reference? Alluding obliquely to this obliquely allusive poet, Quintus, in an aptly Callimachean way, ensures that this is an association to be unlocked.

There are further cues to encourage this unlocking. The choice of the verb θῆκατ', in this inspiratory context, may seem at first sight surprisingly flat. In epic formulations, Muses do not normally simply 'put' ideas in poets' heads. In Homer they are asked to sing their themes and to tell them;[48] and on that single Iliadic occasion where they are described rather than just summoned, they are characterised with verbs of being, knowing, remembering:

> ἔσπετε νῦν μοι Μοῦσαι 'Ολύμπια δώματ' ἔχουσαι·
> ὑμεῖς γὰρ θεαί ἐστε πάρεστέ τε ἴστέ τε πάντα,
> ἡμεῖς δὲ κλέος οἶον ἀκούομεν οὐδέ τι ἴδμεν·
> ...   'Ολυμπιάδες Μοῦσαι Διὸς αἰγιόχοιο
> θυγατέρες μνησαίαθ' ὅσοι ὑπὸ "Ιλιον ἦλθον·
>
> Il. 2.484–6; 91–2

Tell me now, Muses that have dwellings on Olympus – for you are goddesses and present here and know all things, whereas we hear but a rumour and do not know anything.
(Did not) the Muses of Olympus, daughters of Zeus that bears the aegis, call to my mind all of those who came beneath Ilium.

Unlike in Hesiod, whose Theogonic invocation includes an elaborate prosopography of his Heliconian Muses (*Theog.* 2–34), this backstory is one of epistemology, not events.

---

[47] For a critical survey of this quotation history, see Cameron (1995): 104–32.
[48] Cf. the obvious and fundamental paradigms here, *Il.* 1.1 (ἄειδε θεά) and *Od.* 1.1 (ἔννεπε, Μοῦσα). In his own imperative in this proem (ἔσπεθ', 307), Quintus echoes this practice.

170 When Homer Quotes Callimachus: The Proem (not) in the Middle

Imperial Greek epic often followed suit. In the *Sack of Troy* Triphiodorus summons his Muse with a Homeric-imitative style imperative (ἔννεπε, Καλλιόπεια, 4); and even Nonnus, who with typical multifariousness evokes the Muses no fewer than seven times in the *Dionysiaca*, and uniquely gives them descriptive adjectives to match the stories they are about to introduce (Κορυβαντίδες, *Dion.* 13.46, μαχήμονες, 21.73, Λιβανηίδες, 41.11, Ὁμηρίδες, 32.184), still maintains the traditional Homeric emphasis on simply who the Muses are, omitting wider background narrative.[49] In comparison with such treatments, Quintus' vocabulary, and his mini Muse-backstory, sticks out.

A particularly 'close' imperial comparison strengthens this sense of difference. *The Vision of Dorotheos*, whose speculative biographical (af) filiation with the *Posthomerica* we first considered in Chapter 1, contains among its many similarities in diction with Quintus' epic a verse suggestively reminiscent of his statement on the Muses:[50]

καὶ ἐν στή[θεσσιν ἀ]οιδὴγ/παντοίην ἐνέηκε. *Vision of Dorotheos* 340–1[51]

And in my heart, he has sent song of various kind.

The similarity, however, serves to highlight the deviations: whilst replacing the traditional epic Muses with the inspirational voice of the Christian God, the Quintan 'son' has also erased the 'paternal' τίθημι to opt for the more conventionally 'inspirational' ἐνίημι.[52]

Why, therefore, are Quintus' Muses so pragmatic, so transactional? Why is the verb so flat? We shall shortly turn to how in the Muse-call itself (12.306–7) Quintus moves away from a purely Homeric style of summoning to give a Callimachean feel to the art of invocation. Yet it must be noted first that the specific choice of τίθημι could function as a specific if muted nod to this same line of influence. For τίθημι is precisely the verb in the more literal handover of Callimachus' first initiation, the celebrated scene where Apollo speaks to him as he first 'placed the writing tablet on (his) knees':

πρώτιστον ἐμοῖς ἐπὶ δέλτον ἔθηκα/γούνασιν,
Aet. fr.1.21–2

---

[49] On the Nonnian Muses, see particularly Geisz (2017): ch. 4. I defer further discussion of imperial Muse-calls to the next section of this chapter: the aim of these initial observations is as a contextualisation of the significance of Quintus' specific verb choice in θήκατε.

[50] The echo is contentious – see Camplani (2015) – but fully possible.

[51] Text from Kessels and Van Der Horst (1987).

[52] The *Iliad*, for example, frequently uses ἐνίημι to mean 'implant' or 'inspire'. Cf. e.g. ἐνῆκε δέ οἱ μένος ἠΰ *Il.* 20.80; καί οἱ μυίης θάρσος ἐνὶ στήθεσσιν ἐνῆκεν 17.570; τοῖσιν κότον αἰνὸν ἐνήσεις 16.449.

One Continuous Song

The use of this line in a different Homeric impersonation adds valence to the possibility of its presence here. The *Batrachomyomachia* begins with its own provocative statement of programmatics: testing from the outset the limits of its pseudo-Homeric self-position with a material book and, again, an act of placing, *theka*:

> Ἀρχόμενος πρώτης σελίδος χορὸν ἐξ Ἑλικῶνος
> ἐλθεῖν εἰς ἐμὸν ἦτορ ἐπεύχομαι εἵνεκ᾽ ἀοιδῆς,
> ἣν νέον ἐν δέλτοισιν ἐμοῖς ἐπὶ γούνασι θῆκα,
>
> *Batrachomyomachia* 1–3

As I begin on my first column, I pray for the chorus from Helicon to come into my heart for the song that I have just set down on tablets on my knees.[53]

The opening of the mice-battle thus provides another instance of how allusion to Callimachus works both to create and to articulate a boldly anachronistic agenda. Here too, 'Homer' knowingly veers outside of himself; both historically – where Quintus has Homer cite Homeric biography, this author gives him a hymnic gesture (*arkhomai*) and a column of a papyrus role to write on – and poetically, by referencing Hesiod (via his Muses) and Callimachus.[54] The clear use of *this* verse from the *Aetia* to create such effects encourages a reading of a specifically Callimachean θήκατε in Quintus own statement of 'origin', which in turn bolsters the potential resonance of ἓν ἄεισμα διηνεκές in his conception of his 'whole song' in this phrase. In our Quintan proem, the echo of the Apollo initiation is once again less direct, and the effects are more subtle: in keeping with the tone of the poem, humour is less obviously part of the objective. However, in terms of Homeric self-reflection, and topsy-turvy Callimacheanism, the game is the same.

If we can thus perceive the Callimachean phrase embedded in this sense of πᾶσαν ... ἀοιδήν, then the question of its interpretation acquires even further dimensions, not least since the meaning of ἓν ἄεισμα διηνεκές in the *Aetia* itself is notoriously contentious and complex. Formally connected or unified in subject matter? Linear narrative or cyclic chronicling? Temporal or thematic unity?[55] What – if anything – is really being

---

[53] Translation from West (2003a).

[54] On these aspects and their anachronistic effect, see Peirano (2012): 64–6, with Sens (2006) and Kelly (2009).

[55] On these and other enemy camps of interpretation, see Heath (1989); Brink (1946); Pfeiffer (1968); Lyne (1984) as synthesised by Cameron (1995): 342. Hunter (1993): Appendix also offers a convincing possible reading of the knowing paradoxicality of the term, via the Telchines as myopic literary theorists who knew 'poetry only as a set of stylistic criteria and not as a creative act' (ibid. 191). Harder's interpretation ((2012, vol. 2): 18–22), as discussed in the note below,

172 When Homer Quotes Callimachus: The Proem (not) in the Middle

disdained?[56] The most relevant potential definitions for our purposes are those which relate the phrase specifically to epic. Callimachus *could* be interpreted as speaking of a long (ἐν πολλαῖς ἤνυσα χιλιάσιν, fr.1.4) continuous narrative, an uninterrupted epic poem, with ἕν signifying the unity for which Aristotle admired Homer and Callimachus rejected imitation of him.[57] It has, however, been pointed out that not all epics do consist of uninterrupted, continuous narrative: most conspicuously, the two grandest and most famous, the *Iliad* and *Odyssey*, do not fit this mould.[58] But now, with Quintus' ἀοιδή, they do. Taken as an embedded antithesis of ἓν ἄεισμα διηνεκές as Quintus takes it, πᾶσαν . . . ἀοιδήν thus presents a vision of exactly what the *Posthomerica* is doing: like Tatian in the *Diatessaron*, he is creating one unified narrative which joins (in Quintus' case) the two Homeric poems into one narrative. But the conceit stretches further. Within the frame of the poem's claim to Homeric identity, the μοι here (ὑμεῖς γὰρ πᾶσάν μοι ἐνὶ φρεσὶ θήκατ᾽ἀοιδήν) refers to Homer himself. In the comment that the Muses inspired this poet with one 'entire' song, Quintus thus performs a preposterous restructuring of the original Homeric corpus,[59] turning it *into* one continuous poem, moving still further away from Callimachean concepts of disunity and affirming the structural cohesiveness of the Homeric epic narrative by actually creating it.

And yet this rendering of πᾶσαν ἀοιδήν is only part of its possible significance. πᾶς can also, of course, mean 'all' or 'every'; and although singing in the *Posthomerica* usually has a context-specific application, the

---

offers a fresh synthesis, and in some aspects a fresh take on these continual contentions. It is not my intention here to re-summarise these positions in full, nor to offer any new suggestion on the 'original' meaning of the phrase. I seek rather to use such possibilities as routes through which to consider how Quintus, as a reader and interpreter, could have thought about and mobilised its meanings.

[56] Cf. (with both seriousness and humour) Cameron (1995): 118: 'While we need not doubt the basic seriousness of the sentiments expressed in the *Aetia* prologue, it is essential not to overlook the humour that is never far from the surface in Callimachus. Unfortunately, [it] has been treated with almost unrelieved seriousness by modern Telchines more interested in poetics than poetry.'

[57] E.g. Pfeiffer (1968): 13: 'the new poetical school of Callimachus and his followers was ostentatiously anti–Aristotelian. Rejecting unity, completeness and magnitude, it consciously aimed at a discontinuous form'. To these readings should now be added the excellent discussion by Harder (2012, vol. 2): 18–22, who argues that whilst ἕν for Aristotle signified a unity of plot, and for Callimachus is probably numerical ('one single'), the *Aetia* phrase engages with the Aristotelian definition in that it presents a means by which the poet circumvents its charge.

[58] Cameron (1995): 342 is particularly strong in this objection. Cf. also Hunter (1993): Appendix on how Apollonius, by the logic of Hunter's reading of the Callimachean phrase, is also neither 'one' nor 'continuous', in that although the narrative proceeds continually, its author and his characters reject the practice of telling stories 'continuously' (e.g. 1.649, 2.391, 3.401).

[59] On 'preposterous', see Chapter 7.

One Continuous Song   173

pointed choice of ἀοιδήν offers another possibility. If θῆκατ' provides an 'echo' (conventionally understood) of Callimachus – a rare allowed moment of 'direct' mirroring in a passage which otherwise mirrors opacity – then ἀοιδή clearly does not operate in the same way. To define his song, Quintus chooses instead a term which is, unlike ἄεισμα, comfortably Homeric and used frequently throughout the Greek tradition as a designator for poetry.[60] However, Quintus *only* uses it here: this is the sole occurrence of ἀοιδή in the entire poem. This unique presence of the noun, in the accusative, at the end of its line, makes it point quite directly to the Theogonic invocation (22),[61] where it refers more unequivocally to the art of song in general:[62]

> αἵ νύ ποθ' Ἡσίοδον καλὴν ἐδίδαξαν ἀοιδήν,

> And one day they taught Hesiod glorious song. *Theog.* 22

Under this system of meaning the phrase insinuates that 'all song' was originally placed in Homer's breast. πᾶσαν underscores the notion of each and every song that he has written – the *Iliad*, the *Odyssey*, the current poem-in-the-middle – and also encompasses everything in between.

This notion is in itself no polemical rallying cry. A number of works and traditions in Late Antiquity cite Homer as the container for all cultural and intellectual production. Pseudo-Plutarch's *Essay on the Life and Poetry of Homer* presents the poet as ἡ ἀρχή of all things, from politics to medicine, drama and literature. The writers of Neoplatonist allegoresis sought to reconcile the views of their two heroes, Homer and Plato, by conceiving of Homer as a divine sage privy to the most fundamental forms of philosophical truth.[63] Callimachus himself, whose poetics is based on the premise that it is artistic death to attempt direct imitation of Homer

---

[60] To take one obviously relevant line of examples, cf. Callimachus himself, fr.1.1 ἀοιδῆι , which Harder (2012, vol. 2): 20, following Gow-Page (1965) on *HE* 1297), argues is pointedly reminiscent of Herodotus (καὶ δὴ καὶ ἄεισμα ἕν ἐστι, Λίνος, ὅσπερ ἕν τε Φοινίκῃ ἀοίδιμος ἐστι, Hdt. 2.79.1).

[61] ἀοιδήν in this specific case and position is very commonly employed as a gesture, via Hesiod, to poetic composition. Take e.g. Callimachus himself: *Aet.* fr.1.19–20: μηδ' ἀπ' ἐμεῦ διφᾶτε μέγα ψοφέουσαν ἀοιδήν/τίκτεσθαι. . .). And for another rather different example, cf. the opening proem of the anthology of Stephanus of Meleager: Μοῦσα φίλα, τίνι τάνδε φέρεις πάγκαρπον ἀοιδάν (*Anth. Pal.* 4.1.1). The proem goes on to list the poets to be anthologised in the collection, analogising each of them with a flower. In this explicitly literary catalogue – poetry about poetry – the Hesiodic ἀοιδήν (in its Doric alternative) makes a strong statement of intent.

[62] Cf. *Theog.* 32: τά τ'ἐσσόμενα πρό τ'ἐόντα. Hence the translation of the Quintan phrase by Campbell (1981): 103 'all song', accepted by Maciver (2012b): 34 n.124.

[63] For Pseudo-Plutarch, see Keaney and Lamberton (1996); Pontani (2005). On the Neoplatonic Homer, see discussion and references in Chapter 1.7.

174 When Homer Quotes Callimachus: The Proem (not) in the Middle

precisely because of his insurmountable authority, would certainly have been unperturbed by a presentation of him as figurehead of all later song.

In this second meaning of the phrase, Quintus seemingly places his poem within this all-encompassing tradition. However, in the combination of these claims – the two senses of πᾶσαν ἀοιδήν – he also reveals his sting. Acknowledging Homer as the benefactor of all subsequent poetry, he does not deviate deferentially from this almighty source. Rather, he channels this authority into his own attempt at writing traditional epic: presenting an all-encompassing vision of Homer's poetry at the same time as composing a work which claims to be continuing it. It is apposite then that this pivotal word ἀοιδήν in fact combines all three alluded-to poets: taken from the Hesiodic proem, also found in Callimachus' prologue, (fr. 1.19–20: μηδ' ἀπ' ἐμεῦ διφᾶτε μέγα ψοφέουσαν ἀοιδήν/τίκτεσθαι ...) now refracted back into this Homeric-Quintan song.

A further hint in these lines could encourage this image of the poetic whole. The adjective πολυχανδής (307), an Alexandrian neologism, is used with unprecedented frequency in the *Posthomerica*,[64] often to describe a huge space containing smaller composite parts: lions' stomach crammed with prey (1.527); a coffin containing the scorched bones of Achilles (3.731); the cave housing all the gore of Philoctetes' seeping wound (9.390); and twice the hollow stomach of the Wooden Horse ready to be filled with heroes (also at 13.138).[65] This sense of πολυχανδής is stressed and stretched in the present horse-description. The separateness of 306 gives way to an image of conglomeration: καθ' ἕκαστον yields to ὅσοι, and the preposition κατά, which in the phrase καθ' ἕκαστον stressed the individuality of each hero, is redeployed as a prefix to a verb which they perform all together (κατέβησαν).

Now, in contrast to the other reflexive terms in this proem, πολυχανδής does *not* have a rich metaphorical tradition. In the majority of its uses in imperial poetry, and in Theocritus and Nicander, it has a very literal, spatial sense and does not convey statements of poetics.[66] And yet Quintus attaches the word to an object which is steeped in just such a history of double meaning. The inherent duplicity of the Wooden Horse – benign

---

[64] Cf. Bär (2007): 57–8.

[65] Compare the similar 'pregnant' connotations of the adjective in Oppian's *Halieutica* 5.331–2, describing the cavernous belly of the whale; and Triphiodorus, also of the Wooden Horse at 412 (δέμας πολυχανδέος ἵππου), and 536.

[66] The only two known Hellenistic occurrences are κρωσσός Theoc. 13.46; ὅλμος Nic. *Ther.* 951. Cf. the discussions by Livrea (2000) and Franchi (2013) on the term in Nonnus' *Paraphrase*.

Muses and Knowledge 175

offering and hidden disaster, artificial yet seemingly alive –[67] lends it great symbolic potency, and it often stands for the art of heroic storytelling itself. When Menelaus recalls in the *Odyssey* how Helen circled the horse and named each of the Greeks hiding inside, she becomes through this act a creative participant in the Trojan War tradition: by 'describing' the horse, she moulds our judgements of the characters contained within it (*Od.* 4.274–8).[68] By merging the usually literal πολυχανδής with the intricate and multidimensional horse, Quintus may thus be introducing a metaphorical reading for the term: his πολυχανδής ἵππος can symbolise *his* chosen method of (re)telling this heroic tale.[69] If so, then as a picture of his poetry it provides a fitting visualisation of the πᾶσα ἀοιδή that the *Posthomerica* seeks to create – one amassed work of art, which contains within it many aspects and influences, so that an Alexandrian neologism is made to contribute to the defence of traditional, Homeric-style epic.

Read in this way, these two lines (306–7) and their contentious pivotal phrase provide an intense paradigm for the paradoxical self-positioning being articulated in this proem. As Callimachus is echoed in a Callimachean manner against Callimachean claims, and as an Alexandrian coinage comes to uphold the 'original' Homeric form, Quintus' multiple literary positions are activated and conveyed. These positions do not shift, take turns or cancel one another out. They are brought into an unflinching simultaneity.

4.4 Muses and Knowledge

The symbolic weight of πᾶσαν ἀοιδήν also vitalises the meaning of the lines which precede it: the allusion to Callimachus heightens expectation of further Callimachean allusion. If in the bathetic backstory with τίθημι Quintus strikes a discordant note with the standard Homeric language of Muse descriptions, then in his actual instructions to the Muses (12.306–7) he continues to build this significant change in tone. Beyond the superficial similarities to the Iliadic call,[70] there is a clear shift of emphasis in these lines, away from the Muses and their power onto the poet's own desire for knowledge and clarity of information. This shift has been read as a nod to

---

[67] Cf. the ekphrasis at Q.S.12.122–56. Triphiodorus' version (57–98) is even more playful with the competing claims of artifice and *enargeia*.

[68] See Worman (2001): 19–37.

[69] This potential thus also applies to Triphiodorus in that he also uses the adjective for the Wooden Horse.

[70] Detailed discussion of these echoes in Bär (2007): 41–5.

176 *When Homer Quotes Callimachus: The Proem (not) in the Middle*

the Hesiodic influence on these lines.[71] And yet, the infiltration of the archaic concept of the Muses by the personal curiosity of the narrator is better read also as a distinctive marker of Callimachean poetics. Fragments of the dialogue which frames Books 1–2, though scanty, show how in extending the single question-and-answer into a two-way conversation, the *Aetia* challenges the convention of the Muses as the source of all knowledge, as the goddesses encounter an eager and erudite human interlocutor who adds his own insight into the mix.[72]

This new emphasis is taken up with gusto in many imperial Muse-calls: these epics may preserve the linguistic structure of traditional hexameter invocations, but they deliver them in a very different tone of voice. Triphiodorus' bossy demand for Calliope to hurry up (1–5), for example, is a far cry from Homeric *or* Hesiodic demurral and wonder. The author of an ethopoeia fragment from third-/fourth-century CE Egypt – 'What Hesiod would have said when inspired by the Muses' – goes so far as to rewrite the Hesiodic call itself to emphasise such narrator-centred elements (*POxy.* 3537). In this 'creative expansion' of the *Theogony*, Hesiod speaks, feels the presence of the Muse and asks her in person to inspire him with his poems. Bidding farewell to the rustic verse and bucolic pipe – both of which were traditionally the hallowed gifts of the Muses –[73] he presents himself not as a humbled peasant enraptured by his inspirers, but a grand poet unfolding the facts of his own song.[74]

Quintus' invocation also reveals its close affinity with this Callimachean brand of curiosity. The sense of awe at the Muses and their power is eroded in line 306 and replaced by a more 'secular' search for knowledge. The Μοῦσαι are deprived of any elaborating formula, such as the *Iliad*'s Ὀλύμπια δώματ' ἔχουσαι, or Hesiod's laudations at the opening of the *Theogony*, and in the place of such archaic compliments comes a strident emphasis on the manner in which they should convey their information: immediately (νῦν), specifically (καθ' ἕκαστον) and clearly (σάφα).[75] ἀνειρομένῳ (306) may also hint at a dialogue.[76] The construction μοι ἀνειρομένῳ usually occurs during the inquiry section of a two-way

---

[71] Campbell (1981): 103–4; Bär (2007): 43 and 45–7.   [72] Cf. e.g. fr.7c; fr.43.18ff.
[73] Cf. e.g. Vergil *Ecl.* 6.69f.
[74] The author also rejects the Augustan *recusatio* at 25ff. and in the use of hexameter techniques shows close familiarity with Callimachean practice. For the very fragmentary remains of the piece, see Parsons (ed.) (1983): 61–4.
[75] Maciver (2012b): 34 also suggests that this desire for precision indicates rivalry with previous catalogues on this topic – Quintus wants *this* version to be the right one.
[76] Hopkinson (2018 ad loc.) takes up this hint in his translation 'Now inform me clearly, Muses, as I ask you...'

Muses and Knowledge 177

exchange, to refer reflexively to the questioner who expects answers from his informants – as in the Platonic dialogues[77] or the *Odyssey's* question and answer games.[78] That such an exchange is only faintly implied in Quintus' invocation may make a connection with the extended conversations of the *Aetia* seem unlikely. However, the possibility is strengthened by the line's similarity to an epigram describing these very discussions:

> ἆ μέγα Βαττιάδαο σοφοῦ περίπυστον ὄνειαρ,
>   ἦ ῥ' ἐτεὸν κεράων οὐδ' ἐλέφαντος ἔης·
> τοῖα γὰρ ἄμμιν ἔφηνας, ἅτ' οὐ πάρος ἀνέρες ἴδμεν,
>   ἀμφί τε ἀθανάτους ἀμφί τε ἡμιθέους,
> εὖτέ μιν ἐκ Λιβύης ἀναείρας εἰς Ἑλικῶνα
>   ἤγαγες ἐν μέσσαις Πιερίδεσσι φέρων·
> αἱ δέ οἱ εἰρομένωι ἀμφ' ὠγυγίων ἡρώων
>   Αἴτια καὶ μακάρων εἶρον ἀμειβόμεναι.
>
> Adesp. *Anth. Pal.* 7.42[79]

O great and widely known dream of the clever Battiad, truly you were of horn and not of ivory, for such things you showed us, which we men did not know before, about the immortals and about half-gods, when you lifted him up from Libya and brought him to Mt. Helicon, placing him in the middle of the Pierian Muses; and they told him in answer to his questions the *Aetia* about the ancient heroes and blessed gods.

If, as Harder suggests, these lines owe something to the *Aetia* itself,[80] then Quintus' phrasing may once again recall such specific sections of the poem, imparting a specifically Callimachean flavour to his request.

Quintus may use Callimachus' techniques, then, but he resists his invocation being read simply as a reflection of his aesthetics. For our poet embeds this confident emphasis on inquiry into the lines of the proem which most closely repeat the second Iliadic call (*Il.* 2.484–7), with matching imperative (ἔσπεθ'), immediacy (νῦν) and catalogue-style subject (ὅσσοι for the Homeric οἵ τινες). The invocation is at its least Homeric whilst at its most. On the one hand, this echo is hardly earth-shattering: when attempting a heroic catalogue, what better passage for the hyper-Homeric poet to reach for than this? Nonnus acknowledges the blatancy of

---

[77] Cf. L.S.J. s.v. ἀνέρομαι: acc. pers., inquire of, question. E.g. *Od.* 4.420; Soph.*OC.* 210, cf. *Aj.* 314, Pl. *Ap.* 20a.
[78] Cf. e.g. *Od.* 15.293.   [79] Harder T 6 = *test.* 27 et 1, p. 11 Pf.
[80] Beckby (1965, vol. 2) and Harder (2012, vol. 2): 4–5 and 93 support Pfeiffer's suggestion of a Byzantine date for the epigram. The epigram entered also The Database of Byzantine Book Epigrams (DBBE), compiled at the Universiteit Gent: www.dbbe.ugent.be/type/view/id/2604/9 (date last accessed 13.04.20).

178 When Homer Quotes Callimachus: The Proem (not) in the Middle

such a move. In introducing his own catalogue of armies in the Indian war, he wryly marks his indebtedness with an excruciatingly obvious gesture:

οὐ γὰρ ἐγὼ τόσα φῦλα δέκα γλώσσῃσιν ἀείσω
οὐδὲ δέκα στομάτεσσι χέων χαλκόθροον ἠχώ,
ὁππόσα Βάκχος ἄγειρε δορυσσόος, ἀλλὰ λιγαίνων
ἡγεμόνας καὶ Ὅμηρον ἀοσσητῆρα καλέσσω.

Dion. 13.47–50

For I could not tell so many peoples with ten tongues, not if I had ten mouths pouring a voice of bronze, all those which Bacchus gathered for his spear-chasing. Yet I will loudly name their leaders, and I will call Homer to my aid.[81]

And yet on the other hand, as Nonnus reminds us, the Iliadic catalogue is also the site of the rare narratorial 'ego' in Homer, who famously could not name the mass of men 'even if I had ten tongues and ten mouths, an unbreakable voice and a heart of bronze' (*Il.* 2.488–90). So, in imitating *this* invocation, Quintus also echoes the moment where Homer himself comes closest to voicing a poetic I, as Hesiod and Callimachus would later do so expansively. Recycled in this proem, surrounded and re-contextualised by Callimachean and Hesiodic nodes, the Iliadic passage becomes a site for reflection on how compatible Homer's first-person hiccough has become with later, more explicitly self-centred invocations. As a symbol for the tradition of poetic initiation, the Quintan call thus eradicates the divide between the archaic and the Alexandrian approaches, taking their contrasting facets of distance and closeness, deferral and authority and transforming them into a composite whole.

4.5 Youth

Quintus goes on to describe the timing of his inspiration, which occurred during his youth (309). Youth and childhood have long been recognised as running themes in the *Aetia*.[82] The Telchines accuse Callimachus of writing παῖς ἅτε (fr.1.6), and he refutes them with the claim that 'whomsoever the Muses did not look askance at as a child they will not reject as a friend when he is old' (Μοῦσαι γὰρ ὅσους ἴδον ὄθματι παῖδας/μὴ λοξῷ, πολιοὺς οὐκ ἀπέθεντο φίλους, fr.1.37–8). The old poet then falls asleep[83] and his young counterpart meets the Muses in a dream, where, a scholion

---

[81] On the explicit naming of Homer here, see Chapter 6.   [82] Cf. e.g. Cameron (1995): 129–32.
[83] For this intervening narrative, see Kerkhecker (1988): 16–24; Harder, Regtuit and Wakker (1993): 96; Cameron (1995): 129–31.

Youth

relates, he is ἀρτιγένειος, 'sprouting his first beard'.[84] This imagery has often been connected to the innovating intentions of Callimachus' poetry, his aim to traverse paths yet untrodden and create something fresh and new.[85]

In Quintus' image of down spreading on the young shepherd's cheeks, there can be little doubt of the presence of Callimachus' youthful inspiration.[86] Again, however, as soon as we notice the Callimachean intensity of this line, it is simultaneously re-asserted that Homer is supposedly speaking it. In Book 11 of the *Odyssey*, Odysseus describes his sighting in the underworld of Otus and Ephialtes, who were slain by Apollo 'before down covered their cheeks with a beard' (...πρίν σφωιν ὑπὸ κροτάφοισιν ἰούλους/ἀνθῆσαι πυκάσαι τε γένυς ἐυανθέι λάχνῃ, *Od.* 11.319–20).[87] This verse was well known in antiquity and gave rise to a host of imitations.[88] By evoking it here, Quintus again collides Homeric quotation and Callimachean theme, and connects the latter to Homer's voice, imagined as using elements from his formulaic repertoire to describe his initial inspiration.

But Quintus does not just reclaim a Callimachean topos: he competes with his youthful reminiscence. Whereas the poet of the *Aetia* is old as he dreams of his inspiration,[89] 'Homer' here is no such geriatric. Although Quintus states that he was young when he received his first initiation, he does not specify how old he is now.[90] This ambiguity is particularly pointed if read against the ancient tradition that the *Odyssey* was the work of Homer's old age. Pseudo-Longinus evinces this idea most spiritedly, comparing Homer's second poem to the setting sun, since 'as great inspiration fades away old age naturally leans towards the fantastical' (ἴδιόν ἐστιν ἐν γήρᾳ τὸ φιλόμυθον) (*De. Sub.* 9.11–12). Quintus' self-portrayal as no longer young, but not specifically old, can thus reflect the

---

[84] fr.2d = Σ Flor.15–20. For further discussion of this adjective and its subsequent imitation – suggesting that the scholion phrasing may owe something to the text of Callimachus – see e.g. Cameron (1995): 131 and Harder (2012, vol. 2): 144. Harder's translation, however, 'while he was still a young man' (2012, vol. 1): 128 does not capture the specificity of the word.

[85] Cf. Bär (2007): 48 n. 66.

[86] The connection has been noted: Campbell (1981): 104; Bär (2007): 48; Boyten (2010): 278; Carvounis (2014): 183. It is how Quintus uses it that requires reconsideration.

[87] On this scene, see further discussion in Chapter 6.

[88] Examples listed by Campbell (1981): 104.

[89] A contrast to be drawn with the caution advised by Cameron (1995): 174–84 in his discussion of the flexibility of ancient ideas about age and ageing.

[90] Boyten's suggestion (2010: 277) that, by implying that he is not beardless anymore, Quintus insinuates that he is an old man is not supported by the text and neglects the possibility of this connection with Homer's supposed stages of composition.

180 When Homer Quotes Callimachus: The Proem (not) in the Middle

position of his composition in the Homeric *oeuvre* – a post-Iliadic, pre-Odyssean, middle age. His stage of beardedness is also one phase earlier than Callimachus' ἀρτιγένειος (πρίν ἔτ' ... κατασκίδνασθαι): Homer gains literal as well as literary earliness. Youth is thus not merely evoked as a Callimachean nod. It is transformed into a competitive symbol; a reminder that in Quintus' hands, the founding source of the poetic tradition is also revitalised and ever new.

We have considered the crucial importance of 'objectified tradition' to the creative capabilities of imperial Greek texts: only through their feted and 'fixed' position could Homer's epics become re-animated and changed from within. We have also seen how compositions like the verse ethopoeia on *Iliad* 1 and Lucian's new Homeric hexameters on the Island cynically distort and exploit the paradoxes of this position, as Homer must always be canonical and old in order to become destabilised and new. In his image of Homer's facial hair, Quintus gives his own bold visualisation of this conceit. Rather than an eerie old man lurking in a ghostly posthumous state, Quintus 'resurrects' Homer into his younger, more vigorous phase of life – as the trope of ancient youth is made to stand for the elasticity of Homer's antiquity as it was imaginatively reconceived in imperial Greece.

4.6 Topography and Grandeur

The final section of the proem depicts where this inspiration took place (310–13). The impression of locational precision firstly anchors this description to Homeric (auto)biography. Yet in a passage so charged with self-consciousness, the specific place names also have a role in the proem's symbolic system.

Quintus describes his location as τρὶς τόσον Ἑρμοῦ ἄπωθεν, ὅσον βοόωντος ἀκοῦσαι (311). Wherever this formula-type is found in Homer, it stresses one or both of two points: a great distance, and a loud volume and amplitude.[91] Quintus activates both senses of the expression here. The adverb ἄπωθεν – not found in any of the Homeric examples – intensifies the sense of vastness. The Hermus provides another distance marker. Achilles names the river in the *Iliad* as he kills Iphition, citing his birthplace 'by the eddying Hermus' to emphasise sneeringly how far away from this homeland he will perish (*Il.* 20.392). Equal emphasis is thrown on noise and clamour, through the juxtaposition of βοόωντος ἀκοῦσαι

[91] E.g. *Od.* 5.400–3; *Od.* 6.293–4.

and the substitution of γέγωνε, common in the Homeric formula, for a more explicit verb of hearing.

We have seen how Callimachus' imagery of noisy thunder could be adopted by imperial poets to advance their aesthetic statements, articulating an anxious or competitive stance towards the powerful hexameters of Homer. In his doublet of vastness and volume, Quintus reorients this image. Harnessing the Callimachean connection between length and bombastic style[92] he asserts that this is precisely the type of ἀοιδή that he *will* write. As a poet composing in the style, subject and *persona* of Homer, his work will be vast, and it will be loud and booming.

The proem then zooms in further on this setting: near the Temple of Artemis, in the Garden of Liberty (312). Many attempts have been made to identify these features. West's conjecture for the garden – Ἐλευθερίος (*sc.* Διός) – is recorded in Vian's apparatus and accepted by many scholars.[93] Elsewhere in the literary tradition, however, the garden is a space frequently employed as a metaphor for poetic art.[94] Taken in a symbolic rather than geographical sense, Quintus' κῆπος of Liberty – of free spirit, free speaking, or free thinking –[95] builds on this symbolic potential. It serenely accommodates both the terrestrial and the lofty (by virtue of its proximity to the temple) and advocates freedom from rigidity or restraint.[96] But set within these stylistic sites of size and grandeur – the noise and distance and temple – the garden asserts that for Quintus, this is a freedom not to deviate from Homeric epic, but to continue it.

The hill with which the proem concludes, 'neither excessively high nor too low' (313), has already been interpreted as an aesthetic symbol. Hopkinson has taken it as a reference to the middle style of the *Posthomerica* within the *genera dicendi*: 'neither sublime nor pedestrian ... Quintus' motto here and elsewhere is μηδὲν ἄγαν'.[97] It has, however, been countered that the type of traditional heroic epic which Quintus is writing belongs by nature to the *genus grande*, precluding a reading of humble self-deprecation.[98] If, however, we read the hill within the poem's framing conceit, its claims become more reconcilable. That is, if this οὖρος is a

---

[92] Harder (2012, vol. 2): 53–4 demonstrates how Callimachus evokes the literary-critical connotations of ψόφος, and makes μέγα mean both 'loudly' and echo the μεγάλη γυνή of fr.1.12.

[93] See e.g. Carvounis (2014): 182 n. 11. On Artemis, see n. 26 above.

[94] E.g. Pindar *Ol.* 9.27; Plato *Ion* 534a.   [95] Cf. LSJ s.v. ἐλευθέριος.

[96] Bär (2007): 61 considers the garden as a symbol for poetic art, but not in relation to Quintus' Homeric imitation.

[97] Hopkinson (1994b): 106–7. Related discussion by Bär (2007): 59–6; Maciver (2012b): 36.

[98] James (2004): xviii.

182 When Homer Quotes Callimachus: The Proem (not) in the Middle

comment on poetic style, then it is a comment on Homer's poetic style, which Quintus seeks to take up.

In ancient discussions of aesthetics, the concept of the middle style was often evoked in relation to Homer's mode of expression. Quintilian views Homer as a model for language, characterisation, organisation and speech techniques (*hic enim, quenadmodum ex Oceano dicit ipse omnium amnium fontiumque cursus initium capere, omnibus eloquentiae partibus exemplum et ortum dedit, Inst.* 10.1.46), offering another variant on the notion of Homer as a container for all later knowledge. He pits this Homeric form against that of Hesiod, who by contrast represents the middle style. Also called *floridum* or ἀνθηρόν (12.10.58) this style, the third of Quintilian's *genera* (10.1.58–9) is characterised by 'a well-structured composition (*compositione aptus*) and sweetness (*dulcis*) of *sententiae*; like a gentle river translucent but shaded on both sides by verdant river banks' (*Inst.* 12.10.60).[99] When, however, he turns to the question of which of these styles is most desirable, Quintilian concludes that in the end, no one would hesitate to choose the Hesiodic one (12.10.63) – but he cites *Homer* as the basis for this claim:

> nam et Homerus breuem quidem cum iucunditate et propriam, id enim est non deerrare uerbis, et carentem superuacuis eloquentiam Menelao dedit, quae sunt uirtutes generis illius primi, et ex ore Nestoris dixit dulciorem mele profluere sermonem, qua certe delectatione nihil fingi maius potest.[100]
> *Inst.* 12.10.64

> Homer gave Menelaus an eloquence which is concise, pleasing and precise (this is what he means by 'not straying in speech') and without any superfluities: those are the virtues of the first type. From Nestor's lips, he tells us, flowed speech sweeter than honey; which we can conceive no greater pleasure than that.

Since Quintilian has already made clear his conception of Homer as the source of every 'spring' of poetic diction, attributing the origins of this classification to him may at first seem unremarkable – even, as Hunter puts it, 'inevitable'.[101] However, to make any such statement also requires a

---

[99] For further discussion of these stylistic descriptions, see Hunter (1997): 23–6; (2012b): 155–61; and (2014a): 286–7.

[100] Translation adapted from Russell (2001). Quintilian goes on to discuss Odysseus as the third Homeric exemplum, to whom, he says, Homer grants, the 'supreme gift of eloquence' (*summam expressurus in Ulixe facundiam et magnitudinem*) which in this case is conveyed in the power and force of a voice (*Inst.* 10.12.64).

[101] Hunter (2014a): 287.

Topography and Grandeur 183

familiar slippage between poetic traditions. Homer is retroactively consulted to illustrate from within his epic Hesiod's later poetic style, even using the same 'language' to describe it as this present Roman treatise (in Quintilian's translation of the famous Iliadic passage [*Il.* 1.247–9] Homer's *dulcior* matches the *dulcis* in his own initial typology [12.10.60]), and, in an ironic replaying of their traditional *Certamen*[102] the bard is made to concede and even affirm the superiority of his 'rival's' stylistic mode.[103] Dionysius of Halicarnassus also contrasts Homer with Hesiod stylistically: but for him, it is Homer who is crowned with holding the middle or 'mixed' ground (εὔκρατος), in that his epics lie somewhere in between the 'austere' (αὐστηρά) and the 'smooth' style (γλαφυρὰ σύνθεσις) modelled by Hesiod (*Comp.* 23.2–7).[104]

Quintus' portrait of the hill has much in common with these rhetorical configurations. He shares in the metaphorical language of Quintilian, in which a feature of nature functions as an image of style, and even as an image for Homer.[105] And by crowning this style neither excessively high nor low, he concurs with Dionysius that Homer occupies the privileged middle ground. However, whilst these treatises pit Homer against the aesthetic traditions which came after him, Quintus avoids such diachronic dichotomies. Taking far further Quintilian's amalgamation of Homer's honey and Hesiod's 'sweetness', his version of Homer's style blends within it a number of different parts – including the proto-Hesiodic and even the proto-Alexandrian. This expansive notion of the Homeric *genus dicendi*, which refuses to conform to a

---

[102] The *Certamen Homeri et Hesiodi*, probably dated to the second century CE, but whose original core possibly dates back to Alcidamas of Elea, the fourth-century sophist and pupil of Gorgias, is a vibrant part of the Homeric biographical tradition. Expanding the remark in Hesiod's *Works and Days* in which the poet describes his participation in a poetic contest (650–62), the text constructs an imagined poetical *agōn* between Homer and Hesiod, in which both poets spar off one another creatively, with Homer vying to solve the challenges and riddles which Hesiod poses; the winning tripod is awarded to Hesiod, whose poetry is also deemed to be of more value to the *polis* than Homer's tales of war. Recent critical edition and commentary in Bassino (2018). For more on the biographical facets which this work brings to light (the piece starts with details about Homer's birth and parents), see Graziosi (2002) esp. 83–4, 172–3 and 211–2.

[103] Precisely due to this long history of rivalry between the poets, it seems likely to me that Quintilian is indeed knowingly tapping this conceit, pitching Homer and Hesiod against one another *as* archetypes for their styles, despite the caveats of Hunter (2014a): 287, following Russell (1964) xxxiv–xxxvii not to accept too readily this conflation of ancient categories of style onto individual authors, 'whatever claims the proponents of these categories might make'.

[104] As Hunter notes (2014a: 286), this category of the εὔκρατος in Dionysius has much in common with Quintilian's version of the middle style: another way in which we can consider the knowing slippage between Homer and Hesiod in their ancient rhetorical conceptions.

[105] As per Quintilian's Ocean at *Inst.* 10.1.46.

184 When Homer Quotes Callimachus: The Proem (not) in the Middle

rigid set of criteria, is perfectly represented by a hill which defies precise categorisation.[106]

However, whilst ὕψος was a common metaphor for the grand style in antiquity,[107] χθαμαλός is not its usual antithesis.[108] Why then should Quintus use it, forfeiting a more recognisable doublet?[109] The answer may lie in the complex associations of χθαμαλός with Ithaca.[110] When Odysseus describes his homeland to the Phaeacians, the adjective creates a difficult juxtaposition:

> αὐτὴ δὲ χθαμαλὴ πανυπερτάτη εἰν ἁλὶ κεῖται
> πρὸς ζόφον. . .
>
> *Od.* 9.25–6

Ithaca itself lies low in the sea, highest of all towards the dark. . .

Ithaca's simultaneous status as χθαμαλή and πανυπερτάτη perplexed ancient commentators. The scholia ask πῶς χθαμαλή; πῶς πανυπερτάτη; and make various attempts to reconcile the concepts, and Strabo dedicates a lengthy excursus to attempting to resolve the 'incongruities' (ἀπεμφάσεις) in Homer's phraseology (Strabo 10.2.12).[111] By employing the word in his own description of a space that is at once high and low, Quintus can invite an association with the simultaneous height and lowliness of Ithaca – and, by transferral, the well-known stylistic highs and lows within the *Odyssey* itself.[112] ὕψος, conversely, in its adverbial and compound forms, is often used to describe the *Iliad*'s spatial setting and

---

[106] In contrast to the specificity of the rest of the proem, the hill's lack of name and pinpointed location heightens its ability to stand for something which precludes compartmentalisation.

[107] Cf. LSJ s.v. τὸ ὕψος (4); and the Περὶ ὕψους of Pseudo-Longinus. Further discussion by Bär (2007): 59.

[108] The more common metaphorical terminology for the *genus humile* was ἰσχνότης. Cf. LSJ s.v. ἰσχνός (5).

[109] Bär's suggestion (2007): 59 n. 122, that with χθαμαλός Quintus aims at a translation of the Latin *humilis*, is possible, but would be an unusual move for Quintus and seems less likely to me than his interaction with the Odyssean connotations of the word, and at any rate does not preclude it.

[110] The word occurs only four times in the poem, always to describe topographical features (the other instances are: 10.196, Circe's island as Odysseus describes it to his comrades before his recce; 10.212 [in the comparative], Circe describing the lower-lying cliff which conceals Charybdis; and 11.194, a lowly bed of leaves. This sparsity of Homer's use of the term suggests, as it did to Strabo (10.2.12), that it has, or came to acquire, a particular salience in the passage where it is used so confusingly for Ithaca.

[111] Cf. Σ *Odyssey* ad loc. For the persistence of such uncertainty, cf. LSJ s.v. χθαμαλός, (2).

[112] On 'low' material in the *Odyssey* conceived in this way see, for example, Hutchinson (1988): 12–13. That Quintus agrees with such a reading of the *Odyssey* (as characterised by the presence of such material) must remain of course on one level highly speculative: however, the particular use of this adjective in the context of *this* passage, crammed as it is with other symbolic markers of 'high' epic diction, makes it suggestively possible

Topography and Grandeur

subject matter: the lofty towers of Troy and the fighting that takes place beneath them.[113] It is a word connected to Iliadic heights. Read against these precedents, Quintus' doublet thus makes the literal, thematic and stylistic possibilities of the words combine into a reading of the Homeric canon.

ὑψόθι is also frequently applied in poetry to describe Zeus and the gods, as in the Homeric phrase ὑψόθ᾽ ἐόντι Διί[114] and Callimachus' *Hymn to Zeus* (εἶπε καὶ ἀντανύσασα θεὴ μέγαν ὑψόθι πῆχυνπλῆξεν ὄρος σκήπτρῳ... [30]). If, by leaving thundering to Zeus, Callimachus in the *Aetia* links his rejection of the high, grand style to a prudent avoidance of *hubris*, and if Nonnus flirts with this danger through Typhon's kleptomaniac usurpation, then by juxtaposing such loftiness with tokens of Homeric 'humility', Quintus removes the sting from such associations. Homeric epic itself, as Quintus reads and presents it, successfully incorporates both the high and the low. Therefore, to imitate and to continue this epic is not an arrogant attempt at greatness, but the logical harnessing of a style which will always best encapsulate the middle way.

We have seen how later writers' engagement with the biographical stories of their models is often taken to be a clear-voiced signal of their supplementary position. In her portrait of the fake as a work of reception, Peirano argues that the ancient biographical tradition itself is in fact a crucial instance of 'creative supplementation', filling in the gaps of an authorial narrative.[115] Through the double function of these location details in our proem – each feature now operates both as a marker of Homer's life story *and* as an embedded comment on his style – we can see most clearly how Quintus reverses this line. Homeric biography, in this poetics, is no longer just a part of the supplementary, the marker of a later, contested tradition: redrafted as a statement by Homer about Homer, it becomes a proud proclamation not just of the continuation, but of the *continual*.

---

[113] ὑψίπυλος is twice used as an epithet for Troy (*Il.* 21.544 and 16.698), and after the *Teichoscopia* Aphrodite finds Helen πύργῳ ἐφ᾽ ὑψηλῷ (*Il.* 3.384). The related adverbs ὕψι and ὑψοῦ are most frequently employed in the *Iliad* to describe battle tactics, positions or situations: the striking of a blow (e.g. *Il.* 13.140), the mooring of Achaean ships (*Il.* 1.486; *Il.* 14.77), a dust cloud rising from the battlefield (*Il.* 16.374) or the Achaeans lifting the corpse of Patroclus (*Il.* 17.723).

[114] E.g. *Il.* 10.16.

[115] Peirano (2012): 10–11 and ch. 2. Cf. e.g. her comments on the so-called biographical fallacy (11): 'to the extent that authors insert autobiographical statements in their own writing, the process of reconstructing their lives outside of the text will always be a process of supplementing their work with biographical sequels and prequels to that authoritative first narrative'. Related discussion on this position of Peirano's in this book's Chapter 2.1.

186 When Homer Quotes Callimachus: The Proem (not) in the Middle

4.7 Tending Famous Sheep

In our final self-reflexive marker, set within these topographical details, Quintus depicts his former self tending περικλυτὰ μῆλα (310). Through its double allusion to Hesiod's *Theogony* and Callimachus' Hesiod in the *Somnium*, this phrase more than any other emphasises its multiple strands of intertextuality. Maciver has shown how the adjective κλυτά, which has a double meaning of either 'excellent/of quality' or 'famous/renowned',[116] is elsewhere used by Quintus to comment on his poetry and its place in the chain of literary forerunners; a 'footnote' suggesting the sort of subtle and learned use of his models akin to that of the Alexandrian poets.[117] περικλυτά in the proem, he argues, replays this significance on a more intense level, pointing to a perceived superiority in comparison:

> The shepherd of the passage has sheep which are of superior quality to other sheep. Quintus' poetry is of eminently superior quality to other poetry, and, by implication, the poetry of the three he embeds in this passage: Homer, Hesiod and Callimachus.[118]

However, there is another flock of sheep – of κλυτὰ μῆλα – neglected in Maciver's discussion, which significantly affects the symbolism of this image. During his *Apologoi*, Odysseus describes the rams of Polyphemus, under whose fleeces he and his crew make their escape:

> ἦμος δ' ἠριγένεια φάνη ῥοδοδάκτυλος Ἠώς,
> καὶ τότε πῦρ ἀνέκαιε καὶ ἤμελγε κλυτὰ μῆλα,
> πάντα κατὰ μοῖραν, καὶ ὑπ' ἔμβρυον ἧκεν ἑκάστη.
> *Od.* 9.307–9

As soon as early Dawn appeared, the rosy-fingered, he rekindled the fire and milked his fine flocks all in turn, and beneath each dam placed her young.

It is generally considered that of the two possible meanings of κλυτός, fine or famous, the former is employed in this passage. The sheep are splendid and fine-looking in appearance, in a miniature focalisation of Polyphemus' admiration for them.[119] And yet this visual sense of the adjective is usually

---

[116] Cf. *Lexikon des Frühgriechischen Epos* s.v. κλυτός (A) and (B); LSJ s.v. κλυτός (1)/(2).

[117] Maciver (2012a): 54–5 and 66. Maciver focuses on the term's presence in a series of bee similes, centrally at Q.S.6.322–7, where the phrase κλυτὰ φῦλα (6.324) he argues, reflects and comments upon the poem's 'imitative template'.

[118] Maciver (2012b): 37.

[119] Cf. the translations by Campbell (1981): 104 'of outstanding quality' and Murray (1919) ad loc.: 'goodly'.

Tending Famous Sheep

restricted in Homer to inanimate objects such as armour or houses;[120] and nowhere else in Homeric epic is κλυτά used of animals except here.[121] This all suggests that 'fine-looking' is only part of the meaning in Odysseus' phrase. Polyphemus is surrounded by his sheep during his daily routine, and is particularly fond of his large ram, to whom he will later speak with affection, unaware that Odysseus is hiding beneath (*Od.* 9.447–60). The sheep are thus 'fine' at *Od.* 9.308 from an internal perspective, but they are *famous* from an external one, thanks to their role in the adventure being narrated. Their true significance unfolds as the tale progresses, revealed in the crew's spectacular exit. Odysseus thus mobilises the second meaning of κλυτά as a nod to his retroactive self-awareness as a narrator, a reminder of his privileged knowledge and position as the teller of this epic tale.[122]

This doubleness of the Odyssean sheep has important implications for Quintus' allusion. Referring to an episode so centred on identity, anonymity and self-articulation (Οὖτις ἐμοί γ' ὄνομα, *Od.* 9.366, 'φάσθαι Ὀδυσσῆα πτολιπόρθιον ἐξαλαῶσαι', *Od.* 9.504) Quintus does indeed, as Maciver suggests, 'name' his poetic self in light of his literary predecessors. But by taking up Odysseus' expression, and harnessing its ironic double-meaning, he does so from a *Homeric* perspective. In a dizzying proleptic game, Quintus' sheep are actually Homer's sheep: they are the sheep in the *Odyssey*, which, within the conceit of the poem, has not yet been composed, described in the same reflexive way as Homer's most loquacious character will 'later' depict them. The subsequent poetic traditions acknowledged by the intertextuality of this line do not diminish the importance of the Homeric original. Rather, Quintus employs the same retroactive foresight as Odysseus to write them into this superlative fame. It is thanks to the efforts of these later poets that Homer's 'sheep' (his poetry) have become κλυτά, even περικλυτά.[123] So through the act of continuing this poetry, Quintus himself is now able to tend this most celebrated flock. Posing as Homer grants him access to material of the highest quality and renown.

---

[120] References in Maciver (2012a): 54 n. 6.

[121] When Maciver (2012a): 54 states that 'nowhere in either Homer or Quintus is κλυτά used of animals or insects, except at Q.S.6.324 [μελισσάων κλυτά φῦλα]' he omits this important instance.

[122] κλυτός is frequently used in the *Odyssey* as an epithet of a bard: cf. *Od.* 1.325, 8.83, 8.367, 8.521 (so Bär (2007): 51), strengthening the possibility that its use here is indicative of Odysseus' status as internal teller of this tale.

[123] The prefix περι-, which may have been selected by the poet for metrical reasons, could nonetheless also carry connotations of a 'perceived superiority', as Maciver suggests. But what is crucial is that the superiority belongs to Homer and is not set against him.

4.8 Conclusions: Declassifying Quintus

In these duplicitous sheep, we find encapsulated the approach to Alexandrian programmatics in the proem's encoded statements. Claiming – or better, reclaiming – the retrojecting anachronistic moves so typical of Alexandrian poetry, Quintus adopts the games of the *Aetia* to validate the Homeric nature of his undertaking: his own literary game. The invocation thus lays bare the deep intertextual implications of the 'doubleness' of the Quintan agenda, as the *Posthomerica* establishes its Homeric-ness both against, but also by means of, Alexandrian, Callimachean poetics.

I began by suggesting that the proem functions as a template for the imitative strategies of the poem. We have already seen how so many of these strategies – the formulaic switches, stylistic preferences, and the range of narrative and literary interactions – are too often polarised in discussions of this epic: read as either Homeric or un-Homeric, Alexandrian or non-Alexandrian, in the persistent desire to categorise Quintus. The late proem, as this chapter has understood it, provides perhaps the strongest incentive to rethink this current mode of rethinking. Acutely aware of the literary manoeuvres available to him and the innovative pressures of his time, Quintus advocates here a different answer to charges of bland imitation: a symbolic discourse which declares the value of a poetic endeavour not in terms of deviation from traditional epic, but through explicit dependence upon it. In this *post* post-Homeric proem, the polarising statements of the *Aetia* become the new Telchines, against whose charges the voices of Homer, and Hesiod, and Callimachus can chime in the polyphony of the Quintan song.

CHAPTER 5

Selective Memory and Iliadic Revision

Homer knew the truth but changed much of it to suit the subject he
had chosen.

– Philostratus Heroicus, 43.16

Truth? What is that?

– John 18:38

5.1 Introduction

In the previous chapter we examined with close scrutiny a passage which
emblematically and programmatically looks backwards: to the original
moment of inspiration; to the Homeric foundations of Callimachean
games; to the multiple and overlapping origins of Quintus' new-old epic
song. Summoning the Muses for the first and only time in the poem –
those daughters of *Mnemosyne*, goddess of remembrance – Quintus performs his most explicit act of literary recollection.

For the poet of the interval, the notion of recollection offers a particular
set of challenges. As has been variously emphasised by the wealth of recent
scholarship focused on memory and history, to remember is always to
enter into a jagged, refractive, revisionary relationship with the past and
'the truth'.[1] In its multiple iterations and permutations – from the inertial
tug of tradition, to the narratives of personal introspection, to the

---

[1] Few topics in recent years have elicited as much interest among historians as the relationship between
memory and history. These introductory remarks are intended to offer a brief and necessarily
selective glance at this vast topic. They owe much to the synthesis of recent scholarship on
memory and history by Hutton (2000). Central and significant are Nora's monumental study of
Lieux de memoire (1984–92, 3 vols.); Rousso (1991) and Vidal-Naquet (1992) on the 'assassination'
of memory in post-war Europe; Matsuda (1996) on memory and the 'modern'; Friedlander (1991)
and, on re-making public memory (with a focus on modern America); Bodnar (1992) and Kammen
(1991). Further introductory material in Wachtel (1986). For the overbearing exertion of Freud on
such formulations and re-formulations of collective memory, Ricoeur's philosophy of the
psychoanalytic (1970) remains vital and rewarding. For the Freudian dialectic with Halbwachs,

189

190   Selective Memory and Iliadic Revision

accelerating speed with which collective memories are evoked and obliterated in modern cultures of the instantaneous – memory is a construct formed and informed by processes of contradiction, conversion and retransmission. In what can offer a stark, miniature acknowledgement of how these paradoxes play out in the very *language* of memory, the Torah contains a *mizvot* which explicitly commands: 'Do not forget to blot out the memory of Amalek from under heaven' (*Deut.* 25:19). The disorienting notion of being ordered to remember to forget lays bare the lurking duplicities inherent in so many paradigms of remembering, as those who claim to have 'the greatest memory of all time' pursue policies of manipulative amnesia and 'lest we forget' always really means 'lest we remember the wrong parts'.

These vignettes, designedly 'un' imperial-Greek and cross-chronological in range, seek to bring into sharper focus the relevance of memory as a *concept* for Quintus' project. We have seen how Homer formed a crucial part of the literary, educative and textual fabric of imperial Greece, occupying a unique and privileged place in its collective cultural memory. In his act of Homeric impersonation, Quintus demands of his reader, constantly, to remember Homer, but also to remember Homer differently, as something expanded and revived – a part of *this poet*, in the imperial now. In the distinctive temporality of this epic, the act of looking backwards, as we have seen in the proem and will see differently later, also entails a move forwards: to new vocabulary or formulae; to the *Odyssey* that 'Homer' has not yet composed; or to Hesiod or Callimachus, as analepsis folds into the proleptic. Homeric doubleness, in other words, requires the suspension of disbelief, but also the willingness to *misremember*, as Quintus-as-Homer ἴσκε ψεύδεα πολλὰ λέγων ἐτύμοισιν ὁμοῖα (*Od.* 19.203).[2]

In this chapter, I shall consider how Quintus forms this new Homeric memory by looking directly at his use of memory as a *literary* device – a trope operating within the poem and featuring heavily in its plot. Characters in the *Posthomerica* make frequent recourse to remembrance: strikingly often, the heroes are said explicitly to recall events from earlier stages of the Trojan War. A number of these memories correspond to episodes from the primary narrative of the *Iliad*: in narratological terms,

---

see Halbwachs trans. Coser (1992) with further bibliography. All of these varied strands, ostensibly far removed from the realm of imperial Greek epic, will underpin and inform this chapter's topic.

[2] Odysseus of course here is *lying*, rather than just selectively remembering. It is precisely this permeable boundary between memory and truth in poetry which will be crucial to Quintus' game as this chapter reads it.

Introduction

they are 'analepses' to that poem.[3] Seven times, these analepses are expressed through the narrator reporting the memories of characters.[4] On twelve occasions, a character recalls in direct speech an Iliadic event from his or her past.[5] In each of these cases, the relationship to the relevant Homeric passage is signalled by close verbal recapitulations: memory meets with allusion. And yet the Iliadic material is often changed as it is recalled: new details are added, other aspects are omitted, or emphases are skewed.

These moments reveal the *Posthomerica*'s own distinctive take on the relationship between memory and Homeric 'history'. What does it mean when characters who are 'still in the *Iliad*' remember their Homer incorrectly? Beginning with this question, the central claim of this chapter is that through the poem's narrative recollections of the *Iliad*, Quintus significantly redrafts the relationship between Homeric poetry, history and truth. Rather than offering a correction of the *Iliad*'s version of events, our poet uses the pliability of memory as a retrospective allusive device to defend and *continue* Homer's own practice of poetic selectivity. By demonstrating the partiality of any poetic account of events at Troy, he provides a response to charges of Homer's lying and deceit prevalent in the imperial era.

There is, however, a further layer to this response. By countering specific arguments about Homer's historical reliability, Quintus brings his epic into direct contact with a number of contemporary *prose* works from his time. This contact returns us directly to the issue of poetry 'versus' prose in the imperial era, which, as we saw in Chapter 1, held back the serious study of imperial Greek epic for so long. If the conventional view once maintained that poetry in the Roman era was 'annexed' by prose, and if the *Posthomerica* is still often deemed to be 'indebted [primarily] to Homer and the post-Homeric poetic tradition, rather than ... prose writings',[6] then Quintus' treatment of memory also becomes a pressing issue of form. Harnessing the device of remembering, Quintus provides poetry's answer to, as he presents it, a prosaic mode of reading Homer. Pitting new Homeric poetry against these criticisms, the *Posthomerica* makes a case for the superiority of responding to Homer in verse.

---

[3] On analepsis, see the summary of scholarship in de Jong (1987a): 81–90. On analepses and prolepses in the *Posthomerica*, see the chapter by Schmitz (2007b) dedicated to this topic.

[4] Q.S.1.9–15; 1.710–12; 5.400–3; 7.378–81; 9.24–5; 13.267–9; 14.121–42.

[5] Q.S.1.574–95; 1.759–65; 2.431–46; 3.48–9; 3.80–2; 3.253–62; 5.201–9; 5.211–14; 5.270–5; 5.275–7; 5.311–6; 13.276.

[6] Maciver (2012b): 18. Maciver, of course, does not deny the influence of prose writings on the *Posthomerica*. His emphasis on the poetic tradition is here levied as another argument against reading Quintus' epic as a straightforwardly 'second sophistic' text, showing how, in terms of categorisation (both of the *Posthomerica* and the second sophistic 'period') old habits of association die hard...

5.2 Selective Memory and Poetic Selectivity

There are two intersecting frameworks which are central to this approach: first, the modern theoretical discourse on memory and literary allusion; and second, the ancient historicist method of reading and correcting Homer.

We began this chapter by noting the heightened scholarly interest in memory as a complex conveyor of history. There is also a strong literary version of this discourse, where the question becomes how memory is used to document, and distort, the *literary* past. In the impressive body of recent work dedicated to the subject of poetic memory in the ancient world, scholars have focused on how textual allusion provides a particularly effective mechanism for poets to guide readers through negotiations of memory,[7] and, in turn, how memory itself, as a trope within a poetic narrative, can provide a vehicle for the act of reflexive annotation. A major instance of what in Hinds' typology would be a 'tendentious annotation' – a covert, coded means for authors to allude to an earlier model – memory has been revealed as a particularly common signal of literary reference in Latin poetry.[8] Characters' recollections of events from their past, in other words, can unveil the textual 'memories' of the literary layers which inform them. To take one enduringly illustrative example, in Conte's famous reading of Ovid's *Fasti*, the word *memini* in the mouth of Ariadne tropes the intertexts of Catullus 64 which lie behind her speech:[9]

> *en iterum, fluctus, similis audite querellas!*
> *en iterum lacrimas accipe, harena, meas!*
> *dicebam, memini, 'periure et perfide Theseu!' –*
> Ovid, *Fasti*. 3.471–3

Behold, again, you waves, how you hear my complaint! Behold again you sands, how you receive my tears! I remember I used to say: 'Lying, faithless Theseus!'

---

[7] On Late Antiquity, in particular, I have found extremely useful the studies of later Latin literature by Pelttari (2014) and, especially, Hartman (diss.) (2016), who offers a stimulating account of allusion and cultural memory in Ausonius, Prudentius, and Claudian.

[8] See Conte (1986), Barchiesi (1986), Miller (1993), with discussion in Hinds himself at (1998): 3–4. Other scholars have recently rightly stressed the Hellenistic origins of the trope: the poetry of Callimachus and Apollonius in particular is replete with models and vocabulary of literary reminiscence which anticipate and influence later imitations. On this topic, see Van Tress (2004) and Faber (2017).

[9] Conte (1986): 60–3. Related discussion in Barchiesi (1986) and (1993); Miller (1993); Hinds (1998): 3–4.

Ovid's Ariadne has 'lived her experience as a poetic self, in Catullus' poem', and thus she remembers the tears she wept there.[10] The emphasis here is on the gap between fiction and reality, revealed through the space between the 'then' (distant past) and 'now'. Ovid temporarily extracts Ariadne from his world of narrative events, giving her an allusive power which extends beyond his narrative convention, and by so doing attracts attention to the artifice of his own poetic world, 'unmask[ing] its basically imaginative nature'.[11] Memory thus helps to articulate Ovid's characteristic self-consciousness; the drive, as Hardie puts it, 'to realise a maximum of immediate presence in his poetry at the same time as he self-consciously unmasks the reality effects'.[12] Memory thus conceptualised represents another major example of the pattern that we have been tracing throughout this book: Alexandrian-inflected allusivity adopted with creative vigour by Roman poets. Unsurprisingly, given this pattern, the trope is also now being increasingly associated with the poetry of imperial Greece.

Imperial Greek epic, certainly, was alert to this allusive potential in the act of remembering. In the mythological poems focused on events before Homer's segment of the Trojan War, memory provides a particularly useful tool for emphasising the simultaneous earliness and lateness at play. To take a pronounced example, in Colluthus' Homeric prequel, when Eris begins the destructive proceedings, as we have seen, by 'remembering' her golden apples (χρυσέων ἐμνήσατο μήλων, *Abduction of Helen* 59),[13] the verb ἐμνήσατο assertively acknowledges the well-known nature of this scene – *those* apples, *that* wedding – as Colluthus embeds his narrative firmly within the mythological always-already. Later in the poem, when Helen first encounters Paris, she enquires about his lineage by listing the heroes of whom she has already heard. With repeated verbs of knowing and learning, she discloses her literary as well as literal memory, which she 'later' articulates again in the *teichoscopia* of *Iliad* 3:[14]

> ἀλλὰ τεὴν οὐκ οἶδα παρ᾽ Ἀργείοισι γενέθλην.
> πᾶσαν Δευκαλίωνος ἀμύμονος οἶδα γενέθλην·
> οὐ Πύλον ἠμαθόεσσαν ἔχεις, Νηλήιον οὖδας,
> —Ἀντίλοχον δεδάηκα, τεὴν δ᾽ οὐκ εἶδον ὀπωπήν
> οὐ Φθίην χαρίεσσαν, ἀριστήων τροφὸν ἀνδρῶν·
> οἶδα περικλήιστον ὅλον γένος Αἰακιδάων,

---

[10] Conte (1986): 61.   [11] Conte (1986): 62.   [12] Hardie (2002): 15.

[13] See discussion of this passage in Chapter 1.3.

[14] *Il.* 3.121–44. Colluthus' scene makes many intertextual links to this Iliadic episode, confirming how memory is used to configure allusion in this epic. The trope is there...

194   Selective Memory and Iliadic Revision

ἀγλαΐην Πηλῆος, ἐυκλείην Τελαμῶνος,
ἤθεα Πατρόκλοιο καὶ ἠνορέην Ἀχιλῆος.

Abduction of Helen 270–7

But your family, among the Argives, I do not know. I know all the family of blameless Deucalion. Not in sandy Pylus, the land of Neleus, do you have your dwelling: Antilochus I know, but you face I have not seen; not in gracious Phthia, nurse of chieftains; I know the whole renowned race of the sons of Aeacus, the beauty of Peleus, the fair fame of Telamon, the gentleness of Patroclus and the prowess of Achilles.

In his own restaging of the cycle, Quintus anticipates and outdoes Colluthus in his attention to memory. The sheer number and range of recollections in the *Posthomerica* is immediately striking. There are, to be precise, 47 memories in the narrative and 57 in character speech.[15] A number of these occurrences align with the functions of memory found in Homer's epics (set out most clearly in Bakker's recent typology):[16] namely, exhortations in a battlefield context (in formulae such as ὁ δ᾽ οὔπω λήθετο θυμοῦ or ἀλκῆς μνησώμεσθα);[17] appeals to paternal *menos*;[18] recollections of a person;[19] and evocations of a generalised past.[20] As Schmitz has argued in his fine discussion of analepses and prolepses in the *Posthomerica*, through the very use of these methods of anachrony, Quintus is showcasing his inheritance of these fundamental devices from Homer, affirming his status as 'heir to Homer's narrative technique'.[21] However, Quintus also makes far greater recourse than Homer to describing events *as* memories: both those from within the narrative (internal analepses)[22] and those outside of it (external analepses).[23] Thus, when Homer's Nestor speaks in the

---

[15] In determining what constitutes a memory, I have relied on the presence of certain verbal markers within the text: words denoting cognitive faculties (μιμνήσκω and λανθάνω, and also certain uses of οἶδα, ἀκούω, νομίζω, ἐπίσταμαι etc.), and other terms which, when read in context, denote reference to the characters' past (e.g. ὁππότε, πάρος). These aim to cover the broadest possible range of reminiscences.

[16] Bakker (2008).

[17] Q.S.3.139; 4.380; 5.353–4; 1.218; 1.413; 3.138–9; 4.380; 6.607–8; 8.265–6; 9.86; 13.119–20; 14.67–8; 14.345.

[18] Q.S.6.304; 9.50; 14.227.

[19] Q.S.1.116; 1.379; 2.293–4; 3.404; 3.517; 4.498–9; 7.725–7; 7.633; 7.695–7; 10.319; 10.408–10; 10.454–5; 13.454–5; 13.518; 13.522–3; 14.408.

[20] Q.S.1.332; 1.361–2; 1.734–5; 2.661; 5.163–4; 7.243–4; 10.298; 10.406–7; 12.255; 14.166–8; 14.235–45.

[21] Schmitz (2007b): 65–6.

[22] Q.S.4.118–68; 5.135–6; 5.288–9; 5.292–305; 5.362; 7.46–50; 7.207–9; 7.378–83; 9.315–6; 10.157; 12.11–18; 13.267–9; 14.125–42l; 14.274–5; 14.435–9.

[23] Q.S.1.9–15; 1.574–95; 1.711–2; 1.759–63; 2.62; 2.94; 2.431–46; 3.48–9; 3.80–2; 3.98–117; 3.253–62; 3.463–89; 3.628–30; 4.118–68; 4.306–12; 4.313–22; 5.191–4; 5.195–6; 5.198–9; 5.201–9; 5.211–14; 5.267–75; 5.275–8; 5.278–81; 5.311–16; 5.338–9; 5.400–3; 5.538–43;

Selective Memory and Poetic Selectivity

opening Iliadic assembly, he roots the authority of his advice in his knowledge of great men and battles from the past (*Il.* 1.245–84), but he does so by describing what happened, what he *did* (ἐγὼ καὶ ἀρείοσιν ἠέ περ ὑμῖν/ ἀνδράσιν ὡμίλησα..., 260–1) not what he remembers: μιμνήσκω does not occur once in this speech. And memory in the future in Homeric epic – events that *will have* occurred and will be remembered – is most frequently expressed in the language of *kleos* and song: things that will be said and heard, not explicitly what is remembered.[24] When Penelope famously characterises Phemius' bardic knowledge, her frictional juxtaposition of the *kleos* of song and the *penthos* of recollection show how, in this system, to be *aoidimos* is not always the same as to be remembered. Her personal memory of Odysseus, and of her loss of him, is constant, and so she does *not* want him, via his deeds,[25] to be commemorated statically in song:

> Φήμιε, πολλὰ γὰρ ἄλλα βροτῶν θελκτήρια οἶδας,
> ἔργ' ἀνδρῶν τε θεῶν τε, τά τε κλείουσιν ἀοιδοί·
> τῶν ἕν γέ σφιν ἄειδε παρήμενος, οἱ δὲ σιωπῇ
> οἶνον πινόντων· ταύτης δ' ἀποπαύε' ἀοιδῆς
> λυγρῆς, ἥ τέ μοι αἰεὶ ἐνὶ στήθεσσι φίλον κῆρ
> τείρει, ἐπεί με μάλιστα καθίκετο πένθος ἄλαστον.
> τοίην γὰρ κεφαλὴν ποθέω μεμνημένη αἰεί,
> ἀνδρός, τοῦ κλέος εὐρὺ καθ' Ἑλλάδα καὶ μέσον Ἄργος.
>
> *Od.* 1.337–44

Phemius, you know many other things to charm mortals, deeds of men and gods which minstrels make famous. Sing them one of these, as you sit here, and let them drink their wine in silence. But cease from this woeful song which ever torments my heart, for upon me above all women has come a sorrow not to be forgotten. I always remember him with longing, my husband, whose fame is wide through Hellas and mid-Argos.

Quintus' emphatic and quantitative language of memory, therefore, becomes part of his core process of redrafting the terms of Homeric poetics 'from within': in line with the penchants of his contemporary epic composers, his explicit and specific use of this recollective language distinguishes himself sharply from Homer in terms of what poetic discourse is now.[26]

6.61–2; 7.59–61; 7.642–52; 9.400–1; 7.378–83; 9.226–7; 9.491–2; 10.365–6; 10.396; 13.267–9; 13.275–6; 13.294–5; 13.519–22; 14.125–42; 14.152–3; 14.174; 14.210–12.

[24] So, paradigmatically, does Helen remark: οἷσιν ἐπὶ Ζεὺς θῆκε κακὸν μόρον, ὡς καὶ ὀπίσσω/ ἀνθρώποισι πελώμεθ' ἀοίδιμοι ἐσσομένοισι, *Il.* 6.358–9.

[25] Such deeds of course being the topic of the song that Phemius has just completed.

[26] Schmitz acknowledges this second function of analepsis in the *Posthomerica*, arguing that 'Quintus' text is constantly looking back to prior [Iliadic] events. This means that many intertextual references are also analepses since the narrator is reminding his audience of what happened before and why this

196   Selective Memory and Iliadic Revision

And yet when narrative memory is used to express allusion to Homer in the *Posthomerica*, this process of 'self-distinguishing' becomes cloudier and more claustrophobic. The Contean model needs to be augmented for Quintus, or, perhaps better, its emphasis reversed. For whilst a system of exposed artifice undoubtedly holds true for poets such as Ovid, who delight in saying *me specta*[27] and revealing the skill behind their literary hand, memory as an allusive trope can also produce the opposite effect: to conceal rather than expose authorial artifice. After all, if a literary reference is encased within a character's recollection, then it is not the allusion which is ostentatiously 'marked' but the mythological *illusion*:[28] the poetic quotation of a text is subsumed in to the image of a character recalling a genuine experience, like 'the tears she wept'.[29] In Quintus' poem it is this sense of illusion that is foregrounded: the heroes remain in the same mythological world as they occupied in Homer's poem, they are 'waiting' (ἔμιμνον, 1.3), trapped within its narrative space, and in remembering the *Iliad* they are recalling events from their *recent* past, which continue to influence their present. And whereas Conte's Ovid reveals his poetic persona as 'not Catullus' by marking out the gap between fiction and reality, Quintus' interest, as I have continued to argue, is in eroding this gap, subsuming his poetic persona into Homer. His characters' allusive memories, therefore, cannot be comprehended in the same way as those of Ovid or Colluthus.

This is particularly the case when Quintus appears to allow his characters to remember the *Iliad* in an *un*-Homeric way. On the one hand, these additions, suppressions or changes represent purposeful amendments on the characters' part: drawing from their lived experience, they reconfigure an event in the way that best befits their current situation. They display, in other words, a selective memory of their Iliadic past, contradicting, converting and re-transmitting that past, subconsciously or all too willingly. But the reader, of course, also knows that this is a poem and that it is really the poet who gives the characters their material to recall. By impersonating

---

caused the current state of events' (2007b): 66. He does not, however, consider the significance of the use of memory to convey these intertextual references, nor pay due attention to the 'still Homer' temporality at play.

[27] Ov. *Am.* 1.4.17.

[28] For discussion of the theory and practice of illusion in literary, dramatic and rhetorical contexts, see Chapter 2 on 'doubleness'.

[29] As Hinds points out (1998): 4, even in the case of Ariadne the memory is spoken '"in character", and its suspension of the artistic illusion is covert rather than overt'.

Selective Memory and Poetic Selectivity 197

the Homeric poet, Quintus also transfers the notion of selective memory from the Homeric characters onto Homer himself.[30]

On the one hand, this notion of tactical selectivity is already widely perceived and readily exemplified in the Homeric epics. Thus in the Odyssean description of Demodocus constructing his song (a passage which, as discussed in Chapter 2, takes on central importance in Quintus' version of this process), we are told how the bard takes up his tale from a specific mid-point in the war narrative (ἔνθεν ἑλὼν ὡς οἱ μὲν ἐυσσέλμων ἐπὶ νηῶν/βάντες ἀπέπλειον, πῦρ ἐν κλισίῃσι βαλόντες,/Ἀργεῖοι... *Od.* 8.500–2). Odysseus' own narrative selectivity, always suspected in the *Apologoi*, is laid bare in his potted recollection of this recollection to his wife (*Od.* 23.310–44), which shamelessly omits the more erotic details of his adventures.[31] And so too in the *Iliad*, when Odysseus reports to Achilles Agamemnon's catalogue of gifts (*Il.* 9.260–99), within the overwhelming 'block' repetition of a large chunk of Agamemnon's previous speech, he also omits and subtracts various lines and changes certain phrases. As a result, he withholds and refracts the terms of Agamemnon's self-admission, 'important language which Achilles never receives':[32] Odysseus the messenger is carefully, calculatedly, selective.

However, these paradigms of Homeric cut and pasting, guarded and occlusive revelation, are *not* presented as memories: in line with the pattern that we have traced above, the explicit language of memory is largely absent from these characters' selective (and, often, deceptive) treatments of the past. Remembering vocabulary, for instance, does not occur at all in this way in Odysseus' transformative recapitulation of Agamemnon's list:[33] he does not 'recollect' the terms and the gifts. Odysseus only resorts to memory vocabulary once, in the negative, as he chastises Achilles for forgetting the advice of his father (ὣς ἐπέτελλ' ὁ γέρων, σὺ δὲ λήθεαι... *Il.* 9.259).

---

[30] On the difference, and potential overlap, between quotations or (in our case) recollections given by the author and those given by their characters, see Kruchió (2018) in respect of the Greek novels, which make great use, so he argues, of 'actorially motivated' quotations.

[31] Odysseus does not mention Nausicaa at all, speaks only of Circe's 'wiles' and boasts of his endurance of Calypso's propositions and refusal of her promises, omitting the longevity of his stay with the nymph, during which he complied, begrudgingly or otherwise, to her lusts (cf. e.g. *Od.* 5.152–3: κατείβετο δὲ γλυκὺς αἰών/νόστον ὀδυρομένῳ, ἐπεὶ οὐκέτι ἥνδανε νύμφη).

[32] So, for example, the cataloguing verb καταλέγω is shifted from its position in Agamemnon's admission of *ate* to the catalogue of gifts (*Il.* 9.263). See Lynn-George (1988): 91–2 for a full list of changes, and insightful analysis of Odysseus' process of redrafting of Agamemnon's speech.

[33] This is despite the fact that Odysseus would have had to memorise the contents of the lengthy offer to fulfil his task in the embassy of communicating it. See Tsagarakis (1979): 237.

198 Selective Memory and Iliadic Revision

In Quintus' reformulation, therefore, the well-established Homeric practice of selectivity is combined with the un-Homeric emphatic language of remembrance. That new details are now added to these characters' 'still-Homeric' narrative past, and other aspects taken away, *specifically formed as recollections*, opens up the possibility that Homer himself is turning now to employ a different mode of memory in his epic. Framing past events more explicitly through the language of memory to undertake a wilful act of re-transmission, he knew more, or different, information about the Trojan War than that which appears in the *Iliad*, and only now, in this contin-uation poem, is he choosing to commit this material to verse.[34]

This possibility brings us to the second crucial framework for this chapter: the ancient trend of historically based revision of Homer. The tradition of correcting Homer's narrative of the Trojan War, as old as Stesichorus, Herodotus and Euripides, takes the fundamental tenets of the Homeric account – most centrally, the capture of Helen, the crucial and contested *casus belli* – and sees them defiantly undermined and creatively reversed: Helen never went to Troy, or a ghost went in her place – the Homeric version of events is based on a spectre, a misrecognition and/or a *lie*. Herodotus famously suggests the potentially insidious motivations behind the Homeric tale: after hearing the real story from the Egyptian priests, he delivers his verdict on why, in Homer's account, things went awry:

Ἑλένης μὲν ταύτην ἄπιξιν παρὰ Πρωτέα ἔλεγον οἱ ἱρέες
γενέσθαι· δοκέει δέ μοι καὶ Ὅμηρος τὸν λόγον τοῦτον
πυθέσθαι· ἀλλ' οὐ γὰρ ὁμοίως ἐς τὴν ἐποποιίην εὐπρεπὴς ἦν
τῷ ἑτέρῳ τῷ περ ἐχρήσατο, ἑκὼν μετῆκε αὐτόν, δηλώσας
ὡς καὶ τοῦτον ἐπίστατο τὸν λόγον. δῆλον δέ, κατὰ
κατὰ [γὰρ] ἐποίησε ἐν Ἰλιάδι (καὶ οὐδαμῇ ἄλλη ἀνεπόδισε ἑωυτόν)
πλάνην τὴν Ἀλεξάνδρου, ὡς ἀπηνείχθη ἄγων Ἑλένην τῇ τε δὴ
ἄλλη πλαζόμενος καὶ ὡς ἐς Σιδῶνα τῆς Φοινίκης ἀπίκετο.

Hdt. 2.116.1–2

This, the priests said, was how Helen came to Proteus. And, in my opinion, Homer knew this story, too; but seeing that it was not so well suited to epic poetry as the tale of which he made use, he rejected it, showing that he knew it. This is apparent from the passage in the *Iliad* (and nowhere else does he return to the story) where he relates the wanderings of Alexander, and shows how he

---

[34] My interest here is not in exploring whether Quintus perceives any actual historical accuracy in Homer's poetry, but in the ancient responses to this question of historical accuracy with which the *Posthomerica* engages.

Selective Memory and Poetic Selectivity

and Helen were carried off course, and wandered to, among other places, Sidon in Phoenicia.[35]

As Herodotus proceeds to quote, in fact, three passages from the *Iliad* and *Odyssey* which prove this point,[36] Homer's epic selectivity is presented as an act of wilful concealment; and the culprit for this concealment is clear. It is *poetry* which drove Homer's omissions: the truth was not suitable for the epic verse form (οὐ γὰρ ὁμοίως ἐς τὴν ἐποποιίην εὐπρεπὴς ἦν).

This thorny issue of the relationship between history and poetry as representational forms,[37] paradigmatically illustrated by Aristotle's discussion in the *Poetics* (where the distinction is defined as the contrast between actual events – τὰ γενόμενα – and plausible ones – οἷα ἂν γένοιτο καὶ τὰ δυνατὰ κατὰ τὸ εἰκὸς ἢ τὸ ἀναγκαῖον, *Poet.* 1451a36–8), is traceable through a range of ancient responses. Amongst the plethora of post-Aristotelian discourses on this topic, we may consider *exempli causa* the stingingly pithy critique of Gorgias in his famous, fiendish opening to the *Encomium of Helen*. In the programmatic first word κόσμος – meaning 'goodness', but also nodding, via the word's other well-known meaning, to the Thucydidean accusation of poetic 'embellishment';[38] the refutation of the punning poets' incredulous character portraits (2); and the daring, challenging definition of poetry as λόγον ἔχοντα μέτρον (8) – Gorgias continually pits the motivations and form of poetry against the *Encomium*'s own stylised textuality.[39] Or, to turn to a far later antique response, distinctive too is the stance advanced by the historian Agathias in the age of Justinian, who states in his own beginning to the *Histories* that he has been persuaded by his friends to write verse history, because history is not in fact 'far removed from poetry, but both are kindred and related disciplines, differing radically perhaps only in the matter of metre'. (prf. 12.[40]).

---

[35] Trans. adapted from Godley (1920).

[36] *Il.* 6.289–92; *Od.* 4.227–30; *Od.* 4.351–2. Bibliography on Herodotus and Homer, and this passage as a *locus classicus* for the relationship, is formidable. Particularly helpful starting points in Pelling (2006) with targeted further bibliography.

[37] This issue is of course mammoth and multiplex, and one which this brief 'scene setting' can only touch upon. A word is needed to delineate my focus: I am not now dealing primarily in this chapter with lying and truth *within* poetry (*qua*, for instance, Odysseus in Homer, as we have previously discussed, and the Muses in Hesiod) nor with theories and practices of fiction (*muthos, plasma* and their related discourses) – though such topics inform my discussions. My chief concern is about form: poetry as a *medium* to convey such ideas.

[38] Emblematically at Thuc. 1.21.

[39] See e.g. Ford (2002), Wardy (1996) and (2018), Allen (2001).

[40] See Kaldellis (1997), Averil Cameron (1970): 57–111; Goldhill (2020). The factors – both theoretical and cultural-historical – affecting Agathias' discourse on poetry and history in his century go beyond my scope here. But whilst his excursus, as with all the examples above, must

200   Selective Memory and Iliadic Revision

This poetry–prose relationship, however, is also crucial to charting the particular approach to correcting Homer in the imperial Greek period more specifically: the stretch of time, that is, which falls in between the 'first sophistic' rhetorical epoch of Gorgias and the contentious, Christian environment of Agathias in the 'last Roman century.'[41] For the revisionist mode found a host of exceptionally boisterous, cynical new advocates in Quintus' own era. Its popularity in this particular period is in one sense not surprising. In light of the much-hailed hegemony of Homer in this era's education and culture, here was a way for the most learned, ludic members of this culture to engage more irreverently with this hyper-Homericity: *paideia* served with the tongue in the cheek.

This imperial brand of Homeric correction took many forms. The so-called 'Homeric Games' – prose accounts like those of Dictys of Crete and Dares of Phrygia – purported to give the 'true story' of the war based on newly uncovered or more reliable evidence predating the Homeric poems.[42] But there also survive a number of texts which construct a more direct dialogue with Homer. In his lucid account of imperial Homeric revision, Larry Kim identifies three works from the second sophistic as distinctive in their efforts to argue against the poet. Dio's *Trojan Oration*, Lucian's *True Histories* and Philostratus' *Heroicus* (alongside which is discussed the *Vita Apollonii*), he argues, form a distinct group within the field of Homeric rewritings owing to their shared interest in the historical 'truth' of Homer's account, explicit and detailed discussion of Homeric poetry, and centralisation of the figure of Homer himself.[43]

In these texts, therefore, concern with Homer's historical veracity is redeployed to articulate an interest in the *poetic* process driving the so-called lies: Homer's sources, his allegiances and his agenda in turning this story to song. This emphasis, which has been rightly understood against the background of ancient critical discussions such as those in Book 1 of Strabo,[44] sets forward a vision of myth as based on a core truth and a corresponding image of Homer as a tendentious, selective poet, who knew more about this truth than he put in his verses, transforming it in, and

---

be appreciated as a product of its own time, his comments serve to show the enduring relevance of these issues of form across the post-Aristotelian centuries.

[41] Maas (2005). More discussion in this vein in the conclusion to this chapter.

[42] See Merkle (1994): 183–96; Cameron (2004): 136–7; Kim (2010): 15–16 and 175–81.

[43] Kim (2010): esp. 17–18. Artificial as this grouping is – needless to say, there is no indication that any contemporary reader would have approached the texts in such terms – Kim is right to highlight the specific combination of Homeric interests on display, and this combination offers a fruitful test-site for Quintus' approach.

[44] See Kim (2010): 47–84; Hunter (2009): 44–6.

Selective Memory and Poetic Selectivity

therefore *by*, his poetry. The Herodotean motif of Homer's poetry as the driving factor for his falsity and Aristotelian and post-Aristotelian theories of poetry and history are elevated to central importance by these authors, literalised and formalised in their projects. And thus whereas Euripides and Stesichorus provide early instances of Homeric alternativising in verse, Lucian, Dio, Philostratus and co. take pains to associate Homer's lying directly with his medium of poetry and therefore, by transferral, claim the process of correcting him as an exclusive activity for *prose*.

We have seen that the modern scholarly vision of imperial Greece as a literary world dominated by prose is misguided: that those critics who deem that poetry was 'dead' in this period take too seriously, perhaps, the witty self-posturing of such treatise writers. Given the loud voice that poetry did have in the literary culture of this time, we must ask what was its reaction to these anti-Homeric revisions, championed so loudly in (and now *as*) prose? In this constructed contest of form, how did imperial epic cope?

Two epics offer direct answers to this question. In the third book of the *Sibylline Oracles*[45] the Sibyl rounds on Homer aggressively,[46] claiming her stake in exactly these sorts of (anti) Homeric games:

> καί τις ψευδογράφος πρέσβυς βροτὸς ἔσσεται αὖτις
> ψευδόπατρις· δύσει δὲ φάος ἐν ὀπῇσιν ἑῇσιν   (420)
> νοῦν δὲ πολὺν καὶ ἔπος διανοίαις ἔμμετρον ἕξει,
> οὐνόμασιν δυσὶ μισγόμενον· Χῖον δὲ καλέσσει
> αὐτὸν καὶ γράψει τὰ κατ' Ἴλιον, οὐ μὲν ἀληθῶς,
> ἀλλὰ σοφῶς· ἐπέων γὰρ ἐμῶν μέτρων τε κρατήσει·
> πρῶτος γὰρ χείρεσσιν ἐμὰς βίβλους ἀναπλώσει   (425)
> αὐτὸς δ' αὖ μάλα κοσμήσει πολέμοιο κορυστάς,
> Ἕκτορα Πριαμίδην καὶ Ἀχιλλέα Πηλείωνα
> τούς τ' ἄλλους, ὁπόσοις πολεμήια ἔργα μέμηλεν.
> καί γε θεοὺς τούτοισι παρίστασθαί γε ποιήσει,
> ψευδογραφῶν κατὰ πάντα τρόπον, μέροπας κενοκράνους. (430)
> καὶ θανέειν μᾶλλον τοῖσιν κλέος ἔσσεται εὐρύ
> Ἰλίῳ· ἀλλὰ καὶ αὐτὸς ἀμοιβαῖα δέξεται ἔργα.
>
> *Or. Sib.* 3.411–32

---

[45] The dating of the Oracles is a continually contentious issue. On the collection, see Lightfoot (2007) and, on Book 3 in particular, Collins (1974), Amir (1985), Buitenwerf (2003) and Hornblower (2015): 126–35. The third book is usually predominantly in the Ptolemaic period, with newer later sections appended at the beginning and towards the end. The passage under discussion here is generally considered to be among the later material, due to its conspicuous references to Rome and knowledge of Hellenistic modes of Homeric critique. I offer a new analysis of this passage in Greensmith (forthcoming b).

[46] For the unusual move of naming Homer in Greek epic, see Greensmith (forthcoming b), with related discussion for the *Posthomerica* in Chapter 6 of this book.

202 Selective Memory and Iliadic Revision

And then there will be a certain false writer, an old mortal, who has a false fatherland. The light in his eyes will go out. He will be very wise and have a speech suitable for his thoughts which will be joined under two names. He will call himself an inhabitant of Chios. He will write the story of Ilium, not truthfully, but cleverly. For he will have mastered *my* verses and metres, since he will be the first to open my books with his hands. He will highly embellish the helmed men of war. And he will make gods, in fact empty-headed people, to stand by them, writing falsely in every respect. And it will be a great honour for them to die at Troy. But he will also receive retribution.

In this fiery confrontation, Homer becomes not only a liar but a thief. As the Sibyl makes prioritising claim to the hexameter medium – and the Alexandrian bookish culture which cultivated it – this author appropriates the methods and vocabulary of prosaic and historiographical criticisms of Homer and verse (engaging again, for example, the language of κοσμέω and various facets of Homer's biographical tradition) only to reverse them, by turning Homeric correction (back) into a fundamentally poetic matter. Three centuries later, Nonnus gives a potted version of the same poeticised revision. Quoting a famous *gnome* from the *Iliad* (*Il.* 13.636–9) – that device which, as we have seen, provides a prism for challenging the universal authority of Homer – he performs a glib, eroticised reduction of the wryly high-stake claims made by Lucian, Dio and Philostratus. Whereas those authors debate Homer's lies about Trojan history, Nonnus' concern is how Homer got it wrong about love:

> πάντων γὰρ κόρος ἐστὶ παρ' ἀνδράσιν, ἡδέος ὕπνου
> μολπῆς τ' εὐκελάδοιο καὶ ὁππότε κάμπτεται ἀνὴρ
> εἰς δρόμον ὀρχηστῆρα· γυναιμανέοντι δὲ μούνῳ
> οὐ κόρος ἐστὶ πόθων· ἐψεύσατο βίβλος Ὁμήρου.
>
> *Dion.* 42.178–81

For all things can cause satiety in men, sweet sleep and melodious song and when a man spins in the rush of the dance – but only one man about women can never get tired of his longing: the book of Homer lied![47]

Both Nonnus and the Sibyl, therefore, respond to prosaic criticism of Homer's veracity by offering poetic versions of the same attacks. Harnessing that overtly paradoxical temporality characteristic of the mythological poetry of this time, they show how epic can be perfectly compatible with

---

[47] The full Iliadic *gnome* in question here is: πάντων μὲν κόρος ἐστὶ καὶ ὕπνου καὶ φιλότητος/μολπῆς τε γλυκερῆς καὶ ἀμύμονος ὀρχηθμοῖο (*Il.* 13.636–7). Brief discussion of the Nonnus passage in Bannert and Kröll (2016): 484–5, although in general it has attracted surprisingly little comment among Nonnian critics.

the imperial trend of Homeric revision: by purporting to pre-date Homer (*qua* Dares and Dictys) and explicitly correcting him, they transfer the 'prosaic' material of Homeric historicism into their own Homerically derived hexameter.

Quintus, however, does not play this game. In his approach to this issue – how to challenge, in Homerising poetry, the challenges of Homeric criticism – we can perceive once again our poet's distinctive stance. Although the *Posthomerica* too makes claim to retrojecting Homeric chronology (this time the claim is to be 'still Homer' rather than pre-Homer), Quintus does not use this position to prove his model wrong. Instead, under the pretence of Homeric authorship, by adding new details to Iliadic recollections, he is able to *disarm* claims regarding some of Homer's most severe omissions. Nonnus and the Sibyl, in other words, make Homeric revisionism compatible with new hexameter epic. Quintus instead makes Homeric revisionism compatible with Homeric epic itself. In this alternative response by poetry to the charges levied against it, here is Homer answering back.

The central part of this chapter will now focus on how these two frameworks – the literary trope of memory and second sophistic criticism of Homer on the basis of historical truth – are persistently combined in the *Posthomerica*. Characters' memories become the primary vehicle for Quintus' pro-Homeric 'back-chat'. If memory always involves a complex practice of transmission, and if allusivity always involves an engagement with the politics of cultural memory, then in his textual recollections of the *Iliad*, by expanding the space between narrative 'history' and poetic 'fiction', Quintus displays his own Homeric *lieu de mémoire*.

5.3   Reported Memories: Homer *et cetera*

One of the foremost examples of Homer's 'deceptive' poetic selectivity was where he chose to begin his epic tale. The question of why the *Iliad* starts with the *mēnis* of Achilles instead of narrating the entirety of the Trojan War was a prevalent discussion point in antiquity (in, for example, Arist. *Poet.* 1459a 30–7 and Horace's famous phrase *medias in res*): the *Iliad* was, in this respect, the original, problematic poem of the interval. The answer found was that, unlike his competitors, Homer selected the climactic phase for his subject matter and incorporated the antecedents by way of analepsis.[48]

---

[48]   See e.g. Σ. β. *Il.* 2.494–877 *ex.* Erbse (1969): 288. Cf. Nünlist (2009a) and (2009b).

204 Selective Memory and Iliadic Revision

This much-praised feature of Homeric narrative,[49] however, could also be cynically reframed. Dio's *Trojan Oration* tilts the concept of Homeric anastrophe so that it becomes a total subversion of events rather than a particular order of telling (11.24–5):[50] like prosecutors in court who 'lie skilfully' (μετὰ τέχνης ψεύδονται), Homer used a haphazard structure (οὐκ εὐθὺς ἤρξατο ἀπὸ τῆς ἀρχῆς, ἀλλ᾽ ὅθεν ἔτυχεν) to evade the truth more easily. Evading all discussion of the beginning or end of the war beyond the 'incidental' and 'brief' (παρέργως καὶ βραχέως), the poet deliberately confused his audience with this entangled, distorted sequence. In Lucian's *True Histories* Homer admits during his interview that he began with the wrath of Achilles simply because he felt like it (*Ver. Hist.* 2.20): here the most famous storytelling architecture is radically reduced to nothing more than a personal, spontaneous whim. Such conceits were also echoed in visual responses to Homer: on the Iliadic mural in our Casa di Octavius,[51] the story pointedly zigzags across the frieze, changing narrative trajectory between the east and west walls so as to mimic, perhaps, the disorienting effects of the 'haphazard' Homeric text from which it is drawn.[52]

When Quintus recapitulates the *Iliad* by reporting the memories of his characters, he marks his acute awareness of these types of discussions. However, rather than augmenting his narrative to incorporate them, he refuses to bow to their pressure. He revels in the fact that there is more to this Trojan story than a poet commits to tell, nodding to more material than has been included and at the same time justifying the process of selection that Homer originally undertook.

The *Posthomerica*'s own 'non-opening' lays the foundations for this technique. I began this book by discussing how Quintus uses his initial lines to instantiate and interrogate his epic's status as a direct Iliadic continuation. He even continues the Homeric practice of beginning in the middle – this time, of course, the *res* in which he is *in medias* involve not just the timespan of the Trojan story, but the start and end points represented by the *Iliad* and *Odyssey*. Faced with this entirely Homeric predicament, Quintus also follows Homer's 'solution': he incorporates the

---

[49] Cf. e.g. the gushing praise of Heraclitus (*Quaest. Hom.* 36.4) on *Il.* 8.16: 'Homer gives us the measure of the sphere of the universe in a single line.'

[50] On the ancient concept of anastrophe, see e.g. Nünlist (2009a): 67–9. On this aspect of Dio's *Trojan Oration*, see the excellent discussion by Hunter (2009): 51–3.

[51] See previous discussion of this house in Chapter 1 and Chapter 2.

[52] See the helpful diagram of this patterning in Squire (2011): 147 (fig. 48). For analysis, see Lorenz (2013) and Squire (2011): 145–6. For similar games with narrative order on the Iliac Tablets, see Squire (2011): especially ch. 4.

Reported Memories: Homer et cetera

'antecedents' (here, the end of the *Iliad*) through analepsis. However, this opening analepsis is also formed as a memory: the initial and intrinsic connection between Quintus' poem and the *Iliad* is conveyed through the reported recollections of those still trapped inside Troy's walls (μνησάμενοι προτέρων, ὁπόσων ἀπὸ θυμὸν ἴαψεν Θύων Ἰδαίοιο περὶ προχοῆσι Σκαμάνδρου.../τῶν οἵ γε μνησθέντες ἀνὰ πτολίεθρον ἔμιμνον Q.S.1.9; 15). Quintus therefore also uses his opening to establish his intensified interest in the language of memory, a departure from the emphasis of his Homeric model.

So let us now return to these loaded opening lines and read them not just as a statement of literary continuation, but also, and entirely relatedly, as a discourse on poetic memory. The interaction between narrative memory and textual allusion in this sequence is immediately palpable. Maciver's analysis of the passage makes this relationship clear: after first pointing out those many intertextual links with the *Iliad*,[53] he then considers the perspective on the poem's Homeric self-positioning that such connections bring to bear.[54] For Maciver, however, these intertexts denote a severance with the Iliadic past to which they refer: in a comfortably Contean reading, Quintus is seen to display the space between Homer's 'then' and his 'now':

> The situation and place on the mythological timescale is not the *Iliad's* plot: that is signalled as past, and thus the *Posthomerica* begins with the past, the passive aorist δάμη denotes this.[55]

> [Quintus] meta-poetically encodes the epic distance the *Posthomerica* has from Homer and therefore bespeak(s) the imitative program which Quintus, as a poet of the Imperial period, creates.[56]

However, as we have seen, the 'past' here is really *not* so complete. Through careful, intricate wordplay, Quintus anchors his opening Homeric recapitulation *not* to the distant literary or mythological past, but to the pressing, continuous present. And it is in fact in the opening's 'still Homeric' context, in which the *Iliad* is stressed as being in fact part of

---

[53] See Chapter 1.1 for my own analysis of these and other intertexts.
[54] Maciver (2012b): 29–33. ('it is to the opening lines of the *Posthomerica* that the reader looks for an index to the poem's aims and meanings.', ibid. 29).
[55] Maciver (2012b): 31. See also Schmitz (2007b): 66 (my italics): 'Quintus' text is constantly looking *back* to these prior (Iliadic) events.' But the point is that Quintus is not (just) 'constantly looking *back*' to prior events at Troy: he is also looking at them differently from within the ongoing Trojan timeframe of his poem.
[56] Maciver (2018): 71. The fact that this remains Maciver's position more than a decade after his first groundbreaking publications on Quintus shows the weight that such a reading continues to exert.

206   Selective Memory and Iliadic Revision

the poem's ongoing narrative reality, that the content of the Trojans' memories here must be understood. For the events which the Trojans are described as recalling do indeed echo the end of the *Iliad*, but they are not confined to it. As Quintus describes the Trojans remembering ὁπόσων ἀπὸ θυμὸν ἴαψεν ... ἠδ᾽ <ὁπ>όσους[57] φεύγοντας/ὑπὸ μέγα τεῖχος ὄλεσσεν (9–11), he augments the direct links to the *Iliad* with a note of unspecified vastness. Closely reminiscent of the ὅσοι φύγον αἰπὺν ὄλεθρον of the *Odyssey*'s own opening (and the *closing* lines of the *Posthomerica*: ὅσους διὰ χεῖμα κέδασσεν· ... ὅσσοι ὑπὲρ πόντοιο λυγρὰς ὑπάλυξαν ἀέλλας, 14.656–8), this statement expands the range of its possible heroic antecedents: are these casualties just the ones that we heard about in Homer? ὁπόσος, it could be countered, is a simple poetic shorthand, not a pointed note of expansion. But it is less easy to explain away the temporal tilt which accompanies it:

> ἄλλους θ᾽ ὡς ἐδάϊξε δι᾽ ἀκαμάτοιο θαλάσσης
> ὁππότε δὴ τὰ πρῶτα φέρε Τρώεσσιν ὄλεθρον.
>
> Q.S.1.13–14

The Trojans recall when Achilles 'first' brought death to the people of Troy. In the *Iliad*, of course, we do not witness these initial feats. When in *Il.* 9.328–9 Achilles boasts of how he sacked twelve cities by sea, he voices what Genette would call a 'completing external analepsis': in simple terms, he refers back to an event which took place before the timeframe of this narrative.[58]

The opening memories also contain a slight factual variation on the Iliadic version of events. The statement at 1.12 that Hector's body was dragged 'around the city' does not quite accord with any of Homer's descriptions of the desecration in the *Iliad* (*Il.* 22.395–404, 463–5; 24.14–21).[59] This 'change', it has been suggested, offers the first example of how Quintus seeks to correct Homer's account, exemplifying his 'willingness to depart from Homeric authority'.[60] And yet if he really wished to signal the start of a programme of Homeric correction, why opt for something so understated, so unspecific? In fact, in all three of the

---

[57] Some manuscripts preserve ὅσσους here; see Vian (1963): 12.

[58] Genette (1980): 51–61. Cf. also the analeptic feats in Nestor's song in Q.S.4, as discussed, with parallels, in Chapter 2.

[59] Cf. James (2004): 269. This change is also attested in earlier literature. Cf. e.g. Euripides' *Andromache* 107–8.

[60] James (2004): 269. See also Bär (2010) who reads the change as a 'second sophistic' style correction of Homer's account.

Reported Memories: Homer et cetera

relevant Iliadic passages, Achilles is described as moving the corpse in a slightly different place: before the city, towards the ships and around Patroclus' mound.[61] Quintus' ἀμφείρυσσε πόληι can thus just as easily be taken as an encapsulation of all of these different locations: an inclusive reading rather than a revision of the Iliadic terms, according to the programme of stylistic 'moderation in change' which this epic carefully constructs.

We should therefore consider another agenda behind these opening recollections. Rather than correcting Homer's account, the Trojans' reported memories constitute an initial, instigative example of Quintus' process of Homeric expansion: an incorporative re-animation of the material already contained within his model's poems. For whereas Maciver speaks of a distinction between the past of the *Iliad* and the present of Quintus, he neglects the fact that so much of the *Iliad's* plot was itself already past, its anastrophic tendencies famed in ancient critical discussions. By using the device of memory, Quintus intensifies and 'psychologises' this process: the *Iliad* becomes part of the characters' lived experience as well as the readers' literary one. In a few neat verses, Quintus thus defines the parameters of his pretence. This poet, 'still Homer', is continuing the Iliadic practice of using analepsis to give his story a wider perspective and he is about to tell more of this story now.

The device of reported memory is thus given a prominent and programmatic place in this narrative of continuation. As the narrative progresses, it continues to be used to articulate the re-transmission of a range of events from the Iliadic recent past. After the death of Penthesilea, Ares' rage is abated when he recalls that Zeus too had failed to save his own children when they were slain in battle:

> πολλὰ δὲ πορφύροντα θοὸς νόος ὀτρύνεσκεν
> ἄλλοτε μέν Κρονίδαο μέγ᾽ ἀσχαλόωντος ἐνιπὴν
> σμερδαλέην τρομέοντα πρὸς οὐρανὸν ἀπονέεσθαι,
> ἄλλοτε δ᾽ οὐκ ἀλέγειν σφετέρου πατρός, ἀλλ᾽ Ἀχιλῆι
> μῖξαι ἐν αἵματι χεῖρας ἀτειρέας. ὀψὲ δέ οἱ κῆρ
> μνήσαθ᾽, ὅσοι καὶ Ζηνὸς ἐνὶ πτολέμοισι δάμησαν
> υἱέες οἷς οὐδ᾽ αὐτὸς ἐπήρκεσεν ὀλλυμένοισι.
> τοὔνεκ᾽ ἀπ᾽ Ἀργείων ἑκὰς ἤιεν· ἦ γὰρ ἔμελλε
> κεῖσθαι ὁμῶς Τιτῆσι δαμεὶς στονόεντι κεραυνῷ,
> εἰ Δ<ι>ὸς ἀθανάτοιο παρὲκ νόον ἄλλα μενοίνα.
>
> Q.S.1.706–15

---

[61] Respectively *Il.* 22.395–404 and 24.16

208   Selective Memory and Iliadic Revision

As Ares pondered the matter, his mind veered between feeling that he should return cowed to heaven in obedience to the grim warning he had received from the wrathful son of Cronus and, on the other hand, the urge to ignore his father and soak his tireless hands in the blood of Achilles. But eventually he remembered that even Zeus had lost sons in the fighting and had not interfered to help them; and so he moved back from the Argives. Had he opposed the will of immortal Zeus, he would have been laid low like the Titans by the agonising thunderbolt.

To any reader who knows their Homer, Ares' reminiscence evokes *Il.* 16.431–61, where Zeus accepts Hera's advice to allow Sarpedon to be killed by Patroclus in accordance with the will of Fate. Quintus on the one hand steers the reader carefully towards that scene. Ares' fluctuation over two courses of action (πολλὰ δέ πορφύροντα θοὸς νόος ὀτρύνεσκεν, 706) re-enacts Zeus' own deliberation (διχθὰ δέ μοι κραδίη μέμονε φρεσὶν ὁρμαίνοντι, *Il.* 16.435), and the choice and position of the verb δάμησαν (711) balances the prediction of Sarpedon's death, first by Zeus (μοῖρ' ὑπὸ Πατρόκλοιο Μενοιτιάδαο δαμῆναι., *Il.* 16.434)[62] and then by Hera (χέρσ' ὕπο Πατρόκλοιο Μενοιτιάδαο δαμῆναι, *Il.* 16.452). As was the case in the opening sequence, memory is used to encase a 'direct' Iliadic allusion.

On the other hand, however, the *Iliad* is stretched as it is remembered: the directness of the allusion is misdirected in its details. There is first a delay in Ares' thought process: his mind darts to many different places (πολλὰ ... ἄλλοτε ... ἄλλοτε) before arriving at this detail. ὀψέ (710) acknowledges the postponement: this Iliadic analepsis is an afterthought, extracted eventually from his mass of memories. In terms of the content of the memory, although the reader may well think of Sarpedon and recognise the intertexts, the wording is pointedly non-explicit. Ares recalls ὅσοι υἱέες of Zeus have perished. Sarpedon's name is not mentioned and he is subsumed into the more generic group of 'the sons of Zeus'. This is, of course, a group of which Ares himself can also claim membership. This episode is the only place in the poem where the narrative refers to the god as Zeus' son (ὣς Διὸς ὄβριμος υἱὸς Ἄρης ἀέκοντί γε θυμῷ, Q.S.1.702):[63] Zeus' list of children is so long that it includes even the one who rails against him now.

Like the Trojans' broad opening recollections (Q.S.1.9–11), Ares remembers (an undefined amount) more than was disclosed in the *Iliad*. However, the temptation to read this expansion as an extra-Homeric amendment is again precluded by the framing conceit of the poem. If

---

[62] Cf. also the final line of Zeus' speech, ἢ ἤδη ὑπὸ χερσὶ Μενοιτιάδαο δαμάσσω, *Il.* 16.438.
[63] The only other instance occurs in character speech, Q.S.1.189.

Memories in Speech: Self-Motivated Selections   209

Zeus' fatherly sadness, as Ares recounts it, encompasses more than just the death of Sarpedon, then it is the Homeric narrator who acknowledges that now. Ares' recollection 'at last' thus doubles as an image of the poet's own delayed recall of material from his repertoire: 'Homer' now – ὀψέ – adds more.

5.4   Memories in Speech: Self-Motivated Selections

These examples suggest how Quintus uses reported memories of Iliadic events to justify the notion of poetic selectivity: no narrator, be it the poet of the *Iliad*, the (still Homeric) poet of this continuation, or an internal singer of heroic deeds,[64] includes all of the material which is available to them: they must select from it and present only a snapshot. When characters are permitted to speak Homeric memories in their own voice, the potential for this defensive discourse is heightened. Epic characters are both doers and speakers of deeds: they participate in as well as comment on the action of the plot. When a character remembers, therefore, he or she often activates their prior involvement in the event which they are recalling. Yet such character speech is equally motivated by a speaker's *current* concerns. A memory is evoked with an agenda: to persuade, provoke, self-aggrandise, or comfort. In a number of speeches in the *Posthomerica*, in order to achieve such effects, an Iliadic event is manipulated – changed as the speaker recalls it.

The differences from the *Iliad* are usually subtle, a matter of tone or of emphasis. For example, as Achilles vaunts to Penthesilea (Q.S.1.575–91) he asserts the limitless size of his exploits at the Xanthus with another indeterminate ὅσος (ἢ οὔπω τόδ' ἄκουσας, ὅσων ὑποκάππεσε γυῖα... Q.S.1.588). As he kills Thersites, he reminds him of Odysseus' previous castigation of his babbling (Q.S.1.759–63),[65] but readjusts the focus to suggest Odysseus' lightness of touch ('Οδυσσῆος ταλαὸν κῆρ ... καὶ οὐκέτι χειρὶ βαρείῃ/πληξάμενος... 759; 762–3). Then, when struck by Apollo's arrow, he recalls Thetis' premonitions about his death (Q.S.3.78–82), which he also related in *Il.* 21.276–8, but now includes the detail of the setting by Scaean gates, which he learned in the *Iliad* from Hector, not from his mother (*Il.* 22.359–60).[66] There are, however, some

---

[64] Compare here the cyclic songs of Nestor and the bards after the sack of Troy (Q.S.4.118–68; Q.S.14.121–42) as discussed in Chapter 2.
[65] Cf. *Il.* 2.243–69.
[66] For the absence of Paris, one of Achilles' killers in Hector's prophecy, see discussion in Chapter 7.2.

210   Selective Memory and Iliadic Revision

cases when the adaptations seem more drastically distortive: when Quintus' characters recall events as they did *not* happen in the *Iliad* and the poet appears to break with the practice established in the opening lines, of including nothing incompatible with Homer's account.

Achilles, as the above examples suggest, voices the largest number of Homeric memories of all Quintan characters. Whilst at the end of the *Iliad* he was the central doer of deeds – and his is the μένος from which the Trojans at the start of this poem still shrink in fear – his status as this narrative continues begins to wane. Delayed into action (Q.S.1.376–9), soon to meet his death (Q.S.3.1–185), he is confined thereafter to a spectral half-presence and his former self, is available only in fleeting glimpses, reconjured through original Homeric formulae. As a hero moving into the past tense, Achilles is thus forced into a position more familiar to the likes of Nestor, in which he must increasingly rely on evoking the memory of his former accomplishments to assert his authority. When his ghost entreats Neoptolemus to make the Greeks do his bidding (Q.S.14.185–222), he does so precisely by reminding them of his exploits during the war (14.210–1): let them do as he says, if they still (μέμνηνθ' – perfect tense) remember.[67]

The adaptations which Achilles makes to these recalled Iliadic feats can be read as driven by this desire for self-perpetuation: he edits his Homeric memories so that they continue – and through them, he continues – to matter. The majority of these adaptations, as we have seen, are subtle: he reorients an episode to create an even more Achilles-centred version of the *Iliad*. On one occasion, however, he attempts something more extreme. In a flyting speech to Memnon (Q.S.2.429–50), Achilles asserts the reasons why Thetis is held in the greatest honour among the gods:

ὅς σέο φέρτερός εἰμι βίῃ γενεῇ τε φυῇ τε
Ζηνὸς ὑπερθύμοιο λαχὼν ἀριδείκετον αἷμα
καὶ σθεναροῦ Νηρῆος, ὃς εἰναλίας τέκε κούρας
Νηρεΐδας, τὰς δή ῥα θεοὶ τίουσ' ἐν Ὀλύμπῳ,
πασάων δὲ μάλιστα Θέτιν κλυτὰ μητιόωσαν,
οὕνεκά που Διόνυσον ἑοῖς ὑπέδεκτο μελάθροις,
ὁππότε δειμαίνεσκε βίην ὀλοοῖο Λυκούργου,
ἠδὲ καὶ ὡς Ἥφαιστον ἐύφρονα χαλκεοτέχνην
δέξατο οἷσι δόμοισιν ἀπ' Οὐλύμποιο πεσόντα,
αὐτόν τ' Ἀργικέραυνον ὅπως ὑπελύσατο δεσμῶν·

---

[67] Further analysis of this passage in Chapter 6.

Memories in Speech: Self-Motivated Selections 211

τῶν μιμνησκόμενοι πανδερκέες Οὐρανίωνες
μητέρ' ἐμὴν τίουσι Θέτιν ζαθέῳ ἐν Ὀλύμπῳ.

Q.S.2.433–44

I am superior to you in strength, in birth, and in stature. I am of the glorious bloodline of mighty Zeus and great Nereus, father of the Nereids, those sea nymphs honoured by the Olympian gods. And they especially honor Thetis, famed for her shrewd intelligence: she sheltered Dionysus in her halls when he feared the violent and murderous Lycurgus; she welcomed into her home the civilising bronze-smith Hephaestus; and she contrived to release the father of the bright lightning himself from his bonds. It is in gratitude for these actions that the all-seeing heavenly gods on high Olympus honour my mother Thetis.

The examples are instantly recognisable from the *Iliad*, and the links are once again cemented by verbal recapitulations. Dionysus' escape from Lycurgus (Q.S.2.438–9) was narrated by Glaucus to Diomedes at *Il.* 6.130–7; with ὑπέδεκτο μελάθροις (Q.S.2.437) reflecting ὑπεδέξατο κόλπῳ (*Il.* 6.137), the verbs in symmetrical penultimate position. Thetis' aid to Hephaestus (Q.S.2.440–1) was recalled by Hephaestus himself at *Il.* 18.394–405 and Quintus' χαλκεοτέχνην (Q.S.2.440) offers a variant of the Iliadic compound-epithet in that scene (Ἥφαιστον κλυτοτέχνην, *Il.* 18.391).[68] And the story of Thetis releasing Zeus from bondage (Q.S.2.442) was recounted to Thetis by Achilles at *Il.* 1.396–406; here Quintus, breaking from his usual practice, preserves a near-precise Homeric formula from that passage (ὑπελύσατο δεσμῶν, Q.S.2.442; ὑπελύσαο δεσμῶν *Il.* 1.401). Again, the Iliac Tablets provide an instructive parallel for this sort of repackaging: the upper frieze of the Capitoline Tablet representing the first book of the *Iliad* ends with Thetis' supplication of Zeus – the same passage with which Achilles ends his speech here. In the tablet's depiction of this tale, Zeus is looking behind him as Thetis makes her request, back, in fact, to the pictorial events of *Iliad* 24. This glance, as Squire argues, 'quite literally points the viewers to his verdict, and hence to the conclusion of the poem … we are invited to see connections across individual books that – verbally speaking – must go unstated'.[69] Through his own 'looking back' to different reported events from across the *Iliad*, Quintus' Achilles makes these sorts of cross-poem connections come alive *verbally* too.

---

[68] Achilles includes no mention of Eurynome, Hephaestus' co-saviour in the Iliadic version: a deft omission, given his desire to present Thetis as μάλιστα … κλυτά (Q.S.2.437).

[69] Squire (2011): 170.

212 Selective Memory and Iliadic Revision

However, by *merging* these different Iliadic stories, Achilles also 'remembers' deeds of Thetis which according to his speech in *Iliad* 1 his mother had not told him about.[70] In his new version of this recollection, Achilles also condenses the tale told by his Homeric character over ten frantic lines into one neat verse, missing out all but the most essential details.[71] If we were to explore this speech using the concept of memory and allusion as conventionally understood, then Achilles invested with extra-narrative power would function as a kind of Homeric editor: with the panache of an imperial sophist, he collates all of the deeds of Thetis from the *Iliad* and refashions them into something new. But for Quintus, this is not quite the system at play. For these Iliadic memories are not in fact Achilles' own: deeds in which he participated and is now tendentiously recalling to boost his renown. These are the *gods'* memories which he is citing (μιμνησκόμενοι πανδερκέες Οὐρανίωνες) and events which, even when they were discussed in the *Iliad*, were already 'completing external analepses' belonging to a more distant past.

Achilles, however, is not a god.[72] His description of divine memory cannot be so authoritative. Despite his boasts about his parentage from Thetis, it is this mortal status which is subtly foregrounded in this speech. His choice of epithet for the gods, πανδερκέες (443) provides an ironical contrast with, and perhaps even unwitting prolepsis to, his death in the next book of the poem: the gods here are 'all-seeing', when it is precisely Achilles' lack of superhuman vision which leads to his downfall:[73]

> ἀμφὶ δὲ παπτήνας ὀλοὸν καὶ † ἄκρατον † ὁμόκλα·
> 'τίς νύ μοι αἰνὸν ὀιστὸν ἐπιπροέηκε κρυφηδόν;'
>
> Q.S.3.67–8

He stared all about him and gave a terrible cry: 'Who has secretly launched this dread arrow at me?'

Quintus thus points over his character's head to the gap between mortal and divine, which Achilles' bold assertions attempt to deny. In the image

---

[70] Cf. *Il.* 1.396–8: ἄκουσα εὐχομένης ὅτ' ἔφησθα κελαινεφέϊ Κρονίωνι/οἴη ἐν ἀθανάτοισιν ἀεικέα λοιγὸν ἀμῦναι. In other words, in his Iliadic speech, Achilles based his knowledge on Thetis' own testimony to him. No such testimonies are given now.

[71] There is no mention, for instance, of Hera, Poseidon and Athena's role (cf. *Il.* 1.399–400), nor of the part played by Briareus/Aegaeon (*Il.* 1.404–5).

[72] Not at this stage of the *Posthomerica*. For Achilles 'divine' afterlife later in the poem, see Chapters 3 and 6. Discussion also in Maciver (2017) and Carvounis (2019).

[73] The epithet is not strictly true of the gods either, who frequently miss things throughout the epic tradition, but Achilles' use of it in this context seems intended to provoke the divine/mortal contrast.

Memories in Speech: Self-Motivated Selections 213

of Achilles *appropriating* divine memory, assuming the position of one who knows for certain much more than his narrative experience would permit him, Quintus offers another model for poetic selectivity. It is part of the claim of revisionists like Dio that Homer, because of his exceptional place in Greek education and culture, is also exceptional in his distortion of the true events at Troy – he marks the start of the chain of deception and inaccuracy that has led to such stories being mistaken for truth.[74] By presenting Achilles – a character operating within the events at Troy, famed for his honesty and straightness –[75] as distorting his stories too, Quintus removes the *ad hominem* sting from this charge. As the reader recognises the slippage between what Achilles can know and what he purports to, we must acquiesce with the potential unreliability of *any* descriptive recollection, even one which asserts itself so confidently, and accept the ubiquity of self-motivated adaptation.

Quintus also depicts his characters manipulating the memory of events in which they *did* participate. In Phoenix's lament for Achilles (Q.S.3.463–89) his account of how he came to be the protégé of Peleus and was entrusted with rearing his son is based, obviously and closely, on his speech in *Iliad* 9 (444–95). But an important part of that account is omitted, namely that Phoenix left home condemned to childlessness by his father's curse, so that he came to regard Achilles as a surrogate son. For James, this omission 'exemplifies Quintus' readiness to simplify a story'.[76] But this explanation fails to acknowledge that we are in character speech and Phoenix is activating a personal memory.[77] From this perspective, the recollection is not simplified; it is selective.

In contrast to the situation in *Iliad* 9, Phoenix is not seeking to persuade Achilles; he is mourning him. The background of being condemned to childlessness, which at the embassy heightened the pathos of his cause and created affinity with his primary addressee, is no longer what is critically at stake. Instead, Phoenix focuses on the bond that had existed between himself and the fallen hero: a key feature of lamentation.[78] The part of

---

[74] See particularly Kim (2010): 6–10; 17–8; 219–20.

[75] Cf. e.g. *Hippias Minor* 365b, as discussed in Chapter 3. [76] James (2004): 285.

[77] Uniquely in the examples which this chapter discusses, Phoenix does not use the specific vocabulary of memory in this recapitulation: his speech, in this way, adheres more closely to the 'original' practice of Homeric epic. I am including it firstly because of the closeness with which it replays the Iliadic scene and the stark nature of the additional details. It thus constitutes a thoroughly Homeric recollection of an un-Homeric part of this past.

[78] An emphasis readily perceptible in, for instance, the equivalent heroic lamentation scenes in the *Iliad*: those for Hector, especially Hecuba at *Il.* 24.746–9 and Helen at *Il.* 24.765–75. On Greek lamentation more broadly, see especially Alexiou (1974).

214   Selective Memory and Iliadic Revision

the story as it was told in the *Iliad* which is most relevant for *this* purpose is
the memorable image of Achilles as a spluttering infant:

> οὔτ᾽ ἐς δαῖτ᾽ ἰέναι οὔτ᾽ ἐν μεγάροισι πάσασθαι,
> πρίν γ᾽ ὅτε δή σ᾽ ἐπ᾽ ἐμοῖσιν ἐγὼ γούνεσσι καθίσσας
> ὄψου τ᾽ ἄσαιμι προταμὼν καὶ οἶνον ἐπισχών.
> πολλάκι μοι κατέδευσας ἐπὶ στήθεσσι χιτῶνα
> οἴνου ἀποβλύζων ἐν νηπιέῃ ἀλεγεινῇ. . .
>
> *Il.* 9.487–91

For you would not go to the feast with any other or take meat in the hall, until
I had set you on my knees and given you your fill of the savoury morsel cut first
for you, and had put the wine cup to your lips. Often did you wet the tunic on my
chest, sputtering out the wine in your childish helplessness.

Phoenix first homes in on this image, describing Peleus first placing
Achilles in his lap (κόλπῳ ἐμῷ κατέθηκε, Q.S.3.471) and Achilles wetting
his tunic (πολλάκι . . . δίηνας στήθεά τ᾽ ἠδὲ χιτῶνας, Q.S.3.474; 476).
Then he expands it:

> πολλάκι παππάζεσκες ἔτ᾽ ἄκριτα χείλεσι βάζων,
> καί μευ νηπιέῃσιν ὑπ᾽ ἐννεσίῃσι δίην
> στήθεά τ᾽ ἠδὲ χιτῶνας· ἔχον δέ σε χερσὶν ἐμῇσι
> πολλὸν καγχαλόων, ἐπεὶ ἦ νύ μοι ἦτορ ἐώλπει
> θρέψειν κηδεμονῆα βίου καὶ γήραος ἄλκαρ.
>
> Q.S.3.474–8

And many were the times you happily laid in my breast and called me father as
you prattled and spoke half-formed words. Many a time, too, your infant needs
meant that you wetted my breast and my clothing. But I was proud and happy to
hold you in my arms, because I expected that when you grew up you would
defend and look after me in my old age.

That Achilles often used to call Phoenix 'father' (πολλάκι παππάζεσκες,
Q.S.3.474)[79] and his own laughter as he held the child (πολλὸν
καγχαλόων, Q.S.3.477) are details not found in the *Iliad*. And yet in this
new context such additions have great emotive force. The power of
evoking Achilles' infancy at the embassy lay in the intense intimacy which
it engendered. Phoenix aimed not to usurp the role of Peleus, but to create
an entirely unique relationship, paternal in spirit but not actually father-
son.[80] Mourning Achilles now, the old man cements this special role.

---

[79] The verb παππάζω has only two occurrences in the 'real' Homeric epics: Dione to Aphrodite regarding
Diomedes' ill-fated homecoming (*Il.* 5.408) and Nausicaa to her father Alcinous (*Od.* 6.57).

[80] Alden (2000): 222 deems the embassy scene 'unpleasant' due to Phoenix's appropriation of Peleus'
position, surely missing this point.

ἄκριτα ... βάζων, two words which usually denote negative, polemicised speech acts,[81] are now redeployed to become the defining image of young innocence. The transferral of belligerence away from the phrase matches the neutralising nature of the whole scene: Phoenix no longer needs to abate Achilles' anger and so can now focus solely on his childhood charm.

Phoenix recalls his relationship with Achilles a second time in the *Posthomerica*, this time to Neoptolemus as he arrives at Troy (Q.S.7.642–52). The motivations behind his extra-Homeric inclusions here are even more transparent: there is now a new youth who needs persuading. In relating his bond with Achilles to Achilles' own son, Phoenix places an even greater emphasis on the paternal nature of his role: ἔγωγε τυτθὸν ... ἶσον δέ ἑ παιδὶ τίεσκον ... ἶσον ἑῷ πατρὶ τῖεν ἐμὸν κῆρ (Q.S.7.643–8). When the reader encounters another non-Iliadic detail, the addition can be understood as material well-selected by Phoenix to support this emphasis:

> ἔσκεν, ὅπως φήσασκεν ἰδών· ˈΕνὸς αἵματός εἰμεν
> εἵνεχ' ὁμοφροσύνης.ˈ ...
>
> Q.S.7.650–1

When he saw me he would say, 'We must be of one blood, because we are so of one mind!'

No trace of this conversation appeared in Phoenix's speech in the *Iliad*. And yet it is presented as an exchange which happened in the iterative, over and again.[82] Phoenix's inclusion of it has clear relevance to *this* rhetorical context. In stressing a connection achieved by an affiliation in spirit, Phoenix seeks to inflame the filial *thumos* of a young man whose motivation to fight is driven principally by his desire to emulate his father: to achieve, as it were, what Phoenix had with Achilles in reverse – a deep connection with a man with whom he shares a blood bond, but has never met. As a discourse on Homeric veracity, Phoenix's process of Iliadic self-amendment functions as a further model for selective poetic composition and a defence of the rationale behind it. A different setting will call for different facets of a story; new narrative scenarios will permit previously undisclosed aspects to be revealed. Playing at Homer, Quintus looks out over his mask to stake this claim: Homer is not a liar, he is a poet.

---

[81] Cf. *Il.* 4.355; *Il.* 16.207; *Od.* 4.837; *Od.* 11.464. At *Od.* 4.32 Menelaus, censuring Eteoneus, uses βάζω to refer to childlike speech (ἀτὰρ μὲν νῦν γε πάϊς ὣς νήπια βάζεις), but with an insulting rather than a tender force. The Quintan Achilles employs βάζω in this derogatory sense against Thersites: ἀργαλέως ὤρινας ἐλέγχεα μυρία βάζων, Q.S.1.760.

[82] Cf. also ἔσκε δέ μοι μέγ' ὄνειαρ ... ἔσκε νόῳ (646) and πολλάκι παππάζεσκες (3.474).

216 Selective Memory and Iliadic Revision

My final example of this poetics of selective memory is by far the most explosive and returns to the performative space of the *hoplon krisis* (Q.S.5.175–316). In Chapter 2, this passage revealed itself as an important setting for Quintus' culturally inflected agenda of Homeric expansion. Ajax and Odysseus infuse pre-existing Homeric material with new words, lines and scenes, and through these techniques, they were seen not simply to reflect second-sophistic rhetoric or Homeric battle flyting, but rather to enact the processes of the inter-Homeric poet – entirely Homeric *and* 'sophistic'. We must now consider this scene and its dual models – Homeric-poetic and rhetorical – once more. For the contest is also staged as a battle of remembrance. Ajax and Odysseus attempt to surpass one another by brandishing memories of events from their past. The rivals also trade different versions of the same memory: an event is recalled and counter-recalled to suit the designs of the speaker. The framing vocabulary of memory is once again palpably present (thus Ajax: ἠὲ τόδ' ἐξελάθου, ὅτ' ἐς Ἰλίου ἱερὸν ἄστυ/ἐλθέμεναι ἀλέεινες, 191; οὔτ' εὐεργεσίης μεμνημένος, 201) and here it is *combined* with the commemorating discourse of *kleos* (κλυτὸν Ποιάντιον υἷα, 195; μέγα δ' ἔργον ὁμῶς ἐτελέσσαμεν, 255; ἀγακλυτὰ θῆκεν ἄεθλα, 316). In line with the fusing properties of the *agōn* as a whole, these two modes of describing the past – the Homeric and the non-Homeric – are brought into a diptych.

The scene provides the most overt, high-stakes example of the rhetorical pragmatics of selective memory put to work in Quintus' text. Unlike the solipsistic one-on-one of Achilles to Memnon, or the personal, domestic anecdotes of Phoenix' appeals to his 'sons', the contest here is public (ἐν μέσσοισι,178; 180), performative and unapologetically oratorical. Memory becomes part of the show. This performative setting is, as we have seen, a key part of the rhetorical modelling of the *krisis*. As well as imperial sophistic shows, Ajax and Odysseus here can also be aligned with performers from earlier Greek oratory. The arms contest itself was a favourite setting for rhetorical exercises in schools, with its twin speeches offering ripe material for the ever-present desideratum of showing one's ability to argue both sides of an argument equally strongly.[83] Antisthenes' version of the debate (15.4) capitalises on precisely this duality and also, in a very proto-Quintan move, has Odysseus appropriate the chronology of his literary position (as a Homeric character but also the product of a later rhetorical writer) to predict the coming of the *Odyssey*: a 'later poet', he

---

[83] See Bonner (1977) and Maciver (2012 c).

Memories in Speech: Self-Motivated Selections   217

says, will come to defend his merits against Ajax.[84] The particular technique used in this Quintan scene, of combatively recalling and counter-recalling what 'really' happened, also finds ample illustration in the *agōnes* of fourth-century forensic and deliberative oratory. In their famous verbal duels, Aeschines and Demosthenes often construct their character assassinations by trading accounts of events during the conflict with Philip, often drawing explicitly upon the distortive properties of the act of recollection to do so.[85] Demosthenes, for instance, hesitates to recall an incident before Philip's final and absolute victory, which he claims has caused the past to 'vanish, as though obliterated by a flood' (214).[86] And Aeschines often cynically points to the operations of φήμη to exploit listeners' acquittance with local characters and recent events (thus he comments on Demosthenes' notoriety: 'attaching itself to men's life and conduct, talk travels unerringly throughout the city, like a messenger proclaiming to the public at large details of men's private behaviour' –1.127).[87]

In the context of such manoeuvres, this oft-cited 'rhetorical' flavour of Quintus' *krisis* takes on different significance. By exploiting the long-standing oratorical background of this well-known scene, Quintus makes the tricks of memory found there relevant for the *poetic* texture of his new version: the orator's combative use of memory is here applied to Homeric material and transferred to defend a poet's agenda of change.

In this light, let us now consider the memory exchange in detail.[88] Ajax begins by reminding Odysseus of his inferiority and indebtedness to him. He includes two Iliadic analepses: in recalling how ὅς σ' ἐνὶ χάρμῃ/ ἐξεσάωσα πάροιθεν ὑποτρομέοντα κυδοιμόν... (Q.S.5.202–3) he recapitulates the rescue of *Il.* 11.411–88; and when discussing how Odysseus kept his ships 'in the middle' (Q.S.5.212), he evokes the statement in the

---

[84] See the excellent discussion in Maciver (2012 c): 602–3: 'in his conceited Homeric foreshadowing, Antisthenes verbalises what Quintus [here] makes implicit'. On this speech of Antisthenes, see also Lévystone (2005) and Whitmarsh (2001): 97f.

[85] On the different and varied aspects of these character assassinations – which I can here only touch upon, enough to frame my driving interest in the techniques of memory – see Bruns (1896) for the 'foundational' (and variously challenged) pro-Aeschines view of historical bases behind the pair's portraits of one another; Rowe (1966) on the use of Attic comedy; Easterling (1999) on wider and deeper motivations by the 'actors' in this contest.

[86] This *praeteritio* is Demosthenes' version of the paradox of compelling an audience to remember to forget...

[87] On this technique, see V. Hunter (1990), drawing on copious bibliography on the notion of 'gossip' in a fourth-century context.

[88] On the Homeric episodes weaponised by Ajax and Odysseus here, see the discussions of Maciver (2012c) and Bär (2010), who offer convincing readings of the allusivity at play, albeit distractingly encased in their own *agōn* regarding the scene's 'second sophistic context'.

218   Selective Memory and Iliadic Revision

Iliad that Odysseus' ships had been beached in the centre of the camp, whilst those of Ajax and Achilles took the most dangerous positions at either end (*Il.* 8.222–6 = *Il.* 11.5–9). Commingled with this type of recollection are events not found in the *Iliad* at all. Ajax recounts Odysseus' attempt to duck out of the Trojan mission (Q.S.5.191–4), which was neither a part of the Iliadic primary narrative nor referenced in Homer at any point: it is found instead, in extant sources, in the *Cypria* (Proclus *Chrest.* 5 West (2003b)) and Ovid's *Metamorphoses* (13.34–42).[89] Odysseus' role in the abandonment of Philoctetes (Q.S.5.195–6) is also absent from the brief reference to the hero in the Iliadic catalogue (*Il.* 2.718–24). These extra-Iliadic references pave the way for the boldest new recollection:

> οὐκ οἴῳ δ' ἄρα τῷ γε λυγρὴν ἐπεμήσαο λώβην,
> ἀλλὰ καὶ ἀντιθέῳ Παλαμήδεϊ θῆκας ὄλεθρον,
> ὅς σέο φέρτερος ἔσκε βίῃ καὶ ἐΰφρονι βουλῇ.
>
> Q.S.5.197–9

And he is not the only one you have injured with your tricks: you also managed to get godlike Palamedes killed, a man superior to you in both strength and wise counsel.

The mention of Palamedes would have been electric. The story of Palamedes' murder and Odysseus' betrayal seems from our extant sources to have originated in the *Cypria* (fr.30 Bernabé (1987) 2 fr.27 West (2003b) = Paus. 10.31) and is dramatised in a range of reworkings from oratory to Greek tragedy to Roman epic. All three tragic poets composed a drama about him and Gorgias' speech in his defence is still preserved.[90] Ovid, like Quintus, uses the event in his twisty re-staging of the Ajax–Odysseus duel: his Ajax also mobilises Odysseus' role in his death to discredit his opponent and adds the details (not found in the *Posthomerica*) of the false charge and planted evidence with which Odysseus secured Palamedes' conviction (*Met.* 13. 55–60).[91]

It is in imperial Greece, however, that the murder is elevated from a non-Iliadic story to a full-blown Homeric conspiracy. Dictys of Crete reasserts Palamedes' place in the saga.[92] In Philostratus' *Vita Apollonii*, Apollonius meets a gifted unruly boy who is the reincarnated spirit of

---

[89] Whether Quintus is drawing on the *Cypria* or Ovid – or both, or neither – is not the critical issue here, but rather how this material which is not in the *Iliad* is presented in the 'still *Iliad*' illusion. For Quintus' relationship to the Epic Cycle and to Latin literature, see Chapter 1.9.

[90] See Gantz (1993): 603–8; Zeitlin (2001): 250–1.   [91] Cf. James (2004): 297.

[92] See Dictys of Crete 1.1, 1.4, 1.6, 1.16, 1.19 and 2.14–15 on Palamedes, and 2.29 on his murder.

Memories in Speech: Self-Motivated Selections 219

Palamedes and has no interest in learning because 'he found his bitterest enemies in Odysseus and Homer; because Odysseus laid ambush against him, and Homer denied him any place in his epic, while bestowing renown on lesser people' (3.22). When Apollonius then encounters Achilles in an epiphany, he questions him on this omission and visits Palamedes' grave immediately after the interview (4.11–13). The *Heroicus* takes the palm for pro-Palamedes ploys. The vinedresser, armed with the knowledge of his hero-guru Protesilaus, reveals to the Phoenician merchant that Homer ignored Palamedes on purpose, so that he would not have to record Odysseus' shameful role in his murder, as the result of a necromantic bargain struck with the ghost of Odysseus himself (24.2).[93] In these accounts, therefore, the act of narrative supplementation of Homer (the inclusion in the *Cypria* and later sources of a character who does not feature in his epics) is merged with the re-animating drives of Homeric biography to become a tale *about* Homer, *involving* Homer and offering devastating evidence for his wilful distortion of Trojan history.

By including a reference to this hero, Quintus is on the one hand participating in this extra-Homeric tradition. However, this participation must also be considered in light of the presentation of this reference as a memory. Palamedes is a part of these characters' mythological past. Odysseus seeks to block him out, selectively to 'forget' him (τόδ' ἐξελάθ(ε), Q.S.5.191) and Ajax provides the reminder because it helps his rhetorical strategy to do so: he aims to discredit Odysseus by evoking the darker details of his past, and what better example of his ἀτάσθαλα ἔργα (Q.S.5.190) than this? Palamedes, for Ajax, is the φέρτερος hero (Q.S.5.199)[94] – and his superiority is in strength *and* intelligence (βίῃ καὶ εὔφρονι βουλῇ,). Anticipating Odysseus' self-presentation in his counter-argument,[95] Ajax hails Palamedes as the true embodiment of epic heroism, the brains and the brawn. In this single reference, he thus both draws attention to his opponent's ignominy and offers an alternative contender for his heroic identity.

On another level, however, the level on which Philostratus plays, it was really Homer and his *Iliad* who 'forgot' Palamedes. In having Ajax mention him, Quintus thus also issues a reminder of his own, erasing Homer's

---

[93] For full discussion of Philostratan precedents for the Palamedes story, which Quintus may also have known, see Grossardt (2006).

[94] Cf. *Il.* 1.280–1. Compare Achilles' use of the adjective against Memnon in the *agōn* about Thetis (Q.S.2.432).

[95] Odysseus focuses on the mutual necessity of strength and wisdom in his counter–speech (Q.S.5.239–316), and even uses the same term εὐφροσύνη (Q.S.5.263).

220 Selective Memory and Iliadic Revision

paradigmatic omission by including Palamedes and drawing brief attention to Odysseus' fault. The exclusion of Palamedes from the *Iliad* is thus transformed from an insidious 'cover-up job' to a more neutral act of selectivity, driven by the compulsions of narrative. It is crucial to this neutralising process that this mention of Palamedes – the only time that he features in the poem – is pointedly brief. This Homer-in-the-middle does not issue a full-blown apology for his 'previous' Iliadic amnesia. Palamedes does not get a lengthy excursus, discussion or fleshed-out retrospective description. Instead, in fewer verses and with less detail than Ovid, introduced by the bathetic ἀλλὰ καί, he is casually slipped (back) into the Homeric plot. The epithet which he is granted – ἀντίθεος (196) – adds to this slipperiness. We saw in Chapter 3, when the epithet was discussed in relation to Achilles, how Quintus harnesses the polyvalent potential of this term discernible from Homeric exegesis to offer a critical re-reading of the (still) Homeric character: Achilles can be like a god and contrary to the gods at all once. In the mouth of Ajax, the word can convey the pivot between Palamedes' honourable conduct in life (translate 'godlike') and the vicious injustice of his death (transfer to Odysseus, translate: 'contrary to the gods'). But by giving Ajax the adjective, Quintus can also use the term to convey to the reader the fundamental subjectivity of *any* hero's reception and the necessary choices involved in poetically describing their presence or absence, their actions or their faults. The *Iliad*, therefore, did not discuss Palamedes, but its characters do remember him, and in this continued poetic portrayal of their experiences, 'Homer' now self-corrects without conceding and allows him a place in his epic.

Odysseus soon bites back. He combats Ajax's defamations with some Homeric memories of his own (Q.S.5.268–90). He first counter-interprets the Iliadic analepses (268–78): he was not rescued from battle, but withstood alone (268–75); and his ships were not placed ἐς μέσσον (275) out of cowardice, but due to strategy. These are *re*-interpretations of Iliadic events. Although he states that what Ajax says is untrue (σὺ δ' οὐκ ἄρ' ἐτήτυμα βάζεις,[96] 272), Odysseus does not claim that these things did not happen. Rather, he contends that they happened for different reasons from those which Ajax proposes – it is Ajax's emphasis which is οὐκ ἄρ' ἐτήτυμα. In staging the argument over these specific Homeric memories, Quintus selects two incidents about which the *Iliad* is conspicuously inconclusive. In the simile which describes how Menelaus and Ajax found him, Odysseus the wounded stag is, as Ajax suggests, fearful and fleeing:

[96] Note how here βάζω regains its usual, derogatory sense, unlike at Q.S.3.474.

Memories in Speech: Self-Motivated Selections

εὗρον ἔπειτ᾽ Ὀδυσῆα διίφιλον· ἀμφὶ δ᾽ ἄρ᾽ αὐτὸν
Τρῶες ἕπονθ᾽ ὡς εἴ τε δαφοινοὶ θῶες ὄρεσφιν
ἀμφ᾽ ἔλαφον κεραὸν βεβλημένον, ὅν τ᾽ ἔβαλ᾽ ἀνὴρ
ἰῷ ἀπὸ νευρῆς· τὸν μέν τ᾽ ἤλυξε πόδεσσι
φεύγων, ὄφρ᾽ αἷμα λιαρὸν καὶ γούνατ᾽ ὀρώρῃ·

Il. 11.473–7[97]

Then they found Odysseus, dear to Zeus, and round about the Trojans beset him, like tawny jackals in the mountains about a horned stag that has been wounded, that a man has struck with an arrow from the string; from him the stag has escaped and flees swiftly so long as the blood flows warm and his knees are quick.

But in the narrative outside of the simile, an equally strong case could be made for Odysseus' version of events. Beset on all sides, he valiantly defends himself and exhibits a leonine strength of his own:

ὣς ῥα τότ᾽ ἀμφ᾽ Ὀδυσῆα δαΐφρονα ποικιλομήτην
Τρῶες ἕπον πολλοί τε καὶ ἄλκιμοι, αὐτὰρ ὅ γ᾽ ἥρως
ἀΐσσων ᾧ ἔγχει ἀμύνετο νηλεὲς ἦμαρ.

Il. 11.482–4

So then did the Trojans, many and valiant, beset Odysseus on all sides, the wise and crafty-minded; but the warrior darting out with his spear warded off the pitiless day of doom.

Likewise, in the Iliadic description of the location of the ships, both of the contenders' interpretations are possible. The middle position of Odysseus' fleet is certainly described as strategic, not explicitly cowardly: στῆ δ᾽ ἐπ᾽ Ὀδυσσῆος μεγακήτεϊ νηὶ μελαίνῃ/ἥ ῥ᾽ ἐν μεσσάτῳ ἔσκε γεγωνέμεν ἀμφοτέρωσε, *Il.* 8.222–3 = *Il.* 11.5–6). And yet the reasons given for Ajax and Achilles drawing up their ships at the outer ends – ἠνορέῃ πίσυνοι καὶ κάρτεϊ χειρῶν (*Il.* 8.226 = *Il.* 11.9) – could allow for an implicit contrast with Odysseus' choice, to suggest that he selfishly opted for safety. Just as we saw in the opening description of the dragging of Hector, Quintus draws attention to the ambiguity already inherent within certain Homeric statements. But rather than trying to settle these questions, *qua* the angry rebuttals of the Sibyl or Nonnus' erotic gnomic refutation, he opens them up even further. This commitment to Iliadic uncertainty serves to highlight the deep connection between poetry and subjectivity. If the same events can be redeployed to support such diametrically opposed

---

[97] This simile is arguably focalised from Ajax and Menelaus' perspective (εὗρον ἔπειτ᾽ Ὀδυσῆα Διῒ φίλον·...). But compare the similar tone in the narrator's own description of Odysseus' move to withdraw: αὐτὰρ ὅ γ᾽ ἐξοπίσω ἀνεχάζετο, αὖε δ᾽ἑταίρους, *Il.* 11.461.

222 Selective Memory and Iliadic Revision

conclusions, then being told 'what happened' may bring us no closer to the truth.[98]

Homer's poetic spin, as we have seen, could be corrected by appealing to the superior witness of those who were 'actually there'. Autopsy, however, comes with its own problems. As Thucydides states – a notion on which Dio's *Trojan Oration* self-deprecatingly plays –[99] the reports which an eyewitness offers are themselves susceptible to distortion, determined by each person's 'prejudice or memory' (Thuc. 1.22.3). As characters participating in the Trojan War – who were, and still are, there – Ajax and Odysseus competitively trade recollections in a manner which oratorically manipulates the potential for this kind of distortion. As the poet who compiles this *agōn*, Quintus thus suggests that if poetry is the carapace for conceit, eyewitness accounts would be little better.

The *Posthomerica*, finally, does not only justify this concept of poetic selectivity; it ensures that it continues. Towards the end of his first speech, Odysseus claims that he slaughtered many more Trojans than Ajax in the battle for Achilles' corpse (Q.S.5.285). This event happened 'just now' (νῦν δέ, 285). The members of the internal audience watching this debate (τῶν δ' ἄρ' ἀναινομένων Τρώων ἐρικυδέες υἷες/ἕζοντ' ἐν μέσσοισι δορύκτητοί περ ἐόντες, 5.177–8) should, therefore, be able to judge via 'independent checks'[100] whether Odysseus' claims about it are true. The external audience – we the readers – who have 'just now' encountered this part of the narrative ourselves, should also be able to verify the story. But in poetry, Quintus shows, that is not how it has to work. In the description of their verdict (Q.S.5.317–22), we are not told what the internal audience makes of this claim: the eyewitnesses do not help us. And as we 'recall' the narrative account of the battle, conclusive proof for believing or disbelieving Odysseus eludes us there too:

> Αἴας δ' αἰὲν ἐμάρνατ' ἀλίγκιος ἀστεροπῇσι,
> κτείνων ἄλλοθεν ἄλλον, . . .
>
> Q.S.3.293–4

Ajax continued to strike his foes like lightning: killing one and then another from elsewhere.

---

[98] Further examples of distortions of Iliadic memories in this exchange are found at Q.S.5.279–81, on the timing of Odysseus' self-disfigurement and entry into Troy, and Q.S.5.310–11, where Odysseus claims to have won the wrestling match with Ajax at Patroclus' funeral games, when according to the *Iliad* (23.735–9), the outcome was judged a tie.

[99] See Hunter (2009): 49–51; Kim (2010): 108–12.

[100] I borrow this phrase from Crotty (1994): 126 on what makes a storyteller *epistamenos* in Homer: 'in the unusual instance where a member of the audience happens to have participated in the narrated event, there is an independent check on the accuracy of the poet's song'.

Conclusions

> ἀλλ’ ἐδάμη παλάμῃσιν Ὀδυσσέος, ὅς τε καὶ ἄλλων
> πολλῶν θυμὸν ἔλυσεν ὑπ’ ἔγχεϊ μαιμώωντι
> κτείνων ὅν κε κίχῃσι περὶ νέκυν. . . .
>
> Q.S.3.306–8

He died at the hands of Odysseus. Many others, too, lost their lives to his raging spear as he killed whomever he could around the corpse.

Ajax killed ‘another from elsewhere’. Odysseus killed ‘many others’. Like the Iliadic ambiguity over the dragging, the rescue and the positioning of the ships, this poetic account refuses to confirm or deny the more positivist claims made by Odysseus in his speech. Acknowledging that there is more behind an epic verse – more kills in *aristeiai*, more heroes to be mentioned, or ‘facts’ to be disclosed – Quintus does not set out to fill in all of Homer's gaps. Rather, impersonating Homer the selective poet, he continues unapologetically to flaunt the choices of his poetry and reclaims these choices as a strength. Alluding to additional points in his repertoire of knowledge, he asserts that poetry must always be about more than fact: it cannot, and should not, give an answer to those wishing to know it all.

5.5   Conclusions

We began this chapter with a glance at the *Torah*'s potted illustration of the loaded paradoxes of reminiscence: remember in order to blot out memory. Homer, seen through the facetious eyes of certain second-sophists, could be accused of blotting out Greek cultural memory: his epics, and the hegemony which they achieved, manipulated posterity to make it forget the ‘real’ events at Troy. That the *Posthomerica* refutes rather than simply reflects such accusations sheds light upon how Homerising poetry might seek to incorporate these clever revisionist deconstructions into its own agenda. Now, direct links between the *Posthomerica* and such works must remain, on one level, speculative: Quintus certainly knew of the Palamedes tradition, but whether he knew of what the *Heroicus* did with it is difficult to determine for certain.[101] But the poem does display a profound engagement with this *style* of Homeric response and participates critically in the imperial Greek fascination with the nature of Homeric truth, lies and fiction.

That this participation has not before been systematically considered may be due to ostensible differences in tone. There is after all an obvious humour shared by the corrections in Dio's *Trojan Oration*, Lucian's *True*

---

[101]   In Chapter 6 I discuss different examples which point to a direct intertextual engagement between Quintus and Philostratus’ *Vita Apollonii*.

224 Selective Memory and Iliadic Revision

Histories, Philostratus' two Homeric epiphanies and the aptly nicknamed 'Homeric Games': a self-irony which pervades each text, in different ways, on every level. Quintus' poem by contrast has generally been characterised as straight and austere, often to its detriment, and devoid of any such parody or play. If, however, this chapter has succeeded in suggesting that Quintus aims to display, and to continue, Homeric selectivity from mythological material, then the *Posthomerica* goes some way to pervert the perverters and reveals an ironic reflexivity of its own. 'Trapped' in a revisionist game which has been devised, championed and played unceasingly by others (from Homer's earliest critics to and beyond Agathias), the inter-Homeric poet finds a way to use the confines of this particular strand of inherited tradition to his advantage. It may be clever, and funny, to point out Homer's omissions, to hijack the story behind his poetry and to reassemble it as the 'truth', but in the end, it is precisely this poetry – aware of more, expertly selecting to fit the context, editing to persuade and delight – which has the last laugh.

The trope of memory thus provides another significant example of how Quintus' position as 'still Homer' paradoxically affirms his own confident identity. It also, more broadly, shows how the *Posthomerica* offers a distinctive contribution to discussions about the role of poetry in the literary culture of its time; not only a powerful reminder (should we still need one) that this period was not 'arrogated by prose',[102] but an illustration of the *multiple* possible relationships which could be conceived between the forms. Quintus advocates a more reflective, reactionary response to the compulsions of genre and the choices of composition, neither simply supersessionist (prose over poetry) nor synthetic (prose using poetry, or poetry making the same moves as prose).

We saw how by the time of Agathias' *Histories*, poetry and prose could be configured as representing competing claims to be the voice of the authoritative past. Such a position is further affirmed and challenged through multiple, diverse channels across the Christian and Christianising years of Late Antiquity: from, to take just a few selective cases, Nonnus' imperatives to 'remember' in his Dionysiac and Biblical transformations in verse;[103] to Augustine's dual fascination with memory and reading in the Latin tradition;[104] to the polemics of the epigrams arranged in the *Palatine*

---

[102] For this particular wording, see Bowie (1989a): 209.
[103] On this point, with examples, see Goldhill (2020): ch. 4.
[104] On Augustine's philosophy and theology of memory, particularly in the *Confessions*, a crucial site for these issues, see from a vast bibliography, particularly the influential Ricoeur (1984) and more recently the book-length exploration by Hochschild (2012) and the succinct chapter by Teske (2001).

Anthology: the Early Christian poems of the first book, a bold Byzantine preface announces, will speak out and take precedence, 'even if the pagans are displeased' (τὰ τῶν χριστιανῶν προτετάχθω εὐσεβῆ τε καὶ θεῖα ἐπίγραμματα κἂν οἱ Ἕλληνες ἀπαρέσκωνται, *Anth. Pal.* 1. prf.); and in the third book, the same temple frieze is described in an oscillating sequence of epigrammatic poems and (later added) prose introductions, as a single site is 're-read as a double collection, a double vision of what is on display'.[105] Through such dialectics of medium, it is clear that as the vast waves of political, religious and social change continued to reverberate through the later Greek and Roman world, the construction of cultural tradition – its aesthetics and modes of expression, literally *how* it was written – became a crucial vehicle for self-assertion and affiliation.[106]

Quintus' third-century composition, so reticent towards overt self-posturing, and, of course, as we have seen throughout this book, devoid of any conspcious (anti-) Christian discourse, may seem far away from these later, more directly, culturally inflected polemics. And yet the *Posthomerica* displays its own intense interest in memory on the one hand and form on the other, and it places these issues in a consistent and challenging dialogue, as mutually informed responses to the reconstruction of Homer, who was in the third century and continued to be a central part of this contested inheritance. Seated on the cusp of the most extreme 'trans-formations' of Late Antiquity, the *Posthomerica*'s use of memory thus constitutes another example of the critical significance of its interval position: under Quintus' treatment, memory of Homer can offer a sub-versive reflection on second sophistic claims to the authority of prose and a suggestive forerunner to Christian, Agathian-style poetic declarations. Asserting poetry's voice in the contentious redrafting of the Homeric tradition *as poetry*, Quintus carves out its, and by extension his, irreducible place in the playground – or battleground – of imperial cultural criticism. If Homeric verse is to have the last laugh, it will be a Quintan achievement.

---

[105] Goldhill and Greensmith (forthcoming). The original date of these poems is intensely debated: see Demoen (1988) with bibliography. I am referring in these comments to the act of compiling and placing these poems in this structure in the Byzantine era.

[106] These examples to which I once again 'selectively' gesture here have been chosen because they represent explicit and also seemingly very un-Quintan examples of how the twin issues of memory and compositional form can be articulated across different times and spaces in Late Antiquity. For my overall stance on Quintus and Christianity, see Chapter 1.

CHAPTER 6

Prodigal Poetics
Filiation and Succession

> My concern is only with strong poets, major figures with the persistence to wrestle with their strong precursors, even to the death. Weaker talents idealise; figures capable of imagination appropriate for themselves.
>
> – Harold Bloom, *The Anxiety of Influence*: 5

> When a thing has been said and said well have no scruple. Take it and copy it.
>
> – Anatole France

Quintus' response to Homer, in all of the strands explored so far, is based fundamentally upon a relationship: between two poets, figures and literary systems. Charting and defining this relationship – the *Posthomerica*'s self-articulated position alongside and against its primary source and model – is key to unlocking the poetics of the interval. In this chapter, then, we turn to Quintus' treatment of a symbolic marker which visualises 'relationships' in the most direct terms. The imagery of filiation – children and parents, generational continuation or conflict – has long been recognised as a salient metaphor for poets' struggles against their literary predecessors. Recent work has shown how father-son symbolism was particularly dominant in the Latin epic of the Augustan and post-Augustan period, where it was used to express anxieties about dynastic as well as poetic succession. Yet it recurs again forcefully in the poetry of imperial Greece. Considered against the absence (so far as we can see) of extensive filial metaphors in the programmatic poetry of Alexandria,[1] this trope appears to bring imperial Latin and imperial Greek poetics into a particularly close diptych: does

---

[1] For all of Callimachus' musings on childhood and youth (on which see discussion in Chapter 4), his extant poetry does not obsess over successional dynamics in any comparable way, nor, to take a more generically close comparison, does such symbolism feature heavily in Apollonius, who is not, in this sense at least, a 'Bloomian' poet (see e.g. Hutchinson (1988) who takes this line strongly). This apparent absence makes filiation stand in contrast to the tropes that we have considered so far, all of which have both an Alexandrian *and* (subsequently) silver Latin genealogy.

226

filiation (re)-emerge as the metaphor for the Roman Empire? To answer this question, however, we must also confront what is distinctive about the trope as it appears in a later Greek context – in a world radically different from that inherited by Vergil and his successors. The presence of successionist poetics in the *Posthomerica* raises such issues sharply. Quintus' poem is filled with family dynamics and succession so often appears to be the axiomatic motif for the heroic discourse on display. And yet if, as I have argued, Quintus seeks constantly to eschew the distance between himself and his primary model Homer, how can his epic accommodate imagery whose power conventionally *insists* on a gap between old and new, predecessor and inheritor?

It is my aim in this chapter to suggest how the *Posthomerica* makes extensive use of the symbolism of filiation – but a new and expanded version of this symbolism, reworked to accord with the aims of Homeric impersonation. The first part considers how the poem's enlarged heroic environment creates space for this expansion: the post-Homeric world decentralises linear, antagonistic modes of succession and explores alternative models of continuation and different types of relationship. The second part moves to analyse these models, outlining the ways in which Quintus deftly sidesteps the idea that the only kind of succession is the replacement of one generational figure by the next. The poem's most successful successors adopt impersonating approaches to their predecessors reflective of the text's own mimetic ambitions and political-cultural energy. What will emerge from this reading is a poet acutely aware of the pliant potential of filiation as a literary symbol, and who offers a compendium of different ways to reconfigure it, in which positive and assimilatory systems can coexist with the anxious and disruptive. Filial imagery is thereby reclaimed for a different era of poetics *and* politics, and impersonation revealed as a valid, creative response to the age-old predicament of 'coming after'.

6.1 The Ever-Present Anxiety?

In order to focus on the use of filiation in the *Posthomerica*, we must first consider its background, the occurrence of the imagery in earlier poetry and its discussion in modern literary criticism. By way of this consideration, this section will return directly to one of my central literary critical concerns: the issues at stake in drawing analogies between the poetics of imperial Latin and those of imperial Greek.

Whilst often particularly associated with Latin poetry, the motif of generational continuity and conflict can of course be traced to much earlier

228   Prodigal Poetics: Filiation and Succession

in the epic tradition.[2] Homeric epic is itself centred on the family. The
Iliadic *mēnis* is released by a father weeping for a son, and a son weeping
for a father,[3] and famous scenes such as the *agōn* of Agamemnon and
Diomedes (*Il.* 4.364–403) make clear the theme of generational decline:
few men are greater than their fathers, most are worse (τοῖος ἔην Τυδεὺς
Αἰτώλιος· ἀλλὰ τὸν υἱὸν/γείνατο εἷο χέρεια μάχῃ, 399–400).[4] The *Odyssey*
is replete with its own heavy family discourse. Beginning with the paradigm of ancestral crime and filial revenge, its plot is as much about the
reunion of father and son as husband and wife, in which tensions of power
are negotiated through filial aggression and its avoidance: the son who
almost shoots the bow, the precarious authority of the father who holds
him back.[5] The political-cultural dimension of filiation is also perceptible
in this early phase of its history. In a literary-generic sense, the theme of
succession helps to articulate the demands of an oral tradition based self-
consciously on notions of repetition and self-perpetuation. As has been
noted, the *Homeridai* of Pindar's *Nemean* 2 make explicit the sense of
generational replacement inherent in the rhapsodic art: called the sons of
Homer, the members of this guild see themselves as the guardians and
successors of Homeric epic, a chain reaction, as we have seen, continued by
the Pindaric singer himself.[6] More broadly still, the fact that the plots of
both the *Iliad* and *Odyssey* concern 'the restoration of order within the
small-scale structure of the family'[7] reflects upon how the crucial relationship in archaic social and political structures is that of father to son. Issues
of individualism and loyalty, duty to the collective versus private pride and
vengeance which the Homeric poems' family scenarios so powerfully
convey can thus have deep political consequences, even though they are
not tightly connected with a given regime.

Filiation therefore was an image acutely able to express multiple types of
power relation. This potential made the image particularly valent for the

---

[2] Bowlby's concept of 'Freudian mythologies' (2007) excellently captures this point. See also Hardie
(1993): 88–91.
[3] I use the word 'release' to capture both the dissolution of Achilles' rage during this exchange (see
discussion of *lusis* in a related sense in Chapter 7) and its continued unleashing, shown in his fiery
response to Priam at *Il.* 24.559–71.
[4] The aggrieved response of 'Capaneus' son' (*Il.* 4.404–10) – claiming that they are emphatically and
demonstrably better than their rash Theban fathers, who 'perished through their own blind folly'
(*qua Od.* 1.7) – shows the tense circularity of such genealogically rooted arguments.
[5] Cf. Goldhill (1984): 191 and Hardie (1993): 119. Bibliography is vast on paternity in Homeric epic.
See particularly Redfield (1975); Finlay (1980); Griffin (1980); Lynn-George (1996); Felson (1999)
and (2002); Mills (2000); Pratt (2007).
[6] See especially Hardie (1993): 14–8 and 99; and Nagy (1996): 62. Cf. my discussion in Chapter 2.
[7] Hardie (1993): 88.

The Ever-Present Anxiety?

Latin poetry composed during the construction of the empire under Augustus, and its tense continuation after him. As the construction, legitimisation and contestation of imperial power in the Augustan and post-Augustan age unfolded its jagged and fractured narrative, the epic plots of the *Aeneid* and its successors duly appropriated and expanded the language of filiation to explore and explain such issues. This Latin epic poetics, in other words, now gave generational imagery a specific, created-for-purpose political context. As scholars have extensively explored, generational themes become a principal means for reflecting critically on the coming of the Principate and the driving necessity for dynastic succession. Thus the generational triumvirate of Anchises, Aeneas and Ascanius is given a central role in the *Aeneid's* narrative: literalised viscerally in the memorable image of Aeneas clutching both his father and son, along with the household gods – the physical and spiritual manifestation of the family unit – as he runs from burning Troy (*Aen.* 2.721–9). And yet when Anchises in turn is left behind – he dies in Drepanum, stuck in Book 3 along with the failed replicas of Troy, and Aeneas swiftly excludes him, as a living presence at least, from his story (*Aen.* 3.709 –11) – the reader is forced to confront the impossibilities of this threefold family model: for all the need to legitimise through the father, it is the sons in this story who go forward. The importance of creating Augustan genealogy is thus complicated by the fact that newness cannot be achieved by recourse to the past alone, as through the tragic figure of Marcellus, the *future* heir that would have been, lingering in the world of the dead, the chain of linear succession is portrayed as fractured and frayed before it is formed at all. In the decades to come, the Silver Latin poets Statius, Lucan and Valerius Flaccus, who all so programmatically 'exploit the energies and tensions called up but not finally expended or resolved in the *Aeneid*'[8] focus attention centrally on these *problems* of succession lying latent in the Vergilian vision, using the family as the symbolic place within which political conflicts of power develop.[9]

The literary aspect of filiation also assumes a new importance in post-Vergilian Latin epic: it becomes closely connected to these poets' driving desire to prove themselves worthy of the *Aeneid*, the epic model in whose footsteps they follow so closely. It is thus perhaps no great surprise that

---

[8] Hardie (1993): xii.
[9] Hardie (1993) remains seminal. Lee (1979) is a book-length study of fathers and sons in the *Aeneid*. See also Chaudhuri (2014) and Rosati (2005). I shall not further recapitulate the detailed case studies in these accounts, but shall draw on relevant details in what follows.

230 Prodigal Poetics: Filiation and Succession

silver Latin has become the epoch of classical literature most tightly and tirelessly associated with Harold Bloom's (in)famous model of literary family rivalry. If Telemachus' lurking potency already exemplifies 'the essential mode of human growth in [Freud's] Oedipal triad'[10], then Bloom's notion of the 'Anxiety of Influence' rings particularly true for these later Latin poets, with their intense reverence and intense rivalry with their close and canonical predecessor so frequently and forcefully conveyed. The family imagery at the heart of Bloom's psychoanalytical model – 'Laius and Oedipus at the crossroads. . .father and son as mighty opposites'[11] – thus describes the antithesis central to later Latin poetics in symbolic language with which it was wholly familiar.

'The Anxiety of Influence' has indeed become so inseparable from literary analysis of Roman epic that for some scholars, it is a critical cliché in itself. In his second edition of *A Theory of Poetry*, Bloom vents his own frustration with hyperbolised Bloomian rhetoric: 'I never meant by "the Anxiety of Influence"', he laments, 'a Freudian Oedipal rivalry, despite a rhetorical flourish or two'[12]; and the same bent towards self-misreading, as we have seen, is palpable in certain silver Latin critical discourse, so eager to distance itself from the tedious language of 'metapoetics'. Such protestations, of course, serve to underscore rather than undermine the importance and ubiquity of such symbolic readings, and filiation provides one of the strongest examples of how so: a network of images employed persistently and distinctively by the poets of this era, where adversarial imitation is practised on a vast scale.

What is less certain, however, is the applicability of this model to the *Greek* epic of the Roman Empire. And yet of all the critical apparatus borrowed from silver Latin that we have now examined, the concept of filial anxiety has been the most consistently cross-applied, read as metaphorising the concerns of poets who seek this time directly to take on Homer himself. The penchants of later Greek epic which we have traced in the first two chapters – the 'return to Troy', and close adaptation of Homeric theme, style and subject – are perceived to find a perfect metaphor in filial imagery, now mobilised to illustrate the obsession with *this* most foundational literary relationship. The imperial Greek

---

[10] Goldhill (1984): 191.   [11] Bloom (1997): 11.

[12] Bloom (1997): xxii. However much irony we may choose to see in this autobiographical misprision (cf. e.g. Bloom's follow-up to this follow-up, *The Anatomy of Influence* (2011), which the author, prematurely or proleptically, described as his 'virtual swansong' to the western canon), though I myself remain dubious as to whether there is any true self-deprecation at all, its parodic force as a piece of self *reception* is indefatigable.

The Ever-Present Anxiety?

mythological epics are indeed full of generational material, continuing the focus on the family already established in Homer. Triphiodorus opens with a series of elderly laments for fallen sons (17–39) – a generational stagnation reflective of the 'old' war which his epic aims to rejuvenate – and throughout his poem makes ample use of the imagery of childbirth, particularly in the Wooden Horse, depicted as a pregnant mother filled with heroic offspring.[13] Colluthus begins with one wedding (to Thetis), and narrates the contest won by the promise of another (to Helen), and centres his story on the interactions between parents and children: Aphrodite and the Loves (86, 99–100); Hyacinthus (241) and – a character to whom we shall shortly return – Hermione, the deserted daughter of Helen (327–86).[14]

Nonnus is the most overt Greek practitioner of filial poetics. The *Dionysiaca* is filled with multiform and multifarious births: Ampelus reborn from vine (*Dion.* 12), baby Zagreus climbing on to Zeus' throne (5.155–205), Achilles' grandfather contrasted anachronistically with his more famous grandson (22.354–90). The word νόθος, a key term in the poem, works as a tag for this generational waywardness, all set within the driving discourse of Dionysus' own competitive emulation of his father Zeus. This competition is crystallised during the visit to the court of King Staphylus, when after hearing stories of Zeus' mythological achievements, Dionysus' 'ears bewitched, and he wished for a third and greater victory to rival Cronides' (18.309–13). In the second proem Nonnus glosses this extensive filial metaphor;[15] dramatising in the most direct terms his own relationship with his literary forbearer:

> ἀλλὰ θεά με κόμιζε τὸ δεύτερον ἐς μέσον Ἰνδῶν
> ἔμπνοον ἔγχος ἔχοντα καὶ ἀσπίδα πατρὸς Ὁμήρου,
> μαρνάμενον Μορρῆι καὶ ἄφρονι Δηριαδῆι
> σὺν Διὶ καὶ Βρομίῳ κεκορυθμένον·...
>
> *Dion.* 25.264–7[16]

Then bring me, O goddess, into the midst of the Indians again, holding the inspired spear and shield of Father Homer, while I attack Morrheus and the folly of Deriades, armed by the side of Zeus and Bromius!

---

[13] E.g. Triphiodorus 200, 415, 533–4, 389–90.
[14] See Morales (2016), to whose reading of Colluthus we return later in this chapter.
[15] Cf. discussion of *Dion.* 1.431–2 in Chapter 4.
[16] Shorrock's reading of Nonnus–Homer/Dionysus–Zeus, (2001): 152–6, demonstrates how strongly the links between silver Latin and imperial Greek poetics have been drawn specifically in discussions of filiation.

232   Prodigal Poetics: Filiation and Succession

Even non-narrative imperial Greek epic learns to (re)play the filial game. The sixth-century Neoplatonising poet Christodorus constructs a remarkable set of hexameter descriptions of the statues in the Baths of Zeuxippus at Constantinople (which have survived for us as Book 2 of the *Palatine Anthology*).[17] Paternity is a driving trope in this poem, used to instantiate the connections and differences between the distant past of so many of the statue subjects and the author's own contemporary world. Thus for instance the statues of mythological heroes are said to look 'exactly like' their fathers (Ajax and Telemon 271–6; Sarpedon 280–2; Neoptolemus 56–8); the poet figures are frequently described using the language of family bonds (Homer is called πατὴρ ἐμός, [320], probably an echo of Nonnus; Vergil is described as the Roman Homer because he has different parents [414–6]); and the image of Pompeius Magnusis is introduced as 'the father of the emperor Anastasius' (403–5, one of the poem's rare overt references to its sixth-century context).[18] Mythological, poetic and political filiation thus form the veneer for the text's resolutely past-facing viewpoint, whilst allowing glimpses of its subtle connectivity with Christodorus' more elusive present.

I have argued in Chapter 1 that the stylistic and chronological diversity of imperial Greek epics makes alignment with silver Latin dubious and even misleading. In the case of generational poetics, these problems are particularly pressing. Whereas, as we have seen, Vergil's silver successors all wrote within a short time period of one another and of Vergil, for these poets of Troy, Homer was a distant ancestor, a (great) grand-father, a monument and a mystery.[19] Given the contextual uncertainties surrounding many of these epics, an overt politicisation of their family narratives is also far more difficult to assert: in many cases, we simply do not have the information to construct a 'specific, created-for-purpose, political context'. Finally, it is clear even from the limited information available about these poets that the era in which they wrote was simply not characterised by the linear dynastic succession which preoccupied post-Augustan Rome. The Greek empire in the opening five centuries CE was dominated instead by

---

[17] See Bassett (1996) and (2004); Tissoni (2000); Kalldelis (2007); Whitby (2017); Bär (2012); and Middleton (2019).

[18] On this connection, see especially Croke (2009).

[19] Cf. Porter (2002) and related discussion in Chapter 1 to this book. Vergil, of course, also acquired a form of monumentality in his imperial reception (cf. e.g. Rosati (2005) on how Statius 'turns the *Aeneid* into a museum piece'). But the 'deep antiquity' of Homer, and his status as the avatar of Greek education and culture, makes such conceptions of him operate on an altogether different scale.

The Ever-Present Anxiety?   233

shifting modalities of power: new political centres,[20] oscillating leadership, contested *loci* of authority.[21] In the third century more specifically, within this so-called 'era of crisis', no fewer than twenty-five different emperors ruled between 235 and 284 CE; a situation characterised by 'a bewildering list of pretenders, usurpers and short-lived emperors; breakaway kingdoms in both the west and the east; porous and threatened frontiers; and widely different regional histories and economies.'[22] A far cry from direct, dynastic progression, the relationship between participants in this era was far messier and more overlapping.

In both a literary and a political sense, therefore, paradigms of linear succession do not fit well with the Greek third century. Given these fundamental differences, a silver Latin model for Greek filiation will only ever offer a weaker reading. To understand the continued – or revived – relevance of filial poetics in this era of epic, these examples must be approached on their own terms.

The *Posthomerica* is a crucial site for beginning this re-evaluation. The poem is replete with filial imagery. Heroic fathers killed in conflict are succeeded by heroic sons; younger warriors are described with elaborate genealogies; and gods argue in dramatic family stand-offs. The 'Anxiety of Influence' has also seemed to be the overwhelmingly obvious model for characterising the poem as a whole: neatly, if drearily,[23] encapsulating Quintus' relationship to Homer. 'It hardly needs a Bloom to articulate Quintus' literary vision',[24] suggests Kneebone; and Schmitz asks whether this particular Oedipus at the crossroads 'was-particularly brave and clever or particularly stupid and ingenuous to pick this fight against an adversary so much greater than himself.'[25]

---

[20] The centrality of Greece was contested, or at least relativised, by Rome, of course, but also by Alexandria and (in Jewish and Christian traditions) Jerusalem, in the imagination at least.

[21] Greek culture was never centralised in the way that Roman culture was (i.e. there was no single 'Greek capital') and had less investment in narratives of empire and control. This fundamental difference was thus sharpened, rather than created, in the imperial phase of Greek history. For a recent take on the dynamic multiplicity of identity formation and expression in the empire, and the role of the individual and the institution in shaping it, see Vanacker and Zuiderhoek (2017) (an engaging focus on the importance of ritual to these processes), whose introduction also synthesises the current state of the field surrounding the Romanisation debate and theoretical frameworks concerning identity in the Roman Empire.

[22] Clarke (2012). The sense of diversity that these emperors represent in terms of their relationships to their predecessors can be seen from an overview of the different 'types' of emperor as they are commonly categorised: Barrack, Gallic, Illyrian, Britannic. Scholarship on the third-century crisis is vast and this summary does not seek to resurvey it. Among the most lucid recent synoptic accounts are those of Hekster (2008) and Ando (2012), as discussed in Chapter 1.6.

[23] *Qua* Leigh (2006): 238.   [24] Kneebone (2007): 289   [25] Schmitz (2007b): 65.

234   Prodigal Poetics: Filiation and Succession

And yet this model does *not* in fact do justice to the dynamics of our text. The generational poetics of the *Posthomerica*, in diverse and dramatic ways, in fact adamantly *rejects* the Bloomian correlation between 'strong' creative poets and filial anxiety, and redrafts the heroic family model to serve the aims not of literary rivalry, but of constructive impersonation. Given the inherently 'politicised' nature of this model – that filial imagery as far back as Homer has been used to convey structural and political 'relationships' in dialogue with literary ones – this redrafting is key to continuing to grasp Quintus' engagement with 'contemporary' issues in his text. We have seen in the previous chapters how the multiplicity of relationships between Greece and Rome could be a central part of what drives the poetics of interval: how, for all the 'extremes of prejudice, gestures of exclusion and self-assertion' that one can find in imagined narratives of *Graecia Capta*, all terms of identification and categorisation – Homeric and post-Homeric *and*, relatedly, Greek, Roman, Latin (and all ways in which these oppositions can be further divided) – are always 'synchronically and diachronically shifting and repeatedly in a dynamic relation with each other and their own history'.[26] In Quintus' politically evasive poem[27] the extensive use of the filiation trope provides the strongest incentive yet to connect these narratives: to give this literary self-positioning towards Homer a sharply politicised edge. For as the Greek world in the third century was increasingly characterised by the removal of linearity in a dynastic sense, and a more diffuse network of cultural relationships more broadly, then Quintus' rejection of linear paradigms of succession in his epic represents his profound meditation on this new societal space. The interval poet harnesses the conventional associations between familial, political and poetic succession and reworks them to make sense for his contemporary world.

The *Homeridai*, in fact, already offer a model for this reworking. Descendants of Homer who continue the real Homeric song, in

---

[26] Goldhill (forthcoming a) who evocatively captures the complexities of this Graeco-Roman 'relationality'. Further discussion of this standpoint, and the initial markers of Quintus' engagement with its dynamics, in Chapters 2 and 3.

[27] See Chapter 1.5. I use this phrase to acknowledge that the argument to follow does not seek to deny the (pointed) evasiveness regarding contemporary politics pursued by Quintus' text, nor the real opaqueness produced by the contextual uncertainties surrounding his and other imperial Greek epics, which means, as I have repeatedly emphasised so far, that we cannot always construct political readings in a satisfyingly direct way. By making the case for Quintus' engagement with these third-century dynamics in his filial poetics, I am interested in continuing to explore how different politicised (not straightforwardly 'political') readings are indeed possible and productive for this literature, if the terms of engagement are changed.

Epic Ecology: Quintus' Successional Space 235

competition not with their founding source but with one another, theirs is filiation based on impersonation, in which succession becomes possible without the attendant process of supersession. By exploring such a possibility on a vast scale, Quintus' approach to filiation rewrites this literary imagery for his own mimetic agenda; reconciling ideas about succession with claims to embody Homer, and thereby offering a poetic image of his expanded, pluralistic imperial environment.

6.2 Epic Ecology: Quintus' Successional Space

Quintan Troy is a sterile space, filled with geriatric decay and impotence. Old men take up narrative room but are refused narrative action,[28] and the reverse side of the generational spectrum is eerily empty. In contrast to the fecundity of many other imperial Greek mythological epics, no one is born in Quintus' poem and young children only ever appear at the moment of their deaths.[29] This stagnation creates a youthful void, ostensibly ready to be filled. Throughout the course of the poem, a series of new heroic contenders arrive to fill the gap left by Hector, who is set up as the major Iliadic absence at the dawn of the poem,[30] and Achilles, whose death in Book 3 creates a parallel deficiency on the Greek side, a lacuna deeply felt.[31] Such newcomers offer the chance to lift the poem's sagging demographic and reinvigorate heroic life. And yet they also come already fully

---

[28] Quintus, like Triphiodorus, frequently focuses on aged characters, who get involved in martial action even less than Homer's elderly generation at Troy. These characters are prone to discussing their limitations (particularly Nestor, who decries his enforced passivity on three occasions: Q.S.2.301–18; 4.118–26; 12.260–73) and suffer and die throughout the course of the narrative: Illioneus at the hands of Diomedes (13.181–205) and Priam by Neoptolemus (Q.S.13.213–50). For further observations on the older characters in the poem, see Boyten (2010): ch. 3.

[29] Notably Laocoön's sons (12.444–99); the Trojan infants killed during the sack (13.123–30; 443–56); and Astyanax hurled from the tower (13.251–66), without any accompanying living role akin to the touching exchange of *Il.* 6.466–82. Boyten (2010): 166–70 focuses on the pathos of these infant deaths, but overemphasises the role played by young children in the poem as a whole. The only other narrative passages featuring young children are Q.S.9.115–44 and the escape of Ascanius (Q.S.13.300–32). In general, children's presence in the *Posthomerica* is a prelude to their absence.

[30] The death of Hector is, as we have seen in our analysis of the poem's opening in the previous chapter, the primary and stated reason for the Trojan's claustrophobic fear, as they 'remain' huddled inside the city of Troy.

[31] Consider for example the lengthy fight for Achilles' corpse (Q.S.3.389–400), which is described explicitly as motivated by the magnitude of Achilles' heroic efforts (ὅ σφιν ὄνειαρ/ἔπλετ' ἐνὶ πτολέμοισιν ἑῷ μέγα κάρτεϊ θύων./τοὔνεκά μιν βασιλῆες ἀπὸ πτολέμου ἐρύσαντες, 3.383–5), and the even lengthier sequence of initial laments for him (3.401ff.). In a very different way to the situation in the *Iliad*, the Achilles of the *Posthomerica* is himself delayed in his arrival to the Quintan battlefield: he and Ajax mope around the tomb of Patroclus [Q.S.1.376–84] – a scene to which we shall turn in 6.3 – and throughout Quintus' epic he is experienced as an absence for far longer than he exists as a living presence.

236   Prodigal Poetics: Filiation and Succession

formed. They are not born in the war, nor do they grow up in Troy, but are superimposed ready-made onto the narrative. The symbolism of this type of character may well lie close to the surface. In the delayed proem Quintus aligns himself with a Homeric 'middle age', presenting himself as a poet who is neither young and immature nor old and 'over-the-hill'.[32] In this portrait of young but developed heroes we may thus see the poet's continued musings on the correct route to literary arrival: the successful (heroic, literary) newcomer does not need to begin from scratch; they can achieve their renown and impose their innovation by continuation – taking up and moving on from the situation inherited from times before.

The striking feature of all of these new heroes, however, is their substitutability: their *lack* of centrality to the plot. The Trojan allies Penthesilea, Memnon and Eurypylus are all marked by transience. Their doomed fates are underscored as soon as they come to Troy and they die soon after their arrival. The new participants on the winning side, Neoptolemus and Philoctetes, are also subjected to forms of narrative displacement. Their summoning, arrivals and *aristeiai* occur sequentially to one another – they have to share their narrative space –[33] and neither new victor takes on *the* central role in the sack.[34]

This sense of heroic impermanence is underscored by the poem's structure. Each book is centred around a different character or event, with minor themes interwoven accordingly.[35] As the chronological sequence of the story progresses, it becomes clear that there is in fact no single character unifying the whole construction of this epic plot. This structure has been frequently cited as 'episodic' and a 'non-Homeric' feature of the poem. Certainly, the contrast with the plots of the *Iliad* and *Odyssey*, which concentrate on a central section of the Trojan story and are shaped around the actions of a central hero,[36] is stark. It is equally incongruous with Apollonius, where a central hero still dominates in what is the most vast and teleological of journey narratives. Nor is the *Posthomerica* akin to post-Vergilian Latin epic, where the theme of heroic substitution is also extensively explored.[37] In those epics, even if character supremacy is challenged, or switched (Pompey and Caesar, Hannibal versus Scipio),

---

[32] See Chapter 4.   [33] Neoptolemus in Q.S.7–8; Philoctetes in Q.S.9–10.
[34] Calchas' prophecy about Philoctetes' pivotal importance to the sack (Q.S.7.323–32) is not reflected by any major role in the event itself.
[35] I return to the structure of the poem from a different perspective in Chapter 7.
[36] The concentration on a central hero is not the same as structuring an epic around one character's life story, which Aristotle warns against (*Poet.* 1451a).
[37] See particularly Hardie (1993): 37.

Epic Ecology: Quintus' Successional Space 237

the fight *for* supremacy still unifies the plots, which remain organised around the notion of heroic centrality – ideal, conceptualised, thwarted – however difficult it becomes ultimately to achieve. In this sense, a very different text from this Roman corpus may appear to offer a closer model. Ovid's *Metamorphoses* is of course defiantly non-linear in its narrative strategy: built on a pattern of oscillating, colliding episodes and characters, this multiplicitous epic has no central hero, as it proudly announces in the proem, other than change itself (*In noua fert animus mutatas dicere formas corpora, Met.* 1.1–2); and, as Hardie notes, 'largely avoids putting the theme of generational continuity at [its] centre'.[38] However, what makes the *Posthomerica* so striking is that it resists this centralising move in a text which in all other ways is profoundly *non* 'metamorphic': Quintus introduces this shift into heroic epic, traditionally plotted; a realm previously so dominated by the Aristotelian mould.[39]

It is, therefore, perhaps unsurprising that this un-Homeric, un-Apollonian, 'un-silver' structure has traditionally been catalogued amongst the poem's many failings as an epic. In the same way that Aristotle criticised the cyclic poems for their piecemeal plot arrangements (*Poet.* 1459a–b), the *Posthomerica* has been accused of ploddingly narrating one event, sequence and hero after another.[40] In that redemptive turn that characterises recent scholarship on the poem, various moves have been made to counter this criticism. Scholars have proposed concentric plot-structure designs,[41] or promoted certain heroes to the dominant position in the narrative,[42] thus making the poem conform more closely to the (Homeric) epic norm. That no such model has proved durable or convincing as a means of re-structuring the poem is telling: as we saw with the lexical frameworks into which recent scholars have tried and fail to wrestle the poem,[43] Quintus adamantly refuses to be contained by these moulds. It should therefore be considered instead that the *difficulty* in selecting a central figure for the poem is its driving structural impact. Taken seriously, the absence of an overarching, unifying character can be understood as a discourse *on* heroic substitutability, in its most insistent form.

---

[38] Hardie (1993): 94.

[39] In what follows, therefore, I am consciously approaching Quintus' structure in terms of the Aristotelian plot model, because it is Homeric epic, the archetype of this model (and *not* non-conformers such as Ovid or the cyclic poems) with which the *Posthomerica* most explicitly engages.

[40] See James (2004): 239–65 and Maciver (2012b): 20–1 on this negative reception.

[41] E.g. those of Maciver (2012b): 20–4.

[42] E.g. James (2004): xxx. Further discussion in 6.4. Related discussion in Scheijnen (2018): 31–5.

[43] Homeric *koine* versus Alexandrian contrast imitation, as analysed in Chapter 3.

238   Prodigal Poetics: Filiation and Succession

The process of centralisation in epic (of a segment of a story, or a hero in a plot), after all, is always geared towards producing certain effects. In the case of the Homeric poems, the focus on one part of the whole has been connected as far back as Aristotle to notions of economy and amplitude.[44] In the *Iliad* in particular, the technique of exploring large-scale issues in a tight narrative space allows its poetics of 'aestheticised, concentrated power' to take shape.[45] It remains therefore to find a means of characterising Quintus' alternative, un-centralised structure and the effects that it in turn can produce.

If Aristotelian forces of economy and amplitude provide a conceptual framework for comprehending the Homeric plot, and those epics which replicated these features of its shape, then Quintus' structural texture requires a vocabulary which moves away from a focus on 'the centre' and towards more relational forms of interaction: a means of grasping the spaces *in between* the constructed polarities of the heroic-narrative core and the periphery. Recent theories of distributed agency, prevalent in fields as wide-ranging as art criticism,[46] social anthropology[47] and object-orientated ontology, take as their starting point precisely this shift outwards from the centre towards a more holistic view of engagements between, for example, humans, objects or spaces.[48] To take as a pointed illustration one recent and particularly bold contribution, Eduardo Kohn's account of a 'posthuman ecology of living things' in the Ecuadorian Amazon, *How Forests Think*, aims not to do away with the human but to open it up, by focusing on the relationships between human and non-human forms as communicators and representors of the world.[49] To comprehend these relationships, he argues, 'linear thinking' may no longer be adequate. Thus, to take an example to whose significance we shall shortly return, Kohn describes a local man's 'bad dream' involving an encounter with a white policeman, which turned out to prophesy his own successful hunting venture the very next day:

---

[44] See especially Lowe (2000).   [45] For this phrasing, see Quint (1993): 3–4.

[46] Gell (1998) remains seminal, and has stimulated much productive counter-criticism (e.g. Layton (2003) with further references).

[47] Two areas which have made particular advances in this area are actor-network theory (pioneered by Latour (2005)) and posthumanism, for an overview of which see Braidotti (2013): ch. 1.

[48] It would be far beyond the scope of this chapter (and book) to attempt any overview of the vast and varied approaches to relationality in the social sciences and well beyond. I cite here those ventures which have proven most stimulating to my own thinking about relationality and Quintan epic, but which are intentionally based on case studies far afield from the Greek third century. For the factors shaping this methodology (and approach towards 'theory' and the social sciences), see Chapter 1.8 and 1.10.

[49] Kohn (2013). He terms this system an 'anthropology beyond the human'.

Epic Ecology: Quintus' Successional Space

Was Oswaldo the policeman, or had he become prey? Who is that frightening figure that is also so familiar? How can a policeman, a being so threatening and foreign, also be oneself? This uncanny juxtaposition reveals something important about Oswaldo's ongoing struggle to be and become, in relation to the many kinds of others he encounters in the forests that make him who he is.[50]

In the early centuries CE of the Roman Empire – a world which, as we have seen, was by the third century characterised by the substitutability of its own leading figures – 'linear thinking' also came under intense pressure. The relevance of this not-so 'post-modern' vocabulary of distributed agency to this particular ancient space becomes sharply apparent, as many imperial Greek commentators reveal an acute interest in the alternative options available to a centralised conception of the world. Pausanias, for example,[51] when discussing the building programme of Hadrian, subtly engages with the fact that the emperor himself was not singularly responsible for all of the monuments attributed to him. In his account of the Temple of Olympian Zeus (1.18.6–9), as Whitmarsh has productively explored, he gestures towards the multiple chronological strata underlying the present-tense building and thereby evokes the imperial project[52] 'to distinguish prior and present time using spatial demarcation, merging temporality and space into a single symbolic expression'.[53] In the deceptively simple remark that Hadrian 'dedicated' (ἀνέθηκε) the Temple, Pausanias also both masks and draws attention to the whole question of where the agency lies in the construction of imperial architecture: who orders the buildings, who pays for them, the crude mechanics of supply, craft and design.[54] In the third century more specifically, the culture of 're-animation' which we have explored in detail is also crucially informed by and expressive of such modes of relationality. The doubleness expounded by sophistic ethopoetics, Homeric performances and the 'close encounters' in Philostratus and Lucian each put forward the possibility of a more substitutable relationship between figures from different temporal layers, in which a new performer, writer or text could stand contemporaneously with an old one, operating in a continuum which allows room for both.

---

[50] Kohn (2013): ch. 6, with quotation at 191.

[51] The presence of these ideas in Pausanias' writings suggests that relationality has important resonances in discussions which pre-date the 'third century crisis' and which are not unrelated to those which emerge during it.

[52] Institutionalised by Hadrian by his arch, which Pausanias does not mention: a telling omission, as Whitmarsh (2015): 53 remarks.

[53] Whitmarsh (2015): 53.   [54] Mitchell (1987), discussed by Whitmarsh (2015): 53–4.

240   Prodigal Poetics: Filiation and Succession

Much can be brought to bear on Quintus' heroic structure by considering it as a profound contemplation on these relational ideas.[55] For if epic's conventional plot is articulated through one central man, and if through this 'one manthropocentrism' the expectations of linear succession arise (the hero departs, and must return, or be removed, or be replaced), then the *Posthomerica*'s structure is different because it defies these impulses: to centralise and to move only forwards, in a straight line. Whilst still amply anthropocentric, Quintan Troy is a post-*one*-human environment. By constructing this environment, a forceful obfuscation of his genre's conventional structure, Quintus thus offers a more capacious way to think about epic's human relationships. There is no longer a straightforward answer to the question of who succeeds from whom, and how.

In this way, the symbolism of the heroic successors which I suggested lies close to the surface can also be adjusted and expanded. As representations and representors of the possible routes of succession, the poem's multiple heroic newcomers enact Quintus' *de*-centralisation of the singular poetic self and perform the plurality of ways in which the literary past can be conjoined with its later inheritors. By carefully signalled analogy, extension and reflection, the many different Greek identity stances 'under' Rome, the continual and contested relationality of erudite Greeks towards many kinds of others and towards themselves is articulated and examined through this epic . . . and ultimately, exalted.

6.3   Antagonising Antagonism

We turn first to the routes of succession not taken in the *Posthomerica*: the more 'conventional' attempts by heroic children to rival, usurp and better 'either respectfully or violently'[56] their fathers and forerunners. The opening books of the poem present a number of portraits of this antagonistic type of relationship, and Quintus frequently draws attention to their metaphorical potential, exploring their themes of anxiety and competition in a literary as well as literal sense. It indeed 'hardly needs a Bloom' to perceive these adversarial paradigms in Quintus' opening construction of

---

[55] This model, to be clear, does not seek to deny the continued role of individualism on a local and personal-political scale, and the centuries of single ownerships that paid for and produced the wit, erudition and confidence of poets such as Quintus and his imperial Greek epic cohort (on which see further discussion and references in Chapter 1.3–5). A focus on pluralism as an alternative political narrative in this era aims to nuance, not replace, this picture.

[56] *Qua* Bloom (1997) *passim*.

Antagonising Antagonism

his poetic vision. However, what is crucial, but never acknowledged by critics who read Quintus' anxiety of influence in this way, is that these paradigms *fail*. The disruptive filial heroes do not achieve lasting narrative success or permanent epic power. In narrating their failure, with heavy irony and even distain, Quintus identifies them with an older, out-dated set of literary conventions, better suited to the type of epic space from which his decentralised concept of epic – and empire – seeks to move away.

Opening Contenders: Penthesilea, Achilles, Ajax

Penthesilea is the first of these failed successors. Frequently characterised by her genealogy, she is described multiple times as the daughter of Ares.[57] During her first encounter with Achilles and Ajax, she boasts about this divine lineage (Q.S.1.560–2). Their response is derisive: οἱ δ' ἐγέλασσαν (563).[58] Achilles, however, responds with his own ancestral self-promotion, which focuses on Zeus:

> οἳ μέγα φέρτατοί εἰμεν ἐπιχθονίων ἡρώων·
> ἐκ γὰρ δὴ Κρονίωνος ἐριγδούποιο γενέθλης
> εὐχόμεθ' ἐκγεγάμεν·...
>
> Q.S.1.577–9

We are the best heroes on earth, claiming descend from the Thunderer, Zeus son of Cronus. . .

Shortly before this exchange, Ajax rouses Achilles into action using the same sort of rhetoric: οὐ γὰρ ἔοικε Διὸς μεγάλοιο γεγῶτας/αἰσχύνειν πατέρων ἱερὸν γένος (1.502–3). However, as the heroes charge into battle, the narrative complicates this positive relationship to Zeus:

> Ἀργεῖοι δ' ἐχάρησαν, ἐπεὶ ἴδον ἄνδρε κραταιὼ
> εἰδομένω παίδεσσιν Ἀλωῆος μεγάλοιο,
> οἳ ποτ' ἐπ' εὐρὺν Ὄλυμπον ἔφαν θέμεν οὔρεα μακρὰ
> Ὄσσαν <τ'> αἰπεινὴν καὶ Πήλιον ὑψικάρηνον,
> ὅππως δὴ μεμαῶτε καὶ οὐρανὸν εἰσαφίκωνται·
> τοῖοι ἄρ' ἀντέστησαν ἀταρτηροῦ πολέμοιο
> Αἰακίδαι, μέγα χάρμα λιλαιομένοισιν Ἀχαιοῖς,
> ἄμφω ἐπειγόμενοι δηίων ἀπὸ λαὸν ὀλέσσαι.

---

[57] Q.S.1.206; 1.318; 1.461 and the examples in character speech discussed above.
[58] Way's addition of a verse which would make Penthesilea laugh first – (1913) *ad.* 1.563–4: ἦ, μέγα καγχαλόωσα κατὰ φρένας – is unconvincing as well as unnecessary. Hence the text retained by Vian (1963): 34.

242 Prodigal Poetics: Filiation and Succession

πολλοὺς δ' ἐγχείῃσιν ἀμαιμακέτῃσι δάμασσαν·
ὡς δ' ὅτε πίονα μῆλα βοοδμητῆρε λέοντε
εὑρόντ' ἐν ξυλόχοισι φίλων ἀπάνευθε νομήων
πανσυδίῃ κτείνωσιν, ἄχρις μέλαν αἷμα πιόντες
σπλάγχνων ἐμπλήσωνται ἑὴν πολυχανδέα νηδύν·
                                                    Q.S.1.515–27

The Argives were overjoyed to see that powerful pair; they looked like the sons of great Aloeus who once threatened to stack two high mountains, lofty Ossa and Pelicon's high peak, on top of broad Olympus when they were madly minded to get up to heaven. Just so those descendants of Aeacus took their stand in the grim fighting, a joyful answer to the prayers of the Achaeans as they hastened to kill the enemy host. Many were the victims they vanquished with their raging spears: just as when in the thickets a pair of lions that prey on oxen come across some plump ewes which have strayed far from their shepherds' care and set about slaughtering them with all speed, until they have quaffed the black blood and sated their appetites with the entrails.

Achilles' ambivalent kinship to Zeus has a lengthy mythico-literary tradition. Spurred by the prophecy that Thetis would bear a son greater than his father, Zeus' arrangement of her marriage to Peleus sought to prevent this catastrophic threat to his power. Despite their consequently distant relationship (great-great grandfather and grandson), Achilles' connection to Zeus still became a central part of his literary identity, as the threat-and-aversion narrative was replaced by an emphasis on Zeus' unfulfilled *intention* to engender a son by Thetis, and how the hero was thus 'almost' parented by this most powerful father. For Statius' young Achilles, for instance, the self-description as *genitum ... paene Ioui* (*Achil*.1.650–1) is both a boastful self-promotion and a wistful glance at this family tree that could have been.

Quintus' scene reflects Achilles' desire to emphasise his biological closeness to Zeus. However, it also reasserts the anxiety which led to their more distant relationship. In comparing Achilles and Ajax to παῖδες Ἀλωῆος (516) Quintus aligns the two heroes with the monsters who really did threaten to debase Zeus' authority. Odysseus' account of the gigantomachy in the *Odyssey* describes Otus and Ephialtes wandering despondently in the underworld, having been slain by Apollo for their botched attempt to usurp the gods (*Od.* 11.305–20). We have seen in Chapter 4 how Quintus makes close use of this particular Odyssean vignette in the delayed proem. The same passage is also closely echoed in this earlier scene: the use of dual (cf. ἀλλ' ὄλεσεν Διὸς υἱός, ὃν ἠύκομος τέκε Λητώ,/ἀμφοτέρω, *Od.* 11.318–9); the aorist infinitive θέμεν (517; as per *Od.* 11.315: Ὄσσαν ἐπ' Οὐλύμπῳ μέμασαν θέμεν); and the language of

Antagonising Antagonism 243

boasting (cf. οἵ ῥα καὶ ἀθανάτοισιν ἀπειλήτην ἐν Ὀλύμπῳ/φυλόπιδα στήσειν πολυάικος πολέμοιο, *Od.* 11.313–4) all connect Achilles and Ajax with this specific duo from Homer. Gigantomachic comparisons recur frequently in the *Posthomerica*: as he dies in fiery rage, Ajax is likened to the burning of the giant Enceladus (Q.S.5.641–9), as too is Locrian Ajax when he meets his own (self)-destructive end (Q.S.14.582–5). And after the description of the shield of Achilles, another miniature ekphrasis on his helmet unveils Zeus' victory in the related story of the Titonomachy:[59]

> τῇ δ' ἄρα παρκατέκειτο κόρυς μέγα βεβριθυῖα·
> Ζεὺς δέ οἱ ἀμφετέτυκτο μέγ' ἀσχαλόωντι ἐοικώς,
> οὐρανῷ ἐμβεβαώς· περὶ δ' ἀθάνατοι πονέοντο
> Τιτήνων ἐριδαινομένων Διὶ συμμεμαῶτες·
> τοὺς δ' ἤδη κρατερὸν πῦρ ἄμφεχεν· ἐκ δὲ κεραυνοὶ
> ἄλληκτοι νιφάδεσσιν ἐοικότες ἐξεχέοντο
> οὐρανόθεν· Ζηνὸς γὰρ ἀάσπετον ὤρνυτο κάρτος·
> οἳ δ' ἄρ' ἔτ' αἰθομένοισιν ἐοικότες ἀμπνείεσκον.
> Q.S.5.102–9[60]

Next to it lay the helmet, one of great weight. On it was depicted Zeus looking very wrathful in the height of heaven; all around him the other immortals were joining their efforts with his against the rebellious Titans, who were already engulfed by fearsome fire as bolts of lightning poured down ceaselessly from heaven thick as snowflakes, now that Zeus' immense power had been roused; they seemed on fire, even though they were still breathing.

Crucially, all of these other Quintan examples are, like the Odyssean scene, post-polemical: that is, they describe the aftermath of the attempted assault on Zeus, the consequences of sparking his anger, and the dark, eternal punishment for this futile act of violent usurpation. The helmet scene marks this temporality sharply: ἤδη (5.106) combines the enargeic presentism of ekphrasis with a nod to the tale's knowingly retrospective stance:

---

[59] Other occurrences at Q.S.1.179 (Penthesilea compared to Athena fighting the giants); 2.517–8 (Memnon and Achilles imagined as fighting like the Titans or Giants); Q.S.8.461–9 (Nestor describing Zeus' victory over the Titans as a warning to the Greeks to heed signs of his anger); and Q.S.11.415–9 (Aeneas compared to fighting like Zeus himself as he triumphed over the Giants).

[60] James (2004): 270 notes the 'natural association between the battles with Giants and the Titans … as symbolizing the struggle between order and chaos' reflected here, as is emphasised directly at Q.S.2.518–19, where Achilles and Memnon are compared to τε Γίγαντας ἀτειρέας ἠὲ κραταιούς/ Τιτῆνας… However, where James (ibid.) argues for a resultant 'confusion' between the two mythical stories, I would suggest a more invested act of conflation, as Quintus seeks to capitalise on the related symbolism between the two mythological confrontations of Zeus and his authority.

244 Prodigal Poetics: Filiation and Succession

mythically speaking, these rebellious Titans were always-already defeated. The Ajax and Achilles simile is therefore unique in the *Posthomerica* in that it describes the gigantomachic threat still in action: their destructive potential is not yet realised and not yet extinguished. And yet this detail serves only to heighten the ironic prolepsis at play. For the readers' pre-stored mythic knowledge confirms that both Achilles and Ajax soon meet their own ends in this section of the Trojan story: like the Odyssean giants and Quintus' Enceladus and Titan comparanda, they too will be destroyed by their egos and arrogance.[61] Quintus also stresses this part of the connection: the sheep in the simile of 524–7 foreshadow Ajax's frenzied stabbing of the flock before his suicide (Q.S.5.433–50), as Ajax in this killing spree slays men 'like' sheep, a comparison which gets literalised and reversed once his madness takes hold.

We are thus encouraged to read Achilles' boasts to Penthesilea in light of this darker para-narrative of monstrosity and attempted, thwarted take-over. The very language of this boast takes on new significance when refracted through this earlier comparison. His own use of a lion simile (1.587–8) for example, now evokes for the reader, via 1.524 (ὡς δ᾽ ὅτε πίονα μῆλα βοοδμητῆρε λέοντε), the leonine threat that he and Ajax posed as giants. And his mention of Zeus' patronymic Κρονίων (578) provides a passing recap of Zeus' own parricidal history: this magnificent ancestor posed and actually carried out the threat to his father which, in the gigantomachic comparison, Achilles threatened to represent to him.

Through this reminder of the latent danger lurking behind claims of filial admiration, Quintus activates the ambivalent theme of *poetic* ambition. We also saw in our discussion of the delayed proem how Quintus uses topographical features as metaphors for poetic style: the hill neither too high nor too low, the river Hermus and the spacious garden of liberty all represent the 'grand style' that Callimachus claimed to be avoiding. This passage has close lexical connections to the proem. As well as the shared allusions to the Odyssean underworld scene, the words μῆλα (1.524) and πολυχανδέα (1.527) also offer proleptic links to the proem (the words occur respectively in 12.308 and 310), where the terms play central symbolic roles. This intertextual dialogue between the two passages further encourages a symbolic reading of the imagery used here: Quintus is tapping the same web of associations that, in his later, most programmatic

---

[61] The comparison of Ajax again to a Giant at the moment of his actual death (Q.S.5.641–9) strengthens this point and, read in conjunction with this earlier simile, stresses the sense of ironic prolepsis found here.

Antagonising Antagonism 245

moment, he expands in full. Thus, the οὔρεα μακρά (517) which the giants attempted to scale suggests the connection between height and literary arrogance.[62] ὑψικάρηνον (518) is a Homeric *hapax* (*Il.* 11.132) re-mobilised by Callimachus (fr.309 Pf. = *Hec.* fr.119 H) meaning high-topped or lofty,[63] which provides a further image of largeness which can be equated, via Callimachean symbolism, with poetic size. However, whilst Quintus' proem used this symbolic language to articulate how his Home-rising poem strived, unlike Callimachus' polemically retractive *Aetia*, to accommodate these poetic heights, the negative portrayal of such grandeur here – its association with the *hubris* and failure of the giants – may seem to signal on the contrary a Bloomian moment of anxiety: Quintus leaving thundering to Zeus and stepping away from the dangers of 'picking a fight with an adversary so much greater than himself'.[64] However, the way in which this ambitious language is shown to be both applicable and futile *to both sides*, as Achilles and Ajax mock Penthesilea unaware of their own equally precarious filial ambitions, suggests that this portrait of competi-tiveness is contemplated by Quintus at a critical, even cynical, distance. Activated but not venerated, confined to the realm of mythological giants and similes, anxiety is only the start, not the end, of the poet's story.

Memnon and Achilles: Flyting against Filiation

Memnon, Penthesilea's heroic substitute, engages in his own generational flyting match with Achilles (Q.S.2.411–51). We saw in the previous chapter how this stand-off becomes a battle of literary reminiscence and quotation, as the contenders scour the *Iliad* for material to affirm their superiority. But the scene also offers a strong example of successionist poetics, as the tropes of memory and filiation work together to produce its symbolism.

From this perspective, the gendered aspect of this *agōn* is immediately striking. Although patronymics frame the speech-introduction formulae (μόλε σχεδὸν Αἰακίδαο, 388; πάϊς Αἰακίδαο, 430), its content is concerned with the female side of the family: Dawn versus Thetis. Both speeches contain multiple maternal tags, and the word 'mother' itself is repeated like a mantra (μητρός, 416; μητέρα δῖαν, 421; μητέρ' ἐμήν 444). In contrast to his emphasis on Zeus in Book 1, Achilles now passes over this male Olympian ancestor quickly (ὃς σέο φέρτερός εἰμι βίῃ γενεῇ τε φυῇ τε/Ζηνὸς

---

[62] Cf. οὔρεϊ οὔτε λίην χθαμαλῷ οὔθ' ὑψόθι πολλῷ (Q.S.12.313).   [63] Cf. LSJ s.v. ὑψικάρηνος.
[64] Cf. Schmitz (2007b): 65.

246   Prodigal Poetics: Filiation and Succession

ὑπερθύμοιο λαχὼν ἀριδείκετον αἷμα 2.433–4),[65] in order to assert instead his mother's side, and he exemplifies her prowess not with exempla of military might, but by recounting her pacifying achievements. This 'mother-off' at once destabilises traditional epic battle rhetoric, which usually focuses strongly on the father.[66] Heroes do not usually compete using their mums. It also stands in contrast with the roles of Thetis and Dawn as mothers *in* the narrative: at the moments where they appear as characters in the action, it is to perform the more conventional epic motherly moves of fearing for and weeping over their short-lived sons. Dawn is so bereft over the loss of Memnon that, like an elemental Demeter, she temporarily refuses to do her job and give light to the earth (Q.S.2.634–66); and upon the death of Achilles, Thetis, with her proleptic mourning in the *Iliad* now fulfilled, collapses in 'dreadful sadness' (3.631) and is consoled only by the words of another immortal mother, Calliope, who also lost her son, Orpheus (3.631–5). In the words of their sons in this flyting scene, however, these mothers acquire a different valence: objects of triumph rather than voice-pieces of despair, weaponised for wartime self-promotion not just the aftermath of lament. Conventional filial roles and speech structures are here distorted and reversed: the sons 'prattle on' about their mothers, rather than mothers about their sons.

This shift adds another important note of alternativism to Quintus' building portrayal of filiation. That the *Posthomerica*'s expanded heroic 'ecology' (and chosen segment of the Trojan story) includes a large roll-call of female participants is clear from even a casual reading of the poem.[67] In Penthesilea, the series of heroic contenders in fact starts with a woman. The continuation of the Helen and Paris story is also titled towards the female. The emphasis on Helen's two husbands in the Homeric tale is replaced by a reminder that Paris also had two wives: Oinone gets a large share of Quintus' narrative space, and when she kills herself following her refusal to prevent Paris' death, they are described as buried facing away from one another (Q.S.10.483–9) – marital strife in death as in life. Salient too is the emphasis on other women specifically as mothers. The account

---

[65] A wise move, given that Memnon too can claim descent from Zeus (c.f. Q.S.2.524). Comparing and contrasting their mothers is a better way of 'splitting hairs' in this contest.

[66] As is found throughout the *Iliad* and in the flyting match with Penthesilea discussed above. On flyting in Homeric and post-Homeric epic contexts, see Whitman (1958), Adkins (1969), Martin (1989), Alden (2000), Hesk (2006) and, centrally for Quintus' use of the convention, Maciver (2012c).

[67] Of course, no true impersonator of Homer could be purely masculine in their narrative demographic: as has been emphasised and analysed by scholarship too vast to condense here, Homer epic itself had already made it impossible to ignore the female voice.

Antagonising Antagonism 247

of Neoptolemus' summoning to Troy is told largely through the focalisation of his mother Deidamia (Q.S.7.169–434): as Odysseus and Diomedes fetch him from Skyros, Quintus narrates how Deidamia weeps, Penelope-style (as we have seen, with the same simile of melting snow, 7.229–31) for the double loss of her 'husband' and her soon-to-be-absent son.

This emphasis must affect our comprehension of the filial poetics of this work. The mother's role in successionist poetics has been consistently undervalued: Bloom's parricidal model of the *Wunderkind* completely ignores the female. In this *agōn*, Quintus does not. Why, we must ask, does he take this gendered turn? The role of the mother as a figure of particular influence and significance in Late Antiquity from a *Christian* perspective is extremely well-documented. The emerging centrality of Mary as the mother of Christ,[68] the prominence of and discourse surrounding female ascetics, and the complex, changing legislation on issues surrounding marriage, rape and female morality[69] are, to take just a few examples, part of what makes the Christianising environment of the later empire a fertile ground for disputing the connected questions of maternity, virginity, sexuality and seclusion.[70] These issues also find voice in the Greek poetics of the period, as those authors who took on classical themes and forms could refashion their conventional material to reflect such new types of female subject.[71]

---

[68] Consider also the 'analogously' central role of Helena Augusta, the mother of the first Christian Emperor. See the book-length study of Drijvers (1992) for context, overview and ample bibliography.

[69] See e.g. Arjava (1998) for a book-length study of women and the law in Late Antiquity. Specific discussion of the laws on abduction under Constantine and Justinian (in relation to Colluthus) in Morales (2016): 82–4.

[70] These brief comments and bibliographic examples do not intend to chart in any detail the manifold issues surrounding gender in Late Antiquity, but rather to suggest a potential discourse which may be important, in its most general and nascent terms, for reconsidering this unique maternal moment in Quintus. For broad discussions of Late Antique gender, I have found Clark (1993) and Cooper (2007a) particularly helpful starting points. On female asceticism, see Burrus (2008), Cloke (1995), Coon (1997), Elm (1994) and Kitchen (1998). On virginity and marriage, Hastrup (1978) and Cooper (1996) and (2007a), with further bibliography.

[71] I am focusing specifically on Greek verse examples from the vast pool of literary articulations, which have most obvious and immediate relevance for Quintus' manoeuvres. Motherhood, of course, plays a central role in Greek and Latin literature across antiquity, as synthesised in Petersen and Salzman-Mitchell (2012) with cross-chronological and generic overviews and bibliography. For the relevance of motherhood to 'silver Latin' discourse – and the prominent roles played by mothers in Ovid's *Metamorphoses*, Statius and Seneca – see the excellent study by McAuley (2016). My point here is that these later Greek poets reflect the shifting, *different* significance of the mother figure in the imperial (and) Christian world.

248   Prodigal Poetics: Filiation and Succession

Colluthus, to take an imperial epic example, redrafts the story of Helen's departure from Sparta to focus on the abandonment experienced by her daughter Hermione, who dreams of her mother on the night that she leaves (372–8) and grieves inconsolably once she perceives that she is gone (326–32). Morales has drawn attention to Colluthus' innovation in elevating this mother-daughter bond to a central feature of the Helen tale[72] and has attempted to tease out the darker connotations of this focus. As Morales reads it, this intense relationship both portrays the traumatic consequences of abandonment – a critique of Helen's reprehensible motivations for leaving her child, viewed against the positive incentive, in some Christian circles, for mothers to leave in order to pursue ascetic life – and, more chillingly still, suggests the process of sexual substitution, as Hermione takes her mother's place not only in the narrative at Sparta, but also in Menelaus' bed (375).[73] Whilst some may challenge the necessarily incestuous connotations of Hermione's new sleeping space – the poignant image of a bereft young child clinging to their remaining parent to assuage the horrors of night-time is another possible interpretation – it is clear, as Morales well elucidates, that Colluthus' maternal vision of filiation must be comprehended within the gender politics of his time.

Another such vision is found in the remarkable series of epigrams by Gregory Nazianzus, two centuries earlier than Colluthus, dedicated to his mother Nonna, who died whilst praying at church (*Anth. Pal.* 8. 24–74). With self-conscious hyperbole and repetition (8.30 comments explicitly on the performance and form of excessiveness: τοὔνεκα καὶ σὲ τόσοις ἐπιγράμμασι, μῆτερ, ἔτισα) Gregory establishes his mother as the central figure of his family network – a political and theological structure constructed *as* an extended family – and aligns her with a complex, contradictory range of figures: from Mary mother of Jesus (8.28) to Sarah, mother of Isaac (8.27, 52); from a masculinised *Christoforos* more virile than Heracles or Empedocles (8.29), to a sacrificial victim slain at the altar of Christ (8.41,49, 73).[74] Setting the despair of

---

[72] Morales (2016): 70: 'Hermione is usually a footnote in Helen's drama; here, as a child, she is an integral part of it.' Cadau (2015), the only English language book-length study of Colluthus, has disappointingly little to say on this aspect of the poem (as pointed out by Gilka (2015)). Fresh discussion of the scene, and its role in the epyllion as a whole, in Goldhill (2020).

[73] See esp. Morales (2016): 72–3.

[74] This image is bizarre, particularly when set against Christian hostility towards pagan sacrificial practices (although this one is emphasised as being 'bloodless' [8.49]) and could connect Nonna further with Jesus himself, via the rhetoric of the 'lamb of God'. On this and other aspects of this fascinating series of poems, see Goldhill and Greensmith (forthcoming), with further bibliography.

personal grief against the commemorative power of the epigram,[75] this son also, like Quintus' Achilles and Memnon, self-glorifies and self-memorialises through his mother,[76] as the praise of the ideal Christian mother becomes the perfect carapace to convey this Church *Fathers'* theological agenda.[77]

If Colluthus' epyllion and Gregory's epigrams thus suggest, in their own late imperial and Christian contexts, the poetic capabilities of a *maternally* driven 'anxiety of influence', then the presence of this mother-based boasting-match in Quintus offers another example of his earlier, pre- and non-Christian, flirtation with such ideas. If the portrtayal of Penthesilea can reveal, as it has done for some recent scholars, Quintus' investment in 'late antique' concerns over gender roles, the erotics of viewing and the politics of virginity,[78] then the emphasis on *motherly* prowess – heroic and mythological status achieved precisely by embracing, not rejecting, the act of rearing a child – must constitute his engagement with an alternative aspect of this nexus of ideas. In an era on the cusp of a Christian teleology of meaning, the displacement of fathers in favour of mothers in this most traditional and 'stock' epic scene reveals how Quintus too saw in the female an alternative way to conceptualise familial, political and literary structures. In the epic without one man, an otherwise conventional passage of ancestral flaunting eschews the normal paradigms of masculinity and allows influence to be configured in a different way.

Achilles' closing remarks make explicit the self-consciously different nature of this generational conflict:

---

[75] Another form of with which Gregory comforts himself that his mother is now enjoying, having returned to the father in paradise (cf. e.g. 8.66).

[76] Gregory strongly gives the sense that his mother's greatest achievement of all was giving birth to him (see e.g. 8.32) and so many of these maternal epigrams also or actually centralise him, the author and son, above his mother-cum-subject. This mixture of filiation and narcissism also neatly fits the flyting context in the Quintan scene: Achilles and Memnon use their mothers' achievements to instantiate their own.

[77] The *Christus Patiens*, once thought to be the work of Gregory of Nazianzus but now more commonly dated to the Byzantine period (c. eleventh century CE), also deserves mention as a later and highly explicit example of this refashioning of classical paradigms (narrative and structural) to centralise a hyper-Christian maternal subject. The cento begins with the long and impassioned speech of Mary as she watches her son suffer on the cross, and the figure of Mary throughout the poem, as Bryant Davies (2017) has convincingly outlined, is constructed using a complex amalgamation of tragic 'mothers' – Medea, Agave and Musa – 'creating a narrative of fragmentation through clashes between centonic form, tragic sources and Christian subject'.

[78] See particularly Lovatt (2013): 267 and 306–9, and Greensmith (forthcoming c). Relevant discussion, albeit from a mainly intertextual perspective, also in Maciver (2012b): 135–52, Bär (2009): 324–8 and Scheijnen (2018): 47–76.

250 Prodigal Poetics: Filiation and Succession

ἀλλὰ τί νηπιάχοισιν ἐοικότες ἀφραδέεσσιν
ἕσταμεν ἡμετέρων μυθεύμενοι ἔργα τοκήων
ἠδ᾽ αὐτῶν; ἐγγὺς καὶ Ἄρης, ἐγγὺς <δὲ> καὶ ἀλκή.

Q.S.2.449-51

But why are we standing here prattling on about ourselves and our parents like silly children? War is near, prowess must be close at hand.

Achilles reflexively characterises the act of Homeric epic flyting in which he is participating. His words (and the entire scene) are closely modelled on his Iliadic stand-off with Aeneas: the Quintan Achilles mimics his old antagonist, who prefaced his own excessively long family history with the same paraleptic gesture:

τὸν δ᾽ αὖτ᾽ Αἰνείας ἀπαμείβετο φώνησέν τε·
Πηλεΐδη μὴ δὴ ἐπέεσσί με νηπύτιον ὣς
ἔλπεο δειδίξεσθαι, ἐπεὶ σάφα οἶδα καὶ αὐτὸς
ἠμὲν κερτομίας ἠδ᾽ αἴσυλα μυθήσασθαι.
ἴδμεν δ᾽ ἀλλήλων γενεήν, ἴδμεν δὲ τοκῆας
πρόκλυτ᾽ ἀκούοντες ἔπεα θνητῶν ἀνθρώπων·

Il. 20.199-204

Then Aeneas answered him and said: 'Son of Peleus, do not expect to frighten me with words, as if I were a child, since I know well how to utter both taunts and proper words. We know each other's lineage, we know each other's parents, for we have heard the words told of old by mortal men.'

The image of standing around and talking about one's genealogies also pithily evokes the famous Iliadic *tête-à-tête* between Glaucus and Diomedes. Beyond the explicit echo of the Lycurgus story (Q.S.2.448–9) Achilles' scornful ἕσταμεν is also suggestive of the pause created in Homer's narrative as the two warriors stop to talk in the middle of a raging battle (*Il.* 6.119–20). The repeated ἐγγύς also rewrites the σχεδὸν ἦσαν used in both of these Homeric scenes (*Il.* 6.121 and *Il.* 20.176). These parallels operate on two levels. The *Iliad's* narrative frequently enjoys exploiting the paradoxes surrounding proximity and stasis. As Achilles withdraws from the fighting, his tense location so near and yet so far from the action is often expressed in terms of movement; through the ironic contrast between his most characteristic epithet – 'swift footed' – and his sedentary state for two-thirds of the story.[79] In the same way the

---

[79] Cf. e.g. *Il.* 2.688–9 (κεῖτο γὰρ ἐν νήεσσι ποδάρκης δῖος Ἀχιλλεὺς/κούρης χωόμενος Βρισηΐδος ἠϋκόμοιο) to take just one example of where Homer's epithet system draws this contrast directly. For this paradox as a key site for debates surrounding Homeric formular economy, see Dunkle (1997) with full references on both sides. For this book's treatment of epithets, see Chapter 3.

Glaucus and Diomedes scene exercised critics (ancient and modern) because of its own incongruous mixture of close combat and inactivity.[80] As a discourse on narrative structure, Quintus' Achilles here collapses and curtails these tendencies: standing still is pointless when *this* epic battle is near.

This self-deprecation, however, can also function as a comment on literary *agōnes*: the *poetic* prattling on about inheritance. The explicit citation of literary predecessors became increasingly popular in post-Alexandrian epic: a genre that was famously reluctant to name began to confront its poetic heritage openly and directly. Whilst this naming of poets is particularly associated with Late Antique Latin hexameters,[81] the first century CE Statius also names his political and poetical models in the epilogue to the *Thebaid* (12.810–19): in his (faux) deprecating, highly Bloomian statement of deferral, he evokes both 'Caesar' and Vergil, his mighty source, along with his *magnum opus*,[82] and, via the 'footsteps', adopts the metaphor still so common in modern critical writing about living up to one's models:

> *durabisne procul dominoque legere superstes,*
> *o mihi bissenos multum uigilata per annos*
> *Thebai? iam certe praesens tibi Fama benignum*
> *strauit iter coepitque nouam monstrare futuris,*
> *iam te magnanimus dignatur noscere Caesar,*
> *Itala iam studio discit memoratque iuuentus.*
> *uiue, precor; nec tu diuinam Aeneida tempta,*
> *sed longe sequere et uestigia semper adora,*
> *mox, tibi si quis adhuc praetendit nubila liuor,*
> *occidet, et meriti post me referentur honores.*
> *Theb.* 12.810–19

My Thebaid, on whom I have spent twelve wakeful years, will you long endure and be read when your master is gone? Already, 'tis true, Fame has strewn a kindly

---

[80] According to Aristarchus (Arn/A) 'some transpose this composition elsewhere', because of its interruptive and intrusive nature. See also Kirk (1990): 171: 'the whole episode is inorganic, and Hector's arrival at Troy could follow directly on 118 ... (however) whilst there is no good reason for regarding the episode itself or its position as un-Homeric... at the same time the abbreviated style suggests that Homer is drawing on longer and earlier versions'. Further in Kirk (1962): 164–6.

[81] For example, in the preface to his *Iohannis* (7–16), Corippus puts himself into the tradition of epic poets by alluding to Homer covertly (via Smyrna, as Quintus does) but also by naming Vergil directly. Juvencus also compares his epic to those of Homer and Vergil (Iuuenc. 1–27). Venantius Fortunatus lists his poetic models (including Sedulius, Prudentius and Iuuencus) in Mart. 1.14–25.

[82] The *Aeneid* is also named in Statius' *Silvae* (2.7.80), which is addressed to Lucan's widow, Polla, and deals directly with Lucan's own emulation of Vergil's epic. Ovid provides the first surviving use of the *Aeneid*'s title when, at *Tr.* 2.533, addressing Augustus, he speaks of *tua Aeneidos*.

252   Prodigal Poetics: Filiation and Succession

path before you and begun to show the new arrival to posterity. Already great-hearted Caesar deigns to know you, and the studious youth of Italy learns you and recites. Live, I pray; and essay not the divine Aeneid, but ever follow her footsteps from afar in adoration. Soon, if any envy still spreads clouds before you, it shall perish, and after me you shall be paid the honours you deserve.[83]

On the Greek side, Nonnus four centuries later catalogues his plethora of sources in the second proem, where he references Homer, as we have seen, but also Pindar – the lyric poet who himself loved to name:

οἶδα, πόθεν κτύπος οὗτος· ἀειδομένη τάχα Θήβη
Πινδαρέης φόρμιγγος ἐπέκτυπε Δώριος ἠχώ.

Dion. 25. 20–1

I know where that sound comes from: surely it is the Dorian tune of Pindar's lyre sounding for Thebes.

This explicitness has no place in Quintus' poetics. Committed to his Homeric conceit, he opts instead, as we continue to see, for more covert ways of charting his literary inheritance. Achilles' speech acknowledges this deviation. First indulging and then dismissing a direct citation of influence, it aims to move past the trend for such overt statements of debt. In this double statement of difference – the emphasis on the mother and the rejection of direct filial self-discussion beyond this alternative female strain – Quintus continues to construct an image of what his 'poetic vision' is *not*. The straight and clean handover from (just) father to (just) son appears increasingly incompatible with the messy, more entangled world of relationships through which our poet is conditioned and which his narrative forcefully conveys.

Eurypylus: Grandpaternal Poetics

In the figure of Eurypylus, the final failed heroic candidate on the Trojan side, Quintus focuses on another problematic aspect of linear generational succession: the temporal distance involved in engaging with a predecessor from the distant literary past. The son of Telephus and grandson of Heracles, Eurypylus is introduced via a tangled web of family connections:

τὸν δὲ Πάρις δείδεκτο, τίεν δέ μιν Ἕκτορι ἶσον·[84]
τοῦ γὰρ ἀνεψιὸς ἔσκεν, ἰῆς τ᾽ ἐτέτυκτο γενέθλης·

---

[83] Trans. adapted from Shackleton Bailey (2003).

[84] This welcoming of Eurypylus in an equal way to Hector also enacts another instance of the chain-like heroic succession (one replacement hero coming after another) on the Trojan side.

Antagonising Antagonism

> τὸν γὰρ δὴ τέκε δῖα κασιγνήτη Πριάμοιο   (135)
> Ἀστυόχη κρατερῇσιν ὑπ' ἀγκοίνῃσι μιγεῖσα
> Τηλέφου, ὅν ῥα καὶ αὐτὸν ἀταρβέι Ἡρακλῆι
> λάθρῃ ἑοῖο τοκῆος ἐυπλόκαμος τέκεν Αὔγη·
> καί μιν τυτθὸν ἐόντα καὶ ἰσχανόωντα γάλακτος
> θρέψε θοή ποτε κεμμάς, ἑῷ δ' ἴσα φίλατο νεβρῷ   (140)
> μαζὸν ὑποσχομένη βουλῇ Διός· οὐ γὰρ ἐῴκει
> ἔκγονον Ἡρακλῆος ὀιζυρῶς ἀπολέσθαι.
>
> Q.S.6.133–42

He was welcomed by Paris and honoured like Hector, whose cousin he was: they were from the same divine stock, since Eurypylus was born from Priam's divine sister Astyoche after she had felt the powerful embrace of Telephus, whom beautiful-haired Auge likewise bore to fearless Heracles without the knowledge of her father; and when he was an unwearied infant he was suckled by a swift hind which Zeus had planned should give him the breast and cherish him like her own fawn: it would not have been right for a child of Heracles to suffer a pitiful death.

Paris later draws upon the pride in this illustrious family tree to motivate Eurypylus into battle (Q.S.6.298–307). However, this introduction also makes clear the differences between the generations: particularly, between Eurypylus' father and his far mightier grandfather. Telephus' birth is recounted with heavy proleptic irony: he was saved as a baby because it was not fitting that Heracles' offspring should die a miserable death, which is of course exactly what *does* happen to Eurypylus soon.[85] The Trojans, unaware of these future failings as an ἔκγονος Ἡρακλῆος, continue to obsess over Eurypylus' genealogical prowess; and to them, it is his connection to his grandfather that really counts. Eurypylus' shield is covered in the feats of Heracles (Q.S.6.191–293); the ekphrastic images emphasise his superlative strength and fearlessness even as a baby (202–3), and the ease with which he defeated seemingly indefatigable enemies (265). After seeing Eurypylus in this armour, Paris says nothing of Telephus, and instead continues to stress these parallels with Heracles. Like an interpreter of a painting, he looks at the images on the shield and meticulously matches them with the qualities of its new bearer:

> Ἀλλὰ σύ, πρὸς μεγάλοιο καὶ ὀβρίμου Ἡρακλῆος
> τῷ μέγεθός τε βίην τε καὶ ἀγλαὸν εἶδος ἔοικας,
> κείνου μνωόμενος φρονέων τ' ἀντάξια ἔργα.
>
> Q.S.6.302–4

---

[85] The feats of Eurypylus at Troy were narrated in the *Little Iliad*, and his death at the hands of Neoptolemus is relayed by Odysseus at *Od.* 11.517–21. The loaded βουλῇ Διός (Q.S.6.141) makes clear the inevitability of this outcome.

254   Prodigal Poetics: Filiation and Succession

I entreat you, in the name of Heracles, that great and mighty hero whom you resemble in stature, in strength and in beauty – think of him and aim for exploits just as worthy.

If the welcoming sequence implicitly focused on the differences in fortune between father and son, these scenes aim to create a more positive picture of Eurypylus by moving one more step back through the generations. Although his success in the war is short-lived, it is in his ability to echo his grandfather, whose image and memory have already entered into the mythological, ekphrastic tradition, and not his more recent relation, that Eurypylus achieves his most tangible if temporary success.

Now, the evocation of distant lineage is a commonplace in the epic tradition. Just as the Homeric Achilles is frequently connected to Zeus, so too do Vergil and his successors lace their heroes' backstories with far-stretching genealogies.[86] But this sense of generational retrospect received sharpened attention in the later Greek poetry which returned so directly to the mythological deep past. In Christodorus' statues, Neoptolemus is introduced as the 'great- grandson of Aeacus' (56–8). Nonnus, again offering the starkest demonstration of this trend, expands upon Aeacus' potential as the Iliadic grandfather *par excellence*. Halfway through the Indian campaign, he introduces Aeacus as a full-blown character, who is serving as a solider in Dionysus' army. As he describes this older hero's own fight with the Scamander, a competitive rehearsal of Achilles' later performance in the *Iliad*, Nonnus erupts into a burst of topsy-turvy anachronism:

> οὐδ' ἀθεεὶ πολέμιζε καὶ Αἰακός· ἀντιβίους γάρ,
> ὡς γενέτης Πηλῆος, ἔσω ποταμοῖο δαΐζων
> ἰκμαλέον μόθον εἶχε καὶ ὑδατόεσσαν Ἐνυώ,
> οἷα προθεσπίζων ποταμοῦ περὶ χεῦμα Καμάνδρου
> φύλοπιν ἡμιτέλεστον ἐπεσσομένην Ἀχιλῆϊ·
> καὶ μόθον υἱωνοῖο μόθος μαντεύσατο πάππου.
>
> *Dion.* 22.384–9

Not without divine help did Aeacus also fight. As befitted the father of Peleus, he slew his enemies in the river, a watery battle, a conflict among the waves, as if to foretell the unfinished battle for Achilles in time to come at the river Scamander: the grandfather's battle prophesied the grandson's conflict.

---

[86] Even the isolated figure of Lucan's Caesar, for example, is given a debased version of this lineage. His visit to Troy is presented as a dark homage to his ancestral gods, a distant inheritance for him to trample over.

Antagonising Antagonism

In his own re-staging of Troy, Quintus more obliquely centralises this theme of grandpaternity. Just as the narrative space of the *Posthomerica* is filled with elderly characters, so too does the poem's language often favour the older generation. In terms of epithets – that key marker of Quintus' creative reconstruction of the Homeric text – the grand-patronymic Αἰακίδης is used thirty-nine times,[87] more than it occurs in the *Iliad* and *Odyssey* combined.[88]

This focus on the age gap has obvious relevance to these epics, which evoke Homer so closely in subject and style, but write at such a distance from him in literary chronology. Grandpaternity helps to capture the tension between closeness and remoteness inherent to this act of Homeric re-engagement. But if Nonnus' Aeacus episode revels in this tension, Quintus here offers a more critical account of its effects. As a temporary heroic success case, Eurypylus demonstrates the benefits of stretching further back for one's emulative material. But his ultimate failure, like that of Achilles, Ajax and Penthesilea, also hints at the limitations of this kind of grasping. By showing how glibly Paris and the Trojans ignore the crucial differences between older and younger generations,[89] Quintus lays bare the sense of distance that such linear ancestral approximations are not able to overcome. It no longer suffices simply to reach for the same famous models again and again. If his epic is to engage with Homer directly *and* successfully, Quintus' own ἀντάξια ἔργα need to find a way to eschew the divide between himself and his model more permanently: to bridge, not just display, the poetic generation gap.

Taking their place within the episodic environment of the *Posthomerica*, these early contenders provide three different ways of modelling linear succession. As figures standing for Quintus' poetic response, they offer options that he could have employed to achieve his takeover of Homer: competitiveness, man-to-man antagonism and overtly expressed desire to emulate or to rebel. In his *critical* exploration of these characters, however, Quintus shows that his epic will not be limited to these approaches: adversarial succession becomes the route that his poem does not take. The narrative now moves away from these violent models and suggests what else can be put forward in their place.

---

[87] Q.S.1.4, 331, 392, 496, 508, 520–1, 548, 825; 2.99, 388–9, 409, 430; 3.16, 34, 66, 119, 212, 244, 399, 418, 461, 522–3, 602, 697, 701, 743; 4.476, 595; 5.5, 225, 423; 7.403, 689, 727, 8.37; 9.211, 236–7; 12.74.

[88] It occurs twenty-six times in total in Homer and only twice in the *Odyssey,* both in the underworld scene (*Od.* 11 471 and 11.538), when Achilles is already dead.

[89] Differences also suggested by the proleptic hints at Eurypylus' downfall in Q.S.6.131–42.

6.4 Alternative Relations: Succession through Impersonation

Neoptolemus plays the crucial role in this alternative vision of succession. For those commentators who wish to see a more unified, traditional plot structure in the *Posthomerica*, Achilles' son is often hailed as the epic's 'main character': its late but central hero, whose arrival finally breaks the heroic stagnation and provides a successful replacement for Achilles. 'Thus', claims Maciver 'the second half of the poem, despite the episodic nature of its parts, is unified by a central character, in a similar way to the original Homeric poems.'[90] Neoptolemus has also been centrally identified with the poet figure Quintus, his takeover from Achilles read as a consummation of the epic's Bloomian poetics, as Quintus too aims to take the place of his literary forebear, diverging from him and creating himself anew.[91] An identification between character and poet is indeed suggested from Neoptolemus' earliest appearances. The description of him at Skyros as ἔτι παιδνός, ἔτ' ἄχνοος (Q.S.7.357) associates him with the age poetics troped by Quintus in the proem, with the repeated ἔτι perhaps another pre-echo of that passage (cf. πρίν γε μοι ἔτ' ἀμφὶ παρειὰ κατασκίδνασθαι ἴουλον, Q.S.12.309). We may here see in this young hero a mirror of Quintus the Homeric poet, naïve and beardless when he first received his inspiration, now growing up into his post-Iliadic maturity.

As an image of Quintan poetics, however, Achilles' son cuts a more complex emblematic figure if he is not promoted to 'the' dominant character in the epic, centralised at the expense of the other heroes, but rather if he is considered symbiotically alongside them. Read as the latest in the poem's relentless series of comers-next, his symbolic significance lies not in his singularity, but in his relationship to the other models of succession offered in the preceding books.

The most distinctive feature of Neoptolemus as such a successor is his connection to Achilles: which reveals itself to be far more multi-layered than simply 'father and son'. Despite the fact that they never meet, Neoptolemus' relationship to his father is indeed the most dominant aspect of his character. He is called the son of Achilles sixty-one times and is frequently compared with, mistaken for or identified as him. Hera swiftly substitutes him at the moment of Achilles' death (Q.S.3.118–22); Achilles' famous horses are compelled to wait for his arrival, static and motionless until he releases them (3.743–65); and in Skyros, Odysseus and Diomedes are immediately struck, like the viewer of Christodorus' statue,

---

[90] Maciver (2012b): 21. [91] Cf. Kneebone (2007); Boyten (2010).

Alternative Relations: Succession through Impersonation 257

by his likeness to his father's image (7.176–7). This persistent comparison might be presumed to foster a sense of competition – the young newcomer aims to better the one whom he succeeds so directly and closely. This is certainly the line taken by existing treatments of Neoptolemus.[92] Focusing on his characterisation – his heroic personality, qualities and actions in the epic – critics have stressed the substantial differences between the son and his (post-) Homeric father: taciturn (Quintus' Neoptolemus is a man of surprisingly few words),[93] restrained and pragmatic,[94] he appears to promote a pointedly different ethos to the fiery, excessive Achilles of the *Iliad* and – particularly – the early books of this continuation.[95] However, when Neoptolemus arrives at Troy, entering the stagnant space and confronting the ghost of his father's legacy, any assumed notions of competitiveness are in fact displaced. His similarity to Achilles instead increases in intensity, to become a form of *embodiment*.

In his *conceptual* identity – his relationship to Achilles is not as a 'character', but as a heroic and poetical model, and a marker of tradition – Neoptolemus' succession is profoundly rooted in imitation: he does not aim to break away from his heroic or paternal inheritance, but his newness is achieved precisely *by repetition*. The depiction of Neoptolemus slips knowingly throughout the poem between two ontological states: that of being closely identified with Achilles and being the actual incarnation of him. This slippage maps closely on to Quintus' own techniques of poetic impersonation, and so it is rather in this respect that Neoptolemus should be identified with the poet's voice. The question of where to locate the difference between 'being like' and 'being' is actively interrogated through Neoptolemus: he emerges as a figure through which Quintus explores the potential fuzziness between the two positions, so important to a work which claims to be both Homeric and non-Homeric in its essence. It is here too that the contemporary factors driving Quintus' filial poetics assume a central role. Whereas the epic's earlier portraits of failed, rivalrous linear succession drew heavily on paradigms from distant mythology, in his depiction of Neoptolemus' filial triumph Quintus employs ideas about

---

[92] See the extensive discussion by Boyten (2007) and (2010): 183–237, who centrally examines Neoptolemus' heroic characterisation, with further treatment in Scheijnen (2018): 156–225.

[93] On Neoptolemus' brevity as a speaker throughout the *Posthomerica*, in relation to Achilles' 'taciturnity' (*qua* e.g. Feeney (1983): ch. 8) see Boyten (2010): 185–7

[94] During the wooden horse trick, Neoptolemus initially resists the resort to *dolos* to win the war, but is persuaded by the divine omen that follows Odysseus' proposition (Q.S.12.66–103).

[95] Boyten (2010): 115–27 has shown how Quintus exaggerates these violent, emotive tendencies of Homer's Achilles in his own portrait of the character, thus moving Neoptolemus even further away from this type of heroic identity, by the starkness of the contrast.

258 Prodigal Poetics: Filiation and Succession

mimetic re-animation closely derived instead from his own third-century discourse. Neoptolemus – the major witness to the different possible relationships between 'model' and 'imitator', 'tradition' and 'innovation', and the opportunities offered by intense, non-rivalrous emulation – emerges as the hero most conspicuously constructed by and expressive of the Quintan now.

Armour and the Mimetic Double

Once Neoptolemus lands in Troy, he puts on his father's famous arms. (Q.S.7.435–51). As he does so, he seems to become a version of Achilles: 'resembling him entirely' (φαίνετο πάμπαν ἀλίγκιος, 446). When he 'easily' lifts the spear that only Achilles could lift ('Ρηιδίως, 451), we see 'a sword-in-the-stone type moment of pre-ordained potential fulfilled'.[96] This likeness appears wholly convincing: as he enters battle, the Trojans freeze with terror, assuming that they are seeing Achilles himself (Q.S.7.526–41). Arming, however, is an inherently duplicitous act, as much a vehicle for concealment as for identification, with a long literary history of enshrining difficult questions of identity. In this sequence Quintus alludes to this potential for falseness. The entire scene has echoes of the Iliadic Patroclus, who also dressed in Achilles' arms to confront the Trojans, and confounded them in terms similar to Neoptolemus here (Il. 16.278–83). Patroclus of course is famously and fatally not Achilles, and his dress-up game directly leads to his death. Quintus evokes these darker connotations of arming in order to subvert them. He presents Neoptolemus as the antidote to Patroclus' false mimetic ambitions – one who is successful in his attempts at Achillean imitation, able to harness the transformative power of arming to greater and more lasting effect.

The details of the Quintan arming scene make clear how Neoptolemus reverses this failure:

> ἔνθ' ἐσθλὸς μὲν ἔδυ καλὰ τεύχεα, τοὶ δὲ χέρεια   (440)
> δῦσαν ὅσοις ἀλαπαδνὸν ὑπὸ κραδίῃ πέλεν ἦτορ·
> αὐτὰρ Ὀδυσσεὺς δύσαθ' <ἅ> οἱ Ἰθάκηθεν ἔποντο·
> δῶκε δὲ Τυδείδῃ Διομήδεϊ κάλλιμα τεύχη
> κεῖνα τὰ δὴ Σώκοιο βίην εἴρυσσε πάροιθεν·
> υἱὸς δ' αὖτ' Ἀχιλῆος ἐδύσετο τεύχεα πατρός,   (445)
> καί οἱ φαίνετο πάμπαν ἀλίγκιος· ἀμφὶ δ' ἐλαφρὰ
> Ἡφαίστου παλάμῃσι περὶ μελέεσσιν ἀρήρει,
> καί περ ἐόνθ' ἑτέροισι πελώρια· τῷ δ' ἅμα πάντα

---

[96] Maciver (2012b): 182.

Alternative Relations: Succession through Impersonation   259

φαίνετο τεύχεα κοῦφα· κάρη δέ οἱ οὔ τι βάρυνε
πήληξ <οὐ παλάμῃσιν ἐπέβρισεν δόρυ μακρὸν
Πηλιάς>, ἀλλὰ ἑ χερσὶ καὶ ἠλίβατόν περ ἐοῦσαν   (450)
ῥηιδίως ἀνάειρεν ἔθ' αἵματος ἰσχανόωσαν.

Q.S.7.440–51[97]

Then the best men put on the fine armour, and those with timid hearts put on the worse. Odysseus put on the things he had brought with him from Ithaca, and he gave to Diomedes son of Tydeus the fine armour which he had once stripped from mighty Socus. The son of Achilles put on the armour of his father, so that he became his very image; and, thanks to Hephaestus' craftsmanship, it fitted him well, though it was far too big for anyone else: the whole panoply seemed light to him; the helmet did not feel heavy on his head ... <nor did the spear from Pelion seem heavy to him:> he was easily able to raise that still bloodthirsty spear in his hands, for all its huge size.

Neoptolemus' 'sword in the stone moment' corrects the one crucial failing of Patroclus: he takes the spear which Patroclus had to leave behind because he could not lift it (*Il.* 16.141–4). Ῥηιδίως thus works as a provocative aside: what was impossible for Patroclus is now *easily* achievable.[98] Even before entering battle, Neoptolemus has come one step closer to assuming Achilles' military totality.

In the detail that ἔνθ' ἐσθλὸς μὲν ἔδυ καλὰ τεύχεα, τοὶ δὲ χέρεια/δῦσαν, ὅσοις ἀλαπαδνὸν ὑπὸ κραδίῃ πέλεν ἦτορ (440–1), Quintus engages another salient Iliadic passage, where on Poseidon's orders the Greeks are commanded to switch armour, so that ἐσθλὰ μὲν ἐσθλὸς <ἔδυνε>, χέρεια δὲ χείρονι δόσκον (*Il.* 14.382). This incident struck Hellenistic scholars as curious. The scholiasts opt for pragmatic explanations: it befits battle preparations to hand over weapons in this chain-formation,[99] or it makes sense for the *aristoi* to have the best weapons, so that they can face the danger more boldly.[100] There is, however, the possibility that the swap

---

[97] The text here has a double fault. See Vian (1963): 223; (1966): 122–3. I have used Zimmerman's conjecture for the lacuna at 449–50, also adopted by Way (1913) ad loc. and to inform Hopkinson's translation (2018): 383.

[98] As 'easily' as Odysseus strings the bow (*Od.* 21.407). For a related reading of the adverb in the *Posthomerica*, concerning the relationship between Zeus and Fate, see Maciver 2012b: 117 (on Q.S.14.98–9:), *pace* Gärtner (2007): 219 and Wenglinsky (2002): 191 on the same passage. Maciver aptly points out that ῥηιδίως there can be read 'as a signpost, an ironic marker. However, his reading that what it marks is that 'Zeus is (and was in the *Iliad*) unable, lightly as it seemed in the *Iliad*, to dispense with the destinies allotted to characters by Fate' seems to me to run contrary to the general connotations of the word as denoting easiness, leisure, *ability* (in the Quintan passage, Zeus is 'not able easily to thrust Fate away': that is different from him being 'unable, lightly, to thrust Fate away'.). I offer further discussion of ῥηιδίως in Chapter 7.

[99] Σ A ad loc.

[100] Σ bT ad loc. This commentator is perturbed by why the warriors would attempt the dangerous task of changing weapons in the midst of battle.

260 Prodigal Poetics: Filiation and Succession

could also have prompted less literal interpretations. As we have seen, imperial Greek performance culture was often fascinated by the ability of costume to signify the ethos of the character being portrayed. The series of masks donned by pantomime actors enabled the same performer to play a number of different parts.[101] And the increased use of costumes and stage props by the *homeristai* meant that performing Homer involved looking like the bard or his characters. The stage-door inscription at Aphrodisias which describes how a *homeristes* 'became Alexander' also refers explicitly to the equipment (διασκευή) used to achieve this transformation:[102] armour makes the Homeric man.

Read against this background, Quintus' scene reworks the Iliadic passage to enhance its status as a reflection on costume and character. In his version, the match up of the best arms for the best men, and the worst for the feeble, is not presented as an order, but a pre-established fact (note the almost casual tone struck by ἔνθ', 440) inherent now in the epic process of arming. Taking up an idea already found in Homer, Quintus emphasises armour's power to provide a genuine index to the self in order to encourage us to believe in the possibility of the true mimetic transformation of Neoptolemus once he appropriates this outfit.

The Trojans' reaction reveals how this transformation was received: they function as readers of the filial impersonation.

> Οἳ δ' ἄρ' ἀμηχανίη βεβολημένοι ἔνδοθεν ἦτορ
> Τρῶες ἔφαντ' Ἀχιλῆα πελώριον εἰσοράασθαι
> αὐτὸν ὁμῶς τεύχεσσι· καὶ ἀμφασίην ἀλεγεινὴν
> κεῦθον ὑπὸ κραδίῃ, ἵνα μὴ δέος αἰνὸν ἵκηται
> ἐς φρένα Κητείων μηδ' Εὐρυπύλοιο ἄνακτος.
>
> Q.S.7.537–41

Shocked and helpless in their hearts, the Trojans thought it was mighty Achilles the man, armour and all, that they could see. But they kept their horror hidden in their hearts so as not to infect with fear and dread the minds of the Cetaeans and their leader Eurypylus.

In our discussion of epithets in Chapter 3, we perceived how the Trojans 'see' Achilles in his original Homeric form, emphasised through the rare retention of his traditional Homeric adjective πελώριος. The use of the same epithet in the previous arming scene (πελώρια, 7.448 referring to τεύχεα) now suggests how the word also works as a note of cohesion between father and son. The weapons are huge to others, but

---

[101] Cf. e.g. Libanius *On Behalf of Dancers* 113 as discussed in Chapter 2.
[102] On this inscription, see Roueché (1993): 18.

Alternative Relations: Succession through Impersonation 261

Neoptolemus serenely puts them on and, through them, he absorbs this Achillean adjective as a part of himself.

Unlike their sighting of Patroclus, this Trojan reading of Neoptolemus-as-Achilles is not violently proven wrong. Rather, as the war carries on, despite some attempts at disentanglement,[103] the identity collusion continues:

> Τρῶες δ᾽ οὐκέτ᾽ ἔφαντο πρὸ τείχεος αἰπεινοῖο
> στήμεναι ἐν πολέμῳ· μάλα γὰρ δέος ἔλλαβε πάντας
> ζώειν ἐλπομένους ἐρικυδέα Πηλείωνα·
>
> Q.S.9.5–7a

As for the Trojans, they were no longer prepared to stand before their lofty walls and do battle: they were all afraid, imagining that the glorious son of Peleus was alive.

The arming sequence thus begins to develop an alternative 'vision of Quintus' literary ambition'.[104] His text will not be a Patroclus, a false pretender thwarted by failed attempts at identity deception. Instead it will both 'appear to be' and actually 'be' the model in whose clothing it dresses.

Filial Speech: against 'Source Citation'

Neoptolemus also provides his own discussions of the type of succession he represents. When he meets with Phoenix, the old man's appeal (Q.S.7.642–6l), as we have seen, is filled with the language of pseudo-paternity.[105] In his exhortations for Neoptolemus to live up to his father (ἀλλ᾽ ἄγε Μυρμιδόνεσσι καὶ ἱπποδάμοισιν Ἀχαιοῖς/τειρομένοις ἐπάμυνε μέγ᾽ ἀμφ᾽ ἀγαθοῖο τοκῆος... τοῦ γὰρ ὑπέρτερός ἐσσι καὶ ἔσσεαι, ὅσσον ἀρείων/σεῖο πατὴρ κείνοιο πέλεν μογεροῖο τοκῆος.᾽, Q.S.7.661–6) Phoenix provides another version of the generational perorations favoured by the early heroes of the poem. Neoptolemus' response, however, cuts short this conventional rhetorical circuit:

> ῾ὦ γέρον, ἡμετέρην ἀρετὴν ἀνὰ δηιοτῆτα
> Αἶσα διακρινέει κρατερὴ καὶ ὑπέρβιος Ἄρης.᾽
> ὣς εἰπὼν αὐτῆμαρ ἐέλδετο τείχεος ἐκτὸς
> σεύεσθ᾽ ἐν τεύχεσσιν ἑοῦ πατρός...
>
> Q.S.7.668–71

---

[103] Cf. the speech of Deiphobus at Q.S.9.97–9.
[104] *Qua*, again but differently, Kneebone (2007): 289.   [105] See Chapter 5.

262   Prodigal Poetics: Filiation and Succession

'As for my prowess, old man, almighty Fate and irresistible Ares will be the judges of that as I fight the enemy.' So he spoke, eager to charge at the enemy there and then wearing his father's armour.

Neoptolemus replies – characteristically – only briefly and, despite Phoenix's laboured comparisons,[106] does not mention Achilles at all. Instead, in ἡμετέρην ἀρετήν, the first-person *plural*, he echoes lexically the assimilation into his father that he has achieved by putting on his arms.[107] His unspoken thoughts (670–1) then return directly to the theme of armament. It is as if Neoptolemus is trying to get out of the clichéd world of generational oratory, to erase the need for comparisons with Achilles and to get on with simply being him. After this moment, Neoptolemus hardly ever evokes Achilles or voices his desire to live up to him.[108]

During the final confrontation with Eurypylus, this alternative filial rhetoric is put to the test, as Neoptolemus' sense of paternal embodiment is pitted against Eurypylus' more traditional boastings (Q.S.8.138–45).[109] When questioned about his lineage, Neoptolemus again puts a blunt end to this competitive discourse:

> τίπτε μ᾽ ἐπισπεύδοντα ποτὶ κλόνον αἱματόεντα
> ἐχθρὸς ἐὼν ὡς εἴ τε φίλα φρονέων ἐρεείνεις
> εἰπέμεναι γενεήν, ἥν περ μάλα πολλοὶ ἴσασιν·
> υἱὸς Ἀχιλλῆος κρατερόφρονος, ὅς τε τοκῆα   (150)
> σεῖο πάροιθ᾽ ἐφόβησε βαλὼν περιμήκεϊ δουρί·
> καί νύ κέ μιν θανάτοιο κακαὶ περὶ Κῆρες ἔμαρψαν,
> εἰ μή οἱ στονόεντα θοῶς ἰήσατ᾽ ὄλεθρον.
> ἵπποι δ᾽ οἵ φορέουσιν ἐμοῦ πατρὸς ἀντιθέοιο,
> οὓς τέκεθ᾽ Ἅρπυια Ζεφύρῳ πάρος εὐνηθεῖσα,   (155)
> οἵ τε καὶ ἀτρύγετον πέλαγος διὰ ποσσὶ θέουσιν
> ἀκρονύχως ψαύοντες, ἴσον δ᾽ ἀνέμοισι φέρονται.
> νῦν δ᾽ ἐπεὶ οὖν γενεὴν ἐδάης ἵππων τε καὶ αὐτοῦ,
> καὶ δόρατος πείρησαι ἀτειρέος ἡμετέροιο

---

[106] At Q.S.7.653–4 and 665–6.

[107] The plural could of course be simply poetic, but given the wider assimilatory impression that Quintus creates for Neoptolemus, it seems to me that it could have a more interpretative function, as an indication of his unity with Achilles. I have made the broader case for Quintus' tendency to invest 'decorative' poetic words with this sort of interpretative potential in Chapter 3.

[108] The only occasion on which Neoptolemus compares *himself* to Achilles is to Agamemnon immediately after this exchange (Q.S.7.700–4).

[109] Euryplyus does not include his own parentage in his boasts, but with his brags about his superlative success record in battle and the amount of slaughters he has achieved, he places himself firmly in the conventional realm of epic flyting discourse (οὐ γάρ τίς μ᾽ ὑπάλυξεν ἐν ἀργαλέῃ ὑσμίνῃ·/ἀλλά μοι ὅσσοι ἔναντα λιλαιόμενοι μαχέσασθαι/δεῦρο κίον, πάντεσσι φόνον στονόεντ᾽ ἐφῆκα/ἀργαλέως, πάντων δὲ παρὰ Ξάνθοιο ῥέεθρα/ὀστέα τε σάρκας τε κύνες διὰ πάντ᾽ ἐδάσαντο., 140–4).

Alternative Relations: Succession through Impersonation   263

γνώμεναι ἀντιβίην · γενεὴ δέ οἱ ἐν κορυφῇσι   (160)
Πηλίου αἰπεινοῖο, τομὴν ὅθι λεῖπε καὶ εὐνήν.

Q.S.8.147–61

You are an enemy, and I am eager for bloody battle: why are you acting like a friend and asking me my lineage, which is known to so many? I am the son of strong-hearted Achilles, who once put your father to flight with a blow from his long spear; and the malign spirits of doom would have snatched him off to death if my father had not swiftly healed his mortal wound. The horses that carry me are my godlike father's, offspring of Harpyia and sired by Zephyrus: they can gallop over the barren sea barely touching it with their hooves, borne along quick as the wind. But now that you know my own lineage and that of my horses, it is time you became acquainted with my tireless spear face to face; its lineage goes back to lofty Pelion's peaks, where it left behind its embedded stump.

This *praeteritio* has much in common with Achilles' earlier critique of conventional genealogical flyting (Q.S.2.449–51). Like his father's remark that he and Memnon were 'prattling like silly children about the deeds of their parents', Neoptolemus derides the game of generational question-and-answer as pointless and inappropriate. Despite his moment of clarity, Achilles – the obsessive almost-son of Zeus, the flyter in spite of himself – remained ultimately stuck in the old epic world of anxious rivalry. Neoptolemus' self-identification as his father offers a way to circumvent this process more permanently. As he speedily dispatches the details of his paternity – 'known to very many', like Aeneas' πρόκλυτ'... ἔπεα θνητῶν ἀνθρώπων (*Il.* 20.204), already so deeply embedded in the heroic tradition that we do not need to ask about them – he focuses instead on the features that he and his father now share: the horses and the spear, once again in the not-just-poetic plural (δόρατος ἡμετέροιο).

For Bloom, poetic anxiety may or may not be externalised by the later writer, because either way, 'the strong poem *is* the achieved anxiety'.[110] As his characters trade and, in Neoptolemus' case, reject traditional boasts about their predecessors, Quintus suggests how impersonation can take anxiety's place in this sort of formulation: forgoing spiels about rivalry or similarity with Homer, his poem *is* the achieved assimilation. In a text without an opening proem, which closely emulates a revered model without ever naming him directly, Neoptolemus' speech provides a fitting statement of a poetics which seeks to eschew earlier Statian or later Nonnian-style proclamations of an 'external' relationship to the literary father. Like the doubling ethopoetic creations and Homeric performances

---

[110] Bloom (1997): xxiii.

264   Prodigal Poetics: Filiation and Succession

at large in the Greek third century, and like Pausanias' accommodation of the Temple's multiple architectural agents into one metonymic tag, the Posthomeric poet 'both conceals and draws attention to' the different literary and chronological strata which underlie his project, and rather than tearing down or carving over these earlier layers, he builds his new epic *into* them, recombining them into one 'strong' structure.

Necromancy and Filial Possession

Through the act of arming and his self-presentation in speech, Neoptolemus thus reflects and reflects upon the methods for successful impersonation. His final scene in the poem provides the most radical of these methods; one which aims not to bridge the gap between model and inheritor like arming did, but to remove this gap altogether. In the closing book of the epic, the linearity inherent to succession is most provocatively overturned, and Neoptolemus' assimilatory stance towards Achilles comes closest to total possession.

As the Greeks prepare to leave Troy, Neoptolemus comes face to face with the ghost of his father. Achilles appears in a dream, giving a hortatory speech to his son about how to conduct himself and ends by telling him what to command the Argives to do: sacrifice Polyxena, or incur his anger (Q.S.14.179–256).[111] This ghostly encounter, the only moment of direct interaction between father and son, functions on multiple levels as a scene of transmission and instruction. Achilles' advice, it has been noted, echoes the extended allegory of the Mountain of *Arete* on his shield:

> κεῖνος δ' οὔ ποτ' ἀνὴρ Ἀρετῆς ἐπὶ τέρμαθ' ἵκανεν
> ᾧ τινι μὴ νόος ἐστὶν ἐναίσιμος· οὕνεκ' ἄρ' αὐτῆς
> πρέμνον δύσβατόν ἐστι, μακροὶ δέ οἱ ἄχρις ἐπ' αἴθρῃ
> ὄζοι ἀνηέξηνθ'· ὁπόσοισι δὲ κάρτος ὀπηδεῖ
> καὶ πόνος, ἐκ καμάτου πολυγηθέα καρπὸν ἀμῶνται
> εἰς Ἀρετῆς ἀναβάντες ἐυστεφάνου κλυτὸν ἔρνος.
>
> Q.S.14.195–200

No man ever reached the top-most height of Virtue unless he had a righteous mind: her tree is hard to climb, and her branches extend far into the sky. But whoever is strong and struggles hard gathers a delightful fruit after his efforts, once he has climbed that famous tree of fair-crowned Virtue.

> αἰπύτατον δ' ἐτέτυκτο θεοκμήτῳ ἐπὶ ἔργῳ
> καὶ τρηχὺ ζαθέης Ἀρετῆς ὄρος· ἐν δὲ καὶ αὐτὴ

---

[111] See Chapter 3 for this passage in relation to *gnomai*.

Alternative Relations: Succession through Impersonation

εἰστήκει φοίνικος ἐπεμβεβαυῖα κατ' ἄκρης
ὑψηλή, ψαύουσα πρὸς οὐρανόν· ἀμφὶ δὲ πάντη
ἀτραπιτοὶ θαμέεσσι διειργόμεναι σκολόπεσσιν
ἀνθρώπων ἀπέρυκον ἐὺν πάτον, οὔνεκα πολλοὶ
εἰσοπίσω χάζοντο τεθηπότες αἰπὰ κέλευθα,
παῦροι δ' ἱερὸν οἶμον ἀνήιον ἱδρώοντες.

Q.S.5.49–56

The god's crowning effort was a representation of the mountain of holy Virtue, very high and hard to climb; the goddess herself stood high atop a palm tree, her head touching the sky. All the paths were full of thorn bushes to prevent easy access, so that most people retreated, deterred by the steepness of the path, and only a few sweated their way to the top of that sacred route.

The connection with the shield imagery has long been noted. Byre, who teases out the Neopythagorean content of the allegory on virtue,[112] takes the two scenes as 'allegorical cognates', suggesting that the details which Achilles adds – for instance, what awaits the climbers after their struggle – show what must have been presupposed in the earlier scene by the imperial reader.[113] For Maciver, the close correlation between the Ἀρετῆς ... ἔρνος here (14.200) and the mountain in the ekphrasis suggests that 'Achilles expounds, with modification, what was narrated in *Posthomerica 5*' – explaining the allegory on the shield both to his son and to us as readers.[114] ἀρετή, certainly, is a key term in the *Posthomerica*: its Neopythagorean and Stoic significations can function as a programmatic signal of the ethics and philosophical tenets of the epic.[115] By inheriting this shield and its discourse on ἀρετή Neoptolemus thus cements his status as an embodiment and an emblem of these wider ethical standpoints.

Scant attention, however, has been paid to Neoptolemus' methods of *receiving* this message. And yet the whole encounter is also highly unusual from the dreamer's perspective. Dreams in the *Posthomerica*, as in Homer,

---

[112] Byre (1982), following Kakridis (1962), identifies two parallel but originally independent thematic strands in the *Arete* allegory: that of the mountain of *Arete* and the difficulty of the road leading to her; and that of *Arete* atop the palm tree. On the second theme, the palm, in the shield of Achilles, which is unique to Quintus in the surviving works of antiquity – Byre then posits a number of possible influences and sources (see specially ibid. 190–1). By tracing its connections with the tree (which is not a palm tree) in this speech of Achilles in Q.S.14, he argues that 'the ultimate source of the image is to be found in the Pythagorean Y tradition, that is intimately bound up with depicting the two ways and their opposite goals'.

[113] Byre (1982): 191f.   [114] Maciver (2012b): 79–83.

[115] On the 'Stoic undercurrent' of the allegory, and the related possibility for the shield to function as a *mise en abyme* for the Stoic inheritance of the Quintan text, see chiefly Maciver (2007) and (2012b): 39–86. I offer my own reading of the allegory in the *Posthomerica*, from the alternative perspective of personification, in Greensmith (forthcoming a).

266   Prodigal Poetics: Filiation and Succession

are usually based on disguise, distance and intangibility. To take two examples, the deceitful dream sent to Penthesilea (Q.S.1.125–37) takes the shape of her father, and its message is reported to the reader indirectly. In Athena's dream visit to Epeius (Q.S.12.106–21) she is disguised as a tender maiden, and her instructions are again described in indirect speech. Here instead Achilles appears to Neoptolemus οἷος ἔην περ ζωὸς ἐών (Q.S.14.181) and speaks to him directly and at length. This lack of disguise closely resembles the way in which Patroclus appeared to Achilles in the *Iliad* (πάντ' αὐτῷ μέγεθός τε καὶ ὄμματα κάλ' ἐικυῖα/καὶ φωνήν, καὶ τοῖα περὶ χροΐ εἵματα ἔστο·, *Il.* 23.66–7). There are, however, two telling differences between these encounters. Firstly, the fact that Patroclus appears 'like his very self' is readily affirmable by Achilles: thanks to their intense relationship throughout the war, he would, we can imagine, have instantly and viscerally recognised this vision as the true image of his friend. But Neoptolemus has never set eyes on Achilles: like a Telemachus without the reunion, he grew up with an invisible father, an absent presence. How could he *know* that it was him? That this difficulty is glossed over in the Quintan passage – Neoptolemus seems immediately able to recognise his dream visitor, and is even left 'warmed by his father's memory' (μνήσατο πατρὸς ἑοῖο·νόος δέ οἱ ἠὺς ἰάνθη, 227) – serves to decrease the sense of separation between father and son, by aligning them with the more 'logical' intimacy of the Iliadic model.[116]

And secondly, in the Iliadic scene, Achilles reaches out to touch Patroclus, but, in a move widely imitated in the later epic tradition,[117] is not able to grasp anything ("Ὣς ἄρα φωνήσας ὠρέξατο χερσὶ φίλῃσιν/οὐδ' ἔλαβε· ψυχὴ δὲ κατὰ χθονὸς ἠῦτε καπνὸς/ᾤχετο τετριγυῖα·... *Il.* 23.99–101). There is by contrast a remarkable physicality to the Quintan ghost. He does not merely touch Neoptolemus, but kisses him on the neck and eyes (Κύσσε δέ οἱ δειρὴν καὶ φάεα μαρμαίροντα/ἀσπασίως,... Q.S.14.183–4). Neoptolemus is often kissed by his elders in the

---

[116] It may of course be objected that there is nothing in the Quintan line (181) that suggests Achilles' close resemblance to his living self is necessarily focalised through Neoptolemus (i.e. that it is rather his words, where he self-announces as his father [185–6], which secure the identification). However, the fact that this unusual detail evokes the Achilles-Patroclus scene so specifically – a relationship which, as we have seen, is so crucial to charting Neoptolemus' imitative approach to his father throughout the *Posthomerica* – suggests that this *is* a form of visual intimacy being intimated, which pointedly, rather than carelessly, defies how much Neoptolemus could be expected to know. 'Logic', in other words, is always a dubious concept to apply to mythological narrative, but here it is an incongruity which has strong interpretative purpose.

[117] Most famously Odysseus' meeting with Anticlea in *Od.* 11.150–224 and Aeneas' encounters at *Aen.* 2.730–95 and 6.700–3.

Alternative Relations: Succession through Impersonation   267

Posthomerica:[118] but to be kissed by a ghost, that chilly insubstantial form traditionally incapable of touch, is a highly debased version of this act of affection. This intensity of physical contact is in fact almost unique to Quintus' epic dream. Even Ovid's Morpheus, the phantom most skilled in human imitation, appears to Alcyone exactly like Ceyx in terms of image and movements, but stops short of any somatic engagement. Alcyone, like Achilles, Odysseus and Aeneas before her, can only embrace the thin air (*Met.* 11.650–80).

Through these two signals of closeness, Neoptolemus' vision thus seems less like a shady epic sleep and more a spiritual encounter – 'a kind of mystical communion, halfway between a dream reverie and an epiphany'.[119] We have seen how such uncanny encounters were a prevalent feature of imperial Greek re-animating culture.[120] Testimonies from the period suggest how dreams could provide a vehicle for this sort of intimate experience. Colluthus' account of Helen's dream appearance to her daughter has already offered one paradigm for the particular intensity that dream encounters could be used to provide: Hermione's dream is closely commingled with the possibility of an actual vision appearing before her (as she 'wanders among the deceits of dreams' she thinks that she really sees her mother [369]), where the lines between fiction and reality, tangible and intangible interaction are dramatised and blurred. In a more 'clinical' excursus, Artemidorus records his clients' dreams of kissing complete with analogical interpretations and, in more extreme cases, discusses what to do if someone dreams about having sexual intercourse with gods and goddesses (*Oneir.* 1.80).[121] Whilst there is no implication (or at least, no indication...) of sexualisation in Quintus' episode,[122] the kiss between dream and dreamer is a pointedly non-epic/heroic element of its fabric and is more akin to contemporary dream accounts.[123]

Quintus further stresses the closeness of this transmission by appealing to contemporary ideas about *waking* encounters of an otherworldly kind.

---

[118] Boyten (2010): 187–8.
[119] Zeitlin (2001): 235. My point is not that these 'close encounters' which Zeitlin and others discuss necessarily involve physical interaction, but rather that Quintus uses physical interaction to add a sense of closeness to his dream scene; making clear that this is no usual epic version of this sequence.
[120] Cf. Chapter 1.5 and Chapter 2.
[121] See Lane Fox (1986): ch. 4 on divine dreams in Late Antiquity. For ancient love dreams, see Plastira-Valkanou (1999).
[122] I discuss the (a-) sexuality of Quintus' epic centrally in Greensmith (forthcoming c).
[123] Quintus here also eschews the distance inherent to another conventional setting for a son receiving advice from his deceased parent – the *katabasis* to the underworld, as per the scenes of *Od.* 11 and *Aen.* 6.

268 Prodigal Poetics: Filiation and Succession

We have seen how a number of works from the second sophistic describe necromantic resurrections of figures from heroic cults and explore the possibilities for intense, time-transcendent interactions that such rituals could provide.[124] The two most extensive and relevant surviving accounts come from Philostratus' *Heroicus* and the *Vita Apollonii*.[125] The second of these texts includes details which are tellingly close to Quintus' dream sequence here. In the fourth book of the *Vita*, Apollonius spends a night at Troy by Achilles' tomb and summons the hero with a prayer. Achilles duly rises from the dead, laments the neglect of his cult and gives the philosopher advice. Quintus' Neoptolemus also visits Achilles' tomb (at Q.S.9.46–62 he weeps beside it and kisses it) and, when he and the Greeks approach it to sacrifice Polyxena, offers prayer to Achilles' shade (Q.S.14.309–12).

Achilles' dream-speech also has strong similarities to his conversation in Philostratus with Apollonius (*V A.*4.16.3). Offering alternative versions of the same myth,[126] both exchanges discuss the possibility of new Achillean anger which will surpass the Iliadic *mēnis*: Quintus' Achilles warns that he is now angrier than he was over Briseis (μᾶλλον ἔτ᾽ ἢ τὸ πάρος Βρισηίδος, Q.S.14.216) and in Philostratus he threatens that his anger would cause the Thessalians to perish more than the Greeks did (καὶ μηνίειν μὲν οὔπω ἀξιῶ, μηνίσαντος γὰρ ἀπολοῦνται μᾶλλον ἢ οἱ ἐνταῦθά ποτε Ἕλληνες, *V A* 4.16.3). Both speeches combine this anger with paradoxically gentle advice (ξυμβουλίᾳ δὲ ἐπιεικεῖ χρῶμαι, *V A* 4.16.3). They also share an emphasis on Achilles' distinctive egotism: he boasts to Apollonius that the Trojans lost many noble men by his hands, and yet the Thessalians do not pay sacrifice to him (Τρώων, οἳ τοσοῦσδε ἄνδρας ὑπ᾽ ἐμοῦ ἀφαιρεθέντες δημοσίᾳ τε θύουσί μοι καὶ ὡραίων ἀπάρχονται καὶ ἱκετηρίαν τιθέμενοι σπονδὰς αἰτοῦσιν, *V A* 4.16.3), which chimes with his demand to Neoptolemus that the Greeks must offer sacrifice, if they remember ὅσσ᾽

---

[124] Cf. Chapter 1.5 and Chapter 2.

[125] These are not, of course, the only exempla of necromancy from the imperial Greek era: other accounts such as the necromancy performed by the witch of Bessa in Heliodorus' *Aethioipica* 6.15 (on which, see especially Hilton (2017)) and a papyrus fragment from Book 18 of Julius Africanus' *Kestoi* , which adds a hymn in hexameter verse to Homer's account of Odysseus' consultation of the dead, further testify to the renewed interest in necromancy, particularly the Homeric variety, in the third century. I am zooming in on the Philostratean accounts because of their strong textual (as well as thematic) connections to this dream scene in the *Posthomerica*, but wider discourses and treatments of 'resurrection' of this kind must remain firmly part of the picture.

[126] Philostratus' 'romantic' version maintains that Polyxena was not sacrificed at Achilles' tomb but killed herself there out of love for him.

Alternative Relations: Succession through Impersonation 269

ἐμόγησα περὶ Πριάμοιο πόληα,/ἠδ' ὅσα ληισάμην πρὶν Τρώιον οὖδας ἱκέσθαι (Q.S.14.211–12).

Quintus' engagement with the *Vita Apollonii* has not been considered by the scholars who have pondered over this puzzling scene.[127] And yet it became clear in the previous chapter that Quintus covertly polemicises precisely this type of sophistic prose account for rewriting Homer's version of the Trojan War.[128] The similarities with Philostratus in this dream scene suggest that Quintus could be engaging with such texts again; here, harnessing their theme of necromantic interaction to make Neoptolemus' encounter even 'closer', establishing, in a way that his contemporary readership would recognise clearly, the idea of a direct, epiphanic ritual linking father to son.[129]

Quintus' scene thus puts the focus on the connective potential of the dream experience. Like Kohn's account of the 'bad dream' where predator becomes blurred with his prey, this description sets up Neoptolemus' dream as a device that can closely enmesh and even elide its participants, 'aligning the situated points of view of beings that inhabited different worlds'.[130] Now, the *poetic* tradition, as far back as Hesiod, used dreams symbolically to describe poetic inspiration and explain authorial choices. The *Anacreontea*, as we have discussed, begin with a dream featuring Eros and Anacreon: a neat means of emphasising the collection's literary indebtedness to the Anacreontic poet, but also its ontological distinction from him. In silver Latin epic, necromantic encounters are also used for such self-reflexive purposes. Both Silius and Lucan express their belatedness through otherworldly meetings with dead poets or their societies. In Book 13 of the *Punica* (778–97) Scipio encounters the shade of Homer transformed back into a youth,[131] and the *Pharsalia* stages its

---

[127] For such interaction to be plausible Quintus would have to have written after the 220s CE, a likelihood which this book broadly accepts (see Chapter 1.5). If Quintus is indeed deliberately reworking the Philostratean passage, the intertext would have implications for affirming these dating parameters too.

[128] Philostratus' Apollonius poses a series of 'Homeric questions' similar to those of Lucian in *Ver. Hist.* 2. See Zeitlin (2001): 242–55.

[129] Another way to test the strength of these similarities is to consider other treatments of Achilles' appearance to the Greeks before Polyxena's sacrifice: Euripides' *Hecuba* 37–9 and 109–15 and Ovid's *Metamorphoses* 13.439–41. In both of these versions, Achilles expresses a similar indignation at the lack of honour paid by the Greeks to his services during the war. However, Quintus' version is different in that it turns this command into an extended direct speech to just one listener, rather than to all the Greeks, and it adds the indications of a necromantic summoning via prayer: Ovid's Achilles, for instance, just 'suddenly springs from the ground', *Met.* 13.441–2.

[130] Kohn (2013): 141. Kohn includes lengthy discussion of dreams – 'that second life' with which everyday life in Ávila is entangled (13) – as a crucial medium for his type of relationality.

[131] See Hardie (1993): 115; Tipping (2010): 194–6.

270   Prodigal Poetics: Filiation and Succession

confrontation of traditional epic on the actual site of Troy, featuring real spirits of the dead. It is, however, the *start* of the Latin epic tradition which provides the most radical version of this symbolism and uses the image of the dream encounter in a way particularly relevant to Quintus' claims.

'Ennius' *Annals* famously begins with the account of a dream in which the ghost of Homer tells the poet that his soul has transmigrated into his body.[132] As scholars have rightly emphasised, this Pythagorean conceit, an *elevatio ad absurdum* of the association between dreams and poetic inspiration, is an extremely bold means of authorising the poet's ambitions and the cultural transfer embodied in his undertaking: 'in place of a literary dependence on earlier ancestors, (this is) a Homer *rediuiuus* ... a direct transmission from Greek to Latin through the physical mechanism of a rebirth into another's body',[133] in which 'there is no sense of a struggle required to take over the old and make it one's own and new, nor even the distance involved in the natural succession of poetic son to father, but instead the limiting case of poetic identity: Ennius is Homer'.[134]

Pythagorean concepts of metempsychosis remained popular in the literary output of Quintus' era. The *Vita Apollonii* again provides an instructive example. Before his meeting with Achilles, Apollonius discusses with the seer Iarchus the possibility of becoming the Homeric heroes through transmigration, a belief which they both share.[135] In the closeness of Neoptolemus' dream encounter, Quintus offers his version of this process. In an alternative note of potential (neo)pythagorean engagement, merging dreams' connective potential with their conventional poetic associations, he works to denote in a very 'Ennian',[136] but very covert, manner that the son is now possessed by the spirit of his father – a metaphorical account of the poet's own move towards complete Homeric embodiment.

This sense of possession, first suggested by the closeness between dream and dreamer, is most strongly asserted during Neoptolemus' interpretation of the meeting. After Achilles leaves, he conveys his father's message to the

---

[132] *Ann.* 1.5–10 (Goldberg and Manuwald (2018), vol. I).   [133] Zeitlin (2001): 236.

[134] Hardie (1993): 103. The only other surviving example of this poetic transmigration is given by Antipater of Thessalonica (74 Gow-Page (1968)) who describes how in the breast of Stesichorus, 'in accordance with the philosophical pronouncement of Pythagoras, the soul that used to belong to Homer made a second home'.

[135] On the topic, cf. also Lucian's *Gallus*.

[136] It is worth repeating here the allusive methodology established in Chapter 1: that, whilst there is no direct evidence that Quintus knew Ennius, (Vergilian intertextuality has proven contentious enough, before factoring in Vergil's earlier fragmentary model), in line with the maximalist approach that this book adopts to Quintus' literary-cultural engagement, his activation of this theme in a specifically Ennian form is a possibility worth pursuing.

Alternative Relations: Succession through Impersonation   271

troops, in what appears to be a shortened précis of the dream speech, omitting the personal advice and all mention of the allegory of virtue.[137]

> 'κέκλυτέ μευ, φίλα τέκνα μενεπτολέμων Ἀργείων,
> πατρὸς ἐφημοσύνην ἐρικυδέος, ἥν μοι ἔνισπε
> χθιζὸς ἐνὶ λεχέεσσι διὰ κνέφας ὑπνώοντι·
> φῆ γὰρ ἀειγενέεσσι μετέμμεναι ἀθανάτοισιν·
> ἠνώγει δ' ὑμέας τε καὶ Ἀτρείδην βασιλῆα,
> ὄφρα οἱ ἐκ πολέμοιο γέρας περικαλλὲς ἄροιτε   (240)
> τύμβον ἐπ' εὐρώεντα Πολυξείνην εὔπεπλον·
> καί μιν ἔφη ῥέξαντας ἀπόπροθι ταρχύσασθαι·
> εἰ δέ οἱ οὐκ ἀλέγοντες ἐπιπλώοιτε θάλασσαν,
> ἠπείλει κατὰ πόντον ἐναντία κύματ' ἀείρας
> λαὸν ὁμῶς νήεσσι πολὺν χρόνον ἐνθάδ' ἐρύξειν.'   (245)
> ὣς φαμένου πίθοντο,[138] καὶ ὡς θεῷ εὐχετόωντο.
>
> Q.S.14.235–46

'Dear children of the Argives, stalwart in battle, let me tell you of the command which my renowned father gave me as I slept last night in my bed. He said that he is now numbered among the immortals who live for ever. He commanded you, and the son of Atreus, your king, in particular, to bring fair-robed Polyxena to his vast tomb as a handsome reward for his services in the war, to sacrifice her, and then to give her separate burial. And he threatened that if you neglect to do this before you set out on your voyage, he will raise the waves of the sea against you and detain the army and the ships here for a long time.' They obeyed his words and prayed as though to a god.

Neoptolemus ostensibly maintains a sense of separation from his father, by designating his message as reported speech. The audience's reaction, however, makes no such distinction. The compressed wording of line 246 does not specify by whose speech the army was persuaded: that of Neoptolemus, or that of Achilles, which he has related to them. Nor is it stated to whom the Greeks are praying, when they pray 'as (though) to a god': to the father, who is now among the gods, and thus deserving (and demanding) of worship;[139] or to the son, who is like a god but mortal? The ὡς leaves room for both readings. The first-person plural in Neoptolemus' earlier speeches is here transformed into a striking singularity: with father

---

[137] This omission could well be interpreted as a personal as well as poetic choice: from Neoptolemus' perspective, the information concerning ἀρετή was for him only – a communication of the deep and intrinsic ethical concerns of the poem, the safeguarded domain of only the poet's voice, Achilles, his son and the readers. It is not, therefore, for wider 'dissemination' among the army. I discuss this prospect further in Greensmith (forthcoming a).

[138] Vian (1969): 186 prints ὡς φαμένοιο πίθοντο, following Zimmerman.

[139] Cf. e.g. Hopkinson's recent translation (2018: 691), which is too unequivocal here: 'they offered up prayers to Achilles as if he were a god'.

272   Prodigal Poetics: Filiation and Succession

and son sharing the same syntax and engendering an identical response. We saw how the idea of Achilles' potentially monstrous struggle against Zeus' paternalistic authority was activated through the Titan scene on his helmet. Now decked in his father's armour, Neoptolemus holds the potential to be 'titanomachic' – violent, agonistic and threatening – in his own hands (and on his head).[140] But he does not use it: a 'worthy heir' to the shield's ethics and poetics, he also rejects the more aggressive connotations included in its earlier ekphrastic vision.

In this light, we can reinterpret Neoptolemus' synopsis of his father's words. His seemingly simple speech describes Achilles' message in terms reminiscent of poetic inspiration: μοι ἔνισπε (236) is a phrase often found in the imperative form in pleas for information from the Muse.[141] Then in his account of the revealed knowledge, he maintains the essence of Achilles' words, but substitutes the language and formulae in which he presents it. He turns Achilles' ἐπεὶ μακάρεσσι θεοῖσιν (14.186) into ἀειγενέεσσι μετέμμεναι ἀθανάτοισιν (14.238) and reconfigures his description of the storm threat (14.216–18 vs. 243–5). He also employs some recognisable Homeric epithets (μενεπτολέμων Ἀργείων, Πολυξείνην εὔπεπλον) but applies them to different characters than those for whom they are used in the Homeric poems. In other words, through these techniques Neoptolemus offers a miniature, emblematic version of Quintus' own re-composition of Homeric epic, in which he is inspired, like the rhapsode or *homeristes*, to become the primary bard, but selects which Homeric elements to emphasise and conveys a Homeric impression using different formulaic combinations – a creative re-animation of the original poet's voice.

If Ennius committed the boldest conceit by suggesting that his Latin hexameters could be taken as still the work of Homer, then through Neoptolemus Quintus offers his own realignment of this claim. With embedded hints at literary possession rather than overt metempsychosis, coming at the end of the epic rather than the start, and concerning a poem which does not transmit Greek into Latin but closely continues Homer's subject matter and uses many of his original words, the theme of possession for Quintus does not *announce* poetic authority, or justify the poem that is to come. Rather, it represents the most extreme, totalising version of a Homeric closeness, a cultural *connection*, not transfer, which is already there, troped in different ways throughout the poem in its extensive exploration of succession.

---

[140] Cf. κάρη γε μὲν οὔτι βάρυνε/πήληξ… Q.S.7.448–9.
[141] Cf. the μοι ἔ?ννεπε of *Od.* 1.1; *Il.* 2.761.

Alternative Relations: Succession through Impersonation   273

In his own discussion of necromancy, Bloom claims another victory for the adversarial poets:

> In ways that need not be doctrinal, strong poems are always omens of resurrection. The dead may or may not return, but their voice comes alive, paradoxically *never by mere imitation*, but in the agonistic misprision performed upon powerful forerunners by only the most gifted of their successors.[142]

Neoptolemus' paternal reincarnation helps to overturn this false dichotomy. Rather than through agonism, this dead father comes alive precisely *by* imitation. Possession becomes a way for the new Homeric writer to bypass the straight chronology of competitive succession, presenting instead a simultaneous view of literary reception in which the old poet never stopped composing.

Wayward Athena: Concluding Succession

The closing scene of the whole epic contains a compendious summation of these redrafted successionist tropes, as Quintus takes his new vision of filiation away from the human plane and recasts it on a cosmic, universal scale.

As the Greeks set sail, Athena petitions Zeus to allow her to exact revenge for the offence committed by Locrian Ajax. Zeus agrees and lends her his thunderbolt with which she unleashes the storm, stirring into motion the shipwreck which will cause the Greeks all of their Odyssean troubles (Q.S.14.419–65). Athena and Zeus are two of the most active gods in the *Posthomerica*: Zeus appears eighteen times and Athena seventeen, the highest roll calls of any of the poem's divinities. Yet it is only here that they interact specifically as πατήρ and τέκος: the epic's final and most extensive divine exchange is framed in specifically filial terms.[143] The image of Zeus handing over his weapons to his daughter has obvious metapoetic potential: it mixes 'silver-Latin-style' language of filiation with the Callimachean imagery of thunder as a symbol for traditional epic poetry and its authority. This symbol – the adversarial trope *par excellence* – provides the perfect material for Quintus' closing statement of succession.

---

[142] Bloom (1997): xxiv, my italics.
[143] Cf. Q.S.14.427 (Ζεῦ πάτερ. . .) and 444–5 (προσέειπε πατήρ . . . ὦ τέκος). This is also the longest divine exchange in the *Posthomerica* and represents the only (extant) dramatisation of the gestation of the storm, as is alluded to in *Od.* 4. 499–511 and the opening of Euripides' *Troades*.

274 Prodigal Poetics: Filiation and Succession

Alluding to the traditional connotations of conflict with dominant authority, his Athena reveals how such rivalrous images can be rebranded as symbols of unity.

Athena's petition (Q.S.14.426–48) reads like an anthology of antagonistic motifs. She connects Ajax's offence to the wider assault on the sanctity and power of the gods by all mankind (Q.S.14.427–33), and presents him as a type of theomach:

> υἱὸς ᾿Οιλῆος μέγ᾿ ἐνήλιτεν, οὐδ᾿ ἐλέαιρε
> Κασσάνδρην ὀρέγουσαν ἀκηδέας εἰς ἐμὲ χεῖρας
> πολλάκις, οὐδ᾿ ἔδδεισεν ἐμὸν μένος, οὐδέ τι θυμῷ
> ᾐδέσατ᾿ ἀθανάτην, ἀλλ᾿ ἄσχετον ἔργον ἔρεξε.

Q.S.14.436–9

The son of Oïleus committed a great crime in my temple: he had no pity for Cassandra as she kept stretching
out her innocent hands to me, and he felt no shame in my divine presence as he performed that unbearable crime.

In the assertion that Ajax had no respect for her divinity, Athena echoes Quintus' earlier presentation of Achilles, whose arrogance towards Apollo is explained in similar hubristic terms (τοὔνεκ᾿ ἄρ᾿ οὐκ ἀλέγιζε θεοῦ Q.S.3.45). Scholars have recently pursued such connections: King has compared Quintus' Achilles to the famous silver Latin *theomach*, Statius' Capaneus;[144] and Carvounis has likened the description of Locrian Ajax at the moment of his death (Q.S.14.559–89) to Statius' and Aeschylus' gigantomachic depictions of the character.[145] In her presentation of Ajax, Athena thus appropriates these literary models to present him as just this sort of threat – a usurper representing a violent attack against the whole divine order.

In these attempts at manipulation, however, Athena also becomes a type of theomachic rival herself: she has the potential to carry out the violence and disruption to Zeus' authority that she ostensibly warns him against:

> ...ἔγωγε μὲν οὔτ᾿ ἐν ᾿Ολύμπῳ
> ἔσσομαι, οὔτ᾿ ἔτι σεῖο κεκλήσομαι, εἰ μὴ ᾿Αχαιῶν
> τίσομ᾿ ἀτασθαλίην...

Q.S.14.433–5

I declare that I shall renounce Olympus and your claim to be my father if I cannot punish the reckless sins of the Achaeans.

---

[144] King (1987): 133–7.   [145] Carvounis (2007): 251.

Alternative Relations: Succession through Impersonation 275

Now theomachy, as has been finely analysed by Chaudhuri, is often employed by ancient poets to articulate the struggle against various types of authoritative systems.[146] In a literary sense, part of the metaphorical language of thundering and weapon theft, it can symbolise authors' attempts to challenge their powerful poetic predecessors. Quintus has already offered us an oblique version of this image in his opening description of Achilles and Ajax as the giants who threatened Zeus (Q.S.1.515–27). Here he returns to the theme more directly. In the layering of different versions of this challenge, Quintus' Athena merges the theomachic threat with a filial one,[147] instantiating multiple examples of the dangers posed to the superiority of the father.

As soon as Zeus responds, however, all of these threats become unfulfilled and counterfactual:

> ὣς φαμένην προσέειπε <πατὴρ> ἀγανοῖς ἐπέεσσιν·
> '⟨ὦ⟩ τέκος, οὔ τοι ἔγωγ' ἀνθίσταμαι εἵνεκ' Ἀχαιῶν,
> ἀλλὰ καὶ ἔντεα πάντα, τά μοι πάρος ἦρα φέροντες
> χερσὶν ὑπ' ἀκαμάτοισιν ἐτεκτήναντο Κύκλωπες
> δώσω ἐελδομένῃ· σὺ δὲ σῷ κρατερόφρονι θυμῷ
> αὐτὴ χεῖμ' ἀλεγεινὸν ἐπ' Ἀργείοισιν ὄρινον.'
>
> Q.S.14.443–8

So she spoke; and her father replied with kindly words: "My child, I do not stand in your way on account of the Achaeans. If you like, I shall even let you have those weapons once forged in my honour by the Cyclopes' tireless hands. In your mighty anger go and raise a cruel storm against the Argives yourself.'

Zeus' gentle words quash each of Athena's challenges to his hegemony. By agreeing to punish Ajax's rebellion, he also prevents his daughter from ever attempting hers.[148] Far from a Nonnian-style thunder theft, the handover of the weapons is presented as the divine father's own idea. The καί in 445 turns the donation into an inspired piece of improvisation on Zeus' part ('I shall even give you all my weapons …'). Rather than succumbing to his daughter's manipulation, he voluntarily improves upon her original plan.

As he pledges these weapons, Zeus breaks off into a story about their gestation (445–7). Hesiod's *Theogony* describes how the Cyclopes were the personifications of thunder and lightning, and also gave these elements to Zeus when they manufactured his thunderbolt:

---

[146] Chaudhuri (2014).   [147] Athena, unlike Achilles, is a real child of Zeus.
[148] The injustice felt by mankind at collective suffering is, of course, a mythological ellipsis, which, as the prologue of the *Odyssey* makes clear, soon finds new outlets through which to unleash itself.

276 Prodigal Poetics: Filiation and Succession

γείνατο δ' αὖ Κύκλωπας ὑπέρβιον ἦτορ ἔχοντας,
Βρόντην τε Στερόπην τε καὶ Ἄργην ὀβριμόθυμον,
οἳ Ζηνὶ βροντήν τε δόσαν τεῦξάν τε κεραυνόν.
οἱ δ' ἤτοι τὰ μὲν ἄλλα θεοῖς ἐναλίγκιοι ἦσαν,
μοῦνος δ' ὀφθαλμὸς μέσσῳ ἐνέκειτο μετώπῳ.
Κύκλωπες δ' ὄνομ' ἦσαν ἐπώνυμον, οὕνεκ' ἄρα σφέων
κυκλοτερὴς ὀφθαλμὸς ἔεις ἐνέκειτο μετώπῳ·
ἰσχὺς δ' ἠδὲ βίη καὶ μηχαναὶ ἦσαν ἐπ' ἔργοις.

Theog. 139–46

Then she bore the Cyclopes, who have very violent hearts, Brontes (Thunder) and Steropes (Lightning) and strong-spirited Arges (Bright), those who gave thunder to Zeus and fashioned the thunderbolt. These were like the gods in other regards, but only one eye was set in the middle of their foreheads; and they were called Cyclopes (Circle-eyed) by name, since a single circle-shaped eye was set in their foreheads. Strength and force and contrivances were in their works.[149]

Hesiod makes clear the threatening potential of these creatures. He centralises the Cyclopes' might and craftiness, and also suggests just how like the gods they were, in all respects apart from the physical aberration. Quintus' Zeus removes all of these menacing hints and focuses instead only on their desire to win his favour. If Athena played literary-scholar to present Ajax as an epic theomach, her father now performs some source adaptations of his own in order to neutralise such claims. Rewriting the Hesiodic myth, Zeus turns the monsters who were once his rivals into figures of peace and providers of a service to *him*.

Quintus' narrative continues this Hesiodic rewriting. When Athena takes the weapons and crashes in the sky, her aegis is described in a mini-ekphrasis:

ἐν γάρ οἱ πεπόνητο κάρη βλοσυροῖο Μεδούσης
σμερδαλέον· κρατεροὶ δὲ καὶ ἀκαμάτου πυρὸς ὁρμὴν
λάβρον ἀποπνείοντες ἔσαν καθύπερθε δράκοντες·
ἔβραχε δ' αἰγὶς ἅπασα περὶ στήθεσσιν ἀνάσσης,
οἷον ὅτε στεροπῇσιν ἐπιβρέμει ἄσπετος αἰθήρ.

*Q.S.*14.454–8

On it was worked the image of grim Medusa's hideous head surmounted by mighty serpents violently breathing out a powerful blast of unceasing fire. The entire aegis rang out on its mistress' breast like the crash of lightning in the vast sky.

The choice of fire-breathing snakes on the one hand accords with the usual portrayal of Gorgon Medusa: an obvious image to reach for to depict a

---

[149] Translations of the *Theogony* adapted from Most (2007).

Alternative Relations: Succession through Impersonation 277

monstrous female threat.[150] But on the other, the specific combination of power (κρατεροί), fire (πυρός) and serpents (δράκοντες) once again evokes the *Theogony*, this time its dramatic description of the monster Typhon:

> ἦν ἑκατὸν κεφαλαὶ ὄφιος, δεινοῖο δράκοντος,
> γλώσσῃσιν δνοφερῇσι λελιχμότες, ἐκ δέ οἱ ὄσσων
> θεσπεσίης κεφαλῇσιν ὑπ' ὀφρύσι πῦρ ἀμάρυσσεν·
>
> *Theog.* 825–8

And from his shoulders there were a hundred heads of a snake, a terrible dragon's, licking with their dark tongues; and on his prodigious heads fire sparkled from his eyes under the eyebrows, and from all of his heads fire burned as he glared.

In Hesiod's account, Typhon is explicitly figured as a terrible danger to Zeus. Predicting the scenario which was later dramatised by Nonnus, Hesiod describes what would have happened had Zeus not been able to conquer him:

> καί νύ κεν ἔπλετο ἔργον ἀμήχανον ἤματι κείνῳ
> καί κεν ὅ γε θνητοῖσι καὶ ἀθανάτοισιν ἄναξεν,
> εἰ μὴ ἄρ' ὀξὺ νόησε πατὴρ ἀνδρῶν τε θεῶν τε.
>
> *Theog.* 836–8

And on that very day an intractable deed would have been accomplished, and he would have ruled over mortals and immortals, if the father of men and of gods had not taken sharp notice.

Quintus' depiction of Athena at first gestures towards this nightmare scenario. As in Hesiod, we witness a supernatural force gilded with serpents and breathing out fire, rising up to wield its power, as natural and cosmic confusion ensues. This time, however, Zeus simply smiles at the sight, a reminder of his serene endorsement of the handover, and he maintains this control by further colluding with his impersonator:

> λάζετο δ' ἔντεα πατρὸς ἅ περ θεὸς οὔ τις ἀείρει
> νόσφι Διὸς μεγάλοιο· τίναξε δὲ μακρὸν Ὄλυμπον·
> σὺν δ' ἔχεεν νεφέλας τε καὶ ἠέρα πᾶσαν ὕπερθε·
> νὺξ δ' ἐχύθη περὶ γαῖαν, ἐπήχλυσεν δὲ θάλασσα·
> Ζεὺς δὲ μέγ' εἰσορόων ἐπετέρπετο· κίνυτο δ' εὐρὺς
> οὐρανὸς ἀμφὶ πόδεσσι θεῆς· περὶ δ' ἔβραχεν αἰθήρ,
> ὡς Διὸς ἀκαμάτοιο ποτὶ κλόνον ἐμμεμαῶτος.
>
> Q.S.14.459–65

She took up her father's arms, which no god wields but great Zeus; she made high Olympus shake and put in confusion the clouds and the whole of the upper air; night enfolded the land and the sea grew misty; and Zeus took great pleasure in

---

[150] Cf. James (2004): 345.

278   Prodigal Poetics: Filiation and Succession

the sight. The broad heavens shook at her every step, and the sky rang out all around as if unwearying Zeus himself were charging into battle.

As Athena grasps the weapons which no god other than Zeus can carry, shaking Olympus just as Zeus does with a nod (μέγαν δ’ ἐλέλιξεν Ὄλυμπον, *Il.* 1.530), Quintus shows in this divine father and child the same assimilatory mimesis as Neoptolemus achieved when he put on Achilles’ arms. The effects on the audience are equally convincing:[151] it is ‘as though [ὡς] invincible Zeus himself rushes into battle’ (465). ὡς here first points to its own fictive function: it may *seem as though* Zeus is taking part in the storm, but in fact he is sitting and watching, one step removed from the action. And yet we have seen how similes in the *Posthomerica* tend to favour closeness over contrast, between vehicle and tenor, narrative and comparison. And so it is here, as the link between daughter and father is closely reflected in the final narrative scenes, where Athena no longer just acts ‘like’ Zeus but acts with him and they really do charge into the sky together:

> ἥ ῥα καὶ αὐτὴ ὕπερθεν ἀμείλιχα μαιμώωσα
> θῦνε μετ’ ἀστεροπῇσιν· ἐπέκτυπε δ’ οὐρανόθεν Ζεὺς
> κυδαίνων ἀνὰ θυμὸν ἑὸν τέκος . . .
>
> Q.S.14.509–11

She herself was rushing and raging mercilessly up in the sky, wielding her lightning; and from the heavens Zeus provided an accompaniment of thunder because he wished to lend glory to his daughter.

> ἡ δ’ ἄρ’ ἀπ’ Οὐλύμποιο βαρύκτυπος Ἀτρυτώνη
> οὔ τι καταισχύνεσκε βίην πατρός· ἀμφὶ δ’ ἄρ’ αἰθὴρ
> ἴαχεν. . .
>
> Q.S.14.530–2

From Olympus, deep-thundering Atrytone wielded her mighty weapons in a way worthy of her father, and the sky was filled with noise.

What began as potential conflict ends in the most powerful portrait of family co-operation.

6.5 Conclusions

A central and driving claim of this book is that imperial Greek poetics must be moved away from the model of silver Latin, because it cannot be

---

[151] As Neoptolemus merged into Achilles in the perception of the Trojans (Q.S.7.526–41) so here does Athena merge into Zeus in the ‘perception’ of the reader.

Conclusions   279

telling the same story. This chapter has attempted to tell Quintus' story of succession: not a tale of filial struggle against dynastic or literary lineage, but a world narrative in which the relationship between old and new is more profoundly entangled, and multiple actors operate as 'interrelated but not interchangeable'[152] parts. It is, ironically, only through this gesture of *separation* – of Quintan filial discourse from the Statian, Lucanian, or even the Ovidian – that the real connectedness of the *Posthomerica* can be disclosed.

This connectedness is, like so much of the text's poetics, twofold: it is a 'doubleness.' Quintus firstly reveals his relationship to imperial Greek political self-constructions: beneath and within his programmatic occlusiveness, there lies an intense interaction with the inherently plural succession scenarios of the imperial third century. And secondly, he conveys his relations of a more poetic kind: the epic suggests manifold connections and divergences not just with its Greek or Latin forerunners in filial metapoetics, but also with its close, or even not yet born, siblings. We have seen, for instance, how Nonnus rejects Quintus' rejection of naming, but seems to share in his abandonment of direct succession in favour of anachronistic, upside-down relationships. And Colluthus continues and expands Quintan moments of maternal emphasis, but puts them to work for a new, fifth-century Christian matrix. For all of their differences in approach, these works all saw in familial imagery a means to convey the nature of their specific ambitions and times. For such later Greek poets, filiation was a living image, and a pliant one, appropriated with a brazenness and irony which has not before been fully appreciated. If, for Bloom, 'authentic high literature relies upon a turning away not only from the literal but from prior tropes',[153] then these epics all turn back *towards* the prior trope of succession, and reauthenticate it for new and unprecedented purposes. Handled with dexterity, the imagery in the *Posthomerica* strikes at the core of the bond between Quintus and Homer inherent in its impersonating claims. Above all, this is a poetics defined by closeness. As we navigate through the epic which continues the *Iliad* and approaches the *Odyssey*, we are made to appreciate the intensity of this relationship. Father and son are so close that they touch.

---

[152] *Qua* Kohn (2013) *passim.*   [153] Bloom (1997): xix.

CHAPTER 7

Temporality and the Homeric Not Yet

A story has no beginning or end; arbitrarily one chooses that moment
of experience from which to look back or from which to look ahead.
— Graham Greene, *The End of the Affair*

We have not yet come to the end of our trials, but still hereafter there
is to be measureless toil, long and hard, which I must fulfil to the end.
— *Odyssey* 23.248–50

'It's about time. All literature is about time. Yet concern with time in
literature today is untimely. It comes at the wrong time.'

So begins J. Hillis Miller, as he attempts in a recent article to re-tackle –
with a healthy dose of self-irony – the formidable topic of 'time in
literature'.[1] These two succinct contradictory positions, he argues, govern
the paradox at the heart of all contemporary reflections on the literary
treatment of time. On the one hand, an enormous and continually
augmenting corpus of secondary scholarship exists on the subject:[2] it has
long been accepted and continues to be stressed how any study of any
literature requires an awareness of and reflection on time – 'nature's time,
the time of writing, reading's time'[3] and its pliant, permeable possibilities.
Yet on the other hand, the topic is in a sense *so* ubiquitous, so all-
engulfing, that its direct analysis can seem 'these days somewhat out-
moded, old hat, *vieux jeu*'.[4] I begin this book's final chapter with Hillis

[1] Hillis Miller (2003), quotation at 86.
[2] Hillis Miller provides his own selective summary of (then) recent scholarship at ibid. 86. It is not the
purpose of this chapter to attempt a potted or expanded summary of a topic of such gargantuan
vastness; rather, specific examples pertaining to our imperial epic subject matter will be highlighted
where relevant in what follows. For an ambitious attempt to entwine more systematically the history
of scholarship on literary time and Late Antique temporal conceptions, see Goldhill (forthcoming c):
part I.
[3] McMillin (2000): 138.
[4] Hillis Miller (2003): 86. His own examples of how this is so (the focus these days on 'class, race and
gender', which would make such a subject as time seem too artificial and formulaic to be worth
pursuing, or the alignment of time studies with a now faded concept of modernism) can of course be

280

Temporality and the Homeric Not Yet

Miller's sketch not to provide light relief or critical distance from a series of reflexive themes which always run the risk of 'taking themselves too seriously',[5] but rather because his knowing caricature of the hermeneutic state of play has particular resonance with my final area of focus.

For these two opposing principles also map closely onto an area which may seem to fall far afield from Hillis Miller's Heideggerian, semiotic subjects of interest:[6] time in imperial Greek epic. For on the one hand, the centrality of time to ancient epic and its scholarly analysis is deeply established and vastly explored. The penchant for the subject and style of the deep past – the 'return to Troy' and close resurrection of the Homeric idiolect – has also made temporal issues in the Greek hexameter of the Roman Empire particularly attractive and pressing. It is thus perhaps unsurprising that, in the growing scholarly attention paid to this era of poetry, 'temporality' is now emerging as another central talking point, a means of communicating the value, interest and vitality of these works once considered to lie outside the bounds of mainstream classical interest.[7] Scholarly output in the past five years alone provides ample illustration of this trend. Thematic work has appeared and is about to appear, to take just a few examples, on 'Temporality and Late Antique Epic';[8] 'Trojan Temporality and the Materiality of Literary History';[9] 'Untimeliness' and 'Anachronicity' in Late Antique literature and its reception.[10] And a number of the studies of individual poets – and here again Nonnus is a favourite and a frontrunner – also focus on techniques and treatments of time.[11]

Yet on the other hand, given the perennialism of discourses of time to 'all literature', and especially to all epic, one may feasibly question how distinct is this late epic sense of temporality. Is there a unique dynamic to

---

readily challenged and unpicked. I use the quotation rather as it was probably composed: as a caricature from which to launch our central areas of enqiuiry.

[5] *Qua* the discussion of metapoetics and its cynics in Chapter 1.10.

[6] Thus Hillis Miller (2003): 87: 'The basic issue for me now is the question of how words can be used to represent the subjective experience of lived time, in a different way for each work. The basic object of literary study is therefore linguistic in nature.'

[7] Along with, one might summarise, erotics, 'visuality' and the stylistic concerns outlined in Chapter 3. On erotics and imperial Greek epic, see the synthesis of scholarship in Greensmith (forthcoming c); on visuality, Roberts (1989), Elsner (1995) and Cadau (2015).

[8] Goldhill (forthcoming c) will be a book-length treatment of this topic.

[9] Desmond (2016). On 'Untimeliness' see also The Postclassicisms Collective (2020): section 2.8.

[10] See the various chapters in Malm and Cullhed (2018) which focus explicitly on such concepts in the Latin tradition but have much to offer to (and against), and have already sparked much interest for, the study of imperial Greek.

[11] See examples and discussion in 7.1.

282   Temporality and the Homeric Not Yet

imperial Greek epic time? Does it, and how does it, differ radically from that of the previous generic tradition? In light of such questions, temporality offers for these works not only a central talking point, but the epicentre of one of the major challenges with which this book has been concerned: the level of self-definition, canonicity and coherence within the multifarious imperial Greek epics: how far we can really 'join the dots' and consider these works as a discrete literary unit.[12]

Despite the burgeoning interest in imperial Greek epic and time, the *Posthomerica* has so far fallen outside of this particular furore.[13] And yet in many ways, this book's narrative of Quintus' interval poetics has already been intrinsically about time. The opening account of 'enlarging the space' showed how in the *Posthomerica*, and imperial Greek culture more broadly, the processes expressive of time and space (as Heidegger himself famously recognised)[14] entwine closely: imperial 'doubleness' involves both a temporal continuum conceived between the distant past and contemporary present, and a pliant textual area (the fixed, closed Homeric epics) able to be expanded within demarcated limits. The readings of the preceding chapters – Homer quoting Callimachus; the *Iliad* misremembered; necromantic encounters where the poetic father becomes the poetic son – then focused on defining how Quintus creates this self-reflexively open relationship between Homeric tradition and his own imperial chronology.

To end this narrative, this final chapter will confront directly the nature and function of Quintan time. Through the intense, focused thematisation of specific aspects of narrative time – changes of pace, counterfactuals, anachrony and motifs of closure – Quintus attempts a bold reconfiguration of linear models of epic temporality, combining and collapsing different forms (the teleological and the cyclical, the closed and the open-ended) and refracting them back into Homeric epic itself. By bringing to the surface the temporal flexibility already available in the fixed Homeric poems, Quintus definitively reconceptualises the time as well as the space in between his model texts, moving the *Iliad* and *Odyssey*, and the whole Trojan cycle, into his new πᾶσα ἀοιδή.

---

[12] We return to these issues, which I here use Hillis Miller to open up, centrally in 7.1.

[13] One way of appreciating this problem is the fact that none of the above-mentioned studies of late antique temporality discuss Quintus (with the exception of very brief discussion in Goldhill (forthcoming c)) and none of the existing studies of Quintus discuss temporality.

[14] Heidegger (1927) (1996 trans.) on how the words and figures for temporality in Western languages are primarily spatial.

7.1 Imperial Timing

The shape of time in epic can be outlined in a number of ways. It may be viewed as foundational or genealogical, centripetal or centrifugal, the clock in a game of chess[15] or the contours on a map.[16] Central to all these conceptions are two related ideas: the notion of boundedness and the issue of closure. Thus the *Iliad* and *Odyssey*, as many ancient and modern scholars have noted, are considered paradigmatically strong teleological narratives, whose central components are linearity, causal connection, boundedness and closure.[17] How these components are manifested in the two epics, however, is drastically different. The *Iliad* is seen as marking its end by the topos of the burial of Hector and the formal device of ring composition of a father coming to hostile territory to reclaim his child, while closure is effected through the conversation between Achilles and Priam, sworn enemies who for a brief moment are reunited by being mortal.[18] The *Odyssey*, however, delights first in 'aimless' episodes of wandering and digression before allowing itself to be organised by a quest that, however much it may be deferred by adventure, will finally achieve its goal.[19] For Lowe, it is Homer's second poem which therefore demonstrates for all time, 'that an arbitrarily open story universe can accommodate a narrative world-structure that is fully and classically closed'.[20] And yet by the same vein – a point to which we shall soon return – the *Odyssey* also reveals how 'full and classical closure' can be anticipated, and even overshadowed, by competing temporal forces: narrative movements and impulses which are more fluid, kaleidoscopic and less reassuringly 'complete'.

This twin discourse of time in and across Homer's texts was, of course, essential to their influence on later methods of temporal narration. 'Homer's epics', as Goldhill writes, 'are foundational not merely because they functioned as an educational, social and literary origin, but also because of the model of memorialization they perform.'[21] Not only, that is, are the poems, as we have explored in the opening chapter, artefacts of

---

[15] Lowe (2000): esp. 36–41.

[16] Purves (2010) who uses the distinction of 'protocartographic' versus 'countercartographic' modes of narrative time.

[17] So for Aristotle (*Poet.* 7–14). See particularly Lowe (2000) and Fowler (1997). On how the *Odyssey*, with its wandering first half, fits this model in its second half, see discussion below.

[18] See also de Jong (2014): 90.

[19] On this way of conceptualising the *Odyssey*'s temporality, see Quint (1993): 9 (whence comes 'aimless') and Lowe (2000): 151.

[20] Lowe (2000): 130.   [21] Goldhill (forthcoming c).

284 Temporality and the Homeric Not Yet

time – integral markers of Greek culture's sense of objectified tradition – but as narratives *on* time, they also present a brutal awareness 'of the abyss of time and the struggle of humans to transcend their own passing'.[22] The influence of this Homeric model, and this Homeric sense of awareness, can and has been charted in an enormous number of ways.[23] It underpins the temporal mechanisms of historiography (a vast arena at which I glance only briefly here) and the recalibration of the past undertaken therein: the recourse to what Grethlein and Krebs dub the 'plupast' – 'the shift to times "past of the past" to support or destabilize the dynamic and themes of the chosen historical subject or of readers' views of character' –[24] is often profoundly analogous to and reactive against Homeric epic's representation of its own place in tradition.[25] And it is of course directly manifest in the subsequent epic genre, as hexameter texts plotted their own response to this double pull of Homer as time and Homer on time. Apollonius, to take what is now the most extensively discussed example, shapes his entire voyaging epic around a twofold approach to the Homeric past. On the one hand, the *Argonautica* is focused on constructing distinct layers of embedded, distant time. As the proem announces its epigonal subject matter – the topic of 'earlier singers' (*Argon.* 1.18–19), and a story already old for Homer (cf. *Od.* 12.69–70) – we find the Apollonian version of the plupast; but here it is the *epic* world which is put into the pluperfect, 'the absolute past',[26] an 'always already distanced model of excellence'.[27] But at the

---

[22] Ibid.

[23] This necessarily brief exploration of some paradigmatic examples, focused on particular strands of the epic tradition (with historiography an essential point on this roadmap), does not seek to disregard the ways in which Homeric time was also manipulated in other strands of the genre, or indeed other genres. As, for example, the thirty chapters of the ambitiously titled volume *Time in Ancient Greek Literature* (de Jong and Nünlist (2007)) – which stretch from Homer to Heliodorus, but with many questionable omissions along the way – demonstrates, any large-scale attempt to chart this topic will be selective. I have chosen this focus primarily because, in line with the argument outlined in the previous chapters, my aim is to delineate the ways in which these different and chronologically close *imperial* epic traditions – Greek and Latin – diverge in their treatment of the same themes.

[24] Grethlein and Krebs (2012). Quotation from the review of Grethlein and Krebs by Lateiner (2012). See also Grethlein (2014) and (2015). The usefulness and precision of this expression for characterising the varied ways in which ancient literature engages with a 'past embedded within a past' may be questioned (see, for instance, the valid conclusion of Lateiner (2012): '[the term] articulates a newly titled but ancient phenomenon'), but it has nonetheless proven a popular and durable contribution to the field.

[25] Thus for instance the *Odyssey's* songs-within-song, which are read explicitly as analogous to the historian's metahistorical sense of the plupast: stories recalled by characters, and, by extension, the historians' own narrative: 'though writing history differs from recalling the past, both the historian's narrative and his characters' recall constitute acts of memory… Even Thucydides' accuracy, hailed though it has been as the foundation of critical historiography, is ultimately owed to his intention to provide his readers with useful knowledge' (Grethlein and Krebs (2012): 8–9).

[26] Bakhtin (1981): 16.   [27] Goldhill (1991): 284.

Imperial Timing 285

same time, through the towering presence of the quasi-eternal god Apollo, from whom the narrator 'begins' (*Argon.* 1.1), the proem – and, as it continues, the poem – also points 'to the essential *continuity* of the past, rather than its being absolutely walled off from the present'.[28]

This brief overview does not aim to offer in any sense 'a brief history of epic time'. Rather, it begins to suggest a further distinction, lurking in the margins of these examples. It is not simply 'Homeric epic' that was foundational to such later reworkings and treatments, but rather, the Homeric *epics*. This monumental(ising) influence of Homer was also based on a tension, the binary between the temporality of his two poems – a split between the two parts of the foundational Greek canon. We have already seen in brief how this split can be perceived in the different approach to teleology and closure offered by the two narratives. The most pertinent exposition of the effects of this difference derives from the Latin tradition: and here we must return directly to Quint's *Epic and Empire*, with whose readings this book began.[29] In his account of how Homer's forms of temporality were adopted and redrafted by Latin epics, Quint centralises precisely the notion of a division between the *Iliad* and *Odyssey* as contrastive models of time, and brings to the fore the *political* uses to which such a division could be put. Splitting, as we have seen, the history of the epic genre in the western tradition into two political strands – the Vergilian epics of conquest and empire that take the victors' side[30] and the countervailing epics of the defeated and of republican liberty –[31] Quint shows how the works within these strands draw on the plot models offered by the *Iliad* and *Odyssey* to produce opposing ideas of historical narrative: a linear, teleological narrative that belongs to the imperial conquerors; and an episodic and open-ended narrative identified with the defeated:

---

[28] Klooster (2007): 64.

[29] Quint's magnum opus on this topic (1993) has recently been bolstered by his new work on the *Aeneid* exclusively, *Virgil's Double Cross* (2018), which returns again to how form is used to reflect the poem's ideological work. This time he proposes that the rhetorical figure of chiasmus and the effects of chiastic reversal, which he terms 'double cross', have a profound impact on the epic's large- and small-scale design. The book's main argument is that the two figures both encourage and undermine the poem's pro-Augustan, pro-empire message.

[30] Quint (1993) focuses on the *Aeneid* itself, Camões' *Lusíadas*, Tasso's *Gerusalemme liberata*.

[31] Lucan's *Pharsalia*, Ercilla's *Araucana* and d'Aubigné's *Les tragiques*. On politicised time in Lucan, see also Masters (1992).

286   Temporality and the Homeric Not Yet

'The victors experience history as a coherent, end-directed story told by
their own power; the losers experience a contingency that they are powerless
to shape their own ends.'[32]

Those who sought to rewrite Homeric time could thus do so not only by
defining themselves against his models, but by defining these models
against *one another*. In their use of linearity and delay, teleology and
episode, open and closed readings, the *Iliad* and *Odyssey* stand – or are
made to stand – in cutting contraposition.

Now, this binary between the closed and open epic has long been
challenged by scholars concerned with the literary criticism of closure,
most successfully in Fowler's second thoughts on the subject, which warn
against subscribing too uncritically to the 'big myths' surrounding closure,
which posit an oversimplifying contrast between determined and ambiguous narratives.[33] However, such caveats also confirm that a sense of
contrast *is* there to be deconstructed and was a particularly strong aspect
of the epic tradition. Fowler himself acknowledges the importance of the
epic teleology that plays itself out in the *Aeneid* and its silver-age successors, and concedes that real linkages exist in these texts between closure
and the imposition of power. Hardie's study of closure in Latin epic
affirms this point, showing how the classic instance of ambiguous closure
in the ending of the *Aeneid* has its issues taken up again in the ostensibly
'rounded-off' conclusions of the *Thebaid* and the *Punica*.[34] The split
between open and closed temporal narratives is indeed thus established
and explored in these works, proving meaningful Martindale's formulation that the 'refusal of closure is a discourse on closure';[35] and such
readings are right to stress the cultural contingencies on which this split is
based.[36]

I have dedicated time to outlining this model of dichotomised, politicised Homeric time because whilst it has proven durable for the study of
the western phases of the epic tradition, it has not in any detail been
considered against the epic of imperial Greece. In a curious critical scenario, none of the above-discussed analyses of ancient Greek temporality
have included any imperial Greek verse; and, perhaps more surprisingly,[37]
none of the recent treatments of temporality *in* imperial Greek epic have

[32] Quint (1993): 9.   [33] Fowler (1997).   [34] Hardie (1997), expanding on Hardie (1993).
[35] Martindale (1993): 38.   [36] Fowler (1997) uses the phrase 'cultural segmentation.'
[37] Or at least, less predictably, given the previous situation of critical neglect of imperial verse material,
as synthesised in Chapter 1 of this book.

Imperial Timing

considered any such political dimensions in their readings.[38] And yet the mythological works from this era must present a principal test-case for such 'thoughts on closure'. These works, we know, are intensely concerned with issues of temporality; and they pair this concern with that conspicuously close appropriation of Homeric narrative and style that has come to characterise them so strongly. As 'epics of empire', they are also, as we have seen in detail in the previous chapter, written on the cusp of an imperial world in various stages of transition. These texts, therefore, stand – and must be made to stand – as major inheritors of Homer's awareness of time: and for these poets too, there is the possibility of a 'real linkage' between Homeric form, textual closure and imperial power.

In this light, let us consider more closely some of the contrasting examples of imperial Greek temporality which have, unlike the *Posthomerica*, attracted recent scholarly attention. Triphiodorus' epyllion is, as we saw in Chapter 1, in many ways programmatically and overwhelmingly teleological: he cannot end his poem fast enough. The very first word, amusingly and paradoxically, is τέρμα: meaning both the 'end' and a turning point, *qua* the post in a chariot race.[39] The request that follows, that Calliope πολὺν διὰ μῦθον ἀνεῖσα (3) can be taken to acknowledge the many *muthoi*, or the single long one,[40] previously expounded on the topic of the Trojan War: as belated adopter of this theme, the poet is determined not to linger. And in asking the Muse to release her theme in swift song – ταχείη λῦσον ἀοιδῇ (5) – Triphiodorus points more technically to the swift resolution of a plot: *lusis* since Aristotle denoted a term for literary closure.[41] Tomasso's account of Triphiodorus' reflexively accelerative, 'fast and furious' poetics[42] connects this pace of the poem directly to its miniature aesthetics and 'epyllionic' form: for Triphiodorus too, as he reads him, the vocabularies expressive of narrative time and textual space are made to converge.

Other later Greek epics are less temporally straight- (or fast-) forward. The swirling, convoluted timeframe of Nonnus' *Dionysiaca* resolutely

---

[38] The one partial exception is Goldhill (2015) who suggests a contemporary religious textuality to contextualise Nonnus' temporal style. There remain, however, to my knowledge no readings specifically focused on the politics of *empire* in any existing literature on imperial Greek temporality.

[39] Cf. the discussion of this vocabulary in Chapter 4.

[40] Depending on whether one takes πολύς here more literally, to mean 'many', or more conceptually, meaning 'great'. Cf. the discussion of Quintus' own use of πᾶς along these lines in Chapter 4.

[41] Arist. *Poet.* 1454a33–1454b9; a point to which we return in 7.3.

[42] Tomasso (2012). Further and sharper discussion of the relationship between Triphiodorus' temporality and form in Goldhill (forthcoming a).

288   Temporality and the Homeric Not Yet

defies a linear chronology. The hugely extended battle narrative between Dionysus and the Indians winds its way forwards and back through Dionysiac pre-births,[43] analepses within prolepses within analepses,[44] delays and double proems, and then suddenly ends in a flash. Goldhill has identified this style of narrative with a form of typological texturing, 'the redrafting of linear time into a swirl of mythic and literary paradigms … a wilful playfulness with temporal order', which he aptly terms, with due attention to etymology, a 'preposterous poetics'.[45] Kneebone has analysed these dynamics through the poem's representation of Time itself, arguing that the personified Aion in the *Dionysiaca* encapsulates much of the universal, cyclical or non-linear quality of Nonnian temporal poetics.[46]

Colluthus' *The Abduction of Helen*, heavily indebted to Nonnus, may be seen as equally, if differently 'preposterous'. We considered in Chapter 1 the epyllion's programatically pre-Homeric focus, marked in the proem by foregrounding gestures of primordiality and inception. Colluthus expands this focus throughout the poem through a particular narrative shaping: the story is made to unfold in a series of expanded and contracted episodes. In the opening scene, for instance, the poet gives very few details about the wedding of Peleus, but instead treats his reader to a mythically learned roll call of famous attendees (17–40). When Paris travels to Sparta, many lines are dedicated to describing the famous sights that he sees during his journey (211–30), but we hear nothing of his impressions when he first looks at Helen, Greek literature's most famously beautiful woman (253–8).[47] This tendency to condense and suppress major moments, and shift perspective instead onto 'off-piste' details, can be read as Colluthus' method of recalibrating a story whose trajectory is predetermined and well-known, creating alternative techniques of a suspense in a plot that has already worked itself out.

Oppian's *Halieutica* – though neither mythological nor narrative epic – destabilises time in another drastic way.[48] The sea is established at the start of the poem as a counter-genealogical space, unknowable and unending:

---

[43] Namely Zagreus in *Dion.* 6.155–204. On this episode, see Greensmith (forthcoming d).

[44] Examples include the inset tale of Aphrodite's weaving contest with Athena recalled in song by Leucus at the end of *Dion.* 24; the two omens foretelling Dionysus' victory (*Dion.* 38); and Heracles' account of the founding of Tyre (*Dion.* 40).

[45] Goldhill (2015): 158.

[46] Kneebone (2016). We return to Aion from a Quintan perspective in 7.2.

[47] Helen 'suddenly' (ἐξαπίνης, 255) appears and she is described as gazing at Paris (κόρον δ' οὐκ εἶχεν ὀπωπῆς, 259), not the other way around.

[48] I have included the *Halieutica* in this survey despite the fact that it is not mythological narrative epic (cf. e.g. Bowie 1989b) firstly due to its close engagement with Homeric mythological and literary themes and secondly, and most importantly, because of the strong intertextual relationship between Oppian and Quintus, which I discuss in detail below. It represents, I shall argue, an important

Imperial Timing

μυρία μὲν δὴ φῦλα καὶ ἄκριτα βένθεσι πόντου
ἐμφέρεται πλώοντα· τὰ δ' οὔ κέ τις ἐξονομήναι
ἀτρεκέως· οὐ γάρ τις ἐφίκετο τέρμα θαλάσσης·
ἀλλὰ τριηκοσίων ὀργυιῶν ἄχρι μάλιστα
ἀνέρες ἴσασίν τε καὶ ἔδρακον Ἀμφιτρίτην.
πολλὰ δ' (ἀπειρεσίη γὰρ ἀμετροβαθής τε θάλασσα)
κέκρυπται, τά κεν οὔ τις ἀείδελα μυθήσαιτο
θνητὸς ἐών· ὀλίγος δὲ νόος μερόπεσσι καὶ ἀλκή.

Hal. 1.80–7

Infinite and beyond reckoning are the tribes that move and swim in the depths of the sea, and none could name them certainly; for no man has reached the limit of the sea, but unto three hundred fathoms less or more men know and have explored the deep. But, since the sea is infinite and of unmeasured depth, many things are hidden, and of these dark things there is nothing that a mortal can tell; for small is the knowledge and strength of men.[49]

As the epic goes on to expound this unexpoundable topic, the didactic voice repeatedly establishes teleologies, taxonomies and structures only to deconstruct them once again. The fish all have individual end-points – each species from the tiny prawn to the mighty sea-monster gets its own 'life cycle' – but the poem which contains them does not end so neatly. The death of the κῆτος at the start of Book 5 (5.71–349) – a scene to which we shall return – is crammed with teleological language, set up clearly to be the poem's grand finale, only for this expectation to be undermined. The poem continues for more than 300 lines after this episode ends, and we find that there are still more fish-cycles to come.

These examples serve to show how in and across these epics, the relationship between the teleological and the episodic and the opposition between open and closed narratives is not so easy to map. In their use of the two models of time offered by Homer – the determined and the ambiguous – there is no straightforward dichotomy as pursued by the texts of Quint's analysis, but nor are these principals disregarded or proven false in the way imagined by Fowler. These poets instead seem, extremely self-consciously, to make use of multiple, competing models of time *at the same time.* The Trojan poems in particular revel in the contradictions of their 'ante-Homeric' positions, setting forth a knowing, at times ironic, *synchronic* approach to deep mythological time that could not be more different from the discreteness of the 'plupast' of Grethlein and Krebs'

---

model for certain aspects of the *Posthomerica*'s treatment of epic time. Kneebone (2020) will be the most substantial and original treatment of the *Halieutica* to date.

[49] Translations adapted from Mair (1928).

290   Temporality and the Homeric Not Yet

historiographers and bringing to the fore the clash between chronological earliness and literary lateness that such an approach entails.

The previous chapters have argued that the *Posthomerica* provides a critical focal point for comprehending the driving concerns and connective themes of imperial Greek epic. It is my central claim in this chapter that this is most acutely true for issues of temporality. If filial discourse provided our strongest incentive yet for an 'imperially' strong reading of the *Posthomerica* – for viewing our poem as actively engaged with the literary and political energies of its time – then temporality adds a new dimension to this engagement and pushes it to its limits. Quintus shows a forceful awareness of the different models of epic time available to him, and, as the Homerising poet *par excellence* (his Homeric past is, far more drastically than the 'continuity' of Apollonius, also the immediate 'still present'), draws these models specifically and explicitly from the *Iliad* and *Odyssey*. Thematising delay, acceleration, beginnings and ends as a self-reflexive commentary[50] the *Posthomerica merges* cyclic[51] and teleological frameworks in ways, directly comparable with the other imperial Greek texts discussed here. However, once again, the Homeric impersonation – the defining feature of this epic, whose central importance this book has constantly stressed – profoundly affects how we interpret these manoeuvres. Through his narrative position in the *middle* of the two Homeric plots, Quintus too takes up the different modes of narrative offered via the *Iliad* and *Odyssey* in the way that Quint suggests for his authors, but rather than contrasting them,[52] he suggests their fundamental consistency by making them operate within one, unified text. The poem thus removes the

---

[50] To use the language which Fowler (1997) applies to the texts on which his volume focuses.

[51] It must be stressed here, and will be stressed throughout this chapter, that 'cyclic' in relation to the *Posthomerica* does not mean the open-ended *oral* nature of the Homeric poems in their pre-fixation form; rather, it will be taken to refer to the possibilities for expansion and repetition as they are found in the fixed, final and written forms of the Homeric poems, in light of the framework outlined in Chapter 2.

[52] Cf. e.g. Quint's account of the *Aeneid* in this respect, (1993): 50, a poem which, of course, also makes use of both the narrative forms in one text but in a contrastive way: 'the poem falls into two halves . . . the first, modelled on the *Odyssey*, recounts the romance wanderings that detain Aeneas. The second, modelled on the *Iliad*, tells of the epic warfare from which they emerge victorious and will eventually lead to the foundation and history of Rome [i.e. *imperium . . . sine fine*]. The process by which the Trojans go from being losers to winners thus matches the movement in the poem from one narrative form to another, from romance to epic.' Likewise in his recent book (2018), ch. 2, Quint argues that through, for instance, Aeneas' status as a narrator of the fall of Troy, Vergil offers the reader a new perspective, that of the defeated; and thus the epic genuinely reflects on what Roman conquests might mean for the conquered. My argument here will be that unlike (Quint's) *Aeneid*, the *Posthomerica* does not progress or transition or flip perspective from one Homeric or ideological model to another, but rather amalgamates them continually into one inseparable whole.

Pacing: Acceleration and Delay

dichotomy between linear and open-ended models by re-reading time as it appears in Homeric epic itself. The effects of this process offer the final illustration of how the *Posthomerica* represents a different, more positive response to the challenges of this particular imperial period of identity negotiation. If, for Quint, closed epic belongs to the victors, and open-ended narratives to the conquered, then considered as a product of 'Greek culture under Rome', the *Posthomerica*'s unified view of Homeric time unsettles both sides of this equation, to reclaim an open *and* closed narrative for so-called *Graecia capta*. For *this* Greek present, Quintus' temporality of the interval articulates most resoundingly an active, accepting and constructive vision of imperial subjectivity, whose exposition reveals itself to be extremely timely.

7.2 Pacing: Acceleration and Delay

An acute preoccupation with time as a structural and thematic feature is revealed from the outset of the poem. We have seen how its first word is, unusually and programmatically, a temporal connective (εὖτε). From here on in, major moments in the narrative are often accompanied by explicit discussion and images of time. To begin with three striking examples. Before the arrival of Philoctetes, a key turning point in the narrative trajectory, Deiphobus remarks upon how everything changes in time:

> ἦ οὔ πω τόδε οἴδατ' ἀνὰ φρένας, ὡς ἀλεγεινοῖς
> ἀνδράσιν ἐκ καμάτοιο πέλει θαλίη τε καὶ ὄλβος,
> ἐκ δ' ἄρα λευγαλέων ἀνέμων καὶ χείματος αἰνοῦ
> Ζεὺς ἐπάγει μερόπεσσι δι' ἠέρος εὔδιον ἦμαρ,
> ἔκ τ' ὀλοῆς νούσοιο πέλει σθένος, ἔκ τε μόθοιο
> εἰρήνη; τὰ δὲ πάντα χρόνῳ μεταμείβεται ἔργα.
>
> Q.S.9.104–9

You must have realized by now that happy days and prosperity come after suffering for wretched mortals; that Zeus brings mankind clear skies after hurricanes and violent storms; and that health comes after a dangerous sickness, peace after war. All things are change in the course of time.

What begins as a familiar sort of reflection on the mutability of man's fortune in the hands of the gods and the metaphorical language of storm[53] ends by refocusing attention away from Zeus and his elements and onto

---

[53] Most famously enshrined, of course, in Odysseus' 'philosophical' speech to the suitor Amphinomus (*Od.* 18.125–54). The use of weather changes to evoke this sentiment is also a frequent tragic topos: see for instance Eurip. *HF.* 101–2; Soph. *Aj.* 670–5.

292   Temporality and the Homeric Not Yet

the more subtle, less solipsistic power of Chronos, who stands here as the un-personified, teleological and totalising agent through (or in) which all things are really transformed.

During the construction of the Wooden Horse, the narrator himself reflects on how the contraption will be an object of wonder – in more than one time:

> καί ῥά οἱ ἔργον ἔτευξεν ἐπιχθονίοισιν ἀγητὸν
> πᾶσιν, ὅσοι μιν ἴδοντο καὶ οἳ μετόπισθε πύθοντο.
>
> Q.S.12.155–6

And Athena made his work an object of wonder to all mortal men – to those who saw it and to those who heard tell of it in later times.

The brazen contradistinction between two forms of knowledge – the seeing-is-believing affirmation of οἶδα versus the learning-through-enquiry process of πυνθάνομαι –[54] on the one hand makes clear the fundamental difference between the wonder to be acquired in the future and that enjoyed in the here and now.[55] And yet such a difference in time and perspective is disoriented by the consistency of aspect: the seeing of the horse in the present *and* the learning of the future (both aorist) are, syntactically as mythologically, 'completed'. This deceptively simple sentence drives home the paradox that, thanks to the familiarity of mythology and the antiquity of literary Troy, even information designated for 'later' discovery is always already realised.

In the same scene, Zeus puts an end to divine conflict by arriving on his chariot, which was made by a particular character of Time:

> οὐ λάθον ἠὺ νόημα· λιπὼν δ' ἄφαρ Ὠκεανοῖο
> χεύματ' ἐς οὐρανὸν εὐρὺν ἀνήιε· τὸν δὲ φέρεσκον
> Εὖρος καὶ Βορέης, Ζέφυρος δ' ἐπὶ τοῖσι Νότος τε,
> τοὺς ὑπὸ θεσπέσιον ζυγὸν αἰόλος ἤγαγεν Ἶρις
> ἅρματος αἰὲν ἐόντος, ὅ οἱ κάμεν ἄμβροτος Αἰὼν
> χερσὶν ὑπ' ἀκαμάτοισιν ἀτειρέος ἐξ ἀδάμαντος.
>
> Q.S.12.190–5

Although Zeus was at the ends of the earth, they did not escape his notice. He left the streams of Ocean and ascended to the broad heaven, borne by Eurus and Boreas together with Zephyrus and Notus, brought by many-hued Iris under the divine yoke of his imperishable chariot made out of adamant by immortal Time's unwearying hands.

---

[54] See LSJ s.v. πυνθάνομαι 1–6.

[55] An initial difference also bolstered by the use of ἀγητός to denote this wonder: an adjective so often associated specifically with physical appearance and form (εἶδος). Cf. LSJ s.v. ἀγητός.

Pacing: Acceleration and Delay 293

Like the un-personified Chronos in Deiphobus' speech, Time is once again placed in a complex agential relationship with Zeus: now not only eclipsing his glory – stealing the final line in this display of power – but also cast as the architect of his ascent. Here, however, the 'Temporal Agent' is not Chronos but Aion. A word which spans archaic Greek, astrological, Orphic and Christian traditions, and whose meanings can include 'age', 'epoch', 'space of time' or (most commonly in Homer), the lifespan of an individual, Aion came increasingly to signify a broader, more all-encompassing concept: it was in the imperial period increasingly identified not with human lifetime or (like Chronos) linear time, but eternal, cyclical or seasonal time – universal and potentially *endless*.[56] We have already touched on how these capacious capacities caught the attention of one imperial poet. Aion is, as Kneebone's work has explored, widely used and heavily personified in Nonnus' *Dionysiaca*, where it plays an active role as a character in the poem. Aion, for example, is the god whose supplication of Zeus for a 'saviour' of mankind leads to the birth of Dionysus himself (*Dion.* 7.9ff.), instigating the long-awaited, twice-born hero of the poem, who himself keeps 'beginning again'.[57] Aion appears far less dramatically in the *Posthomerica*. Whilst the term is used fourteen times – once in almost every book of the poem – it is only in isolated phrases (not, like in Nonnus, lengthy descriptions and vignettes); it has fewer occurrences than Chronos; and, like Chronos in Quintus, is never fully personified.[58] And yet, just as we saw for Homeric buzzwords like *polytropos*, Nonnus' exuberance does more than show up Quintus as reluctant and conservative by contrast. By making a rare reference to Aion *here* – and, only here, with suggestive hints of a personification ('divine' epithet and human[ised] hands) which never, in this poem, becomes fleshed out to the full – Quintus suggests the significance of this more uncontainable temporal concept to this particular epic juncture. At the very point where the famous Homeric theomachy is replayed – as the *Iliad* is being 'completed'

---

[56] On the changing connotations of αἰών, see Keizer (2010). On Aion in Nonnus with wider context, see Chuvin (1972), Vian (1963): 46–51; Spanoudakis (2012); Stegemann (1930). On literary and visual representations of Aion in the imperial period, see Levi (1944); Zuntz (1988) and (1992); Porter (2013).

[57] The other appearances of Aion in Nonnus' poem are: *Dion.* 6.371–2; 12.25; 24.265–7; 25.23–4; and 38.90–5.

[58] It is used fourteen times (Q.S.2.206, 544; 3.319, 569; 5.477, 555; 6.586; 8.433; 10.341, 440; 11.485; 12.194; 14.256, 2.506), compared with eighteen instances of χρόνος (Q.S.2.344, 256; 3.479; 6.426; 7.458, 612, 630; 9.22, 109, 281; 10.23, 29, 32; 12.14, 59, 365; 14.219, 245). We return to certain of these references below; however, the present passage offers the most expansive, and literarily suggestive, use of the term in the *Posthomerica* and is thus the centre point of my comments on this topic here.

294   Temporality and the Homeric Not Yet

(with the construction of the horse) but also, through this set-piece, returned to, and done all over again – Quintus encases universal time into a singular literary moment. The scene thus provides a neat encapsulation of how the poet merges different ways of envisaging time as a force working upon his epic: Homeric back-reference, Olympian plot-determination[59] and cyclical temporality are here brought together in one sweeping allusion.

These miniature excursuses on time – expressed through the primary voice pieces of the poem, in its narrative and character speech – highlight two crucial aspects of the *Posthomerica*'s approach to epic temporality. Firstly, they suggest a deep connection between explicit discussion of time and pivotal moments in the inter-Homeric plot: time is most actively 'characterised', brought to the dramatic foreground, at narrative turning points, wartime climaxes and extreme cases of Homeric recapitulation. Secondly, they reveal Quintus' tendency to use such discussions of time to merge and muddy a number of acutely competing ideas: divine authority versus divine submission; Time humanised and personified or an external agent of momentum; the immediate experience of the present with the always-anticipated discoveries of the future. These aspects find their most expansive expression in the poem's structure, where such merging is paralleled on the largest of scales. We have seen in the previous chapter how the narrative is constructed around a particular form of episodicity. Thus, with the exception of two simultaneously occurring scenes[60] and analepses flashing back to past events, the action unfolds in a linear, straightforward manner: from hero to hero, battle to battle, the story moves with each book closer to the pre-determined fall – to achieving the narrative closure which, the opening lines lead us to assume, will come with the capture of Troy (ὡς ἤδη στονόεντι καταιθομένης πυρὶ Τροίης, Q.S.1.17). This sense of linearity, however, is set in stark contrast with another, competing vector of time: the force of delay and exhaustion, which is also pursued extensively, as the pace constantly shifts between sharp acceleration and lethargic slowing down, pausing over the inconsequential, almost grinding to a halt.

On the one hand, such variation of speed is a standard prospect in all good storytelling. The opposition of *diegesis* and *ekphrasis*, the advance of the storyline versus delay through description, is a hallmark of structuralist

---

[59] Zeus acts here to prevent the plot from losing focus on the momentum of the sack, in the way described for divine counterfactuals in section 7.3 of this chapter.
[60] The voyages to Skyros and Lemnos, in Q.S.7.169–345 and 9.353–445.

Pacing: Acceleration and Delay 295

literary criticism, and, as we have seen, is certainly at home in ancient epic. And yet as the examples of Triphiodorus, Oppian, Nonnus and Colluthus make clear, an interest in matters of pace became sharpened in later Greek mythological poetics, where it can be viewed as a means of adumbrating a storyline whose central components and ultimate outcome are otherwise far too steady – anticipated and accepted. So too for the visual poetics of the Trojan tale. The Iliac Tablets, as we have already seen, show a ludic and serious concern with temporal juxtaposition and narrative (dis)order. Thus the duplicate organisation of the Capitoline Tablet (mirrored on a number of the other fragments), both offers a single snapshot of Troy at the time of its destruction and constructs a number of other, discrete narrative moments, each unfolding in time rather than merely in space; a strategy intended to 'invite viewers to make sense of the image *both* synchronically *and* in linear sequence'.[61]

Quintus' poem does not simply offer a further example of this trend. It also offers a critical commentary *on* such techniques of visualised time and narrative movement, pursued to their extremes. Acceleration and delay are promoted to central narrative strategies in the *Posthomerica* and contraposed relentlessly. There are three areas where this tug between speed and sluggishness is at its most insistent and which also best suggest the interpretative effects of this contrast: battle scenes, prophesies and descriptions of disembodiment. Such moments become the underlying basis for comprehending Quintus' new, amalgamative approach to the models of Homeric time: our poet uses pace variation to establish his work as both strictly linear (with the sack as *telos*) *and* 'wandering and random' (with the sack not the *telos* at all). In an epic which begins with the assertion that Troy has already fallen, the blending of speed and delay works to undermine this foregone sense of closure, as the poem uses its very structure to begin to interrogate both sides of the 'dichotomy' of epic time.

The heroic battle is the perfect stage for the dramatisation of pacing. In the successive series of duels, Quintus centralises competing notions of balance and unevenness: the warriors seem at certain points to be completely matched in their prowess and at others to be entirely uneven – one destined inevitably to triumph over the other. This oscillation is of course another common feature of epic battle descriptions,[62] but it

---

[61] Squire (2011): 163.
[62] The dizzying chases between Achilles and Hector (*Il.* 22.130–305) and Aeneas and Turnus (*Aen.* 12.697–918) are among the most famous examples. For discussions of the technique in Quintus, see Duckworth (1936) and Schmitz (2007b).

296 Temporality and the Homeric Not Yet

becomes especially pronounced in the *Posthomerica*, where it also maps closely onto ideas of narrative speed. Each fight can be read as both swift and quickly resolved, with a predetermined endpoint shown by the obviously superior fighter, and, in the moments where things seem to be evenly matched and static, as elongated and capable of dragging on interminably. In this sense, the individual battles can provide miniature visions of the Trojan War itself: the epic subject which, as Quintus' opening shows, has already been won, but is also continually reiterated and stretched back out.

The extended standoff between Achilles and Memnon once again provides a clear example of this strategy.[63] Memnon's arrival includes a proleptic reference to his impending defeat:

> ὣς φάθ'· ὃ δ' ἐκ δόρποιο μεθίστατο· βῆ δὲ πρὸς εὐνὴν
> ὑστατίην. ...
>
> Q.S.2.161–2

With these words he rose from the meal and went to bed – for the last time.

This type of fatalistic forward glance is also perfectly common in epic.[64] But here it is used specifically to mark as especially 'pointless' the drawn-out battle to come: a battle which, as we have seen, goes on to be narrated in the most eye-wateringly elongated terms – including with the longest cluster simile in the entire epic. In the confrontation itself (Q.S.2.458–513) terms for evenness, balance and equality abound: ἀμφοτέροισι, πολλάκις..., ἄμφω...; ἀπειρέσιον πονέεσθαι/δῆριν ἀνὰ στονόεσσαν· Ἄρης δ' οὐ λῆγε φόνοιο, set in contrast with competing words for speed (e.g. θοῶς, 509). This contrast is continued through digression. Whilst the Olympians look on and take sides (another manifestation of balance), the narrative breaks off into a vista of zodiac constellations:

> δεῖδιε δ' Ἠριγένεια φίλῳ περὶ παιδὶ καὶ αὐτὴ
> ἵπποις ἐμβεβαυῖα δι' αἰθέρος· αἳ δέ οἱ ἄγχι
> Ἠελίοιο θύγατρες ἐθάμβεον ἑστηυῖαι
> θεσπέσιον περὶ κύκλον, ὃν Ἠελίῳ ἀκάμαντι
> Ζεὺς πόρεν εἰς ἐνιαυτὸν ἐὺν δρόμον, ᾧ περὶ πάντα
> ζώει τε φθινύθει τε περιπλομένοιο κατ' ἦμαρ
> νωλεμέως αἰῶνος ἑλισσομένων ἐνιαυτῶν.
>
> Q.S.2.500–6

---

[63] Cf. the discussions of this passage in Chapters 5 and 6.

[64] As displayed, e.g. the prolepses of this sort discussed for Penthesilea, Memnon and Eurypylus in Chapter 6.

Pacing: Acceleration and Delay 297

The daughters of the sun, her companions, stood amazed in that sacred circle which Zeus gave to tireless Helius for his noble yearly course, and which controls all that lives and perishes, as day by day time slowly progresses and the years go round.

As the stalemate is finally broken, and the 'endless' fight is about to come to an end (Zeus 'speedily' dispatches the heroes' two fates, Q.S.2.507–13), our attention is focused on an image which offers an analogous expression of the competing types of time in this scene: unstoppable linearity versus unending, universal cyclicality. The linearity comes in the first instance through the teleological life of man: the phrase πάντα ζώει τε φθινύθει contains the whole progression of human life – from start to end – soon to be completed in the mortal battle at hand. And yet, as with all Quintan language, the statement gains further dimensions from its embedded Homeric inheritance. The overall sentiment is, of course, highly reminiscent of Glaucus' speech to Diomedes in the *Iliad*, and its (in)famous simile about the progression of mankind:[65]

> οἵη περ φύλλων γενεὴ τοίη δὲ καὶ ἀνδρῶν.
> φύλλα τὰ μέν τ' ἄνεμος χαμάδις χέει, ἄλλα δέ θ' ὕλη
> τηλεθόωσα φύει, ἔαρος δ' ἐπιγίγνεται ὥρη·
> ὡς ἀνδρῶν γενεὴ ἣ μὲν φύει ἣ δ' ἀπολήγει.
>
> *Il.* 6.146–9

Like the generations of leaves are those of men. The wind blows and one year's leaves are scattered on the ground, but the trees bud and fresh leaves open when spring comes again. So a generation of men is born as another passes away.

Refracted through this Iliadic sentiment – left unelaborated in Quintus' sentence (there are just general 'things' [πάντα], not races; there is no explicitly replenishing imagery, no nature simile) – the phrase also bespeaks a cyclical quality: as one race of men passes away, another springs up in its place, so that the teleology inherent in the ending of one life is overcome by the pluralistic, circular rejuvenations of the races yet to come.

This cyclic essence is bolstered by the heavy emphasis on circles on all levels of the passage: both the overall shape which the description narrates – the circle of the sun occupied by the Heliades, also outlined in Aratus' *Phaenomena* (544–52) and which occurs again later in this book of the

---

[65] That Quintus' line evokes this famous Iliadic simile, despite a lack of direct verbal mirroring and the condensed nature of the thought, is both clear from the context – remarking gnomically on the transience-cum-renewal of human life in the heat of a battle – and in keeping with Quintus' general policy of employing multiple methods of Homeric engagement (see Chapter 1.10, for this policy outlined in full).

298 Temporality and the Homeric Not Yet

Posthomerica (2.594–62), where the seasons too are described explicitly in terms of their association with the circle – and the image of the κύκλος, the rolling years. Another mention of Aion acts as a hinge between the twofold types of motion – the straight line and the circle – at play here. The term, accompanied here by the harsh, almost bitter adverb νωλεμέως seems on the surface to be deployed in a more 'conventional', archaic-Homeric sense: directly applied to man's life through to death, relentlessly passing through. However, read in conjunction with other, more elaborate appearances of Aion – such as his later, quasi-personified role as the craftsman of Zeus' chariot – this choice of time-term also hints at its more cyclical, 'imperial' connotations: endless time too can be relentless in its force. The 'shape' of this vista, and the 'interminable' battle which the digression further stretches out, thus encapsulates many of the linear *and* non-linear qualities of Quintan poetics – his own exhortation to his readers to 'make sense of his story *both* synchronically *and* in linear sequence'[66] – and drives these features into explicit textual contact.[67]

Heroic death provides another, brutal means of visualising pace in the poem, most notably the death of Achilles – the thematically drastic but mythically inevitable removal of the *Iliad*'s central hero (Q.S.3.60–177). Shot by Apollo's arrow, Achilles falls at once, with framing adverbs for swiftness, aorist verbs of completion, and a simile denoting total collapse:

> ἠέρα δ᾽ ἐσσάμενος στυγερὸν προέηκε βέλεμνον
> καί ἑ θοῶς οὔτησε κατὰ σφυρόν· αἶψα δ᾽ ἀνῖαι
> δῦσαν ὑπὸ κραδίην· ὃ δ᾽ ἀνετράπετ᾽ ἠύτε πύργος,
> ὅν τε βίη τυφῶνος ὑποχθονίη στροφάλιγγι
> ῥήξῃ ὑπὲρ δαπέδοιο κραδαινομένης βαθὺ γαίης·
> ὣς ἐκλίθη δέμας ἠὺ κατ᾽ οὔδεος Αἰακίδαο.
>
> Q.S.3.61–6

And cloaked in this way in mist Apollo loosened a bitter arrow which struck him straight on the ankle. At once agony entered his heart; he fell backward like a tower razed to the ground by the force of a subterranean whirlwind which makes the earth quake in its depths: just so the noble figure of Aeacides collapsed on the ground. He stared all about him and gave a terrible cry.

---

[66] *Qua* Squire (2011): 163 of the Iliac Tablets, as discussed above in this section.
[67] Other passages useful for cross-comparison in this regard include Q.S.8.133–220 – where Neoptolemus and Euryalus fight with an evenness similar to that found here (see discussion of this passage in Chapter 6) – and the boxing match at Q.S.4.215–83, which offers a 'comic' miniature of the same dynamics.

Pacing: Acceleration and Delay

The simile (ἠΰτε πύργος...63) also contains a prolepsis – the reference to a tower points forwards to the ultimate destruction of Troy –[68] which encourages a connection between the categorical death of this hero and the 'finality' of the fall.

This is, however, a false *telos*. Immediately after he is struck, Achilles speaks (68–83) and refers back, as we have seen, to the Iliadic prophecy at the Scaean gates. This recollection on the one hand serves as a reminder of the inevitability of the hero's early death, prescribed and predicted in the earlier literary tradition (a tradition here marked as τὸ πάροιθε, 80). However, on the other hand, it paradoxically provides a means of delaying this death, through the very narrative time taken up by giving this speech. Though dying, Achilles still finds time to allude to the *Iliad*, pausing to resurrect conversations from the literary 'before'. What is more, the Iliadic prophecy to which he refers predicted that he would be killed 'by Paris *and* Phoebus Apollo' (*Il.* 22.359). In the surprise created by the absence of Paris here, the forward onslaught of the plot is derailed by this disorientating literary misdirection.

The sense of suspension continues in the second phase of the episode, as the narrative lens shifts to a conversation between an incensed Hera and the recalcitrant Apollo (Q.S.3.91–138). Hera's rebuke of the god for what he has done suspends Achilles' death still more to look further backwards – to the wedding of Peleus – and yet also to propel everything forwards, as her speech also foretells the imminent arrival of Neoptolemus (υἱὸς ἀπὸ Σκύροιο θοῶς ἐς ἀπηνέα δῆριν/Ἀργείοις ἐπαρωγὸς ἐλεύσεται εἴκελος ἀλκὴν/πατρὶ ἑῷ... 120–2). She thereby predicts the next phase of the Quintan process of hasty heroic substitution, but by discussing this arrival, she also delays the reader from reaching the point in the narrative where this process is fulfilled.

Achilles then steals the narrative space back: in the half-line at 138 he reasserts himself into the very syntax of the poem:

> κρύβδ' Ἥρης· πάντες γὰρ ἐναντίον Οὐρανίωνες
> ἅζοντ' ἀσχαλόωσαν. ὃ δ' οὔ πω λήθετο θυμοῦ
> Πηλείδης·...
>
> Q.S.3.137–9

They hid their feelings from Hera, since all the gods in heaven feel awe in her presence when she is out of temper. The son of Peleus, meanwhile, had not yet forgotten his warlike spirit...

---

[68] For Troy's frequent association with towers, see discussion in Chapter 4.

300   Temporality and the Homeric Not Yet

As he rages on, a simile compares him to a lion struck by a shaft (...εὐτελέοντος/ἀγρόταιἐνξυλόχοισιτεθηπότες) Q.S.3.142–3. Lions, of course, are one of the most frequent Homeric comparanda for Achilles, used in the *Iliad* to emphasise both his fearsome violence and his swift-footed speed. The simile during the interview with Priam links these two characteristics directly. As his *mēnis* is momentarily reignited, Achilles is described as lionlike in his leap:

> ὣς ἔφατ', ἔδεισεν δ' ὁ γέρων καὶ ἐπείθετο μύθῳ.
> Πηλεΐδης δ' οἴκοιο λέων ὣς ἆλτο θύραζε...
>
> *Il.* 24.571–2

The old king, gripped by fear, was silent. Then like a lion the son of Peleus sprang up like a lion outside of the tent.

In Quintus' comparison, Achilles has shifted from the hunted lion to the wounded prey but as the main narrative resumes, we find reminders of his former agility: the lion in the vehicle and the language in the tenor come together to evoke the Achilles of *Iliad* 24:[69]

> ὣς ἄρα Πηλείδαο χόλος καὶ λοίγιον ἕλκος
> θυμὸν ἄδην ὀρόθυνε· θεοῦ δέ μιν ἰὸς ἐδάμνα.
> ἀλλὰ καὶ ὣς ἀνόρουσε καὶ ἔνθορε δυσμενέεσσι...
>
> Q.S.3.147–9

Just so Pelides' wrath and his fatal wound were enough to rouse his warlike spirit. Gradually the god's arrow was taking effect; but even so he leaped up and sprang on the foe brandishing his mighty spear.

As his limbs finally grow cold, still Achilles lingers on (164–9). His *thumos* ebbs away (ἀπήιε θυμός, 164), a slow, eked-out withdrawal, in contrast to the crashing fall of the opening of the scene. He also speaks even more (167–9), threatening the Trojans and continuing the fear which caused their paralysis at the poem's opening. Like the zodiac digression during the battle with Memnon, Achilles' death sits awkwardly and pointedly in the middle of two modes of narrative pace: he is rewound and raced forward with disorienting simultaneity.

In his own poetics of delay, Oppian plays a comparable game with frustration and finality. His story's frightening heroic monster – the gargantuan κῆτος – is brought down by the skill of the human fishers in the closing book of the poem, where building language of termination (the

---

[69] This provides another example of Quintus' techniques of refocusing Homeric similes as outlined in Chapter 3.

Pacing: Acceleration and Delay

death is described explicitly as a μόρου τέλος, [*Hal.* 5.293], and the fishers sing a paean of victory [*Hal.* 5.294], as though the 'war' is over) encourages the reader to elide the end of this creature with the end of the epic: the poem, it seems, will crash out with it.

However, Oppian also works to extend the episode beyond this expected and anticipated endpoint, as the κῆτος killed but still, still does not *die* and ultimately undercuts this episode's status as the *telos* of the epic:

> ...ἀλλ' ὅτε χέρσῳ
> ἐμπελάσῃ, τότε δή μιν ἐτήτυμος ὦρσεν ὄλεθρος
> λοίσθιος ἀσπαίρει τε διαξαίνει τε θάλασσαν
> σμερδαλέαις πτερύγεσσιν, ἅτ' εὐτύκτῳ περὶ βωμῷ
> ὄρνις ἑλισσομένη θανάτου στροφάλιγγι κελαινῇ.
>
> *Hal.* 5.304–8

But when he comes near the land, then real and final destruction urges him on, and he struggles and lashes the sea with his terrible fins, like a bird upon the well-built altar tossing in the dark struggle of death.

> πλῆσεν δ' ἠόνα πᾶσαν ὑπ' ἀπλάτοις μελέεσσι
> κεκλιμένοις, τέταται δὲ νέκυς ῥίγιστος ἰδέσθαι.
> τοῦ μέν τις φθιμένοιο καὶ ἐν χθονὶ πεπταμένοιο
> εἰσέτι δειμαίνει πελάσαι δυσδερκέϊ νεκρῷ
> ταρβεῖ τ' οὐκέτ' ἐόντα καὶ οἰχομένοιό περ ἔμπης...
>
> *Hal.* 5.317–21

Even when he is killed and laid upon the land they still dread to approach his corpse, dreadful to see, and fear him when he is no more.

The parallels here with Quintus' dying Achilles are striking. Oppian's monster also rails against a death which has been categorically dispensed to it. And the fear induced by its corpse mirrors the Trojan's reaction to Achilles' body after his final collapse (seeing the dead monster fills the humans with dread [*Hal.* 5.318] just as seeing the dying Achilles torments the Trojans: οἱ δ' ἔτι θυμῷ/δήιοι εἰσορόωντες ἀπειρέσιον τρομέεσκον Q.S.3.179–80). Now, it has often been suggested that the *Posthomerica* shows some knowledge of Oppian's sea poem. Baumbach and Bär, as we have seen, emphasise three allusions to the *Halieutica* to strengthen the likelihood of a first century *terminus post quem* for its date of composition.[70] Kneebone, draws attention specifically to the Oppianic quality of one of Quintus' 'more unusual' similes on fishing (Q.S.7.569–95), which become a vehicle for expressing the night-time

---

[70] Baumbach and Bär (2007): 3, as discussed in Chapter 1.7.

302 Temporality and the Homeric Not Yet

subterfuge of the *dolos* needed to win the war.[71] The temporal moves shared by these scenes surely suggest a more dynamic interconnection between the two works. Reading the Oppianic κῆτος *as* a symbol for protracted epic death, Quintus elevates these techniques to central poetic importance at this stage of his plot, using them for a character whose death most strongly indicates a move away from the *Iliad* into a new heroic space. The Homeric hero of speed, and the paradigmatic figure of delay (who spends eighteen books of the *Iliad* refusing to fight and begins this epic delayed into battle, loitering around Patroclus' tomb), is in his final moments transformed by Quintus into an expression of both of these forces at once, revealing how they are put to work together in this epic.

However, this connection also highlights a number of moments in Oppian's sequence which themselves seem more suited to a blazing battlefield than a fishing trip at sea. Once the κῆτος is eventually brought down, the victory song of its conquerors (οἱ δὲ μέγαν νίκης παιήονα κυδαίνοντες, *Hal.* 5.294) elevates the killing of this fish to a military conquest – they sing just as Herodotus' Perinthians sing (Herod. 5.1.3) and Thucydides' Peloponnesians sing (Thuc. 2.91); and just as the jubilant Greeks in the *Posthomerica* sing, once Troy is finally laid low:

Ἀργεῖοι δ᾽ ἐπὶ νῆας ἔβαν μέγα καγχαλόωντες
μέλποντες Νίκης ἐρικυδέος ὄβριμον ἀλκήν.
Q.S.14.85–6

The Argives went to their ships in great exultation, now celebrating in song the might and power of glorious Victory.

Just as Achilles resembles the κῆτος, so too, through the re-harnessed language of battle song, does Oppian's κῆτος look proleptically Quintan. By removing the rigid linearity so inherent, as we have seen, in traditional schemes of intertextuality, but inadequate for assessing the modes of engagement in these 'difficult' imperial texts,[72] we can place Quintus' Achilles and Oppian's whale into a provocative diptych. Their narrative techniques produce a mutually enriching conversation, which bespeaks a shared interest in exploiting the connection between narrative closure and poetic protraction – as the thrashing in the sea helps to construct the stretched-out liminality of Achilles' last monstrous moments of epic life.

Against this sense of delay, however, Quintus sets the equal and opposite force: an acute acceleration past events of potentially critical importance to the plot. After the death of Paris, the narrative shifts to another

---

[71] Kneebone (2007): 285–306.   [72] See the intertextual methodology outlined in Chapter 1.10.

Pacing: Acceleration and Delay

celestial vista (Q.S.10.334–443). The maidens of Hera discuss events which are to take place in the near future, conveyed to the reader via reported speech (343–60): the marriage of Helen to Deiphobus; Helenus' jealous rage; how the Achaeans will capture Helenus, and how Diomedes and Odysseus will scale the walls of Troy; the subsequent death of Alcathus; and finally the theft of the Palladium, the image 'which had protected the city and the people' (354).[73]

These events are later marked by Quintus as highly significant to the story which the *Posthomerica* is telling. As Menelaus hacks his way through Troy, he encounters Deiphobus in bed with Helen and takes revenge on the marriage which was predicted by these very prophecies (Q.S.13.354–73). The Palladium's importance for the capture of Troy is confirmed when Odysseus sets out his plan for the *dolos* of the horse (Q.S.12.25–45). He suggests that the appeasement of Athena's anger will provide the excuse for offering the gift to the Trojans:

> ὅς τις ὑποκρίναιτο βίην ὑπέροπλον Ἀχαιῶν
> ῥέξαι ὑπὲρ νόστοιο λιλαιομένων ὑπαλύξαι,
> ἵππῳ ὑποπτήξας εὐεργέι τόν ῥ’ ἐκάμοντο
> Παλλάδι χωομένῃ Τρώων ὕπερ αἰχμητάων·
>
> Q.S.12.35–9

He is to say that the Achaeans wanted to sacrifice him in return for reaching home, but that he escaped their brutal violence by hiding underneath that well-made horse, which they had put together with much effort to appease Pallas' anger on behalf of the spearmen of Troy.

The remark makes implicit allusion, as is stated more directly in Vergil's *Aeneid* (2.162–88), to the theft of the Palladium which triggered her rage in the first place. The gap, however, between the maidens' prophecies and their narrative fulfilment is left starkly open. The events are subjected to a leap in time: foretold in the future during this celestial conversation, they then move immediately into the past tense. Athena has already been made angry by the time Odysseus gives his speech, and when Menelaus enters Troy, Deiphobus and Helen are already married, found in bed together before revenge is taken. Quintus thus denies these turning points a place in his primary narration. This 'curious' situation,[74] in which crucial events

---

[73] As James (2004): 321 notes, all of these events, except the killing of Alcathus which is not otherwise attested, were included in the *Little Iliad*, but not in the same order, nor (so far as we can tell) as a connected sequence. What interests me here is not that Quintus includes these well-known events, but how he includes them, as part of his poetics of pacing.

[74] Duckworth (1936): 65. He notes that there are no such extensive unfulfilled forecasts in Homer, Apollonius or Vergil (cf. ibid. 1933).

304 Temporality and the Homeric Not Yet

are forecast and foreshadowed but *not* narratively fulfilled, has long perplexed Quintan commentators. Some have suggested that a lacuna must be
the answer: these moments were surely described by Quintus, but a long
passage has fallen out after Book 11.[75] For others, the explanation lies not
in corruption but incompetence: in line with the conventional down-
playing of Quintus' skills in poetic decision-making, these lines represent
'a summary of events that Quintus thought unwise to incorporate at
length in a poem already growing too long'.[76] Such solutions attempt to
smooth out a moment of temporal texturing which is in fact motivated
and marked, emphatically abstract and tellingly indirect. Like Homer
himself in his Odyssean bardic songs, Quintus knows that the best way
to include 'crucial' cyclic information is to *report* another 'author' telling it.
In light of the text's wider interest in varying storytelling speed, the
'omission' of these prophesised events ought to be read as a crucial, self-
reflexive manoeuvre on the part of the poet's voice.

The poetics of acceleration in later Greek epic, as we have seen, is
usually and most predominantly associated with the epyllion. As is revealed
in Colluthus' compression of the major facts of the Paris myth, or
Triphiodorus' amusingly explicit sense of haste, the 'little epic' form well
accommodates discussions of speed, methods of condensing and shifting
perspectives. This prophecy sequence in Quintus – suggests that these ideas
also find voice in his larger-scale project. Whilst for Triphiodorus speed is *the*
programmatic statement of authorial agenda, in the *Posthomerica* the concept
of rushing is worked to achieve a different, more contrastive effect. The fact
that the narrative zooms past such major events throws even more emphasis
on just how drawn-out other moments of the story are (the pointless battle,
the slow death of swift Achilles). Working together, these alternative impulses
help to create the varied temporal texture of the poem, where speed *and*
delay, linearity and circumvention both claim a driving role.

The final aspect of this texture shows how these two types of pace can be
more jarringly juxtaposed. Immediately before the turning point of the
horse ruse, Quintus dedicates an entire book to the continued fighting
between the Trojans and Greeks (Q.S.11). This is a section of the epic
where, in one sense, many things happen. The Trojans are roused by
Apollo (139), one of only two times a god talks directly to mortals in the
poem.[77] Aeneas is snatched away from harm (289–97), while Odysseus
attempts to break the stalemate by inventing a new weapon formation

---

[75] Thus Kehmptzow (1891): 39–41 supported by Duckworth (1936): 66.   [76] Paschal (1904): 77.

[77] The only other instance is the hubristic exchange with Achilles of Q.S.3.40–59.

Pacing: Acceleration and Delay

(358–414) – two loaded moments of intervention to whose significance we shall later return. And the Greek soldier Alcimedon climbs the Trojan wall and gets within peeping distance of the city (446–73), coming desperately close, like the Iliadic Patroclus (*Il.* 16.698–72), to pushing forward the Greek attack. In another sense, however, nothing happens at all. These points of action are foiled by equal and stagnating reactions. Neoptolemus is kept away from Aeneas; Odysseus' plan is categorically foiled; and Alcimedon, again mirroring the brutal end to Patroclus' wall-scaling story, is killed before completing his climb.

This is a book based on stasis; the action stands us still. We know that the sack is coming, that the *dolos* is around the narrative corner, a fact stressed at the opening of the following book, as Calchas cries μηκέτι πὰρ τείχεσσιν ἐφεζόμενοι πονέεσθε,/ἀλλ᾽ ἄλλην τινὰ μῆτιν ἐνὶ φρεσὶ μητιάασθε/ ἢ δόλον δόλον (Q.S.12.8–10). And yet despite such assertions of momentum, in this sequence we are made to indulge the feeling of endlessness, as delay is promoted to the dominant component of the narrative. The language itself is filled with terms for both stoppage and acceleration. The battle is repeatedly described as endless (μάχη δ᾽ οὐ λῆγε φόνοιο, (4); ...οἱ δ᾽ οὔτι κακοῦ παύοντο μόθοιο, (162); ἑκάτερθε ἴσην ἐτάνυσσεν Ἐνυὼ ὑσμίνην... (237–8); ἀλλὰ καὶ ὡς μάρναντο (251)); but Aeneas is also snatched away quickly (ἥρπασεν ἐσσυμένως, 291), the Argives leap with fast fury (ἐν γάρ σφιν θήρεσσιν ἐοικότες ὠμοβόροισιν/ἔνθορον Ἀργεῖοι μέγα μαιμώωντες Ἄρηι 300–1) and slaughtered warriors die at once (ταχὺς δ᾽ ἄμ᾽ ἀπέπτατο θυμός, 59). This contrast concentrates the lexical tensions between speed and lethargy found in the earlier scenes of the poem, and enacts on the level of language the characters' thwarted attempts to break the stalemate, as the narrative resists its own attempts to hurry on.

Delay is also expressed in this book through the image of disembodiment. On four occasions, Quintus describes body parts bluntly severed from their owners, but which retain signs of life. Nirus' tongue is cut clean from his jaw (πέρησε, 28, another aorist completed verb),[78] but it still 'speaks with a human voice' (γλῶσσάν τ᾽ αὐδήεσσαν, 29). A Trojan soldier Pyrasos is deprived of his head, which rolls away still eager to talk (κάρη δ᾽ ἀπάτερθε κυλινδομένη πεφόρητο/φωνῆς ἱεμένοιο... 58–9). The arm of Hellos is sliced off, but it wants to carry on working (70–8). And most elaborately, an anonymous Argive (τις Ἀργείων, 184) is killed by

---

[78] Cf. Q.S.3.62–6.

306 Temporality and the Homeric Not Yet

Agenor, but when his body falls over his horse, a hand remains attached to the reins:

> ...βίη δ' ὑπόειξε σιδήρου
> ὀστέον οὐταμένοιο βραχίονος· ἀμφὶ δὲ νεῦρα
> ῥηιδίως ἤμησε· φλέβες δ' ὑπερέβλυσαν αἷμα·
> ἀμφεχύθη δ' ἵπποιο κατ' αὐχένος, αἶψα δ' ἄρ' αὐτὸς
> κάππεσεν ἀμφὶ νέκυς<σι>· λίπε<ν> δ' ἄρα χεῖρα κραταιὴν
> στερρὸν ἔτ' ἐμπεφυυῖαν ἐυγνάμπτοιο χαλινοῦ,
> οἵον ὅτε ζώοντος ἔην· μέγα δ' ἔπλετο θαῦμα,
> οὕνεκα δὴ ῥυτῆρος ἀπεκρέμαθ' αἱματόεσσα
> Ἄρεος ἐννεσίῃσι φόβον δηίοισι φέρουσα·
> φαίης κεν χατέουσαν ἔθ' ἱππασίης πονέεσθαι·
> σῆμα δέ μιν φέρεν ἵππος ἀποκταμένοιο ἄνακτος.
>
> Q.S.11.190–200

The bone of his wounded arm yielded to the iron's force; the surrounding tendons were easily cut through; and the veins gushed out copious blood. He collapsed over his horse's neck; then his body fell among the dead, leaving his stout hand firmly gripping the curved bit just as it did while he was alive: it was a shocking sight, this bloody arm dangling from the reins, Ares' way of frightening the foe. You would have thought it was still at work and wanting horsemanship; and the horse bore it along as a sign of its murdered master.

Here again the agency of anatomical parts is emphasised, but this is agency of a different sort to the eager tongue and severed arm. The Argive's hand only *seems* to be living still (οἵη ἔτι ζώοντος ἔην); it is the object of analogy and comparison (φαίης κεν); and its real destiny is to become a cause of wonderment and a σῆμα of its master.[79] The gruesome relic of the hand thus commemorates an otherwise insignificant character and grants him lasting space in this book of inaction.

Such disembodied imagery has clear epic precedent. Heads roll on the point of speaking in many Iliadic *aristeiai*;[80] and during the Odyssean battle in the banquet-hall, the suitor Antinous is struck down 'on the point of raising the wine goblet to his lips' (*Od.* 22.8–12). It was also a markedly popular subject in imperial rhetorical culture. Polemo, for example, gives an extended, gruesome description of the hand of a Greek soldier which remains attached to a ship after it has been cut off.[81] However, even as

---

[79] A proleptic echo is created here with the Wooden Horse, later also described, as we have seen in 7.2, as a commemorative monument.

[80] Particularly those of *Iliad* 5 (e.g. Aeneas' sliced hip-skin at *Il.* 5.304–10).

[81] Polemo, *Declamation* 1: 10–11, in Reader (1996): 104–5. On Quintus' relationship to this rhetorical culture, see Chapter 2.

Pacing: Acceleration and Delay 307

versions of such topoi, Quintus' severed parts focus particularly acutely on the paradoxes of detachment and remaining, and this duality can help to express the pace that his epic is concerned with establishing. The immediacy of instant dismemberment is set against the expansion of time produced by the parts' continued half-life, which forms an index of the competing drives towards closure which characterise the wider plotting.

The final lines of the book encapsulate these drives:

> νωλεμέως· οὐ γάρ τι κακοῦ παύοντο μόθοιο·
> οὐδέ σφιν μάλα δηρὸν ὑπ᾽ Ἄρεϊ τειρομένοισιν
> ἔσκε λύσις καμάτοιο· πόνος δ᾽ ἄπρηκτος ὀρώρει.
>
> Q.S.11.499–501

Long (this all continued). They never ceased from that cruel conflict, and for a lengthy period they toiled without relief, worn down by Ares: all their efforts were in vain.

Lusis, as we have seen, can evoke the Aristotelian term for the resolution of plot, and was used in this sense by Triphiodorus to kick-start the accelerative tone of his epic. By ending this sequence by *denying* such a *lusis*, Quintus makes a claim instead for the benefits of slowing down. This book without resolution asserts an agenda which will incorporate moments of haste into a more expansive, meandering vision.

In this light, we can add a second act to our imperial Greek epic conversation on time. We have seen in Chapter 1 how the direction of influence between Quintus and Triphiodorus has been much debated by scholars. Here once again, we can see how eschewing the tight constraints of chronological linearity best unlocks the interactive possibilities on display. If the *Posthomerica is* the earlier poem, then by commencing his relentlessly fast epyllion with a pronounced pledge to *lusis*, could Triphiodorus be dismissing not only large-scale traditional epic, but also Quintus' time-taking re-telling? Or, if *The Sack of Troy* comes first, then does Quintus kick back against the obsessive 'resolution' of the epyllionic mode, using the interminable battle of Book 11 (after more verses than any 'little epic' would reach) to reinstitute some breathing space into epic battle narrative? Whichever way the dialogue works (and it does, tellingly, 'work' *both ways*), we can perceive how in their treatment of pace, these two Trojan poets operate in a dynamic interrelation, one which suggests not only direct flows of influence, but also *conceptual* nodes of engagement: diverse, but related, assertions, experiments and concerns. This imperial Greek temporal conversation, thus construed, can also be an *agōn*.

308 Temporality and the Homeric Not Yet

We have so far explored the means by which Quintus charts his preoccupation with issues of time and persistently fuses two different methods of shaping it. Through so doing, we have perceived in these methods the deeply running connections between pacing and plot. Acceleration is used to gesture towards the teleological and linear style of his story – the closure of the sack that has already happened, the certainty of what happens next – and delay works to gesture away from it – towards the wandering, cyclic, or interminable nature of some of the moments within this story pattern. These two vectors thus establish the wide-ranging temporal perspective of the poem. In a self-declared Iliadic continuation (εὖτε... 1.1), which both serves as a prequel to and post-dates the *Odyssey*, this is a narrative texture which insists on confronting what it means to put off the inevitable, a question essential for expanding a literary space whose boundaries are strictly established and known.

This particular take on narrative time is crucial grounding for constructing the 'temporality' of Quintus' *poetic* position. We now move to consider how these techniques are related by Quintus to Homeric epic itself. If, as I began this chapter by discussing, the *Iliad* is seen as the characteristic 'tightly controlled' plot, which marks its end-game strongly, and the *Odyssey* is viewed as its alternative narrative form, whose end-game (also definitely present) is delayed by the seemingly 'aimless' deferrals of adventure; and if many epics expressed their ideological positions by drawing on these epics *as* contrasting ways of figuring time, then Quintus must work to establish both forms as a constitutive part of *the same* Homeric text. There are three specific markers which reveal how he achieves this mammoth task, each of which indicates how the *Posthomerica* combines the temporality found in the *Iliad* and the *Odyssey,* and affirms its own position as a connective between these two story-worlds and the political significations which they convey.

7.3 Straining: Plot Control and the Counterfactual

The device of hypothetical narration has long been recognised as a key technique for analysing alternatives, of exploring different options within teleological story-types. In historical interpretation, as Kennedy argues, the practice of asking 'what if. . .?' ('What if the Emperor Trajan had exploited the steam technology available to him?'[82]), far from being the marginal exercise it is often taken to be, can be central to challenging deterministic

---

[82] Kennedy (2013): 120, who cites this 'elegant' example from Morley (2000).

Straining: Plot Control and the Counterfactual 309

perspectives which underlie mainstream methodologies and form: if the behaviour of historical actors itself is seen already to have a narrative aspect, then even within deterministic systems, specific initial conditions can soon give rise to unpredictable outcomes, so that the shape of historical disclosure suddenly begins to look *non-linear*.[83] In epic, this flirtation with non-linearity can be put to particular and powerful use. When Homer describes how, if Patroclus had indeed scaled the wall of Troy and had not been stopped by Apollo, the Greeks might have taken the city there and then (*Il.* 16.698–712), he flirts with a feat which the audience knows would have short-circuited both Achilles' glory and the recognised mythology surrounding the sack. The counterfactual thus reveals a delicate balance between the glimpse of an opportunity to revolutionise the epic world – by fundamentally changing the plot – and the inevitable prevention of such change by, for example, the gods.[84] It articulates, above all, as Wohl puts it, 'a past that has not happened'.[85]

Quintus makes extensive use of the counterfactual. There are thirty-seven counterfactual scenarios in total,[86] almost all marked with the specific lexical tag εἰ μή. These involve a wide range of 'control agents'[87] – forces which intervene to prevent the alternative scenario from being actualised: the gods, fate, night, mist and even human characters. This range and density suggest a particular significance of the device for this poetics. Through the opportunity to display the seams of a plot decision, to mark the alternative routes that the narrative has not taken, the counterfactual provides the perfect prism for Quintus to gesture towards a more aggressive uprooting of the literary tradition, all the while

---

[83] Kennedy (2013), ch. 4, especially 119–20 (whence the quotations come). Kennedy here is channelling Ferguson (1997): 1–90, who discusses and analyses the recent penchant for 'counterfactual history' (see the two volumes of counterfactual essays, *What If?* and *More What If?* Cowley (2001) and (2002), which tackle topics such as 'what if Pontius Pilate had spared Jesus?' and (an unsurprising and cliched favourite) 'what if the Nazis had won?'). Ferguson (1997): 76–9 interestingly, relates his notion of non-linearity enshrined in the counterfactual to what he sees as its counterpart: chaos theory in physics.

[84] On this process, see the excellent potted discussion by Chaudhuri (2014): 25.

[85] Wohl (2014) e.g. 146. The introduction to Wohl's volume provides an engaging synthesis of the literature – ancient and modern – on the device of the counterfactual and its complex relationship to concepts of hypotheticality from rhetoric, centrally, *to eikos*.

[86] Q.S.1.447–9; 2.305–7; 2.689–91; 2.775–81; 3.25–30; 3.366–8; 3.752–5; 4.563–6; 5.353–64; 5.500–2; 6.422–4; 6.503–6; 6.542–4; 6.570–3; 6.644–8; 7.28–30; 7.142–4; 7.626–30; 8.237–41; 8.340–58; 8.427–30; 9.151–5; 9.255–9; 9.304–23; 9.398–45; 10.103–6; 11.238–42; 11.255–60; 11.273–82; 11.293–5; 11.457–61; 12.93–102; 12.394–8; 13.385–415; 14.419–21; 14.580–1. All marked with εἰ μή except 6.422–4 (=οὐδ᾿ εἴ τοι); 9.304–23; 11.238–42; 11.273–82; 11.293–5. There are, by comparison, sixty-five such clauses (with the εἰ μή marker) in the *Iliad* and *Odyssey* combined and sixteen in Apollonius' *Argonautica*.

[87] Phrase from Lowe (2000): 54.

310 Temporality and the Homeric Not Yet

maintaining the dictates of that tradition, by pointing to his ultimate adherence to the 'rules' laid down by the two parts of Homer's canon.

Let us consider the examples which reveal this process working at its most sustained and self-conscious. In the lead up to his suicide, Ajax contemplates charging at the Argives and taking revenge on Odysseus. The fulfilment of this plan is prevented by Athena:

> καὶ τὰ μὲν ὥς ὥρμαινε, τὰ δὴ τάχα πάντ' ἐτέλεσσεν,
> εἰ μή οἱ Τριτωνὶς ἀάσχετον ἔμβαλε λύσσαν·
>
> Q.S.5.359–60

He would have quickly carried out the result of his deliberations if Tritonis had not afflicted him with irresistible madness.

As is dramatised devastatingly on the tragic stage, Ajax is a hero deeply associated with the counterfactual. What he if had won the contest? What if he had listened to Tecmessa? What if he had stayed in his tent? His famous deception speech on time (Soph. *Aj.* 646–92) ventriloquises with passionate intensity this sense of alternativeness inherent in his conflicted character; as he describes his new-found sense of pity, plan to cleanse away the goddess' wrath and future reconciliation with the Atreids, Ajax performs a mythic self-narrative that cannot be, and already has not happened. And as the chorus rejoice, believing in his change of heart, and erupt into song 'almost hysterical with relief',[88] we are able to glimpse momentarily what this narrative, actualised, would have looked like: Ajax without his tragedy.

In Quintus' miniature narration of his downfall, these possibilities appear to be greatly compressed and condensed: the alternative *telos* to this central aspect of Ajax' story, in which he kills Greeks, not sheep, is quickly forestalled by the intervention of a god. This passage, however, then goes on to articulate a literary motivation behind this rapid forestalling – and shows how it takes place to ensure continuity of a specifically *Homeric* line of events:

> κήδετο γὰρ φρεσὶν ᾗσι πολυτλήτου Ὀδυσῆος
> ἱρῶν μνωομένη τά οἱ ἔμπεδα κεῖνος ἔρεξε·
> τοὔνεκα δὴ μεγάλοιο μένος Τελαμωνιάδαο
> τρέψεν ἀπ' Ἀργείων...
>
> Q.S.5.361–4

---

[88] Crane (1990): 89. Bibliography on this speech – '[than which] perhaps no passage in Greek literature has generated more controversy' (ibid.) – is gargantuan. For a summary of key publications to the article's date, see Crane (1990): 89, n. 1 and, on major positions and receptions, Golder (1990): 10–11.

Straining: Plot Control and the Counterfactual 311

Because of her affection for much-enduring Odysseus and her recalling the sincere sacrifices he had made to her. she therefore deflected the violence of the great son of Telamon away from the Argives.

Athena diverts Ajax's *menos* from all of the Greeks due to her concern for one of them, πολυτλῆτος Ὀδυσσεύς – with the paradigmatic *poly*-compound evoking his characterisation in the *Odyssey* –[89] because she recalls his 'constant' sacrifices to her. Odysseus does not make 'constant' or even frequent sacrifice in the *Iliad*, nor during the *Posthomerica*, but the 'future' Odysseus of the *Odyssey is* characterised by his commitment to divine offerings, as Athena makes clear in her opening petition in that poem, which Quintus' description here (362) echoes closely:

> . . .οὔ νύ τ᾽ Ὀδυσσεὺς
> Ἀργείων παρὰ νηυσὶ χαρίζετο ἱερὰ ῥέζων
> Τροίῃ ἐν εὐρείῃ; τί νύ οἱ τόσον ὠδύσαο, Ζεῦ;
> *Od.* 1.60–2

Did not Odysseus beside the ships of the Argives win your favor by his sacrifices in the broad land of Troy? Why then did you will him such pain, Zeus?

Athena thus acts against Ajax not just on behalf of Odysseus, but also on behalf of the *Odyssey*. She ensures that the points of the mythic plot are maintained which will get us to that poem – to the situation where her special relationship with this hero is realised, and where this concern and favouritism will come to make sense. The counterfactual thus enforces the process of moving across the *Iliad-Odyssey* interval. For when Odysseus and Ajax 'next' meet, the verbose, extended exchanges of the *hoplon krisis* – and Ajax's dominant, imposing speeches in the last hours of his life in Sophocles – are reduced to the uncanny quiet of the underworld: as Ajax famously refuses to speak to Odysseus in death (*Od.* 11.563), he replaces his former verbal and physical violence with a counter gesture of withdrawal. By removing Ajax here, Athena sets in motion the Homeric transition of this relationship from speech to devastating silence.

Athena is the most prevalent counterfactual deity in the *Posthomerica*: she controls five εἰ μή scenarios, all of which occur at decisive moments in the story.[90] Her particular status across Homer's epics explains why. The

---

[89] See the discussion of Quintus' use of *poly*- compounds to mark his Odyssean inheritance in Chapter 3.

[90] Other cases: the arrival of Neoptolemus (Q.S.7.142–4); a double counterfactual in Q.S.8.340–58 in which Athena is first the agent and then the victim of the reining in of the alternative; the silencing of Laocoön to allow the horse to enter Troy (Q.S.12.394–8); and the prevention of the Greeks sailing home from Troy (Q.S.14.419–21) which I discuss next in this chapter.

312   Temporality and the Homeric Not Yet

patron deity of the *Odyssey* who famously and self-consciously changes sides,[91] who acts quasi-unilaterally in the *Iliad*, but whose special relationship with one hero forms the heart of the Odyssean narrative, Athena is the goddess *par excellence* of the Homeric in-between. At the start of the *Iliad*, by preventing Achilles from killing Agamemnon (*Il.* 1.188–222), she also sets up a driving counterfactual of Homer's story, intervening at the point 'where the narrative is poised in the possibility of instant slaying and immediate revenge'; and, as Lynn-George has emphasised, her success in stabilising this intense moment of uncertainty 'rests upon the promise of compensation as a future certainty'.[92] Quintus thus uses her so frequently in his counterfactuals to assert his own commitment to progressing from one side of his interval to the other, a certainty which counterbalances his own moments of possible narrative upheaval.

Athena, and the poem's, final counterfactual further emphasises this drive towards the *Odyssey*:

> καί νύ κεν Ἀργεῖοι κίον Ἑλλάδος ἱερὸν οὖδας
> πάντες ἁλὸς κατὰ βένθος ἀκηδέες, εἰ μὴ ἄρα σφι
> κούρη ἐριγδούποιο Διὸς νεμέσησεν Ἀθήνη.
>
> Q.S.14.419–21[93]

The Argives would all have crossed the deep sea and reached the sacred soil of Hellas untroubled had not Athena, daughter of Zeus the thunderer, been angry with them.

These lines have a rich Odyssean texture. The image of Athena petitioning Zeus evokes the opening assembly of *Od.* 1.22–95; her speech is loaded with thematic language from that poem (ἐπιμηχανόωνται, 428;[94] ἀτασθαλίην, 435); and Zeus' response, as we have seen in the previous chapter, unleashes the storm with which the *Odyssey* begins. Such echoes remind us that the counterfactual achieves the continuation of the Homerically orientated plot: Athena's complaint anticipates and facilitates the progression to the *Odyssey*'s story. But in this example, the move is acknowledged even more reflexively. ἐπιμηχανόωνται (428) is also

---

[91] Cf. e.g. Q.S.14.629–33, discussed in 7.6, and Euripides' *Troades* 59–75.

[92] Lynn-George (1988): 45 (both quotations).

[93] This scene is discussed at length in the final section of Chapter 6.5.

[94] The compound is a rare word itself, which occurs less then fifty times in all extant ancient Greek literature, and not (in this compound form) in Homer at all. However, it is clearly conceptually related to the group of *poly-metis*/*poly-mechanos* compounds which litter the *Odyssey* and in this respect seems almost to emphasise as well as echo the significations of this contrivance-based word-group. This is the *only* occurrence of the verb in the whole of the *Posthomerica*, making its potential Odyssean connectivity here, at this late stage of the epic, especially resonant.

Straining: Plot Control and the Counterfactual 313

evocative, like *lusis*, of ancient critical vocabulary. Aristotle famously despised inorganic inputs into the plot which he termed as working ἀπο μηχανῆς (*Poet.* 1454a33–1454b9).[95] As Lowe argues, in this critique Aristotle seems to be fusing a broad and a narrow sense of the word μηχανή, meaning 'contrivance' but also the technical name used in tragedy for end-of-play divine epiphanies.[96] Functioning here *as* a sort of *dea ex machina* herself, appearing in order to move the plot on towards its 'correct' form of continuation, Athena uses a word with these embedded connotations of construction. If we hear this type of 'metaliterary' μηχανή in her ἐπιμηχανόωνται, then Quintus makes the goddess point to her own role as Homeric plot-facilitator.

The same reflexive awareness informs a further counterfactual scene. After slaying Deiphobus, Menelaus discovers Helen in hiding, terrified that she is next to face his sword (Q.S.13.385–415). Her fears are almost realised, but Menelaus' violence is checked by the intervention of Aphrodite:

> ὥρμαινε κτανέειν ζηλημοσύνῃσι νόοιο,
> εἰ μή οἱ κατέρυξε βίην ἐρόεσσ' Ἀφροδίτη,
> ἥ ῥά οἱ ἐκ χειρῶν ἔβαλε ξίφος, ἔσχε δ' ἐρωήν·
> τοῦ γὰρ ζῆλον ἐρεμνὸν ἀπώσατο, καί οἱ ἔνερθεν
> ἡδὺν ὑφ' ἵμερον ὦρσε κατὰ φρενὸς ἠδὲ καὶ ὄσσων.
> τῷ δ' ἄρα θάμβος ἄελπτον ἐπήλυθεν· οὐδ' ἄρ' <ἔτ'> ἔτλη
> κάλλος ἰδὼν ἀρίδηλον ἐπὶ ξίφος αὐχένι κῦρσαι·
>
> Q.S.13.388–94

The sight of her roused his jealousy so much that he felt driven to kill her. But Aphrodite, goddess of love, restrained his violence, made the sword fall from his hand, and put a stop to his impulse by ridding him of dark jealousy and kindling sweet desire deep in his mind and eyes. He had not expected to be dumbstruck at the sight of her in all her beauty, but he could no longer bring himself to strike her neck with his sword.

In traditional accounts of this meeting, emphasis is placed firmly on Helen, and how she harnesses the disorientating effect of her beauty to save her own skin. In Aristophanes' *Lysistrata*, she bears her breasts in order to preserve herself from Menelaus' anger:

---

[95] Antiphanes was another early critic of the technique, who deemed that the use of the *deus ex machina* was a sign that the playwright was unable to properly manage the complications of his plot (fr.191. 13–17). For discussion of the device in ancient criticism and drama, see Cunningham (1954) and more recently Chondros, Milidonis and Vitzilaios (2013).

[96] Lowe (2000): 76.

314 Temporality and the Homeric Not Yet

ὁ γῶν Μενέλαος τᾶς Ἑλένας τὰ μᾶλά πα
γυμνᾶς παραϊδὼν ἐξέβαλ᾽, οἰῶ, τὸ ξίφος.

Lys. 155–6

When Menelaus saw the apples of the naked Helen, he dropped, I believe, his
sword.

A scholion on the passage reveals that the same version occurred both in
the *Little Iliad* and in Ibycus.[97] The story is also mentioned in Euripides'
Andromache (627–31), where Peleus rebukes Menelaus for being seduced
after seeing Helen's breast. And in early depictions of the encounter in
visual art, Helen is often portrayed as removing her veil, the revelation of
her face an alternative act of seduction.[98] In an adapted version of this
scene in Stesichorus' *Sack of Troy* (Σ Eur. *Or.* 1287) she appears instead in
front of the whole Greek army and somehow, through the power of her
presence, prevents them from stoning her.[99] In all of these versions,
therefore, Helen becomes the dominant force in her own survival scene:
she actively counters the threat to her life by manipulating the male gaze of
which she might otherwise be thought to be the victim.

Quintus' account works differently. He holds the conventional line
regarding Helen's beauty, but removes any direct agency from Helen
and bestows all power onto Aphrodite. Despite the goddess' potentially
allegorical connotations – she could function here as an outward manifestation of Menelaus' desire – there are no reinforcing details of the strength
of this desire as Menelaus as a lover experiences it. Instead, with a generalising *gnome* Quintus asserts the universal inescapability of the goddess'
power: πάντα γὰρ ἡμάλδυνε θεὴ Κύπρις, ἥ περ ἁπάντων/ἀθανάτων
δάμνησι νόον θνητῶν τ᾽ ἀνθρώπων (401–2). Menelaus' personal feelings
are diffused into the wider collective of 'all mortals and immortals', and it
is only through this power that he is suddenly and unexpectedly (ἄελπτον,
393) enraptured. Even once this happens, he gazes not specifically at
Helen's breasts, but at her κάλλος (394), as an abstract concept takes the

---

[97] Σ Ar. *Lys.*155a = p. 12 Hangard (1996); Il. Parv. fr.28 GEF; Ibyc. fr.296 PMGF.
[98] Two of the most famous examples are the early seventh-century Mykonos pithos (Archaeological
museum 2240 = *ArchDelt* 18, A (1963) pl. 22) and an Attic black-figure amphora in Berlin by
Lydos, both of which depict a warrior holding a drawn sword, facing a woman and grasping her
wrist or the hem of her cloak, while she stands before him and holds out the hem of the cloak with
one or both of her hands. See Hedreen (1996) for rich analysis and further reading. That this act
should indeed be understood as a seductive move, see Moret (1975): 31–2 *pace* Clement (1958)
(who argues that it is an attempt to make Menelaus recognise her – surely not, for if he is running
towards the figure in anger, the recognition must already be complete) and Hedreen (1996):
168–70, who considers fear to be a possible motivation for the gesture.
[99] See Davies and Finglass (2014) and Finglass (2018).

Straining: Plot Control and the Counterfactual

place of more explicit anatomical attraction.[100] Menelaus' desire for his wife is thus, sequentially and causally, secondary to this divine intervention. Thanks to this intervention, the outcome of the meeting was inevitable.

The passage, however, then moves to test the limits of this inevitability:

> ἀλλὰ καὶ ὣς θοὸν ἄορ ἀπὸ χθονὸς αὖτις ἀείρας
> κουριδίῃ ἐπόρουσε· νόος δέ οἱ ἄλλ᾽ ἐνὶ θυμῷ
> ὥρματ᾽ ἐσσυμένοιο, δόλῳ δ᾽ ἄρ᾽ ἔθελγεν Ἀχαιούς.
> καὶ τότε μιν κατέρυξεν ἀδελφεὸς ἱέμενόν περ
> μειλιχίοις μάλα πολλὰ παραυδήσας ἐπέεσσι·
>
> Q.S.13.403–7

Even so he picked up his sharp sword again and made a rush at his wife, but acted now with a different intention in his mind: it was a trick to beguile the Achaeans. This time his brother Agamemnon checked his zeal, who used many soothing words to change his mind, for fear that all their efforts should have been for nothing.

Menelaus' rage towards Helen has by now been completely calmed by Aphrodite. However, he pretends otherwise, drawing his sword and running at his wife again 'in order to beguile the Achaeans'. This is a strange turn of events. Why exactly is Menelaus trying to beguile them? The insertion of this moment, without plot requirement or build up, suggests that its importance may lie in its literary currency – its familiarity and recognisability. The scenario of a son of Aretus deceiving the Greeks at a critical point in the war may echo, subtly and implicitly, Agamemnon's famous test of the army in *Iliad* 2. There are hints to support this connection.[101] The very presence of Agamemnon, as the obstructer of Menelaus' plan, could remind us of his role as the instigator of that original test. And the note that Agamemnon checked Menelaus 'with words' (ἐπέεσσι, 407) echoes the king's Iliadic plan to test the Greeks, and for the elders to restrain them, in the same way (πρῶτα δ᾽ ἐγὼν ἔπεσιν πειρήσομαι. . ./ ὑμεῖς δ᾽ ἄλλοθεν ἄλλος ἐρητύειν ἐπέεσσιν. *Il.* 2.72–5). Such a detail may seem inconsequential in isolation (it is, to be sure, a common enough dative plural, particularly in Homeric speech formulae), but in

---

[100] Cf. Achilles' remorse for Penthesilea's ἐρατὸν σθένος (1.719). I treat this Helen passage from an erotic perspective in Greensmith (forthcoming c).

[101] This connection is more conceptual than strictly linguistic. The verb θέλγω is not found in the Iliadic scene; it may thus be countered that, should Quintus have wished to evoke this moment, he would surely gesture towards it more directly. However, as has been much discussed throughout this book, Quintus' allusive strategies towards Homer and his other models span the full spectrum from direct quotation to embedded interaction; and this scene provides our final example of the extremes of that spectrum of engagement.

316 Temporality and the Homeric Not Yet

aggregate the links are suggestive.[102] Such connectivity gains further force when read against a further gesture towards the Iliadic Agamemnon here: when the Trojan captive Adrastus begs Menelaus not to kill him, Menelaus was, Homer tells us, about to let him live, but Agamemnon rushes in and 'sways' him to change his mind, and show no compassion:

> καὶ δή μιν τάχ' ἔμελλε θοὰς ἐπὶ νῆας Ἀχαιῶν
> δώσειν ᾧ θεράποντι καταξέμεν· ἀλλ' Ἀγαμέμνων
> ἀντίος ἦλθε θέων, καὶ ὁμοκλήσας ἔπος ηὔδα·
> 'ὦ πέπον ὦ Μενέλαε, τί ἢ δὲ σὺ κήδεαι οὕτως
> ἀνδρῶν; ἦ σοὶ ἄριστα πεποίηται κατὰ οἶκον
> πρὸς Τρώων; τῶν μή τις ὑπεκφύγοι αἰπὺν ὄλεθρον
> χεῖράς θ' ἡμετέρας, μηδ' ὅν τινα γαστέρι μήτηρ
> κοῦρον ἐόντα φέροι, μηδ' ὃς φύγοι, ἀλλ' ἅμα πάντες
> Ἰλίου ἐξαπολοίατ' ἀκήδεστοι καὶ ἄφαντοι.'
> ὣς εἰπὼν ἔτρεψεν ἀδελφειοῦ φρένας ἥρως
> αἴσιμα παρειπών...
>
> *Il.* 6.52–61

So he spoke, and he tried to persuade the other's heart in his breast, and Menelaus was about to give him to his attendant to lead to the swift ships of the Achaeans, but Agamemnon came running to meet him, and spoke in reproach, saying: "Soft-hearted Menelaus, why do you care for the men? Has, then, some great kindness been done to you in your house by Trojans? Let not one of them escape sheer destruction and the might of our hands, not the man-child whom his mother bears in her womb; let not even him escape, but let all perish together out of Ilios, unmourned and unmarked." So spoke the warrior, and turned his brother's mind, since he advised him fatefully.

The presence of a παρ- compound in this sequence (παρειπών, 61) emphasises the form of the exchange as an act of surprising persuasion, not just speech.[103] Quintus too uses such a compound in this new instance of Agamemnon exerting his influence on Menelaus: παραυδήσας, 407 – a verb for which the *locus classicus* is Achilles' angry rebuke in the underworld, as Odysseus attempts his own persuasive swerve: μὴ δή μοι θάνατόν γε παραύδα, φαίδιμ' Ὀδυσσεῦ., *Od.* 11.488. The choice echoes the effect of the original brotherly scene, but reverses its direction: in the *Iliad* the surprising persuasion led to the death of a suppliant; here it saves a life.

Read against the double frame of the Iliadic trick and the Iliadic 'swerving', these lines alter the entire tone of the counterfactuality at play.

---

[102] The moment also perhaps has resonances with another Homeric scene – Odysseus' charge at Circe in *Od.* 10.322, where he rushes 'as though desiring to kill her' (ὥς τε κτάμεναι μενεαίνων).
[103] See Goldhill (1990).

Straining: Plot Control and the Counterfactual   317

On the one hand, this meeting between Menelaus and Helen, well-known in the literary tradition, moves us forward in the Trojan story: the 'abduction of Helen' is almost over; original husband and wife move closer towards reunion; and the way is paved for the way for the 'future' of *Odyssey* 4 and the dramatic adventures of Helen in tragedy. But on the other, the scene is now *pulled back* by the re-performance of rage, of an episode from the Iliadic past, and one which reminds us precisely of how a 'hoped for' *telos* is *not* always fulfilled. The deceitful dream which prompted Agamemnon's test, after all, made him a 'fool' (νήπιος, *Il.* 2.38) for believing that he would take the city of Priam on that day, 'when really Zeus was to bring many more woes before that' (*Il.* 2.35-40). In Quintus' narrative now, Troy *has* been sacked and Menelaus has quickly forgotten – or rather, been made to forget – his rage at Helen. He has not, however, forgotten how to enact it. As he conducts this pretence, Menelaus performs the effects of the pivotal counterfactual. We know that Helen will not be killed at this point in the story. Myth dictates that she does not die at Troy and she has to play her role in further accounts of the war's aftermath, where she will, as she predicts in the *Iliad*, be the subject of songs to come.[104] As an internal player in this myth, Menelaus 'knows' this too: he is entrapped by this sequence in which he must play his part. By playing with the alternative, in which she *is* rushed at and killed, Quintus thus focuses attention on the transient nature of such attempts to rewrite the story; as the move towards the *Odyssey* is achieved by the repetition of an Iliadic scene and Menelaus' attempts to undo his own conversion are always already false.

Nowhere are these inter-Homeric connotations of the counterfactual more clearly on display than during the return of Philoctetes to Troy (Q.S.9.333–546). This moment is, in accordance with mythic convention, prophesied by Calchas as *the* essential event for achieving the 'closure' of the sack (Q.S.9.325–32).[105] But the intercessions on Lemnos required to get the hero back had a long literary history of being painful, difficult and above all prolonged. Sophocles' surviving version of this agonising quest is most familiar to us, but we know from Dio Chrysostom (*Or.* 52) that

---

[104] *Il.* 6.357–8.
[105] Tellingly, this prophecy is given in indirect speech (οὐ γὰρ δὴ πέπρωτο δαμήμεναι Ἰλίου ἄστυ,/ πρίν γε Φιλοκτήταο βίην ἐς ὅμιλον Ἀχαιῶν/ἐλθέμεναι. . ., 9.327–9) : like the maidens' predictions in Book 10, Quintus compresses this major prediction of a major moment into the margins of his narration.

318 Temporality and the Homeric Not Yet

Euripides and Aeschylus also wrote plays on the subject.[106] In Quintus, Odysseus and Diomedes find Philoctetes writhing in torment from his wound described in ghoulish terms readily reminiscent of Sophocles' version (Q.S.9.354–97). Then, however, Athena simply melts his anger away:

> καί νύ κεν αἶψ' ἐτέλεσσεν, ἅ οἱ θρασὺς ἤθελε θυμός,
> εἰ μή οἱ στονόεντα χόλον διέχευεν Ἀθήνη. . .
>
> Q.S.9.403–4

And he would soon have carried out his bold heart's determination had not Athena dissolved his grief and anger.

> . . . ὃ δ' εἰσαΐων Ὀδυσῆος
> ἠδὲ καὶ ἀντιθέου Διομήδεος αὐτίκα θυμὸν
> ῥηιδίως κατέπαυσεν ἀνιηροῖο χόλοιο,
> ἔκπαγλον τὸ πάροιθε χολούμενος, ὅσσ' ἐπεπόνθει.
>
> Q.S.9.422–5

On hearing this from Odysseus and godlike Diomedes he found it easy to put an end to his anger at once, intensely angry though he had been until then at all he had suffered.

In lines 403–4, a single couplet whitewashes Philoctetes' paradigmatically turbulent anger and transfers the responsibility for changing his mind, as in the Helen and Menelaus scene, entirely onto a goddess. The word ῥηιδίως (424) makes explicit the ease of this conversion. James reads this streamlined sequence as 'a rather facile way of overcoming the resentment of Philoctetes'.[107] Yet far from 'facile' is the way in which this speedy sequence crystallises much of the epic's Stoic philosophical sentiment. Like Sinon before him and Neoptolemus soon to follow him, Philoctetes' swift acceptance of his fate, albeit divinely enacted, also shows how he 'conforms to the ideals of stoic *apatheia*: he comprehends the ethical and philosophical workings presented in the *Posthomerica*, as represented here in the reported words of Odysseus and Diomedes':[108]

> κακῶν δέ οἱ οὔ τιν' Ἀχαιῶν
> αἴτιον ἔμμεν' ἔφαντο κατὰ στρατόν, ἀλλ' ἀλεγεινὰς
> Μοίρας, ὧν ἑκὰς οὔ τις ἀνὴρ ἐπινίσσεται αἶαν,

---

[106] See Jebb (1898): xxii–xl. According to Vian (1966): 172 and James (2004): 315, Quintus does not appear to be influenced by Sophocles' version of the story. It seems to me, however, that the influence of the tragic tradition of resentment as a whole has a very strong, negative, pull on Quintus' choice of emphasis.

[107] James (2004): 318.   [108] Maciver (2012b): 120–1, quotation at 120, n. 42.

Straining: Plot Control and the Counterfactual   319

ἀλλ' αἰεὶ μογεροῖσιν ἐπ' ἀνδράσιν ἀπροτίοπτοι
στρωφῶντ' ἤματα πάντα, βροτῶν γένος ἄλλοτε μέν που
βλάπτουσαι κατὰ θυμὸν ἀμείλιχον, ἄλλοτε δ' αὖτε
ἔκποθε κυδαίνουσαι· ἐπεὶ μάλα πάντα βροτοῖσι
κεῖναι καὶ στονόεντα καὶ ἤπια μηχανόωνται
αὐταὶ ὅπως ἐθέλουσιν.

Q.S.9.414–22

And they said that no one in the Achaean army was to blame for his troubles, but
rather the cruel Fates: no man who treads the earth can escape them: they roam the
world continually, unseen by wretched mortals, sometimes harming the strength of
mortals in their grievous desire, sometimes unexpectedly raising them to glory, since
it is they who plan all pleasure and pain for mortals, just as they wish.

This shift to a 'Stoicising' calm, however, becomes even more complex if
understood less as a removal of the usual histrionics of this moment than a
reversal of them. Through the counterfactual, Quintus transfers the emotion
and subterfuge of the tragic accounts to make way for this 'new' version for
the present, but this transfer is also a movement *back* into an alternative past
(marked again as τὸ πάροιθε) – a past which now 'did not happen' – and
which also returns us to a specifically *Homeric* plot purchase.

For the importance of Philoctetes' arrival for the successful capture of
Troy is also described in the *Iliad*. The brief reference to the hero in the
catalogue of ships makes clear his decisive role in the future course of
action:

τῶν δὲ Φιλοκτήτης ἦρχεν τόξων ἐῢ εἰδὼς
ἑπτὰ νεῶν· ἐρέται δ' ἐν ἑκάστῃ πεντήκοντα
ἐμβέβασαν, τόξων εὖ εἰδότες ἶφι μάχεσθαι.
ἀλλ' ὃ μὲν ἐν νήσῳ κεῖτο κρατέρ' ἄλγεα πάσχων
Λήμνῳ ἐν ἠγαθέῃ, ὅθι μιν λίπον υἷες Ἀχαιῶν
ἕλκεϊ μοχθίζοντα κακῷ ὀλοόφρονος ὕδρου·
ἔνθ' ὅ γε κεῖτ' ἀχέων· τάχα δὲ μνήσεσθαι ἔμελλον
Ἀργεῖοι παρὰ νηυσὶ Φιλοκτήταο ἄνακτος.

Il. 2.718–25

But Philoctetes lay suffering mighty pains on an island, on sacred Lemnos, where
the sons of the Achaeans had left him in anguish with an evil wound from a deadly
water snake. There he lay in grief; but soon the Argives beside their ships would
remember king Philoctetes.

The Homeric account rushes through Philoctetes' story in analepsis and
prolepsis, and emphasises above all the certainty of his involvement in the
later stages of the war. The adverb τάχα, the verb of remembering in the
future tense (μνήσεσθαι: a key term, as we have seen, for marking poetic

320   Temporality and the Homeric Not Yet

referentiality)[109] and the fatalistic ἔμελλον all help to inscribe this sense of preordained importance. A scholion on these lines affirms their sense of certitude: the note records Zenodotus' athetisation of 724–5, but also flags the 'necessity' of the event as the catalogue records it:

> ὅτι Ζηνόδοτος τοῦτον καὶ τὸν ἑξῆς ἠθέτηκεν. ἀναγκαῖον δέ ἐστι γνῶναι ὅτι
> ὕστερον ἀνεκομίσθη ἐκ Λήμνου ὁ Φιλοκτήτης.
>
> Σ A. Il. 2.724a

As he was depicted and read in the *Iliad*, therefore, Philoctetes is a figure of urgency rather than deliberation. Since he is fundamentally a pivot required to move the plot towards the fall of Troy, the details of how and why he returns are left elliptical. This sense of necessity, based on the story in its compressed Homeric form, is marked as central to Quintus' account. Homer's two poems structure and frame Quintus' entire unfolding of the story. First, upon arriving at Lemnos, Odysseus' and Diomedes' attempts at persuasion are reported in extended indirect speech (Q.S.9.410–22). This type of speech, described explicitly as designed to cheer its recipient (οἱ δέ ἑ θαρσύνεσκον, 410), strongly recalls the bardic method of storytelling as characterised in the *Odyssey* (cf. *Od.* 1.340; 347): a far cry from the multiple, oscillating, deliberations of the Sophoclean drama, this new Lemnos pair talk to Philoctetes more as an amenable banqueter than a tragic antagonist.[110] Then, after the three heroes serenely sail to Troy – with the unnerving image of Odysseus enjoying a stress-free sea journey – the reunion with the Greeks (Q.S.9.480–523) replays an Iliadic scene. The meeting with Agamemnon closely evokes the embassy of *Iliad* 9.[111] First Agamemnon waits, ironically like Achilles did, to receive a band of envoys into his hut (καὶ τότ᾽ ἄρ᾽ ἐς κλισίην Ἀγαμέμνονος ἀφνειοῖο/ πάντες ὁμῶς οἱ ἄριστοι ἄγον Ποιάντιον υἷα·, 486–7). However, once they arrive, it is Philoctetes who starts to reperform Achilles' role. He hears Agamemnon's apology for his error (βλαφθέντε νόημα, 492), and his exculpatory excuses;[112] he is promised gifts in recompense (510–11), and he even ventriloquises Achilles' original speech-greeting:

---

[109] See Chapter 5.
[110] On the substitution of Neoptolemus for Diomedes, who is also the second messenger in Euripides' lost play, see James (2004): 315. That Odysseus himself is part of the initial (and, in this case, the only) supplication of Philoctetes – rather than, as per the Sophoclean plot, scheming in advance and then hiding in wait – further suggests a connection with the Odyssean model, where, after Demodocus finishes singing, Odysseus himself takes up the role as the teller of the epic tale.
[111] See Vian (1966): 200, n. 6 for the full parallels, with further discussion at Maciver (2012b): 122, n. 148.
[112] Agamemnon blames first the gods (Q.S.9.491–8) and then Fate (500–8).

Straining: Plot Control and the Counterfactual

ὦ φίλος, οὔ τοι ἐγὼν ἔτι χώομαι, οὐδὲ μὲν ἄλλῳ
Ἀργείων, εἰ <καί> τις ἔτ᾽ ἤλιτεν εἴνεκ᾽ ἐμεῖο. . .

Q.S.9.518–9

My friend, I am no longer angry with you or with any other of the Argives, if there is anyone else who has wronged me.

χαίρετον·[113] ἦ φίλοι ἄνδρες ἱκάνετον ἦ τι μάλα χρεώ.

Il. 9.197

Welcome, you are friends indeed that have come – the need must surely be great.

However, *unlike* Achilles, Philoctetes immediately comes around: he accepts Agamemnon's apology (Q.S.9.520–1) and promptly rejoins the war (535). These parallels with the embassy's dynamics may seem to represent the consummation of the moral smoothening of the Philoctetes scene as a whole. Thus for Schmitz, Quintus invites his readers to 'dwell on the behaviour of Philoctetes as opposed to Achilles, the moral implications of wrath and foregiveness' and thus to see that 'Quintus' heroes are ethically superior to their Homeric predecessors'.[114] And yet the inverse Homeric framing of this episode – first the echoes of the *Odyssey*, and then the replaying of the *Iliad* – suggests why it is in fact thanks to, and because of, Homer that this acceptance can be so quick. Philoctetes' arrival in Troy is the route by which the poetic trajectory can move on from the *Iliad,*and achieve the events necessary for the sack, and therefore for the *Odyssey*, which the Lemnos scene already foreshadows. Quintus thus uses his well-honed technique of pace variation to rush past the emotional twists of the Philoctetes story to achieve the inevitability of the return as it is inscribed in the original Homeric reference. The Quintan ῥηιδίως achieves the Homeric τάχα. Athena's role as 'control agent' in the Lemnos scene underscores this connection: as she did with Ajax, and as she will do again in the storm, the goddess of the *Odyssey* acts to allow the story to continue on its unstoppable Homeric progression.

It is through the narrative of the interval that the eerie calm of this angry tale – the disjuncture between this tranquil heroics embodied by Philoctetes and the continually disturbing, fierce and violent portrayal of war –[115] comes to make fullest sense. Exploiting the space in between

---

[113] The infamous issue with the dual form of address is, of course, no longer at play in the Quintan scene: Philoctetes, unlike the Iliadic Achilles, is afforded the opportunity to address Agamemnon directly and singularly.

[114] Schmitz (2007b): 77.

[115] As in the gruesome severed body parts and bloody battles in Book 11 and elsewhere, as discussed in the previous section. On the bloodiness of Quintan battle scenes, see Ozbek (2007), and most

322　Temporality and the Homeric Not Yet

the *Iliad* and *Odyssey* allows for the gradual removal of the most aggressive epic heroics, while maintaining a focus on virtue and military success. We saw in the discussion of Quintus' portrayal of Sinon how the poet uses Homeric qualities to construct the Stoicising fabric of this character: tapping and exploiting the inherited tradition of reading Odysseus as a proto-Stoic, he turns Sinon's 'new' philosophically oriented *apatheia* into something always-already Homeric.[116] The Quintan Philoctetes, highly Sinon-like in his withstanding of pain and acceptance of fate, activates this connection once again and expands it still further. For the Philoctetes of the *Posthomerica*, like Sinon, *does* suffer: his agony at his wound is emphasised, not downplayed. But he also (unlike Sinon and more akin to Menelaus) *does* rage: his passionate anger is present and its consequences considered. It finds a different route, re-formed through the counterfactual as an embedded, discarded alternative, rather than enacted as an extended, destructive reality. The Homeric τάχα, the Quintan ῥηιδίως and the Stoic *apatheia* – all three are put to work, and made to work *together*, to construct the new ethical heroics of this scene.

The new 'emotional economy' of Philoctetes thus redrafts the normative responses of war, submission and surrender through a positive, united framework. As the product of an epic 'by the conquered', under the Quintan scheme, this story thus told can also metaphorise a more constructive response to Quintus' own position as a Greek citizen of Roman rule. Confronted, as Philoctetes is, by the charged and changed realities of the present, the poet of the interval uses the advancement through Homer's story (from the *mēnis* towards the man) to challenge the role of anger and resistance as the only viable responses to liminality and subjectivity. Violent rage becomes part of the narrative of the might-have-been, trumped by the proud advocation of acceptance, collaboration and return. Philoctetes, in other words, advocates the ideological consequences of the Quintan 'middle way'.[117]

In the most recent, book-length, treatment of counterfactuals, Christopher Prendergast asks not how such scenarios work (e.g. as rhetorical devices, which is Wohl's central question, or as historical methodologies, *qua* Ferguson and Kennedy),[118] but rather, what they *mean*: 'what are

---

　　recently Kauffman (2018). For Hall (2005) 'even readers who thought they were inured to Greek epic carnage may feel as if they were watching a film about the fall of Troy directed by Tarantino'.

[116] See discussion and references in Chapter 3.3.

[117] This notion, which I aim here to introduce and establish in brief, will become central to the analysis in 7.4, and is pursued to the end in this chapter's conclusion.

[118] Wohl (2014) and Kennedy (2013), *qua* Ferguson, as discussed above.

counterfactuals, and what is their point?'[119] The answer that he finds is tellingly ambivalent. It is possible, on the one hand, that they really amount to very little; indicating something that may be true if it happened, but is not true, because it never did, counterfactuals can become as useless as the historians deem them to be: 'parlour game' reductions,[120] a discourse of the irrelevant, even the make-believe.[121] And yet they are also, he argues, a crucial part of actual, and actualised, human thinking and experience, 'richly, albeit sometimes treacherously, present in the everyday human realm of how our lives are both imagined and lived'. Operating in the crossroads scenario of decision-making, they can express the place of regret in retrospective assessments of paths taken and not taken, and, at the outer limit, as the wish not to have been born.[122]

At the crossroads of his own scenarios of decision-making – his choices as Homerising poet, traditional epicist and Greek writer negotiating the role of Greek writing in the Roman world – Quintus' counterfactuals perform his own powerful retrospective assessment. On the one hand, like Menelaus forced to play out the role that mythology has preordained for him, this frequent but temporary entertainment of a plot world that could exist εἰ μή the Homeric canon was so fixed, εἰ μή Quintus' Homerising commitment was so firm, εἰ μή Greek heroic poetics had to confront the Roman imperial 'now' may seem only to reinforce the restrictions of the linear reality that this poet 'knows'. There is no point in dreaming; this is how the story has to go. And yet by making the device such a prominent part of his epic, Quintus gives such 'might have beens' ample narrative space, allowing them to affect the tone of his story without ultimately derailing the inter-Homeric plot. By aligning them so firmly with both parts of the Homeric canon, Quintus shows how the 'status quo' and disruptive, dangerous alternatives to it can not only co-exist, but combine. The counterfactual becomes for our poet an effective device for doubleness, which 'supports the construction of divided and multiple identities' and

---

[119] Prendergast (2019). He describes this focus as 'an "anthropology" of the counterfactual' (4). This excellent book considers the counterfactual in a dizzyingly diverse range of disciplines – including philosophy, history, cosmology, biology, cognitive psychology, jurisprudence, economics, art history, literary theory.

[120] The verdict of E. H. Carr, cited by Kennedy (2013): 120.

[121] See e.g. Prendergast (2019): 3: '*La La Land* can stand as the name of a vast country in the world of counterfactuals, with a correspondingly vast population.'

[122] The significance of the crossroad to this discourse of the counterfactual is explored centrally in Prendergast's fourth chapter.

324   Temporality and the Homeric Not Yet

allows these identities to speak.[123] A further, different means expanding from within, they disclose how 'being on the inside' – of a canon, a story, or an empire – can be cause for celebration, not just regret.

7.4   Bending: Anachrony and Prolepsis

If the grammar of the counterfactual provides a means of joining the *Iliad* and the *Odyssey* by offering alternative views of the epic past, Quintus also explores ways of combining and extending Homeric time by moving it into the future. Once again, this expansion is achieved using a combination of techniques drawn from both of Homer's epics. We discussed in Chapter 5 how in terms of the timespan of the Trojan saga (why Homer did not cover the climax of the war as his primary subject) Homer was the original poet of 'the interval'. However, as was noted by ancient as well as modern scholarship, there are ways in which both of Homer's poems attempt to protrude outwards past these confines of their primary narrative frame. The scholia note the *Iliad's* notorious use of anachronism, transplanting into the tenth year of the war episodes which would more naturally fit in the first.[124] The *Odyssey* does not use such anachronism, but opts instead for more drastic forms of self-extension, most memorably in Tiresias' prophecy (*Od.* 11.90–137) which relates events that will take place in Odysseus' life after the '*telos*' of his return. As has been often discussed, this forward-focus of the prophecy is in keeping with certain other resistances to closure in the poem. In Odysseus' recapitulation of his story to Penelope (*Od.* 23.248–9), the first thing he tells her is that they have not yet reached the endpoint, or boundary (πείρατα), of their trials (248–9). Then as the suitors' families and Odysseus' household are about to meet in battle, in the last lines of Book 24 we are told that 'everyone would have died and not returned home' (literally, been made *nostoi*-less – ἔθηκαν ἀνόστους) if not for the sudden involvement of Athena (*Od.* 24.528): a counterfactual which momentarily derails the poem's

---

[123] Prendergast (2019): 8. His final chapter takes on this topic and explores what it is that enables a writer such as Fernando Pessoa to say of himself 'I am what I am and am not', an inquiry which aligns closely to our discussion of imperial doubleness (being 'not and not not' Demosthenes, for example) in Chapter 2.

[124] The scholia focus particularly on the *teichoscopia* (why wait until the tenth year to have the soldiers identified?). Aristotle adds the catalogue of ships (*Poet.* 1459a30–b2) as discussed productively by Sammons (2010): 140–8, who shows how in his praise of the catalogue, 'Aristotle almost certainly thought, as do modern scholars, that the catalogue evoked an event at the beginning of the war' (140).

Bending: Anachrony and Prolepsis

celebration of Odysseus' homecoming and looks at how it could not have been completed.[125]

In these ways, Homeric epic itself could be read as unstable in its temporality: the rules of epic time, 'made' in Homer, were in Homer already being broken. On a number of occasions Quintus shows himself to be sharply attuned to these ideas. He mobilises them in his own proleptic moments to provide a further means of creating a joined-up vision of Homeric time, stressing its ability to incorporate moments which stretch beyond its otherwise tightly controlled frame.

This process is clearly perceived in the two episodes of the *Posthomerica* conventionally considered by scholars to be the most explicit moments of 'anachrony', where the poem breaks with its Homeric conceit and alludes to events which are incompatible with it. Such moments offer, so it seems, Quintus' own version of what Goldhill has termed for Nonnus the 'preposterous', as he includes, with surprising brazenness, events mythically prior to but chronologically subsequent to the time frame of his inter-Homeric poem.[126] On the first of these occasions, the Greek soldier Antiphus is attacked by Eurypylus, but he escapes because of what is fated in the literary ὕστερον:

> ἐς πληθὺν ἑτάρων· κρατερὸν δέ μιν οὔ τι δάμασσεν
> ἔγχος Τηλεφίδαο δαΐφρονος, οὕνεκ’ ἔμελλεν
> ἀργαλέως ὀλέ<ε>σθαι ὑπ’ ἀνδροφόνοιο Κύκλωπος
> ὕστερον· ὣς γάρ που στυγερῇ ἐπιήνδανε Μοίρῃ.
>
> Q.S.8.124–7

He fled for cover among his comrades; he was not laid low by the warlike Telephides' mighty spear, because he was destined to die a grisly death at a later time at the hands of the Cyclops, murderer of men: such was the pleasure of hateful Fate.

This reference is the poem's clearest allusion of all to the narrative of the *Odyssey*: both to Polyphemus' devouring of the Odyssean crew (*Od.* 9.287–98) and to the grief of Aegyptus, whose presence at the Ithacan assembly is explained by his son's death in the Cyclops' cave (*Od.* 2.15–20). The Quintan scene is also filled with the language of inevitability. οὕνεκ’ ἔμελλεν (125) presents Antiphus' Odyssean experience as

---

[125] See Purves (2010): 74.
[126] The delayed proem as analysed in Chapter 4 provides another example of how Quintus breaks this Homeric conceit. However, the focus there was on intertextual 'lateness', whereas these two examples are anachronistic more specifically because of their *narrative* posteriority to the events depicted in the poem.

326 Temporality and the Homeric Not Yet

something fated (dictated by Μοῖρα).[127] In the narratorial aside ὡς γάρ που (127), we can perceive a verbal eyebrow raise to the process of maintaining literary-mythic convention. The particle που often marks an authorial comment on the narrative choices being made:[128] here again, says Quintus, this is how the story must go. The delayed ὕστερον enshrines this sense of pre-ordainment: we have to wait for this destiny to be realised. Such glances to the future thus both set up the absolute expectation that the *Odyssey* is still to come, and yet also work against the literary chronology – the earliness of the *Odyssey* – required to make the allusion work.

In this clash between the early and the late, Quintus plays heavily on the idea of a source text coming both before and after its poetic inheritor: a technique, we may note, which is much more widespread than is suggested by Goldhill's application of the term exclusively to Nonnus. It finds strong expression across earlier ancient epic, from Apollonius' multi-temporal opening – which, as we have seen, insists upon occupying a place in time where Homer's poems are an old, early 'tradition' and also inherently part of the poem's ongoing present – to, differently, Ovid's treatment of the *Aeneid* in *Metamorphoses* 13–14, where, in Hinds' words, 'rather than constructing himself as an epigonal reader of the *Aeneid*, Ovid makes Vergil a hesitant precursor of the *Metamorphoses*'.[129] In his Odyssean pre-echo, Quintus is thus in one sense writing himself into this long tradition of literary pre- and post-dating. However, he also, very differently from Apollonius, Ovid or Nonnus, turns this manoeuvre into a fundamentally Homeric move. He does so by not only alluding to this specific episode from the *Odyssey*, but also by referring to proleptic passages from Homer which *themselves* look forwards in temporally 'unusual' ways.[130]

The reference to the comrades (ἑτάρων, Q.S.8.124) and the choice of verb ὀλέεσθαι refer in the first instance to the paradigmatic opening of the *Odyssey*:

> ἀλλ' οὐδ' ὣς ἑτάρους ἐρρύσατο, ἱέμενός περ·
> αὐτῶν γὰρ σφετέρῃσιν ἀτασθαλίῃσιν ὄλοντο.
>
> *Od.* 1.6–7

---

[127] Cf. the above discussion of ἔμελλον in *Il.* 2.724.

[128] See particularly Cuypers (2005) for an excellent discussion of this and other 'interactional' particles in Apollonius.

[129] Hinds (1998): 106.

[130] I use 'unusual' in the sense outlined in the opening discussion of this section, as exemplified most broadly by Tiresias' prophecy and the 'non–closure' moments of the final books of the *Odyssey*.

Bending: Anachrony and Prolepsis

Yet even so he did not save his comrades, for all his desire, for through their own blind recklessness they perished.

The inevitable demise of the comrades, and the self-induced nature of their downfall, is of course as much of a question as a statement in the *Odyssey*. How far Odysseus could have saved his companions becomes a live issue throughout the poem, interrogated in the gap between his self-serving narration to the Phaeacians and the unspoken alternatives known and gestured to by the muted poetic voice.[131] Quintus takes these gaps here and pulls them open. Odysseus is notably missing from this scene:

> ἀλλ' ὃ μὲν οὖν ἀπάτερθεν ἔχεν πόνον οὐδ' ἐπαμύνειν
> ἔσθενεν ᾧ θεράποντι δεδουπότι·...
>
> Q.S.8.114–5

Odysseus himself was hard at work some distance away, and he was not able to defend his fallen comrade.

The hero's absence from this point of danger aligns with his strategic self-distancing as he recounts his comrades' catalogue of errors to the Phaeacians: asleep when they let out Aeolus' winds (*Od.* 10.31–55); on a separate mission as they stumble into Circe's lair (*Od.* 10.145–213); and otherwise engaged as they fatally steal the sacred cattle (*Od.* 12.327–73) – he was preoccupied when they committed their *atasthalia*, powerless, unpresent, to stop them.

The choice of Antiphus further evokes this exculpatory rhetoric. Of all the comrades eaten by Polyphemus in the *Odyssey*, it is only Antiphus who is named. But the naming comes not from Odysseus as secondary narrator, but from Homer the primary one: it is in the earlier episode of the assembly, as Homer describes Antiphus' father Aegyptus' motivations for speaking out against the suitors, that he is given a genealogy, a backstory and an epithet:

> τοῖσι δ' ἔπειθ' ἥρως Αἰγύπτιος ἦρχ' ἀγορεύειν,
> ὃς δὴ γήραϊ κυφὸς ἔην καὶ μυρία ᾔδη.
> καὶ γὰρ τοῦ φίλος υἱὸς ἅμ' ἀντιθέῳ Ὀδυσῆι
> Ἴλιον εἰς εὔπωλον ἔβη κοίλης ἐνὶ νηυσίν,
> Ἄντιφος αἰχμητής· τὸν δ' ἄγριος ἔκτανε Κύκλωψ
> ἐν σπῆι γλαφυρῷ, πύματον δ' ὡπλίσσατο δόρπον.
>
> *Od.* 2.15–20[132]

---

[131] On these gaps, see e.g. Goldhill (1991): ch. 1; de Jong (2001).

[132] Homer goes on to say that Aegyptus has three sons, but only names a further one of them (negatively, because of his collusion with the suitors), a contrast which further heightens the

328 Temporality and the Homeric Not Yet

Then among them the hero Aegyptius was the first to speak, a man bowed with age and wise with wisdom untold. Now he spoke, because his dear son, the spearman Antiphus, had gone in the hollow ships to Ilium, famed for its horses, in the company of godlike Odysseus. But him the savage Cyclops had slain in his hollow cave, and made of him his latest meal.

In Odysseus' *Apologoi* – later in the narrative, earlier in the story – he is reduced to a number, re-anonymised completely (τοὺς δὲ διὰ μελεϊστὶ ταμὼν ὡπλίσσατο δόρπον, *Od.* 9.291), with the use of the same phrase ὡπλίσσατο δόρπον as in the Aegyptus scene (*Od.* 2.20) reminding the audience of the more personal previous account. By giving him back his name, and, via the weapon that almost kills him (ἔγχος Τηλεφίδαο δαΐφρονος, Q.S.8.125), re-evoking his spearman epithet, Quintus brings to the surface the difference between these two *Odyssey* accounts – between where in the poem they come, who the narrator is, what details they give and what motivations the 'speakers' have (a father described as mourning his son; a *polytropos* adventurer saving his own reputation) – and shows how the same event can be manipulated across different levels of Odyssean time. Quintus' 'anachrony' here, therefore, is *in keeping* with Homer's, and our poet uses Antiphus to break the rules of time according to the rules that he has resolved to follow.

This process becomes even more effective when Quintus alludes not just to the literary but to the political 'future'. We arrive here at the most explicit illustration of the ideological consequences of interval temporality which the Quintan counterfactuals first began to construct, as the poet himself glosses the imperial analogies which lie behind his amalgamative vision of Homeric time. During the sack of Troy, Aeneas is led from the burning city by Aphrodite, clutching his father and son. Calchas stops the Greeks in their pursuit of the family by foretelling Aeneas' Roman destiny:

> καὶ τότε δὴ Κάλχας μεγάλ᾽ ἴαχε λαὸν ἐέργων·
> Ἴσχεσθ᾽ Αἰνείαο κατ᾽ ἰφθίμοιο καρήνου
> βάλλοντες στονόεντα βέλη καὶ λοίγια δοῦρα.
> τὸν γὰρ θέσφατόν ἐστι θεῶν ἐρικυδέι βουλῇ
> Θύμβριν ἐπ᾽ εὐρυρέεθρον ἀπὸ Ξάνθοιο μολόντα
> τευξέμεν ἱερὸν ἄστυ καὶ ἐσσομένοισιν ἀγητὸν
> ἀνθρώποις, αὐτὸν δὲ πολυσπερέεσσι βροτοῖσι
> κοιρανέειν· ἐκ τοῦ δὲ γένος μετόπισθεν ἀνάξειν
> ἄχρις ἐπ᾽ Ἀντολίην τε καὶ ἀκαμάτον Δύσιν ἐλθεῖν·

strength of Antiphus' personalised characterisation at this moment in the story (τρεῖς δέ οἱ ἄλλοι ἔσαν, καὶ ὁ μὲν μνηστῆρσιν ὁμίλει,/Εὐρύνομος, δύο δ᾽ αἰὲν ἔχον πατρώια ἔργα. – *Od.* 2.21–2).

Bending: Anachrony and Prolepsis

καὶ γάρ οἱ θέμις ἐστὶ μετέμμεναι ἀθανάτοισιν,
οὕνεκα δὴ πάις ἐστὶν ἐϋπλοκάμου Ἀφροδίτης.'

Q.S.13.333–43

Then Calchas gave a loud shout restraining the army: "Stop hurling your deadly missiles and murderous spears at mighty Aeneas' head! By the glorious will of the gods he is destined to leave Xanthus and go to Tiber's broad streams, there to found a holy city that will be a marvel even to future men; he himself shall be ruler of a people far and wide, and his descendants shall be lords of an empire extending from the tireless sun's eastern rising to where it sets in the west. And it is right that he should have a place among the immortals, since he is the son of Aphrodite of the beautiful tresses.

This speech has been hailed as one of the clearest and most important indications of the poem's imperial context.[133] Through the 'safe space' of a prophecy about the future, Quintus comes closest to positioning himself in the context of Roman rule, as the prediction describes the poet and his readers' lived present. Calchas' words also offer a near-direct expression of Roman hegemony in a political sense, as the scene now not only points, in general terms, to the myth of Rome's origins, but also to the mythologised genealogy of the Julian imperial family and its complex legacies in Quintus' own time.[134]

For this transportation of a Trojan narrative into a Roman aetiological space, we can return for a final time to the Iliac Tablets, which again become a telling interlocutor. Aeneas is at the centre of three of the surviving tablets, and on the Capitoline Tablet, among the various Homeric and extra-Homeric scenes, the largest image, in pride of place, is this very episode: Aeneas guiding his father and son through the carnage, accompanied by Hermes. The sack of Troy, and the accompanying *Greek* inscribed texts,[135] now demand to be interpreted through an image with 'a defiantly Roman aetiology'.[136] In his analysis of the scene, Squire makes clear the ideological consequences of this representational twist:

---

[133] See e.g. Baumbach and Bär (2007): 3, James (2004): xviii–xix. The two other 'firm' markers are the description of the use of wild beasts for executions in the amphitheatre in the simile at Q.S.6.532–6 and Odysseus' *testudo* trick (Q.S.11.358–414), on which, see discussion below.

[134] See especially Hadjittofi (2007): 362–5.

[135] Here the intermedial quality of the tablets helps to convey these competing Greek and Roman influences even more forcefully: as Squire suggests (2011: 154) 'there is no place for [e.g.] Vergil amid the references to Homer, Stesichorus, Arctinus and Lesches. But the rival pull between text and image is set against a parallel tension between Greek and Roman.'

[136] Squire (2011): 148. It is relevant too that most of the tablets, where their provenances can be determined, were discovered in or around Rome. There are also similar debates to those ongoing for Quintus and Triphiodorus surrounding the extent to which Vergil's *Aeneid* specifically informs this central representation – see ibid. 155f for further discussion and references.

330 Temporality and the Homeric Not Yet

At the literal and metaphorical heart of this tablet is a visual emblem that reframes the Greek epic panorama in more subjective Roman terms. The world of Greek epic is repackaged as the prequel to a distinctly Roman cultural, social and literary history: where the Trojan cycle traditionally ends with the homecoming of Odysseus,[137] it is *Aeneas* who is turned into a prototypical wandering hero.[138]

Quintus takes up all of these potential pulls between Greek and Roman enshrined in the scene. However, he moves (from) the resultant tension very differently. For once again, and here more than anywhere, we can see how the obsessive search for contemporary signs in the *Posthomerica* downplays the significance of two types of *Homeric* texturing at work.[139] The first is the close engagement with the *Iliad*'s own prophecy regarding Aeneas, in which Poseidon prevents Achilles from killing him because of his future role as the salvation of Priam's race:

> ἀλλ᾽ ἄγεθ᾽ ἡμεῖς πέρ μιν ὑπὲκ θανάτου ἀγάγωμεν,
> μή πως καὶ Κρονίδης κεχολώσεται, αἴ κεν Ἀχιλλεὺς
> τόνδε κατακτείνῃ· μόριμον δέ οἵ ἐστ᾽ ἀλέασθαι,
> ὄφρα μὴ ἄσπερμος γενεὴ καὶ ἄφαντος ὄληται
> Δαρδάνου, ὃν Κρονίδης περὶ πάντων φίλατο παίδων
> οἳ ἕθεν ἐξεγένοντο γυναικῶν τε θνητάων.
> ἤδη γὰρ Πριάμου γενεὴν ἔχθηρε Κρονίων·
> νῦν δὲ δὴ Αἰνείαο βίη Τρώεσσιν ἀνάξει
> καὶ παίδων παῖδες, τοί κεν μετόπισθε γένωνται.
>
> *Il.* 20.300–8

Come, let us lead him away from death, lest the son of Cronos grow angry in any way, if Achilles slays him; for it is fated for him to escape, so that the race of Dardanus will not perish without seed and be seen no more – of Dardanus whom the son of Cronos loved above all the children born to him from mortal women. For at length the son of Cronos has come to hate the race of Priam; and now truly shall the mighty Aeneas be king among the Trojans, and his sons' sons that shall be born in days to come.

This prophecy – brief, vague and, of course, 'un-Roman' – may seem an unlikely primary model for the *Posthomerica*'s account.[140] Yet Quintus,

---

[137] This is not in fact true of the ending of the Cycle, as we shall discuss below.

[138] Squire (2011): 154. Petrain (2014): 118f also convincingly argues that Theodorus has given his material on this tablet 'a uniquely Roman cast': by foregrounding the flight of Aeneas, he makes the future founder of the Roman people into the most important figure in the Epic Cycle.

[139] Cf. the similar argument made for Quintus' stylistic techniques in Chapter 3, with which this present discussion should be read in dialogue.

[140] Or at least, a model which Quintus updates entirely. Other versions which may, in my view, less programmatically, lie behind the prophecy include the prophecies in *Homeric Hymn to Aphrodite*

Bending: Anachrony and Prolepsis 331

once again, anchors his version structurally, thematically and lexically to this specific Iliadic moment of prolepsis. He mimics its fundamental form of an intervention speech by a divinelyconnected figure in the midst of a heated battle.[141] His emphasis on γένος suggests Poseidon's repeated γενεή, γενεήν and θέσφατόν ἐστι reworks the god's fatalistic warning μόριμον δέ οἷ εστ'. The mention of the Xanthus (Q.S.13.337), with its strong associations with Achilles' *aristeia*,[142] also evokes by transferral Achilles' own role in Poseidon's prophecy, where it is from his rage specifically that Aeneas is saved.

Calchas then adds a second reason why Aeneas must be allowed to escape:

> καὶ δ' ἄλλως τοῦδ' ἀνδρὸς ἑὰς ἀπεχώμεθα χεῖρας,
> οὕνεκά οἱ χρυσοῖο καὶ ἄλλοις ἐν κτεάτεσσιν
> 143
> ἄνδρα σαοῖ φεύγοντα καὶ ἀλλοδαπὴν ἐπὶ γαῖαν,
> τῶν πάντων προβέβουλεν ἑὸν πατέρ' ἠδὲ καὶ υἷα·
> νὺξ δὲ μί' ἧμιν ἔφηνε καὶ υἱέα πατρὶ γέροντι
> ἤπιον ἐκπάγλως καὶ ἀμεμφέα παιδὶ τοκῆα.
>
> Q.S.13.344–9

For another reason, too, we should offer this man no violence: instead of all his gold and other possessions <...> which might keep an exile safe even in a foreign land, he preferred his father and his son: this one night has shown us the extraordinary piety of a son toward his father and the blameless love of a parent toward his son.

On the one hand, this praise of Aeneas' paternal and filial piety is in keeping with the Roman context of the scene: it affiliates Quintus' Aeneas with the idealised family figure familiar from Augustan politics and rhetoric, which was, as we have seen, so often centred on the promotion of generational continuity and the importance of producing and maintaining the family.[144] But the family-centredness as specifically expressed in these lines is reminiscent not just of Augustan Rome, but also of the Homeric Greek world.[145] For the image of a hero who is simultaneously a father and

---

and Lycophron's *Alexandra*. See James (2004): 337 and, for a more positive assessment of the importance of this Iliadic scene, Hadjittofi (2007): 359–60.

[141] This time an inspired prophet rather than an Olympian.

[142] A connection also made much of in Nonnus during Aeacus' fight with the river (*Dion.* 22, particularly 384–9).

[143] On the probable lacuna here, see Vian (1969): 142.   [144] Cf. Chapter 6.

[145] On the reformulation of the myth of Troy in Greece and Rome more broadly, see Erskine (2001), from whose ideas my reading of this passage greatly benefited.

a son finds earlier parallel in the figure of Odysseus, whose story starts with a son's anguished search for his father and ends with an anguished father's reunion with his son, and where the image of a filial triad is instantiated in the final book, which provides the first and only scene where the three generations act together (*Od.* 24.359–64).

Calchas' speech in fact alludes most strongly to this Odyssean paradigm, turning the Roman image of Aeneas as a father-and-son back into a Homeric one. The theme of fleeing and entering a foreign land is, we are reminded linguistically, an original topos of Odysseus' wandering. ἀλλοδαπός (Q.S.13.346), a word which, as we have seen in Chapter 3, is employed with unknowing proleptic irony in Priam's exhortatory *gnome* (it is better to perish bravely, he claims, than ζώειν ἀλλοδαποῖσι παρ' ἀνδράσιν αἴσχε' ἔχοντας, Q.S.2.40), is found most frequently in the *Odyssey* in the context of the central hero's own wayward travelling.[146] The reference to gold also evokes Odysseus' interaction with Laertes, where he discusses the prospect of gifts whilst 'cruelly' testing him (χρυσοῦ μέν οἱ δῶκ' εὐεργέος ἑπτὰ τάλαντα, *Od.* 24.274). And in the mention of Ascanius as a παῖς (Q.S.13.349) we may hear Odysseus' recollection of himself as a child during this same conversation with his father (παιδνὸς ἐών, *Od.* 24.338) – another moment where his double status as grown hero and emergent son are starkly combined. By making such connections, Quintus reverses the implications of the prototyping that Squire reads on the tablet; he also establishes Aeneas as a proto-Odyssean figure, but shows how this relationship can *work both ways*: to have a renewed Greek, as well as 'new' Roman, subjective effect. Aeneas' famously 'Augustan' father-son duties here find literary precedent, but mythic *fulfilment*, in the workings of the *Odyssey*.

This moment must be read with a further instance of combination between Odysseus and Aeneas, which takes place during the standstill of Book 11. During this fighting, as we have seen, Odysseus devises a trick which tries – and ultimately fails – to break the stalemate. Considering now the specificities of this trick, his plan involves the soldiers arranging their shields in an interlocking formation, 'placing them above their heads to overlap with each other, all joined in a single movement' (Q.S.11.358–61). Now, this description in one sense echoes Apollonius'

---

[146] Odysseus uses the adjective in direct speech (to describe himself or others he has met) at *Od.* 8.211, 9.36 and 14.231; and it is used about him at *Od.* 9.255 and 17.485. The only other occurrences are at *Od.* 3.74, 20.220 and 23.219.

Bending: Anachrony and Prolepsis

account of how the Argonauts used shields and helmets to protect themselves from the birds on the Island of Ares (*Argon.* 2.1047–89). However, the exact formation as described here is also quintessentially Roman: Quintus is depicting the *testudo*, the device whereby a body of soldiers covered themselves with shields interlocked above their heads. The description is, more specifically, closely analogous with the two mentions of this very tactic in the *Aeneid*: in Book 2 (438–44) the Greeks attack Priam's palace in such a configuration; and in Book 9 (505–18), the Trojan defenders first fail and then succeed against a Volscian *testudo*.[147]

The passage therefore does appear to act as a straightforward 'contemporary nod', a deliberately out of place detail, inserted to remind the reader of the imperial context, and later Vergilian inheritance, underlying the superficial Homeric tenor. Then, however, Quintus again steers this 'tense' scene in a different way:

> ὥρμηναν δὲ πύλῃσι θεηγενέος Πριάμοιο
> ἀθρόοι ἐγχριμφθέντες ὑπ᾽ ἀμφιτόμοις πελέκεσσι
> ῥῆξαι τείχεα μακρά, πύλας δ᾽ εἰς οὖδας ἐρεῖσαι
> θαιρῶν ἐξερύσαντες. ἔχεν δ᾽ ἄρα μῆτις ἀγαυὴ
> ἐλπωρήν· ἀλλ᾽ οὔ σφιν ἐπήρκεσαν οὔτε βόειαι
> οὔτε θοοὶ βουπλῆγες, ἐπεὶ μένος Αἰνείαο
> ὄβριμον ἀμφοτέρῃσιν ἀρηρότα χείρεσι λᾶαν
> ἐμμεμαὼς ἐφέηκε, δάμασσε δὲ τλήμονι πότμῳ,
> ἀνέρας οὓς κατέμαρψεν ὑπ᾽ ἀσπίσιν ...
>
> Q.S.11.388–96

They meant to approach all together the gates of Priam, descendant of the gods, to smash the great walls with their double-edged axes, and to demolish the gates by tearing them from their hinges. This admirable plan held hopes of success; but neither their ox-hide shields nor their fast-moving axes availed them when the mighty Aeneas picked up a great rock in both hands and furiously flung it at them, and a wretched death befell the men whom he caught unawares beneath their shields.

---

[147] On the matter of the scene's sources, see Keydell (1954): 294–5 and James (2004): 32–6, who stress more adamantly (only) the *Argonautica* intertext. On the *Aeneid testudos*, see e.g. Austin (1964) ad. 441 (*pace*, incredulously, Camps (1965): 180); Horsfall (2008) 341–2 (who references the Quintus passage); and Lendon (2005): 124; and, for their possible influence on Quintus, see Gärtner (2005): 243–51 and Tomasso (2010): 142–6, both of whom are hampered by an over-tentative position regarding the Latin question (cf. e.g. Tomasso (2010): 'it is exceedingly difficult to prove that a poet from one language influenced a text written in another in terms of diction' [and yet, of course, we have no issue with Homer and Vergil...]). For my position on this issue, see discussion in Chapter 1.9, with additional suggestions in Chapter 6.

334 Temporality and the Homeric Not Yet

The *testudo* is now given vocabulary of an Odyssean flavour.[148] With μῆτις Quintus uses another paradigmatic noun associated with Homer's cunning hero[149] and the epithet ἀγαυός is most often used in the *Odyssey* for the suitors, who are also destroyed by Odysseus' wiles.[150] The device is also linked via foreshadowing to Odysseus' later, successful weapon-trick at Troy: the Wooden Horse itself, the subject of the next book of the *Posthomerica*. This link is forged firstly through the symmetry of the image produced by the devices – the individual heroes are joined in the *testudo* into one animalistic formation (361) just like, the delayed proem and catalogue will soon tell us, they will be in the horse –[151] and secondly by that loaded word μῆτις. After its use in this passage, the noun next occurs to describe Odysseus' plan that results in the construction of the horse: τῷ νῦν μή τι βίῃ πειρώμεθα Τρώιον ἄστυ/περσέμεν, ἀλλ᾽ εἴ πού τι δόλος καὶ μῆτις ἀνύσσῃ, Q.S.12.19–20.

This deep association between Roman stratagem and Homeric Odysseus makes starker the fact that Quintus attributes the *failure* of this plan to Aeneas. The founder of Rome and the hero of the *Aeneid* discovers this trick, and learns how to counter it, by watching Odysseus create it. A definitive Roman military invention is thus retrojected into an instance of Odyssean *dolos*, and it is through this context that it enters into Aeneas' proto-Roman ideology. The forces of foreshadowing and retrospection are here most defiantly collapsed into one another, as Aeneas *learns how to be Roman* through copying Homer's hero at Troy.

This interplay between Odysseus and Aeneas provides perhaps the strongest indication of Quintus' engagement with teleology in an imperial, ideological form. If, according to Quint, myth could be co-opted to serve either an '*Aeneid*-based' or an '*Odyssey*-derived' framework, then by co-opting their two representative heroes, the *Posthomerica* juxtaposes these two different forms of inevitability, and ultimately reconciles them, emphasising the Aeneas story as the thread connecting Greek and Roman cultural aetiologies. We therefore do not need to pursue further the 'Quintus as epigonal reader of Quint' framework (although, later and differently, still we shall) to see how the *Posthomerica* recognises and

---

[148] The storm scene of Q.S.14, as will be discussed in 7.5, is also given Odyssean language, but with that scene, the thematic connection with the *Odyssey* is more apparent and so such echoes are more expected.

[149] In the carefully selective way that Quintus redeploys Homeric epithets of this kind outlined in Chapter 3. Cf. also the discussion in 7.3 of πολυτλήτος in Q.S.5.361.

[150] *Od.* 2.209, 247; 4.681; 14.180; 17.325; 18.99; 19.488, 496; 21.58, 174, 213, 232; 22.171; 23.63.

[151] Cf. the discussion in Chapter 4 of Q.S.12.307 (ὅσοι κατέβησαν ἔσω πολυχανδέος ἵππου).

Unravelling ... or Un-Ending   335

recalibrates the political implications of an open versus closed, Greek-conquered versus Roman-conqueror conception of epic time. The way in which this scene collides the Roman (Vergilian) and the Odyssean – characters, inventions, plots – provides in fact not the poem's most overt 'contemporary' nod, but rather (or perhaps, a better understanding of the 'contemporary' for Quintus) its most epitomical expression of the possibilities for incorporation between the imperial Greek obsession with the 'past' and the realities of the Roman present. This collision reaches its climax in the epic's final scenes, as the poem of the interval is forced to confront directly the issues associated with its own closure.

7.5   Unravelling ... or Un-ending

If, therefore, the *Iliad* and *Odyssey* not only present different forms of closure, but also find different ways to resist such closure altogether, and if this resistance is crucial to Quintus' amalgamative reading of their ideologies of time, then how our poet chooses to close his own work becomes a final, fundamental question. We have seen how Quintus seems to signal the end-game of his epic as early as in its opening lines, foreshadowing the fire of Troy which is soon really to occur. As the text does draw to its close, however, this signal is revealed to be false. The *Posthomerica* does not end with the sack of Troy. The city falls, but, just like after Achilles' 'sudden' death, the poem continues on its way: the Greeks celebrate, Achilles necromantically returns, the Greeks plan their *nostoi*, and their serene homecoming is thwarted by the storm with which the narrative actually concludes (the final word is ἀέλλας).

Quintus makes clear in his account of the sack its status as a false climax. As the city burns, the lens shifts to the perspective of an anonymous onlooker, who watches the destruction from afar:

> φλὸξ δ' ἄρ' ἐς ἠέρα δῖαν ἀνέγρετο, πέπτατο δ' αἴγλη
> ἄσπετος· ἀμφὶ δὲ φῦλα περικτιόνων ὁρόωντο
> μέχρις ἐπ' Ἰδαίων ὀρέων ὑψηλὰ κάρηνα
> Θρηικίης τε Σάμοιο καὶ ἀγχιάλου Τενέδοιο·
> καί τις ἁλὸς κατὰ βένθος ἔσω νεὸς ἔκφατο μῦθον·
> 'ἤνυσαν Ἀργεῖοι κρατερόφρονες ἄσπετον ἔργον
> πολλὰ μάλ' ἀμφ' Ἑλένης ἑλικοβλεφάροιο καμόντες,
> πᾶσα δ' ἄρ' ἡ τὸ πάροιθε πανόλβιος ἐν πυρὶ Τροίη
> καίεται οὐδὲ θεῶν τις ἐελδομένοισιν ἄμυνε.
> πάντα γὰρ ἄσχετος Αἶσα βροτῶν ἐπιδέρκεται ἔργα·
> καὶ τὰ μὲν ἀκλέα πολλὰ καὶ οὐκ ἀρίδηλα γεγῶτα

336 Temporality and the Homeric Not Yet

κυδήεντα τίθησι, τὰ δ' ὑψόθι μείονα θῆκε·
πολλάκι δ' ἐξ ἀγαθοῖο πέλει κακόν, ἐκ δὲ κακοῖο
ἐσθλὸν ἀμειβομένοιο πολυτλήτου βιότοιο.'

Q.S.13.464–77

Flames mounted into the divine air, and an intense brightness extended over the city: it was visible to the neighbouring peoples as far as the lofty peaks of Ida's mountains, Samothrace and sea-girt Tenedos; and out on the deep sea sailors on board ship would say: 'The formidable Argives have brought their huge enterprise to an end after their long struggle over the seductive Helen; and the once prosperous city of Troy is in flames. They hoped for help from the gods, but none came: irresistible Destiny surveys all the deeds of men, making famous things originally without fame and obscure, and making low the mighty. As life goes by with all its changes and sufferings, good many a time gives way to evil, evil to good.'

This episode looks back closely to the poem's opening. φλόξ actualises in glowing colour the prophetic καταιθομένης πυρὶ Τροίης (Q.S.1.17). πέπ-τατο repeats the early grief which winged its way around Troy (Q.S.1.16), a despair now given new gravity by the downfall which at that stage was only predicted. Such echoes create a tight ring composition between the start of the poem and the close of this book, setting up the image of Troy in flames as a neat, symmetrical point on which the story could end. The motif of the 'view from afar' was a popular end-point for other imperial Greek epics. Triphiodorus imagines, like Quintus does in his account of the sack, how 'even now' smoking Troy made a great monument (μέγα σῆμα) to her citizens (Triph. 682). And Colluthus leaves us with Cassandra gazing down from the acropolis, watching the Trojans unbar their gates to the 'newcomer' Helen, welcoming in their doom (Coll. 391–4). By concluding with such expansive vantage points, Triphiodorus and Colluthus find a fitting antithesis to the compressed epyllionic form: such vistas become these poems' final play with different modes of perspective. Such panoramas in these tiny poems also offer, perhaps, a way of conceptualising the possible modes of viewing an empire on offer to these Greek poets in their various 'Roman' environments: an empire on the cusp of rising, changing or (like Troy) even always already falling. Just as Scipio, as described by Diodorus Siculus,[152] cried out quoted verses from Homer as he watched the destruction of Carthage from a distance, ἔσσεται ἦμαρ ὅτ'ἄν ποτ'ὀλώλη Ἴλιος ἱρὴ/καὶ Πρίαμος καὶ λαός, 'A day will come when

---

[152] Via the now-lost report of Polybius in his *Histories* and preserved in the *Excerpta Constantiniana*.

Unravelling ... or Un-Ending   337

holy Troy will fall, and Priam and his people' (32.24) – a moment which, as Feeney and Goldhill have recently discussed, offers a deeply layered sense of the transience of empires ('He sees the fate of Rome in Carthage and Troy is the model for both') –[153] so too for these writers of imperial Greece, the vista of the fall of Troy is used 'in order to imagine [one's own] empire's future destruction, as a necessary stage in the history of empires'.[154]

In Quintus, however, this symmetry with the opening and use of the 'external viewer' motif only make more emphatic the 'surprise' that this is not *his* end, nor his fall, at all.[155] The poem instead pushes us outwards, with ἔσω in line 471 denoting a movement in time as well as space. The onlooker's gnomic remarks (469–79) move Troy already into the past tense, marked with a final τὸ πάροιθε tag, and the subsequent scene-change hurries, with Quintus' characteristic blending of speed and delay, onto a new episode (καὶ τότε, 496), another book and a further story.[156] Enacting in his own text Aristarchus' and Aristophanes' infamous verdict about the ending of the *Odyssey* – offering a neater, more 'satisfying' *telos* in the penultimate book, only to go on elliptically and 'uncomfortably' far beyond it – Quintus makes clear the significance of the fact that this poem, and, this vision of empire, is far from over.

This whole process of extending his epic past the false closure of the sack seems on the one hand to fit perfectly with Quintus' agenda as a poet in the Homeric middle: the narrative continues past the fall of Troy to bring the reader up to the start of the *Odyssey*, achieving the final stage of the linear Homeric progression which the epic has signalled its obsession with achieving. Indeed, not only the storm scene but also this final book as a whole is marked by an increase in Odyssean allusions: *poly*-compounds,[157] ἀτασθαλίην (Q.S.14.435) and multiple terms for cunning and contrivance (ἐπιμηχανόωνται, 427; ἐμήδετο, 559; πινυτόφρονος, 631). The last lines

---

[153] Feeney (2007): 55.
[154] Goldhill (forthcoming d). This use of Homer to look to the future of the fall of Rome via the sack of Troy also has resonances with the apocalyptic predictions in the third book of the *Sibylline Oracles*, as discussed in Chapter 5.
[155] Oppian also uses the device in his depiction of the death of the κῆτος: he imagines some goatherd or shepherd standing on a cliff 'far away' and watching and listening to the din in amazement (*Hal.* 5.247–54), another possible way in which Quintus connects his temporal dynamics to the *Halieutica* – here, by using the 'teleological' device of the onlooker, along with, as we have seen, the victory song of the conquerors, as false indications of the end.
[156] In this instance, the meeting of Aithra and her grandsons (Q.S.13.496–563).
[157] Discussion and statistics in Chapter 3.

338 Temporality and the Homeric Not Yet

of the whole poem, as we have seen in Chapter 1.1, also read as a preparatory gloss on the start of the *Odyssey* (*Od.* 1.11–12). In all such respects, Quintus' false tease of the sack-as-*telos* perfectly accords with his much-signalled, meticulously contrived, inter-Homeric agenda.

However, Quintus also makes another, competing claim with this final book, which derails this tidy explanation: that his poem does *not* end with the *Odyssey* at all.[158] In terms of plot, the *nostoi* signalled as already complete in the *Odyssey*'s opening narrative (οἴκοι ἔσαν, πόλεμόν τε πεφευγότες ἠδὲ θάλασσαν... *Od.* 1.12) still have to happen before we get to that start of the *Odyssey*: this Iliadic continuation, in other words, requires another continuation in order really to fill the Homeric gap. Quintus emphasises this point in other imagery and language which lace his final scenes: the heavy Odyssean texture that we have charted in the closing book so far is dappled with alternative, unsettling, voices.[159] The parting image of the storm, whilst on the surface a clear pre-echo of the *Odyssey*'s central drama, in fact creates a sense of transition, not completion. Tempests in epic are most often used to *turn* the narrative, or mark a point of changed direction: not only Odysseus, but also Aeneas, Jason, and even Paris are all blown onto new heroic courses by them.[160] Here, however, we do not get to this new heroic course: the storm just rages on as we wait for the *Odyssey* still. Quintus also includes more of his signifying words for pluralisation and endlessness: πάντας (592), πᾶσαν (610), ἀπείρονος (598) all suggest, as we saw in Chapter 5, that there is more to this story than what is being narrated here. And in the final *tis* speech, the specific catastrophe of the storm which triggers the *Odyssey* is refracted back into the wider history of myth:

> καί τις ἔφη· 'τάχα τοῖον ἐπέχραεν ἀνδράσι χεῖμα,
> ὁππότε Δευκαλίωνος ἀθέσφατος ὑετὸς ἦλθε,
> ποντώθη δ' ἄρα γαῖα, βυθὸς δ' ἐπεχεύατο πάντῃ.'
> Q.S.14.602–4

And someone said: 'It must have been a storm like this which was unleashed on mankind when Deucalion's mighty deluge came to inundate the earth and cover everything with deep waters!'

---

[158] In this respect, my opening discussion of the final lines of the *Posthomerica* in Chapter 1.1 was, designedly, not the full story: the ellipsis there echoes the Quintan ellipsis in his own non-ending.

[159] For the purposes of this discussion, I am taking the 'final scenes' of the poem to be the events in 419–658: that is, all those which occur after the pivotal counterfactual at Q.S.14.419–21. On this section of the poem, and its rich intertextual layering, see the detailed discussion in Carvounis (2007): 255–6.

[160] For Paris as a storm-tossed voyager, see Colluthus 206–10.

Unravelling ... or Un-Ending 339

The reference to Deucalion marks a deep sense of antiquity[161] and removes some of the directness of the recourse to the *Odyssey* in this elemental turn of events: like the storm passing to calm in Deiphobus' earlier reflections on time (Q.S.9.105), this has all happened before and will happen again.

In the final mention of Athena, we are told of her profound ambivalence at the havoc which she has caused:

$$\text{... αὐτὰρ Ἀθήνη}$$
ἄλλοτε μὲν <θυμῷ> μέγ' ἐγήθεεν, ἄλλοτε δ' αὖτε
ἄχνυτ' Ὀδυσσῆος πινυτόφρονος, οὕνεκ' ἔμελλε
πάσχειν ἄλγεα πολλὰ Ποσειδάωνος ὁμοκλῇ·

Q.S.14.628–31

Meanwhile Athena's feelings veered between great joy and her concern for Odysseus, that man of good sense, who was destined to suffer many troubles from the wrath of Poseidon.

The patron goddess of the *Odyssey* and the deity of Homeric transition ends this poem completely torn. She both rejoices in the present, pre-Odyssean Greek turmoil and expresses concern for the hero she is destined to help in the future, with πάσχειν ἄλγεα πολλά echoing line 4 of the *Odyssey*'s proem and the loaded ἔμελλε marking again the sense of literary inevitability. Her split emotion mirrors our own sense of stasis as we end the poem as readers: we are left suspended in the aftermath of the climax, hanging between the end of the sack and the next turning point in the cyclic story.

So, in one sense Quintus ends with a flagrant self-contradiction, in that he seems to undermine the notion of tight Homeric interstitiality upon which he has built the poetics and towards which so many of these temporal manoeuvres are aimed. The *Posthomerica* now both is and is not the poem in the Homeric middle. However, the final scenes also show how these two competing ideas about Quintus' *own* text – of bridging Homer's works in a linear, teleological sense and leaving them open in a more elliptical way – can be powerfully reconciled. Our poet achieves this reconciliation once again by using material drawn from Homer himself: the final storm becomes the most intense site for Homeric modes of overturning as much as establishing the idea of 'full and classical closure'. By pushing these modes to their limits, Quintus turns his finale into a probing discussion of his model's continual defiance of a *telos*: for the

---

[161] Such stories of Deucalion as are found in, e.g., Hesiod *Cat.* fr.2–7 and 234; Ap. Rhod. *Argon.* 3.1087; Verg. *G.* 1.62; Ov. *Met.* 1.318ff., 7.356; Strabo, *Geog.* 9.4 and Nonnus *Dion.* 3.211; 6.367.

340 Temporality and the Homeric Not Yet

Posthomerica truly to claim its place as Homer in the middle, it is essential that Homer does not yet end.

Quintus' ending harnesses two major moments of closure-resistance from the *Odyssey*: yet again engaging the temporality of the epic which the narrative – now most emphatically – does not yet quite reach. When Telemachus visits Menelaus' palace, he hears stories of the Greek returns which the king acquired from Proteus (*Od.* 4.332–592). Quintus draws closely on the 'facts' of this reported tale in his concluding sequence. His account of the death of Locrian Ajax (Q.S.14.559–89), for instance, maintains Poseidon's role in the episode: his anger at Ajax's scornful boasting and even smaller details such as the location of the Gyrae rock (as at *Od.* 4.500–1 and 506–7). Now, Menelaus' speech marks the point where the *Odyssey* incorporates the *nostoi* into its own narrative. By using it, Quintus thus announces how he can continue his continuation using material already found within the Homeric source.

The closing scenes also contain an echo of the *Odyssey*'s own problematic final book: after provoking in his readers, through the false-ending tease of Book 13, the scholiasts' dissatisfaction with the continuation of the *Odyssey* past the reunion *telos* of *Od.* 23, Quintus now definitively engages with the 'aftermath' book of Homer's epic:

> . . .ἀλλὰ τὰ μέν που
> ἀθανάτων ἐτέλεσσε κακὸς νόος· οἳ δ' ἐνὶ νηυσὶν
> Ἀργεῖοι πλώεσκον ὅσους διὰ χεῖμα κέδασσεν·
>
> Q.S.14.654–6

Such it seems was the result of the immortal gods' resentment. Meanwhile those Argives still aboard ship sailed on, scattered by the storm.

This statement evokes Athena's attempts to enact closure on the *Odyssey*'s last battle: the goddess' appeal to Zeus' νόος, lamentation about the πόλεμον κακόν (*Od.* 24.473) and intervention to bring about a peaceful *telos* (*Od.* 24.502) are all signalled in Quintus' ἀθανάτων ἐτέλεσσε κακὸς νόος – with που once again present to denote a moment of strong authorial self-awareness about the allusivity of this scene. As we have seen, this resolution in the *Odyssey* is not neatly achieved. The counterfactual at *Od.* 24.528 suggested how things could have gone another way; and in Odysseus' final act in the poem, the danger that his rage will continue is at least partially fulfilled:

> σμερδαλέον δ' ἐβόησε πολύτλας δῖος Ὀδυσσεύς,
> οἴμησεν δὲ ἀλεὶς ὥς τ' αἰετὸς ὑψιπετήεις.
>
> *Od.* 24.537–8

Final Conclusions 341

Then much enduring, godlike Odysseus roared terribly; and gathering himself together he swooped upon them like an eagle lofty in flight.

The closing speech of Homer's most silver-tongued speaker is an inarticulate roar. This outburst jars with the narrative's attempts to reassure us of a final peace (*Od.* 24.545–8) and provides a parting reminder of what was stressed in Tiresias' prophecy: that the *nostos* is not the end of Odysseus' turbulent adventures, but he must go a-roving again. By ending his own work with an allusion to these upheavals, Quintus asserts that in disrupting the closure of his epic he is doing something entirely Homeric: not ending properly with the *Odyssey* is, ultimately, an Odyssean form of ellipsis, a resounding final coda of the driving paradox of Quintan doubleness.

The *Posthomerica* thus affirms its status as a poem of the Homeric interval and at the same time radically redefines what this interval is. Beginning where the *Iliad* leaves off, it finishes not with the start of the *Odyssey*, but with the ever-elusive 'end': and where this ending is going to be, even in the written, bounded Homeric texts, is presented as continually open for negotiation. The space between Homer's poems is thus not just expanded, but revealed to *already be expansive*, as Quintus brings to the fore his model's own lack of containment and expands his conclusion using the profound plurality of Homeric ends.

7.6   Final Conclusions

Throughout this final chapter, Quint and Quintus have struggled against one another – narrators of time, made to stand as constant sparring companions. Quint's own thoughts on endings must comprise the closing phase of this contest. It is, of course, the 'losers' who in *Epic and Empire* most fiercely cling to the idea of open-ended conclusions: the epics composed under imperial conquest lay claim in their narrative structures to 'unending endings'. This claim is a crucial part of their resistance. Thus when Ercilla in the sixteenth century strives in the *Araucana* – which also (un)ends with an indomitable storm (15.58ff.) – to contest repeatedly the idea of narrative closure, specifically opposing the model of the *Aeneid* and channelling the 'aimlessness' of Lucan, he inscribes, we are told, a powerful message of political defiance:

> The *Pharsalia*'s resistance to narrative teleology and closure had contained ... an injunction to the defeated republican cause to keep up the fight even after an apparently decisive victory of imperial tyranny. This

342 Temporality and the Homeric Not Yet

may have been largely wishful thinking on Lucan's part, but the Araucanian wars provided a living example of a people who, no matter how many times they might be vanquished, refused to give up their struggle for liberty ... the *Araucana* writes the story of a losing side's unending resistance.[162]

Is it here, in the end, that the analogy between principate Latin and imperial Greek, 'Rome under Rome' and 'Greece under Rome', reaches its loudest crescendo after all? There is much that would suggest so. In their own ongoing aftermath of a swiftly concluded war, living out the 'decisive victory' of Roman rule, the imperial Greeks' performance of the past, that not-so-post-Latourian interrogation of the forward arrow of time, can readily be read as a narrative of resistance. The reality of Greek conquest in the early centuries CE, its crushing sense of teleology and closure is rejected or masked, with creative 'wishful thinking', by the retrojecting polemic of *paideia*; the linear onslaught of 'captive' time is thwarted by the cyclic return to the past and the re-enactment of the classical glory days. More than 2000 years after Horace unleashed the indefatigable phrase *Graecia Capta* upon the world, the tale, as we have seen, is still so often told in these terms: *Being Greek Under Rome, The Politics of Imitation, Bildung und Macht, The Struggle for Identity* ... tradition objectified and weaponised has become this losing side's never-ending story of unending opposition.[163]

As with his lexica and style, his Callimacheanism, his approach to Iliadic revision and his discourse of filiation, Quintus resists this narrative of resistance. His own open-ending does not perpetuate a struggle or oppose the teleology of victory, and it actively encourages the processes of advancement and fulfilment: first of the *Odyssey*, then – via Aeneas, the *testudo*, the future-present that *does* happen – of Rome. The 'unending ending' of the *Posthomerica* thus forms instead the final phase of the poem's sustained redrafting of the language of openness, cyclicality and non-linearity, as the removal of closure is used to unify rather than to divide opposing positions and sides: emotional anger with serenity and restraint; Greek anteriority with Roman appropriation; the *Iliad* and the *Odyssey*, Homer and the *Aeneid*. The temporality of the interval triumphs by displaying the condition of possibility for existing, at times with wistfulness, at times with difficulty, *in between* these polemicising poles.

---

[162] Quint (1993): 160–1.
[163] Respectively, the titles of: Goldhill (2001); Whitmarsh (2001); Schmitz (1997) and Schmitz and Wiater (2011). The list is of course intended to be illustrative of a particular trend and not exhaustive. For further discussion of these books and their positions, see Chapter 1.4–5.

Final Conclusions

It is through assessing this condition that we can perceive most clearly the connection which we have traced throughout this book, between the poetics of the *Posthomerica* and the politics of its day – the ramifications, in other words, of 'Quintus on time' and 'Quintus as time'.[164] Let us end with some brief summative reflections on both of these strands. First, as a comment on his own time, this poet's treatment of temporality can speak to an alternative way of conceptualising Greek identity formations in the particular environment of the third century. We discussed in the first two chapters how moments of crisis in particular evoke a tendency to imitate one's forebears closely. And yet, as we have continued to see, the intense and dramatic crisis points which characterised the first 200 years of Roman rule had also by the third century given way to a subtler, shifting and, above all, multivalent *modus vivendi*. The existence of the emperor and the reality of imperial rule was established, but the *holders* of this role oscillated variably; the total destruction of the battle of Corinth was now moving into the realm of recent history, and the next phases of total overhaul and upheaval – the religious 'conversion' of the empire, the shift of power to Constantinople – were still part of the future not yet (quite) realised. Quintus' interval temporality can thus reflect this particular state of imperial subjectivity: not a crisis or a concession, not a beginning or an end of conflict, but a dynamic occupation of the transitional space in the middle. Now in one sense, of course, this is a liminality that can only fully emerge with retrospect: unlike the relentless, preordained narrative advancement of the *Odyssey*, Quintus, bluntly put, could not see all of these 'future' changes coming. And yet the tone of the poem's temporality, as this chapter has understood it, does suggest a strong internal reflexivity about the current imperial state of play. In a period when an empire was neither being made nor defeated, the *Posthomerica*'s united Homeric structure, its anti-agonistic use of tradition, reveals the opportunities of accepting multiple types of 'middle ground'. This literary world view, not a statement of passivity or resignation, but a polemic *against* aggression and supersession, sets forward a *modus scribendi* in which the (Homeric) past is not used to blot out or ameliorate the present, but to convey – paradoxically – the living energy of the here and now.

Secondly, and finally, as a poetic portrait *of* time, the Quintan interval offers a significant opportunity to other epic composers engaged in thinking through the ideological impacts of Homeric narrative on their own

---

[164] For this way of conceptualising the question, see the 'double pull' of Homer discussed in these terms in 7.1.

imperial realities. As we have seen in this chapter's interactions with Oppian, Triphiodorus and Nonnus, the *Posthomerica* speaks loudly to the engagements with time undertaken by other hexameter voices in Late Antiquity. As the empire continued to twist and turn on its uncertain collision course, its transition from modes of construction to destruction gradually and unevenly unfolding, could the *Posthomerica*'s positive approach to its own third-century status quo offer a new archetype for other, later Trojan poets, as they too re-worked the teleology-openness divide into their Homerically inspired, imperially inflected texts? As we once more regard with retrospect Quintus standing in the middle of this fluid canon of works, so does this literary 'middleness' have a more self-generative force too. As a central and self-conscious player in imperial epic time, the *Posthomerica* offered to its successors a new brand of response, which itself could be taken up, adapted or rejected in turn. Through the unifying programme of the πᾶσα ἀοιδή – the poem's most direct statement of literary principle and also, we now see, a symbol of its imperially incorporative agenda – Quintus gave to Greek poetics a new way to go forward by going back: a model to manipulate, a provocative challenge, or even a call to arms.

Bibliography

Accorinti, D. (ed.) (2016) *Brill's Companion to Nonnus of Panopolis.* Leiden: Brill.

Acosta-Hughes, B. (2016) 'Composing the Masters: An Essay on Nonnus and Hellenistic Poetry' in Accorinti (ed.): 507–28.

Adams, J. (2003) *Bilingualism and The Latin Language.* Cambridge: Cambridge University Press.

Adams, J., Janse, M. and Swain S. (eds.) (2002) *Bilingualism in Ancient Society: Language Contact and The Written Text.* Oxford: Oxford University Press.

Adkins, A. (1969) 'Threatening, Abusing and Feeling Angry in the Homeric to Poems.; in *JHS* 89: 7–21.

Agosti, G. (2006) 'La voce dei libri: dimensioni performative dell'epica greca tardoantica' in E. Amato, A. Roduit and M. Steinrück (eds.) *Approches de la Troisième Sophistique: hommages à Jacques Schamp.* Brussels: Latomus: 35–62.

Ahl, F. (1984a) 'The Art of Safe Criticism in Greece and Rome' in *AJPh* 105 (2): 174–208.

(1984b) = 'The Rider and the Horse: Politics and Power in Roman Poetry from Horace to Statius' in *ANRW* II 32.1–40.

Ahrens, E. (1937) *Gnomen in griechischer Dictung.* Halle: Martin-Luther-Universität.

Alcock, S. E. (1993) *Graecia Capta: The Landscapes of Roman Greece.* Cambridge: Cambridge University Press.

(ed.) (1997) *The Early Roman Empire in the East.* Oxford: Oxbow.

Alden, M. J. (2000) *Homer Beside Himself: Para-Narratives in the Iliad.* Oxford: Oxford University Press.

Alexiou, M. (1974) *The Ritual Lament in Greek Tradition.* Cambridge: Cambridge University Press.

Allen, D. S. (2001) 'Gorgianic Figures' in T. O. Sloane (ed.) *Encyclopaedia of Rhetoric*, vol. I. Oxford: Oxford University Press: 321–3.

Allen, T. W. (1924) *Homer and the Origins of Transmission.* Oxford: Clarendon Press.

Amato, E. and Schamp, J. (eds.) (2005) *Ethopoiia. La représentation de caractères entre fiction scolaire et réalité vivante à l'époque impériale et tardive.* Salerno: Helios Editrice.

346 Bibliography

Amir, Y. (1985) 'Homer und Bibel als Ausdrucksmittel im 3. Sibyllenbuch' in *Studien zum Antiken Judentum*. Frankfurt: 83–100.

Anderson, G. (1978) 'Patterns in Lucian's Quotations' in *Bulletin of the Institute of Classical Studies*, 25: 97–100.

(1993) *The Second Sophistic: A Cultural Phenomenon in the Roman Empire*. London and New York: Routledge.

Ando, C. (2012) *Imperial Rome AD 193 to 284: The Critical Century*. Edinburgh: Edinburgh University Press.

Appel, W. (1993) 'Die homerischen *hapax legomena* bei Quintus Smyrnaeus' in *Adverbien in Glotta* 71: 178–88.

(1994a) *Die homerischen hapax legomena in den Posthomerica des Quintus Smyrnaeus*. Toruń.

(1994b) 'Zur Frage der *interpretatio Homeri* bei den späteren Dichtern' in *ZPE* 101: 49–52.

Arjava, A. (1998) *Women and Law in Late Antiquity*. Oxford.

Aurigemma, F. (1953) 'Appendice: tre nuovi cicli di figurazioni ispirate all'Iliade in case della Via dell'Abbondanza in Pompei' in V. Spinazzola (ed.) *Pompei alla luce degli scavi nuovi di Via dell'Abbondanza (anni 1920–23)*. Rome: Libreria della Stato: 867–1008.

Austin, R. (1964) *P. Vergili Maronis Aeneidos Liber Secundus*. Oxford: Clarendon Press.

Autenrieth, G. (1876) *Homeric Dictionary*. Richmond: Duckworth.

Bachmann, L. (ed.) (1835) *Scholia in Homeri Iliadem*. Leipzig: Kollmann.

Bakhtin, M. (1981) 'Epic and Novel' in *The Dialogic Imagination* (ed. and introduction by M. Holquist). Austin: University of Texas Press: 3–40.

Bakker, E. J. (2008) 'Epic Remembering' in A. Mackay (ed.) *Orality, Literacy, Memory in the Ancient Greek and Roman World*. Leiden: Brill: 65–78.

Bannert, H. and Kröll, N. (2016) 'Nonnus and the Homeric Poems' in Accorinti (ed.): 479–506.

Bär, S. (2007) 'Quintus Smyrnaeus und die Tradition des epischen Musenanrufs' in Baumbach and Bär (eds.): 29–64.

(2009) *Quintus Smyrnaeus Posthomerica 1. Die Wiedergeburt des Epos aus dem Geiste der Amazonomachie. Mit einem Kommentar zu den Versen 1–219*. Göttingen: Vandenhoeck & Ruprecht.

(2010) 'Quintus of Smyrna and the Second Sophistic' in *HSPh* 105: 287–316.

(2012) '"Museum of words": Christodorus, the Art of Ekphrasis, and the Epyllic Genre', in Baumbach and Bär (eds.): 447–71.

Barchiesi, A. (1986) 'Problemi d'interpretazione in Ovidio: continuità delle storie, continuazione dei testi' in *MD* 16: 77–107.

(1993) 'Future Reflexive: Two Modes of Allusion in Ovid's *Heroides*' in *HSCP* 95: 333–6.

Barnouw, E. (ed.) (1989) *International Encyclopaedia of Communications*. Oxford: Oxford University Press.

Bibliography 347

Barthes, R. (2001) 'The Death of the Author'. Translated by Stephen Heath in V. B. Leitch, *The Norton Anthology of Theory and Criticism*. New York: WW Norton & Company: 1466–70.

Bartsch, S. (1994) *Actors in the Audience*. Cambridge, MA: Harvard University Press.

Bassett, S. (1921) *Hysteron proteron Homērikōs (Cicero, Att. I, 16, I)*. Boston.

(1925) 'The Laocoon Episode in Quintus Smyrnaeus' in *AJPh* 46 (3): 243–252.

(1996) 'Historiae custos: Sculpture and Tradition in the Baths of Zeuxippos', *AJA* 100: 491–506.

(2004) *The Urban Image of Late Antique Constantinople*. Cambridge: Cambridge University Press.

Bassino, P. (2018) *The "Certamen Homeri Et Hesiodi": A Commentary*. Berlin: de Gruyter.

Baumbach, M. and Bär, S. (eds.) (2007) *Quintus Smyrnaeus: Transforming Homer in Second Sophistic Epic*. Berlin: de Gruyter.

(eds.) (2007) 'An Introduction to Quintus' Smyrnaeus' Posthomerica' in Baumbach and Bär (eds.): 1–26.

(eds.) (2012) *Brill's Companion to Greek and Latin Epyllion and Its Reception*. Leiden: Brill.

(2015) 'The Epic Cycle and Imperial Greek Epic' in M. Fantuzzi and C. Tsagalis (eds.) *The Greek Epic Cycle and Its Ancient Reception: A Companion*. Cambridge: Cambridge University Press: 604–22.

Beall, S. (2001) '*Homo fandi dulcissimus*: the Role of Favorinus in the Attic Nights of Aulus Gellius' in *AJPh* 122: 87–106.

Beck, D. (2014) 'The First Simile of the *Aeneid*' in *Vergilius* 60: 67–83.

Beckby, H. (ed.) (1965) *Anthologia Graeca*, Vol. II. Munich: Heimeran.

Bekker, I. (ed.) (1833) *Apollonii Sophistae: Lexicon Homericum Recensuit Immanuelelis Bekkeri*. Hildesheim: Georg Olms.

Belfiore, E. (1984) 'A Theory of Imitation in Plato's *Republic*' in *TAPA* 114: 121–46.

Benoit, W. (1982) 'The Most Significant Passage in Aristotle's *Rhetoric*' in *Rhetoric Society Quarterly*, 12: 2–9.

(1987) 'On Aristotle's Example' in *Philosophy & Rhetoric* 20 (4): 261–7.

Bergen, A. (1983) 'Odyssean Temporality: Many (Re)Turns' in C. A. Rubino and W. Shelmerdine (eds.) *Approaches to Homer*. Austin: University of Texas Press: 38–73.

Bernabé, A. (1987) (ed.) *Poetarum epicorum Graecorum testimonia et fragmenta*, pt. 1. Leipzig: Teubner.

Billerbeck, M. and Zuber, C. (2000) *Das Lob der Fliege von Lukian bis L.B. Alberti*. Bern: Peter Lang.

Blondell, R. (2002) *The Play of Character in Plato's Dialogues*. Cambridge: Cambridge University Press.

Bloom, H. (1975) *A Map of Misreading*. New York: Oxford University Press.

348 *Bibliography*

(1997) *The Anxiety of Influence: A Theory of Poetry*. New York and Oxford: Oxford University Press. New Haven: Yale University Press.

(2011) *The Anatomy of Influence: Literature as a Way of Life*. New Haven: Yale University Press.

Bodnar, J. (1992) *Remaking America: Public Memory, Commemoration, and Patriotism in the Twentieth Century*. New Jersey: Princeton University Press.

Boeke, H. (2007) *The Value of Victory in Pindar's Odes: Gnomai, Cosmology and the Role of the Poet*. Leiden: Brill.

Bonner, S. (1977) *Education in Ancient Rome: From the Elder Cato to the Younger Pliny*. London: Routledge.

Bowersock, G. W. (1990) *Hellenism in Late Antiquity*. Cambridge: Cambridge University Press.

Bowie, E. (1989a) 'Greek Sophists and Greek Poetry in the Second Sophistic' in *ANRW* II 33 (1): 209–58.

(1989b) 'Poetry and Poets in Asia and Achaia' in Averil Cameron and S. Walker (eds.) *The Greek Renaissance in the Roman Empire* (ICS Bulletin Supplement 55). London: University of London, Institute of Classical Studies: 198–205.

(1990) Greek Poetry in the Antonine Age' in D. Russell (ed.) *Antonine Literature*, Oxford: 53–90.

Bowlby, R. (2007) *Freudian Mythologies: Greek Tragedy and Modern Identities*. Cambridge: Cambridge University Press.

Boyten, B. (2007) 'More "Parfit Gentil Knyght" than "Hyrcanian Beast": The Reception of Neoptolemus in Quintus Smyrnaeus' Posthomerica' in Baumbach and Bär (eds.): 307–36.

(2010) *Epic Journeys: Studies in the Reception of the Hero and Heroism in Quintus Smyrnaeus' Posthomerica*. PhD Diss. at University College London (published online: discovery.ucl.ac.uk/1310146/1/1310146.pdf. Date last accessed: 07.04.20).

Bradshaw, E. and Berenson Maclean, J. K. (2004) *Philostratus's Heroikos: Religion and Cultural Identity in the Third Century C.E.* Atlanta: Society of Biblical Literature.

Braidotti, R. (2013) *The Posthuman*. Cambridge: Polity Press.

Braune, J. (1935) *Nonnos und Ovid. Greifswalder Beiträge zur Literatur – und Stilforschung*. Greifswald: Dallmeyer.

Brilliant, R. (1984) *Visual Narratives: Story-telling in Etruscan and Roman Art*. Ithaca, NY: Cornell University Press.

Brink, K. (1946) 'Callimachus and Aristotle: an Inquiry into Callimachus' ΠΡΟΣ ΠΡΑΞΙΦΑΝΗΝ' in *CQ* 40: 11–26.

Bruns, I. (1896) *Das literarische Porträt der Griechen im fünften und vierten Jahrhundert vor Christi geburt*. Olms.

Bryant Davies, R. (2017) 'The Figure of Mary Mother of God in Christus Patiens: Fragmenting Tragic Myth and Passion Narrative in a Byzantine Appropriation of Euripidean Tragedy' in *JHS* 137: 188–212.

Buffière, F. (1956) *Les myths d'Homère et la pensée grecque*. Paris: Les Belles Lettres.

Bibliography

349

Buitenwerf, R. (2003) *Book III of the Sibylline Oracles and Its Social Setting.* Leiden: Brill.

Burgess, J. S. (2001) *The Tradition of the Trojan War in Homer and the Epic Cycle.* Baltimore and London: Johns Hopkins University Press.

Burkitt, C. (1935) 'The Dura Fragment of Tatian' in *JThS* 36: 255–9.

Burrus, V. (2000) *Begotten, Not Made: Conceiving Manhood in Late Antiquity* (Figurae: Reading Medieval Culture). Stanford.

(2008) *The Sex Lives of Saints: An Erotics of Ancient Hagiography, Divinations: Rereading Late Antique Religion.* Philadelphia.

Butler, H. (trans.) (1921) *The Institutio Oratoria of Quintilian.* Cambridge, MA: Harvard University Press.

Byre, C. (1982) '*Per Aspera (et Arborem) ad Astra*: Ramifications of the Allegory of *Arete* in Quintus Smyrnaeus *Posthomerica* 5.49–68', in *Hermes* 110: 184–95.

Cadau, C. (2015) *Studies in Colluthus's* Abduction of Helen. Leiden: Brill

Caizzi, F. (ed.) (1966) *Antisthenis Fragmenta.* Milan: Cisalpino.

Campbell, M. (1981) *A Commentary on Quintus Smyrnaeus, Posthomerica XII. Mnemosyne Supplement 71.* Leiden: Brill.

(1985) *A Lexicon to Triphiodorus.* Hildesheim.

Camplani, A. (2015) 'Per un profilo storico-religioso degli ambienti di produzione e fruizione dei Papiri Bodmer: contaminazione dei linguaggi e dialettica delle idee nel contesto del dibattito su dualismo e origenismo', in A. Camplani and A. Cacciari (eds.) *Adamantius* 21.

Cameron, Alan (1995) *Callimachus and His Critics.* Princeton, NJ: Princeton University Press.

(2004) *Greek Mythography in the Roman World.* Oxford: Oxford University Press.

(2016) *Wandering Poets and Other Essays on Late Greek Literature and Philosophy.* Oxford: Oxford University Press.

Cameron, Averil (1970) *Agathias.* Oxford: Clarendon Press.

Camps, J. (1965) Review of Austin (1964) in *The Classical Review* 15 (2): 178–80.

Carlson, M. (1996) *Performance: A Critical Introduction.* London and New York: Routledge.

Carvounis, K. (2005) *Transformations of Epic: Reading Quintus of Smyrna, Posthomerica XIV.* DPhil Diss. at the University of Oxford.

(2007) 'Final Scenes in Quintus of Smyrna, *Posthomerica 14*' in Baumbach and Bär (eds.): 241–57.

(2014) 'Landscape Markers and Time in Quintus' *Posthomerica*' in M. Skempis and I. Ziogos (eds.) *Geography, Topography, Landscape: Configurations of Space in Greek and Roman Epic.* Berlin: de Gruyter: 181–208.

(2019) *A Commentary on Quintus of Smyrna, Posthomerica 14.* Oxford: Oxford University Press.

(forthcoming) 'Poetry, Performance and Quintus' *Posthomerica*' in S. Bär, E. Greensmith and L. Ozbek. (eds.) *Writing Homer Under Rome: Quintus of Smyrna in and Beyond the Second Sophistic.*

350   *Bibliography*

Cavallo, G. (2007) 'Places of Public Reading in Late Antiquity' in T. Derda, T. Markiewicz and E. Wipszycka (eds.) *Alexandria. Auditoria of Kom el-Dikka and Late Antique Education.* Warsaw: Journal of Juristic Papyrology: 151–6.

Chaudhuri, P. (2014) *The War with God: Theomachy in Roman Imperial Poetry.* Oxford: Oxford University Press.

Chondros, T., Milidonis, K., Vitzilaios, G. and Vaitsis, J. (2013) '"Deus-Ex-Machina" Reconstruction in the Athens Theater of Dionysus' in *Mechanism and Machine Theory.* 67: 172–91.

Chrysafis, G. (1985) 'Pedantry and Elegance in Quintus Smyrnaeus' *Posthomerica*' in *Corolla Londiniensis* 4: 17–42.

Chuvin, P. (1972) *Nonnos de Panopolis. Les Dionysiaques*, III. Paris: Les Belles Lettres.

Clark, G. (1993) *Women in Late Antiquity: Pagan and Christian Lifestyles.* Oxford: Clarendon Press.

(2012) Review of Ando (2012) in *BMCR* 2012.11.31.

Clarke, J. (1991) *The Houses of Roman Italy, 100 BC – AD 250: Ritual, Space and Decoration.* Berkeley: University of California Press.

Clauss, J. (2007) Review of Hunter (2006) in *BMCR* 2007.07.51.

Clay, J. S. (1997) *The Wrath of Athena: Gods and Men in the* Odyssey. London: Rowman and Littlefield (Originally published 1983: Princeton, NJ: Princeton University Press).

Clement, P. (1958) 'The Recovery of Helen' in *Hesperia* 27: 47–73.

Cloke, G. (1995) *This Female Man of God: Women and Spiritual Power in the Patristic Age, AD 350-450.* London: Routledge.

Collins, D. (2001) 'Improvisation in Rhapsodic Performance' in Stehle (ed.): 11–28.

(2004) *Master of the Game: Competition and Performance in Greek Poetry.* Washington: Center for Hellenic Studies, Trustees for Harvard University.

Collins, J. J. (1974) *The Sibylline Oracles of Egyptian Judaism.* Missoula: Society for Biblical Literature.

Connolly, J. (2001a) 'The Problems of the Past in Imperial Greek Education' in Y. L. Too (ed.) *Education in Greek and Roman Antiquity.* Leiden, Brill: 339–72.

(2001b) 'Reclaiming the Theatrical in the Second Sophistic' in Stehle (ed.): 75–95.

Conte, G. (1986) *The Rhetoric of Imitation: Genre and Poetic Memory in Virgil and Other Latin Poets.* Ithaca: Cornell University Press.

(1992) 'Proems in the Middle' in F. M. Dunn and T. Cole (eds.) *Beginnings in Classical Literature.* Cambridge, Cambridge University Press: 147–59.

Coon, L. (1997) *Sacred Fictions: Holy Women and Hagiography in Late Antiquity.* Philadelphia: University of Pennsylvania Press.

Cooper, K. (1996) *The Virgin and the Bride: Idealized Womanhood in Late Antiquity.* Cambridge, MA: Harvard University Press.

(2007a) 'Gender and the Fall of Rome', in P. Rousseau (ed.), *A Companion to Late Antiquity, Blackwell Companions to the Ancient World* Oxford: 187–200.

Bibliography

(2007b) *The Fall of the Roman Household*. Cambridge: Cambridge University Press.

Cowley, R. (2001) *What If?* New York: G. P. Putnam's Sons.

(2002) *More What If?* New York: G. P. Putnam's Sons.

Crane, G. (1990) 'Ajax, the Unexpected, and the Deception Speech' in *Classical Philology* 85 (2): 89–101.

Crawford, M. (2015) '"Reordering the Confusion": Tatian, the Second Sophistic, and the So-called Diatessaron' in *Zeitschrift für Antike und Christentum* 19: 209–36.

(2016) 'The Diatessaron, Canonical or Non-canonical? Rereading the Dura Fragment' in *New Testament Studies* 62 (2): 253–77.

Cribiore, R. (1999) Review of Morgan (1998) in *BMCR* 1999.05.22.

(2001): *Gymnastics of the Mind: Greek Education in Hellenistic and Roman Egypt*. Princeton, NJ: Princeton University Press.

Croke, B. (2009) 'Poetry and Propaganda: Anastasius as Pompey' in *GRBS* 48: 447–66.

Crotty, K. (1994) *The Poetics of Supplication: Homer's Iliad and Odyssey*. Ithaca: Cornell University Press.

Cunningham, M. (1954). 'Medea ΑΠΟ ΜΗΧΑΝΗΣ' in *Classical Philology* 49 (3): 151–60.

Cuypers, M. (2005) 'Interactional Particles and Narrative Voice in Apollonius and Homer' in A. Harder and M. Cuypers (eds.) *Beginning from Apollo. Studies in Apollonius Rhodius and the Argonautic Tradition*. Leuven: Peeters.

Dällenbach, L. (1989) *The Mirror in the Text*. Chicago: University of Chicago Press.

Dausque (1614) 'Notes on Quintus Calaber, Coluthus, and Triphiodorus', attached to L. Rhodomann, *Quinti Calabri Paraleipomena, Id est, Derelicta ab Homero, XIV*. Hanover.

Davies, M. (1989) *The Greek Epic Cycle*. Bristol: Bristol Classical Press.

Davies, M. and Finglass, P. J. (eds.) 2014. *Stesichorus: The Poems*. Cambridge Classical Texts and Commentaries, 54. Cambridge: Cambridge University Press.

de Jong, I. (1987a) *Narrators and Focalizers: The Presentation of the Story in the Iliad*. Amsterdam: Grüner.

(1987b) 'The Voice of Anonymity: *Tis*–speeches in the *Iliad*' in *Eranos* 85: 69–84.

(2001) *A Narratological Commentary on the* Odyssey. Cambridge: Cambridge University Press.

(2014) *Narratology and Classics: A Practical Guide*. Oxford: Oxford University Press.

de Jong, I. and Nünlist, R. (eds.) (2007) *Time in Ancient Greek Literature: Studies in Ancient Greek Narrative, Volume Two*. Leiden: Brill.

de Stefani, C. and Magnelli, E. (2011) 'Callimachus and Late Greek Poetry' in B. Acosta–Hughes, L. Lehnus and S. Stephens (eds.), *Brill's Companion to Callimachus*. Leiden: Brill 534–65.

Bibliography

Deckers, J. G. (1986), 'Dionysos der Erlöser? Bemerkungen zur Deutung der Bodenmosaiken im "Haus des Aion" in Nea-Paphos auf Cypern durch W.A. Daszewski' in *RQA* 81: 145–72.

Demoen, K. (1988) "The Date of the Cyzicene Epigrams. An Analysis of the Vocabulary and Metrical Technique of *AP* III', in *AC* 57: 231–48.

Dench, E. (2017) 'Ethnicity, Culture, and Identity' in D. Richter and W. Johnson (eds.) *The Oxford Handbook to the Second Sophistic*. Oxford: Oxford University Press: 99–114.

Desmond, M. (2016) 'Trojan Temporality and the Materiality of Literary History': Paper given at The Cambridge Classical Reception Seminar Series, Faculty of Classics, University of Cambridge, 21 January 2016.

Detienne, M. and Vernant, J. (1974) *Les ruses de l'intelligence: la mètis des Grecs.* Paris: Flammarion.

D'Ippolito, G. (1994) *Studi nonniani: L'epillio nello* Dionisiache. Palermo: Presso L'Accademia.

Dominik, W. (1994) *The Mythic Voice of Statius: Power and Politics in the Thebaid.* Leiden: Brill.

Doroszewski, F. (2016) *Orgie słów. Terminologia misteriów w „Parafrazie Ewangelii wg św. Jana" Nonnosa z Panopolis.* Toruń: seria Monografie FNP.

Drijvers, J. (1992) *Helena Augusta: The Mother of Constantine the Great and the Legend of her Finding the True Cross.* Leiden: Brill.

Dubielzig, U. (1996) Τριφιοδώρου Ἰλίου Ἅλωσις. *Triphiodor. Die Einnahme Ilions.* Tübingen.

Duc, T. (1990) 'La question de la cohérence dans les *Dionysiaques* de Nonnos de Panopolis' in *RPh* 64: 181–91.

Duckworth, G. (1933) 'Foreshadowing and Suspense in the *Posthomerica* of Quintus of Smyrna', in *AJPh* 57: 58–86.

(1936) *Foreshadowing and Suspense in Homer, Apollonius, and Vergil.* Princeton: Princeton University Press.

Dunkle, R. (1997) 'Swift-Footed Achilles' in *Classical World* 90: 227–34.

Dunn, G. (2004) *Tertullian.* London: Routledge.

Easterling, P. (1999) 'Actors and Voices: Reading between the Lines in Aeschines and Demosthenes' in Goldhill and Osborne (eds.): 154–66.

Edwards, C. (2002) 'Acting and Self-actualisation in Imperial Rome: Some Death scenes' in P. Easterling and E. Hall (eds.) *Greek and Roman Actors: Aspects of an Ancient Profession.* Cambridge: Cambridge University Press: 377–94.

Edwards, M. W. (1991) *The Iliad: A Commentary, Vol. 5, Books 17–20.* Cambridge: Cambridge University Press.

(2007) 'Severan Christianity' in Swain, Harrison and Elsner (eds.): 401–18.

Elm, S. (1994) *Virgins of God: The Making of Asceticism in Late Antiquity.* Oxford: Oxford University Press.

Elsner, J. (1995) *Art and the Roman Viewer: The Transformation of Art from the Pagan World to Christianity.* Cambridge: Cambridge University Press.

(2004) 'Late Antique Art: The Problem of the Concept and the Cumulative Aesthetic' in S. Swain and M. Edwards (eds.) *Approaching Late Antiquity:*

The Transformation from Early to Late Empire. Oxford: Oxford University Press: 271–309.

    (2017) 'Late Narcissus Classicism and Culture in a Late Roman Cento' in Elsner and Hernández Lobato (eds.): 176–205.

Elsner, J. and Hernandez Lobato, J. (eds.) (2017) *The Poetics of Late Latin Literature.* Oxford: Oxford University Press.

Enos, R. L. (2008) *Roman Rhetoric: Revolution and The Greek Influence.* West Lafayette: Parlor Press.

Erbse, H. (1969) (ed.) *Scholia Graeca in Homeri Iliadem (Scholia Vetera). Volumen Primum, Praefationem et Scholia ad Libros A-A continens.* Berlin: de Gruyter.

Erskine, A. (2001) *Troy between Greece and Rome: Local Tradition and Imperial Power.* Oxford: Oxford University Press.

Eshleman, K. (2012) *The Social World of Intellectuals in the Roman Empire: Sophists, Philosophers, and Christians.* Cambridge: Cambridge University Press.

Faber, R. A. (2017) 'The Hellenistic Origins of Memory as Trope for Literary Allusion in Latin Poetry' in *Philologus* 161 (1): 77–89.

Fantham, E. (2002) 'Orator and/et Actor' in Easterling and Hall (eds.): 362–76.

Fantuzzi, M. (2012) *Achilles in Love. Intertextual Studies.* Oxford: Oxford University Press.

Fantuzzi, M. and Hunter, R. (2004) *Tradition and Innovation in Hellenistic Poetry.* Cambridge: Cambridge University Press.

Fantuzzi, M. and Tsagalis, C. (eds.) (2015) *The Greek Epic Cycle and Its Ancient Reception: A Companion.* Cambridge: Cambridge University Press.

Feeney, D. (1983) 'The Taciturnity of Aeneas' in *The CQ* 33 (1): 204–19.

    (1991) *The Gods in Epic: Poets and Critics of the Classical Tradition.* Oxford: Clarendon Press.

    (2007) *Caesar's Calendar: Ancient Time and the Beginnings of History.* Berkeley: University of California Press.

    (2014) 'First Similes in Epic' in *TAPA* 144 (2): 189–228.

Felson, N. (1999) *Paradigms of Paternity: Fathers, Sons, and Athletic/Sexual Prowess in Homer's Odyssey* in J. N. Kazazis and A. Rengakos (eds.) *Euphrosyne: Studies in Ancient Epic and Its Legacy in Honor of D. N. Maronitis.* Stuttgart: F. Steiner: 89–98.

    (2002) 'Threptra and Invincible Hands: The Father–Son Relationship in *Iliad* 24' in *Arethusa* 35: 35–5.

Ferguson, N. (1997) *Virtual History: Alternatives and Counterfactuals.* London; Oxford: Macmillan.

Fernandelli, M. (2012) *Catullo e la rinascita dell'epos: dal carme 64 all'Eneide.* Spudasmata, Bd 142. Hildesheim; Zürich; New York: Georg Olms Verlag.

Ferreccio, A. (2014) *Commento al libro II dei Posthomerica di Quinto Smirneo.* Rome: Edizioni di Storia e Letteratura.

Finglass, P. (2018) 'Gazing at Helen with Stesichorus' in A. Kampakoglou, and A. Novokhatko (eds.), *Gaze, Vision, and Visuality in Ancient Greek Literature.* (Trends in Classics Supplements; Vol. 54). Berlin: de Gruyter: 140–59.

Bibliography

Finlay, R. A. (1980) 'Patroklos, Achilleus and Peleus: Fathers and Sons in the *Iliad*' in *CW* 73: 267–73.

Finn, R. (2007) 'Almsgiving for the Pure of Heart: Continuity and Change in Early Christian Teaching' in Swain, Harrison and Elsner (eds.): 419–29.

Fiorenza, E. S. (1979) ''Women in the Early Christian Movement', in C. P. Christ (ed.), *Womanspirit Rising: A Feminist Reader in Religion*. San Francisco, CA.

Fisher, E. A. (1982) 'Greek Translations of Latin Literature in the Fourth Century A.D.' in *Yale Classical Studies* 27: 173–215.

Foerster, R. (1963 edn.) *Libanii Opera*, Leipzig: Teubner.

Ford, A. (2002) *The Origins of Criticism: Literary Culture and Poetic Theory in Classical Greece*. New Jersey: Princeton University Press.

Fournet, J. L. (1992) 'Une éthopée de Caïn dans le Codex des Visions de la Fondation Bodmer' in *ZPE* 92: 254–66.

Fowler, D. (1997) 'Second Thoughts on Closure' in D. Roberts, F. M. Dunn and D. Fowler (eds.) *Classical Closure: Reading the End in Greek and Latin Literature*. Princeton, NJ: Princeton University Press: 3–22.

(2000) *Roman Constructions: Readings in Postmodern Latin*. Oxford: Oxford University Press.

Franchi, R. (2013) *Nonno di Panopoli. Parafrasi del Vangelo di S. Giovanni: Canto Sesto*. Bologna: EDB.

Frangoulis, H. (1999) *Nonnos de Panopolis. Les Dionysiaques, XIII: Chant XXVII*. Paris: Les Belles Lettres.

Fränkel, H. (1997) 'Essence and Nature of the Homeric Similes' in P. Jones and G. Wright (eds.) *Homer: German Scholarship in Translation*. Oxford: Oxford University Press: 103–23.

Fratantuono, L. (2016) 'The Penthesilead of Quintus Smyrnaeus: A Study in Epic Reversal' in *Wiener Studien* 129: 207–31.

Friedlander, S. (1991), *Probing the Limits of Representation: Nazism and the 'Final Solution'*. Cambridge, MA: Harvard University Press.

Gangloff, A. (2010) 'Rhapsodes et poètes épiques à l'époque impériale' in *REG* 123: 51–70.

Gantz, T. (1993) *Early Greek Myth: A Guide to Literary and Artistic Sources*. Baltimore and London: Johns Hopkins University Press.

Gärtner, U. (2005) *Quintus Smyrnaeus und die "Aeneis": Zur Nachwirkung Vergils in der griechischen Literatur der Kaiserzeit*. Munich: C.H. Beck.

(2007) 'Zur Rolle der Personifikationen des Schicksals in den Posthomerica des Quintus Smyrnaeus' in Baumbach and Bär (eds.): 211–40.

(2014) 'Schicksal und Entscheidungsfreiheit bei Quintus Smyrnaeus', in *Philologus* 58 (1): 97–129.

Geisz, C. (2017) *A Study of the Narrator in Nonnus of Panopolis' Dionysiaca: Storytelling in Late Antique Epic*. Leiden: Brill.

Gell, A. (1998) *Art and Agency: An Anthropological Theory*. Oxford: Clarendon Press.

Bibliography

Genette, G. (1980) *Narrative Discourse: An Essay in Method.* Translated by J. Lewin. Oxford: Blackwell.

Gerlaud, B. (1982) *Triphiodore, La Prise d'Ilion. Texte établi et traduit.* Paris: Les Belles Lettres.

Gibson, C. A. (trans.) (2008) *Libanius's Progymnasmata: Model Exercises in Greek Prose Composition and Rhetoric.* Atlanta: Society of Biblical Literature.

Gilka, M. (2015) Review of Cadau (2015) in *BMCR* 2015.12.2.

Giuliano, F. (1995) 'L'Odisseo di Platone: uno ζήτημα omerico nell'Ippia Minore', in G. Arrighetti (ed.), *Poesia greca.* Pisa: Giardini: 9–57.

Gleason, M. (1995) *Making Men: Sophists and Self-Presentation in Ancient Rome.* Princeton, NJ: Princeton University Press.

Godley, A. (1920) *Herodotus, with an English Translation.* Cambridge, MA: Harvard University Press.

Goldberg, S. and Manuwald, G. (eds. and trans.) (2018) *Fragmentary Republican Latin, Volume I: Ennius, Testimonia. Epic Fragments.* Cambridge, MA: Harvard University Press.

Golder, H. (1990) 'Sophocles' *Ajax*: Beyond the Shadow of Time', in *Ario*, 3rd series (1): 9–34.

Goldhill, S. (1984) *Language, Sexuality, Narrative: The Oresteia.* Cambridge: Cambridge University Press.

(1988) 'Doubling and Recognition in the *Bacchae*' in *Metis* 3: 137–56.

(1990) 'Supplication and Authorial Comment in *Iliad* Z 61–2' in *Hermes* 118 (3): 373–6.

(1991) *The Poet's Voice: Essays on Poetics and Greek Literature.* Cambridge: Cambridge University Press.

(2001) (ed.) *Being Greek under Rome. Cultural Identity, The Second Sophistic and the Development of Empire.* Cambridge: Cambridge University Press.

(2002a) *The Invention of Prose.* Greece and Rome New Surveys in the Classics No. 32. Oxford: Oxford University Press.

(2002b) *Who Needs Greek? Contests in the Cultural History of Hellenism.* Cambridge: Cambridge University Press.

(2015) 'Preposterous Poetics and the Erotics of Death' in *Eugestea* 5: 154–77.

(forthcoming a) 'Latin on Greek' in C. Whitton and R. Gibson (eds.) *Cambridge Critical Guide to Latin Literature.* Cambridge: Cambridge University Press.

(2020) *Preposterous Poetics: The Ideology and Aesthetics of Form in Late Antiquity.* Cambridge: Cambridge University Press.

(forthcoming c) *Playing God with Time.*

(forthcoming d) 'Homer and the Precarity of Tradition: Can Jesus be Achilles?'

Goldhill, S. and Greensmith, E. (forthcoming) in *The Cambridge Classical Journal.* 'Gregory of Nazianzus and the Palatine Anthology: The Poetics of Christian Death', in *The Cambridge Classical Journal.*

González, J. M. (2013) *The Epic Rhapsode and His Craft: Homeric Performance in a Diachronic Perspective.* Boston and London: Center for Hellenic Studies.

Bibliography

Gow, A. and Page, D. (1965) *Hellenistic Epigrams*. Cambridge: Cambridge University Press.

(eds. and trans.) (1968) *The Greek Anthology: Garland of Philip and some Contemporary Epigrams*. (2 vols.). Cambridge: Cambridge University Press.

Graziosi, B. (2002) *Inventing Homer: The Early Reception of Epic*. Cambridge: Cambridge University Press.

Greene, T. (1963) *The Descent from Heaven: A Study in Epic Continuity*. New Haven and London: Yale University Press.

Greensmith, E. (2018) 'When Homer Quotes Callimachus: Allusive Poetics in the Proem of the *Posthomerica*' in *CQ* 68 (1): 257–74.

(forthcoming a) 'Saying the Other: The Poetics of Personification in Later Antique Epic', in B. Verhelst and T. Scheijnen (eds.) *Walking the Wire: Greek and Latin Poetry in Dialogue*.

(forthcoming b) 'The Wrath of the Sibyl: Homeric Reception and Contested Identities in the *Sibylline Oracles* 3' in J. Konig and N. Wiater (eds.) *Late Hellenistic Literature in Context*. Cambridge: Cambridge University Press.

(forthcoming c) 'A-Sexual Epic? Consummation and Closure in the Posthomerica' in S. Bär, E. Greensmith and L. Ozbek (eds.) *Writing Homer under Rome: Quintus of Smyrna in and beyond the Second Sophistic*.

(forthcoming d) 'The Miracle Baby. Zagreus and Nonnus' Poetics of Mutation' in B. Verhelst (ed.) *Nonnus of Panopolis in Context* IV: *Poetry at the Crossroads*. Peeters: *Orientalia Lovaniensia Analecta* (Bibliothèque de Byzantion).

Grethlein, J. (2014) '"Future Past": Time and Teleology in (Ancient) Historiography', in *History and Theory* 53 (3): 309–30.

(2015) *Experience and Teleology in Ancient Historiography: "Futures Past" from Herodotus to Augustine*. Cambridge: Cambridge University Press.

Grethlein, J. and Krebs, C. B. (eds.) (2012) *Time and Narrative in Ancient Historiography: The 'Plupast' from Herodotus to Appian*. Cambridge: Cambridge University Press.

Griffin, J. (1980) *Homer on Life and Death*. Oxford: Clarendon Press.

Grossardt, P. (ed. and trans.) (2006) *Einführung, Übersetzung und Kommentar zum Heroikos von Flavius Philostrat*. Basle: Schwabe AG Verlag.

Habicht, C. (1985) *Pausanias' Guide to Ancient Greece*. Berkeley, Los Angeles and London: University of California Press

Hadjittofi, F. (2007) '*Res Romanae*: Cultural Politics in Quintus and Nonnus' in Baumbach and Bär (eds.): 357–78.

Halbwachs, M. (ed. and trans. L. Coser) (1992) *Collective Memory*. Chicago: University of Chicago Press.

Halliwell, S. (1988) *Plato Republic Book 10: With Introduction, Translation, and Commentary*. Oxford: Aris and Phillips.

(2011) *Between Ecstasy and Truth: Interpretations of Greek Poetics from Homer to Longinus*. Oxford: Oxford University Press.

Hall, E. (2005) 'Offstage Iliads' (review of James 2004) in *TLS*, October 7: 4–6.

Hangard, J. (1996) *Scholia in Aristophanis Lysistratam*. Groningen: Forsten.

Bibliography

Harder, M. A. (ed. and trans.) (2012) *Callimachus Aetia Vol. 1: Introduction, Text and Translation*. Oxford: Oxford University Press.

  (ed. and trans.) (2012) *Callimachus Aetia Vol. 2: Commentary*. Oxford: Oxford University Press.

Harder, M. A., Regtuit, R. and Wakker, G. (1993) *Callimachus* (Hellenistica Groningana 1). Groningen: Egbert Forsten.

Hardie, P. (1993) *The Epic Successors of Virgil: A Study in the Dynamics of a Tradition*. Cambridge: Cambridge University Press.

  (1997) 'Closure in Latin Epic' in Roberts, Dunn and Fowler (eds.): 139–62.

  (2002) *Ovid's Poetics of Illusion*. Cambridge: Cambridge University Press.

  (2007) 'Polyphony or Babel? Hosidius Geta's 'Medea' and the poetics of the cento' in Swain, Harrison and Elsner (eds.): 168–76.

Harmon, A. (trans.) (1913) *Lucian Volume 1*. Cambridge, MA: Harvard University Press.

Harries, B. (1994) 'The Pastoral Mode in the Dionysiaca' in Hopkinson (ed.): 63–85.

Harrison, S. (1988) 'Virgil on Kingship: The First Simile of the *Aeneid*' in *Proceedings of the Cambridge Philological Society* 34: 55–9.

Hartman, J. (2016) *Allusion and Cultural Memory in Late Antiquity: Ausonius, Prudentius, and Claudian*. PhD Diss. at the University of Washington.

Haslam, M. (1994) '*The Homer 'Lexicon of Apollonius Sophista: I. Composition and Constituents'* in *Classical Philology* 89 (1): 1–45.

  (1994) 'The Homer Lexicon of Apollonius Sophista: II. Identity and Transmission' in *Classical Philology* 89 (2): 107–19.

Hastrup, K. (1978) 'The Semantics of Biology: Virginity', in S. Ardener (ed.), *Defining Females: The Nature of Women in Society*. London.

Havell, H. (trans.) (1890) *Longinus on the Sublime*. London and New York: Macmillan.

Havelock, E. A. (1963) *Preface to Plato*. Cambridge, MA: Harvard University Press.

Heath, M. (1989) *Unity in Greek Poetics*. Oxford: Oxford University Press.

Hedreen, G. (1996) 'Image, Text, and Story in the Recovery of Helen' in *Classical Antiquity* 15 (1): 152–84.

Heidegger M. (1996). *Being and Time. A Translation of "Sein und Zeit"*. Translated by J. Stambaugh (7th ed.). Albany, New York: SUNY Press.

Heinze, R. (1915) *Virgils epische Technik*. Leipzig: Stuttgart.

Hekster O. (2008) *Rome and Its Empire, AD 193–284. Debates and Documents in Ancient History*. Edinburgh: Edinburgh University Press.

Henderson, J. (1987) ' Lucan/The Word at War' in *Ramus* 16 (1–2): 122–64.

Heseltine, M. (1975 rev. ed.) *Petronius:* Satyricon*; Seneca:* Apocolocyntosis. Cambridge, MA: Harvard University Press.

Hesk, J. (2006) 'Homeric Flyting and How to Read It: Performance and Intratext in *Iliad* 20.83–109 and 20.178–258' in *Ramus* 35: 4–28.

Hillgruber, M. (1994, 1999) *Die pseudoplutarchische Schrift De Homero* (2 vols.). Stuttgart and Leipzig.

358   Bibliography

(2000) 'Homer im Dienste des Mimus. Zur künstlerischen Eigenart der Homeristen.' in *ZPE* 132: 63–72.

Hillis Miller, J. (2003) 'Time in Literature' in *Daedalus* 132 (2): 86–97.

Hilton, J. (2017) 'Egyptian Necromancy in Heliodorus *Aethiopica* (6.12–15) and the Witch of Endor Narrative (1 Sam 28)' in Evans, R. (ed.) *Prophets and Profits: Ancient Divination and Its Reception.* Routledge.

Hinds, S. (1998) *Allusion and Intertext: Dynamics of Appropriation in Roman Poetry.* Cambridge: Cambridge University Press.

(2014) 'The Self-Conscious Cento' in M. Formisano and T. Fuhrer (eds.) *Decadence or "Other Antiquity".* Heidelberg: Winter: 171–98.

Hochschild, P. E. (2012) *Memory in Augustine's Theological Anthropology.* Oxford: Oxford University Press.

Hoekstra, A. (1965) *Homeric Modifications of Formulaic Prototypes: Studies in the Development of Greek Epic Diction.* Amsterdam: Noord–Hollandsche Uitg.

Hopkinson, N. (ed.) (1988) *A Hellenistic Anthology.* Cambridge.

(1994a) 'Nonnus and Homer' in Hopkinson (ed.) *Studies in the Dionysiaca of Nonnus.* Cambridge Philological Society: Supplementary volumes (17): 9–42.

(ed.) (1994b) *Greek Poetry of the Imperial Period.* Cambridge: Cambridge University Press.

(ed. and trans.) (2018) *Quintus Smyrnaeus* Posthomerica. Cambridge, MA: Harvard University Press.

Hornblower, S. (2015) *Lykophron:* Alexandra. *Greek Text, Translation, Commentary, and Introduction.* Oxford: Oxford University Press.

Horsfall, N. (2008) *Virgil, Aeneid 2.* Leiden: Brill.

Householder, F. W. (1941) *Literary Quotation and Allusion in Lucian.* New York: King's Crown Press.

Hunter, R. (1993) *The Argonautica of Apollonius: Literary Studies.* Cambridge: Cambridge University Press.

(1997) 'Longus and Plato' in M. Picone and B. Zimmermann (eds.) *Der antike Roman und seine mittelalterliche Rezeption.* Basle: Birkhäuser.

(2006) *The Shadow of Callimachus. Studies in the Reception of Hellenistic Poetry at Rome.* Cambridge: Cambridge University Press.

(2009) 'The Trojan Oration of Dio Chrysostom and Ancient Homeric Criticism' in J. Grethlein and A. Rengakos (eds.), *Narratology and Interpretation: The Content of Narrative Form in Ancient Literature.* Berlin: de Gruyter: 43–62.

(2012a) 'The Songs of Demodocus: Compression and Extension in Greek Narrative Poetry' in Baumbach and Bär (eds.): 81–109.

(2012b) *Plato and the Traditions of Ancient Literature: The Silent Stream.* Cambridge: Cambridge University Press.

(2014a) *Hesiodic Voices. Studies in the Ancient Reception of Hesiod's Works and Days.* Cambridge: Cambridge University Press.

(2014b) 'The Rhetorical Criticism of Homer' in F. Montanari, S. Matthaios and A. Rengakos (eds.) *Brill's Companion to Ancient Greek Scholarship*: 673–705.

(2015) 'Eustathian Moments: Reading Eustathius' Commentaries' in F. Pontani, V. Katsaros and V. Sarris (eds.) *Reading Eustathios of Thessalonike*. Berlin: de Gruyter.

(2016) 'The *Hippias Minor* and the Traditions of Homeric Criticism' in *The Cambridge Classical Journal* 62: 85–107.

Hunter, R. and Carvounis, K. (eds.) (2008) *Signs of Life? Studies in Later Greek Poetry* (*Ramus* 37.1 and 2).

Hunter, V. (1990) 'Gossip and the Politics of Reputation in Classical Athens' in *Phoenix* 44 (4): 299–325.

Husson, G. (1993) 'Les homéristes' in *Journal of Juristic Papyrology* 23: 93–9.

Hutchinson, G. (1988) *Hellenistic Poetry*. Oxford: Oxford University Press.

Hutton, P. (2000) 'Recent Scholarship on Memory and History' in *The History Teacher* 33 (4): 533–48.

Irwin, W. (2004) 'Against Intertextuality' in *Philosophy and Literature* 28: 227–42.

Jacobson, H. (1974) *Ovid's Heroides*. New Jersey: Princeton University Press.

James, A. (ed. and trans.) (2004) *Quintus of Smyrna, The Trojan Epic*. Baltimore and London: Johns Hopkins University Press.

(2006) Review of Gärner (2005) in *The Classical Review* 56: 328–9.

(2007) 'Quintus of Smyrna and Virgil: a Matter of Prejudice' in Baumbach and Bär (eds.): 285–306.

James, A. and Lee, K. (2000) *A Commentary on Quintus of Smyrna, Posthomerica V. Mnemosyne Supplement* 208. Leiden: Brill.

Jameson, F. (1991) *Postmodernism or, The Cultural Logic of Late Capitalism*. North Carolina: Duke University Press.

Jebb, R. C. (1898) *Sophocles: The Plays and Fragments with Critical Notes, Commentary and Translation in English Prose, Part IV: The Philoctetes* (2nd ed.). Cambridge: Cambridge University Press.

Johnson, W. (1987) *Momentary Monsters: Lucan and His Heroes*. Ithaca, NY: Cornell University Press.

Jones, P. (1985) Review of Strauss Clay (1983) in *The Classical Review* 35 (1): 177–8.

Joosten, J. (2001) 'Tatian's *Diatessaron* and the Old Testament Peshitta' in *Journal of Biblical Literature* 120: 501–23.

(2017) 'Le Diatessaron syriaque' in J. Haelewyck (ed.) *Le Nouveau Testament en syriaque*. Paris: Geuthner: 55–66.

(1996) 'The Independent Heroes of the *Iliad*' in *JHS* 116: 108–18.

Jordanova, L. (1989) *Sexual Visions: Images of Gender in Science and Medicine between the Eighteenth and Twentieth Centuries*. Wisconsin: University of Wisconsin Press.

Kakridis, Ph. I. (1962) Κόιντος Σμυρναῖος. Γενικὴ μελέτξ τῶν Μεθ᾽ Ὅμηρον καὶ τοῦ ποιητῆ τους. Athens.

Kaldellis, A. (1997) 'Agathias on History and Poetry', in *GRBS* 38: 295–306.

(2007) 'Christodoros on the Statues of the Zeuxippos Baths: A New Reading of the Ekphrasis.' in *GRBS* 47: 361–83.

360 *Bibliography*

Kaletsch, H. (1998) 'Hermos (Ἑρμός) [2]' in *DNP* 5: 452–3.

Kammen, M. (1991) *Mystic Chords of Memory: The Transformation of Tradition in American Culture*. New York: Knopf.

Kauffman, N. (2018) 'Slaughter and Spectacle in Quintus Smyrnaeus' Posthomerica' in *CQ* 68 (2): 634–48.

Kayachev, B. (2013) Review of Peirano (2012) in *BMCR* 2013.11.52.

Keaney, J. and Lamberton, R. (eds. and trans.) (1996) *Essay on the Life and Poetry of Homer (Plutarch)*. Atlanta: Scholars Press.

Kehmptzow, F. (1891) *De Quinti Smyrnaei fontibus ac mythopoeia*. Diss. Kiel.

Keizer, H. (2010) *Life Time Entirety. A Study of AION in Greek Literature and Philosophy, the Septuagint and Philo*. PhD Diss. 1999, Amsterdam: published as ebook in 2010.

Kelly, A. (2009) 'Parodic Inconsistency: Some Problems in the *Batrakhomyomakhia*' in *JHS* 129: 45–51.

Kennedy, D. (2013) *Antiquity and the Meanings of Time*. London; New York: I.B. Tauris.

Kerkhecker, A. (1988) 'Ein Musenanruf am Anfang der Aitia des Kallimachos' in *ZPE* 71: 16–24.

Kessels, A. and Van Der Horst. P. (1987) 'The Vision of Dorotheus: Edited with Introduction, Translation and Notes' in *Vigiliae Christianae* 41,(4): 313–59.

Keydell, R. (1931) 'Die griechische Poesie der Kaiserzeit' in *Bursians* 231: 41–161.

(1954) 'Quintus von Smyrna und Vergil' in *Hermes* 82: 254–6.

(1961) Review of Vian (1959a) in *Gnomon* 33: 278–84.

(1963) 'Quintus von Smyrna' in *RE* XXIV.1: 1271–96.

Kim, L. (2010) *Homer between History and Fiction in Imperial Greek Literature*. Cambridge: Cambridge University Press.

Kindstrand, J. F. (1973) *Homer in der zweiten Sophistik: Studien zu der Homerlektüre und dem Homerbild bei Dion von Prusa, Maximos von Tyros und Ailios Aristeides*. Uppsala: Acta Universitatis Upsaliensis.

King, K. C. (1987) *Achilles. Paradigms of the War Hero from Homer to the Middle Ages*. Berkeley: University of California Press.

Kirk, G. S. (1962) *Songs of Homer*. Cambridge: Cambridge University Press.

(1990) *The* Iliad*: A Commentary. Vol II: Books 5–8*. Cambridge: Cambridge University Press.

Kitchen, J. (1998) *Saints' Lives and the Rhetoric of Gender: Male and Female in Merovingian Hagiography*. Oxford: Oxford University Press.

Klooster, J. (2007) 'Apollonius of Rhodes' in de Jong and Nünlist (eds.): 63–80.

Kneebone, E. (2007) 'Fish in Battle? Quintus of Smyrna and the Halieutica of Oppian', in Baumbach and Bär (eds.): 285–306.

(2020) *Oppian's Halieutica: Charting a Didactic Epic*. Cambridge: Cambridge University Press.

(2016) 'Circling Time: *Aion* in Nonnus' Dionysiaca': paper given at The Society for Classical Studies 147th Annual Meeting, San Francisco, 9 January 2016.

Knox, P. E. (1988) 'Phaethon in Nonnus and Ovid' in *CQ* 38 (2): 536–51.

Bibliography

(ed.) (1995) *Ovid. Heroides: Select Epistles.* Cambridge: Cambridge. University Press.

Köchly, H (1850) *Quinti Smyrnaei Posthomericorum libri XIV. Relegit Armenius Koechly. Accedit index nominum a Francisco Spitznero confectus.* Leipzig: Teubner.

König, J. (2005) *Athletics and Literature in the Roman Empire.* Cambridge: Cambridge University Press.

Kohn, E. (2013) *How Forests Think: Toward an Anthropology Beyond the Human.* Berkeley: University of California Press.

Konstan, D. and Saïd, S. (eds.) (2006) *Greeks on Greekness: Viewing the Greek Past under the Roman Empire,* Cambridge: Cambridge Philological Society (29).

Kraeling, C. (1935) *A Greek Fragment of Tatian's Diatessaron from Dura. Studies and Documents 3.* London: Christophers.

Kristeva, J. (1969) *Desire in Language: A Semiotic Approach to Literature and Art.* Translated by Leon Roudiez. New York: Columbia University Press.

Kruchió, B. (2018) 'Heliodorus' Postsophistica: Homeric Intertextuality and Its Cultural Implications: paper given at the conference 'Heliodorus in New Contexts', Faculty of Classics, University of Cambridge, 12 December 2018.

Lada–Richards, I. (2002) 'The Subjectivity of Greek Performance' in P. Easterling and E. Hall (eds.). *Greek and Roman Actors: Aspects of an Ancient Profession.* Cambridge, Cambridge University Press: 395–418.

Lamberton, R. (1986) *Homer the Theologian: Neoplatonist Allegorical Reading and the Growth of the Epic Tradition.* Berkeley: University of California Press.

Lane Fox, R. (1986) *Pagans and Christians.* Harmondsworth: Viking.

Lardinois, A. (1997) 'Modern Paroemiology and the Use of Gnomai in Homer's *Iliad*' in *Classical Philology* 92: 213–34.

Lasek, A. (2016) 'Nonnus and the Play of Genres' in Accorinti (ed.): 402–21.

Lateiner, D. (2012) Review of Grethlein and Krebs (eds.) (2012) in *BMCR* 2012.11.43.

Latour, B. (1993) *We Have Never Been Modern.* Translated by Catherine Porter. Cambridge, MA: Harvard University Press.

(2005) *Reassembling the Social: An Introduction to Actor-Network-Theory.* Oxford: Oxford University Press.

Layton, R. (2003) 'Art and Agency: A Reassessment' in *The Journal of the Royal Anthropological Institute* 9 (3): 447–64.

Lear, G. (2011) 'Mimesis and Psychological Change in *Republic* III,' in P. Destree, and F. Herrmann (eds.), *Plato and the Poets.* Leiden: Brill: 195–216.

Lee, D. (1964) *The Similes of the Iliad and Odyssey Compared.* Melbourne: Melbourne University Press.

Lee, O. (1979) *Fathers and Sons in Virgil's* Aeneid: *tum genitor natum.* Albany: State University of New York Press.

Leigh, M. (2006) 'Statius and the Sublimity of Capaneus' in M. J. Clarke, B. Currie and R. O. A. M. Lyne (eds.) *Epic Interactions: Perspectives on Homer, Virgil, and the Epic Tradition, Presented to Jasper Griffin by Former Pupils.* Oxford: Oxford University Press: 217–42.

362 *Bibliography*

Lelli, E. et al. (eds.) (2013) *Quinto di Smirne: il seguito dell'Iliade di Omero.* Milan: Bompiani.

Lendon, J. (2005) *Soldiers and Ghosts: A History of Battle in Classical Antiquity.* New Haven: Yale University Press.

Levi, D. (1944) 'Aion' in *Hesperia* 13: 269–314.

Lévystone, D. (2005) 'La figure d'Ulysse chez les Socratiques: Socrate polutropôs' in *Phronesis* 50: 181–214.

Liapis, V. (2016) 'On the Hector of Astydamas', in *AJPh* 137: 61–89.

Liebert, R. (2013) 'Pity and Disgust in Plato's Republic: The Case of Leontius' in *Classical Philology* 108 (3) 179–201.

Lightfoot, J. (2007) *The Sibylline Oracles: With Introduction, Translation, and Commentary on the First and Second Books.* Oxford: Oxford University Press.

Livrea, E. (2000) *Nonno di Panopoli, Parafrasi del Vangelo di S. Giovanni, Canto B.* Bologna: EDB.

Lloyd–Jones, H. (1969) Review of Combellack (1968) in *Classical Review* 19: 101.

Lorenz, K. (2013) 'Split Screen Aficionados: Heracles on Top of Troy in the Casa di Octavius Quartio in Pompeii' in H. Lovatt and C. Vout (eds.) *Epic Visions.* Cambridge: Cambridge University Press: 218–47.

Lovatt, H. (2013) *The Epic Gaze: Vision, Gender and Narrative in Ancient Epic.* Cambridge: Cambridge University Press.

Lowe, N. J. (2000) *The Classical Plot and the Invention of Western Narrative.* Cambridge: Cambridge University Press.

Lyne, R. O. A. M. (1984) 'Ovid's Metamorphoses, Callimachus and l'art pour l'art', in *MD* 12: 9–34.

 (1987) *Further Voices in Vergil's* Aeneid. Oxford: Oxford University Press.

 (1989) *Words and the Poet: Characteristic Techniques of Style in Vergil's Aeneid.* Oxford: Clarendon Press.

 (1994) 'Vergil's *Aeneid*: Subversion by Intertextuality. Catullus 66. 39–40 and Other Examples' in R.O.A.M. Lyne and S. Harrison (eds.) *R.O.A.M. Lyne: Collected Papers on Latin Poetry.* Oxford: Oxford University Press.

Lynn-George, M. (1988) *Epos: Word, Narrative, and the Iliad.* London: Humanities Press International.

 (1996) 'Structures of Care in the *Iliad*' in *CQ* 46 (1): 1–26.

Ma, J. (2007) 'The Worlds of Nestor the Poet' in Swain, Harrison and Elsner (eds.): 83–113.

Maas, M. (ed) (2005) *The Cambridge Companion to the Age of Justinian.* Cambridge: Cambridge University Press.

Maciver, C. A. (2007) 'Returning to the Mountain of *Arete*: Reading Ecphrasis, Constructing Ethics in Quintus' Smyrnaeus' *Posthomerica*' in Baumbach and Bär (eds.): 259–84.

 (2012a): 'Representative Bees in Quintus Smyrnaeus' *Posthomerica*' in *Classical Philology* 107 (1): 53–69.

 (2012b) *Quintus Smyrnaeus' 'Posthomerica': Engaging Homer in Late Antiquity.* Leiden: Brill.

Bibliography 363

(2012c) 'The Flyte of Odysseus: Allusion and the *hoplōn krisis* in Quintus Smyrnaeus, *Posthomerica* 5' in *AJPh* 133.4: 601–28.

(2016) 'Nonnus and Imperial Greek Poetry' in Accorinti (ed.): 529–48.

(2017) 'Netherworld Destinations in Quintus Smyrnaeus' *Posthomerica*: Some (Homeric) Problems', in I. Tanaseanu–Döbler, A. Lefteratou, G. Ryser and K. Stamatopoulos (eds.) *Reading the Way to the Netherworld. Education and Representations of the Beyond in Later Antiquity*. Göttingen: Vandenhoeck and Ruprecht: 123–37.

(2018) 'Program and Poetics in Quintus of Smyrnaeus' *Posthomerica*' in R. Simms (ed.) *Brill's Companion to Epic Continuations, Prequels and Sequels*. Leiden: Brill: 71–89.

(2020) 'Triphiodorus and the Poetics of Imperial Greek Epic', in *Classical Philology* 115 (2): 164–85.

Mackie, H. (1997) 'Song and Storytelling: An Odyssean Perspective' in *TAPA* 127 (7): 77–95.

Madden, E. (1952) 'The Enthymeme: Crossroads of Logic, Rhetoric, and Metaphysics' in *The Philosophical Review* 61 (3): 368–76.

Mair, A. (trans.) (1928) *Oppian, Colluthus, Tryphiodorus*. Cambridge, MA: Harvard University Press.

Malm, M. and Cullhed, S. (eds.) (2018) *Reading Late Antiquity. The Library of the other Antiquity*. Heidelberg: Universitätsverlag C. Winter.

Mansur, M. W. (1940) *The Treatment of Homeric Characters by Quintus of Smyrna*. New York: Columbia University.

Maronitis, D. (1973) *Αναζήτηση και νόστος του Οδυσσεά: η διαλεκτική της Οδύσσειας*. Athens: Papazēsē.

Martin, R. (1989) *The Language of Heroes: Speech and Performance in the Iliad*. Ithaca: Cornell University Press.

Martindale, C. (1993) *Redeeming the Text: Latin Poetry and the Hermeneutics of Reception*. Cambridge: Cambridge University Press.

Martínez, J. (ed.) (2014) *Fakes and Forgeries in Classical Literature*. Leiden: Brill.

Masters, J. (1992) *Poetry and Civil War in Lucan's Bellum Civile*. Cambridge: Cambridge Classical Studies.

Matsuda, M. K. (1996) *The Memory of the Modern*. New York: Oxford University Press.

McAuley, M. (2016) *Reproducing Rome: Motherhood in Virgil, Ovid, Seneca and Statius. Oxford Studies in Classical Literature and Gender Theory*. Oxford; New York: Oxford University Press.

McMillin, T. (2000) *Our Preposterous Use of Literature: Emerson and the Nature of Reading*. Chicago: University of Illinois Press.

Mehler, J. (1961) 'Quintus Smyrnaeus' in *Hermeneus* 33: 34–41.

Merkle, S. (1994) 'Telling the True Story of the Trojan War: the Eyewitness Account of Dictys of Crete', in J. Tatum (ed.) *The Search for the Ancient Novel*. Baltimore and London: Johns Hopkins University Press: 183–98.

Bibliography

Middleton, F. (2019) 'The Poetics of Later Greek Ecphrasis: Christodorus Coptus, the *Palatine Anthology* and the *Periochae* of Nonnus' *Dionysiaca*', *Ramus* 47, 216–38.

Miguélez Cavero, L. (2008) *Poems in Context: Greek Poetry in the Egyptian Thebaid 200–600 AD. Sozomena. Studies in the Recovery of Ancient Texts 2.* Berlin: de Gruyter.

(2013) *Triphiodorus,* The Sack of Troy: *A General Introduction and a Commentary.* Berlin: de Gruyter.

Miller, J. F. (1993) 'Ovidian Allusion and the Vocabulary of Memory' in *MD* 30: 153–74.

Mills, S. (2000) 'Achilles, Patroclus and Parental Care in Some Homeric Similes' in *Greece & Rome* 47 (1): 3–18.

Mitchell, S. (1987) 'Imperial Building in the Eastern Roman Provinces' in *Harvard Studies in Classical Philology* 91: 333–65.

Montiglio, S. (2011) *From Villain to Hero: Odysseus in Ancient Thought.* Michigan: University of Michigan Press.

Morales, H. (2000) 'Sense and Sententiousness in the Ancient Greek Novels' in A. Sharrock and H. Morales (eds.) *Intratextuality: Greek and Roman Textual Relations.* Oxford: Oxford University Press: 67–88.

(2004) *Vision and Narrative in Achilles Tatius' Leucippe and Clitophon.* Cambridge: Cambridge University Press.

(2016) 'Rape, Violence, Complicity: Colluthus's *Abduction of Helen*' in *Arethusa* 49.1: 61–92.

Moret, J. M. (1975) *Ilioupersis dans la céramique italiote: Les mythes et leur expression figurée au IVe siècle.* Rome: Bibliotheca Helvetica Romana.

Morgan, T. (1998) *Literate Education in the Hellenistic and Roman Worlds.* Cambridge: Cambridge University Press.

(2007) *Popular Morality in the Early Roman Empire.* Cambridge: Cambridge University Press.

Morley, N. (2000) 'Trajan's Engines' in *Greece and Rome* 47: 197–210.

Most, G. (trans.) (2007) *Hesiod: Theogony, Works and Days, Testimonia*, vol. I. Cambridge, MA: Harvard University Press.

Moulton, C. (1977) *Similes in the Homeric Poems.* Göttingen: Vandenhoeck und Ruprecht.

Mullen, A. and James, P. (eds.) (2012) *Multilingualism in the Graeco-Roman Worlds.* Cambridge: Cambridge University Press.

Mullen, A and Elder, O. (eds.) (2019) *The Language of Letters: Bilingual Roman Epistolography from Cicero to Fronto.* Cambridge: Cambridge University Press.

Murray, A. (1919) *Homer Iliad 1–12 (vol. 1) and 13–24 (vol. 2).* Revised by W. Wyatt 1999. Cambridge, MA: Harvard University Press.

(revised by G. Dimock) (1998) *Homer Odyssey Vols. 1 & 2.* Cambridge, MA: Harvard University Press.

Naddaff, R. (2002) *Exiling the Poets: The Production of Censorship in Plato's Republic.* Chicago and London: University of Chicago Press.

Bibliography

Nagy, G. (1990) *Pindar's Homer: The Lyric Possession of an Epic Past*. Baltimore and London: Johns Hopkins University Press.

(1996) *Poetry as Performance: Homer and Beyond*. Cambridge: Cambridge University Press.

(1997) 'Homeric Scholia' in I. Morris and B. Powell (eds.) *A New Companion to Homer*. Leiden: Brill: 101–22.

Nehamas, A. (1982) 'Plato on Imitation and Poetry in *Republic* 10' in J. Moravcsik, and P. Temko (eds.) *Plato on Beauty, Wisdom, and the Arts*. Totowa: Rowman and Littlefield: 47–78.

Newby, Z. (2007) 'Art at the Crossroads? Themes and Style in Severan Art' in Swain, Harrison and Elsner (eds.): 201–49.

Ní Mheallaigh, K. (2014) *Reading Fiction with Lucian. Fakes, Freaks and Hyperreality*. Cambridge: Cambridge University Press.

Nora, P. (ed)., (1984–1992) *Les Lieux de mémoire* (3 vols.). Paris: Gallimard.

Nünlist, R. (2009a) 'Narratological Concepts in Greek Scholia' in Grethlein and Rengakos (eds.): 63–86.

(2009b) *The Ancient Critic at Work: Terms and Concepts of Literary Criticism in Greek Scholia*. Cambridge: Cambridge University Press.

Ojeda, E. J. L. (2002) *La adjetivación en las Dionisíacas de Nono de Panópolis: tradición e innovación. Hapax absolutos y no absolutos*. PhD. Diss. at the University of Málaga.

O'Nolan, K. (1978) *Doublets in the Odyssey*. Cambridge: Cambridge University Press.

Ozbek, L. (2007) 'Ripresa della tradizione e innovazione compositiva: la medicina nei *Posthomerica* di Quinto Smirneo' in Baumbach and Bär (eds.): 159–83.

Pappas, N. (2017) 'Plato's Aesthetics' in E. Zalda (ed.) *The Stanford Encyclopedia of Philosophy* (Fall 2017 ed.).

Paratore, E. (1976) 'Il problema degli pseudepigrapha' in *Romane Litterae* (reprinted from 1971). Rome: 5–32.

Parker, D., Taylor, D. and Goodacre, M (eds.) (1999) 'The Dura-Europos Gospel Harmony' in D. G. K. Taylor (ed.) *Studies in the Early Text of the Gospels and Acts*. Atlanta: Society of Biblical Literature: 192–228.

Parker, P. (1987) *Literary Fat Ladies: Rhetoric, Gender, Property*. London and New York: Methuen.

Parry, A. (ed.) (1971) *The Making of Homeric Verse: The Collected Papers of Milman Parry*. New York and Oxford: Oxford University Press.

Parsons, P. (ed.) (1974) *The Oxyrhynchus Papyri, vol. xlii*. London: Bloomsbury.

(ed.) (1983) *The Oxyrhynchus Papyri, L*. London: Egypt Exploration Society.

(2012) 'Homer: Papyri and Performance' in G. Bastianini and A. Casaova (eds.) *I papyri omerici. Atti del convengo internazionale di studi*. Florence: Istituto papirologico.

Paschal, G. W. (1904) *A Study in Quintus of Smyrna*. Diss. at the University of Columbia.

Paton, W. (trans.) (1918) *The Greek Anthology* (5 vols.) Cambridge, MA: Harvard University Press.

Bibliography

Pavese, C. O. (1998) 'The Rhapsodic Epic Poems as Oral and Independent Poems' in *Harvard Studies in Classical Philology* 98: 63–90.

Peirano, I. (2012) *The Rhetoric of the Roman Fake: Latin Pseudepigrapha in Context*. Cambridge: Cambridge University Press.

Pelling, C. (2006) 'Herodotus and Homer' in M. J. Clarke, B. G. F. Currie and R. O. A. M. Lyne (eds.), *Epic Interactions: Perspectives on Homer, Virgil, and the Epic Tradition Presented to Jasper Griffien by Former Pupils*, Oxford: Oxford University Press: 75–104.

Pelttari, A. (2014) *The Space That Remains: Reading Latin Poetry in Late Antiquity*. Ithaca, NY: Cornell University Press.

Perret, J. (ed.) (1977) *Virgile Énéide Livres I–IV*. Paris: Les Belles Lettres.

Petersen, L. and Salzman-Mitchell, P. (eds.) (2012). *Mothering and Motherhood in Ancient Greece and Rome*. Austin: University of Texas Press.

Petersen, W. (1994) *Tatian's Diatessaron. Its Creation, Dissemination, Significance and History in Scholarship, Vigiliae Christianae* Supplement 25. Leiden: Brill.

Petrain, D. (2014) *Homer in Stone: The 'Tabulae Iliacae' in their Roman Context. Greek Culture in the Roman World*. Cambridge: Cambridge University Press.

Pfeiffer, R. (ed.) (1949) *Callimachus* 1. Oxford: Clarendon Press.

(1968) *History of Classical Scholarship from the Beginnings to the End of the Hellenistic Age*. Oxford: Clarendon Press.

Piccardi, D. C. (2016) 'Nonnus' Poetics', in Accorinti (ed.): 422–42.

Plastira-Valkanou, M. (1999) 'Love-dreams in the Anthology' in *AC* 68: 275–82.

Plooij, D. (1934/1935) "A Fragment of Tatian's Diatessaron in Greek," in *ExpTim* 46: 471–6.

Pontani, F. (2005) *Sguardi su Ulisse. La tradizione esegetica greca all'Odissea*. Rome: Edizioni di storia e letteratura.

(ed.) (2007) *Scholia graeca in Odysseam. Pleiadi : 6*. Rome: Edizioni di storia e letteratura.

Porter, J. (2002) 'Homer the Very Idea' in *Arion* 10 (2): 57–86.

(2010) *The Origins of Aesthetic Thought in Ancient Greece: Matter, Sensation, and Experience*, Cambridge: Cambridge University Press.

Porter, S. (2013) 'What Can We Learn about Greek Grammar from a Mosaic'? in S. Porter and A. Pitts (eds.) *The Language of the New Testament: Context, History and Development*. Leiden: Brill: 29–41.

Postclassicisms Collective (2020) *Postclassicisms*. Chicago: University of Chicago Press.

Pöschl, V. (1970) *The Art of Vergil*. Translated by G. M. Seligson. Ann Arbor: University of Michigan Press.

Powell, B. (1997) Review of Nagy (1996) in *BMCR* 97.3.21.

Pratt, L. (2007) 'The Parental Ethos of the *Iliad*' in *Hesperia Supplements* 41 (Constructions of Childhood in Ancient Greece and Italy): 24–40.

Prendergast, C. (2019) *Counterfactuals: Paths of the Might Have Been*. London; New York: Bloomsbury.

Pucci, J. (1998) *The Full Knowing Reader. Allusion and the Power of the Reader in the Western Literary Tradition*. New Haven: Yale University Press.

Purves, A. (2010) *Space and Time in Ancient Greek Narrative*. Cambridge: Cambridge University Press.

Quint, D. (1993) *Epic and Empire*. Princeton, NJ: Princeton University Press.

  (2018) *Virgil's Double Cross: Design and Meaning in the Aeneid*. Princeton: Princeton University Press.

Rea, J. (1972) 'Triphiodorus, Fall of Troy, 391–402' in *POxy*. 46: 9–10 [publication of *POxy*. 2946].

Reader, W. W. (ed.) (1996) *The Severed Hand and the Upright Corpse: The Declamations of Marcus Antonius Polemo*. Atlanta: Society of Biblical Literature.

Redfield, J. (1973) 'The Making of the *Odyssey*' in A. Yu (ed.) *Parnassus Revisited: Modern Critical Essays on the Epic Tradition*. Chicago: University of Chicago Press: 141–54.

  (1975) *Nature and Culture in the Iliad: the Tragedy of Hector*. Chicago and London: University of Chicago Press.

Remijsen, S. (2015) *The End of Greek Athletics in Late Antiquity*. Cambridge: Cambridge University Press.

Rengakos, A. (1993) *Der Homertext und Die Hellenistischen Dichter*. Stuttgart: Franz Steiner.

  (1994) *Apollonios Rhodios und die antike Homererklärung*. Munich: C.H. Beck.

Richardson, N. J. (1993) *The Iliad. A Commentary*, vol. VI, books 21–4. Cambridge: Cambridge University Press.

Richter, D. and Johnson, A. (eds.) (2017) *The Oxford Handbook of the Second Sophistic*. Oxford; New York: Oxford University Press.

Ricoeur, P. (1970) *Freud and Philosophy: An Essay in Interpretation*. Translated by D. Savage. New Haven: Yale University Press.

  (1984), *Time and Narrative, Vol. I*. Translated by K. McLaughlin and D. Pellauer. Chicago: Chicago University Press.

Robert, W. (1936) 'Ἀρχαιολόγος' in *Revue des études grecques* 49: 235–54.

Roberts, M. (1989) *The Jeweled Style: Poetry and Poetics in Late Antiquity*. Ithaca and London: Cornell University Press.

Rosati, G. (2005) 'Statius, Domitian and Acknowledging Paternity: Rituals of Succession in the *Thebaid*' in R. R. Nauta, H. Dam and J. J. L. Smolenaars (eds.) *The Poetry of Statius*. Leiden: Brill: 175–94.

Rosenmeyer, P. (1992) *The Poetics of Imitation: Anacreon and the Anacreontic Tradition*. Cambridge: Cambridge University Press.

Roueché, C. (1993) *Performers and Partisans at Aphrodisias in the Roman and Late Roman Periods. A Study based on Inscriptions from the Current Excavations at Aphrodisias in Caria*. London: Society for the Promotion of Roman Studies.

Rousso, H. (1991) *The Vichy Syndrome: History and Memory in France since 1944*. Translated by Arthur Goldhammer. Cambridge, MA: Harvard University Press.

Rowe, G. (1966) 'The Portrait of Aeschines in the Oration on the Crown' in *TAPA* 97: 397–406.

368   *Bibliography*

Russell, D. (1964) *Longinus, On the Sublime*. Oxford: Clarendon Press.
(ed. and trans.) (2001) *Quintilian, The Orator's Education* (5 vols.). Cambridge, MA: Harvard University Press.
Rüter, K. (1969) *Odysseeinterpretationen. Untersuchungen zum ersten Buch und zur Phaiakis*. Göttingen: Vandenhoeck u. Ruprecht.
Sammons, B. (2010) *The Art and Rhetoric of the Homeric Catalogue*. Oxford: Oxford University Press.
(2017) *Device and Composition in the Greek Epic Cycle*. Oxford: New York: Oxford University Press.
Sánchez-Ostiz, A. (2013) 'Cicero Graecus: Notes on Ciceronian Papyri from Egypt' in *ZPE* 187: 144–53.
Sandnes, K. (2011) *The Gospel 'According to Homer and Virgil': Cento and Canon*. Leiden: Brill.
Schechner, R. (1985) *Between Theater and Anthropology*. Philadelphia: University of Pennsylvania Press.
Scheijnen, T. (2018) *Quintus of Smyrna's Posthomerica: A Study of Heroic Characterization and Heroism*. Leiden: Brill.
Schenk, P. (1997) 'Handlungsstruktur und Komposition in den *Posthomerica* des Quintus Smyrnaeus' in *RhM* 140: 363–85.
Schmid, U. (2013) 'Tatian's Diatessaron' in B. Ehrman, M. Holmes (eds.), *The Text of the New Testament in Contemporary Research: Essays on the Status Quaestionis*, 2nd ed., Leiden: Brill: 115–42.
Schmidt, T. and Fleury, P. (eds.) (2011) *Perceptions of the Second Sophistic and Its Times*. Toronto and London: University of Toronto Press.
Schmitz, T. (1997) *Bildung und Macht. Zur sozialen und politischen Funktion der zweiten Sophistik in der griechischen Welt der Kaiserzeit*. Munich: C.H. Beck.
(1999) 'Performing History in the Second Sophistic' in M. Zimmermann (ed.) *Geschichtsschreibung und politischer Wandel im 3. Jh. N. Chr.* Stuttgart: Franz Steiner.
(2007a) *Modern Literary Theory and Ancient Texts. An Introduction. Translation of 2002 German edition*. Malden, MA: Blackwell Publishing.
(2007b) 'The Use of Analepses and Prolepses in Quintus Smyrnaeus' *Posthomerica*' in Baumbach and Bär (eds.): 65–84.
Schmitz, T. and Wiater, N. (eds.) (2011) *The Struggle for Identity: Greeks and Their Past in the First Century BCE*. Stuttgart: Franz Steiner Verlag.
Scott, W. (2009) *The Artistry of the Homeric Simile*. Dartmouth: Dartmouth College Press.
Segal, C. (1982) *Dionysiac Poetics and Euripides' Bacchae*. Princeton, University Press.
(1994) *Singers, Heroes and Gods in the Odyssey*. Ithaca: Cornell University Press.
Sens, A. (2006) 'Tipte genos toumon zeteis? The *Batrachomyomachia*, Hellenistic Epic Parody and Early Epic' in F. Montanari and A. Rengakos (eds.) *La Poésie Epique Grecque*. Geneva: 215–48.
Shackleton Bailey, D. R. (2003) *Statius. Vol. 2: Thebaid, Books 1–7; Vol. 3: Books 8–12*. Cambridge, MA: Harvard University Press.

Bibliography

Shorrock, R. (2001) *The Challenge of Epic: Allusive Engagement in the* Dionysiaca *of Nonnus*. Leiden: Brill.

(2008) 'The Politics of Poetics: Nonnus' *Dionysiaca* and the World of Late Antiquity' in Carvounis and Hunter (eds.): 99–113.

(2011) *The Myth of Paganism: Nonnus, Dionysus and the World of Late Antiquity*. London: Bristol Classical Press.

Skutsch, O. (1985) (eds.) *The Annals of Q. Ennius*. Oxford: Clarendon Press.

Snell, R. and Kannicht, S. (eds.) (1986) *Tragicorum Graecorum Fragmenta*, I^2. Göttingen: Vandenhoeck & Ruprecht.

Sörbom, G. (1966) *Mimesis and Art. Studies in the Origin and Early Development of an Aesthetic Vocabulary*. Stockholm: Scandinavian University Books.

Sowers, B. (2020) *In Her Own Words: The Life and Poetry of Aelia Eudocia*. Cambridge, MA: Harvard University Press.

Snipes, K. (1988) 'Literary Interpretation in the Homeric Scholia: The Similes of the *Iliad*' in *AJPh* 109: 196–222.

Spanoudakis, K. (2012) 'Aiwnos Litai (Nonn. Dion. 7.1–109)' in *Aitia* 2: 1–32.

(2014a) (ed.) *Nonnus of Panopolis in Context: Poetry and Cultural Milieu in Late Antiquity with a Section on Nonnus and the Modern World*. Berlin: de Gruyter.

(2014b) (ed.) *Nonnus of Panopolis Paraphrasis of the Gospel of John XI*. Oxford: Oxford University Press.

Spawforth, A. (1989) 'Agonistic Festivals in Roman Greece' in *Bulletin Supplement (University of London. Institute of Classical Studies)* 55: 'The Greek Renaissance in the Roman Empire: Papers from the Tenth British Museum Classical Colloquium': 193–7.

Speyer, W. (1971) *Die literarische Fälschung im heidnischen und christlichen Altertum. Ein Versuch ihrer Deutung*. Munich, C.H. Beck.

Squire, M. (2011) *The Iliad in a Nutshell: Visualizing Epic on the Tabulae Iliacae*. Oxford: Oxford University Press.

(2014) 'The *Ordo* of Rhetoric and the Rhetoric of Order', in Meyer, M. and Elsner, J. (eds.) *Art and Rhetoric in Roman Culture*. Cambridge: Cambridge University Press: 353–417.

Stanford, W. (1950) 'Homer's Use of Personal πολυ–Compounds' in *Classical Philology* 45: 108–10.

Starr, R. J. (1987) 'Trimalchio's *Homeristae*' in *Latomus* 46: 199–200.

Stefanou, D. (2006) *Darstellungen aus dem Epos und Drama auf kaiserzeitlichen und spätantiken Bodenmosaiken. Eine ikonographische und deutungsgeschichtliche Untersuchung*. Munster: LIT Verlag.

Stegemann, V. (1930) *Astrologie und Universalgeschichte: Studien und Interpretationen zu den Dionysiaka des Nonnos von Panopolis*. Leipzig: Berlin.

Stehle, E. (ed.) (2001) *Unmasked Performances: Staging Identities in Greece and Rome (Helios 28.1)*.

Steiner, G. (1989) *Real Presences: Is There Anything in What We Say?* London: Faber.

Stephens, S. A. (2002) 'Linus Song' in *Hermathena* 173: 13–28.

Bibliography

Strauss Clay, J. (1983) *The Wrath of Athena: Gods and Men in the Odyssey.* Princeton, NJ: Princeton University Press.

Strenger, J. (2004) *Poetische Argumentation. Die Funktion der Gnomik in den Epinikien des Bakchylides.* Berlin: de Gruyter.

Swain, S. (1989) 'Favorinus and Hadrian' in *ZPE* 79: 150–8.

(1991) 'The Reliability of Philostratus's "Lives of the Sophists"' in *Classical Antiquity* 10 (1): 148–63.

(1996) *Hellenism and Empire. Language, Classicism and Power in the Greek World AD 50–250.* Oxford: Clarendon Press.

(2007) 'Introduction' in Swain, Harrison and Elsner (eds.): 1–26.

Swain, S., Harrison, S. and Elsner, J. (eds.) (2007) *Severan Culture.* Cambridge: Cambridge University Press.

Tarrant, R. J. (1989) 'The Reader as Author: Collaborative Interpolation in Latin Poetry' in J. N. Grant (ed.) *Editing Greek and Latin Texts.* New York: 121–62.

Teske, R. (2001) 'Augustine's Philosophy of Memory' in N. Kretzmann and E. Stump (eds.) *The Cambridge Companion to Augustine.* Cambridge: Cambridge University Press: 148–58.

Thalmann, W. (1984) *Conventions of Form and Thought in Early Greek Poetry.* Baltimore and London: Johns Hopkins University Press.

Tipping, B. (2010) *Exemplary Epic: Silius Italicus'* Punica. Oxford: Oxford University Press.

Tissoni, F. (2016) 'The Reception of Nonnus in Late Antiquity, Byzantine and Renaissance Literature' in Accorinti (ed.): 671–91.

(2000) *Cristodoro: Un'introduzione e un comment.* Alessandria: dell'Orso.

Tomasso, V. E. (2010) *'Cast in Later Grecian Mould', Quintus of Smyrna's Reception of Homer in the Posthomerica.* Diss. at the University of Stanford.

(2012) 'The Fast and the Furious: Triphiodorus' Reception of Homer in The Capture of Troy' in Baumbach and Bär (eds.): 369–409.

Too, Y. L. (ed.) (2001) *Education in Greek and Roman Antiquity.* Leiden: Brill.

Tsagalis, C. C. (2007) *The Oral Palimpsest: Exploring Intertextuality in the Homeric Epics.* Washington and London: Center for Hellenic Studies, Trustees for Harvard University.

Tsagarakis, O. (1979) 'Phoenix's Social Status and the Achaean Embassy' in *Mnemosyne,* 32: 221–42.

Tychsen, T. (1807) *Quinti Smyarnaei Posthomericorum libri XIV.* Strasbourg.

Usher, M. (1998) *Homeric Stitchings: The Homeric Centos of the Empress Eudocia.* Lanham, MD: Rowman & Littlefield.

Van der Valk, M. (1949) *Textual Criticism of the* Odyssey. Leiden: A. W. Sijthoff.

(ed.) (1971) *Eustathii Archiepiscopi Thessalonicensis Commentarii ad Homeri Iliadem Pertinentes.* Leiden: Brill.

Van Minnen, P. (2016) 'Nonnus' Panopolis' in Accorinti (ed.): 54–74.

Van Tress, H. (2004) *Poetic Memory: Allusion in the Poetry of Callimachus and the Metamorphoses of Ovid.* Leiden: Brill (*Mnemosyne Supplement* 258).

Bibliography

Vanacker, W. and Zuiderhoek, A. (eds.) (2017) *Imperial Identities in the Roman World*. London; New York: Routledge.

Verhelst, B. and Scheijnen, T. (eds.) (forthcoming) *Walking the Wire: Greek and Latin Poetry in Dialogue*.

Vernant, J. (1980) *Myth and Society in Ancient Greece*. Translated by Janet Lloyd. London: Methuen.

Vian, F. (1954) 'Les comparaisons de Quintus de Smyrne' in *RPh* 28: 30–51; 235–43.

    (1959) *Recherches sur les 'Posthomerica' de Quintus de Smyrne*. Paris: Les Belles Lettres.

    (ed. and trans.) (1963) *Quintus de Smyrne, 'La suite d'Homère'*. Tome 1. Paris: Les Belles Lettres.

    (ed. and trans.) (1966) *Quintus de Smyrne, 'La suite d'Homère'*. Tome 2. Paris: Les Belles Lettres.

    (ed. and trans.) (1969) *Quintus de Smyrne, 'La suite d'Homère'*. Tome 3. Paris: Les Belles Lettres.

    (1976) *Nonnos de Panopolis. Les Dionysiaques*. Tome 1. Chants 1–2. Paris: Les Belles Lettres.

    (1985) 'A propos de la "Vision de Dorothéos"' in *ZPE* 60: 45–9.

    (1994) 'Théogamies et sotériologie dans les *Dionysiaques* de Nonnos' in *JSav*: 197–233.

    (2001) 'Echoes and Imitations of Apollonius Rhodius in Late Greek Epic' in Th. D. Papanghelis and A. Rengakos (eds.) *A Companion to Apollonius Rhodius*. Leiden: Brill.

Vian, F. and Battegay, E. (1984) *Lexique de Quintus de Smyrne*. Paris: Les Belles Lettres.

Vidal-Naquet, P. (1992) *Assassins of Memory: Essays on the Denial of the Holocaust*. Translated by Jeffrey Mehlman. New York: Columbia University Press.

Visser, E. (1987) *Homerische Versifikationstechnik: Versuch einer Rekonstruktion*. Frankfurt: Peter Lang.

Vivante, P. (1982) *The Epithets in Homer: A Study in Poetic Values*. New Haven and London: Yale University Press.

Von Möllendorff, P. (2016) Review of ní Mheallaigh (2014) in *Mnemosyne* 69 (6): 1059–69.

Von Reden, S. and Goldhill, S. (1999) 'Plato and the Performance of Dialogue' in Goldhill, S. and Osborne, R. (eds.) *Performance Culture and Classical Athens*. Cambridge: Cambridge University Press: 267–92.

Vout, C. (2007) *Power and Eroticism in Imperial Rome*. Cambridge: Cambridge University Press.

Wachtel, N. (1986) 'Memory and History: An Introduction' in *History and Anthropology* 2: 207–24.

Walz, C. (ed.) (1832) *Rhetores Graeci*, vol. I. Stuttgart and London: J.G. Cotta and Black, Young & Young.

Wardy, R. (1996) *The Birth of Rhetoric: Gorgias, Plato and Their Successors*. London: Routledge.

(2018) 'Antique Authority' in J. Bryan, R. Wardy and J. Warren (eds.) *Authors and Authority in Ancient Philosophy*: Cambridge: Cambridge University Press: 313–29.

Watson, F. (2013) 'Harmony or Gospel? On the Genre of the (so-called) Diatessaron'. SNTS Christian Apocryphal Literature Seminar, Perth.

Way, A. S. (trans.) (1913) *Quintus Smyrnaeus: The Fall of Troy*. Cambridge, MA: Harvard University Press.

Webb, R. (2001) 'The *Progymnasmata* as Practice' in Too (ed.): 289–316.

(2006) 'Fiction, Mimesis and the Performance of the Past in the Second Sophistic' in Konstan and Saïd (eds.): 27–46.

(2008) *Demons and Dancers. Performance in Late Antiquity*. Cambridge, MA, and London: Harvard University Press.

Weidemann, H. (1989) 'Aristotle on Inferences from Signs (*Rhetoric* I 2, 1357b1–25)' in *Phronesis* 34: 343–51.

Wenglinsky, M. H. (1999) 'Response to the Philological Criticism of the Portrayal of the Gods: The *Posthomerica* of Quintus of Smyrna' in *Ancient Philosophy* 19: 77–86.

(2002) *The Representation of the Divine in the Posthomerica of Quintus of Smyrna*. Diss. at the University of Columbia.

West, M. (1993) *Carmina Anacreontea*. Stuttgart and Leipzig: Teubner.

(2003a) (trans) *Homeric Hymns. Homeric Apocrypha. Lives of Homer*. Cambridge, MA: Harvard University Press.

(2003b) (trans) *Greek Epic Fragments*. Cambridge, MA: Harvard University Press.

(2013) *The Epic Cycle: A Commentary on the Lost Trojan Epics*. Oxford: Oxford University Press.

Whitby, M. (1994) 'From Moschus to Nonnus: The Evolution of the Nonnian Style' in Hopkinson (ed.): 99–154.

(2017) 'Christodorus of Coptus on the Statues in the Baths of Zeuxippus at Constantinople. Text and Context' in H. Bannert and H. Kröll (eds.) *Nonnus of Panopolis in Context II: Poetry, Religion, and Society*. Leiden: Brill (Mnemosyne Supplement 408): 271–88.

Whitman, C. (1958) *Homer and the Heroic Tradition*. Cambridge, MA: Harvard University Press.

Whitmarsh, T. (2001) *Greek Literature and the Roman Empire: The Politics of Imitation*. Oxford: Oxford University Press.

(2004) *Ancient Greek Literature*. Cambridge: Polity.

(ed.) (2005) *The Second Sophistic*. Oxford: Oxford University Press.

(2007) 'Prose Literature and the Severan Dynasty' in Swain, Harrison and Elsner (eds.): 29–51.

(2013) *Beyond the Second Sophistic: Adventures in Greek Postclassicism*. Berkeley and London: University of California Press.

(2015) 'The Mnemology of Empire and Resistance: Memory, Oblivion, and Periegesis in Imperial Greek Culture' in K. Galinsky and K. Lapatin (eds.)

Cultural Memories in the Roman Empire. Los Angeles: J. Paul Getty Museum: 49–65.

Wiemken, H. (1972) *Der griechische Mimus: Dokumente zur Geschichte des antiken Volkstheaters*. Bremen: Carl Schünemann Universitätsverlag.

Williams, G. (1983) *Technique and Ideas in the Aeneid*. New Haven: Yale University Press.

Wills, J. (1997) 'Homeric and Virgilian Doublets: The Case of *Aeneid* 6.901' in *Materiali e discussioni per l'analisi dei testi classici* 38: 185–202.

Wohl, V. (ed.) (2014) *Probabilities, Hypotheticals, and Counterfactuals in Ancient Greek Thought*. Cambridge: Cambridge University Press.

Worman, N. (2001) 'This Voice Which Is Not One: Helen's Verbal Guises in Homeric Epic' in A. Lardinois and L. McClure (eds.) *Making Silence Speak: Women's Voices in Greek Literature and Society*. Princeton, NJ: Princeton University Press: 19–37.

Zeitlin, F. (1985) 'Playing the Other: Theater, Theatricality and the Feminine in Greek Drama', in *Representations* 11: 63–94.

(1996) *Playing the Other. Essays on Gender and Society in Classical Greek Literature*. Chicago: University of Chicago Press.

(2001) 'Visions and Revisions of Homer' in S. Goldhill (ed.) *Being Greek under Rome*. Cambridge: Cambridge University Press: 195–268.

Zuntz, G. (1988) 'Aion Plutonios (Eine Gründungslegende von Alexandria)' in *Hermes* 116: 291–303.

(1989) *Aion, Gott des Römerreichs* (Abhandlungen der Heidelberger Akademie der Wissenschaften, Philosophisch-historische Klasse). Heidelberg: Winter-Verlag.

(1992) *AIWN in der Literatur der Kaiserzeit* (Wiener Studien Beihefte 17, Arbeiten zur antiken Religionsgeschichte 2). Vienna: VÖAW.

Index Locorum for *Resurrection of Homer*

Achilles Tatius, *Leucippe and Clitophon* 3.20: 71
Aeschylus, *Ag.*, 1482: 66
Aethiopis, fr.1 W: 37
Agathias, prf.12.: 199
Anth. Pal.
  1.prf.: 225
  2.56–8: 232, 254
  2.271–6: 232
  2.280–2: 232
  2.320: 232
  2.403–5: 232
  2.414–6: 232
  7.42: 177
  8.24–74: 248
  11.130: 161
Antisthenes, 15.4: 216
Apollodorus
  Bibl.
    1.7.10: 63
    1.86: 63
Apollonius Rhodius
  Argon
    1.1: 285
    1.18–19: 284
    2.1047–89: 333
Apollonius the Sophist, *Lexicon Homericum*
  116
Aratus, *Phaen.* 544–52: 297
Aristophanes
  Ach. 400–1: 50
  *Lys.*155–6: 314
Aristotle
  Poet.
    1451a36–8: 199
    1454a33–145429: 313
    1459a–b: 237
  Rh. 1394a22f: 127
Artemidorus Daldianus, *Oneir.*1.80: 267

Batrachomyomachia,1–3: 171

Callimachus
  Aet.
    1 fr.19–20: 163
    1 fr.26–8: 163
    1.21–2: 170–1
    fr.1.19–20: 174
    fr.1.3: 169
    fr.1.37–8: 178
    fr.1.6: 178
    fr.2.1–2: 6
  Epigr. 540.3: 66
  fr. 309 Pf. = Hec.fr.119 H
    244–5
  Hymn 1 (*Zeus*), 30: 185
  Hymn 4 (*Del.*), 26: 66
Colluthus
  Abduction of Helen
    17–40: 288
    59–61: 14
    211–30: 288
    253–8: 288
    270–7: 193–4
    326–32: 248
    372–8: 248
    375: 248
    391–4: 336
Cypria
  fr.30 (Bernabé 2 fr.27 West = Paus. 10.31):
    218
  Proclus, *Chrest.*5 West: 218

Dio Chrysostom
  Or.
    2, 3: 60
    4: 60
    52: 317–18
  Trojan Oration, 11.24–5: 204
Diodorus Siculus, 32.24: 336–7
Dionysus of Halicarnassus, *Comp.* 23.2–7:
  183

Index Locorum

375

Euripides
Andr. 627–31: 314
Tro.
  154–61: 106
  585: 106
*Schol. Eur. Or.*1287: 314

Heliodorus, *Aeth.* 4.4: 129
Herodotus
Hdt., 2.116.1–2: 198–9
Hdt., 5.1.3: 302
Hesiod
Theog.
  2–34: 169
  22: 173
  22–8: 159
  139–46: 276
  825–8: 277
  836–8: 277
Hom. Hymn Herm,. 4.13: 119
Hom. Hymn Art., 9.1–4: 166
Homer
Il.
  1.4.118: 63
  1.7: 115
  1.85: 62
  1.9–91: 62
  1.92: 62
  1.188–222: 312
  1.207–14: 66
  1.245–84: 195
  1.247–9: 183
  1.249: 62
  1.280–1: 67
  1.396–406: 211
  1.401: 211
  1.530: 278
  2.6: 112
  2.20: 112
  2.35–40: 317
  2.38: 317
  2.72–5: 315
  2.87–90: 139
  2.91–2: 169
  2.144–9: 139
  2.216: 62
  2.217–8: 102
  2.484–6: 169
  2.484–7: 177
  2.484–92: 159
  2.484–93: 79
  2.718–24: 218
  2.718–25: 319
  3.212–6: 82
  4.364–403: 228

6.51–61: 316
6.119–20: 250
6.121: 250
6.130–7: 211
6.137: 211
6.145–9: 297
6.466–71: 151
6.474: 151
7.409–10: 132
8.222–3 = 11.5–6: 221
8.222–6 = 11.5–9: 218
8.226 = 11.9: 221
9.14–16: 147
9.197: 321
9.259: 197
9.260–99: 197
9.328–9: 206
9.444–95: 213
9.488–91: 214
9.670: 86
10.445–62: 102
11.132: 245
11.137: 114
11.411–88: 91, 217
11.473–7: 221
11.482–4: 221
13.636: 129
13.636–9: 202
14.115: 63
14.382: 259
14.425: 86
16.2–4: 147–8
16.94: 75
16.141–4: 259
16.278–83: 258
16.431–31: 208
16.434: 208
16.435: 208
16.452: 208
16.698–712: 305
16.698–715: 309
17.32: 75
18.250: 130
18.284–314: 131
18.391: 211
18.394–405: 211
18.569–72: 84–5
20.176: 250
20.198: 75
20.199–204: 250
20.204: 263
20.300–8: 330
20.392: 180
21.97–102: 114
21.276–8: 209

Index Locorum

Homer (cont.)
22.194: 75
22.197 75
22.220: 26
22.345–54: 133
22.359: 299
22.359–60: 210
22.395–404: 206
22.463–5: 206
22.466–7: 101
23.106: 75
23.66–7: 266
23.759: 98
23.845: 98
23.99–101: 266
24.14–17: 133
24.14–21: 206
24.257: 85
24.486: 75
24.559–71: 133
24.571–2: 300

Od.
1.1: 109
1.6–7: 326–7
1.11–12: 4, 338
1.12: 338
1.13: 4
1.60–2: 311
1.70: 116
1.229: 135
1.302: 67
1.337–44: 195
2.15–20: 325, 327–8
2.20: 328
4.211: 135
4.274–8: 175
4.332–592: 87, 340
6.317: 86
8.500: 84
8.500–2: 197
9.25–6: 184
9.287–98: 325
9.291: 328
9.307–9: 186
9.477–60: 187
9.504: 187
10.31–55: 327
10.145–213: 327
10.330: 109
11.90–137: 324
11.305–20: 242
11.315: 242
11.318–9: 242
11.319–20: 179

11.364; 123
11.441: 135
11.444–6: 135
11.487: 316
11.563: 311
12.327–73: 327
17.463–5: 137
19.203: 190
19.205–9: 148
22.8–12: 306
23.239–50: 324
23.247–250: 280
23.310–44: 197
24.274: 332
24.338: 332
24.473: 340
24.502: 340
24.528: 324, 340
24.537–8: 340–1
24.545–8: 341

Schol. Hom.
ABT, 3.212–6: 82
Il. 2.724a: 320
*Od.*1 l Pontani = Antisthenes fr.51 Caizzi
110

Horace, *Epist.*, 2.1.156: 32–3

Libanius
On Behalf of Dancers, 113: 53
Prog. Enc.
1.2: 63
3.12: 61–2
4.1: 62
Prog. Psog.
1.11: 62
1.2: 62
1.3: 63
Lucian
Salt. 83–4: 54
Ver. Hist.
2.20: 77
2.2: 77
2.20: 204
2.24: 77
2.28: 78

New Testament, John 18:38: 189
Nonnus
Dion.
1.14: 120
1.431–2: 163–4
5.155–205: 231
12: 231
13.47–50: 178

Index Locorum

18.309–13: 231
19.59–348: 83
22.354–90: 231
22.387–9: 254
25.20–1: 252
25.265–7: 231–2
42.178–81: 202
42.181: 129–30

Oppian
Hal.
1.80–7: 289
5.71–349: 289
5.293: 301
5.294: 301–2
5.304–8: 301
5.317–21: 301
5.403–9: 140
5.727–8: 140
Or. Sib., 3.411–32: 201–2
Ovid
*Fast.*3.471–3: 192
Met.
1.1–2: 237
13.34–42: 218
13.55–60: 218

Pausanias, 1.18.6–9: 239
Petronius
Sat.
59.2–7: 69
59.3: 71–2
59.4–5: 72
59.7: 72–3
Philostratus
Her.
24.2: 219
43.16: 189
V A
3.22: 219
4.11–13: 219
4.16.3: 268
V S, 489: 57
Plato
Hp. mi.
364c4–7: 109
365b: 118
Ion 533 D: 69
Resp. 4.439e–441b; 51–2
POsl. III., 189: 71
POxy.
2946: 26
3002: 64–5
3537: 176

III 519: 70
VII 1050: 70
Prudentius, *Perist.* 2.357–76: 140–1
Pseudo-Longinus, *De. Sub* 9.11–13:
179

Quintilian
Inst.
8.5.3: 127
10.1.46: 182
10.1.58–9: 182
12.10.58: 182
12.10.63: 182
12.10.64: 182
Quintus of Smyrna
1.1: 86, 146, 308
1.1–17: 1–2
1.5–81: 144
1.9: 205
1.9–11: 208
1.10: 294
1.13–14: 206
1.15: 205
1.16: 336
1.17: 146, 336
1.18–19: 2
1.76–82: 141
1.124–37: 112
1.125–37: 266
1.128–80: 82
1.132: 121
1.376–9: 210
1.502–3: 241
1.515–27: 275
1.524: 244
1.527; 174
1.560–2: 241
1.563: 241
1.575–91: 209
1.577–9: 241
1.587–8: 244
1.588: 209
1.702: 208
1.706–15: 207–8
1.716–824: 63
1.726–28: 120
1.759–63: 209
1.809–10: 132
2.10–25: 129
2.25: 114
2.36–40: 130
2.39–40: 332
2.49–55: 130
2.97: 116

Quintus of Smyrna (cont.)
2.161–2: 296
2.193–234: 142–4
2.411–51: 245
2.433–44: 210–11
2.434–5: 245–6
2.448–9: 250
2.449–51: 250, 263
2.458–513: 296
2.500–6: 296–7
2.507–13: 297
2.594–62: 298
2.634–66: 246
3.1–185: 210
3.45: 274
3.61–6: 298–9
3.67–8: 212
3.78–82: 209
3.91–138: 299
3.118–22: 256
3.137–9: 299–300
3.142–3: 300
3.147–9: 300
3.164–9: 300
3.179–80: 301
3.293–4: 222–3
3.306–8: 223
3.463–89: 213
3.470: 214
3.471: 214
3.474–78: 214
3.476: 214
3.577–81: 146
3.631–5: 246
3.731: 174
3.743–65: 256
4.110–14: 83
4.123–4: 83
4.130: 83
4.130–45: 85
4.131: 83
4.139: 86
4.147: 83
4.147–8: 83
4.148–9: 84, 100
4.154–60: 85
4.156: 86
4.158: 114
4.160: 86
4.160–1: 86
4.161–2: 83, 85
4.162–3: 84
4.378–9: 134
4.379: 134
4.385: 116

4.522: 98
5.49–56: 264–5
5.97–8: 5
5.102–9: 243
5.175–9: 89
5.175–316: 216
5.177–9: 222
5.180–316: 89
5.186–8: 90
5.190: 219
5.191: 219
5.191–4: 218
5.195–6: 218
5.196–8: 91
5.197–9: 218
5.199: 219
5.202–3: 217
5.202–5: 90
5.212: 217
5.222–3: 90
5.232–3: 90–1
5.236–7: 121–2
5.268–90: 220
5.285: 222
5.299: 97
5.305: 116
5.315–6: 91
5.317–32: 222
5.359–60: 310
5.361–4: 310–11
5.433–50: 244
5.641–9: 243
6.133–42: 252–3
6.152: 116
6.191–293: 253
6.298–307: 253
6.302–4: 253–4
6.520–4: 100–1
6.532–6: 26
7.44–55: 136
7.176–7: 257
7.228–31: 146
7.435–51: 258
7.440–51: 258–9
7.501–2: 101–2
7.526–41: 258
7.530–2: 141
7.530–5: 150
7.537–9: 113
7.537–41: 260
7.569–95: 301
7.630–4: 113
7.642–6: 261
7.642–52: 215
7.643–8: 215

Index Locorum

7.650–1: 215
7.661–6: 261
7.668–71: 261–2
7.686: 115
7.769–434: 247
8.114–5: 327
8.124: 326
8.124–7: 325
8.125: 328
8.138–45: 262
8.335: 114
9.6–7: 261
9.46–62: 268
9.104–9: 291
9.105: 339
9.162–6: 141
9.247: 114
9.325–32: 317
9.333–546: 317
9.354–94: 318
9.390: 174
9.403–4: 318
9.410–22: 320
9.422–5: 318
9.518–9: 321
9.520–1: 321
10.306–26: 148
10.334–443: 303
10.415–20: 147
10.483–9: 246
11.139: 304
11.190–200: 306
11.234: 115
11.289–97: 304
11.358–61: 332
11.358–414: 304–5
11.388–96: 333–4
11.446–73: 305
11.499–501: 307
12.4: 305
12.8–10: 305
12.20: 121–2
12.25–45: 303
12.35–9: 303
12.59: 305
12.106–121: 266
12.154–6: 121
12.155–6: 292
12.162: 305
12.169–72: 124
12.19–20: 334
12.190–95: 292
12.237–8: 305
12.251: 305
12.254–8: 104

12.288: 116
12.291: 305
12.300–1: 305
12.306–7: 170
12.306–8: 168
12.306–10: 5
12.306–13: 158–9
12.307: 88
12.309: 256
12.363–6: 137
12.387–8: 136
12.387–91: 123
13.138: 174
13.333–43: 328–9
13.337: 331
13.344–9: 331
13.346: 332
13.349: 332
13.354–73: 303
13.366–41: 26
13.385–415: 313
13.388–94: 313
13.401–2: 314
13.403–7: 315
13.464–77: 335–6
13.595: 116
14.29–31: 131
14.33–6: 141
14.121–42: 87–8
14.131–3: 88
14.136–41: 88
14.139: 88
14.142: 100
14.179–256: 264
14.181: 266
14.183–4: 266
14.185–7: 117
14.185–222: 210
14.186: 272
14.192–4: 134
14.195–200: 264
14.203–4: 134
14.211–12: 268–9
14.216: 268
14.216–18: 272
14.225–6: 117
14.235–46: 271
14.238: 272
14.268: 114
14.271–303: 105
14.272–6: 116–17
14.276: 116
14.289–93: 131
14.289–96: 106
14.304: 115

380 *Index Locorum*

Quintus of Smyrna (cont.)
14.309–12: 268
14.419–21: 312
14.419–65: 273
14.426–48: 274
14.427–33: 274
14.430–2: 278
14.433–5: 274–5
14.436–9: 274
14.443–8: 275
14.454–8: 276
14.459–65: 277–8
14.509–11: 278
14.558–89: 101
14.559–89: 274, 340
14.582–5: 243
14.602–4: 338
14.628–31: 339
14.654–6: 340
14.665–8: 4
14.666–8: 206
14.85–6: 302

Silius, *Pun.* 778–97: 269
Sophocles, *Aj.* 646–92: 310

Statius
Achil. 1.650–1: 242
Theb. 12.810–19: 251–2
Strabo, 10.2.12: 184

Thucydides
1.22.3: 222
2.91: 302
Torah, Deut. 25:19: 190
Triphiodorus
Sack of Troy
220: 123
291: 123
682: 336

Vergil
Aen.
1.148–53: 139
2.438–44: 332–3
2.57–144: 123
2.721–9: 229
3.709–11: 229
9.505–18: 333
G., 3.284: 35
Vision of Dorotheos, 340–1: 170

Subject index for Resurrection of Homer

Page numbers in italics are figure; with 'n' are notes.

Achilles
  death of, 298–300, 302
  epithets, 110–18
  and selective memory, 209–16
  shield of, 5
  and succession, 241–5
    flyting and Memnon, 245–52
    and Neoptolemus, 256, 266–8
Achilles Tatius, *Leucippe and Clitophon*, 71
adoxography, 62–3
Aeneas
  filiation/succession, 229, 250
  temporality, 290n51, 328–35
  see also Vergil, *Aeneid*
Aeschines, 217
Aeschylus, 274, 317–18
  Agamemnon, 66
Aethiopis, 2, 37, 86
Agamemnon, and Menelaus, 315–16
Agathias, *Histories*, 199
Aion (Time), 292–4
Ajax (Locrian), 100–1, 243, 273–6, 340
Ajax (Telamonian)
  arms contest with Odysseus, 89–91
  and Athena, 310–11
  and succession, 241–5
Alcidamas of Elea, 183n102
allegory
  interpretations of Homer
    Neoplatonists, 29, 173
    Pseudo-Plutarch, 173
  Mountain of *Arete*, 265
allusion
  Hinds study of, 9
  as term, 41–3
anachrony, 21, 171, 188, 324–35
  analepsis, 190–1, 194, 203–9, 294
  Dionysiaca (Nonnus), 254–5, 279,
    287–8

prolepsis, 2, 100–3, 194, 212, 244, 298–9,
    319, 324–35
Anacreontea, 24, 269
analepsis, 190–1, 194, 203–9, 294
Antipater of Thessalonica, 270n134
Antiphanes, 313n95
Antiphus, and Eurypylus, 325–8
Antisthenes, 110, 118, 216–17
anxiety, filial, 230, 234
anxiety of influence, 8, 230, 233, 241, 249, 263
Aphrodite, and Menelaus, 313–15
apocrypha, 19, 23
Apollo, 23n87, 299, 304
Apollodorus, 63
Apollonius Rhodius, 8, 138–9
  Argonautica, 284–5, 332–3
Apollonius the Sophist, 110, 115, 326
Appel, W., 97, 101
Aratus, *Phaenomena* ,297
Archilaos relief, 29n120
Areios, 14
Ares, 207–9
Arete (mountain) allegory, 264–5
Aristarchus, 68, 251n80
Aristophanes
  Acharnians, 50
  Lysistrata, 313–14
Aristotle
  enthymemes, 125, 127
  Poetics, 199, 237, 287, 313
armour
  Achilles', 258–61
  see also shields
art *see* visual representations
Artemidorus, 267
Astydamas, *Hector*, 151–2
Athena
  appeasement of anger, 303
  as control agent, 321

381

382   *Subject Index*

Athena (cont.)
  epithet, 121–2
  ethopoeia, 73, 76
  final mention of, 339
  and Odysseus, 311–13
  petition to Zeus, 273–8
Augustan poetry *see* Horace; Ovid; Vergil
Augustine, 224
Augustus, 229
  see also political context

Bär, Silvio, 21, 25, 81, 89, 159, 167, 184n109, 301
Bartsch, Shadi, 50–1, 54
Batrachomyomachia, 23, 24n89, 171
battle scenes
  and pace, 295–8
  see also disembodiment
Bauman, Richard, 52, 89
Baumbach, Manuel, 21, 25, 81, 301
beard imagery, 179–80
bees, simile, 139, 186n117
bilingualism, 38
Bloom, Harold, 263, 273, 279
  The Anxiety of Influence, 226
  A Theory of Poetry, 230
body parts, and disembodiment, 305–7
Bowie, Ewen, 11–12, 79–80
Briseis, simile, 146, 148–9
Byre, Calvin, 265

Calchas, 328–9, 331–2
calendar, 71
Callimachus, 66, 98, 160–7
  Aetia, 6, 188
    and epigram Adesp. *Anth. Pal.*, 177
    and Hesiod, 159
    and Triphiodorus, 162
    and Book 12 proem, 167–75
    youth, 178–80
  and Homeric *hapaxes*, 233–45
  Hymn to Zeus (*Hymn* 1), 185
Cameron, Alan, 33–4n145, 172n56
Capitoline Tablet, 295–340
Carvounis, Katerina, 81, 274
Casa di Octavius Quartio (Pompeii),
  29, 32, 204
Catullus, 64 192–3
cento poetry, 15, 76
  Christus Patiens, 249n77
centralisation, 200, 238, 240
Certamen Homeri et Hesiodi, 183
chariot imagery, 163, 164n22
Chaudhuri, Pramit, 44, 275
Christianity, 16–20
  mother imagery, 247, 249n77

Christodorus, on statues in the Baths of
  Zeuxippus, 232, 254
Christus Patiens, 249n77
circle imagery, 297–8
Claudian, similes, 140–1
closure, 282–7, 335–41
clusters, of similes, 141–6
Collins, D., 69
Colluthus, 162
  Abduction of Helen, 13–14, 193–4, 267
    closure, 336
    filial imagery, 231, 279
    mother imagery, 248
    temporality, 288
competitions
  Odysseus and Ajax, 89–91
  poetic, 81
  rhapsodic, 54, 68–80
Connolly, Joy, 31
Conte, Gian Biagio, 159, 192–3
contrast imitation, 7–20, 34
  see also allusion
'control agents', 309–10
counterfactuals, 308–24, 340
cowering children, simile 150–1
cows, simile, 2–3
culture, imperial Greek, 28–34
  see also visual representations
Cyclopes, 275–6
Cypria, 218

dating, of *Posthomerica*, 12, 25–8
declamation, 30–4, 54–60, 89
Deidameia, simile, 146–9
Demosthenes
  Philostratus' imitation of, 58–60
  selective memory, 217
Detienne, Marcel, 119
Deucalion, 194, 338–9
Dictys of Crete, 218
didacticism, 132
Dio Chrysostom, 60, 201–2, 317–18
  Trojan Oration, 200, 204
Diodorus Siculus, 336–7
Diogenes Laertius, 18
Dionysius of Alexandria, *Periegesis*, 12
Dionysius of Halicarnassus, 183
disembodiment, 305–7
distributed agency, 238–40
divine memory, 212–13
divinity, epithets of Achilles, 115–17
Dorotheus (? son of Quintus), 17
  and *Vision*, 27–8
doubleness, 34–6, 49–56
  and counterfactuals, 323–4

Subject Index

and declamation, 56–60
in epithet of Achilles, 117
and *gnomai*, 129, 137
and Homeric performance, 76, 80
and internal performance, 82
and memory, 190
in *progymnasmata*, 66–7
and rhapsodic shows, 68–80
sheep allusion, 186–8
and simile, 146
and temporality, 282
'doublespeak', 50–1
Iliad, 59–60
dreams, 265–71

eikos, 125
ekphrasis, 96–7n17
Elsner, Jaś, 15
encomium, 61–3
Encomium of Helen (Gorgias), 199
endings *see* closure
Ennius, 270–1n136, 272
Annals, 270
enthymeme, 125
Epic Cycle, 19–37
Aethiopis, 2, 37
epigrams
herms in the *Porta Trigemina*, 79–80
Palatine Anthology, 177
epithets, 107–10
'generic', 118–25
epyllions, 162
Abduction of Helen (Colluthus), 13–14
Sack of Troy (Triphiodorus), 12–13, 38–9
era of crisis, 233
Ercilla, Alonso de, 341–2
ethopoeia, 30, 60–1, 63–7, 87, 176
Euripides, 317–18
Andromache, 314
Bacchae, 52, 57
Troades, 105–6
Eurypylus, 252–5
and Antiphus, 325–8
confrontation with Neoptolemus, 262–3
Eustathius, 26, 138
'external viewer', 337

Fate, 124–5
Favorinus of Arles, 57
Feeney, Denis, 337
filiation, 226–7, 233–4, 278–9
literary background of, 227–35
see also succession
fish image, in *Halieutica* (Oppian), 289
fishing, similes, 301

formulae, 107–10
Fowler, Don, 286
France, Anatole, 226

Garden of Liberty, 181
gentleness, 134–5
ghosts *see* necromancy
gigantomachy, 242–4
Glaucus, speech to Diomedes, 250, 297
glosses, 97–8, 100
gnomai, 125–38
Goldhill, Simon, 283–4, 287n38, 325, 337
Gorgias, *Encomium of Helen*, 199
grandpaternity, 252–5
Graziosi, Barbara, 23
Greene, Graham, 280
Gregory Nazianzus, 248–9
Grethlein, Jonas, 284, 289–90

Habicht, Christian, 10–11
Hadrian, 239
hapax legomena, 97–8
Hippias Minor (Plato), 109
Iliad (Homer), 245
Harder, M. Annette, 171–2n55, 172n57,
172n55, 177
Hardie, Philip, 7–9, 43n182, 193, 237, 286
Helen
Encomium of Helen (Gorgias), 199
and Menelaus scene, 313–15, 317
Helena Augusta, 247n68
Heliodorus, *Aethiopica*, 129
helmet, of Achilles, 243–4
Hera, and Apollo conversation, 299
herms, epigrams, 79–80
Hermus (river), 166, 180–1
Herodotus
on Homer, 198–9
and the Perinthians, 302
Hesiod
compared to Homer, 183
ethopoeia fragment, 176
middle style, 82
and sheep allusion, 186
Theogony
Cyclopes, 275–6
Muses, 169–70, 173, 176
Typhon, 277
Works and Days, 35
hill, in the proem, 181–3
Hillis Miller, J. 280–1
Hinds, Stephen, 7, 9, 34, 167, 192,
196–7n29
history, and memory, 189–91
Hoekstra, A., 107

384   *Subject Index*

Homer
  Iliad
    Achilles
      and Aeneas, 330
      lion simile, 300
      Phoenix's lament for, 213–14
      and Thetis, 211–12
      see also below Patroclus
    and anachronism, 324
    armour-switching scene, 259
    Athena, 312
    and Zeus' weapons, 278
    centralisation, 238
    'doublespeak', 59–60
    ending, 2–3
    filiation imagery, 228
    gnomai, 126–7, 129–34
    Hermus, 180–1
    invocation, 178
    Linus song, 84–5
    Muses, 176
    Palamedes, 219–20
    Patroclus
      in Achilles' armour, 258–9
      appearing to Achilles, 266
    Philoctetes' return, 319–20
    Phoenix's lament for Achilles, 213–14
    selective memory, 194–5, 197, 203–4, 206–8, 217–18
    similes, 147–9, 151–2
    succession, 250–1
    temporality, closure, 283
    topography, 184–5
  Odyssey, 86–7, 280
    and Athena, 311–12
    bardic songs, 82
    Cyclopes, 325
    demise of Odysseus' comrades, 326–7
    and the ending of *Posthomerica*, 337–41
    epithets, 109, 123
    filiation imagery, 228
    gnomai, 126, 135
    and the *Iliad*, 56
    memory, 195, 197
    rams of Polyphemus, 186–7
    simile, 148–50
    succession, 242–3
    temporality, 283, 324
    topography, 184
    Wooden Horse, 175
    youth, 179
  performance, 24–34, 67–80
  and *POxy. ethopoeiae*, 66–7
  and the proem, 165–7
  Q.S. as, 5–6

Quintilian on, 182–4
and temporality, 283–6
visual representations, 29–30
'Homeric Games', 200, 224
Homeridai, 68–9, 228, 234–5
homeristai, 69–76, 260
Hopkinson, Neil, 168, 181
hoplon krisis, 89–91, 122–3, 216–23, 311
Horace, 32–3
Hunter, Richard, 138–9, 161, 182
Hymn to Apollo, 23n87
'hyperreality', 78

Ibycus, 314
Iliac Tablets, 29, 86, 295, 329–30
imperial Greek culture, 28–34
impersonation
  poetic, 23–4
  see also progymnasmata
interstitial, defined, 7n9
intertextuality, use of term, 41–3
interval
  defined, 7n9
  poetics of the, 6–7
invective, of Libanius, 61–3
Isocrates, *Panathenaicus*, 57–8
Ithaca, 184

James, Alan, 108n56, 108–9, 141, 150–1, 168, 213, 243n60, 303n73, 318–19

Kennedy, Duncan, 308–9
Kim, Larry, 28, 200
King, Katherine, 274
Kirk, Geoffrey, 251n80
kisses, Achilles and Neoptolemus, 266–8
Kneebone, Emily, 233, 293, 301–2
knowledge, and proem, 175–8
Kohn, Eduardo, 269
  How Forests Think, 238–9
Konstan, David, 32
Krebs, Christopher, 284, 289–90

Lada-Richards, Ismene, 52–3
Lamberton, Robert, 28–9
Laocoön, simile, 147, 149–50
Latin authors, influence on Quintus, 38–40
Latour, Bruno, 43
  We Have Never Been Modern, 35–6
Lee, Kevin 108n56, 108–9
Leigh, Matthew, 44
Lemnos scene *see* Philoctetes
Lesches of Pyrrha, *Little Iliad*, 86, 303n73, 314

Libanius
  On Behalf of Dancers, 53–4
  use of Iliad in invective and encomium, 61–3
linear thinking, 238–9
linear time, 43, 288, 293
Linus, song, 84–5
lion, simile, 300
lipogrammatic poetry, 14–15
literary inheritance, 251–2
Lowe, Nick, 283, 313
Lucan, Pharsalia, 269–70, 341–2
Lucian, 87, 201–2
  On Dance, 53–4
  True Histories, 77–9, 200, 204
lusis, 307–8, 313
lying
  and Homer, 200–3
  Odysseus, 190n2
Lykaon episode, 114–15

Macellus of Side, 12n35
Maciver, Calum, 21, 25, 34, 37–8, 40, 42, 89,
      94, 127, 131–2, 135–6, 142, 144,
      152, 159, 162, 168, 186–8, 191, 205,
      207, 256, 259n98
maidens of Hera prophecy, 303–4
Mansur, Melvin, 108, 111–12
Martindale, Charles, 7–9, 286
Meles (river), 166
Memnon
  flyting against Achilles, 245–52
  similes, 142–5
memory, and history, 189–91
memory-and-allusion, 212
Menelaus
  and Agamemnon, 315–16
  and Helen, 313–15
metapoetics, 44–5
mētis, 119, 121–2
middle style, 82, 181–3
Miguélez Cavero, Laura, 93–4
mime, 53–6
  see also homeristai
mimesis
  visual representations, 29–32, 34
  see also mime
monster/whale story, Halieutica (Oppian),
      300–2, 337n155
Montiglio, Silvia, 136–7
Morales, Helen, 128, 248
Morgan, Teresa, 128n134
mothers, 245–9
Mountain of Arete, 265
Muses, 169–71
  Aetia (Callimachus), 6, 159

Dionysiaca (Nonnus), 170
epigram on herm, 79
Iliad, 176
Ion (Plato), 69
proem, 158–9, 168, 172
  and knowledge, 175–8
Theogony (Hesiod), 169–70, 173, 176

Nagy, Gregory, 68
necromancy, 268
  Achilles, 115, 134, 210, 264–8
  Homer, 270
  Odysseus, 219
  Patroclus, 75–6
neologisms, 98–9, 103–7, 174–5
Neoplatonists, 29, 173
Neoptolemus, 256–8
  as Achilles, 258–61
  filial speech, 261–4
  and the ghost of Achilles, 264–73
Neopythagoreanism, 265
Nestor
  and age, 235n28
  gnomic sayings, 136
  in Hippias Minor (Plato), 109
  in the Iliad, 62, 194–5
  lipogrammatic Iliad, 14–15
  song 82–7
New Testament, 18–19
Newby, Zahra, 18
Ní Mheallaigh, Karen, 78
Nonnus, 66–7, 224, 279
  awareness of Posthomerica, 26
  Dionysiaca, 14, 16–17, 20–1, 39, 98–9,
      119–20, 129–30n138
    Aion, 293
    and Callimachu,s 163–4
    filial imagery, 231–2
    funeral games, 83
    grandpaternity, 254
    on Homer lying, 202–3
    invocation, 177–8
    invoking the Muses, 170
    and Pindar, 252
    temporality, 287–8
  Paraphrase, 16, 119–20
novels, 128–9

Odysseus
  competes with Ajax for Achilles' arms, 89–91
  and demise of his comrades, 327–8
  lying, 190n2
  memories in speech, 220–3
  as polytropos, 109–10, 118–19
  rams of Polyphemus, 186–7

386 Subject Index

Odysseus (cont.)
  temporality, 332–5
  see also Homer, *Odyssey*
Oinone, simile, 147–8
Oppian
  Halieutica, 25–6
    monster/whale story, 300–2, 337n155
    similes, 139–40
    temporality, 288–9
opposition in imitation *see* contrast imitation
oratory *see* declamation; *gnomai*
Origen, Sermons, 18
ornamentality, 108–9, 119
Ovid
  Fasti, 192–3
  and memory, 196
  Metamorphoses, 39, 218, 237, 267, 326
pacing, 291–308
Palamedes, 218–20, 223
Palatine Anthology, 161, 224–5
  Christodorus, 232–73

pantomime, 53–6
Parry, Adam, 118–19
Parsons, Peter, 66, 76
Patroclus
  and Achilles' armour, 258–9
  appearing to Achilles, 266
Pausanias, 239
Peirano, Irene, 23, 56, 185
Peloponnesians' song, in Thucydides, 302
Penthesilea
  death of, 85–6
  dream (epithets), 112–13
  and succession, 241
performance, 24–34, 67–8
  as being and not being, 49–56
  defined, 52
  internal, 81–92, 284n25
  of the past, 30–4
  rhapsodic shows, 54, 68–80
Perinthians, 302
Petronius, *Satyricon, Cena Trimalchionis*, 69, 71–3
Pfeiffer, Rudolf, 172n57
Philoctetes, return of, 317–22
Philostratus, 18, 201–2
  Heroicus, 189, 200, 219, 223, 268
  imitation of Demosthenes, 58–60
  Vita Apollonii, 218–19, 268–70
Phoenix
  lament for Achilles, 213–16
  meeting with Neoptolemus, 261–4
Pindar
  in *Dionysiaca* (Nonnus), 252
  Nemean, 2 68–9, 228

Pisander, *Heroic Marriage of the Gods*, 14–15
Plato
  Hippias Minor, 109, 118
  Ion, 69
  mimesis, 51–2
plupast, 284–5, 289–90
poetic selectivity, 192–203
poetics of the interval, 6–7
Polemo, Marcus Antonius, 306
political context, 9–10, 328–42
  and performance, 24–34
  and sophists, 56–60
Pollianus, 160–2
poly- epithets, 119–20, 311
  polytropos, 109–10, 118–19, 122–5
Porter, Jim, 166
POxy. 3001, 73–6, 73–5
Prendergast, Christopher 322–3, 324n124
Priam, *gnome*, 129–31
proem of Book 12, 158–60, 165–7,
    188, 236
  famous sheep allusion, 186–8
  Muses and knowledge, 174–5
  and poetic/Homeric unity, 167–75
  topography and grandeur 180–5
  and youth, 178–80
programmatics, 44–5
  Batrachomyomachia, 171
  Dionysiaca (Nonnus), 119–20
  Encomium of Helen (Gorgias), 199
  proem in Book 12, 157–60, 168
  and similes, 139–42
progymnasmata, 61–7
prolepsis, 194, 324–35
prophecy
  and Aeneas, 330–1
  death of Achilles, 299
  maidens of Hera discussion, 303–4
  Tiresias', 324, 341
Prudentius, *Peristephanon* 2, 140–1
pseudepigraphia, 23–4
Pseudo-Longinus, *De.Sub.*, 179
Pseudo-Plutarch, *Essay on the Life and Poetry of Homer* 173
Pucci, Joseph, 41

Quint, David, 9–10, 290–1, 334–5,
    341–2
  Epic and Empire, 285–6
Quintilian, 66n60, 82, 183n104
  gnomai, 127
  on Homer, 182–4

rams, of Polyphemus, 186–7
revision, of Homer, 198–203

Subject Index 387

rhapsodic shows, 54, 68–80
  see also performance, internal
Rosenmeyer, Patricia, 24

Säid, Suzanne, 32
Schechner, Richard, 50
Schmitz, Thomas, 21, 31, 194, 233, 321
scholia, Homer, 82
second sophistic period, 18n64, 25
  declamation, 30–4
selective memory, 189–91, 223–5
  analepsis, 203–9
  and poetic selectivity, 192–203
  in speeches, 209–23
    Achilles, 209–16
    hoplon krisis, 216–23
sheep, 159, 186–8
  and Ajax, 73, 244
shields
  of Achilles, 5, 264–5, 272
  of Eurypylus, 253
  see also armour
Shorrock, Rob, 7–20
Sibylline Oracles, 201–2
Silius, *Punica*, 269, 286
silver Latin, 10–16, 20–2
similes, 125–6, 138–52
  bees, 139, 186n117
  cows, 2–3
  fishing, 301
  Laocoön, 147, 149–50
  lion, 300
  sheep, 244
  snow, 146–8
  tower, 298–9
  wounded stag, 220–1
Sinon, 104–5, 123–4, 322
snow, similes, 146–8
songs
  death and funeral of Achilles, 87–9
  Nestor's, 82–7
  within songs, 49, 81–92
Sophocles, *Ajax*, 310
Squire, Michael, 30–1, 211, 329–30
Statius, 242, 274
  Silvae, and the *Aeneid* (Vergil), 251n82
  Thebaid, 251–2, 286
Stehle, Eva, 53
Stesichorus, *Sack of Troy*, 314
Stoicism, 127, 136–8, 265, 318–19, 322
storm scenes
  and Ajax, 101
  Athena using Zeus' thunderbolt, 4
  ending, 335, 337–40
  Odyssey, 4

Strabo, on Homer, 184, 184n110
stylistics, 93–6, 152–3
  and Achilles, 110–18
  'generic', 118–25
  gnomai, 125–38
  formulae and epithets, 107–10
  language, 96–100
    Homeric rarities, 97, 99–103
    neologisms, 98–9, 103–7
  similes, 125–6, 138–52
succession, 227–9, 233–40
  and Athena, 273–8
  flyting of Memnon and Achilles,
    245–52
  grandpaternity, 252–5
  and Neoptolemus, 256–8
    as Achilles, 258–61
    filial speech, 261–4
    and the ghost of Achilles, 264–73
  Penthesilea/Ajax/Achilles, 241–5
  see also filiation
supplementarity, 8–9, 56, 185, 219
syllogism, 125–6n122

Tatian, *Diatessaron*, 19–20
Teichomachy, 102
Temple of Artemis, 166
Temple of Olympian Zeus, 239
temporality, 34–6, 52, 280–2, 343–4
  anachrony and prolepsis, 324–35
  closure, 282–7, 335–41
  and counterfactuals, 308–24
  and *hapax*, 101–2
  and imperial Greek epic, 283–91
  pacing, 291–308
Tertullian, 17
testudo scene, 40n174, 333–4
Theodorus, 330n138
Thersites, 62–3
Thucydides, 222, 302
thunder, 141, 144, 150, 163–4
  in Callimachus, 181, 185
  and Zeus/Athena, 273–6, 278
Time *see* Aion
Tiresias, prophecy, 324, 341
Tomasso, Vincent, 287
Torah, 190, 223
tower simile, 298–9
Triphiodorus, 93–4, 123
  epyllion, 12–13, 26, 38–9
  pace of, 304
  temporality, 287
  filial imagery, 231
  lipogrammatic *Odyssey*, 14
  Paraphrase of Homer's Similes, 14

Subject Index

Triphiodorus (cont.)
  sack of Troy, 336
  The Sack of Troy, 93–4, 162, 170, 307
    and Callimachus, 162–3
truth *see* selective memory
Typhon
  in *Dionysiaca* (Nonnus), 163–4, 185
  in *Theogony* (Hesiod), 277
Tzetzes, John, 26

variants, Homeric, 97–8
Verae Historiae (Lucian) *see* Lucian, *True Histories*
Vergil
  Aeneid, 39–40, 123, 290n51
    Athena's anger, 303
    and closure, 286
    and filiation imagery, 229
    and *Silvae* (Statius), 251n82
    similes, 139–40
    testudo, 333
  Georgics, 35

Vernant, Jean-Pierre, 119
Vian, Francis 11, 27, 39, 97, 103–4, 106, 108,
    164–5, 168
Vision of Dorotheus, 27–8, 170
visual representations
  Helen and Menelaus, 314
  of Homer, 29–32, 34

weather, 291–2n52
Webb, Ruth, 31, 61, 69–70n76
whale/monster story, *Halieutica* (Oppian),
    300–2, 337n155
Whitmarsh, Tim, 239
Wohl, Victoria, 309
Wooden Horse, 104, 121, 166n34, 174–5, 231,
    292, 334
wounded stag, simile, 220–1

Zeitlin, Froma, 29n120
Zenodotus, and Homeric variants, 98
Zeus, Athena petition to, 273–8

CPSIA information can be obtained
at www.ICGtesting.com
Printed in the USA
LVHW011048030821
694401LV00005B/361